ACURA COUPES AND SEDANS
1994-00 REPAIR MANUAL

CHILTON'S

Covers all U.S. and Canadian models of
Acura Integra, Integra Type R, Legend, Vigor,
2.2CL, 2.3CL, 2.5TL, 3.0CL, 3.2TL and 3.5RL

by Paul T. DeSanto, A.S.E.

CHILTON *Automotive Books*

PUBLISHED BY **HAYNES NORTH AMERICA**, Inc.

Manufactured in USA
© 2000 Haynes North America, Inc.
ISBN 0-8019-9094-7
Library of Congress Catalog Card No. 00-130399
1234567890 9876543210

Haynes Publishing Group
Sparkford Nr Yeovil
Somerset BA22 7JJ England

Haynes North America, Inc
861 Lawrence Drive
Newbury Park
California 91320 USA

ABCDE
FGHIJ
KLMNO

12E1

Contents

Contents

SAFETY NOTICE

Proper service and repair procedures are vital to the safe, reliable operation of all motor vehicles, as well as the personal safety of those performing repairs. This manual outlines procedures for servicing and repairing vehicles using safe, effective methods. The procedures contain many NOTES, CAUTIONS and WARNINGS which should be followed, along with standard procedures to eliminate the possibility of personal injury or improper service which could damage the vehicle or compromise its safety.

It is important to note that repair procedures and techniques, tools and parts for servicing motor vehicles, as well as the skill and experience of the individual performing the work vary widely. It is not possible to anticipate all of the conceivable ways or conditions under which vehicles may be serviced, or to provide cautions as to all possible hazards that may result. Standard and accepted safety precautions and equipment should be used when handling toxic or flammable fluids, and safety goggles or other protection should be used during cutting, grinding, chiseling, prying, or any other process that can cause material removal or projectiles.

Some procedures require the use of tools specially designed for a specific purpose. Before substituting another tool or procedure, you must be completely satisfied that neither your personal safety, nor the performance of the vehicle will be endangered.

Although information in this manual is based on industry sources and is complete as possible at the time of publication, the possibility exists that some car manufacturers made later changes which could not be included here. While striving for total accuracy, the authors or publishers cannot assume responsibility for any errors, changes or omissions that may occur in the compilation of this data.

PART NUMBERS

Part numbers listed in this reference are not recommendations by Haynes North America, Inc. for any product brand name. They are references that can be used with interchange manuals and aftermarket supplier catalogs to locate each brand supplier's discrete part number.

SPECIAL TOOLS

Special tools are recommended by the vehicle manufacturer to perform their specific job. Use has been kept to a minimum, but where absolutely necessary, they are referred to in the text by the part number of the tool manufacturer. These tools can be purchased, under the appropriate part number, from your local dealer or regional distributor, or an equivalent tool can be purchased locally from a tool supplier or parts outlet. Before substituting any tool for the one recommended, read the SAFETY NOTICE at the top of this page.

ACKNOWLEDGMENTS

The publisher expresses appreciation to Honda Motor Co. Ltd, for their generous assistance.

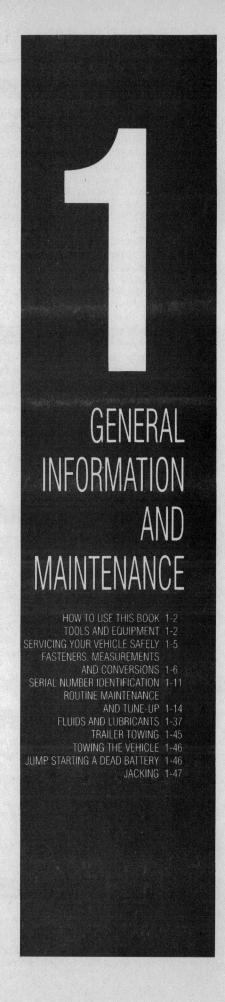

GENERAL INFORMATION AND MAINTENANCE

HOW TO USE THIS BOOK

Chilton's Total Car Care manual for 1994–00 Acura coupes and sedans is intended to help you learn more about the inner workings of your vehicle while saving you money on its upkeep and operation.

The beginning of the book will likely be referred to the most, since that is where you will find information for maintenance and tune-up. The other sections deal with the more complex systems of your vehicle. Operating systems from engine through brakes are covered to the extent that the average do-it-yourselfer becomes mechanically involved. This book will not explain such things as rebuilding a differential for the simple reason that the expertise required and the investment in special tools make this task uneconomical. It will, however, give you detailed instructions to help you change your own brake pads and shoes, replace spark plugs, and perform many more jobs that can save you money, give you personal satisfaction and help you avoid expensive problems.

A secondary purpose of this book is a reference for owners who want to understand their vehicle and/or their mechanics better. In this case, no tools at all are required.

Where to Begin

Before removing any bolts, read through the entire procedure. This will give you the overall view of what tools and supplies will be required. There is nothing more frustrating than having to walk to the bus stop on Monday morning because you were short one bolt on Sunday afternoon. So read ahead and plan ahead. Each operation should be approached logically and all procedures thoroughly understood before attempting any work.

All sections contain adjustments, maintenance, removal and installation procedures, and in some cases, repair or overhaul procedures. When repair is not considered practical, we tell you how to remove the part and then how to install the new or rebuilt replacement. In this way, you at least save labor costs. "Backyard" repair of some components is just not practical.

Avoiding Trouble

Many procedures in this book require you to "label and disconnect . . ." a group of lines, hoses or wires. Don't be lulled into thinking you can remember where everything goes—you won't. If you hook up vacuum or fuel lines incorrectly, the vehicle may run poorly, if at all. If you hook up electrical wiring incorrectly, you may instantly learn a very expensive lesson.

You don't need to know the official or engineering name for each hose or line. A piece of masking tape on the hose and a piece on its fitting will allow you to assign your own label such as the letter A or a short name. As long as you remember your own code, the lines can be reconnected by matching similar letters or names. Do remember that tape will dissolve in gasoline or other fluids; if a component is to be washed or cleaned, use another method of identification. A permanent felt-tipped marker or a metal scribe can be very handy for marking metal parts. Remove any tape or paper labels after assembly.

Maintenance or Repair?

It's necessary to mention the difference between maintenance and repair. Maintenance includes routine inspections, adjustments, and replacement of parts which show signs of normal wear. Maintenance compensates for wear or deterioration. Repair implies that something has broken or is not working. A need for repair is often caused by lack of maintenance. Example: draining and refilling the automatic transmission fluid is maintenance recommended by the manufacturer at specific mileage intervals. Failure to do this can shorten the life of the transaxle, requiring very expensive repairs. While no maintenance program can prevent items from breaking or wearing out, a general rule can be stated: MAINTENANCE IS CHEAPER THAN REPAIR.

Two basic mechanic's rules should be mentioned here. First, whenever the left side of the vehicle or engine is referred to, it is meant to specify the driver's side. Conversely, the right side of the vehicle means the passenger's side. Second, screws and bolts are removed by turning counterclockwise, and tightened by turning clockwise unless specifically noted.

Safety is always the most important rule. Constantly be aware of the dangers involved in working on an automobile and take the proper precautions. See the information in this section regarding SERVICING YOUR VEHICLE SAFELY and the SAFETY NOTICE on the acknowledgment page.

Avoiding the Most Common Mistakes

Pay attention to the instructions provided. There are 3 common mistakes in mechanical work:

1. Incorrect order of assembly, disassembly or adjustment. When taking something apart or putting it together, performing steps in the wrong order usually just costs you extra time; however, it CAN break something. Read the entire procedure before beginning disassembly. Perform everything in the order in which the instructions say you should, even if you can't immediately see a reason for it. When you're taking apart something that is very intricate, you might want to draw a picture of how it looks when assembled at one point in order to make sure you get everything back in its proper position. We will supply exploded views whenever possible. When making adjustments, perform them in the proper order. One adjustment possibly will affect another.

2. Overtorquing (or undertorquing). While it is more common for overtorquing to cause damage, undertorquing may allow a fastener to vibrate loose causing serious damage. Especially when dealing with aluminum parts, pay attention to torque specifications and utilize a torque wrench in assembly. If a torque figure is not available, remember that if you are using the right tool to perform the job, you will probably not have to strain yourself to get a fastener tight enough. The pitch of most threads is so slight that the tension you put on the wrench will be multiplied many times in actual force on what you are tightening. A good example of how critical torque is can be seen in the case of spark plug installation, especially where you are putting the plug into an aluminum cylinder head. Too little torque can fail to crush the gasket, causing leakage of combustion gases and consequent overheating of the plug and engine parts. Too much torque can damage the threads or distort the plug, changing the spark gap.

There are many commercial products available for ensuring that fasteners won't come loose, even if they are not torqued just right (a very common brand is Loctite®). If you're worried about getting something together tight enough to hold, but loose enough to avoid mechanical damage during assembly, one of these products might offer substantial insurance. Before choosing a threadlocking compound, read the label on the package and make sure the product is compatible with the materials, fluids, etc. involved.

3. Crossthreading. This occurs when a part such as a bolt is screwed into a nut or casting at the wrong angle and forced. Crossthreading is more likely to occur if access is difficult. It helps to clean and lubricate fasteners, then to start threading the bolt, spark plug, etc. with your fingers. If you encounter resistance, unscrew the part and start over again at a different angle until it can be inserted and turned several times without much effort. Keep in mind that many parts, especially spark plugs, have tapered threads, so that gentle turning will automatically bring the part you're threading to the proper angle. Don't put a wrench on the part until it's been tightened a couple of turns by hand. If you suddenly encounter resistance, and the part has not seated fully, don't force it. Pull it back out to make sure it's clean and threading properly.

Be sure to take your time and be patient, and always plan ahead. Allow yourself ample time to perform repairs and maintenance. You may find maintaining your car a satisfying and enjoyable experience.

TOOLS AND EQUIPMENT

▶ **See Figures 1 thru 15**

Naturally, without the proper tools and equipment it is impossible to properly service your vehicle. It would also be virtually impossible to catalog every tool that you would need to perform all of the operations in this book. Of course, It

would be unwise for the amateur to rush out and buy an expensive set of tools on the theory that he/she may need one or more of them at some time.

The best approach is to proceed slowly, gathering a good quality set of those tools that are used most frequently. Don't be misled by the low cost of bargain tools. It is far better to spend a little more for better quality. Forged wrenches, 6 or 12-point sockets and fine tooth ratchets are by far preferable to their less expensive counterparts. As any good mechanic can tell you, there are few worse experiences than trying to work on a vehicle with bad tools. Your monetary savings will be far outweighed by frustration and mangled knuckles.

Begin accumulating those tools that are used most frequently: those associated with routine maintenance and tune-up. In addition to the normal assortment of screwdrivers and pliers, you should have the following tools:

• Wrenches/sockets and combination open end/box end wrenches in sizes from ⅛ –¾ in. or 3–19mm, as well as a ¹³⁄₁₆ in. or ⅝ in. spark plug socket (depending on plug type).

➡**If possible, buy various length socket drive extensions. Universal-joint and wobble extensions can be extremely useful, but be careful when using them, as they can change the amount of torque applied to the socket.**

• Jackstands for support.
• Oil filter wrench.

• Spout or funnel for pouring fluids.
• Grease gun for chassis lubrication (unless your vehicle is not equipped with any grease fittings—for details, please refer to information on Fluids and Lubricants, later in this section).
• Hydrometer for checking the battery (unless equipped with a sealed, maintenance-free battery).
• A container for draining oil and other fluids.
• Rags for wiping up the inevitable mess.

In addition to the above items there are several others that are not absolutely necessary, but handy to have around. These include Oil Dry• (or an equivalent oil absorbent gravel—such as cat litter) and the usual supply of lubricants, antifreeze and fluids, although these can be purchased as needed. This is a basic list for routine maintenance, but only your personal needs and desire can accurately determine your list of tools.

After performing a few projects on the vehicle, you'll be amazed at the other tools and non-tools on your workbench. Some useful household items are: a large turkey baster or siphon, empty coffee cans and ice trays (to store parts),

TCCS1200

Fig. 1 All but the most basic procedures will require an assortment of ratchets and sockets

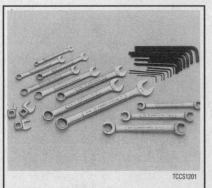

TCCS1201

Fig. 2 In addition to ratchets, a good set of wrenches and hex keys will be necessary

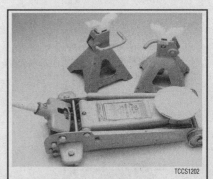

TCCS1202

Fig. 3 A hydraulic floor jack and a set of jackstands are essential for lifting and supporting the vehicle

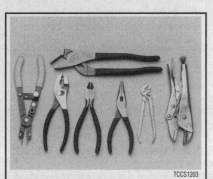

TCCS1203

Fig. 4 An assortment of pliers, grippers and cutters will be handy for old rusted parts and stripped bolt heads

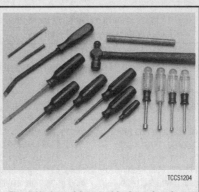

TCCS1204

Fig. 5 Various drivers, chisels and prybars are great tools to have in your toolbox

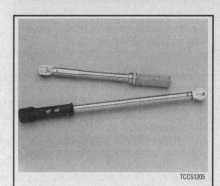

TCCS1205

Fig. 6 Many repairs will require the use of a torque wrench to assure the components are properly fastened

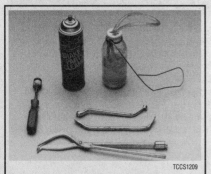

TCCS1209

Fig. 7 Although not always necessary, using specialized brake tools will save time

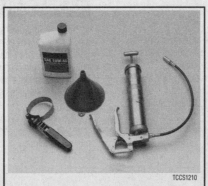

TCCS1210

Fig. 8 A few inexpensive lubrication tools will make maintenance easier

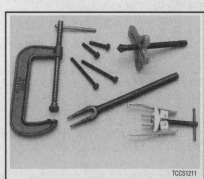

TCCS1211

Fig. 9 Various pullers, clamps and separa-tor tools are needed for many larger, more complicated repairs

Fig. 10 A variety of tools and gauges should be used for spark plug gapping and installation

TCCS1212

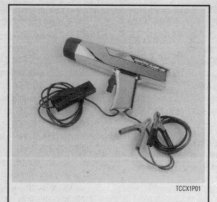

Fig. 11 Inductive type timing light

TCCX1P01

Fig. 12 A screw-in type compression gauge is recommended for compression testing

TCCX1P02

Fig. 13 A vacuum/pressure tester is necessary for many testing procedures

TCCX1P03

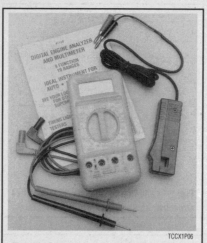

Fig. 14 Most modern automotive multimeters incorporate many helpful features

TCCX1P06

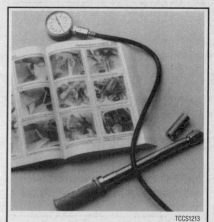

Fig. 15 Proper information is vital, so always have a Chilton Total Car Care manual handy

TCCS1213

ball of twine, electrical tape for wiring, small rolls of colored tape for tagging lines or hoses, markers and pens, a note pad, golf tees (for plugging vacuum lines), metal coat hangers or a roll of mechanic's wire (to hold things out of the way), dental pick or similar long, pointed probe, a strong magnet, and a small mirror (to see into recesses and under manifolds).

A more advanced set of tools, suitable for tune-up work, can be drawn up easily. While the tools are slightly more sophisticated, they need not be outrageously expensive. There are several inexpensive tach/dwell meters on the market that are every bit as good for the average mechanic as a professional model. Just be sure that it goes to a least 1200–1500 rpm on the tach scale and that it works on 4, 6 and 8-cylinder engines. The key to these purchases is to make them with an eye towards adaptability and wide range. A basic list of tune-up tools could include:

• Tach/dwell meter.
• Spark plug wrench and gapping tool.
• Feeler gauges for valve adjustment.
• Timing light.

The choice of a timing light should be made carefully. A light which works on the DC current supplied by the vehicle's battery is the best choice; it should have a xenon tube for brightness. On any vehicle with an electronic ignition system, a timing light with an inductive pickup that clamps around the No. 1 spark plug cable is preferred.

In addition to these basic tools, there are several other tools and gauges you may find useful. These include:

• Compression gauge. The screw-in type is slower to use, but eliminates the possibility of a faulty reading due to escaping pressure.

• Manifold vacuum gauge.
• 12V test light.
• A combination volt/ohmmeter
• Induction Ammeter. This is used for determining whether or not there is current in a wire. These are handy for use if a wire is broken somewhere in a wiring harness.

As a final note, you will probably find a torque wrench necessary for all but the most basic work. The beam type models are perfectly adequate, although the newer click types (breakaway) are easier to use. The click type torque wrenches tend to be more expensive. Also keep in mind that all types of torque wrenches should be periodically checked and/or recalibrated. You will have to decide for yourself which better fits your pocketbook, and purpose.

Special Tools

Normally, the use of special factory tools is avoided for repair procedures, since these are not readily available for the do-it-yourself mechanic. When it is possible to perform the job with more commonly available tools, it will be pointed out, but occasionally, a special tool was designed to perform a specific function and should be used. Before substituting another tool, you should be convinced that neither your safety nor the performance of the vehicle will be compromised.

Special tools can usually be purchased from an automotive parts store or from your dealer. In some cases special tools may be available directly from the tool manufacturer.

SERVICING YOUR VEHICLE SAFELY

▶ See Figures 16, 17, 18 and 19

It is virtually impossible to anticipate all of the hazards involved with automotive maintenance and service, but care and common sense will prevent most accidents.

The rules of safety for mechanics range from "don't smoke around gasoline," to "use the proper tool(s) for the job." The trick to avoiding injuries is to develop safe work habits and to take every possible precaution.

Do's

• Do keep a fire extinguisher and first aid kit handy.

• Do wear safety glasses or goggles when cutting, drilling, grinding or prying, even if you have 20–20 vision. If you wear glasses for the sake of vision, wear safety goggles over your regular glasses.

• Do shield your eyes whenever you work around the battery. Batteries contain sulfuric acid. In case of contact with the eyes or skin, flush the area with water or a mixture of water and baking soda, then seek immediate medical attention.

• Do use safety stands (jackstands) for any undervehicle service. Jacks are for raising vehicles; jackstands are for making sure the vehicle stays raised until you want it to come down. Whenever the vehicle is raised, block the wheels remaining on the ground and set the parking brake.

• Do use adequate ventilation when working with any chemicals or hazardous materials. Like carbon monoxide, the asbestos dust resulting from some brake lining wear can be hazardous in sufficient quantities.

• Do disconnect the negative battery cable when working on the electrical system. The secondary ignition system contains EXTREMELY HIGH VOLTAGE. In some cases it can even exceed 50,000 volts.

• Do follow manufacturer's directions whenever working with potentially hazardous materials. Most chemicals and fluids are poisonous if taken internally.

• Do properly maintain your tools. Loose hammerheads, mushroomed punches and chisels, frayed or poorly grounded electrical cords, excessively worn screwdrivers, spread wrenches (open end), cracked sockets, slipping ratchets, or faulty droplight sockets can cause accidents.

• Likewise, keep your tools clean; a greasy wrench can slip off a bolt head, ruining the bolt and often harming your knuckles in the process.

• Do use the proper size and type of tool for the job at hand. Do select a wrench or socket that fits the nut or bolt. The wrench or socket should sit straight, not cocked.

• Do, when possible, pull on a wrench handle rather than push on it, and adjto prevent a fall.

• Do be sure that adjustable wrenches are tightly closed on the nut or bolt and pulled so that the force is on the side of the fixed jaw.

• Do strike squarely with a hammer; avoid glancing blows.

• Do set the parking brake and block the drive wheels if the work requires a running engine.

Don'ts

• Don't run the engine in a garage or anywhere else without proper ventilation—EVER! Carbon monoxide is poisonous; it takes a long time to leave the human body and you can build up a deadly supply of it in your system by simply breathing in a little every day. You may not realize you are slowly poisoning yourself. Always use power vents, windows, fans and/or open the garage door.

• Don't work around moving parts while wearing loose clothing. Short sleeves are much safer than long, loose sleeves. Hard-toed shoes with neoprene soles protect your toes and give a better grip on slippery surfaces. Jewelry such as watches, fancy belt buckles, beads or body adornment of any kind is not safe working around a vehicle. Long hair should be tied back under a hat or cap.

• Don't use pockets for toolboxes. A fall or bump can drive a screwdriver deep into your body. Even a rag hanging from your back pocket can wrap around a spinning shaft or fan.

• Don't smoke when working around gasoline, cleaning solvent or other flammable material.

• Don't smoke when working around the battery. When the battery is being charged, it gives off explosive hydrogen gas.

• Don't use gasoline to wash your hands; there are excellent soaps available. Gasoline contains dangerous additives which can enter the body through a cut or through your pores. Gasoline also removes all the natural oils from the skin so that bone dry hands will suck up oil and grease.

• Don't service the air conditioning system unless you are equipped with the necessary tools and training. When liquid or compressed gas refrigerant is released to atmospheric pressure it will absorb heat from whatever it contacts. This will chill or freeze anything it touches.

• Don't use screwdrivers for anything other than driving screws! A screwdriver used as an prying tool can snap when you least expect it, causing injuries. At the very least, you'll ruin a good screwdriver.

• Don't use an emergency jack (that little ratchet, scissors, or pantograph jack supplied with the vehicle) for anything other than changing a flat! These jacks are only intended for emergency use out on the road; they are NOT designed as a maintenance tool. If you are serious about maintaining your vehicle yourself, invest in a hydraulic floor jack of at least a 1½ ton capacity, and at least two sturdy jackstands.

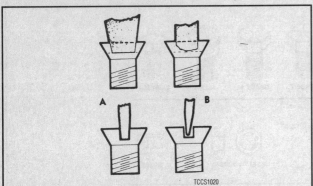

Fig. 16 Screwdrivers should be kept in good condition to prevent injury or damage which could result if the blade slips from the screw

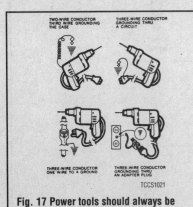

Fig. 17 Power tools should always be properly grounded

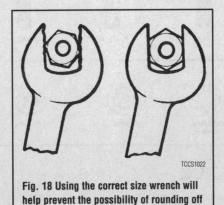

Fig. 18 Using the correct size wrench will help prevent the possibility of rounding off a nut

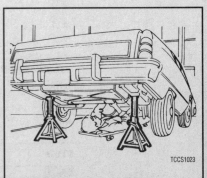

Fig. 19 NEVER work under a vehicle unless it is supported using safety stands (jackstands)

FASTENERS, MEASUREMENTS AND CONVERSIONS

Bolts, Nuts and Other Threaded Retainers

▶ **See Figures 20, 21, 22, 23 and 24**

Although there are a great variety of fasteners found in the modern car or truck, the most commonly used retainer is the threaded fastener (nuts, bolts, screws, studs, etc.). Most threaded retainers may be reused, provided that they are not damaged in use or during the repair. Some retainers (such as stretch bolts or torque prevailing nuts) are designed to deform when tightened or in use and should not be reinstalled.

Whenever possible, we will note any special retainers which should be replaced during a procedure. But you should always inspect the condition of a

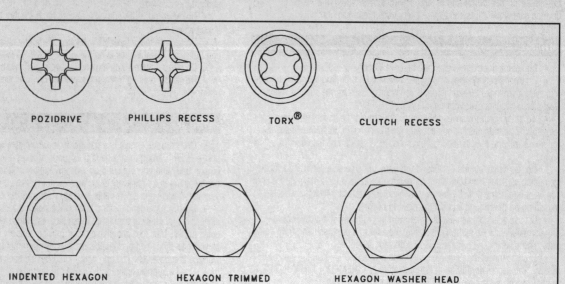

Fig. 20 Here are a few of the most common screw/bolt driver styles

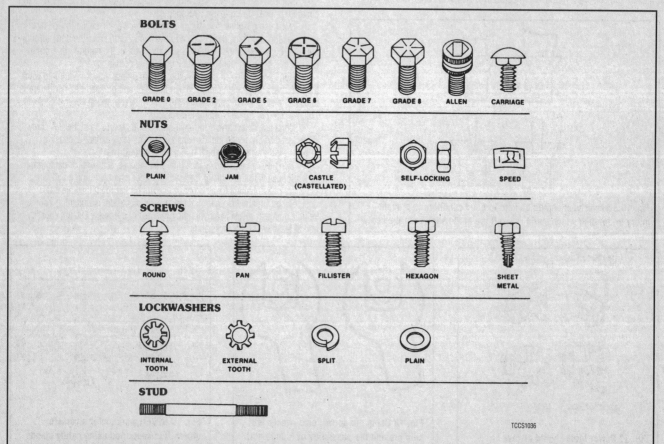

Fig. 21 There are many different types of threaded retainers found on vehicles

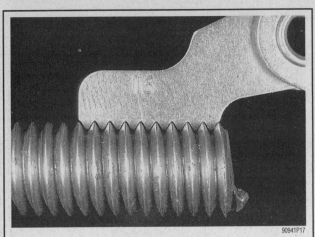

Fig. 22 A thread pitch gauge will allow precise measurement of most bolts

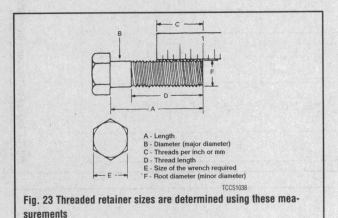

A - Length
B - Diameter (major diameter)
C - Threads per inch or mm
D - Thread length
E - Size of the wrench required
F - Root diameter (minor diameter)

TCCS1038

Fig. 23 Threaded retainer sizes are determined using these measurements

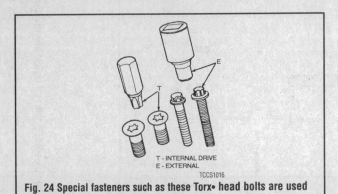

T - INTERNAL DRIVE
E - EXTERNAL

TCCS1016

Fig. 24 Special fasteners such as these Torx• head bolts are used by manufacturers to discourage people from working on vehicles without the proper tools

retainer when it is removed and replace any that show signs of damage. Check all threads for rust or corrosion which can increase the torque necessary to achieve the desired clamp load for which that fastener was originally selected. Additionally, be sure that the driver surface of the fastener has not been compromised by rounding or other damage. In some cases a driver surface may become only partially rounded, allowing the driver to catch in only one direction. In many of these occurrences, a fastener may be installed and tightened, but the driver would not be able to grip and loosen the fastener again. (This could lead to frustration down the line should that component ever need to be disassembled again).

If you must replace a fastener, whether due to design or damage, you must ALWAYS be sure acement. In all cases, a retainer of the same design, material and strength should be used. Markings on the heads of most bolts will help determine the proper strength of the fastener. The same material, thread and

pitch must be selected to assure proper installation and safe operation of the vehicle afterwards.

Thread gauges are available to help measure a bolt or stud's thread. Most automotive and hardware stores keep gauges available to help you select the proper size. In a pinch, you can use another nut or bolt for a thread gauge. If the bolt you are replacing is not too badly damaged, you can select a match by finding another bolt which will thread in its place. If you find a nut which threads properly onto the damaged bolt, then use that nut to help select the replacement bolt. If however, the bolt you are replacing is so badly damaged (broken or drilled out) that its threads cannot be used as a gauge, you might start by looking for another bolt (from the same assembly or a similar location on your vehicle) which will thread into the damaged bolt's mounting. If so, the other bolt can be used to select a nut; the nut can then be used to select the replacement bolt.

In all cases, be absolutely sure you have selected the proper replacement. Don't be shy, you can always ask the store clerk for help.

✳✳ WARNING

Be aware that when you find a bolt with damaged threads, you may also find the nut or drilled hole it was threaded into has also been damaged. If this is the case, you may have to drill and tap the hole, replace the nut or otherwise repair the threads. NEVER try to force a replacement bolt to fit into the damaged threads.

Torque

Torque is defined as the measurement of resistance to turning or rotating. It tends to twist a body about an axis of rotation. A common example of this would be tightening a threaded retainer such as a nut, bolt or screw. Measuring torque is one of the most common ways to help assure that a threaded retainer has been properly fastened.

When tightening a threaded fastener, torque is applied in three distinct areas, the head, the bearing surface and the clamp load. About 50 percent of the measured torque is used in overcoming bearing friction. This is the friction between the bearing surface of the bolt head, screw head or nut face and the base material or washer (the surface on which the fastener is rotating). Approximately 40 percent of the applied torque is used in overcoming thread friction. This leaves only about 10 percent of the applied torque to develop a useful clamp load (the force which holds a joint together). This means that friction can account for as much as 90 percent of the applied torque on a fastener.

TORQUE WRENCHES

▶ **See Figures 25, 26 and 27**

In most applications, a torque wrench can be used to assure proper installation of a fastener. Torque wrenches come in various designs and most automotive supply stores will carry a variety to suit your needs. A torque wrench should be used any time we supply a specific torque value for a fastener. A torque wrench can also be used if you are following the general guidelines in the accompanying charts. Keep in mind that because there is no worldwide standardization of fasteners, the charts are a general guideline and should be used

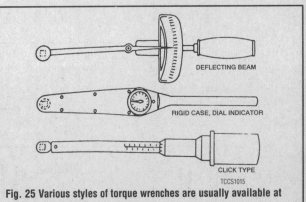

DEFLECTING BEAM

RIGID CASE, DIAL INDICATOR

CLICK TYPE

TCCS1015

Fig. 25 Various styles of torque wrenches are usually available at your local automotive supply store

Class	Diameter mm	Pitch mm	Hexagon head bolt			Hexagon flange bolt		
			N·m	kgf·cm	ft-lbf	N·m	kgf·cm	ft-lbf
4T	6	1	5	55	48 in.-lbf	6	60	52 in.-lbf
	8	1.25	12.5	130	9	14	145	10
	10	1.25	26	260	19	29	290	21
	12	1.25	47	480	35	53	540	39
	14	1.5	74	760	55	84	850	61
	16	1.5	115	1,150	83	—	—	—
5T	6	1	6.5	65	56 in.-lbf	7.5	75	65 in.-lbf
	8	1.25	15.5	160	12	17.5	175	13
	10	1.25	32	330	24	36	360	26
	12	1.25	59	600	43	65	670	48
	14	1.5	91	930	67	100	1,050	76
	16	1.5	140	1,400	101	—	—	—
6T	6	1	8	80	69 in.-lbf	9	90	78 in.-lbf
	8	1.25	19	195	14	21	210	15
	10	1.25	39	400	29	44	440	32
	12	1.25	71	730	53	80	810	59
	14	1.5	110	1,100	80	125	1,250	90
	16	1.5	170	1,750	127	—	—	—
7T	6	1	10.5	110	8	12	120	9
	8	1.25	25	260	19	28	290	21
	10	1.25	52	530	38	58	590	43
	12	1.25	95	970	70	105	1,050	76
	14	1.5	145	1,500	108	165	1,700	123
	16	1.5	230	2,300	166	—	—	—
8T	8	1.25	29	300	22	33	330	24
	10	1.25	61	620	45	68	690	50
	12	1.25	110	1,100	80	120	1,250	90
9T	8	1.25	34	340	25	37	380	27
	10	1.25	70	710	51	78	790	57
	12	1.25	125	1,300	94	140	1,450	105
10T	8	1.25	38	390	28	42	430	31
	10	1.25	78	800	58	88	890	64
	12	1.25	140	1,450	105	155	1,600	116
11T	8	1.25	42	430	31	47	480	35
	10	1.25	87	890	64	97	990	72
	12	1.25	155	1,600	116	175	1,800	130

Specified torque

TCCS1241

Fig. 27 Typical bolt torques for metric fasteners—WARNING: use only as a guide

	Mark	Class
Hexagon head bolt	Bolt head No. 4, 5, 6, 7, 8, 9, 10, 11	4T, 5T, 6T, 7T, 8T, 9T, 10T, 11T
Hexagon flange bolt w/ washer hexagon bolt	No mark	4T
Hexagon head bolt	No mark	4T
Hexagon flange bolt w/ washer hexagon bolt	Two protruding lines	5T
Hexagon head bolt	Two protruding lines	6T
Hexagon head bolt	Three protruding lines	7T
Hexagon head bolt	Four protruding lines	8T

	Mark	Class
Stud bolt	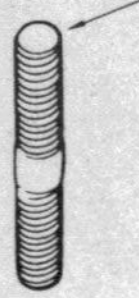 No mark	4T
	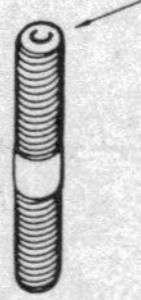 Grooved	6T
Welded bolt	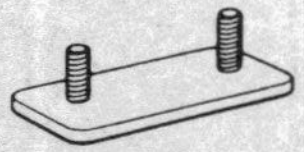	4T

TCCS1240

Fig. 26 Determining bolt strength of metric fasteners—NOTE: this is a typical bolt marking system, but there is not a worldwide standard

with caution. Again, the general rule of "if you are using the right tool for the job, you should not have to strain to tighten a fastener" applies here.

Beam Type

▶ **See Figure 28**

The beam type torque wrench is one of the most popular types. It consists of a pointer attached to the head that runs the length of the flexible beam (shaft) to a scale located near the handle. As the wrench is pulled, the beam bends and the pointer indicates the torque using the scale.

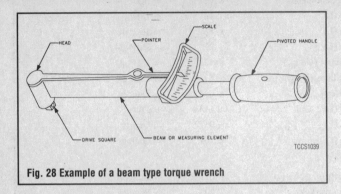

Fig. 28 Example of a beam type torque wrench

Click (Breakaway) Type

▶ **See Figure 29**

Another popular design of torque wrench is the click type. To use the click type wrench you pre-adjust it to a torque setting. Once the torque is reached, the wrench has a reflex signaling feature that causes a momentary breakaway of the torque wrench body, sending an impulse to the operator's hand.

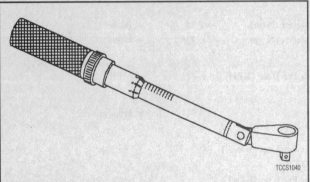

Fig. 29 A click type or breakaway torque wrench—note that this one has a pivoting head

Pivot Head Type

▶ **See Figures 29 and 30**

Some torque wrenches (usually of the click type) may be equipped with a pivot head which can allow it to be used in areas of limited access. BUT, it must be used properly. To hold a pivot head wrench, grasp the handle lightly, and as you pull on the handle, it should be floated on the pivot point. If the handle comes in contact with the yoke extension during the process of pulling, there is a very good chance the torque readings will be inaccurate because this could alter the wrench loading point. The design of the handle is usually such as to make it inconvenient to deliberately misuse the wrench.

➡ It should be mentioned that the use of any U-joint, wobble or extension will have an effect on the torque readings, no matter what type of wrench you are using. For the most accurate readings, install the socket directly on the wrench driver. If necessary, straight extensions (which hold a socket directly under the wrench driver) will have the least effect on the torque reading. Avoid any extension that alters the length of the wrench from the handle to the head/driving point (such as a crow's foot). U-joint or wobble extensions can greatly affect the readings; avoid their use at all times.

Rigid Case (Direct Reading)

▶ **See Figure 31**

A rigid case or direct reading torque wrench is equipped with a dial indicator to show torque values. One advantage of these wrenches is that they can be held at any position on the wrench without affecting accuracy. These wrenches are often preferred because they tend to be compact, easy to read and have a great degree of accuracy.

TORQUE ANGLE METERS

▶ **See Figure 32**

Because the frictional characteristics of each fastener or threaded hole will vary, clamp loads which are based strictly on torque will vary as well. In most applications, this variance is not significant enough to cause worry. But, in certain applications, a manufacturer's engineers may determine that more precise clamp loads are necessary (such is the case with many aluminum cylinder heads). In these cases, a torque angle method of installation would be specified. When installing fasteners which are torque angle tightened, a predetermined seating torque and standard torque wrench are usually used first to remove any compliance from the joint. The fastener is then tightened the specified additional portion of a turn measured in degrees. A torque angle gauge (mechanical protractor) is used for these applications.

Standard and Metric Measurements

▶ **See Figure 33**

Throughout this manual, specifications are given to help you determine the condition of various components on your vehicle, or to assist you in their installation. Some of the most common measurements include length (in. or

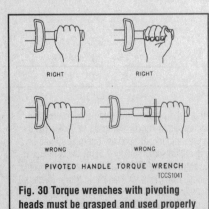

Fig. 30 Torque wrenches with pivoting heads must be grasped and used properly to prevent an incorrect reading

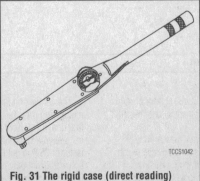

Fig. 31 The rigid case (direct reading) torque wrench uses a dial indicator to show torque

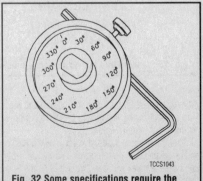

Fig. 32 Some specifications require the use of a torque angle meter (mechanical protractor)

CONVERSION FACTORS

LENGTH–DISTANCE

Inches (in.)	x 25.4	= Millimeters (mm)	x .0394	= Inches
Feet (ft.)	x .305	= Meters (m)	x 3.281	= Feet
Miles	x 1.609	= Kilometers (km)	x .0621	= Miles

VOLUME

Cubic Inches (in3)	x 16.387	= Cubic Centimeters	x .061	= in3
IMP Pints (IMP pt.)	x .568	= Liters (L)	x 1.76	= IMP pt.
IMP Quarts (IMP qt.)	x 1.137	= Liters (L)	x .88	= IMP qt.
IMP Gallons (IMP gal.)	x 4.546	= Liters (L)	x .22	= IMP gal.
IMP Quarts (IMP qt.)	x 1.201	= US Quarts (US qt.)	x .833	= IMP qt.
IMP Gallons (IMP gal.)	x 1.201	= US Gallons (US gal.)	x .833	= IMP gal.
Fl. Ounces	x 29.573	= Milliliters	x .034	= Ounces
US Pints (US pt.)	x .473	= Liters (L)	x 2.113	= Pints
US Quarts (US qt.)	x .946	= Liters (L)	x 1.057	= Quarts
US Gallons (US gal.)	x 3.785	= Liters (L)	x .264	= Gallons

MASS–WEIGHT

Ounces (oz.)	x 28.35	= Grams (g)	x .035	= Ounces
Pounds (lb.)	x .454	= Kilograms (kg)	x 2.205	= Pounds

PRESSURE

Pounds Per Sq. In. (psi)	x 6.895	= Kilopascals (kPa)	x .145	= psi
Inches of Mercury (Hg)	x .4912	= psi	x 2.036	= Hg
Inches of Mercury (Hg)	x 3.377	= Kilopascals (kPa)	x .2961	= Hg
Inches of Water (H_2O)	x .07355	= Inches of Mercury	x 13.783	= H_2O
Inches of Water (H_2O)	x .03613	= psi	x 27.684	= H_2O
Inches of Water (H_2O)	x .248	= Kilopascals (kPa)	x 4.026	= H_2O

TORQUE

Pounds–Force Inches (in–lb)	x .113	= Newton Meters (N·m)	x 8.85	= in–lb
Pounds–Force Feet (ft–lb)	x 1.356	= Newton Meters (N·m)	x .738	= ft–lb

VELOCITY

Miles Per Hour (MPH)	x 1.609	= Kilometers Per Hour (KPH)	x .621	= MPH

POWER

Horsepower (Hp)	x .745	= Kilowatts	x 1.34	= Horsepower

FUEL CONSUMPTION*

Miles Per Gallon IMP (MPG)	x .354	= Kilometers Per Liter (Km/L)
Kilometers Per Liter (Km/L)	x 2.352	= IMP MPG
Miles Per Gallon US (MPG)	x .425	= Kilometers Per Liter (Km/L)
Kilometers Per Liter (Km/L)	x 2.352	= US MPG

*It is common to covert from miles per gallon (mpg) to liters/100 kilometers (1/100 km), where mpg (IMP) x 1/100 km = 282 and mpg (US) x 1/100 km = 235.

TEMPERATURE

Degree Fahrenheit (°F)	= (°C x 1.8) + 32
Degree Celsius (°C)	= (°F – 32) x .56

TCCS1044

Fig. 33 Standard and metric conversion factors chart

cm/mm), torque (ft. lbs., inch lbs. or Nm) and pressure (psi, in. Hg, kPa or mm Hg). In most cases, we strive to provide the proper measurement as determined by the manufacturer's engineers.

Though, in some cases, that value may not be conveniently measured with what is available in your toolbox. Luckily, many of the measuring devices which are available today will have two scales so the Standard or Metric measurements may easily be taken. If any of the various measuring tools which are available to you do not contain the same scale as listed in the specifications, use the accompanying conversion factors to determine the proper value.

The conversion factor chart is used by taking the given specification and multiplying it by the necessary conversion factor. For instance, looking at the first line, if you have a measurement in inches such as "free-play should be 2 in." but your ruler reads only in millimeters, multiply 2 in. by the conversion factor of 25.4 to get the metric equivalent of 50.8mm. Likewise, if the specification was given only in a Metric measurement, for example in Newton Meters (Nm), then look at the center column first. If the measurement is 100 Nm, multiply it by the conversion factor of 0.738 to get 73.8 ft. lbs.

SERIAL NUMBER IDENTIFICATION

Vehicle

♦ **See Figures 34, 35 and 36**

The Vehicle Identification Number (VIN) is located on the instrument panel, close to the windshield on the driver's side of the vehicle. It is visible from outside the vehicle.

Fig. 34 Besides the dashboard, the VIN can also be found on a label under the hood or in the driver's side door jam

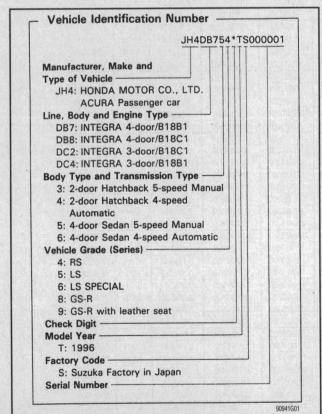

Fig. 35 Vehicle Identification Number (VIN) breakdown—U.S. model shown

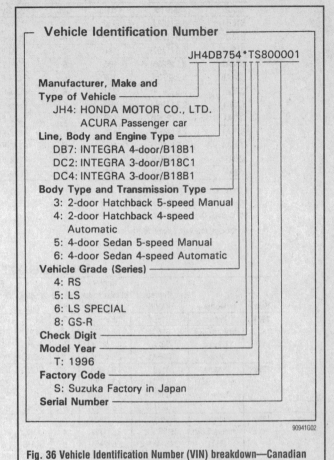

Fig. 36 Vehicle Identification Number (VIN) breakdown—Canadian model shown

The 17-character label contains the following information:
- Digits 1, 2 and 3: Type of Vehicle
- Digits 4, 5 and 6: Line, Body and Engine Type
- Digit 7: Body Type and Transmission Type
- Digit 8: Vehicle Grade (Series)
- Digit 9: Check digit
- Digit 10: Vehicle model year
- Digit 11: Factory Code
- Digits 12 through 17: Serial Number

Engine

♦ **See Figures 37, 38, 39 and 40**

The engine identification code is contained within the VIN as the 8th digit and identifies the engine type, displacement and fuel system. The VIN can be found on the instrument panel. See the Engine Identification chart for engine VIN codes.

The engine serial number is stamped on the clutch casing on all vehicles. This number is also stamped onto the Vehicle/Engine Identification plate mounted on the hood bracket.

VEHICLE IDENTIFICATION CHART

	Engine Code						Model Year	
Code	Liters (cc)	Cu. In.	Cyl.	Fuel Sys.	Eng. Mfg.		Code ①	Year
B18B1	1.8 (1834)	112	4	PGM-FI	Honda		R	1994
B18C1	1.8 (1797)	110	4	PGM-FI	Honda		S	1995
B18C5	1.8 (1797)	110	4	PGM-FI	Honda		T	1996
C32A1	3.2 (3206)	196	6	PGM-FI	Honda		V	1997
C32A6	3.2 (3206)	196	6	PGM-FI	Honda		W	1998
C35A1	3.5 (3474)	211	6	PGM-FI	Honda		X	1999
F22B1	2.2 (2156)	132	4	PGM-FI	Honda		Y	2000
F23A1	2.3 (2254)	138	4	PGM-FI	Honda			
G25A1	2.5 (2451)	150	5	PGM-FI	Honda			
G25A4	2.5 (2451)	150	5	PGM-FI	Honda			
J30A1	3.0 (2997)	183	6	PGM-FI	Honda			
J32A1	3.2 (3210)	196	6	PGM-FI	Honda			

PGM-FI - Programmed Fuel Injection
DOHC- Double Overhead Camshaft
SOHC- Single Overhead Camshaft

① 10th digit of the Vehicle Identification Number (VIN)

90941C01

GENERAL ENGINE SPECIFICATIONS

Year	Model	Engine ID/VIN	Engine Displacement Liters (cc)	No. of Cyl.	Engine Type	Fuel System Type	Net Horsepower @ rpm	Net Torque @ rpm (ft. lbs.)	Bore x Stroke (in.)	Compression Ratio	Oil Pressure @ rpm
1994	Integra	B18B1	1.8 (1834)	4	DOHC	PGM-FI	142@6300	127@5000	3.19x3.50	9.2:1	50@3000
	Integra GSR	B18C1	1.8 (1797)	4	DOHC	PGM-FI	170@7600	128@6200	3.19x3.43	10.0:1	50@3000
	Legend	C32A1	3.2 (3206)	6	SOHC	PGM-FI	200@5500	210@4500	3.54x3.31	9.6:1	50@3000
	Vigor	G25A1	2.5 (2451)	5	SOHC	PGM-FI	176@6300	170@3900	3.35x3.40	9.0:1	50@3000
1995	Integra	B18B1	1.8 (1834)	4	DOHC	PGM-FI	142@6300	127@5000	3.19x3.50	9.2:1	50@3000
	Integra GSR	B18C1	1.8 (1797)	4	DOHC	PGM-FI	170@7600	128@6200	3.19x3.43	10.0:1	50@3000
	Legend	C32A1	3.2 (3206)	6	SOHC	PGM-FI	200@5500	210@4500	3.54x3.31	9.6:1	50@3000
	Vigor	G25A1	2.5 (2451)	5	SOHC	PGM-FI	176@6300	170@3900	3.35x3.40	9.0:1	50@3000
1996	Integra	B18B1/①	1.8 (1834)	4	DOHC	PGM-FI	140@6300	127@5200	3.19x3.50	9.2:1	50@3000
	Integra GSR	B18C1/②	1.8 (1797)	4	DOHC	PGM-FI	170@7600	128@6200	3.19x3.43	10.0:1	50@3000
	2.5TL	G25A4/UA2	2.5 (2451)	5	SOHC	PGM-FI	176@6300	170@3900	3.35x3.40	9.6:1	50@3000
	3.2TL	C32A6/UA3	3.2 (3206)	6	SOHC	PGM-FI	200@5300	210@4500	3.54x3.31	9.6:1	50@3000
	3.5RL	C35A1/KA9	3.5 (3474)	6	SOHC	PGM-FI	210@5200	224@2800	3.54x3.58	9.6:1	50@3000
1997	Integra	B18B1/①	1.8 (1834)	4	DOHC	PGM-FI	140@6300	127@5200	3.19x3.50	9.2:1	50@3000
	Integra GSR	B18C1/②	1.8 (1797)	4	DOHC	PGM-FI	170@7600	128@6200	3.19x3.43	10.0:1	50@3000
	Integra Type R	B18C5/②	1.8 (1797)	4	DOHC	PGM-FI	195@8000	130@7500	3.19x3.43	10.6:1	50@3000
	2.2CL	F22B1/YA1	2.2 (2156)	4	SOHC	PGM-FI	145@5500	147@4500	3.35x3.74	8.8:1	50@3000
	2.5TL	G25A4/UA2	2.5 (2451)	5	SOHC	PGM-FI	176@6300	170@3900	3.35x3.40	9.6:1	50@3000
	3.0CL	J30A1/YA2	3.0 (2997)	6	SOHC	PGM-FI	200@5000	195@4800	3.39x3.39	9.4:1	71@3000
	3.2TL	C32A6/UA3	3.2 (3206)	6	SOHC	PGM-FI	200@5300	210@4500	3.35x3.40	9.6:1	50@3000
	3.5RL	C35A1/KA9	3.5 (3474)	6	SOHC	PGM-FI	210@5200	224@2800	3.54x3.58	9.6:1	50@3000
1998	Integra	B18B1/①	1.8 (1834)	4	DOHC	PGM-FI	140@6300	127@5200	3.19x3.50	9.2:1	50@3000
	Integra GSR	B18C1/②	1.8 (1797)	4	DOHC	PGM-FI	170@7600	128@6200	3.19x3.43	10.0:1	50@3000
	Integra Type R	B18C5/②	1.8 (1797)	4	DOHC	PGM-FI	195@8000	130@7500	3.19x3.43	10.6:1	50@3000
	2.3CL	F23A1/YA3	2.3 (2254)	4	SOHC	PGM-FI	150@5700	152@4800	3.39x3.82	9.3:1	50@3000
	2.5TL	G25A4/UA2	2.5 (2451)	5	SOHC	PGM-FI	176@6300	170@3900	3.35x3.40	9.6:1	50@3000
	3.0CL	J30A1/YA2	3.0 (2997)	6	SOHC	PGM-FI	200@5000	195@4800	3.39x3.39	9.4:1	71@3000
	3.2TL	C32A6/UA3	3.2 (3206)	6	SOHC	PGM-FI	200@5300	210@4500	3.35x3.40	9.6:1	50@3000
	3.5RL	C35A1/KA9	3.5 (3474)	6	SOHC	PGM-FI	210@5200	224@2800	3.54x3.58	9.6:1	50@3000
1999	Integra	B18B1/①	1.8 (1834)	4	DOHC	PGM-FI	140@6300	127@5200	3.19x3.50	9.2:1	50@3000
	Integra GSR	B18C1/②	1.8 (1797)	4	DOHC	PGM-FI	170@7600	128@6200	3.19x3.43	10.0:1	50@3000
	2.3CL	F23A1/YA3	2.3 (2254)	4	SOHC	PGM-FI	150@5700	152@4800	3.39x3.82	9.3:1	50@3000
	3.0CL	J30A1/YA2	3.0 (2997)	6	SOHC	PGM-FI	200@5600	195@4800	3.39x3.39	9.4:1	71@3000
	3.2TL	J32A1/UA5	3.2 (3210)	6	SOHC	PGM-FI	225@5500	216@5000	3.50x3.39	9.8:1	71@3000
	3.5RL	C35A1/KA9	3.5 (3474)	6	SOHC	PGM-FI	210@5200	224@2800	3.54x3.58	9.6:1	50@3000
2000	Integra	B18B1/①	1.8 (1834)	4	DOHC	PGM-FI	140@6300	127@5200	3.19x3.50	9.2:1	50@3000
	Integra GSR	B18C1/②	1.8 (1797)	4	DOHC	PGM-FI	170@7600	128@6200	3.19x3.43	10.0:1	50@3000
	Integra Type R	B18C5/②	1.8 (1797)	4	DOHC	PGM-FI	195@8000	130@7500	3.19x3.43	10.6:1	50@3000
	2.3CL	F23A1/YA3	2.3 (2254)	4	SOHC	PGM-FI	150@5700	152@4800	3.39x3.82	9.3:1	50@3000
	3.0CL	J30A1/YA2	3.0 (2997)	6	SOHC	PGM-FI	200@5600	195@4800	3.39x3.39	9.4:1	71@3000
	3.2TL	J32A1/UA5	3.2 (3210)	6	SOHC	PGM-FI	225@5500	216@5000	3.50x3.39	9.8:1	71@3000
	3.5RL	C35A1/KA9	3.5 (3474)	6	SOHC	PGM-FI	210@5200	224@2800	3.54x3.58	9.6:1	50@3000

PGM-FI - Programmed Fuel Injection

① DB7: 4 door   ② DB8: 4 door (Except Type R)
  DC4: 3 door   DC2: 3 door

90941C02

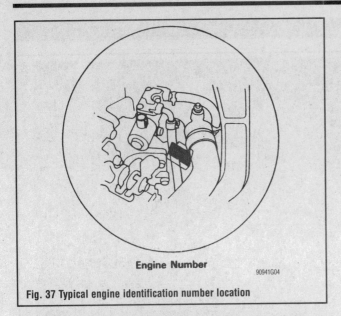

Engine Number

90941G04

Fig. 37 Typical engine identification number location

90941P82

Fig. 38 The engine identification number can be found stamped into the engine casting

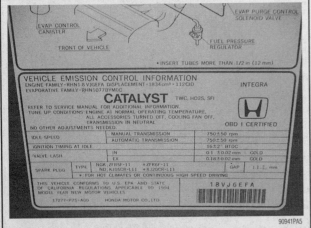

90941PA5

Fig. 39 For vehicle emissions control information consult the catalyst label

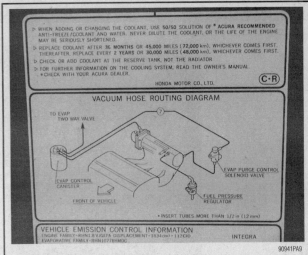

90941PA9

Fig. 40 For vacuum hose routing information you can reference a diagram such as the one shown here

Transaxle

MANUAL

The manual transaxle identification number is found in several locations depending on the model, engine, and transmission type. On Legend and Vigor models, this number is located on the right side of the bellhousing, not far from the firewall. On all other models, including the Integra, the identification number is found on the bell housing, opposite the starter motor.

AUTOMATIC

▶ **See Figure 41**

On all models, except the Legend and Vigor, the automatic transaxle identification number can be found on the right front of the transaxle housing, close to the dipstick. The Legend and Vigor's identification number is found on the right hand side of the bellhousing.

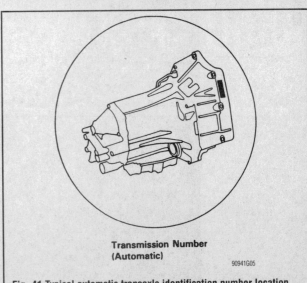

Transmission Number (Automatic)

90941G05

Fig. 41 Typical automatic transaxle identification number location

ROUTINE MAINTENANCE AND TUNE-UP

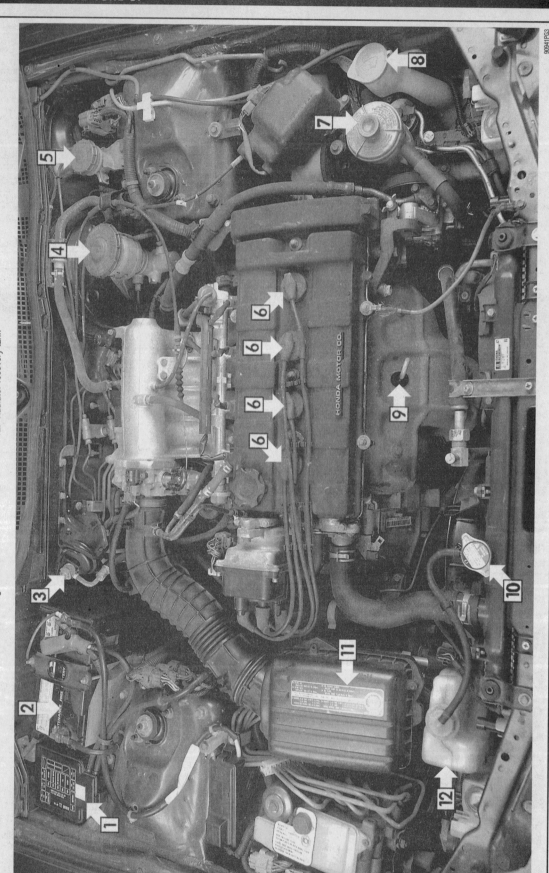

MAINTENANCE COMPONENT LOCATIONS—INTEGRA

1. Fuse box
2. Battery
3. Fuel filter
4. Brake master cylinder
5. Clutch master cylinder
6. Ignition wires
7. Power steering pump reservoir
8. Windshield washer fluid
9. Oil dipstick
10. Radiator cap
11. Air filter box
12. Radiator recovery tank

MAINTENANCE COMPONENT LOCATIONS—3.2TL

1. Fuse box
2. Brake master cylinder
3. Air filter box
4. Battery
5. Oil filler cap
6. Oil dipstick
7. Power steering pump reservoir
8. Windshield washer fluid
9. Radiator cap
10. Radiator recovery tank

Proper maintenance and tune-up is the key to long and trouble-free vehicle life, and the work can yield its own rewards. Studies have shown that a properly tuned and maintained vehicle can achieve better gas mileage than an out-of-tune vehicle. As a conscientious owner and driver, set aside a Saturday morning, say once a month, to check or replace items which could cause major problems later. Keep your own personal log to jot down which services you performed, how much the parts cost you, the date, and the exact odometer reading at the time. Keep all receipts for such items as engine oil and filters, so that they may be referred to in case of related problems or to determine operating expenses. As a do-it-yourselfer, these receipts are the only proof you have that the required maintenance was performed. In the event of a warranty problem, these receipts will be invaluable.

The literature provided with your vehicle when it was originally delivered includes the factory recommended maintenance schedule. If you no longer have this literature, replacement copies are usually available from the dealer. A maintenance schedule is provided later in this section, in case you do not have the factory literature.

Air Cleaner (Element)

REMOVAL & INSTALLATION

▶ See Figures 42, 43 and 44

The air cleaner on all Acura models is located in a housing at the front of the vehicle. The recommended change interval for the air filter is 30,000 miles (48,000 km) under normal circumstances; severe service requires more frequent changes.

Fig. 42 Gently lift up on the air box cover to gain access to the filter

Fig. 43 Lift the air filter element from the air box

Fig. 44 Detach the air filter from the air intake tube

1. Unscrew the bolts and/or spring clips from the air cleaner cover.
2. Remove the air cleaner cover and the air cleaner element. If necessary, disconnect the air intake tube from the air cleaner element.
3. Using a clean rag, wipe out the air cleaner housing.

To install:
4. Install the new air cleaner element. If removed, connect the air intake tube.
5. Install the air cleaner cover and any remaining bolts and/or fasteners.

Fuel Filter

The recommended change interval for the fuel filter on all models is 60,000 miles (96,000 km) under normal service. Severe service will require more frequent changing of the fuel filter.

✳✳ CAUTION

Observe all applicable safety precautions when working around fuel. Whenever servicing the fuel system, always work in a well ventilated area. Do not allow fuel spray or vapors to come in contact with a spark or open flame. Keep a dry chemical fire extinguisher near the work area. Always keep fuel in a container

specifically designed for fuel storage; also, always properly seal fuel containers to avoid the possibility of fire or explosion.

REMOVAL & INSTALLATION

▶ See Figure 45

➡**Many Acura models are equipped with a theft deterrent audio system. Make sure you have the necessary code before disconnecting the battery.**

1. Disconnect the negative battery cable.
2. Properly relieve the fuel system pressure.

➡**On 2.2L and 3.0L engines you may have to remove the engine wire harness bracket and power steering feed hose clamp.**

3. Wrap a shop towel around the fittings and, using a proper flare nut wrench, slowly loosen the fuel line fittings.
4. Remove the banjo bolts from the fuel lines.
5. Remove the fuel filter clamp retaining bolt and the clamp.
6. Remove the filter from the vehicle.

➡**A through cleaning of the high pressure hoses is recommended before installation.**

To install:

✳✳ CAUTION

It is very important that ALL of the fuel line banjo bolt washers be replaced every time the banjo bolts are loosened. If the washers

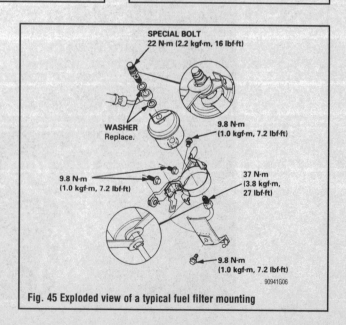

Fig. 45 Exploded view of a typical fuel filter mounting

are not replaced, the fuel lines will leak pressurized fuel causing the risk of fire or explosion.

7. Install the new filter and tighten the clamp mounting bolt to 7 ft. lbs. (10 Nm).

8. Attach the banjo fittings with new washers in place.

9. Tighten the banjo fitting bolts to 25 ft. lbs. (33 Nm).

➡On 2.2L and 3.0L engines you may have to reconnect the engine wire harness bracket and power steering feed hose clamp.

10. Connect the negative battery cable, then start the engine and thoroughly check for leaks.

PCV Valve

The Positive Crankcase Ventilation (PCV) valve is part of a system which is designed to protect the atmosphere from harmful vapors. Blow-by gas from the crankcase, as well as fumes from crankcase oil, are diverted into the combustion chamber where they are burned during engine operation. Proper operation of this system will improve engine performance, as well as decrease the amount of harmful vapors released into the atmosphere.

Each Acura is equipped with a Positive Crankcase Ventilation (PCV) system in which blow-by gas is returned to the combustion chamber through the intake manifold and/or the air cleaner.

The maintenance interval for the PCV valve is 60,000 miles (96,000 km) normal circumstances. Under severe operating conditions, the PCV valve may need to be changed sooner.

REMOVAL & INSTALLATION

▶ See Figures 46, 47 and 48

1. The PCV valve is mounted in the intake manifold and has a hose connected to it from the crankcase breather chamber. The valve is removed by pulling it from the manifold.

2. Check for loose, disconnected or deteriorated tubes and replace if necessary. Make sure the hoses are clean inside, cleaning them with a safe solvent, if necessary. If the system has a condensation chamber attached to the bottom of the air cleaner, unscrew and remove the chamber, clean and replace it; when removing the top gasket from the chamber, note the angle of installation. Reinstall it in the same position to provide proper airflow.

3. Check the valve by pulling it out of the manifold with the engine idling. Cover the open end of the valve with your finger so airflow is stopped. If the valve clicks, it is OK; if not, replace it.

For further information on the servicing of Acura emission control components, see Section 4 of this manual.

4. Install the PCV valve in the reverse order of removal.

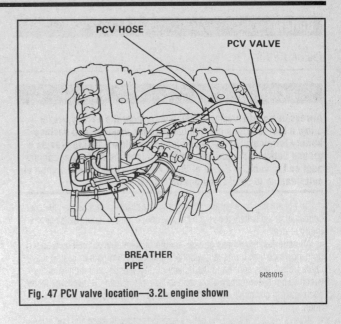

Fig. 47 PCV valve location—3.2L engine shown

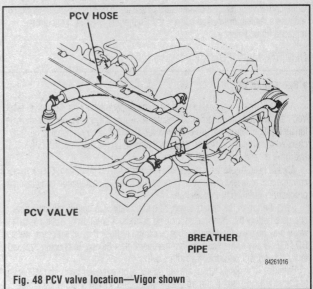

Fig. 48 PCV valve location—Vigor shown

Evaporative Canister

The charcoal canister is part of the Evaporative Emission Control System. This system prevents the escape of raw gasoline vapors from the fuel tank and carburetor.

This system is designed to contain gasoline vapor, which normally escapes from the fuel tank and intake manifold, from discharging into the atmosphere. Vapor absorption is accomplished through the use of a charcoal canister, which stores the vapors until they can be removed and burned in the combustion process.

The charcoal canister is designed to absorb fuel vapors under certain conditions. For a more detailed description and removal and installation, see Section 4 of this manual.

The canister is a coffee can-sized object located in the engine compartment.

SERVICING

The canister does not require periodic replacement. The entire system requires a careful operational check with a vacuum gauge at 60,000 miles (96,000 km). See Section 4 for testing and removal procedures.

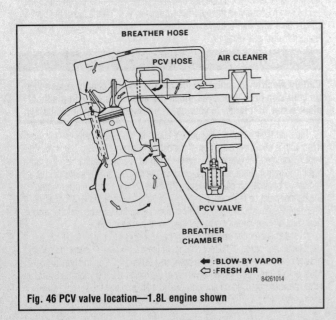

Fig. 46 PCV valve location—1.8L engine shown

Battery

PRECAUTIONS

✳✳ CAUTION

Always use caution when working on or near the battery. Never allow a tool to bridge the gap between the negative and positive battery terminals. Also, be careful not to allow a tool to provide a ground between the positive cable/terminal and any metal component on the vehicle. Either of these conditions will cause a short circuit, leading to sparks and possible personal injury.

Do not smoke, have an open flame or create sparks near a battery; the gases contained in the battery are very explosive and, if ignited, could cause severe injury or death.

All batteries, regardless of type, should be carefully secured by a battery hold-down device. If this is not done, the battery terminals or casing may crack from stress applied to the battery during vehicle operation. A battery which is not secured may allow acid to leak out, making it discharge faster; such leaking corrosive acid can also eat away at components under the hood.

Always visually inspect the battery case for cracks, leakage and corrosion. A white corrosive substance on the battery case or on nearby components would indicate a leaking or cracked battery. If the battery is cracked, it should be replaced immediately.

GENERAL MAINTENANCE

▶ See Figure 49

A battery that is not sealed must be checked periodically for electrolyte level. You cannot add water to a sealed maintenance-free battery (though not all maintenance-free batteries are sealed); however, a sealed battery must also be checked for proper electrolyte level, as indicated by the color of the built-in hydrometer "eye."

Always keep the battery cables and terminals free of corrosion. Check these components at least once a year. Refer to the removal, installation and cleaning procedures outlined in this section.

Keep the top of the battery clean, as a film of dirt can help completely discharge a battery that is not used for long periods. A solution of baking soda and water may be used for cleaning, but be careful to flush this off with clear water. DO NOT let any of the solution into the filler holes. Baking soda neutralizes battery acid and will de-activate a battery cell.

Batteries in vehicles which are not operated on a regular basis can fall victim to parasitic loads (small current drains which are constantly drawing current

from the battery). Normal parasitic loads may drain a battery on a vehicle that is in storage and not used for 6–8 weeks. Vehicles that have additional accessories such as a cellular phone, alarm system or other devices that increase parasitic load may discharge a battery sooner. If the vehicle is to be stored for 6–8 weeks in a secure area and the alarm system, if present, is not necessary, the negative battery cable should be disconnected at the onset of storage to protect the battery charge.

Remember that constantly discharging and recharging will shorten battery life. Take care not to allow a battery to be needlessly discharged.

BATTERY FLUID

Check the battery electrolyte level at least once a month, or more often in hot weather or during periods of extended vehicle operation. On non-sealed batteries, the level can be checked either through the case on translucent batteries or by removing the cell caps on opaque-cased types. The electrolyte level in each cell should be kept filled to the split ring inside each cell, or the line marked on the outside of the case.

If the level is low, add only distilled water through the opening until the level is correct. Each cell is separate from the others, so each must be checked and filled individually. Distilled water should be used, because the chemicals and minerals found in most drinking water are harmful to the battery and could significantly shorten its life.

If water is added in freezing weather, the vehicle should be driven several miles to allow the water to mix with the electrolyte. Otherwise, the battery could freeze.

Although some maintenance-free batteries have removable cell caps for access to the electrolyte, the electrolyte condition and level on all sealed maintenance-free batteries must be checked using the built-in hydrometer "eye." The exact type of eye varies between battery manufacturers, but most apply a sticker to the battery itself explaining the possible readings. When in doubt, refer to the battery manufacturer's instructions to interpret battery condition using the built-in hydrometer.

➡**Although the readings from built-in hydrometers found in sealed batteries may vary, a green eye usually indicates a properly charged battery with sufficient fluid level. A dark eye is normally an indicator of a battery with sufficient fluid, but one which may be low in charge. And a light or yellow eye is usually an indication that electrolyte supply has dropped below the necessary level for battery (and hydrometer) operation. In this last case, sealed batteries with an insufficient electrolyte level must usually be discarded.**

Checking the Specific Gravity

▶ See Figures 50, 51 and 52

A hydrometer is required to check the specific gravity on all batteries that are not maintenance-free. On batteries that are maintenance-free, the specific gravity is checked by observing the built-in hydrometer "eye" on the top of the battery case. Check with your battery's manufacturer for proper interpretation of its built-in hydrometer readings.

✳✳ CAUTION

Battery electrolyte contains sulfuric acid. If you should splash any on your skin or in your eyes, flush the affected area with plenty of clear water. If it lands in your eyes, get medical help immediately.

The fluid (sulfuric acid solution) contained in the battery cells will tell you many things about the condition of the battery. Because the cell plates must be kept submerged below the fluid level in order to operate, maintaining the fluid level is extremely important. And, because the specific gravity of the acid is an indication of electrical charge, testing the fluid can be an aid in determining if the battery must be replaced. A battery in a vehicle with a properly operating charging system should require little maintenance, but careful, periodic inspection should reveal problems before they leave you stranded.

As stated earlier, the specific gravity of a battery's electrolyte level can be used as an indication of battery charge. At least once a year, check the specific gravity of the battery. It should be between 1.20 and 1.26 on the gravity scale. Most auto supply stores carry a variety of inexpensive battery testing hydrometers. These can be used on any non-sealed battery to test the specific gravity in each cell.

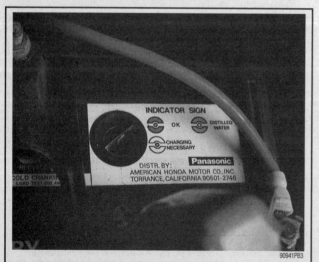

90941PB3

Fig. 49 A typical location for the built-in hydrometer on maintenance-free batteries

Fig. 50 On non-maintenance-free batteries, the fluid level can be checked through the case on translucent models; the cell caps must be removed on other models

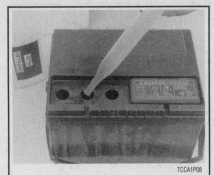

Fig. 51 If the fluid level is low, add only distilled water through the opening until the level is correct

Fig. 52 Check the specific gravity of the battery's electrolyte with a hydrometer

The battery testing hydrometer has a squeeze bulb at one end and a nozzle at the other. Battery electrolyte is sucked into the hydrometer until the float is lifted from its seat. The specific gravity is then read by noting the position of the float. If gravity is low in one or more cells, the battery should be slowly charged and checked again to see if the gravity has come up. Generally, if after charging, the specific gravity between any two cells varies more than 50 points (0.50), the battery should be replaced, as it can no longer produce sufficient voltage to guarantee proper operation.

CABLES

▶ See Figures 53, 54, 55, 56 and 57

Once a year (or as necessary), the battery terminals and the cable clamps should be cleaned. Loosen the clamps and remove the cables, negative cable first. On batteries with posts on top, the use of a puller specially made for this purpose is recommended. These are inexpensive and available in most auto parts stores. Side terminal battery cables are secured with a small bolt.

Clean the cable clamps and the battery terminal with a wire brush, until all corrosion, grease, etc., is removed and the metal is shiny. It is especially important to clean the inside of the clamp thoroughly (an old knife is useful here), since a small deposit of foreign material or oxidation there will prevent a sound electrical connection and inhibit either starting or charging. Special tools are available for cleaning these parts, one type for conventional top post batteries and another type for side terminal batteries. It is also a good idea to apply some dielectric grease to the terminal, as this will aid in the prevention of corrosion.

After the clamps and terminals are clean, reinstall the cables, negative cable last; DO NOT hammer the clamps onto battery posts. Tighten the clamps securely, but do not distort them. Give the clamps and terminals a thin external coating of grease after installation, to retard corrosion.

Check the cables at the same time that the terminals are cleaned. If the cable insulation is cracked or broken, or if the ends are frayed, the cable should be replaced with a new cable of the same length and gauge.

CHARGING

▶ See Figure 58

✳✳ CAUTION

The chemical reaction which takes place in all batteries generates explosive hydrogen gas. A spark can cause the battery to explode and splash acid. To avoid serious personal injury, be sure there is proper ventilation and take appropriate fire safety precautions when connecting, disconnecting, or charging a battery and when using jumper cables.

A battery should be charged at a slow rate to keep the plates inside from getting too hot. However, if some maintenance-free batteries are allowed to discharge until they are almost "dead," they may have to be charged at a high rate to bring them back to "life." Always follow the charger manufacturer's instructions on charging the battery.

REPLACEMENT

When it becomes necessary to replace the battery, select one with an amperage rating equal to or greater than the battery originally installed. Deterioration and just plain aging of the battery cables, starter motor, and associated wires makes the battery's job harder in successive years. The slow increase in electrical resistance over time makes it prudent to install a new battery with a greater capacity than the old.

Fig. 53 Maintenance is performed with household items and with special tools like this post cleaner

Fig. 54 The underside of this special battery tool has a wire brush to clean post terminals

Fig. 55 Place the tool over the battery posts and twist to clean until the metal is shiny

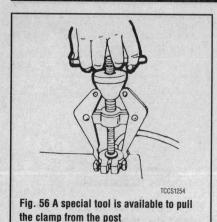

Fig. 56 A special tool is available to pull the clamp from the post

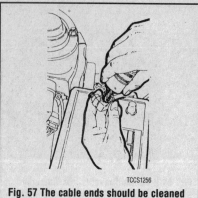

Fig. 57 The cable ends should be cleaned as well

Fig. 58 Always use caution when connecting the clamps of a battery charger

Belts

INSPECTION

See Figures 59, 60, 61, 62 and 63

Inspect the drive belt(s) every 30,000 miles (48,000 km)/24 months for signs of glazing or cracking. A glazed belt will be perfectly smooth from slippage, while a good belt will have a slight texture of fabric visible. Cracks will usually start at the inner edge of the belt and run outward. All worn or damaged drive belts should be replaced immediately. It is best to replace all drive belts at one time, as a preventive maintenance measure, during this service operation.

ADJUSTMENT

◆ See Figures 64 thru 71

Inspect the drive belt(s) every 30,000 miles or 24 months. Determine the belt tension at a point halfway between the pulleys by pressing on the belt with moderate thumb pressure. If the deflection is found to be too much or too little, perform the tension adjustments.

➡On some Acura models it will be necessary to work from beneath the vehicle when servicing the accessory drive belts.

Before adjusting, inspect the belt to see that it is not cracked or worn. Be sure that its surfaces are free of grease and oil. If contamination is present, belt replacement is recommended.

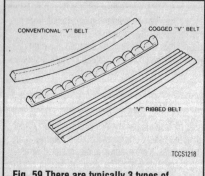

Fig. 59 There are typically 3 types of accessory drive belts found on vehicles today

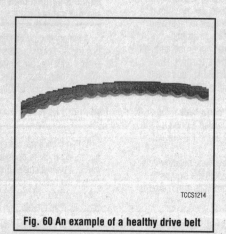

Fig. 60 An example of a healthy drive belt

Fig. 61 Deep cracks in this belt will cause flex, building up heat that will eventually lead to belt failure

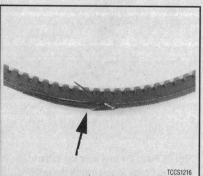

Fig. 62 The cover of this belt is worn, exposing the critical reinforcing cords to excessive wear

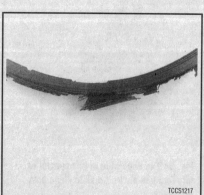

Fig. 63 Installing too wide a belt can result in serious belt wear and/or breakage

Fig. 64 Location of adjusting mechanism for the A/C belt on the Integra's 1.8L engine

1. Push down on the belt halfway between pulleys with a force of about 20 lbs. The belt should deflect: 0.16–0.41 in. (4–11mm)—on Integra and 0.22–0.45 in. (5.5–11.5mm) on all other models.

2. Adjust the belt tension by loosening the adjusting bolts.

3. Next loosen any mounting bolts and/or nuts that may hinder adjustment.

→ **3.0CL models have automatic tensioners therefore no belt adjustment is required.**

4. To adjust the alternator belt tension on Integra, loosen the adjustment lock bolt and move the alternator with a prybar positioned against the front of the alternator housing.

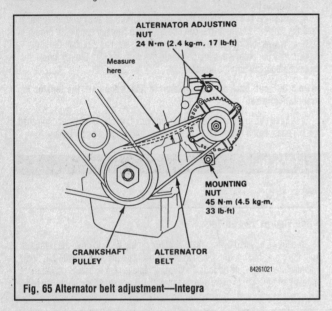

Fig. 65 Alternator belt adjustment—Integra

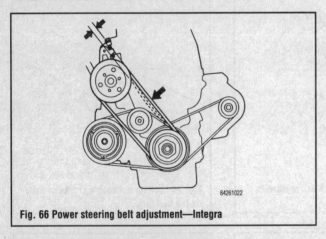

Fig. 66 Power steering belt adjustment—Integra

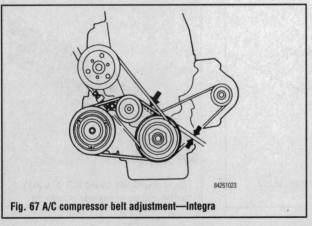

Fig. 67 A/C compressor belt adjustment—Integra

✳✳ WARNING

Do not apply pressure to any other part of the alternator or damage may occur.

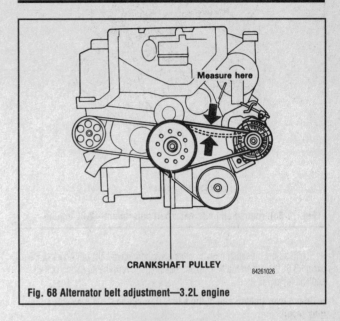

Fig. 68 Alternator belt adjustment—3.2L engine

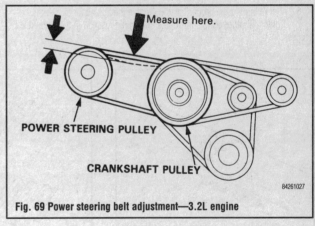

Fig. 69 Power steering belt adjustment—3.2L engine

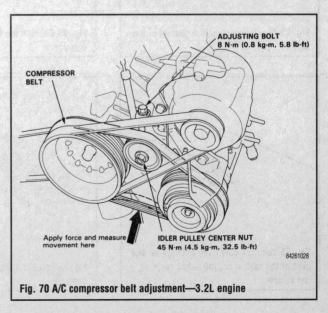

Fig. 70 A/C compressor belt adjustment—3.2L engine

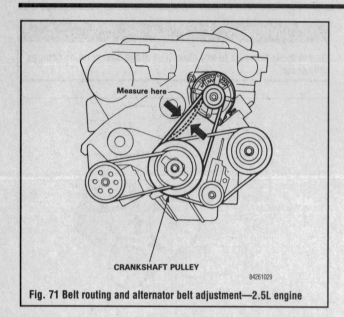

Fig. 71 Belt routing and alternator belt adjustment—2.5L engine

5. To adjust the tension on all other accessory drive belts (all Acura models except 3.0CL), loosen the adjustment lock bolt and turn the adjusting bolt (if applicable) as required.

➡Do not over tighten any of the belts. Damage to the pulley's bearings may result.

6. After obtaining the proper tension, tighten the adjustment lock bolt.
7. Tighten all other bolts and/or nuts that were loosened in the adjustment process.

REMOVAL & INSTALLATION

➡Many Acura models are equipped with a theft deterrent audio system. Make sure you have the necessary code before disconnecting the battery.

1. Disconnect the negative battery cable.
2. Loosen the driven accessory's pivot and mounting bolts.

➡If removing the alternator belt on a 3.0CL, pull back on the belt tensioner with a commercially available tool.

3. Remove the belt.
4. Install the belt by moving the accessory toward or away from the engine until the tension is correct. You can use a wooden hammer handle, or broomstick, as a lever, but do not use anything metallic, such as a prybar. Certain models may utilize an adjusting bolt to do this work for you. Simply loosen the mounting bolt and turn the adjuster.

➡On 3.0CL pull back on the tensioner to install the belt, the tension is automatically set.

5. Tighten the bolts and recheck the tension. If new belts have been installed, run the engine for a few minutes, then recheck and readjust as necessary.

Timing Belt

INSPECTION

◆ See Figures 72 thru 79

All engines covered by this manual utilize timing belts to drive the camshaft from the crankshaft's turning motion and to maintain proper valve timing. Some manufacturers schedule periodic timing belt replacement to assure optimum engine performance, to make sure the motorist is not stranded should the belt

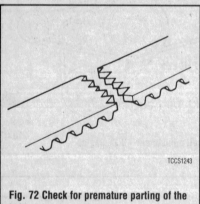

Fig. 72 Check for premature parting of the belt

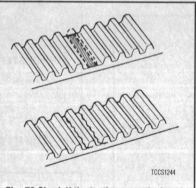

Fig. 73 Check if the teeth are cracked or damaged

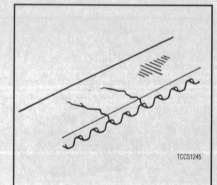

Fig. 74 Look for noticeable cracks or wear on the belt face

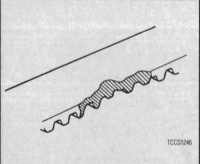

Fig. 75 You may only have damage on one side of the belt; if so, the guide could be the culprit

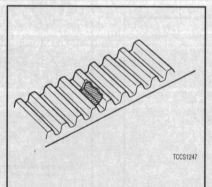

Fig. 76 Foreign materialsh and cause damage

Fig. 77 Inspect the timing belt for cracks, fraying, glazing or damage of any kind

Fig. 78 Damage on only one side of the timing belt may indicate a faulty guide

Fig. 79 ALWAYS replace the timing belt at the interval specified by the manufacturer

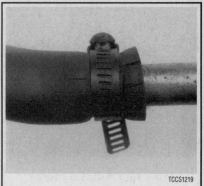

Fig. 80 The cracks developing along this hose are a result of age-related hardening

break (as the engine will stop instantly), and for some (manufacturers with interference motors), to prevent the possibility of severe internal engine damage should the belt break.

Because the engines are classified as interference motors (listed by the manufacturer as an engine whose valves might contact the pistons if the camshaft was rotated separately from the crankshaft), Acura recommends changing the timing belt at 90,000 miles (144,000 km) or 72 months which ever occurs first.

Regardless of whether or not you decide to replace the timing belt, you would be wise to check it periodically to make sure it has not become damaged or worn. Generally speaking, a severely worn belt may cause engine performance to drop dramatically, but a damaged belt (which could give out suddenly) may not give as much warning. In general, any time the engine timing cover(s) is (are) removed, you should inspect the belt for premature parting, severe cracks or missing teeth. Also, an access plug is provided in the upper portion of the timing cover so that camshaft timing can be checked without cover removal. If timing is found to be off, cover removal and further belt inspection or replacement is necessary.

Hoses

INSPECTION

▶ See Figures 80, 81, 82 and 83

Upper and lower radiator hoses, along with the heater hoses, should be checked for deterioration, leaks and loose hose clamps at every oil change or at least every 15,000 miles (24,000 km). It is also wise to check the hoses periodically in early spring and at the beginning of the fall or winter when you are performing other maintenance. A quick visual inspection could discover a weakened hose which might have left you stranded if it had remained unrepaired.

Whenever you are checking the hoses, make sure the engine and cooling system are cold. Visually inspect for cracking, rotting or collapsed hoses, and replace as necessary. Run your hand along the length of the hose. If a weak or swollen spot is noted when squeezing the hose wall, the hose should be replaced.

REMOVAL & INSTALLATION

▶ See Figures 84, 85 and 86

1. Remove the radiator pressure cap.

❊❊ CAUTION

Never remove the pressure cap while the engine is running, or personal injury from scalding hot coolant or steam may result. If possible, wait until the engine has cooled to remove the pressure cap. If this is not possible, wrap a thick cloth around the pressure cap and turn it slowly to the stop. Step back while the pressure is released from the cooling system. When you are sure all the pressure has been released, use the cloth to turn and remove the cap.

2. Position a clean container under the radiator and/or engine draincock or plug, then open the drain and allow the cooling system to drain to an appropriate level. For some upper hoses, only a little coolant must be drained. To remove hoses positioned lower on the engine, such as a lower radiator hose, the entire cooling system must be emptied.

❊❊ CAUTION

When draining coolant, keep in mind that cats and dogs are attracted by ethylene glycol antifreeze, and are quite likely to drink any that is left in an uncovered container or in puddles on the ground. This will prove fatal in sufficient quantity. Always drain coolant into a sealable container. Coolant may be reused unless it is contaminated or several years old.

3. Loosen the hose clamps at each end of the hose requiring replacement. Clamps are usually either of the spring tension type (which require pliers to

Fig. 81 A hose clamp that is too tight can cause older hoses to separate and tear on either side of the clamp

Fig. 82 A soft spongy hose (identifiable by the swollen section) will eventually burst and should be replaced

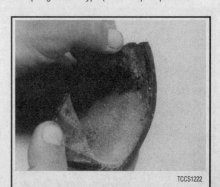

Fig. 83 Hoses are likely to deteriorate from the inside if the cooling system is not periodically flushed

Fig. 84 Use a pair of pliers to grasp the upper radiator hose clamp and squeeze the tabs to release the clamp tension

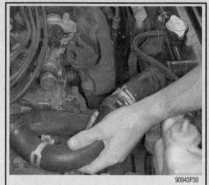

Fig. 85 Slide the clamps back away from the end of the hose . . .

Fig. 86 . . . then disconnect the hose and remove it from the vehicle

squeeze the tabs and loosen) or of the screw tension type (which require screw or hex drivers to loosen). Pull the clamps back on the hose away from the connection.

4. Twist, pull and slide the hose off the fitting, taking care not to damage the neck of the component from which the hose is being removed.

➥**If the hose is stuck at the connection, do not try to insert a screwdriver or other sharp tool under the hose end in an effort to free it, as the connection and/or hose may become damaged. Heater connections especially may be easily damaged by such a procedure. If the hose is to be replaced, use a single-edged razor blade to make a slice along the portion of the hose which is stuck on the connection, perpendicular to the end of the hose. Do not cut deep so as to prevent damaging the connection. The hose can then be peeled from the connection and discarded.**

5. Clean both hose mounting connections. Inspect the condition of the hose clamps and replace them, if necessary.

To install:

6. Dip the ends of the new hose into clean engine coolant to ease installation.

7. Slide the clamps over the replacement hose, then slide the hose ends over the connections into position.

8. Position and secure the clamps at least ¼ in. (6.35mm) from the ends of the hose. Make sure they are located beyond the raised bead of the connector.

9. Close the radiator or engine drains and properly refill the cooling system with the clean drained engine coolant or a suitable mixture of ethylene glycol coolant and water.

10. If available, install a pressure tester and check for leaks. If a pressure tester is not available, run the engine until normal operating temperature is reached (allowing the system to naturally pressurize), then check for leaks.

✳✳ CAUTION

If you are checking for leaks with the system at normal operating temperature, BE EXTREMELY CAREFUL not to touch any moving or

hot engine parts. Once temperature has been reached, shut the engine OFF, and check for leaks around the hose fittings and connections which were removed earlier.

CV-Boots

INSPECTION

◗ **See Figures 87 and 88**

The CV (Constant Velocity) boots should be checked for damage each time the oil is changed and any other time the vehicle is raised for service. These boots keep water, grime, dirt and other damaging matter from entering the CV-joints. Any of these could cause early CV-joint failure which can be expensive to repair. Heavy grease thrown around the inside of the front wheel(s) and on the brake caliper/drum can be an indication of a torn boot. Thoroughly check the boots for missing clamps and tears. If the boot is damaged, it should be replaced immediately. Please refer to Section 7 for procedures.

Spark Plugs

◗ **See Figures 89 and 90**

A typical spark plug consists of a metal shell surrounding a ceramic insulator. A metal electrode extends downward through the center of the insulator and protrudes a small distance. Located at the end of the plug and attached to the side of the outer metal shell is the side electrode. The side electrode bends in at a 90° angle so that its tip is just past and parallel to the tip of the center electrode. The distance between these two electrodes (measured in thousandths of an inch or hundredths of a millimeter) is called the spark plug gap.

The spark plug does not produce a spark but instead provides a gap across which the current can arc. The coil produces anywhere from 20,000 to 50,000 volts (depending on the type and application) which travels through the wires to

Fig. 87 CV-boots must be inspected periodically for damage

Fig. 88 A torn boot should be replaced immediately

Fig. 89 Close up of a typical Acura spark plug

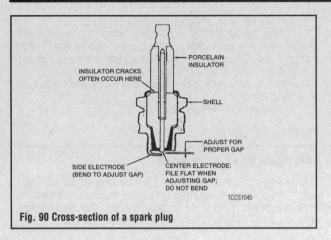

Fig. 90 Cross-section of a spark plug

the spark plugs. The current passes along the center electrode and jumps the gap to the side electrode, and in doing so, ignites the air/fuel mixture in the combustion chamber.

SPARK PLUG HEAT RANGE

▶ **See Figure 91**

Spark plug heat range is the ability of the plug to dissipate heat. The longer the insulator (or the farther it extends into the engine), the hotter the plug will operate; the shorter the insulator (the closer the electrode is to the block's cooling passages) the cooler it will operate. A plug that absorbs little heat and remains too cool will quickly accumulate deposits of oil and carbon since it is not hot enough to burn them off. This leads to plug fouling and consequently to misfiring. A plug that absorbs too much heat will have no deposits but, due to the excessive heat, the electrodes will burn away quickly and might possibly lead to preignition or other ignition problems. Preignition takes place when plug

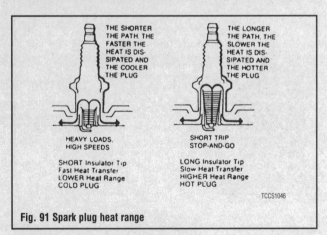

Fig. 91 Spark plug heat range

tips get so hot that they glow sufficiently to ignite the air/fuel mixture before the actual spark occurs. This early ignition will usually cause a pinging during low speeds and heavy loads.

The general rule of thumb for choosing the correct heat range when picking a spark plug is: if most of your driving is long distance, high speed travel, use a colder plug; if most of your driving is stop and go, use a hotter plug. Original equipment plugs are generally a good compromise between the 2 styles and most people never have the need to change their plugs from the factory-recommended heat range.

REMOVAL & INSTALLATION

▶ **See Figures 92, 93 and 94**

A set of spark plugs usually requires replacement after about 30,000 miles (48,000 km), depending on your style of driving. However, some engines today can reach 100,000 miles (161,000 km) before the spark plugs require replacement. In any case, it is recommended that the spark plugs be replaced according to the maintenance interval chart located in the vehicle owner's manual or at the end of this section. In normal operation plug gap increases about 0.001 in. (0.025mm) for every 2500 miles (4000 km). As the gap increases, the plug's voltage requirement also increases. It requires a greater voltage to jump the wider gap and about two to three times as much voltage to fire the plug at high speeds than at idle. The improved air/fuel ratio control of modern fuel injection combined with the higher voltage output of modern ignition systems will often allow an engine to run significantly longer on a set of standard spark plugs, but keep in mind that efficiency will drop as the gap widens (along with fuel economy and power).

When you're removing spark plugs, work on one at a time. Don't start by removing the plug wires all at once, because, unless you number them, they may become mixed up. Take a minute before you begin and number the wires with tape.

1. Disconnect the negative battery cable and, if the vehicle has been run recently, allow the engine to thoroughly cool.

➡**Remove the spark plugs when the engine is cold, if possible, to prevent damage to the threads. If removal of the plugs is difficult, apply a few drops of penetrating oil or silicone spray to the area around the base of the plug, and allow it a few minutes to work.**

2. Using a spark plug socket equipped with a rubber insert to properly hold the plug, turn the spark plug counterclockwise to loosen and remove the spark plug from the bore.

✳✳ WARNING

Be sure not to use a flexible extension on the socket. Use of a flexible extension may allow a shear force to be applied to the plug. A shear force could break the plug off in the cylinder head, leading to costly and frustrating repairs.

To install:
3. Inspect the spark plug boot for tears or damage. If a damaged boot is found, the spark plug wire must be replaced.
4. Using a wire feeler gauge, check and adjust the spark plug gap. When

Fig. 92 Disconnect the spark plug wires one at a time

Fig. 93 Keep track of which cylinder the spark plugs were removed from. This can help when troubleshooting problems later

Fig. 94 To ease installation and removal, apply an anti-seize lubricant to the threads of the spark plug

using a gauge, the proper size should pass between the electrodes with a slight drag. The next larger size should not be able to pass, while the next smaller size should pass freely.

5. Carefully thread the plug into the bore by hand. If resistance is felt before the plug is almost completely threaded, back the plug out and begin threading again. In small, hard to reach areas, an old spark plug wire and boot could be used as a threading tool. The boot will hold the plug while you twist the end of the wire and the wire is supple enough to twist before it would allow the plug to crossthread.

✻✻ WARNING

Do not use the spark plug socket to thread the plugs. Always carefully thread the plug by hand or by using an old plug wire to prevent the possibility of crossthreading and damaging the cylinder head bore.

6. Carefully tighten the spark plug to 13 ft. lbs. (18 Nm).

7. Apply a small amount of silicone dielectric compound to the end of the spark plug lead or inside the spark plug boot to prevent sticking, then install the boot to the spark plug and push until it clicks into place. The click may be felt or heard, then gently pull back on the boot to assure proper contact.

8. If removed, connect the spark plug wire to its corresponding ignition coil or distributor terminal.

9. Connect the negative battery cable.

INSPECTION & GAPPING

♦ See Figures 95, 96, 97, 98 and 99

Check the plugs for deposits and wear. If they are not going to be replaced, clean the plugs thoroughly. Remember that any kind of deposit will decrease the efficiency of the plug. Plugs can be cleaned on a spark plug cleaning machine, which can sometimes be found in service stations, or you can do an acceptable

A **normally worn** spark plug should have light tan or gray deposits on the firing tip.

A **carbon fouled** plug, identified by soft, sooty, black deposits, may indicate an improperly tuned vehicle. Check the air cleaner, ignition components and engine control system.

This spark plug has been **left in the engine too long,** as evidenced by the extreme gap- Plugs with such an extreme gap can cause misfiring and stumbling accompanied by a noticeable lack of power.

An **oil fouled** spark plug indicates an engine with worn poston rings and/or bad valve seals allowing excessive oil to enter the chamber.

A **physically damaged** spark plug may be evidence of severe detonation in that cylinder. Watch that cylinder carefully between services, as a continued detonation will not only damage the plug, but could also damage the engine.

A **bridged or almost bridged** spark plug, identified by a build-up between the electrodes caused by excessive carbon or oil build-up on the plug.

TCCA1P40

Fig. 95 Inspect the spark plug to determine engine running conditions

Fig. 96 A variety of tools and gauges are needed for spark plug service

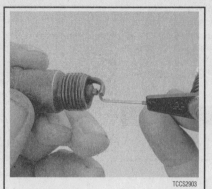

Fig. 97 Checking the spark plug gap with a feeler gauge

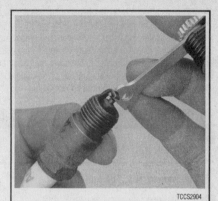

Fig. 98 Adjusting the spark plug gap

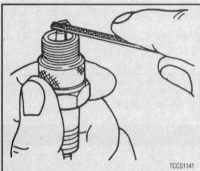

Fig. 99 If the standard plug is in good condition, the electrode may be filed flat—WARNING: do not file platinum plugs

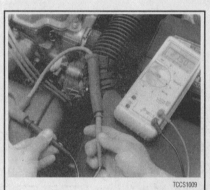

Fig. 100 Checking individual plug wire resistance with a digital ohmmeter

Fig. 101 A hand held tester, such as the one shown, can be used to check for a break in the wire

job of cleaning with a stiff brush. If the plugs are cleaned, the electrodes must be filed flat. Use an ignition points file, not an emery board or the like, which will leave deposits. The electrodes must be filed perfectly flat with sharp edges; rounded edges reduce the spark plug voltage by as much as 50%.

Check spark plug gap before installation. The ground electrode (the L-shaped one connected to the body of the plug) must be parallel to the center electrode and the specified size wire gauge (please refer to the Tune-Up Specifications chart for details) must pass between the electrodes with a slight drag.

➡**NEVER adjust the gap on a used platinum type spark plug.**

Always check the gap on new plugs as they are not always set correctly at the factory. Do not use a flat feeler gauge when measuring the gap on a used plug, because the reading may be inaccurate. A round-wire type gapping tool is the best way to check the gap. The correct gauge should pass through the electrode gap with a slight drag. If you're in doubt, try one size smaller and one larger. The smaller gauge should go through easily, while the larger one shouldn't go through at all. Wire gapping tools usually have a bending tool attached. Use that to adjust the side electrode until the proper distance is obtained. Absolutely never attempt to bend the center electrode. Also, be careful not to bend the side electrode too far or too often as it may weaken and break off within the engine, requiring removal of the cylinder head to retrieve it.

Spark Plug Wires

TESTING

▸ **See Figures 100 and 101**

At every tune-up/inspection, visually check the spark plug cables for burns cuts, or breaks in the insulation. Check the boots and the nipples on the coil or distributor, if equipped. Replace any damaged wiring.

Every 50,000 miles (80,000 km) or 60 months, the resistance of the wires should be checked with an ohmmeter. Wires with excessive resistance will cause misfiring, and may make the engine difficult to start in damp weather. Ignition wire resistance should not be greater than 25 kilohms.

To check resistance, disconnect the spark plug wire from the plug and ignition coil or distributor, then use an ohmmeter to measure the resistance.

If resistance falls outside of specifications, the cable(s) should be replaced with new ones.

REMOVAL & INSTALLATION

▸ **See Figure 102**

➡**As the spark plug wires must be routed and connected properly, if all of the wires must be disconnected from the spark plugs or from the ignition coil pack/distributor at the same time, be sure to tag the wires to assure proper reconnection.**

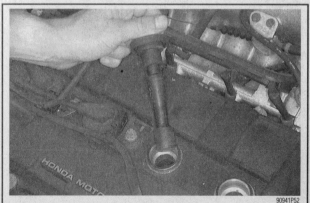

Fig. 102 Always grasp the plug wire at the boot. This will prevent any damage to the ignition wire set

When installing a new set of spark plug wires, replace the wires one at a time so there will be no mix-up. Start by replacing the longest cable first. Twist the boot of the spark plug wire ½ turn in each direction before pulling if off. Install the boot firmly over the spark plug. Route the wire exactly the same as the original. Insert the nipple firmly onto the tower on the ignition coil or distributor, if equipped. Be sure to apply silicone dielectric compound to the spark plug wire boots and tower connectors prior to installation.

Distributor Cap and Rotor

REMOVAL & INSTALLATION

▶ **See Figures 103, 104 and 105**

1. Disconnect the negative battery cable.
2. Tag and disconnect the spark plug (ignition) wires from the cap.
3. Remove the distributor cap attaching bolts.
4. Remove the Allen bolt, attaching the rotor to the shaft.

➡ **Inspect the distributor cap to housing seal for damage and/or cracks.**

To install:
5. Install the rotor onto the distributor and tighten the Allen bolt.

Fig. 103 View of the distributor cap with the spark plug wires still attached

Fig. 104 After disconnect the spark plug wires and remove the retainers, you can remove the distributor cap

Fig. 105 Once the distributor cap is removed, you can access the rotor

6. Install the distributor cap and tighten the attaching bolts..
7. Connect the spark plug cables, following the identification marks made at disassembly.
8. Reconnect the negative battery cable.

INSPECTION

Inspect the distributor cap for cracks or burned electrodes. Inspect the rotor for cracks or a burned electrode. Replace if defective.

Ignition Timing

GENERAL INFORMATION

In timing is the measurement, in degrees of crankshaft rotation, of the point at which the spark plugs fire in each of the cylinders. It is measured in degrees before or after Top Dead Center (TDC) of the compression stroke. Ignition timing is controlled by turning the distributor in the engine.

Ideally, the air/fuel mixture in the cylinder will be ignited by the spark plug just as the piston passes TDC of the compression stroke. If this happens, this piston will be beginning the power stroke just as the compressed and ignited air/fuel mixture starts to expand. The expansion of the air/fuel mixture then forces the piston down on the power stroke and turns the crankshaft.

Because it takes a fraction of a second for the spark plug to ignite the gases in the cylinder, the spark plug must fire a little before the piston reaches TDC. Otherwise, the mixture will not be completely ignited as the piston passes TDC and the full benefit of the explosion will not be used by the engine. The timing measurement is given in degrees of crankshaft rotation before the piston reaches TDC (BTDC). If the setting for the ignition timing is 5 degrees BTDC, the spark plug must fire 5 degrees before that piston reaches TDC. This only holds true, however, when the engine is at idle speed.

As the engine speed increases, the pistons go faster. The spark plugs have to ignite the fuel even sooner if it is to be completely ignited when the piston reaches TDC. To do this, the distributor has a means to advance the timing of the spark as the engine speed increases.

If the ignition is set too far advanced (BTDC), the ignition and expansion of the fuel in the cylinder will occur too soon and tend to force the piston down while it is still traveling up. This causes engine ping. If the engine is too far retarded after TDC (ATDC), the piston will have already passed TDC and started on its way down when the fuel is ignited. This will cause the piston to be forced down for only a portion of its travel. This will result informance and lack of power.

Timing should be checked at each tune-up. It isn't likely to change much. The timing marks consist of a notch on the rim of the crankshaft pulley or vibration damper and a graduated scale attached to the engine front (timing) cover.

There are three basic types of timing lights available. The first is a simple neon bulb with two wire connections. One wire connects to the spark plug terminal and the other plugs into the end of the spark plug wire for the No. 1 cylinder, thus connecting the light in series with the spark plug. This type of light is pretty dim and must be held very closely to the timing marks to be seen. Sometimes a dark corner has to be sought out to see the flash at all. This type of light is very inexpensive. The second type operates from the vehicle battery—two alligator clips connect to the battery terminals, while an adapter enables a third clip to be connected between No. 1 spark plug and wire. This type is a bit more expensive, but it provides a nice bright flash that you can see even in bright sunlight. It is the type most often seen in professional shops. The third type replaces the battery power source with 115 volt current.

Some timing lights have other features built into them, such as dwell meters, or tachometers. These are convenient, in that they reduce the tangle of wires under the hood when you're working, but may duplicate the functions of tools you already have. One worthwhile feature, which is becoming more of a necessity with higher voltage ignition systems, is an inductive pickup. The inductive pickup clamps around the No. 1 spark plug wire, sensing the surges of high voltage electricity as they are sent to the plug. The advantage is that no mechanical connection is inserted between the wire and the plug, which eliminates false signals to the timing light. A timing light with an inductive pickup should be used on Acura systems.

ADJUSTMENT

1.8L, 2.2L, and 2.3L Engines

1. Before servicing the vehicle, refer to the precautions in the beginning of this section.
2. If equipped with an automatic transaxle, place the shifter in Park. If equipped with a manual transaxle place the shifter in Neutral. Set the parking brake and block the drive wheels.
3. Start the engine and hold the engine speed at 3000 rpm, until the radiator fan comes on. The engine should be at idle speed and at normal operating temperature. Be sure all electrical accessories (radio, air conditioning, lights, etc.,) are turned OFF.
4. Locate the Service Check (SCS) connector:
   - 1.8L engines: behind the right kick panel
   - 2.2L and 2.3L engines: centrally located under the dash
5. Connect the SCS service connector part number 07PAZ–0010100 or equivalent.
6. Connect a timing light to the No. 1 ignition wire and point the light toward the pointer on the timing belt cover.
7. Check the idle speed and adjust if necessary.
8. The red mark on the crankshaft pulley should be aligned with the pointer on the timing belt cover.

➡The white mark on the crank pulley is Top Dead Center (TDC).

9. Adjust the ignition timing by loosening the distributor mounting bolts and rotating the distributor housing to adjust the timing. Set as follows:
   - 1.8L engines (Except Type R): 16 degrees Before Top Dead (BTDC) Center at 700–800 rpm
   - 1.8L engines (Type R): 16 degrees BTDC at 750–850 rpm
   - 2.2L engines: 15 degrees BTDC Center at 650–750 rpm
   - 2.3L engines: 12 degrees BTDC Center at 650–750 rpm
10. Tighten the distributor bolts to 17 ft. lbs. (24 Nm) and recheck the timing.
11. Remove the SCS service connector part number 07PAZ–0010100 or equivalent.

2.5L and 3.0L Engines

➡These vehicles have distributors, however the ignition timing is not adjustable. The ignition timing is controlled by the Powertrain Control (PCM) Module and can be checked for diagnostic purposes. If the timing is out of specification, all mechanical and electrical systems should checked for proper operation before replacing the PCM.

1. Before servicing the vehicle, refer to the precautions in the beginning of this section.
2. To check the ignition timing, start the engine and allow it to fast idle at 3000 rpm with all electrical accessories off and the transmission in **N** or **P**. Allow the engine to warm up and reach normal operating temperature. The engine cooling fan should cycle at least one time.
3. Locate the Service Check (SCS) connector out from under the glove box. Connect the service connector tool part number 07PAZ–0010100 or equivalent to the SCS terminals.
4. Check the idle speed and adjust if necessary.
5. Connect a timing light to the No. 1 plug wire. While engine idles, point the light toward the pointer on the timing belt cover.

6. Inspect the ignition timing at idle. The specifications are as follows:
   - 2.5L Engine: 13–17 degrees Before Top Dead (BTDC) Center at 650–750 rpm
   - 3.0L Engine: 8–12 degrees BTDC at 700–800

➡All mechanical and electrical systems should checked for proper operation before replacing the PCM.

7. If the ignition timing is incorrect, replace the PCM.
8. Remove the service connector.

3.2L and 3.5L Engines

♦ See Figures 106 and 107

➡These vehicles have individual ignition coils and the ignition timing is not adjustable. The ignition timing is controlled by the Powertrain Control (PCM) Module and can be checked for diagnostic purposes. If the timing is out of specification, all mechanical and electrical systems should checked for proper operation before replacing the PCM.

1. Before servicing the vehicle, refer to the precautions in the beginning of this section.
2. To check the ignition timing, start the engine and allow it to fast idle at 3000 rpm with all electrical accessories off and the transmission in **N** or **P**. Allow the engine to warm up and reach normal operating temperature. The engine cooling fan should cycle at least one time.
3. Locate the Service Check (SCS) connector under the glove box and connect the service connector tool part number 07PAZ–0010100 or equivalent to the SCS terminals.

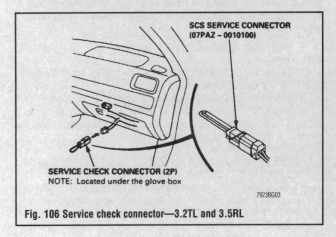

Fig. 106 Service check connector—3.2TL and 3.5RL

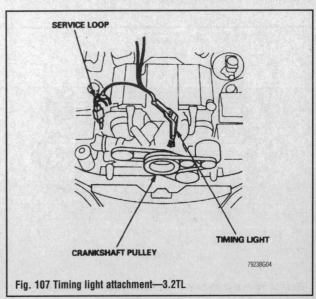

Fig. 107 Timing light attachment—3.2TL

4. Check the idle speed and adjust if necessary.

5. Connect a timing light to the No. 1 plug wire. With the engine idling at normal operating temperature point the timing light toward the pointer on the timing belt cover.

6. Inspect the ignition timing. The specifications are as follows:
- 3.2L Engine: 13–17 degrees Before Top Dead (BTDC) Center at 590–690 rpm
- 3.5L Engine: 13–17 degrees BTDC at 700–800 rpm

➡**All mechanical and electrical systems should checked for proper operation before replacing the PCM.**

7. If the ignition timing is incorrect, replace the PCM. Only replace the PCM as a last resort.

8. Remove the timing light.

9. Disconnect the special tool (SCS service connector) from the service check connector.

Valve Lash

ADJUSTMENT

1.8L (B18B1, B18C1 and B18C5) Engines

▸ **See Figures 108 and 109**

➡**While all valve adjustments must be as accurate as possible, it is better to have the valve adjustment slightly loose rather than too tight. Burned valves may result from overly tight adjustments. Perform the valve adjustment for each cylinder in the same sequence as the firing order: 1–3–4–2.**

1. Before servicing the vehicle, refer to the precautions in the beginning of this section.

2. Be sure the engine is cold; cylinder head temperature must be below 100° F (38° C). Overnight cold is best.

3. Remove the cylinder head cover and the upper timing belt cover.

4. Set the No. 1 cylinder to Top Dead Center (TDC). The word **UP** should appear at the top and the TDC grooves on the pulley should align with the cylinder head surface or the mark on the rear belt cover.

5. Valve clearances are:
   a. B18B1 engine: Intake—0.003–0.005 in. (0.08–0.12mm), Exhaust—0.006–0.008 in. (0.16–0.20mm)
   b. B18C1 and B18C5 Variable Valve Timing and Electronic Lift Control (VTEC) engine: Intake—0.006–0.007 in. (0.15–0.19mm), Exhaust—0.007–0.008 in. (0.17–0.20mm)

6. With the No. 1 cylinder at TDC, adjust the valves of the No. 1 cylinder by performing the following procedures:

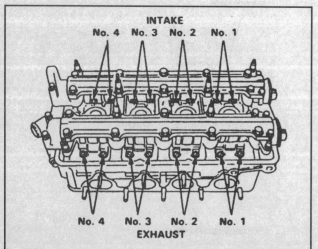

Fig. 108 Valve arrangement—1.8L (B18B1, B18C1, and B18C5) engines

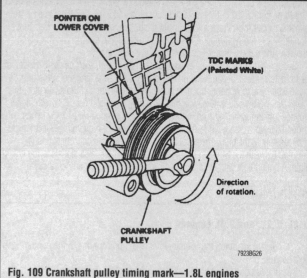

Fig. 109 Crankshaft pulley timing mark—1.8L engines

a. Hold the rocker arm against the valve and place the feeler gauge between the rocker arm and the camshaft lobe. There should be a slight drag on the feeler gauge.

b. If adjustment is required, loosen the valve adjusting the screw locknut.

c. Turn the adjusting screw to obtain the proper clearance.

d. Hold the adjusting screw and tighten the locknut(s) to 18 ft. lbs. (25 Nm).

e. Recheck the clearance.

7. Turn the crankshaft 180 degrees counterclockwise; the cam pulley will turn 90 degrees. With the No. 3 cylinder at TDC, the **UP** marks should be at the exhaust side. Adjust the valves on the No. 3 cylinder.

8. Turn the crankshaft 180 degrees counterclockwise; the cam pulley will turn 90 degrees. With the No. 4 cylinder at TDC, both **UP** marks should be at the bottom. Adjust the valves on the No. 4 cylinder.

9. Turn the crankshaft 180 degrees counterclockwise. The No. 2 cylinder will now be on TDC and the **UP** marks should be at the intake side. Adjust the valves on the No. 2 cylinder.

10. Install the cylinder head cover and upper timing belt cover.

2.3L Engine

➡**The valve should be adjusted only when the engine temperature is below 100°F (38°C). Retighten the crankshaft pulley bolt to 181 ft. lbs. (245 Nm) after adjusting the valves.**

1. Before servicing the vehicle, refer to the precautions in the beginning of this section.

2. Turn the crankshaft so the No. 1 piston is at Top Dead Center (TDC). Be sure the UP mark on the camshaft pulley is at the 12 o'clock position.

3. Adjust the valves on the No. 1 cylinder. To the following specifications:
- Intake—0.010 in. (0.26mm)
- Exhaust—0.012 in. (0.30mm)

4. Tighten the locknut to 14 ft. lbs. (20 Nm).

5. Turn the crankshaft counterclockwise 180degrees. Be sure the UP mark on the camshaft pulley is at the 9 o'clock position.

6. Adjust the valves on the No. 3 cylinder. Tighten the locknut to 14 ft. lbs. (20 Nm).

7. Turn the crankshaft counterclockwise 180 degrees. Be sure the UP mark on the camshaft pulley is at the 6 o'clock position.

8. Adjust the valves on the No. 4 cylinder. Tighten the locknut to 14 ft. lbs. (20 Nm).

9. Turn the crankshaft counterclockwise 180 degrees. Be sure the UP mark on the camshaft pulley is at the 3 o'clock position.

10. Adjust the valves on the No. 2 cylinder. Tighten the locknut to 14 ft. lbs. (20 Nm).

11. Retighten the crankshaft pulley bolt to 181 ft. lbs. (245 Nm) after adjusting the valves.

2.5L Engine

1. Before servicing the vehicle, refer to the precautions in the beginning of this section.
2. Disconnect the negative battery cable.
3. Remove the cylinder head cover and the upper timing belt cover.
4. Rotate the crankshaft to align the white Top Dead Center (TDC) on the crankshaft pulley with the pointer on the cover. Be sure the **UP** mark on the camshaft sprocket is up and the TDC marks align with the edge of the cylinder head.
5. Align the No. 1 mark on the back of the camshaft sprocket with the notch in the camshaft holder.
6. Hold a No. 1 cylinder rocker arm against the camshaft and use a feeler gauge to check the clearance at the valve stem. Intake valve clearance should be 0.010 in. (0.26mm), exhaust valve clearance should be 0.012 in. (0.30mm). The service limit for both intake and exhaust valves is plus or minus 0.0008 in. (0.02mm). Loosen the locknut and turn the adjusting screw to adjust the clearance. Tighten the locknut and recheck the clearance.
7. Rotate the crankshaft counterclockwise to align the TDC marks for each piston with the notch. Adjust the valves of each cylinder. The adjustment order is 1, 2, 4, 5 and 3.
8. Install the cylinder head and timing belt covers.
9. Reconnect the negative battery cable.

3.0L Engine

▶ See Figures 110, 111 and 112

1. Before servicing the vehicle, refer to the precautions in the beginning of this section.
2. Remove the cylinder head cover.
3. Remove the upper front timing belt cover.

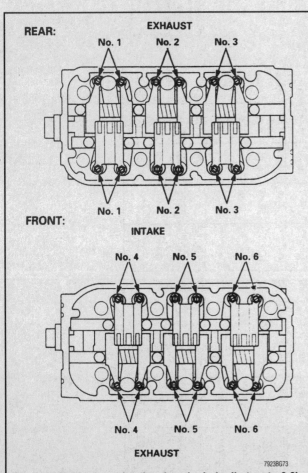

Fig. 110 Adjusting screw locations for valve lash adjustment—3.0L engine

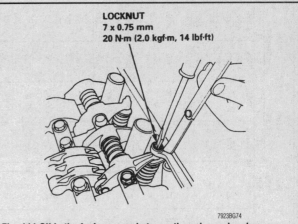

Fig. 111 Slide the feeler gauge between the valve and rocker arm while turning the adjusting screw—3.0L engine

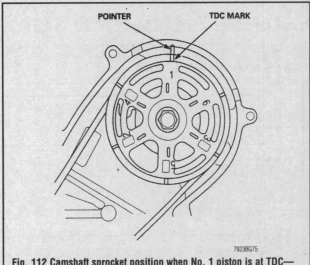

Fig. 112 Camshaft sprocket position when No. 1 piston is at TDC—3.0L engine

4. Rotate the crankshaft so the No. 1 piston is at Top Dead Center (TDC) on compression to adjust the valves for the No. 1 cylinder.
5. Loosen the locknuts and adjust the screws until a slight drag can be felt with the feeler gage when the gage is placed between the valve and rocker arm tip as shown. The specifications are as follows:
   - Intake—0.006–0.007 in. (0.15–0.18mm)
   - Exhaust—0.007–0.008 in. (0.18–0.20mm)
6. Rotate the crankshaft clockwise until the No. 4 on the camshaft sprocket is near the pointer on the rear cover. This is the No. 4 cylinder firing position.
7. Adjust the valves for the No. 4 cylinder while the sprocket is in this position. Tighten the locknuts to 14 ft. lbs. (20 Nm).
8. Continue to rotate the crankshaft and adjust the valves for each cylinder in this manner.
9. Install the timing belt and cylinder head covers.

3.2L and 3.5L Engines

These engines are equipped with hydraulic valve lash adjusters on the rocker arms. No valve clearance adjustments are possible or necessary.

Idle Speed and Mixture Adjustment

Idle speed and mixture for all engines covered by this manual are electronically controlled by a computerized fuel injection system. Adjustments are neither necessary nor possible.

ENGINE TUNE-UP SPECIFICATIONS

Year	Engine ID/VIN	Engine Displacement Liters (cc)	Spark Plug Gap (in.)	Ignition Timing (deg.) MT	Ignition Timing (deg.) AT	Fuel Pump (psi)	Idle Speed (rpm) MT	Idle Speed (rpm) AT	Valve Clearance In.	Valve Clearance Ex.
1994	B18B1	1.8 (1834)	0.041	16B	16B	40-47 [1]	700-800	700-800	0.003-0.005	0.006-0.008
	B18C1	1.8 (1797)	0.049	16B	16B	48-55 [1]	700-800	700-800	0.006-0.007	0.007-0.008
	C32A1	3.2 (3206)	0.043	15B	15B	44-51 [1]	600-700	550-650	HYD	HYD
	C32A6	3.2 (3206)	0.043	15B	15B	44-51 [1]	630-730	580-680	HYD	HYD
	G25A1	2.5 (2451)	0.043	15B	15B	43-50 [1]	650-750	650-750	0.009-0.011	0.011-0.013
1995	B18B1	1.8 (1834)	0.041	16B	16B	40-47 [1]	700-800	700-800	0.003-0.005	0.006-0.008
	B18C1	1.8 (1797)	0.049	16B	16B	48-55 [1]	700-800	700-800	0.006-0.007	0.007-0.008
	C30A1	3.0 (2977)	0.041	15B	15B	46-63 [1]	750-850	700-800	0.006-0.007	0.007-0.008
	C32A1	3.2 (3206)	0.043	15B	15B	44-51 [1]	600-700	550-650	HYD	HYD
	C32A6	3.2 (3206)	0.043	15B	15B	44-51 [1]	630-730	580-680	HYD	HYD
	G25A1	2.5 (2451)	0.043	15B	15B	43-50 [1]	650-750	650-750	0.009-0.011	0.011-0.013
1996	B18B1/[2]	1.8 (1834)	0.039-0.043	16B	16B	40-47 [1]	700-800	700-800	0.003-0.005	0.006-0.008
	B18C1/[3]	1.8 (1797)	0.051	16B	16B	48-55 [1]	700-800	700-800	0.006-0.007	0.007-0.008
	B18C5/[5]	1.8 (1797)	0.039-0.043	16B	-	38-45 [1]	750-850	-	HYD	HYD
	C32A6/UA3	3.2 (3206)	0.039-0.043	-	15B	43-50 [1]	-	590-690	HYD	HYD
	C35A1/KA9	3.5 (3474)	0.039-0.043	-	15B	43-50 [1]	-	600-700	0.003-0.005	0.006-0.008
	G25A4/UA2	2.5 (2451)	0.039-0.043	-	15B	43-50 [1]	-	650-750	0.009-0.011	0.011-0.013
1997	B18B1/[2]	1.8 (1834)	0.039-0.043	16B	16B	40-47 [1]	700-800	700-800	0.003-0.005	0.006-0.008
	B18C1/[3]	1.8 (1797)	0.051	16B	16B	48-55 [1]	700-800	700-800	0.006-0.007	0.007-0.008
	B18C5/[5]	1.8 (1797)	0.039-0.043	16B	-	47-54 [1]	750-850	-	HYD	HYD
	C32A6/UA3	3.2 (3206)	0.039-0.043	-	15B	38-45 [1]	-	590-690	HYD	HYD
	C35A1/KA9	3.5 (3474)	0.039-0.043	-	15B	43-50 [1]	-	600-700	HYD	HYD
	F22B1/YA1	2.2 (2156)	0.039-0.043	15B	15B	38-46 [1]	650-750	650-750	0.009-0.011	0.011-0.013
	G25A4/UA2	2.5 (2451)	0.039-0.043	-	15B	43-50 [1]	-	650-750	0.009-0.011	0.011-0.013
	J30A1/YA2	3.0 (2997)	0.039-0.043	-	10B	41-48 [1]	-	700-800	0.008-0.009	0.011-0.013

90941C03

ENGINE TUNE-UP SPECIFICATIONS

Year	Engine ID/VIN	Engine Displacement Liters (cc)	Spark Plug Gap (in.)	Ignition Timing (deg.) MT	Ignition Timing (deg.) AT	Fuel Pump (psi)	Idle Speed (rpm) MT	Idle Speed (rpm) AT	Valve Clearance In.	Valve Clearance Ex.
1998	B18B1/[2]	1.8 (1834)	0.039-0.043	16B	16B	40-47 [1]	700-800	700-800	0.003-0.005	0.006-0.008
	B18C1/[3]	1.8 (1797)	0.051	16B	16B	48-55 [1]	700-800	700-800	0.006-0.007	0.007-0.008
	B18C5/[5]	1.8 (1797)	0.039-0.043	16B	-	47-54 [1]	750-850	-	0.006-0.007	0.007-0.008
	C32A6/UA3	3.2 (3206)	0.039-0.043	-	15B	38-45 [1]	-	590-690	HYD	HYD
	C35A1/KA9	3.5 (3474)	0.039-0.043	-	15B	43-50 [1]	-	600-700	HYD	HYD
	F23A1/YA3	2.3 (2254)	0.039-0.043	12B	12B	47-54 [1]	650-750	650-750	0.009-0.011	0.011-0.013
	G25A4/UA2	2.5 (2451)	0.039-0.043	-	15B	43-50 [1]	-	650-750	0.011	0.011-0.013
	J30A1/YA2	3.0 (2997)	0.039-0.043	-	10B	41-48 [1]	-	700-800	0.008-0.009	0.011-0.013
1999	B18B1/[2]	1.8 (1834)	0.039-0.043	16B	16B	40-47 [1]	700-800	700-800	0.003-0.005	0.006-0.008
	B18C1/[3]	1.8 (1797)	0.051	16B	16B	48-55 [1]	700-800	700-800	0.006-0.007	0.007-0.008
	C35A1/KA9	3.5 (3474)	0.039-0.043	-	15B	43-50 [1]	-	600-700	HYD	HYD
	F23A1/YA3	2.3 (2254)	0.039-0.043	12B	12B	47-54 [1]	650-750	650-750	0.009-0.011	0.011-0.013
	J30A1/YA2	3.0 (2997)	0.039-0.043	-	10B	41-48 [1]	-	700-800	0.008-0.009	0.011-0.013
	J32A1/UA5	3.2 (3210)	0.039-0.043	-	10B	41-48 [1]	-	630-730	0.008-0.009	0.011-0.013
2000	B18B1/[2]	1.8 (1834)	0.039-0.043	16B	16B	40-47 [1]	700-800	700-800	0.003-0.005	0.006-0.008
	B18C1/[3]	1.8 (1797)	0.051	16B	16B	48-55 [1]	700-800	700-800	0.006-0.007	0.007-0.008
	C35A1/KA9	3.5 (3474)	0.039-0.043	-	15B	43-50 [1]	-	600-700	HYD	HYD
	F23A1/YA3	2.3 (2254)	0.039-0.043	12B	12B	47-54 [1]	650-750	650-750	0.009-0.011	0.011-0.013
	J30A1/YA2	3.0 (2997)	0.039-0.043	-	10B	41-48 [1]	-	700-800	0.008-0.009	0.011-0.013
	J32A1/UA5	3.2 (3210)	0.039-0.043	-	10B	41-48 [1]	-	630-730	0.008-0.009	0.011-0.013

NOTE: The Vehicle Emission Control Information label reflects specification changes during production and must be used if they differ from this chart.
B - Before Top Dead Center
HYD - Hydraulic
[1] At idle, pressure regulator vacuum hose disconnected
[2] D87: 4 door
[3] DC4: 3 door
[5] DB8: 4 door (Except Type R)
   DC2: 3 door

90941C04

Air Conditioning System

SYSTEM SERVICE & REPAIR

➡️**It is recommended that the A/C system be serviced by an EPA Section 609 certified automotive technician utilizing a refrigerant recovery/recycling machine.**

The do-it-yourselfer should not service his/her own vehicle's A/C system for many reasons, including legal concerns, personal injury, environmental damage and cost. The following are some of the reasons why you may decide not to service your own vehicle's A/C system.

According to the U.S. Clean Air Act, it is a federal crime to service or repair (involving the refrigerant) a Motor Vehicle Air Conditioning (MVAC) system for money without being EPA certified. It is also illegal to vent R-134a refrigerant into the atmosphere.

State and/or local laws may be more strict than the federal regulations, so be sure to check with your state and/or local authorities for further information. For further federal information on the legality of servicing your A/C system, call the EPA Stratospheric Ozone Hotline.

➡️**Federal law dictates that a fine of up to $25,000 may be levied on people convicted of venting refrigerant into the atmosphere. Additionally, the EPA may pay up to $10,000 for information or services leading to a criminal conviction of the violation of these laws.**

When servicing an A/C system, you run the risk of handling or coming in contact with refrigerant, which may result in skin or eye irritation, or frostbite. Although low in toxicity (due to chemical stability), inhalation of concentrated refrigerant fumes is dangerous and can result in death; cases of fatal cardiac arrhythmia have been reported in people accidentally subjected to high levels of refrigerant. Some early symptoms include loss of concentration and drowsiness.

Also, refrigerants can decompose at high temperatures (near gas heaters or open flame), which may result in hydrofluoric acid, hydrochloric acid and phosgene (a fatal nerve gas).

R-134a refrigerant is a greenhouse gas which, if allowed to vent into the atmosphere, will contribute to global warming (the Greenhouse Effect).

It is usually more economically feasible to have a certified MVAC automotive technician perform A/C system service to your vehicle. While it is illegal to service an A/C system without the proper equipment, the home mechanic would have to purchase an expensive refrigerant recovery/recycling machine to service his/her own vehicle.

PREVENTIVE MAINTENANCE

Although the A/C system should not be serviced by the do-it-yourselfer, preventive maintenance can be practiced and A/C system inspections can be performed to help maintain the efficiency of the vehicle's A/C system. For preventive maintenance, perform the following:

• The easiest and most important preventive maintenance for your A/C system is to be sure that it is used on a regular basis. Running the system for five minutes each month (no matter what the season) will help ensure that the seals and all internal components remain lubricated.

➡️**Some newer vehicles automatically operate the A/C system compressor whenever the windshield defroster is activated. When running, the compressor lubricates the A/C system components; therefore, the A/C system would not need to be operated each month.**

• In order to prevent heater core freeze-up during A/C operation, it is necessary to maintain a proper antifreeze protection. Use a hand-held coolant tester (hydrometer) to periodically check the condition of the antifreeze in your engine's cooling system.

➡️**Antifreeze should not be used longer than the manufacturer specifies.**

• For efficient operation of an air conditioned vehicle's cooling system, the radiator cap should have a holding pressure which meets manufacturer's specifications. A cap which fails to hold these pressures should be replaced.

• Any obstruction of or damage to the condenser configuration will restrict air flow which is essential to its efficient operation. It is, therefore, a good rule to keep this unit clean and in proper physical shape.

➡️**Bug screens which are mounted in front of the condenser (unless they are original equipment) are regarded as obstructions.**

• The condensation drain tube expels any water, which accumulates on the bottom of the evaporator housing, into the engine compartment. If this tube is obstructed, the air conditioning performance can be restricted and condensation buildup can spill over onto the vehicle's floor.

SYSTEM INSPECTION

Although the A/C system should not be serviced by the do-it-yourselfer, preventive maintenance can be practiced and A/C system inspections can be performed to help maintain the efficiency of the vehicle's A/C system. For A/C system inspection, perform the following:

The easiest and often most important check for the air conditioning system consists of a visual inspection of the system components. Visually inspect the air conditioning system for refrigerant leaks, damaged compressor clutch, abnormal compressor drive belt tension and/or condition, plugged evaporator drain tube, blocked condenser fins, disconnected or broken wires, blown fuses, corroded connections and poor insulation.

A refrigerant leak will usually appear as an oily residue at the leakage point in the system. The oily residue soon picks up dust or dirt particles from the surrounding air and appears greasy. Through time, this will build up and appear to be a heavy dirt impregnated grease.

For a thorough visual and operational inspection, check the following:
• Check the surface of the radiator and condenser for dirt, leaves or other material which might block air flow.
• Check for kinks in hoses and lines. Check the system for leaks.
• Make sure the drive belt is properly tensioned. When the air conditioning is operating, make sure the drive belt is free of noise or slippage.
• Make sure the blower motor operates at all appropriate positions, then check for distribution of the air from all outlets with the blower on **HIGH** or **MAX**.

➡️**Keep in mind that under conditions of high humidity, air discharged from the A/C vents may not feel as cold as expected, even if the system is working properly. This is because vaporized moisture in humid air retains heat more effectively than dry air, thereby making humid air more difficult to cool.**

• Make sure the air passage selection lever is operating correctly. Start the engine and warm it to normal operating temperature, then make sure the temperature selection lever is operating correctly.

Windshield Wiper (Elements)

ELEMENT (REFILL) CARE & REPLACEMENT

▶ **See Figures 113 thru 122**

For maximum effectiveness and longest element life, the windshield and wiper blades should be kept clean. Dirt, tree sap, road tar and so on will cause streaking, smearing and blade deterioration if left on the glass. It is advisable to wash the windshield carefully with a commercial glass cleaner at least once a month. Wipe off the rubber blades with the wet rag afterwards. Do not attempt to move wipers across the windshield by hand; damage to the motor and drive mechanism will result.

To inspect and/or replace the wiper blade elements, place the wiper switch in the **LOW** speed position and the ignition switch in the **ACC** position. When the wiper blades are approximately vertical on the windshield, turn the ignition switch to **OFF**.

Examine the wiper blade elements. If they are found to be cracked, broken or torn, they should be replaced immediately. Replacement intervals will vary with usage, although ozone deterioration usually limits element life to about one year. If the wiper pattern is smeared or streaked, or if the blade chatters across the glass, the elements should be replaced. It is easiest and most sensible to replace the elements in pairs.

If your vehicle is equipped with aftermarket blades, there are several different types of refills and your vehicle might have any kind. Aftermarket blades and arms rarely use the exact same type blade or refill as the original equipment. Here are some typical aftermarket blades; not all may be available for your vehicle:

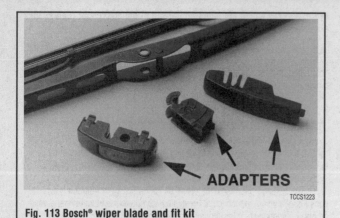

Fig. 113 Bosch® wiper blade and fit kit

The Anco® type uses a release button that is pushed down to allow the refill to slide out of the yoke jaws. The new refill slides back into the frame and locks in place.

Some Trico® refills are removed by locating where the metal backing strip or the refill is wider. Insert a small screwdriver blade between the frame and metal backing strip. Press down to release taining tab.

Other types of Trico® refills have two metal tabs which are unlocked by squeezing them together. The rubber filler can then be withdrawn from the frame jaws. A new refill is installed by inserting the refill into the front frame jaws and sliding it rearward to engage the remaining frame jaws. There are usually four jaws; be certain when installing that the refill is engaged in all of them. At the end of its travel, the tabs will lock into place on the front jaws of the wiper blade frame.

Another type of refill is made from polycarbonate. The refill has a simple locking device at one end which flexes downward out of the groove into which the jaws of the holder fit, allowing easy release. By sliding the new refill through all the jaws and pushing through the slight resistance when it reaches the end of its travel, the refill will lock into position.

Fig. 114 Lexor® wiper blade and fit kit

Fig. 115 Pylon® wiper blade and adapter

Fig. 116 Trico® wiper blade and fit kit

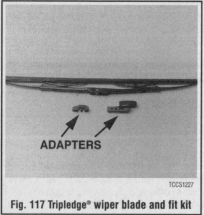

Fig. 117 Tripledge® wiper blade and fit kit

Fig. 118 To remove and install a Lexor® wiper blade refill, slip out the old insert and slide in a new one

Fig. 119 On Pylon® inserts, the clip at the end has to be removed prior to sliding the insert off

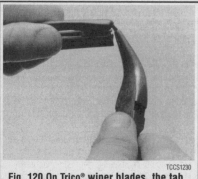

Fig. 120 On Trico® wiper blades, the tab at the end of the blade must be turned up . . .

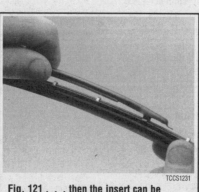

Fig. 121 . . . then the insert can be removed. After installing the replacement insert, bend the tab back

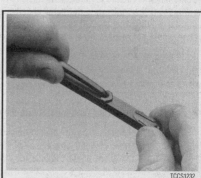

Fig. 122 The Tripledge® wiper blade insert is removed and installed using a securing clip

To replace the Tridon® refill, it is necessary to remove the wiper blade. This refill has a plastic backing strip with a notch about 1 in. (25mm) from the end. Hold the blade (frame) on a hard surface so that the frame is tightly bowed. Grip the tip of the backing strip and pull up while twisting counterclockwise. The backing strip will snap out of the retaining tab. Do this for the remaining tabs until the refill is free of the blade. The length of these refills is molded into the end and they should be replaced with identical types.

Regardless of the type of refill used, be sure to follow the part manufacturer's instructions closely. Make sure that all of the frame jaws are engaged as the refill is pushed into place and locked. If the metal blade holder and frame are allowed to touch the glass during wiper operation, the glass will be scratched.

Tires and Wheels

Common sense and good driving habits will afford maximum tire life. Fast starts, sudden stops and hard cornering are hard on tires and will shorten their useful life span. Make sure that you don't overload the vehicle or run with incorrect pressure in the tires. Both of these practices will increase tread wear.

➡ **For optimum tire life, keep the tires properly inflated, rotate them often and have the wheel alignment checked periodically.**

Inspect your tires frequently. Be especially careful to watch for bubbles in the tread or sidewall, deep cuts or underinflation. Replace any tires with bubbles in the sidewall. If cuts are so deep that they penetrate to the cords, discard the tire. Any cut in the sidewall of a radial tire renders it unsafe. Also look for uneven tread wear patterns that may indicate the front end is out of alignment or that the tires are out of balance.

TIRE ROTATION

▶ **See Figures 123 and 124**

Tires must be rotated periodically to equalize wear patterns that vary with a tire's position on the vehicle. Tires will also wear in an uneven way as the front steering/suspension system wears to the point where the alignment should be reset.

Rotating the tires will ensure maximum life for the tires as a set, so you will not have to discard a tire early due to wear on only part of the tread. Regular rotation is required to equalize wear.

When rotating "unidirectional tires," make sure that they always roll in the same direction. This means that a tire used on the left side of the vehicle must not be switched to the right side and vice-versa. Such tires should only be rotated front-to-rear or rear-to-front, while always remaining on the same side of the vehicle. These tires are marked on the sidewall as to the direction of rotation; observe the marks when reinstalling the tire(s).

Some styled or "mag" wheels may have different offsets front to rear. In these cases, the rear wheels must not be used up front and vice-versa. Furthermore, if these wheels are equipped with unidirectional tires, they cannot be rotated unless the tire is remounted for the proper direction of rotation.

➡ **The compact or space-saver spare is strictly for emergency use. It must never be included in the tire rotation or placed on the vehicle for everyday use.**

TIRE DESIGN

▶ **See Figure 125**

For maximum satisfaction, tires should be used in sets of four. Mixing of different types (radial, bias-belted, fiberglass belted) must be avoided. In most cases, the vehicle manufacturer has designated a type of tire on which the vehicle will perform best. Your first choice when replacing tires should be to use the same type of tire that the manufacturer recommends.

When radial tires are used, tire sizes and wheel diameters should be selected to maintain ground clearance and tire load capacity equivalent to the original specified tire. Radial tires should always be used in sets of four.

✳✳ CAUTION

Radial tires should never be used on only the front axle.

When selecting tires, pay attention to the original size as marked on the tire. Most tires are described using an industry size code sometimes referred to as P-Metric. This allows the exact identification of the tire specifications, regardless of the manufacturer. If selecting a different tire size or brand, remember to check the installed tire for any sign of interference with the body or suspension while the vehicle is stopping, turning sharply or heavily loaded.

Snow Tires

Good radial tires can produce a big advantage in slippery weather, but in snow, a street radial tire does not have sufficient tread to provide traction and control. The small grooves of a street tire quickly pack with snow and the tire behaves like a billiard ball on a marble floor. The more open, chunky tread of a snow tire will self-clean as the tire turns, providing much better grip on snowy surfaces.

To satisfy municipalities requiring snow tires during weather emergencies, most snow tires carry either an M + S designation after the tire size stamped on the sidewall, or the designation "all-season." In general, no change in tire size is necessary when buying snow tires.

Most manufacturers strongly recommend the use of 4 snow tires on their vehicles for reasons of stability. If snow tires are fitted only to the drive wheels, the opposite end of the vehicle may become very unstable when braking or turning on slippery surfaces. This instability can lead to unpleasant endings if the driver can't counteract the slide in time.

Note that snow tires, whether 2 or 4, will affect vehicle handling in all non-snow situations. The stiffer, heavier snow tires will noticeably change the turning and braking characteristics of the vehicle. Once the snow tires are installed, you must re-learn the behavior of the vehicle and drive accordingly.

➡ **Consider buying extra wheels on which to mount the snow tires. Once done, the "snow wheels" can be installed and removed as needed. This eliminates the potential damage to tires or wheels from seasonal removal and installation. Even if your vehicle has styled wheels, see if inexpensive steel wheels are available. Although the look of the vehicle will change, the expensive wheels will be protected from salt, curb hits and pothole damage.**

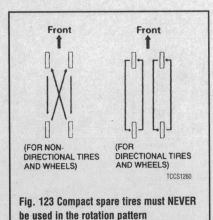

Fig. 123 Compact spare tires must NEVER be used in the rotation pattern

Fig. 124 Unidirectional tires are identifiable by sidewall arrows and/or the word "rotation"

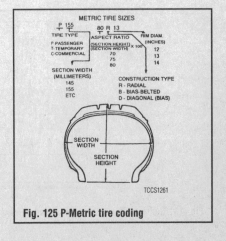

Fig. 125 P-Metric tire coding

TIRE STORAGE

If they are mounted on wheels, store the tires at proper inflation pressure. All tires should be kept in a cool, dry place. If they are stored in the garage or basement, do not let them stand on a concrete floor; set them on strips of wood, a mat or a large stack of newspaper. Keeping them away from direct moisture is of paramount importance. Tires should not be stored upright, but in a flat position.

INFLATION & INSPECTION

♦ See Figures 126 thru 134

The importance of proper tire inflation cannot be overemphasized. A tire employs air as part of its structure. It is designed around the supporting strength of the air at a specified pressure. For this reason, improper inflation drastically reduces the tire's ability to perform as intended. A tire will lose some air in day-to-day use; having to add a few pounds of air periodically is not necessarily a sign of a leaking tire.

Two items should be a permanent fixture in every glove compartment: an accurate tire pressure gauge and a tread depth gauge. Check the tire pressure (including the spare) regularly with a pocket type gauge. Too often, the gauge on the end of the air hose at your corner garage is not accurate because it suffers too much abuse. Always check tire pressure when the tires are cold, as pressure increases with temperature. If you must move the vehicle to check the tire inflation, do not drive more than a mile before checking. A cold tire is generally one that has not been driven for more than three hours.

A plate or sticker is normally provided somewhere in the vehicle (driver door, post, hood, tailgate or trunk lid) which shows the proper pressure for the tires. Never counteract excessive pressure build-up by bleeding off air pressure (letting some air out). This will cause the tire to run hotter and wear quicker.

Fig. 126 The tire information label can usually be found on the driver's side door jam

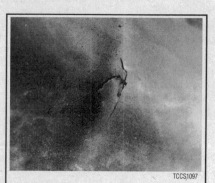

Fig. 127 Tires should be checked frequently for any sign of puncture or damage

Fig. 128 Tires with deep cuts, or cuts which show bulging, should be replaced immediately

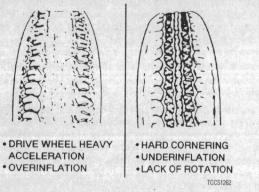

- DRIVE WHEEL HEAVY ACCELERATION
- OVERINFLATION

- HARD CORNERING
- UNDERINFLATION
- LACK OF ROTATION

Fig. 129 Examples of inflation-related tire wear patterns

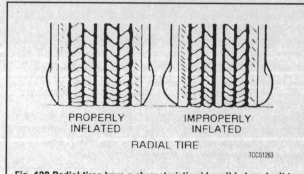

PROPERLY INFLATED

IMPROPERLY INFLATED

RADIAL TIRE

Fig. 130 Radial tires have a characteristic sidewall bulge; don't try to measure pressure by looking at the tire. Use a quality air pressure gauge

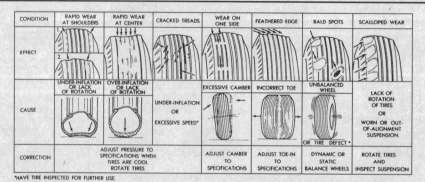

CONDITION	RAPID WEAR AT SHOULDERS	RAPID WEAR AT CENTER	CRACKED TREADS	WEAR ON ONE SIDE	FEATHERED EDGE	BALD SPOTS	SCALLOPED WEAR
EFFECT							
CAUSE	UNDER-INFLATION OR LACK OF ROTATION	OVER-INFLATION OR LACK OF ROTATION	UNDER-INFLATION OR EXCESSIVE SPEED*	EXCESSIVE CAMBER	INCORRECT TOE	UNBALANCED WHEEL OR TIRE DEFECT *	LACK OF ROTATION OF TIRES OR WORN OR OUT-OF-ALIGNMENT SUSPENSION.
CORRECTION	ADJUST PRESSURE TO SPECIFICATIONS WHEN TIRES ARE COOL ROTATE TIRES			ADJUST CAMBER TO SPECIFICATIONS	ADJUST TOE-IN TO SPECIFICATIONS	DYNAMIC OR STATIC BALANCE WHEELS	ROTATE TIRES AND INSPECT SUSPENSION

*HAVE TIRE INSPECTED FOR FURTHER USE.

Fig. 131 Common tire wear patterns and causes

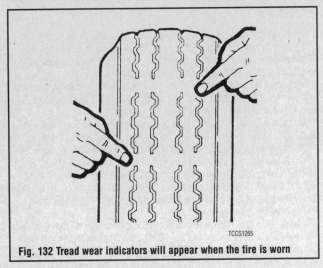

Fig. 132 Tread wear indicators will appear when the tire is worn

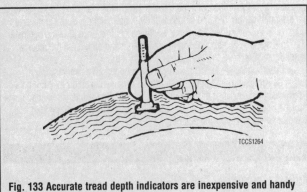

Fig. 133 Accurate tread depth indicators are inexpensive and handy

Fig. 134 A penny works well for a quick check of tread depth

✳✳ CAUTION

Never exceed the maximum tire pressure embossed on the tire! This is the pressure to be used when the tire is at maximum loading, but it is rarely the correct pressure for everyday driving. Consult the owner's manual or the tire pressure sticker for the correct tire pressure.

Once you've maintained the correct tire pressures for several weeks, you'll be familiar with the vehicle's braking and handling personality. Slight adjustments in tire pressures can fine-tune these characteristics, but never change the cold pressure specification by more than 2 psi. A slightly softer tire pressure will give a softer ride but also yield lower fuel mileage. A slightly harder tire will give crisper dry road handling but can cause skidding on wet surfaces. Unless you're fully attuned to the vehicle, stick to the recommended inflation pressures.

All tires made since 1968 have built-in tread wear indicator bars that show up as ½ in. (13mm) wide smooth bands across the tire when 1/16 in. (1.5mm) of tread remains. The appearance of tread wear indicators means that the tires should be replaced. In fact, many states have laws prohibiting the use of tires with less than this amount of tread.

You can check your own tread depth with an inexpensive gauge or by using a Lincoln head penny. Slip the Lincoln penny (with Lincoln's head upside-down) into several tread grooves. If you can see the top of Lincoln's head in 2 adjacent grooves, the tire has less than 1/16 in. (1.5mm) tread left and should be replaced. You can measure snow tires in the same manner by using the "tails" side of the Lincoln penny. If you can see the top of the Lincoln memorial, it's time to replace the snow tire(s).

CARE OF SPECIAL WHEELS

If you have invested money in magnesium, aluminum alloy or sport wheels, special precautions should be taken to make sure your investment is not wasted and that your special wheels look good for the life of the vehicle.

Special wheels are easily damaged and/or scratched. Occasionally check the rims for cracking, impact damage or air leaks. If any of these are found, replace the wheel. But in order to prevent this type of damage and the costly replacement of a special wheel, observe the following precautions:
- Use extra care not to damage the wheels during removal, installation, balancing, etc. After removal of the wheels from the vehicle, place them on a mat or other protective surface. If they are to be stored for any length of time, support them on strips of wood. Never store tires and wheels upright; the tread may develop flat spots.
- When driving, watch for hazards; it doesn't take much to crack a wheel.
- When washing, use a mild soap or non-abrasive dish detergent (keeping in mind that detergent tends to remove wax). Avoid cleansers with abrasives or the use of hard brushes. There are many cleaners and polishes for special wheels.
- If possible, remove the wheels during the winter. Salt and sand used for snow removal can severely damage the finish of a wheel.
- Make certain the recommended lug nut torque is never exceeded or the wheel may crack. Never use snow chains on special wheels; severe scratching will occur.

FLUIDS AND LUBRICANTS

Fluid Disposal

Used fluids such as engine oil, transmission fluid, antifreeze and brake fluid are hazardous wastes and must be disposed of properly. Before draining any fluids, consult with your local authorities; in many areas, waste oil, coolant, etc. is being accepted as a part of recycling programs. A number of service stations and auto parts stores are also accepting waste fluids for recycling.

Be sure of the recycling center's policies before draining any fluids, as many will not accept different fluids that have been mixed together.

Fuel and Engine Oil Recommendations

FUEL

➡**Some fuel additives contain chemicals that can damage the catalytic converter and/or oxygen sensor. Read all of the labels carefully before using any additive in the engine or fuel system.**

All Acura models are designed to run on unleaded fuel. The use of a leaded fuel in a car requiring unleaded fuel will plug the catalytic converter and render it inoperative. It will also increase exhaust backpressure to the point where engine output will be severely reduced. The minimum octane rating of the unleaded fuel being used must be at least 87, which usually means regular unleaded, but some high performance engines may require higher ratings. Fuel should be selected for the brand and octane which performs best with your engine. Judge a gasoline by its ability to prevent pinging, its engine starting capabilities (cold and hot) and general all weather performance.

As far as the octane rating is concerned, refer to the General Engine Specifications chart earlier in this section to find your engine and its compression ratio. If the compression ratio is 9.0:1 or lower, a regular grade of unleaded gasoline can be used in most cases. If the compression ratio is higher than 9.0:1, use a premium grade of unleaded fuel.

The use of a fuel too low in octane (a measure of anti-knock quality) will result in spark knock. Since many factors such as altitude, terrain, air temperature and humidity affect operating efficiency, knocking may result even though the recommended fuel is being used. If persistent knocking occurs, it may be necessary to switch to a higher grade of fuel. Continuous or heavy knocking may result in engine damage.

➡**Your engine's fuel requirement can change with time, mainly due to carbon build-up, which will, in turn, change the compression ratio. If your engine pings, knocks or diesels (runs with the ignition OFF) switch to a higher grade of fuel. Sometimes, just changing brands will cure the problem. If it becomes necessary to retard the timing from the specifications, don't change it more than a few degrees. Retarded timing will reduce power output and fuel mileage, in addition to making the engine run hotter.**

OIL

♦ See Figures 135, 136 and 137

The Society Of Automotive Engineer (SAE) grade number indicates the viscosity of the engine oil and, thus, its ability to lubricate at a given temperature. The lower the SAE grade number, the lighter the oil; the lower the viscosity, the easier it is to crank the engine in cold weather. Oil viscosities should be chosen from those oils recommended for the lowest anticipated temperatures during the oil change interval. With the proper viscosity, you will be assured of easy cold starting and sufficient engine protection.

Multi-viscosity oils (5W-30, 10W-30, etc.) offer the important advantage of being adaptable to temperature extremes. They allow easy starting at low temperatures, yet they give good protection at high speeds and engine temperatures. This is a decided advantage in changeable climates or in long distance driving.

The American Petroleum Institute (API) designation indicates the classification of engine oil used under certain given operating conditions. Only oil designated for Service SJ, or the latest superseding oil grade, should be used. Oils of the SJ type perform a variety of functions inside the engine in addition to their basic function as a lubricant. Through a balanced system of metallic detergents and polymeric dispersants, engine oil prevents the formation of high and low temperature deposits and also keeps sludge and particles of dirt in suspension. Acids, particularly sulfuric acid, as well as other byproducts of combustion, are neutralized. Both the SAE grade number and the API designation can be found on the side of the oil bottle.

Synthetic Oils

There are excellent synthetic and fuel-efficient oils available that, under the right circumstances, can help provide better fuel mileage and better engine protection. However, these advantages come at a price, which can be significantly more than the price per quart of conventional motor oils.

Before pouring any synthetic oils into your car's engine, you should consider the condition of the engine and the type of driving you do. It is also wise to check the vehicle manufacturer's position on synthetic oils.

Generally, it is best to avoid the use of synthetic oil in both brand new and older, high mileage engines. New engines require a proper break-in, and the synthetics are so slippery that they can impede this; most manufacturers recommend that you wait at least 5,000 miles (8,000 km) before switching to a synthetic oil. Conversely, older engines which have worn parts tend to lose more oil; synthetics will slip past worn parts more readily than regular oil. If your car already leaks oil, (due to worn parts or bad seals/gaskets), it may leak more with a synthetic inside.

Consider your type of driving. If most of your accumulated mileage is on the highway at higher, steadier speeds, a synthetic oil will reduce friction and probably help deliver better fuel mileage. Under such ideal highway conditions, the oil change interval can be extended, as long as the oil filter can continue to operate effectively for the extended life of the oil. If the filter can't do its job for this extended period, dirt and sludge will build up in your engine's crankcase, sump, oil pump and lines, no matter what type of oil is used. If using synthetic oil in this manner, you should continue to change the oil filter at the recommended intervals.

Cars used under harder, stop-and-go, short hop circumstances should always be serviced more frequently; for these cars, synthetic oil may not be a wise investment. Because of the necessary shorter change interval needed for this type of driving, you cannot take advantage of the long recommended change interval of most synthetic oils.

Engine

OIL LEVEL CHECK

♦ See Figures 138, 139, 140 and 141

Every time you stop for fuel, check the engine oil, after making sure the engine has fully warmed and the vehicle is parked on a level surface. Because it takes some time for the oil to drain back to the oil pan, you should wait a few minutes before checking your oil. If you are doing this at a fuel stop, first fill the fuel tank, then open the hood and check the oil, but don't get so carried away as to forget to pay for the fuel! Most station attendants won't believe that you forgot.

1. Make sure the car is parked on level ground.
2. When checking the oil level, it is best for the engine to be at normal operating temperature, although checking the oil immediately after stopping will lead to a false reading. Wait a few minutes after turning off the engine to allow the oil to drain back into the crankcase.
3. Open the hood and locate the dipstick, which will be in a guide tube located in the front of the engine compartment. Pull the dipstick from its tube, wipe it clean (using a clean, lint-free rag) and then reinsert it.

Fig. 135 To determine the correct oil viscosity, consult the information label found in the engine compartment

Fig. 136 Look for the API oil identification label when choosing your engine oil

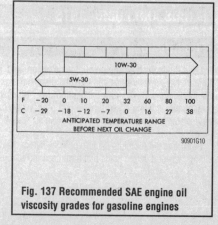

Fig. 137 Recommended SAE engine oil viscosity grades for gasoline engines

Fig. 138 Pull the engine oil dipstick from its tube, which is located at the front of the engine

Fig. 139 The engine oil level should measure between the upper and lower notch marks

Fig. 140 Remove the oil filler cap from the top of the valve cover. Examine the condition of the cap and rubber seal; replace if worn or damaged

4. Pull the dipstick out again and, holding it horizontally, read the oil level. The oil should be between the SAFE and ADD, MIN and MAX or the upper and lower notch marks on the dipstick. If the oil is below the ADD, MIN, or lower notch marks, add oil of the proper viscosity through the capped opening in the top of the valve cover. See the oil and fuel recommendations listed earlier in this section for the proper viscosity and rating of oil to use.

5. Insert the dipstick and check the oil level again after adding any oil. Approximately one quart of oil will raise the level from the ADD, MIN, or lower notch marks to the SAFE, MAX, or upper notch marks. Be sure not to overfill the crankcase. Excess oil will generally be consumed at an accelerated rate and may cause problems.

※※ WARNING

DO NOT overfill the crankcase. It may result in oil fouled spark plugs, oil leaks caused by oil seal failure, or engine damage due to oil foaming.

6. Close the hood.

OIL & FILTER CHANGE

▸ **See Figures 142 thru 150**

※※ CAUTION

The EPA warns that prolonged contact with used engine oil may cause a number of skin disorders, including cancer! You should make every effort to minimize your exposure to used engine oil. Protective gloves should be worn when changing the oil. Wash your hands and any other exposed skin areas as soon as possible after exposure to used engine oil. Soap and water, or waterless hand cleaner should be used.

The manufacturer's recommended oil change interval is 7500 miles (12,000 km) under normal operating conditions. We recommend an oil change interval of 3000–3500 miles (4800–5600 km) under normal conditions; more frequently under severe conditions such as when the average trip is less than 4 miles (6 km), the engine is operated for extended periods at idle or low speed, when towing a trailer or operating in dusty areas.

In addition, we recommend that the filter be replaced EVERY time the oil is changed.

➡**Please be considerate of the environment. Dispose of waste oil properly by taking it to a service station, municipal facility or recycling center.**

1. Run the engine until it reaches normal operating temperature. Then turn the engine **OFF**.

2. Remove the oil filler cap.

3. Raise and safely support the front of the vehicle using jackstands.

4. Slide a drain pan of at least 5 quarts (4.7 liters) capacity under the oil pan. Wipe the drain plug and surrounding area clean using an old rag.

5. Loosen the drain plug using a ratchet, short extension and socket, or a box wrench. Turn the plug out by hand, using a rag to shield your fingers from the hot oil. By keeping an inward pressure on the plug as you unscrew it, oil won't escape past the threads and you can remove it without being burned by hot oil. Quickly withdraw the plug and move your hands out of the way, but be careful not to drop the plug into the drain pan, as fishing it out can be an unpleasant mess. Allow the oil to drain completely.

6. Examine the condition of the drain plug for thread damage or stretching, and replace if necessary. Remove and discard the drain plug gasket.

7. Install the drain plug and new gasket. Tighten the drain plug to 25–33 ft. lbs. (34–44 Nm).

8. Move the drain pan under the oil filter. Use a strap-type or end cap-type wrench to loosen the oil filter. Cover your hand with a rag and spin the filter off by hand, but turn it slowly. Keep in mind that it's holding about one quart of dirty, hot oil.

Fig. 141 Use a funnel to pour in the proper amount of the correct viscosity engine oil

Fig. 142 After the drain pan is in correct position, loosen the oil pan drain plug

Fig. 143 Once loosened, unscrew the plug by hand

Fig. 144 Remove the plug and allow the oil to drain until it stops dripping. Be careful not to drop the plug into the pan

Fig. 145 Always install a new washer on the oil drain plug to ensure a tight, leak free seal

Fig. 146 You can use a cap-type oil filter wrench with a ratchet tool to loosen the oil filter

Fig. 147 During removal, always keep the opening of the filter straight up to prevent any of the old oil, still contained in the filter, from spilling

Fig. 148 Before installing a new oil filter, lightly coat the rubber gasket with clean oil

Fig. 149 Install the oil fill cap, making sure to tighten it securely

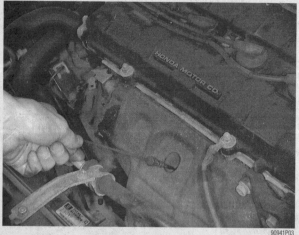

Fig. 150 After the oil change is complete, check to be sure the oil level is OK

➡Be careful when removing the oil filter, because the filter contains about 1 quart of hot, dirty oil.

9. Empty the old oil filter into the drain pan, then properly dispose of the filter.

10. Using a clean shop towel, wipe off the filter adapter on the engine block. Be sure the towel does not leave any lint which could clog an oil passage.

11. Coat the rubber gasket and pour some fresh oil into the new filter before installation; this will lubricate the engine quicker during initial startup. Spin the filter onto the adapter by hand until it contacts the mounting surface, then tighten it an additional ½–¾ turn. Do NOT overtighten the filter.

12. Carefully lower the vehicle.

13. Refill the crankcase with the correct amount of fresh engine oil. Please refer to the Capacities chart later in this section.

14. Install the oil filler cap.

15. Check the oil level on the dipstick. It is normal for the level to be a bit above the full mark until the engine is run and the new filter is filled with oil. Start the engine and allow it to idle for a few minutes.

✳✳ WARNING

Do not run the engine above idle speed until it has built up oil pressure, as indicated when the oil light goes out.

16. Shut off the engine and allow the oil to flow back to the crankcase for a minute, then recheck the oil level. Check around the filter and drain plug for any leaks, and correct as necessary.

When you have finished this job, you will notice that you now possess four or five quarts of dirty oil. The best thing to do is to pour it into plastic jugs, such as milk or old antifreeze containers. Then, locate a service station or automotive parts store where you can pour it into their used oil tank for recycling.

➡Improperly disposing of used motor oil not only pollutes the environment, it violates federal law. Dispose of waste oil properly.

Manual Transaxle

FLUID RECOMMENDATIONS

The recommended fluid for manual transaxles is Honda Manual Transmission Fluid (MTF). As a temporary replacement, you can use engine oil labeled for SG, SH or SJ use. If using engine oil, make sure to use 10W-30 or 10W-40 viscosity; the 10W-40 viscosity is the safer recommendation, especially if driving frequently at high speeds for prolonged periods in hot weather.

LEVEL CHECK

▶ **See Figure 151**

The transaxle fluid should be changed every 30,000 miles (48,000 km) under moderate to severe duty.

1. Remove the oil level check bolt from the side of the transaxle. If oil runs out the fluid level is OK, retighten the bolt to 33 ft. lbs. (45 Nm).

2. If fluid does not run out, the level is low. Loosen the filler plug and pour oil in slowly until it begins to run out via the level check bolt, then, tighten the bolt to 33 ft. lbs. (45 Nm) and filler plug.

DRAIN & REFILL

▶ **See Figures 152 and 153**

1. Raise and safely support the front of the vehicle.
2. Place a fluid catch pan under the transaxle.
3. Remove the upper and lower plugs, then, drain the fluid.
4. Using a new washer, install the bottom plug tightening to 29 ft. lbs. (40 Nm). Refill the transaxle, until the oil is level with the upper filler plug hole. Install the filler plug and tighten to 33 ft. lbs. (45 Nm).

Automatic Transaxle

FLUID RECOMMENDATIONS

All Acura automatic transaxles use Honda approved ATF or Dexron®II automatic transmission fluid.

LEVEL CHECK

The recommended change interval for the fluid in the automatic transaxle is 30,000 miles (48,000 km) or 24 months.

The level is checked with the vehicle on level ground and the engine hot, but off. All models use a standard push in dipstick. Remove the dipstick and wipe it clean, reinstall it in position. Remove the dipstick and check the oil level on the stick, it should be between the upper and lower marks on the dipstick.

If the fluid level is low, use a funnel to add the proper type and amount of transaxle fluid to bring it to the correct level, through the dipstick tube. It generally takes less than a pint. DO NOT overfill the transaxle! If the fluid level is within specifications, simply push the dipstick back into the filler tube completely.

❋❋ WARNING

To avoid getting any dirt or water in the transaxle, always make sure the dipstick is fully seated in the tube.

DRAIN & REFILL

1. Drive the vehicle to bring the transaxle fluid up to operating temperatures.
2. Raise and safely support the front of the vehicle.
3. Place a fluid catch pan under the transaxle.
4. Remove the drain plug, located on the bottom of the transaxle housing, and drain the transaxle.
5. Using a new washer, install the drain plug. Tighten to 29 ft. lbs. (40 Nm) on the Integra, and to 36 ft. lbs. (50 Nm) on all other models.
6. Using Dexron®II automatic transmission fluid refill the transaxle using the transaxle fluid dipstick hole or filler cap, until fluid reaches the FULL mark on the dipstick; DO NOT overfill the transaxle.

➡ **Be sure that the quantity of fluid you add is always slightly less than the specified quantity, due to the remaining fluid left in the transaxle housing recesses.**

7. Start the engine and allow to idle for at least a minute. With the parking brake set and the brakes depressed, move the gear selector through each position, ending in the Park or Neutral position.
8. Check the fluid level and add just enough fluid to bring the level to ⅛ inch (3mm) below the ADD mark.
9. Allow the engine to fully warm up to normal operating temperature, then check the fluid level. The fluid level should be in the HOT range. If not, add the proper amount of fluid to bring it up to that level. If the fluid level is within specifications, simply push the dipstick back into the filler tube completely.

❋❋ WARNING

To avoid getting any dirt or water in the transaxle, always make sure the dipstick is fully seated in the tube.

Cooling System

▶ **See Figure 154**

❋❋ CAUTION

Never remove the radiator cap under any conditions while the engine is hot! Failure to follow these instructions could result in damage to the cooling system, engine and/or personal injury. To avoid having scalding hot coolant or steam blow out of the radiator, use extreme care whenever you are removing the radiator cap. Wait until the engine has cooled, then wrap a thick cloth around the radiator cap and turn it slowly to the first stop. Step back while the pressure is released from the cooling system. When you are sure the pressure has been released, press down on the radiator cap (with the cloth still in position), then turn and remove the cap.

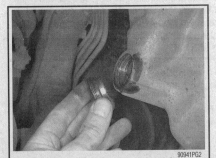

Fig. 151 Remove the level check plug from the side of the manual transmission; if fluid does not run out, the transmission needs to be filled

Fig. 152 To change the oil in the gearbox, use a ratchet or breaker bar to loosen the drain plug . . .

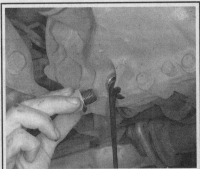

Fig. 153 . . . then remove the drain plug from the lower half of the transmission

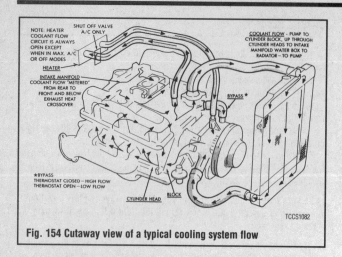

Fig. 154 Cutaway view of a typical cooling system flow

FLUID RECOMMENDATIONS

The cooling system should be inspected, flushed and refilled with fresh coolant at least every 30,000 miles (48,000 km) or 36 months. If the coolant is left in the system too long, it loses its ability to prevent rust and corrosion.

When the coolant is being replaced, use a good quality ethylene glycol or equivalent type antifreeze that is safe to be used with aluminum cooling system components. The ratio of antifreeze to water should always be a 50/50 mixture. This ratio will ensure the proper balance of cooling ability, corrosion protection and antifreeze protection. At this ratio, the antifreeze protection should be good to -34°F (-37°C). If greater antifreeze protection is needed, the ratio should not exceed 70% antifreeze to 30% water.

LEVEL CHECK

▶ See Figures 155, 156 and 157

To check the coolant level, simply determine whether the coolant is up to the FULL line on the expansion tank. Add coolant to the expansion tank if the level is low, being sure to mix it with clean water. Never add cold water or coolant to a hot engine as damage to both the cooling system and the engine could result.

※ CAUTION

Should it be necessary to remove the radiator cap, make sure the system has had time to cool, reducing the internal pressure.

The radiator cap should be removed only for the purpose of cleaning or draining the system.

The cooling system is under pressure when hot. Removing the radiator cap when the engine is warm or overheated will cause coolant to spill or shoot out, possibly causing serious burns. The system should be allowed to cool before attempting removal of the radiator cap or hoses.

Fig. 155 Never open the radiator cap when the vehicle is hot

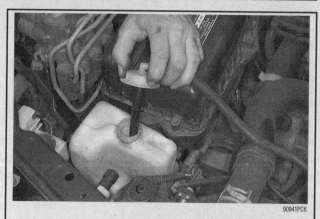

Fig. 156 To remove the cap from the expansion tank, twist as shown

Fig. 157 Make sure the coolant level is between the MAX and MIN marks on the expansion (overflow) tank

➡ If any coolant spills on painted portions of the body, rinse it off immediately.

DRAIN & REFILL

▶ See Figure 158

※ CAUTION

When draining the coolant, keep in mind that cats and dogs are attracted by ethylene glycol antifreeze and are quite likely to drink any that is left in an uncovered container or in puddles on the ground. This will prove fatal in sufficient quantity. Always drain the coolant into a sealable container. Coolant should be reused until it is contaminated or several years old. To avoid injuries from scalding fluid and steam, DO NOT remove the radiator cap while the engine and radiator are still hot.

1. Before draining the cooling system, place the heater's temperature selector to the full WARM position while the engine is running. This will provide vacuum for system operation.
2. Turn the engine **OFF** before it gets hot and the system builds pressure.
3. Make sure the engine is still cool and the vehicle is parked on a level surface.
4. Remove the recovery tank cap.
5. Place a fluid catch pan under the radiator. Turn the radiator draincock counterclockwise to open, then allow the coolant to drain. The coolant should drain out of the recovery tank first.
6. Remove the radiator cap by performing the following:
   a. Slowly rotate the cap counterclockwise to the detent.
   b. If any residual pressure is present, WAIT until the hissing stops.
   c. After the hissing noise has ceased, press down on the cap and continue rotating it counterclockwise to remove it.

Fig. 158 Fill the coolant recovery tank to the proper level after filling the cooling system at the engine. Always use a funnel to avoid spills

7. Allow the coolant to drain completely from the vehicle.
8. Close the radiator draincock.

➡When filling the cooling system, be careful not to spill any coolant on the drive belts or alternator.

9. Using a 50/50 mixture of antifreeze and clean water, fill the radiator to the bottom of the filler neck and the coolant tank to the FULL mark.
10. Install the radiator cap, then place the cap back on the recovery bottle or surge tank.
11. Start the engine. Select heat on the climate control panel and turn the temperature selector to full WARM. Run the engine until it reaches normal operating temperature. Check to make sure there is hot air flowing from the vents.
12. Check the fluid level in the recovery tank, and add as necessary.

FLUSHING & CLEANING

1. Drain the cooling system, as described in the preceding drain and refill procedure.
2. Close the drain valve.

➡A flushing solution may be used. Ensure that it is safe for use with aluminum cooling system components, and follow the directions on the container.

3. If using a flushing solution, remove the thermostat, then reinstall the thermostat housing.
4. Add sufficient water to fill the system.
5. Start the engine and run it for a few minutes. Drain the system.
6. Allow the water to flow out of the radiator until it is clear.
7. Reconnect the heater hose.
8. Drain the cooling system.
9. Reinstall the thermostat.
10. Empty the coolant reservoir or surge tank and flush it.

11. Fill the cooling system, using the correct ratio of antifreeze and water, to the bottom of the filler neck. Fill the reservoir or surge tank to the FULL mark.
12. Install the radiator cap.

Brake Master Cylinder

FLUID RECOMMENDATIONS

Use only ACURA®, or equivalent brake fluid meeting DOT 3 or DOT 4 specifications from a clean, sealed container. Using any other type of fluid may result in severe brake system damage.

❊❊ WARNING

Brake fluid damages paint. It also absorbs moisture from the air; never leave a container or the master cylinder uncovered longer than necessary. All parts in contact with the brake fluid (master cylinder, hoses, plunger assemblies, etc.) must be kept clean, since any contamination of the brake fluid will adversely affect braking performance.

LEVEL CHECK

▶ **See Figures 159, 160 and 161**

It should be obvious how important the brake system is to safe operation of your vehicle. The brake fluid is key to the proper operation of your vehicle. Low levels of fluid indicate a need for service (there may be a leak in the system or the brake pads may just be worn and in need of replacement). In any case, the brake fluid level should be inspected at least during every oil change, but more often is desirable. Every time you open the hood is a good time to glance at the master cylinder reservoir.

To check the fluid level, look on the side of the reservoir to see how high the fluid level is against the markings on the side of the reservoir. The level should be at the MAX mark. If not, remove the reservoir cap, then add the proper amount of DOT 3 or DOT 4 brake fluid to bring the level up to MAX.

When making additions of brake fluid, use only fresh, uncontaminated brake fluid which meets or exceeds DOT 3 standards. Be careful not to spill any brake fluid on painted surfaces, as it will quickly eat the paint. Do not allow the brake fluid container or the master cylinder to remain open any longer than necessary; brake fluid absorbs moisture from the air, reducing the fluid's effectiveness and causing corrosion in the lines.

Clutch Master Cylinder

FLUID RECOMMENDATIONS

▶ **See Figure 162**

When adding or changing the fluid in the hydraulic clutch system, use a quality brake fluid conforming to DOT 3 OR DOT 4 specifications such as HONDA® Brake Fluid, or equivalent. Never reuse old brake fluid.

Fig. 159 When checking the fluid level, the level should be at the MAX line. Add the proper amount of fluid if necessary

Fig. 160 Inspect the inner rubber seal of the reservoir cap for any dirt, and clean as necessary

Fig. 161 Pour in enough DOT 3 quality brake fluid until it reaches the FULL level. Be careful not to spill any brake fluid, as it can damage painted surfaces

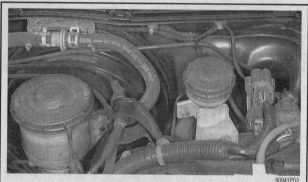

Fig. 162 The clutch master cylinder reservoir is located at the rear of the engine, near the firewall

LEVEL CHECK

▶ See Figure 163

The fluid in the clutch master cylinder is key to the proper clutch actuation on your vehicle. Low levels of fluid indicate a need for service (there may be a leak in the system or the clutch pad lining may just be worn and in need of replacement). In any case, the fluid level should be inspected at least during every oil change, but more often is desirable. Every time you open the hood is a good time to glance at the master cylinder reservoir.

1. Wipe the clutch master cylinder reservoir cap and the surrounding area clean with a shop towel.

2. Inspect the fluid in the reservoir, making sure the fluid is between the MAX and MIN marks.

3. If required, remove the clutch master cylinder reservoir lid, then add fresh fluid to bring the level up to the MAX mark on the reservoir.

When making additions of fluid, use only fresh, uncontaminated brake fluid

Fig. 163 Adding fluid to the clutch master cylinder.

which meets DOT 3 or DOT 4 standards. Do not allow the brake fluid container or the master cylinder to remain open any longer than necessary; brake fluid absorbs moisture from the air, reducing the fluid's effectiveness and causing corrosion in the lines.

✳✳ WARNING

Be careful to avoid spilling any brake fluid on painted surfaces, because the paint coat will become discolored or damaged.

4. Reinstall the lid onto the clutch master cylinder.

Power Steering Pump

FLUID RECOMMENDATIONS

Only genuine Honda power steering fluid or a known equivalent may be used when adding fluid. Acura says that ATF or fluids manufactured for use in other brands of vehicles by their manufacturers or independents are not compatible with the Honda power steering system. The use of any other fluid will cause the seals to swell and create leaks.

LEVEL CHECK

▶ See Figures 164, 165 and 166

The fluid in the power steering reservoir should be checked every few weeks for indications of leaks or low fluid level. Check the fluid with the engine cold and the vehicle parked on a level spot. The level should be between the upper and lower marks. Fluid need not be added right away unless it has dropped almost to the lower mark. DO NOT overfill the reservoir.

When adding fluid, or making a complete fluid change, use only Honda Power Steering Fluid or equivalent; NEVER add automatic transmission fluid. Failure to use the proper fluid may cause hose and seal damage, and fluid leaks.

Unscrew the cap again, then check the fluid level while holding the cap above the tip of the dipstick. If the level is at or below the ADD mark on the dipstick, add fluid until the level reaches the FULL mark. Be careful not to overfill, as this will cause fluid loss and seal damage. A large loss in fluid volume may indicate a problem, which should be inspected and repaired at once.

Body Lubrication and Maintenance

The body mechanisms and linkages should be inspected, cleaned and lubricated, as necessary, to preserve correct operation and to avoid wear and corrosion. Before you lubricate a component, make sure to wipe any dirt or grease from the surface with a suitable rag. If necessary, you can also use a suitable cleaning solvent to clean off the surface. And don't forget to wipe any excess lubricant off the component when finished.

To be sure the hood latch works properly, use engine oil to lubricate the latch, safety catch and hood hinges, as necessary. Apply Honda® or equivalent multi-purpose grease sparingly to all pivot and slide contact areas.

Fig. 164 Fluid level indicator lines can be found on the side of the power steering reservoir

Fig. 165 Twist and pull up on the cap to add fluid

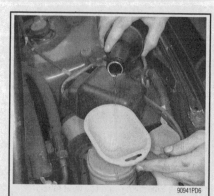

Fig. 166 Use a funnel to avoid spilling the fluid

Use engine oil to lubricate the following components:
- Door hinges—hinge pin and pivot points
- Hood hinges—pivot points
- Trunk lid hinges—pivot points

Use Honda® Lubricate or equivalent on the following components:
- Door check straps
- Ashtray slides
- Fuel fill door latch mechanism
- Parking brake moving parts
- Front seat tracks

TRAILER TOWING

General Recommendations

Trailer towing is generally NOT recommended for Acuras. Your vehicle was primarily designed to carry passengers and cargo. It is important to remember that towing a trailer will place additional loads on your vehicle's engine, drive train, steering, braking and other systems. However, if you decide to tow a trailer, using the proper equipment is a must.

Local laws may require specific equipment such as trailer brakes or fender mounted mirrors. Check your local laws.

❈❈ WARNING

Installing the trailer brakes to the vehicle's brake system lines can place an excessive load and cause a possible failure to the system. If the system fails when the brakes are needed, tragic consequences could result.

Trailer Weight

The weight of the trailer is the most important factor. A good weight-to-horse-power ratio is about 35:1, 35 lbs. of Gross Combined Weight (GCW) for every horsepower your engine develops. Multiply the engine's rated horsepower by 35 and subtract the weight of the vehicle, passengers and luggage. The number remaining is the approximate ideal maximum weight you should tow, although a numerically higher axle ratio can help compensate for heavier weight.

Hitch (Tongue) Weight

♦ See Figure 167

Calculate the hitch weight in order to select a proper hitch. The weight of the hitch is usually 9–11% of the trailer gross weight and should be measured with the trailer loaded. Hitches fall into various categories: those that mount on the frame and rear bumper, the bolt-on type, or the weld-on distribution type used for larger trailers. Axle mounted or clamp-on bumper hitches should never be used.

Check the gross weight rating of your trailer. Tongue weight is usually figured as 10% of gross trailer weight. Therefore, a trailer with a maximum gross weight of 2000 lbs. will have a maximum tongue weight of 200 lbs. Class I trailers fall into this category. Class II trailers are those with a gross weight rating of 2000–3000 lbs., while Class III trailers fall into the 3500–6000 lbs. category. Class IV trailers are those over 6000 lbs. and are for use with fifth wheel trucks, only.

When you've determined the hitch that you'll need, follow the manufacturer's

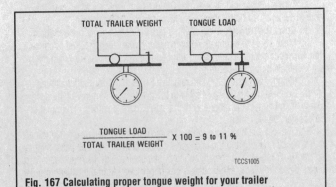

Fig. 167 Calculating proper tongue weight for your trailer

TOTAL TRAILER WEIGHT   TONGUE LOAD

$$\frac{\text{TONGUE LOAD}}{\text{TOTAL TRAILER WEIGHT}} \times 100 = 9 \text{ to } 11 \text{ \%}$$

TCCS1005

installation instructions, exactly, especially when it comes to fastener torques. The hitch will be subjected to a lot of stress and good hitches come with hardened bolts. Never substitute an inferior bolt for a hardened bolt.

Cooling

ENGINE

Overflow Tank

One of the most common, if not THE most common, problems associated with trailer towing is engine overheating. If you have a cooling system without an expansion tank, you'll definitely need to get an aftermarket expansion tank kit, preferably one with at least a 2 quart capacity. These kits are easily installed on the radiator's overflow hose, and come with a pressure cap designed for expansion tanks.

Oil Cooler

Aftermarket engine oil coolers are helpful for prolonging engine oil life and reducing overall engine temperatures. Both of these factors increase engine life. While not absolutely necessary in towing Class I and some Class II trailers, they are recommended for heavier Class II and all Class III towing. Engine oil cooler systems usually consist of an adapter, screwed on in place of the oil filter, a remote filter mounting and a multi-tube, finned heat exchanger, which is mounted in front of the radiator or air conditioning condenser.

TRANSAXLE

An automatic transaxle is usually recommended for trailer towing. Modern automatics have proven reliable and, of course, easy to operate, in trailer towing. The increased load of a trailer, however, causes an increase in the temperature of the automatic transaxle fluid. Heat is the worst enemy of an automatic transaxle. As the temperature of the fluid increases, the life of the fluid decreases.

It is essential, therefore, that you install an automatic transaxle cooler. The cooler, which consists of a multi-tube, finned heat exchanger, is usually installed in front of the radiator or air conditioning compressor, and hooked in-line with the transaxle cooler tank inlet line. Follow the cooler manufacturer's installation instructions.

Select a cooler of at least adequate capacity, based upon the combined gross weights of the vehicle and trailer.

Cooler manufacturers recommend that you use an aftermarket cooler in addition to, and not instead of, the present cooling tank in your radiator. If you do want to use it in place of the radiator cooling tank, get a cooler at least two sizes larger than normally necessary.

➡**A transaxle cooler can, sometimes, cause slow or harsh shifting in the transaxle during cold weather, until the fluid has a chance to come up to normal operating temperature. Some coolers can be purchased with or retrofitted with a temperature bypass valve which will allow fluid flow through the cooler only when the fluid has reached above a certain operating temperature.**

Handling a Trailer

Towing a trailer with ease and safety requires a certain amount of experience. It's a good idea to learn the feel of a trailer by practicing turning, stopping and backing in an open area such as an empty parking lot.

Wheel Bearings

All Acura vehicles are equipped with sealed hub and bearing assemblies. The hub and bearing assembly is non-serviceable. If the assembly is damaged, the complete unit must be replaced. Refer to Section 8 for the hub and bearing removal and installation procedure.

TOWING THE VEHICLE

▶ **See Figure 168**

When towing is required, the vehicle should be flat bedded or towed with the front wheels off of the ground on a wheel lift, to prevent damage to the transaxle. DO NOT allow your vehicle to be towed by a sling type tow truck, if it is at all avoidable. If it is necessary to tow the vehicle from the rear, a wheel dolly should be placed under the front tires.

Regardless of whether the vehicle is equipped with a manual transaxle, push starting the vehicle IS NOT RECOMMENDED under any circumstance.

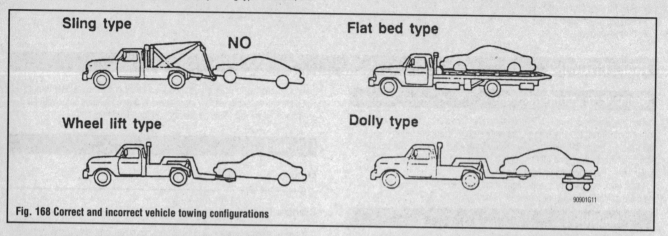

Fig. 168 Correct and incorrect vehicle towing configurations

JUMP STARTING A DEAD BATTERY

▶ **See Figure 169**

Whenever a vehicle is jump started, precautions must be followed in order to prevent the possibility of personal injury. Remember that batteries contain a small amount of explosive hydrogen gas which is a by-product of battery charging. Sparks should always be avoided when working around batteries, especially when attaching jumper cables. To minimize the possibility of accidental sparks, follow the procedure carefully.

❊❊ CAUTION

NEVER hook up the batteries in a series circuit, or the entire electrical system will go up in smoke, including the starter!

Vehicles equipped with a diesel engine may utilize two 12 volt batteries. If so, the batteries are connected in a parallel circuit (positive terminal to positive terminal, negative terminal to negative terminal). Hooking the batteries up in parallel circuit increases battery cranking power without increasing total battery voltage output. Output remains at 12 volts. On the other hand, hooking two 12 volt batteries up in a series circuit (positive terminal to negative terminal, positive terminal to negative terminal) increases total battery output to 24 volts (12 volts plus 12 volts).

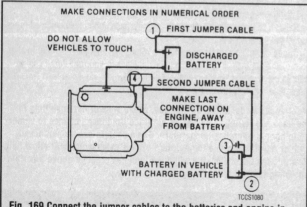

Fig. 169 Connect the jumper cables to the batteries and engine in the order shown

Jump Starting Precautions

• Be sure that both batteries are of the same voltage. Vehicles covered by this manual and most vehicles on the road today utilize a 12 volt charging system.

• Be sure that both batteries are of the same polarity (have the same terminal, in most cases NEGATIVE grounded).

• Be sure that the vehicles are not touching or a short could occur.

• On serviceable batteries, be sure the vent cap holes are not obstructed.

• Do not smoke or allow sparks anywhere near the batteries.

• In cold weather, make sure the battery electrolyte is not frozen. This can occur more readily in a battery that has been in a state of discharge.

• Do not allow electrolyte to contact your skin or clothing.

Jump Starting Procedure

1. Make sure that the voltages of the 2 batteries are the same. Most batteries and charging systems are of the 12 volt variety.

2. Pull the jumping vehicle (with the good battery) into a position so the jumper cables can reach the dead battery and that vehicle's engine. Make sure that the vehicles do NOT touch.

3. Place the transmissions/transaxles of both vehicles in **Neutral** (MT) or **Park** (AT), as applicable, then firmly set their parking brakes.

➡ **If necessary for safety reasons, the hazard lights on both vehicles may be operated throughout the entire procedure without significantly increasing the difficulty of jumping the dead battery.**

4. Turn all lights and accessories OFF on both vehicles. Make sure the ignition switches on both vehicles are turned to the **OFF** position.

5. Cover the battery cell caps with a rag, but do not cover the terminals.

6. Make sure the terminals on both batteries are clean and free of corrosion or proper electrical connection will be impeded. If necessary, clean the battery terminals before proceeding.

7. Identify the positive (+) and negative (−) terminals on both batteries.

8. Connect the first jumper cable to the positive (+) terminal of the dead battery, then connect the other end of that cable to the positive (+) terminal of the booster (good) battery.

9. Connect one end of the other jumper cable to the negative (−) terminal on the booster battery and the final cable clamp to an engine bolt head, alternator bracket or other solid, metallic point on the engine with the dead battery. Try to pick a ground on the engine that is positioned away from the battery in order

to minimize the possibility of the 2 clamps touching should one loosen during the procedure. DO NOT connect this clamp to the negative (–) terminal of the bad battery.

Be very careful to keep the jumper cables away from moving parts (cooling fan, belts, etc.) on both engines.

10. Check to make sure that the cables are routed away from any moving parts, then start the donor vehicle's engine. Run the engine at moderate speed for several minutes to allow the dead battery a chance to receive some initial charge.

11. With the donor vehicle's engine still running at idle, try to start the vehicle with the dead battery. Crank the engine for no more than 15 seconds at a time and let the starter cool for at least 15 minutes between tries. If the vehicle does not start in 3 tries, it is likely that something else is also wrong or that the battery needs additional time to charge.

12. Once the vehicle is started, allow it to run at idle for a few seconds to make sure that it is operating properly.

13. Turn ON the headlights, heater blower and, if equipped, the rear defroster of both vehicles in order to reduce the severity of voltage spikes and subsequent risk of damage to the vehicles' electrical systems when the cables are disconnected. This step is especially important to any vehicle equipped with computer control modules.

14. Carefully disconnect the cables in the reverse order of connection. Start with the negative cable that is attached to the engine ground, then the negative cable on the donor battery. Disconnect the positive cable from the donor battery and finally, disconnect the positive cable from the formerly dead battery. Be careful when disconnecting the cables from the positive terminals not to allow the alligator clips to touch any metal on either vehicle or a short and sparks will occur.

JACKING

▶ **See Figures 170, 171, 172 and 173**

Your vehicle was supplied with a jack for emergency road repairs. This jack is fine for changing a flat tire or other short term procedures not requiring you to go beneath the vehicle. If it is used in an emergency situation, carefully follow the instructions provided either with the jack or in your owner's manual. Do not attempt to use the jack on any portions of the vehicle other than those specified by the vehicle manufacturer. Always block the diagonally opposite wheel when using a jack.

A more convenient way of jacking is the use of a garage or floor jack. Never place the jack under the radiator, engine or transaxle components. Severe and expensive damage will result when the jack is raised. Additionally, never jack under the floorpan or bodywork; the metal will deform.

Whenever you plan to work under the vehicle, you must support it on jackstands or ramps. Never use cinder blocks or stacks of wood to support the vehicle, even if you're only going to be under it for a few minutes. Never crawl under the vehicle when it is supported only by the tire changing jack or other floor jack.

➡ **Always position a block of wood or small rubber pad on top of the jack or jackstand to protect the lifting points finish when lifting or supporting the vehicle.**

Small hydraulic, screw, or scissors jacks are satisfactory for raising the vehicle. Drive-on trestles or ramps are also a handy and safe way to both raise and support the vehicle. Be careful though, some ramps may be too steep to drive your vehicle onto without scraping the front bottom panels. Never support the vehicle beneath any suspension member (unless specifically instructed to do so by a repair manual) or by an underbody panel.

Jacking Precautions

The following safety points cannot be overemphasized:
• Always block the opposite wheel or wheels to keep the vehicle from rolling off the jack.
• When raising the front of the vehicle, firmly apply the parking brake.
• When the drive wheels are to remain on the ground, leave the vehicle in gear to help prevent it from rolling.
• Always use jackstands to support the vehicle when you are working underneath. Place the stands beneath the vehicle's jacking brackets. Before climbing underneath, rock the vehicle a bit to make sure it is firmly supported.

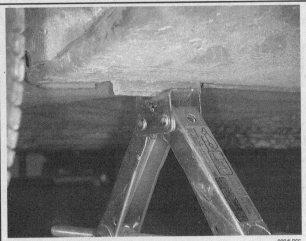

9094LP66

Fig. 170 Always make sure that the vehicle is parked on a level surface with the emergency brake applied when utilizing the emergency jack

9094LP67

Fig. 171 To raise the front of the vehicle, center the jack bracket in the middle of the hydraulic floor jack lift platform

9094LP70

Fig. 172 To raise the rear of the vehicle, place the contact pad of a hydraulic floor jack at the center point of the jack lift platform

9094LP69

Fig. 173 Whenever raising the front or rear of the vehicle, ALWAYS safely support the vehicle with jack stands before getting underneath the vehicle

MANUFACTURER RECOMMENDED MAINTENANCE INTERVALS (NORMAL CONDITIONS)

Component	Procedure	VEHICLE MAINTENANCE INTERVALS															
miles (x1000)		7.5	15	22.5	30	37.5	45	52.5	60	67.5	75	82.5	90	97.5	105	112.5	120
km (x1000)		12	24	36	48	60	72	84	96	108	120	132	144	156	168	180	192
months		12			24		36		48		60		72		84		96
Air cleaner	Replace																✓
Check engine oil	Inspect	Check engine oil level at each fuel stop.															
Coolant level	Inspect	✓	✓	✓	✓	✓	✓	✓	✓	✓	✓	✓	✓	✓	✓	✓	✓
Change coolant	Replace						✓								✓		
Engine oil and filter	Replace	✓	✓	✓	✓	✓	✓	✓	✓	✓	✓	✓	✓	✓	✓	✓	✓
Valve adjustment:																	
1.8L engine	Inspect														✓		
2.2L engine	Inspect				✓										✓		
2.3L engine	Inspect		✓								✓						
2.5L engine	Inspect										✓						
3.0L V-6 engine	Inspect						✓								✓		
3.2L V-6 engine	Inspect						✓								✓		
3.5L V-6 engine	Inspect						✓								✓		
Spark plugs (except V-6)	Replace				✓												✓
Spark plugs (B18C5)	Replace								✓								
Spark plugs (B18B1)	Replace				✓				✓								✓
Spark plugs (V-6)	Replace														✓		
Timing belt	Replace														✓		
Balance shaft belt	Replace														✓		
Water pump	Inspect														✓		
Drive belts	Inspect/Adjust								✓				✓				✓
Idle speed	Inspect/Adjust								✓								✓
PCV valve	Inspect								✓								✓
Transmission fluid	Replace	✓			✓		✓		✓	✓			✓		✓		✓
Front and rear brakes	Inspect		✓		✓		✓		✓		✓		✓		✓		✓
Brake fluid	Replace				✓				✓				✓				✓
Parking brake	Inspect/Adjust		✓		✓		✓		✓		✓		✓		✓		✓
Air conditioner filter	Replace		✓		✓		✓		✓		✓		✓		✓		✓
Tires	Rotate	✓	✓	✓	✓	✓	✓	✓	✓	✓	✓	✓	✓	✓	✓	✓	✓
Tire pressure	Adjust	Check the tire pressure at least once a month.															
Steering box	Inspect		✓		✓		✓		✓		✓		✓		✓		✓
Tie rod ends	Inspect		✓		✓		✓		✓		✓		✓		✓		✓
Steering rack bellows boots	Inspect		✓		✓		✓		✓		✓		✓		✓		✓
Suspension	Inspect		✓		✓		✓		✓		✓		✓		✓		✓
Fluid levels and condition	Inspect		✓		✓		✓		✓		✓		✓		✓		✓
Cooling system	Inspect		✓		✓		✓		✓		✓		✓		✓		✓
Exhaust system	Inspect		✓		✓		✓		✓		✓		✓		✓		✓
CV joint boots	Inspect	✓	✓	✓	✓	✓	✓	✓	✓	✓	✓	✓	✓	✓	✓	✓	✓
Brake lines, fittings and ABS	Inspect		✓		✓		✓		✓		✓		✓		✓		✓
Fuel lines, fittings, and hoses	Inspect		✓		✓		✓		✓		✓		✓		✓		✓
Supplemental restraint	Inspect	10 years after production															

90941C05

MANUFACTURER RECOMMENDED MAINTENANCE INTERVALS (SEVERE CONDITIONS)

Component	Service	VEHICLE MAINTENANCE INTERVALS															
miles (x1000)		7.5	15	22.5	30	37.5	45	52.5	60	67.5	75	82.5	90	97.5	105	112.5	120
km (x1000)		12	24	36	48	60	72	84	96	108	120	132	144	156	168	180	192
months		12			24		36		48		60		72		84		96
Air cleaner	Replace																✓
Check engine oil level	Inspect	Inspect engine oil level at every fuel stop.															
Coolant level	Inspect	✓	✓	✓	✓	✓	✓	✓	✓	✓	✓	✓	✓	✓	✓	✓	✓
Change coolant	Replace						✓								✓		
Engine oil and filter	Replace	Replace every 3,700 miles (6,000 km) or 6 months.															
Valve adjustment:																	
1.8L engine	Inspect														✓		
2.2L engine	Inspect				✓										✓		
2.3L engine	Inspect		✓								✓						
2.5L engine	Inspect										✓						
3.0L V-6 engine	Inspect						✓								✓		
3.2L V-6 engine	Inspect						✓								✓		
3.5L V-6 engine	Inspect						✓								✓		
Spark plugs (except V-6)	Replace				✓												✓
Spark plugs (B18C5)	Replace								✓								
Spark plugs (B18B1)	Replace				✓				✓								✓
Spark plugs (V-6)	Replace														✓		
Timing belt	Replace														✓		
Balance shaft belt	Replace								✓								✓
Water pump	Inspect								✓								✓
Drive belts	Inspect/Adjust				✓				✓				✓				✓
Idle speed	Inspect/Adjust								✓								✓
PCV valve	Inspect								✓								✓
Transmission fluid	Replace				✓				✓				✓				✓
Front and rear brakes	Inspect	✓	✓	✓	✓	✓	✓	✓	✓	✓	✓	✓	✓	✓	✓	✓	✓
Brake fluid	Replace				✓				✓				✓				✓
Parking brake	Inspect/Adjust		✓		✓		✓		✓		✓		✓		✓		✓
Air conditioner air filter	Replace		✓		✓		✓		✓		✓		✓		✓		✓
Check tire pressure	Inspect	Check the tire pressure at least once a month.															
Tires	Rotate	✓	✓	✓	✓	✓	✓	✓	✓	✓	✓	✓	✓	✓	✓	✓	✓
Steering box	Inspect		✓		✓		✓		✓		✓		✓		✓		✓
Tie rod ends	Inspect	✓	✓	✓	✓	✓	✓	✓	✓	✓	✓	✓	✓	✓	✓	✓	✓
Steering rack bellows boots	Inspect		✓		✓		✓		✓		✓		✓		✓		✓
Suspension	Inspect		✓		✓		✓		✓		✓		✓		✓		✓
Fluid levels and condition	Inspect		✓		✓		✓		✓		✓		✓		✓		✓
Cooling system	Inspect		✓		✓		✓		✓		✓		✓		✓		✓
Exhaust system	Inspect		✓		✓		✓		✓		✓		✓		✓		✓
CV joint boots	Inspect	✓	✓	✓	✓	✓	✓	✓	✓	✓	✓	✓	✓	✓	✓	✓	✓
Brake lines, fittings and ABS	Inspect		✓		✓		✓		✓		✓		✓		✓		✓
Fuel lines, fittings, and hoses	Inspect		✓		✓		✓		✓		✓		✓		✓		✓
Supplemental restraint	Inspect	10 years after production															

90941C06

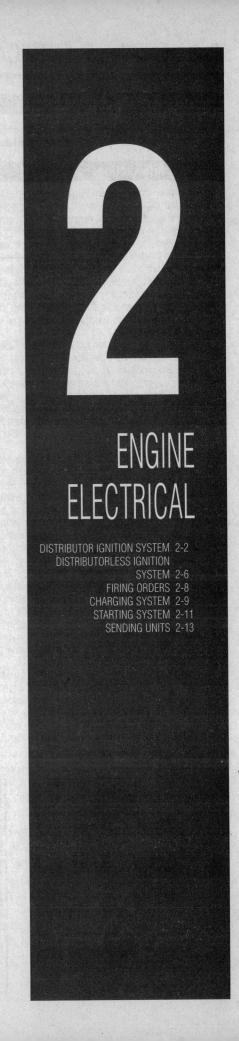

2

ENGINE
ELECTRICAL

DISTRIBUTOR IGNITION SYSTEM

➡**For information on understanding electricity and troubleshooting electrical circuits, please refer to Section 6 of this manual.**

General Information

The distributor ignition system differs from the conventional breaker points system in form only; its function is exactly the same: to supply a spark to the spark plugs at precisely the right moment to ignite the compressed air/fuel mixture in the cylinders and create mechanical movement.

Located in the distributor, in addition to the rotor, is a spoked reluctor which is pressed onto the distributor shaft. The reluctor revolves with the rotor; as it passes a pickup coil inside the distributor body, it breaks a high flux field, which occurs in the space between the reluctor and the pickup coil. The breaking of the field allows current to flow to the pickup coil. Primary ignition current is then cut off by the Powertrain Control Module (PCM), allowing the magnetic field in the ignition coil to collapse, creating the spark which the distributor passes on to the spark plugs.

The distributor ignition system has timing controlled by the Powertrain Control Module (PCM). The standard reference ignition timing data for the engine operating conditions are programmed in the memory of the PCM. The engine conditions (rpm, load and temperature) are detected by various sensors. Based on these sensor signals and the ignition timing data, a signal is sent to interrupt the primary current at the power transistor. The ignition coil is activated and a spark sent through the distributor, down the spark plug wires to the spark plugs. Ignition timing is controlled by the PCM for optimum performance.

The distributor ignition system can be identified by looking for the presence of a distributor (with spark plug wires connecting the distributor cap to the spark plugs). If no distributor is found, it can be assumed that the engine uses a distributorless ignition system. Coverage of the distributorless ignition system is found later in this section. Acura ignition systems are basically comprised of a distributor, an ignition control module, a control box, a high energy coil and related ignition wires. The diss a reluctor mounted on a rotor shaft and a magnet mounted on a base plate. The pick-up coil is located around the rotor shaft but does not rotate with the shaft. The programmed ignition employed on these vehicles, provides optimum control of ignition timing by determining the optimum timing using a microcomputer in response to engine speed and vacuum pressure in the intake manifold, which are transmitted by signals from CRANK/CYL sensor, TDC sensor, throttle angle sensor, coolant temperature sensor and MAP sensor. This system, not dependent on a governor or vacuum diaphragm, is capable of setting lead angles with complicated characteristics which cannot be provided by conventional governors or diaphragms.

The ignition control module contains 3 resistors, 3 diodes and 2 transistors. The transistors act as switches which are activated at a precise voltage. When the ignition is switched **ON**, the switching of the transistors in the ignition control module ensures that no current can flow in the ignition coil primary windings. When the engine is cranked, the reluctor moves through the magnetic field created by the stator and, when the reluctor teeth are aligned with the stator pro-

jections, a small AC voltage is created. The ignition control module amplifies this voltage and uses it to switch the transistors so that an earth path is provided to the primary circuit.

As the reluctor teeth move out of alignment with the stator projections, an abrupt change occurs in the AC voltage. The transistors are switched again and the primary circuit earth path is broken. This induces a high voltage in the ignition coil secondary winding.

A time control circuit in the ignition control module controls the charging time for the ignition coil according to engine speed, this reduces consumption at low engine speeds and prevents secondary voltage drop at high engine speeds.

Diagnosis and Testing

SPARK PLUG CABLE TEST

▶ **See Figure 1**

✸✸ CAUTION

Before beginning this test, be sure to wear rubber gloves and rubber-soled shoes for safety.

1. One at a time, disengage each spark plug wire with the engine idling to check whether the engine's performance changes or not.
2. If the performance does not change, check the resistance of each spark plug and wire. Refer to Section 1 for checking the resistance of the spark plug wires.

SECONDARY SPARK TEST

▶ **See Figures 2, 3, 4 and 5**

1. Remove a spark plug from the engine. Examine the spark plug for cracks in its insulation and replace if necessary.
2. Connect the spark plug to its spark plug wire.
3. Ground the spark plug's outer electrode to the engine (touch the spark plug's metal body to the engine block or other piece of metal on the car).
4. Crank the engine and look for spark across the electrodes of the spark plug.
5. If a strong blue spark exists across the plug electrode, the ignition system is functioning properly.
6. Repeat the test for the remaining cylinders. If one or more tests indicate irregular, weak or no spark, refer to the coil test.
7. If spark does not exist, remove the distributor cap and ensure that the rotor is turning when the engine is cranked.

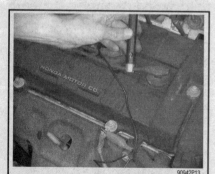

90942P13

Fig. 1 A spark plug wire tester, such as this one, can save much time in the diagnostic process

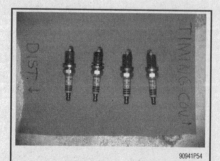

90941P54

Fig. 2 Place the plugs in order on a piece of cardboard. This will aid you in determining the condition of the plugs and their corresponding cylinder

90942P10

Fig. 3 A spark tester can save lots of time in determining an ignition system problem. This model allows you to adjust the gap that the spark has to jump

Fig. 4 To test for spark at the plug, ground the body to a known good ground such as this ground strap bolt

Fig. 5 The use of an anti-seize compound is advised for easy removal and installation of spark plugs

Fig. 6 Testing resistance on the secondary side of the coil

Ignition Coil

TESTING

1.8L, 2.2L, 2.3L Engines

▶ **See Figures 6 and 7**

1. Disconnect the negative battery cable.
2. Remove the black/yellow and white/blue wires from the terminals marked A (+) and B (−).

➡**Resistance will vary with coil temperature; therefore all specification were taken at an ambient temperature of 68°F (20°C)**

3. Measure the resistance between both terminals using an ohmmeter and compare with the following specifications:

   a. For the 1.8L engine, the primary winding resistance should be within 0.6–0.8 ohms. Proper secondary winding resistance is 12.8–19.2 kilohms.

   b. For the 2.2L and 2.3L engines, the primary winding resistance should be 0.45–0.55 ohms. The secondary winding resistance should be 16.8–25.2 ohms.

➡**The Powertrain Control Module (PCM) idle memory must be reset after reconnecting the battery. Start the engine and hold it at 3000 rpm until the cooling fan comes on. Then allow the engine to idle for about five minutes with all accessories OFF and with the transmission in Park or Neutral.**

4. Reconnect the negative battery cable.

Fig. 7 Testing the primary resistance of the ignition coil

2.5L Engine

1. Disconnect the negative battery cable.
2. Remove the four prong connector.
3. Disconnect the ignition coil wire from the coil.
4. Use an ohmmeter to measure the resistance between the terminals as follows:

   a. Measure primary wire resistance between terminals 2 and 3. A result of 0.36–0.44 ohms is within specification.

   b. Resistance between terminals 3 and 4 should be between 2.0–2.3 Kilohms.

➡**The Powertrain Control Module (PCM) idle memory must be reset after reconnecting the battery. Start the engine and hold it at 3000 rpm until the cooling fan comes on. Then allow the engine to idle for about five minutes with all accessories OFF and with the transmission in Park or Neutral.**

5. Reconnect the negative battery cable.

3.0L Engine

1. Disconnect the negative battery cable.
2. Remove the 3 prong connector from the ignition coil.
3. Remove the ignition coil wire.
4. Use an ohmmeter to measure the resistance between the terminals on the coil, and compare with the following:

   a. Resistance between the two outer most terminals should be between 0.34–0.42 ohms. This is the primary winding side of the coil.

   b. The secondary winding resistance is found by measuring across the middle terminal of the coil and the secondary winding terminal. The resistance should be between 17.1–20.9 Kilohms.

➡**The Powertrain Control Module (PCM) idle memory must be reset after reconnecting the battery. Start the engine and hold it at 3000 rpm until the cooling fan comes on. Then allow the engine to idle for about five minutes with all accessories OFF and with the transmission in Park or Neutral.**

5. Reconnect the negative battery cable.

REMOVAL & INSTALLATION

1.8L, 2.2L, 2.3L Engines

▶ **See Figures 8, 9, 10, 11 and 12**

1. Disconnect the negative battery cable.
2. Remove the distributor cap.
3. Mark the position of the rotor to the housing.
4. Remove the ignition rotor.
5. Remove the cap seal.
6. Remove the leak cover.
7. Remove the screws that hold the black/yellow and white/blue wires to the ignition coil.

Fig. 8 Remove the plastic cover from the coil

Fig. 9 Unfasten the screw(s) securing the electrical wiring to the coil

Fig. 10 A Phillips head screw driver may be necessary to remove the attaching bolts from the coil

Fig. 11 Note the length of each screw as you remove them, for they may be different sizes

Fig. 12 Removal of the ignition coil from the Integra's 1.8L engine

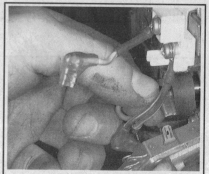

Fig. 13 Removing of the Integrated Control Module (ICM) from the distributor

8. Unfasten the screws that secure the coil, then pull the ignition coil from the housing.
9. Installation is the reverse of the removal procedure.

➡The Powertrain Control Module (PCM) idle memory must be reset after reconnecting the battery. Start the engine and hold it at 3000 rpm until the cooling fan comes on. Then allow the engine to idle for about five minutes with all accessories OFF and with the transmission in Park or Neutral.

2.5L, 3.0L Engines

1. Disconnect the negative battery cable.
2. Detach the electrical connector from the coil.
3. Detach the ignition coil wire.
4. Remove the mounting bolts, then remove the ignition coil.
5. Installation is the reverse of the removal procedure.

➡The Powertrain Control Module (PCM) idle memory must be reset after reconnecting the battery. Start the engine and hold it at 3000 rpm until the cooling fan comes on. Then allow the engine to idle for about five minutes with all accessories OFF and with the transmission in Park or Neutral.

Ignition Module

REMOVAL & INSTALLATION

▸ **See Figures 13 and 14**

1. Disconnect the negative battery cable.
2. Remove the distributor cap, ignition rotor, and protective leak cover.
3. Detach the wires from the Integrated Control Module (ICM).

4. Remove the ICM.
5. Installation is the reverse of the removal procedure.

➡The Powertrain Control Module (PCM) idle memory must be reset after reconnecting the battery. Start the engine and hold it at 3000 rpm until the cooling fan comes on. Then allow the engine to idle for about five minutes with all accessories OFF and with the transmission in Park or Neutral.

Fig. 14 Close up view of the Integrated Control Module (ICM)—Integra shown, others similar

Distributor

REMOVAL & INSTALLATION

➡ **The radio on these vehicles may contain a coded anti-theft circuit. Be sure you have the security code number before disconnecting the battery cable.**

1.8L, 2.2L and 2.3L Engines

▶ **See Figures 15, 16, 17 and 18**

1. Disconnect the negative battery cable.
2. Detach engine wiring harness and connectors from distributor.
3. Tag and disconnect the spark plug wires from distributor cap.
4. If removing the ignition coil, remove the distributor cap, rotor, and cap seal, then remove the leak cover.
5. Remove the 2 screws to disconnect the wires from the coil.
6. Matchmark the position of the distributor housing to the valve cover or another stationary point such as the engine block. This step is done to ensure the distributor can be installed in the exact position from which it was removed.
7. Remove the 2 screws and slide the ignition coil out of the distributor housing.
8. Remove distributor hold-down bolts, and remove distributor from cylinder head.

To install:

9. Use new O-ring on distributor housing. Coat new O-ring with engine oil before installation.

Fig. 15 Unfasten the distributor mounting bolts . . .

10. Slip the distributor into position.
11. Align the matchmarks that were made during the removal process.

➡ **The lugs on the end of the distributor and the matching grooves in the camshaft end are offset to eliminate any possibility of installing the distributor 180 degrees out of time.**

12. Install the hold-down bolts, hand tighten.
13. Slide the ignition coil into the distributor housing and install the 2 mounting screws.
14. Reconnect the 2 wires to the coil and install the 2 screws. Install the leak cover, rotor, cap seal, and cap.
15. Attach the engine wiring harness and connector to distributor.
16. Connect the spark plug wires, as tagged during removal. Reconnect the negative battery cable.
17. Set the timing, using a timing light as outlined in Section 1, then tighten the distributor hold-down bolts to 16 ft. lbs. (22 Nm).

➡ **The Powertrain Control Module (PCM) idle memory must be reset after reconnecting the battery. To perform this, you must start the engine and hold it at 3000 rpm until the cooling fan comes on. Then allow the engine to idle for about five minutes with all accessories OFF and with the transmission in Park or Neutral.**

2.5L and 3.0L Engines

1. Disconnect the negative battery cable.
2. Disconnect the spark plug and coil wires from the distributor cap and mark their positions.
3. Detach the harness connector(s) from the distributor.
4. Matchmark the position of the distributor housing to the valve cover or another stationary point such as the engine block. This step is done to ensure the distributor can be installed in the exact position from which it was removed.
5. Remove the distributor mounting bolts.
6. Remove the distributor from the cylinder head.

To install:

7. Install a new O-ring on the distributor housing. Coat the O-ring with engine oil before installation.
8. Install the distributor into position, verifying that the lugs on the distributor shaft end fit into the grooves on the camshaft end.
9. Align the matchmarks that were made during the removal process.
10. Install the mounting bolts. Tighten the bolt(s) to 13 ft. lbs. (18 Nm).
11. Connect the spark plug and coil wires. Connect the negative battery cable.
12. Check the ignition timing with a timing light, as outlined in Section 1. The timing marks are located on the crankshaft pulley and lower timing cover.

➡ **The Powertrain Control Module (PCM) idle memory must be reset after reconnecting the battery. To perform this, you must start the engine and hold it at 3000 rpm until the cooling fan comes on. Then allow the engine to idle for about five minutes with all accessories OFF and with the transmission in Park or Neutral.**

Fig. 16 . . . then remove the distributor from the engine

Fig. 17 Top view of the distributor from a 1.8L engine

Fig. 18 Use a suitable tool to carefully remove the distributor O-ring and replace with a new one before installation

Crankshaft Position Sensor

Refer to Electronic Engine Controls in Section 4 for information on servicing the crankshaft position sensor.

Camshaft Position Sensor

Refer to Electronic Engine Controls in Section 4 for information on servicing the camshaft position sensor.

DISTRIBUTORLESS IGNITION SYSTEM

General Information

♦ **See Figures 19 and 20**

Many Acura models are equipped with a distributorless ignition system. This system is still considered a Programmed Ignition (PGM-IG) system. The basic difference is that the distributorless system incorporates one ignition coil per cylinder as opposed to the distributor type system, which uses one ignition coil for the entire system. System operation is accomplished when the ignition switch is in the **RUN** or **START** position. Battery current is applied through each of the ignition coils to the ignition control module. The ignition control module acts as a switch to control current through the primary windings of the ignition coils. This module is controlled by the PGM-FI electronic unit. When current to the ignition coil is stopped, a high voltage current flows to the spark plug. The ignition system is controlled by inputs to the PGM-FI electronic control unit. The inputs include; detonation, engine RPM, accelerator position, coolant temperature, ignition timing adjustment, manifold pressure, crankshaft position and exhaust oxygen content. Traction control and the automatic transmission also affect the ignition system.

Diagnosis and Testing

To test the ignition system, perform the test procedures in a particular sequence. Start with the secondary spark test, commence to the coil test (located under the coil procedures later in this section) and, finally, perform the failure-to-start test. Performing the tests in this order will narrow down the ignition system problem in the easiest manner.

SECONDARY SPARK TEST

♦ **See Figure 21**

> ❊❊ **CAUTION**
>
> **The Distributorless Ignition System generates approximately 40,000 volts. Personal injury could result from contact with this system.**

1. Remove the cable from the No. 1 spark plug, then insert a clean spark plug into the spark plug boot.

➡**Due to the high secondary voltage and risk of electrical shock, it is advisable to wrap a thick, dry cloth around the boot before grasping it.**

> ❊❊ **WARNING**
>
> **Spark plug wire damage may occur if the spark plug is moved more than ¼ in. (6mm) away from the engine ground.**

2. Ground the plug to the engine (touch the spark plug metal body to the engine block or other piece of metal on the car).
3. Crank the engine and look for a strong, blue spark across the electrodes of the spark plug.
4. Repeat the test for the remaining cylinders. If there is no spark during all cylinder tests, refer to the failure-to-start test. If one or more tests indicate irregular, weak or no spark, refer to the coil test.

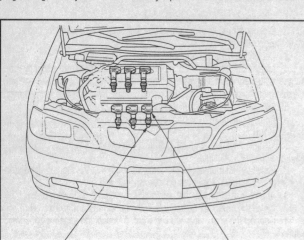

Fig. 19 Ignition system components—3.2L engine shown

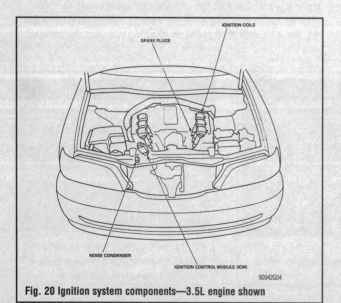

Fig. 20 Ignition system components—3.5L engine shown

Fig. 21 When checking for spark, always ground the plug to a known good source.

Adjustments

The programmed ignition system provides the best control of the ignition timing therefore there is no need for adjustment.

Ignition Coil Pack

TESTING

3.2L Engine

▶ See Figure 22

1. Disconnect the negative battery cable.
2. Remove the ignition coil.

➡In order to get to the ignition coil at the No. 6 cylinder, it may be necessary to remove the A/C suction line mounting bolts to enable the line to be moved over slightly. This will provide adequate access to the coil.

3. Remove the two wire connector that feeds the coil battery voltage.
4. Use an ohmmeter to check the primary coil resistance between the two terminals on the coil. Resistance should be between 0.9–1.1 ohms.

➡The Powertrain Control Module (PCM) idle memory must be reset after reconnecting the battery. Start the engine and hold it at 3000 rpm until the cooling fan comes on. Then allow the engine to idle for about five minutes with all accessories OFF and with the transmission in Park or Neutral.

5. Reconnect the negative battery cable.

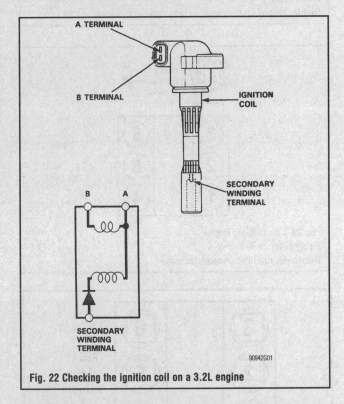

Fig. 22 Checking the ignition coil on a 3.2L engine

3.5L Engine

▶ See Figure 23

1. Disconnect the negative battery cable.
2. Remove the strut brace by unscrewing the 4 nuts and one bolt.
3. Remove the engine cover.
4. Remove the ignition coil.
5. Measure the resistance of the coil between terminals 1 and 2. Primary winding resistance should be between 0.9–1.1 ohms.

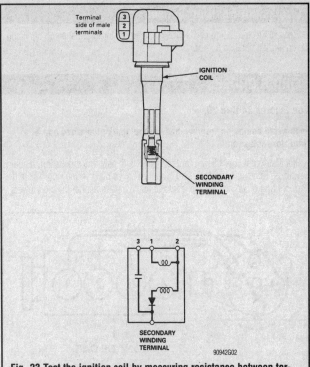

Fig. 23 Test the ignition coil by measuring resistance between terminals 1 & 2—3.5L engine

➡The Powertrain Control Module (PCM) idle memory must be reset after reconnecting the battery. Start the engine and hold it at 3000 rpm until the cooling fan comes on. Then allow the engine to idle for about five minutes with all accessories OFF and with the transmission in Park or Neutral.

6. Reconnect the negative battery cable.

REMOVAL & INSTALLATION

1. Disconnect the negative battery cable.
2. Remove the wiring harness from the coil.
3. Remove the ignition coil wire.
4. Remove the ignition coil by removing the mounting bolts.
5. Remove the ignition coil.
6. Install is the reverse of the removal procedure.

➡The Powertrain Control Module (PCM) idle memory must be reset after reconnecting the battery. Start the engine and hold it at 3000 rpm until the cooling fan comes on. Then allow the engine to idle for about five minutes with all accessories OFF and with the transmission in Park or Neutral.

Ignition Control Module (ICM)

REMOVAL & INSTALLATION

1. Disconnect the negative battery cable.
2. Detach all of the electrical connectors that are located at the top of the Ignition Control Module (ICM).
3. Remove the mounting bolts, then remove the ICM from the vehicle.
4. Installation is the reverse of the removal procedure.

➡The Powertrain Control Module (PCM) idle memory must be reset after reconnecting the battery. Start the engine and hold it at 3000 rpm until the cooling fan comes on. Then allow the engine to idle for about five minutes with all accessories OFF and with the transmission in Park or Neutral.

Crankshaft Position Sensor

Refer to Electronic Engine Controls in Section 4 for information on servicing the crankshaft position sensor.

FIRING ORDERS

See Figures 24 thru 29

➡**To avoid confusion, remove and tag the spark plug wires one at a time, for replacement.**

If a distributor is not keyed for installation with only one orientation, it could have been removed previously and rewired. The resultant wiring would hold the correct firing order, but could change the relative placement of the plug towers

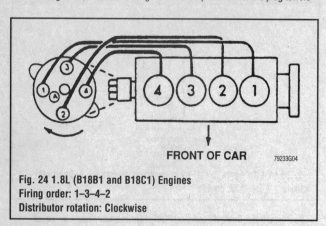

Fig. 24 1.8L (B18B1 and B18C1) Engines
Firing order: 1–3–4–2
Distributor rotation: Clockwise

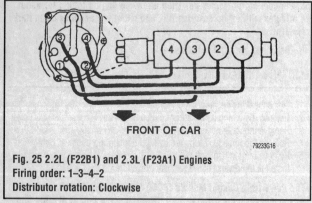

Fig. 25 2.2L (F22B1) and 2.3L (F23A1) Engines
Firing order: 1–3–4–2
Distributor rotation: Clockwise

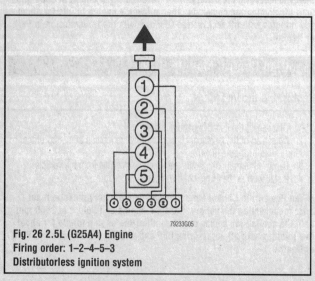

Fig. 26 2.5L (G25A4) Engine
Firing order: 1–2–4–5–3
Distributorless ignition system

Camshaft Position Sensor

Refer to Electronic Engine Controls in Section 4 for information on servicing the camshaft position sensor.

in relation to the engine. For this reason, it is imperative that you label all wires before disconnecting any of them. Also, before removal, compare the current wiring with the accompanying illustrations. If the current wiring does not match, make notes in your book to reflect how your engine is wired.

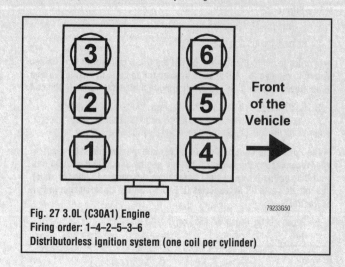

Fig. 27 3.0L (C30A1) Engine
Firing order: 1–4–2–5–3–6
Distributorless ignition system (one coil per cylinder)

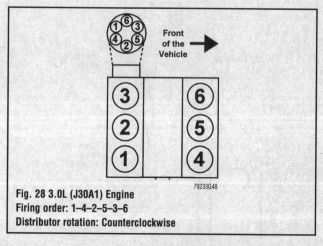

Fig. 28 3.0L (J30A1) Engine
Firing order: 1–4–2–5–3–6
Distributor rotation: Counterclockwise

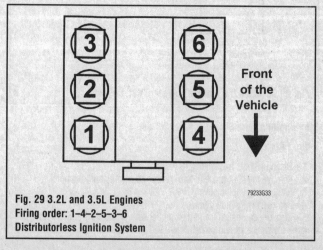

Fig. 29 3.2L and 3.5L Engines
Firing order: 1–4–2–5–3–6
Distributorless Ignition System

CHARGING SYSTEM

General Information

The charging system is a negative (–) ground system which consists of an alternator, a regulator within the Powertrain Control Module (PCM), ignition switch, charge indicator lamp, battery, circuit protection and wiring connecting the components.

The alternator is belt-driven from the engine. Energy is supplied from the alternator to the rotating field through brushes to slip-rings. The slip-rings are mounted on the rotor shaft and are connected to the field coil. This energy supplied to the rotating field from the battery is called excitation current and is used to initially energize the field to begin the generation of electricity. Once the alternator starts to generate electricity, the excitation current comes from its own output, rather than from the battery.

The alternator produces power in the form of alternating current. The alternating current is rectified by diodes into direct current. The direct current is used to charge the battery and power the rest of the electrical system. When the ignition key is turned **ON**, current flows from the battery, through the charging system indicator light on the instrument panel, to the voltage regulator in the PCM, and to the alternator. Since the alternator is not producing any current, the alternator warning light comes on. When the engine is started, the alternator begins to produce current and turns the alternator light off.

As the alternator turns and produces current, the current is divided in two ways: charging the battery and powering the electrical components of the vehicle. Part of the current is returned to the alternator to enable it to increase its output. In this situation, the alternator is receiving current from the battery and from itself. A voltage regulator is wired into the current supply to the alternator to prevent it from receiving too much current, which would cause it to overproduce current. Conversely, if the voltage regulator does not allow the alternator to receive enough current, the battery will not be fully charged and will eventually go dead.

The battery is connected to the alternator at all times, whether the ignition key is turned **ON** or **OFF**. If the battery were shorted to ground, the alternator would also be shorted. This would damage the alternator. To prevent this, circuit protection (usually in the form of a fuse link) is installed in the wiring between the battery and the altbattery is shorted, the circuit protection will protect the alternator.

Alternator Precautions

Several precautions must be observed with alternator equipped vehicles to avoid damage to the unit.

- ALWAYS observe proper polarity of the battery connections; be especially careful when jump starting the car. Reversing the battery connections may result in damage to the one-way rectifiers.
- ALWAYS remove the battery or, at least, disconnect the cables while charging.
- ALWAYS match and/or consider the polarity of the battery, alternator and regulator before making any electrical connections within the system.
- ALWAYS disconnect the battery ground terminal while repairing or replacing any electrical components.
- NEVER use a fast battery charger to jump start a dead battery.
- NEVER attempt to polarize an alternator.
- NEVER use test lights of more than 12 volts when checking diode continuity.
- NEVER ground or short out the alternator or regulator terminals.
- NEVER separate the alternator on an open circuit. Make sure all connections within the circuit are clean and tight.
- NEVER use arc welding equipment on the car with the alternator connected.
- NEVER operate the alternator with any of its or the battery's lead wires disconnected.
- NEVER subject the alternator to excessive heat or dampness (for instance, steam cleaning the engine).
- When utilizing a booster battery as a starting aid, always connect the positive to positive terminals and the negative terminal from the booster battery to a good engine ground on the vehicle being started.

Alternator

TESTING

Voltage Drop Test

➡**These tests will show the amount of voltage drop across the alternator output wire from the alternator output (B+) terminal to the battery positive post. They will also show the amount of voltage drop from the ground (–) terminal on the alternator.**

A voltmeter with a 0–18 volt DC scale should be used for these tests. By repositioning the voltmeter test leads, the point of high resistance (voltage drop) can easily be found. Test points on the alternator can be reached by either removing the air cleaner housing or below by raising the vehicle.

1. Before starting the test, make sure the battery is in good condition and is fully charged. Check the conditions of the battery cables.
2. Start the engine, let it warm up to normal operating temperatures, then turn the engine **OFF**.
3. Connect an engine tachometer, following the manufacturer's directions.
4. Make sure the parking brake is fully engaged.
5. Start the engine, then place the blower on HIGH, and turn on the high beam headlamps and interior lamps.
6. Bring the engine speed up to 2,400 rpm and hold it there.
7. To test the ground (–) circuitry, perform the following:
   a. Touch the negative lead of the voltmeter directly to the positive battery terminal.
   b. Touch the positive lead of the voltmeter to the B+ output terminal stud on the alternator (NOT the terminal mounting nut). The voltage should be no higher than 0.6 volts. If the voltage is higher than 0.6 volts, touch the test lead to the terminal mounting stud nut, and then to the wiring connector. If the voltage is now below 0.6 volts, look for dirty, loose or poor connections at this point. A voltage drop test may be performed at each ground (–) connection in the circuit to locate the excessive resistance.
8. To test the positive (+) circuitry, perform the following:
   a. Touch the positive lead of the voltmeter directly to the negative battery terminal.
   b. Touch the negative lead of the voltmeter to the ground terminal stud on the alternatrminal mounting nut). The voltage should be no higher than 0.3 volts. If the voltage is higher than 0.3 volts, touch the test lead to the terminal mounting stud nut, and then to the wiring connector. If the voltage is now below 0.3 volts, look for dirty, loose or poor connections at this point. A voltage drop test may be performed at each positive (+) connection in the circuit to locate the excessive resistance.
9. This test can also be performed between the alternator case and the engine. If the test voltage is higher than 0.3 volts, check for corrosion at the alternator mounting points or loose alternator mounting.

Output Voltage Test

1. Determine if any Diagnostic Trouble Codes (DTC's) exist, as outlined in Section 4.
2. Before starting the test, make sure the battery is in good condition and is fully charged. Check the conditions of the battery cables.
3. Perform the voltage drop test to ensure clean and tight alternator/battery electrical connections.
4. Be sure the alternator drive belt is properly tensioned, as outlined in Section 1.
5. A volt/amp tester equipped with both a battery load control (carbon pile rheostat) and an inductive-type pickup clamp (ammeter probe) will be used for this test. Make sure to follows all directions supplied with the tester. If you are using a tester equipped with an inductive-type clamp, you don't have to remove the wiring from the alternator.
6. Start the engine and let it run until it reaches normal operating temperature, then shut the engine **OFF**.
7. Make sure all electrical accessories and lights are turned OFF.

8. Connect the volt/amp tester leads to the battery. Be sure the carbon pile rheostat control is in the OPEN or OFF position before connecting the leads.

9. Connect the inductive clamp (ammeter probe), following the instructions supplied with the test equipment.

10. If a volt/amp tester is not equipped with an engine tachometer, connect a separate tachometer to the engine.

11. Fully engage the parking brake.

12. Start the engine, then bring the engine speed up to 2,500 rpm.

✷✷ WARNING

This load test must be performed within 15 seconds to prevent damage to the test equipment!

13. With the engine speed held at 2,500 rpm, slowly adjust the rheostat control (load) on the tester to get the highest amperage reading. Do not let the voltage drop below 12 volts. Record the reading.

➡On certain brands of test equipment, this load will be applied automatically. Be sure to read the operating manual supplied with the test equipment before performing the test.

14. The ammeter reading must meet the minimum test amps specification of 75 amps.

15. Rotate the load control to the OFF position.

16. Continue holding the engine speed at 2,500 rpm. If the circuitry is OK, the amperage should drop below 15–20 amps. With all of the electrical accessories and vehicle lighting off, this could take several minutes of engine operation.

17. After the procedure is complete, remove the volt/amp tester.

REMOVAL & INSTALLATION

1.8L, 2.2L, 2.3L, 2.5L Engines

▶ **See Figures 30, 31 and 32**

1. Disconnect the negative, then the positive battery cable.

2. Detach the four prong connector and the black wire from the rear of the alternator.

3. Remove the alternator adjusting bolt.

4. Remove the locknut.

5. Remove the alternator belt.

6. Remove the alternator assembly.

7. Installation is the reverse of the removal procedure.

✷✷ WARNING

Be sure to adjust the alternator belt to the proper tension or alternator bearing failure may occur.

➡The Powertrain Control Module (PCM) idle memory must be reset after reconnecting the battery. Start the engine and hold it at 3000 rpm until the cooling fan comes on. Then allow the engine to idle for about five minutes with all accessories OFF and with the transmission in Park or Neutral.

3.0L Engine

1. Remove the battery cover.

2. Disconnect the negative, then the positive battery cable.

3. Remove the front engine cover.

4. Remove the accessory drive belt by pulling back on the tensioner.

5. Remove the A/C condenser fan shroud assembly. This is done by disconnecting the fan motor connector and removing the A/C compressor clutch wiring connector from the fan shroud.

6. Disconnect the ground cable

7. Disconnect the wiring from the alternator.

8. Remove the alternator and bracket assembly.

9. Installation is the reverse of the removal procedure.

➡There is no belt tension adjustment due to the use of an automatic tensioner.

➡The Powertrain Control Module (PCM) idle memory must be reset after reconnecting the battery. Start the engine and hold it at 3000 rpm until the cooling fan comes on. Then allow the engine to idle for about five minutes with all accessories OFF and with the transmission in Park or Neutral.

10. Connect the positive, then the negative battery cable.

11. Install battery cover.

3.2L, 3.5L Engines

▶ **See Figures 33 and 34**

1. Disconnect the negative, then the positive battery cable.

2. Remove the necessary mounting and adjusting bolts.

3. Remove the belt from the pulley.

4. On the 3.2L engine, turn the alternator 90°in a counter clockwise direction.

5. Remove the alternator by pulling it towards you.

6. Remove the four prong connector

7. Remove the harness clip and bracket assembly

8. Remove the black wire from the terminal.

9. Lift the alternator from the vehicle.

To install:

10. Connect the black wire to the alternator.

11. Attach the harness clip and bracket assembly.

12. Attach the four prong connector.

13. Install the alternator into the bracket.

14. Install the belt.

15. Adjust the belt tension.

➡The Powertrain Control Module (PCM) idle memory must be reset after reconnecting the battery. Start the engine and hold it at 3000 rpm until the cooling fan comes on. Then allow the engine to idle for about five minutes with all accessories OFF and with the transmission in Park or Neutral.

16. Connect the positive, then the negative battery cable.

Fig. 30 Remove the alternator belt from the pulley

Fig. 31 On some models, the alternator is removed from the under side of the car

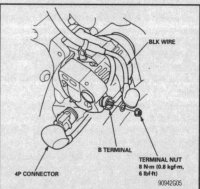

Fig. 32 Alternator mounting—2.2L engine shown

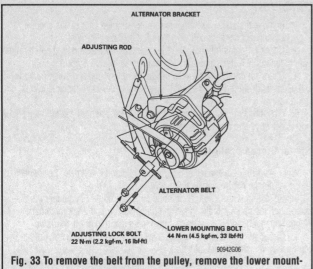

Fig. 33 To remove the belt from the pulley, remove the lower mounting bolt, adjusting lock bolt and adjusting rod

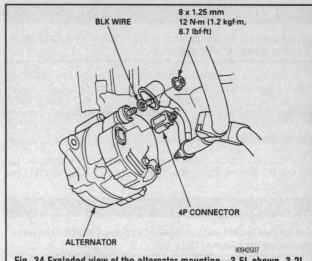

Fig. 34 Exploded view of the alternator mounting—3.5L shown, 3.2L similar

STARTING SYSTEM

General Information

The battery and starting motor are linked by very heavy electrical cables designed to minimize resistance to the flow of current. Generally, the major power supply cable that leaves the battery goes directly to the starter, while other electrical system needs are supplied by a smaller cable. During starter operation, power flows from the battery to the starter and is grounded through the vehicle's frame/body or engine and the battery's negative ground strap.

The starter is a specially designed, direct current electric motor capable of producing a great amount of power for its size. One thing that allows the motor to produce a great deal of power is its tremendous rotating speed. It drives the engine through a tiny pinion gear (attached to the starter's armature), which drives the very large flywheel ring gear at a greatly reduced speed. Another factor allowing it to produce so much power is that only intermittent operation is required of it. Thus, little allowance for air circulation is necessary, and the windings can be built into a very small space.

The starter solenoid is a magnetic device which employs the small current supplied by the start circuit of the ignition switch. This magnetic action moves a plunger which mechanically engages the starter and closes the heavy switch connecting it to the battery. The starting switch circuit usually consists of the starting switch contained within the ignition switch, a neutral safety switch or clutch pedal switch, and the wiring necessary to connect these in series with the starter solenoid or relay.

The pinion, a small gear, is mounted to a one-way drive clutch. This clutch is splined to the starter armature shaft. When the ignition switch is moved to the **START** position, the solenoid plunger slides the pinion toward the flywheel ring gear via a collar and spring. If the teeth on the pinion and flywheel match properly, the pinion will engage the flywheel immediately. If the gear teeth butt one another, the spring will be compressed and will force the gears to mesh as soon as the starter turns far enough to allow them to do so. As the solenoid plunger reaches the end of its travel, it closes the contacts that connect the battery and starter, then the engine is cranked.

As soon as the engine starts, the flywheel ring gear begins turning fast enough to drive the pinion at an extremely high rate of speed. At this point, the one-way clutch begins allowing the pinion to spin faster than the starter shaft so that the starter will not operate at excessive speed. When the ignition switch is released from the starter position, the solenoid is de-energized, and a spring pulls the gear out of mesh, interrupting the current flow to the starter.

Some starters employ a separate relay, mounted away from the starter, to switch the motor and solenoid current on and off. The relay replaces the solenoid electrical switch, but does not eliminate the need for a solenoid mounted on the starter used to mechanically engage the starter drive gears. The relay is used to reduce the amount of current the starting switch must carry.

Starter

TESTING

Testing Preparation

➡The air temperature should be between 59–100°F (15–38°C) before starting any testing.

The starting system consists of an ignition switch, starter relay, neutral safety switch, wiring harness, battery, and a starter motor with an integral solenoid. These components form two separate circuits: a high amperage circuit that feeds the starter motor up to 300 or more amps, and a control circuit that operates on less than 20 amps.

Before commencing with the starting system diagnostics, verify the following:

- The battery top posts, and terminals are clean.
- The alternator drive belt tension and condition is correct.
- The battery state-of-charge is correct.
- The battery cable connections at the starter and engine block are clean and free from corrosion.
- The wiring harness connectors and terminals are clean and free from corrosion.
- Proper circuit grounding.

Starter Feed Circuit

✳ CAUTION

The ignition system must be disabled to prevent accidental engine start while performing the following tests.

1. Connect a volt-ampere tester (multimeter) to the battery terminals.
2. Disable the ignition system.
3. Verify that all lights and accessories are OFF, and the transaxle shift selector is in Park (automatic) or Neutral (manual). Set the parking brake.
4. Rotate and hold the ignition switch in the **START** position. Observe the volt-ampere tester and compare with the following specifications:

- If the voltage reads above 9.6 volts, and the amperage draw reads above 250 amps, go to the starter feed circuit resistance test (following this test).

- If the voltage reads 12.4 volts or greater and the amperage reads 0–10 amps, refer to the starter solenoid and relay tests.

❄❄ WARNING

Do not overheat the starter motor or draw the battery voltage below 9.6 volts during cranking operations.

5. After the starting system problems have been corrected, verify the battery state of charge and charge the battery if necessary. Disconnect all of the testing equipment and connect the ignition coil cable or ignition coil connector. Start the vehicle several times to assure the problem was corrected.

Starter Feed Circuit Resistance

Before proceeding with this test, refer to the battery tests and starter feed circuit test. The following test will require a voltmeter, which is capable of accuracy to 0.1 volt.

❄❄ CAUTION

The ignition system must be disabled to prevent engine start while performing the following tests.

1. Disable the ignition system.
2. With all wiring harnesses and components (except for the coils) properly connected, perform the following:
    a. Connect the negative (–) lead of the voltmeter to the negative battery post, and the positive (+) lead to the negative (–) battery cable clamp. Rotate and hold the ignition switch in the **START** position. Observe the voltmeter. If the voltage is detected, correct the poor contact between the cable clamp and post.
    b. Connect the positive (+) lead of the voltmeter to the positive battery post, and the negative (–) to the positive battery cable clamp. Rotate and hold the ignition switch key in the **START** position. Observe the voltmeter. If voltage is detected, correct the poor contact between the cable clamp and post.
    c. Connect the negative lead of the voltmeter to the negative (–) battery terminal, and positive lead to the engine block near the battery cable attaching point. Rotate and hold the ignition switch in the **START** position. If the voltage reads above 0.2 volt, correct the poor contact at ground cable attaching point. If the voltage reading is still above 0.2 volt after correcting the poor contact, replace the negative ground cable with a new one.
3. Remove the heat shield. Refer to removal and installation procedures to gain access to the starter motor and solenoid connections. Perform the following steps:
    a. Connect the positive (+) voltmeter lead to the starter motor housing and the negative (–) lead to the negative battery terminal. Hold the ignition switch key in the **START** position. If the voltage reads above 0.2 volt, correct the poor starter to engine ground.
    b. Connect the positive (+) voltmeter lead to the positive battery terminal, and the negative lead to the battery cable terminal on the starter solenoid. Rotate and hold the ignition key in the **START** position. eads above 0.2 volt, correct poor contact at the battery cable to the solenoid connection. If the reading is still above 0.2 volt after correcting the poor contacts, replace the positive battery cable with a new one.
    c. If the resistance tests did not detect feed circuit failures, refer to the starter solenoid test.

Starter Solenoid

ON VEHICLE TEST

1. Before testing, assure the parking brake is set, the transmission is in Park (automatic) or Neutral (manual), and the battery is fully charged and in good condition.
2. Connect a voltmeter from the (S) terminal on the solenoid to ground. Turn the ignition switch to the **START** position and test for battery voltage. If battery voltage is not found, inspect the ignition switch circuit. If battery voltage is found, proceed to next step.
3. Connect an ohmmeter between the battery negative post and the starter solenoid mounting plate (manual) or the ground terminal (automatic). Turn the ignition switch to the **START** position. The ohmmeter should read zero (0). If not, repair the faulty ground.
4. If both tests are performed and the solenoid still does not energize, replace the solenoid.

BENCH TEST

1. Remove the starter from the vehicle, as outlined later in this section.
2. Disconnect the field coil wire from the field coil terminal.
3. Check for continuity between the solenoid terminal and field coil terminal with a continuity tester. Continuity (resistance) should be present.
4. Check for continuity between the solenoid terminal and solenoid housing. Continuity should be detected. If continuity is detected, the solenoid is good.
5. If continuity is not detected in either test, the solenoid has an open circuit and is defective and must be replaced.

Starter/Ground Cable Test

When performing these tests, it is important that the voltmeter be connected to the terminals, not the cables themselves.

Before testing, assure that the ignition control module (if equipped) is disconnected, the parking brake is set, the transmission is in Park (automatic) or Neutral (manual), and the battery is fully charged and in good condition.

1. Check voltage between the positive battery post and the center of the B + terminal on the starter solenoid stud.
2. Check voltage between the negative battery post and the engine block.
3. Disconnect the ignition coil wire from the distributor cap and connect a suitable jumper wire between the coil cable and a good body ground.
4. Have an assistant crank the engine and measure voltage again. Voltage drop should not exceed 0.5 volts.
5. If voltage drop is greater than 0.5 volts, clean metal surfaces. Apply a thick layer of silicone grease. Install a new cadmium plated bolt and star washer on the battery terminal and a new brass nut on the starter solenoid. Retest and replace cable not within specifications.

REMOVAL & INSTALLATION

Except 3.5L Engine

▶ See Figure 35

➡ **The factory sound system has a coded theft protection system. It is recommended that you know your reset code before you begin.**

1. Disconnect the negative, then the positive battery cable..
2. Wait at least three minutes before performing any repair.
3. On the 1.8L engine, remove the air intake duct.

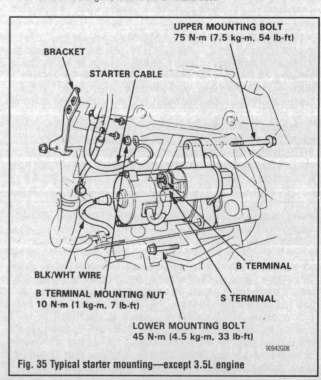

Fig. 35 Typical starter mounting—except 3.5L engine

4. On 2.2L, 2.3L engines, remove the lower radiator hose and the engine wiring harness from the bracket on the starter.

5. On 2.5L engines, remove the intake manifold rear bracket assembly.

6. On 3.0L engines, remove the automatic transmission cooler hose from the bracket on the starter motor.

7. On 3.2L engines, the left drive shaft must be removed. Also separate and remove the exhaust pipe.

8. Remove the starter cable from terminal B located on the back of the solenoid.

9. Remove the black/white wire from the S (solenoid) terminal.

10. Remove the two starter mounting bolts, then remove the starter from the vehicle.

➡The Powertrain Control Module (PCM) idle memory must be reset after reconnecting the battery. Start the engine and hold it at 3000 rpm until the cooling fan comes on. Then allow the engine to idle for about five minutes with all accessories OFF and with the transmission in Park or Neutral.

11. Installation is the reverse of the removal procedure.

➡When installing the starter cable, be sure to place the closed loop connector over the stud on the starter with the crimped side of the connector facing up. This is to ensure a proper fit against the stud.

3.5L Engine

♦ See Figure 36

➡This procedure requires the use of an engine hoist to lift the engine slightly.

1. Obtain the radio anti-theft code if applicable.
2. Disconnect the negative, then the positive battery cable.
3. Lift the coolant reservoir out of the way, then remove the battery and battery base.
4. Remove the alternator and belt.
5. Remove the left exhaust manifold cover from the engine assembly.
6. Remove the damper fork.
7. Disconnect the left lower ball joint from the suspension.
8. Remove the left drive shaft from the hub and transaxle assemblies.

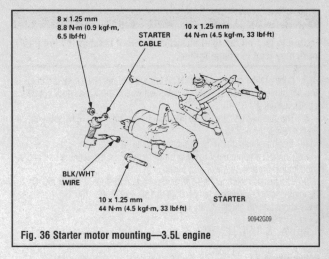

Fig. 36 Starter motor mounting—3.5L engine

9. Remove the transmission stop collar.
10. Remove the exhaust system Y—pipe.
11. Remove the front motor mounting bolts.
12. Attach a suitable engine hoist and slightly lift the engine.
13. Remove the motor mount.
14. Disconnect the starter cable from the attaching stud and black/white wire.
15. Remove the starter.

➡The Powertrain Control Module (PCM) idle memory must be reset after reconnecting the battery. Start the engine and hold it at 3000 rpm until the cooling fan comes on. Then allow the engine to idle for about five minutes with all accessories OFF and with the transmission in Park or Neutral.

16. Installation is the reverse of the removal procedure.

➡Upon installation of the starter cable and the black/white wire, make sure that the crimped side of the connector is facing up.

17. Enter the anti-theft code for the radio.

SENDING UNITS

➡This section describes the operating principles of sending units, warning lights and gauges. Sensors which provide information to the Electronic Control Module (ECM) are covered in Section 4 of this manual.

Instrument panels contain a number of indicating devices (gauges and warning lights). These devices are composed of two separate components. One is the sending unit, mounted on the engine or other remote part of the vehicle, and the other is the actual gauge or light in the instrument panel.

Several types of sending units exist, however most can be characterized as being either a pressure type or a resistance type. Pressure type sending units convert liquid pressure into an electrical signal which is sent to the gauge or warning light. Resistance type sending units are most often used to measure temperature and use variable resistance to control the current flow back to the indicating device. Both types of sending units are connected in series by a wire to the battery (through the ignition switch). When the ignition is turned **ON**, current flows from the battery through the indicating device and on to the sending unit.

Coolant Temperature Sender

The coolant temperature information is conveyed to the instrument panel, through the PCM, from the Engine Coolant Temperature (ECT) sensor. To test and remove the sensor, refer to Section 4. To test the gauge, perform the following testing procedure.

TESTING

♦ See Figure 37

1. Check that the No.1 fuse (10 A) has continuity before testing.
2. With the ignition switch **OFF**, disconnect the yellow/green wire from the gauge sending unit. Then ground it to a place on the engine block (or other known good ground) with a jumper wire.

3. Turn the ignition switch to the **ON** position.

4. Watch the Engine Coolant Temperature (ECT) gauge as it should start moving towards the hot ("H") mark.

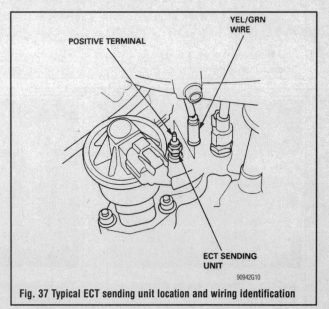

Fig. 37 Typical ECT sending unit location and wiring identification

※※ **WARNING**

Failure to turn off the ignition switch before it reaches the hot ("H") mark may lead to gauge failure.

5. If the pointer does not move at all or moves erratically, check for an open or point of high resistance in the yellow/green wire. If the wires check out OK, replace the gauge.

6. The sending unit should be the next component tested if the above steps did not reveal the problem.

7. Test the sending unit by disconnecting the yellow/green.

8. Connect an ohmmeter to the positive terminal on the sending unit and a good known ground on the engine block.

9. The resistance should be 137 ohms at a temperature of 133°F (56°C). If the engine is hot, and has a temperature of 185–212°F (85–100°C), the resistance should be 46 ohms–30 ohms.

REMOVAL & INSTALLATION

▶ See Figure 37

※※ **CAUTION**

Engine coolant can spray out causing severe burns if the Engine Coolant Temperature (ECT) sending unit is removed from a hot engine without draining the antifreeze first.

1. Locate the engine coolant sending unit on the engine.
2. Remove the negative battery cable.
3. Disconnect the sending unit electrical harness.
4. Drain the engine coolant to a level below the unit.
5. Remove the Engine Coolant Temperature (ECT) sending unit using a pressure switch socket or wrench.

To install:

6. Coat the threads of the sending unit with a suitable sealant. Make sure the sealant is safe for use on sending units and will not impede proper temperature readings.

7. Install the new sensor and tighten to 7 ft. lbs. (10 Nm) using a wrench or sending unit pressure switch socket..

8. Refill the engine with Acura/Honda approved or equivalent coolant.

➡**The Powertrain Control Module (PCM) idle memory must be reset after reconnecting the battery. Start the engine and hold it at 3000 rpm until the cooling fan comes on. Then allow the engine to idle for about five minutes with all accessories OFF and with the transmission in Park or Neutral.**

9. Reconnect the negative battery cable.
10. Start the engine, allow it to reach operating temperature and check for leaks.

Oil Pressure Sender

TESTING

The low oil pressure warning lamp will illuminate when the ignition switch is turned to the **ON** position without the engine running. The lamp also illuminates if the engine oil pressure drops below a safe oil pressure level. To test the system, perform the following:

1. Turn the ignition switch to the **ON** position.
2. If the lamp does not light, check for a broken or disconnected wire around the engine and oil pressure sending unit switch.
3. If the wire at the connector checks out OK, pull the connector loose from the switch and, with a jumper wire, ground the connector to the engine.
4. With the ignition switch turned to the **ON** position, check the warning lamp. If the lamp still fails to light, check for a burned out lamp or disconnected socket in the instrument cluster.

REMOVAL & INSTALLATION

1. Locate the oil pressure sending unit on the engine.
2. Disconnect the negative battery cable.
3. Disconnect the sending unit electrical harness.
4. Using a pressure switch socket, deep-well socket or wrench, loosen and remove the sending unit from the engine.

To install:

5. Install the sending unit in the vehicle and tighten securely.
6. Attach the electrical connector to the sending unit.

➡**The Powertrain Control Module (PCM) idle memory must be reset after reconnecting the battery. Start the engine and hold it at 3000 rpm until the cooling fan comes on. Then allow the engine to idle for about five minutes with all accessories OFF and with the transmission in Park or Neutral.**

7. Connect the negative battery cable.
8. Start the engine, allow it to reach operating temperature and check for leaks.
9. Check for proper sending unit operation.

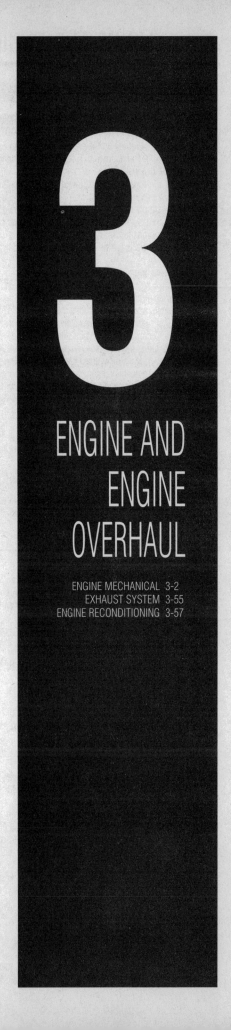

ENGINE AND ENGINE OVERHAUL

ENGINE MECHANICAL 3-2
EXHAUST SYSTEM 3-55
ENGINE RECONDITIONING 3-57

ENGINE MECHANICAL

Engine

In the process of removing the engine, you will come across a number of steps which call for the removal of a separate component or system, such as "disconnect the exhaust system" or "remove the radiator." In most instances, a detailed removal procedure can be found elsewhere in this manual.

It is virtually impossible to list each individual wire and hose which must be disconnected, simply because so many different model and engine combinations have been manufactured. Careful observation and common sense are the best possible approaches to any repair procedure.

Removal and installation of the engine can be made easier if you follow these basic points:

• If you have to drain any of the fluids, use a suitable container.

• Always tag any wires or hoses and, if possible, the components they came from before disconnecting them.

• Because there are so many bolts and fasteners involved, store and label the retainers from components separately in muffin pans, jars or coffee cans. This will prevent confusion during installation.

• After unbolting the transaxle, always make sure it is properly supported.

• If it is necessary to disconnect the air conditioning system, have this service performed by a qualified technician using a recovery/recycling station. If the system does not have to be disconnected, unbolt the compressor and set it aside.

• When unbolting the engine mounts, always make sure the engine is properly supported. When removing the engine, make sure that any lifting devices are properly attached to the engine. It is recommended that if your engine is supplied with lifting hooks, your lifting apparatus be attached to them.

• Lift the engine from its compartment slowly, checking that no hoses, wires or other components are still connected.

• After the engine is clear of the compartment, place it on an engine stand or workbench.

• After the engine has been removed, you can perform a partial or full teardown of the engine using the procedures outlined in this manual.

REMOVAL & INSTALLATION

1.8L Engines

➡The radio may contain a coded theft protection circuit. Always obtain the code number before disconnecting the battery.

1. Before servicing the vehicle, refer to the precautions in the beginning of this section.
2. Disconnect the negative, then the positive battery cables.
3. Mark the positions of the hood hinges on the hood and remove the hood from the vehicle.
4. If equipped, remove the strut brace.
5. Disconnect the battery cables from the under-hood fuse/relay box and under-hood Antilock Brake (ABS) System fuse/relay box.
6. Remove the intake air duct, air cleaner housing assembly and mounting bracket.
7. Remove the evaporative emission control canister hose and vacuum hose from the intake manifold.
8. On B18C5 engines, disconnect the brake booster and fuel return hoses.
9. Tag and detach the engine wiring harness connectors on the right side of engine compartment.
10. Properly relieve the residual fuel system pressure. Relieve the fuel pressure by loosening the service bolt on the fuel filter about one turn. Place a shop towel over the fuel filter to prevent pressurized fuel from spraying over the engine.
11. Disconnect the fuel feed hose, brake booster vacuum hose, and fuel return hose.
12. Remove the throttle cable by loosening the locknut, then slip the cable end out of the accelerator linkage. Be careful not to bend the cable when removing it. Replace the cable if it gets kinked.
13. Remove the engine wiring harness connectors, terminal, and clamps on the left side of engine compartment.
14. Remove the cruise control actuator, and engine ground cable at the body end.
15. Remove the adjusting bolt and mounting bolt, then remove the power steering belt and pump. Do not disconnect the power steering hoses.

16. Loosen the idler pulley bolt and adjusting bolt, then remove the air conditioning compressor belt.
17. On manual transaxle only, remove the clutch slave cylinder and pipe/hose assembly. Do not disconnect the pipe/hose assembly.
18. Remove the transaxle ground cable and hose clamp. Remove the radiator cap.
19. Safely raise and support the vehicle.
20. Remove the front wheels and lower splash shield.
21. Drain the engine coolant, engine oil, and transaxle fluid into sealable containers. Reinstall the drain plugs using new washers. Be careful not to over tighten the drain plugs.
22. Disconnect the upper and lower radiator hoses and the heater hoses from the engine.
23. If equipped with an automatic transaxle, disconnect the automatic transaxle fluid (ATF) cooler hoses.
24. Remove the radiator assembly.
25. Remove the air conditioning compressor mounting bolts and position the compressor out of the way. Suspend the compressor on a wire, do not let it hang by its hoses. Do not disconnect the hoses.
26. Detach the Heated Oxygen (HO2S) sensor connector.
27. Remove the nuts and bolts connecting exhaust pipe A to the catalytic converter. Discard the gasket and the lock nuts.
28. Remove and discard the nuts attaching exhaust pipe A to the exhaust hanger.
29. Remove and discard the lock nuts attaching exhaust pipe A to the exhaust manifold, then remove exhaust pipe A from the vehicle. discard the exhaust gaskets.
30. If equipped with a manual transaxle, disconnect the shift rod and extension rod from the transaxle.
31. If equipped with an automatic transaxle, remove the shift cable cover, then disconnect the shift cable from the transaxle.
32. Remove the right strut fork bolt, discard the nut.
33. Remove the right strut pinch bolt, then remove the strut fork.
34. Disconnect the suspension lower arm ball joints using a suitable ball joint removal tool.
35. Carefully pry the inner CV–joint away from the transaxle to force the set ring at the inner end past the groove. Remove the other CV–joint out of the intermediate shaft. Do not let the halfshafts hang down. Support the halfshafts or hang them from the body with wire and cover the halfshaft ends with plastic bags.
36. Attach a suitable hoist to the engine.
37. Remove the left and right front mounts and brackets, then remove the rear mount bracket.
38. Remove the side engine mount, then remove the transaxle mount.
39. Check that the engine is completely clear of vacuum, fuel and engine coolant hoses, and electrical wiring.
40. Slowly raise the engine approximately 6 in. (150mm). Check to be sure that all hoses, cables and wires are disconnected from the engine.
41. Raise the engine and transaxle assembly all the way and remove it from the vehicle.
42. Separate the engine and transaxle.
To install:
43. Install the transaxle to the engine assembly.
44. If equipped with a manual transaxle, tighten the transaxle housing mounting bolts to 47 ft. lbs. (64 Nm), the two bolts and new washers to the rear mounting bracket to 87 ft. lbs. (118 Nm), and tighten the upper mounting bolts to 47 ft. lbs. (64 Nm).
45. If equipped with an automatic transaxle, tighten the transaxle housing mounting bolts to 43 ft. lbs. (59 Nm), the two bolts and new washers to the rear mounting bracket to 87 ft. lbs. (118 Nm), and tighten the upper mounting bolts to 54 ft. lbs. (74 Nm).
46. If equipped with an automatic transaxle, tighten the bolts attaching the torque converter to the drive plate to 104 inch lbs. (12 Nm).
47. Install the torque converter/clutch cover.
48. Install the rear engine stiffener, tighten the bolts attaching the stiffener to the engine to 17 ft. lbs. (24 Nm). If equipped with a manual transaxle, tighten the bolts attaching the stiffener to the transaxle to 42 ft. lbs. (57 Nm). If equipped with an automatic transaxle, tighten the bolts attaching the stiffener to the transaxle to 32 ft. lbs. (43 Nm).

49. If equipped with the Variable Valve Timing and Electronic Lift Control (VTEC) (B18C1 and B18C5 engines), install the front engine stiffener. Tighten the bolt attaching the stiffener to the engine to 17 ft. lbs. (24 Nm), tighten the bolts attaching the stiffener to the transaxle to 42 ft. lbs. (57 Nm).

50. Install the engine and transaxle into the engine compartment. Install the transaxle mount, then tighten the bolt/nuts on the transaxle side. Leave the mount bolt loose.

51. Install the engine side mount, then tighten the bolt/nuts on the engine side. Leave the mount bolt loose. Tighten the mount bolt on the transaxle mount, then tighten the mount bolt on the side engine mount.

52. Install the rear mount bracket, then tighten the bolts in the proper sequence.

53. Install the right front mount/bracket, then tighten the bolts in the proper sequence.

54. Install the left front mount, then tighten the bolts in the proper sequence.

55. Install the strut fork and pinch bolt.

56. If equipped with an automatic transaxle, connect the shift cable to the transaxle and install the shift cable cover.

57. If equipped with a manual transaxle, connect the shift rod and extension rod to the transaxle.

58. Install the exhaust pipe A to the exhaust manifold and to the catalytic converter.

59. Attach the HO2S sensor connector.

60. Install the air conditioning compressor and mounting bolts.

61. Install the radiator assembly.

62. If equipped with an automatic transaxles, connect the ATF cooler hoses.

63. Connect the upper and lower radiator hoses and the heater hoses to the engine.

64. Install the front wheels and lower splash shield.

65. Install the transaxle ground cable and hose clamp. Install the radiator cap.

66. If equipped with a manual transaxle, install the clutch slave cylinder and pipe/hose assembly.

67. Loosen the idler pulley bolt and adjusting bolt, then install the air conditioning compressor belt.

68. Install the power steering pump, the adjusting bolt and mounting bolt, then install the power steering belt.

69. Install the cruise control actuator, and engine ground cable at the body end.

70. Install the engine wiring harness connectors, terminal, and clamps on the left side of engine compartment.

71. Install the throttle cable. Replace the cable if it gets kinked.

72. Connect the fuel feed hose, brake booster vacuum hose, and fuel return hose.

73. Attach the engine wiring harness connectors on the right side of engine compartment.

74. On B18C5 engines, install the brake booster and fuel return hoses.

75. Install the evaporative emission control canister hose and vacuum hose to the intake manifold.

76. Install the intake air duct, air cleaner housing assembly and mounting bracket.

77. Connect the battery cables to the under-hood fuse/relay box and under-hood ABS system fuse/relay box.

78. If equipped, install the strut brace.

79. Install the hood to the vehicle.

80. Fill the engine coolant, engine oil, and transaxle fluid.

81. Reconnect the battery cables to the fuse/relay boxes and the battery. Connect the positive cable, then the negative cable to the battery.

82. Turn the ignition switch to the **ON** position, (do not operate the starter) so that the fuel pump operates for approximately 2 seconds and the fuel line pressurizes. Repeat this operation 2 or 3 times and check for fuel leakage.

83. Start the engine and check for any fluid leaks.

84. Recheck fluid levels and top off as necessary.

85. Enter the radio security code, then test drive the vehicle.

2.2L, 2.3L and 3.0L Engines

▶ See Figures 1 and 2

1. Obtain the anti–theft code for the radio, then disconnect the battery cables. Be sure to disconnect the negative cable first.

2. Remove the air intake duct.

3. Remove the hood opening struts and support the hood in a vertical position.

4. Detach the negative battery cable and then the positive cable.

5. If equipped with engine compartment covers, remove the covers.

6. Remove the strut brace.

7. Remove the intake air duct assembly.

8. Remove the battery, battery tray and the engine ground cable.

9. If equipped, remove the cosmetic manifold and throttle body covers.

10. Remove the accelerator and cruise control cables from the throttle body and bracket.

11. Remove the battery cables from the under-hood Antilock Brake System (ABS) and under-hood fuse/relay box assemblies and disconnect the engine wiring harness on the right side of the engine.

12. Properly relieve the fuel system pressure, as outlined in Section 5 of this manual.

13. Detach the fuel hoses from the fuel rail.

14. Disconnect the engine wiring harness on the left side of the engine.

15. Tag and disconnect the brake booster vacuum hoses and the canister hoses.

16. Remove the accessory drive belt(s).

17. Remove and support the power steering pump leaving the hoses attached.

18. Remove the bolt securing the power steering hose bracket on the engine.

19. On vehicles equipped with manual transaxles, remove the shift cable, clutch slave cylinder (leaving the hydraulic line attached), and detach the reverse light switch connector.

20. If equipped, remove the cruise control vacuum tank.

21. Remove the radiator cap.

22. Carefully raise the vehicle.

23. Remove the front wheels and lower splash shield.

24. Drain the engine oil, coolant, and transaxle oil (or fluid) into sealable containers and carefully reinstall the drain plugs using new sealing washers.

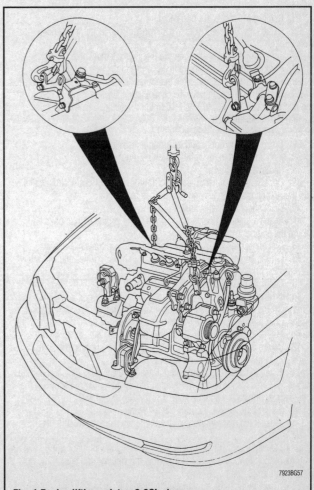

Fig. 1 Engine lifting points—2.3CL shown

7923BG57

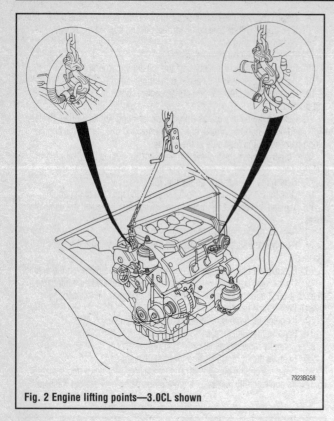

Fig. 2 Engine lifting points—3.0CL shown

7923BG58

25. Remove the center support beam.

26. Detach the Heated Oxygen (HO_2S) sensor connector and remove the front A pipe.

27. On automatic transaxles, remove the shift selector cable.

28. Remove the damper forks and disconnect the lower ball joints.

29. Remove the driveshafts from the transaxle and cover the machined ends.

30. On 3.0L engines, remove the crankshaft pulley, the Variable Valve Timing and Electronic Lift Control (VTEC)/oil filter housing, and A/C compressor leaving the hoses attached.

31. Carefully lower the vehicle.

32. Disconnect the upper and lower radiator hoses.

33. If so equipped, remove the ATF cooler hoses.

34. Remove the radiator.

35. On 2.3L engines, remove the distributor, Idle Air Control (IAC) valve, and the A/C compressor, leaving the hoses attached.

36. Disconnect the heater hoses.

37. Attach a suitable engine lifting hoist to the engine lifting hooks and secure the engine.

38. Disconnect the front, rear, and side engine and transaxle mounts.

39. Lift the engine slightly and check that all hoses, cables and wires have been properly disconnected.

40. Carefully raise the engine from the vehicle.

To install:

41. Lift the engine into position and install the engine mounting brackets. On the 2.3L, tighten the engine mounting bolts and nuts to 40 ft. lbs. (54 Nm). On the 3.0L, tighten the bolts to 28 ft. lbs. (38 Nm).

42. On the 3.0L engine, install the A/C compressor. Tighten the bolts to 16 ft. lbs. (22 Nm).

43. Install the transaxle mounting bracket. On the 2.3L engine, tighten the nuts to 28 ft. lbs. (38 Nm) and the through bolt to 40 ft. lbs. (54 Nm). On the 3.0L engine, tighten the bolts to 28 ft. lbs. (38 Nm).

44. On the 2.3L engine, perform the following:

 • Install the rear mount bracket and tighten the bolts to 40 ft. lbs. (54 Nm).

 • On vehicles with manual transaxles, install the stiffener and tighten the through bolt to 47 ft. lbs. (64 Nm). Install the stiffener and tighten the nut and bolt to 28 ft. lbs. (38 Nm)

 • Tighten the three front mounting bracket bolts to 28 ft. lbs. (38 Nm). Then, tighten the through bolt to 47 ft. lbs. (64 Nm).

 • Install the A/C compressor. Tighten the bolts to 16 ft. lbs. (22 Nm).

45. On the 3.0L engine, perform the following:

 • Install the radius rod bolts. Tighten them to 119 ft. lbs. (162 Nm).

 • Install the front mounting bracket support nut. Tighten it to 40 ft. lbs. (54 Nm).

 • Install the rear mounting bracket nut and bolt. Tighten the nut to 40 ft. lbs. (54 Nm) and the bolt to 28 ft. lbs. (38 Nm).

 • Install the side mounting bracket. Tighten the bolts to 40 ft. lbs. (54 Nm) and the through bolt to 40 ft. lbs. (54 Nm).

46. Assemble the exhaust system.

47. If equipped with an automatic transaxle, connect the shift linkage.

48. The remainder of installation is the reverse of the removal procedure.

49. Refill and bleed the cooling system.

50. Fill the engine and transaxle with the correct amount and type of fluid.

51. Install the battery if removed. Start the engine and check for any fluid leaks.

52. Bring the engine to operating temperature and recheck all fluid levels.

53. Enter the security code for the radio.

2.5L Engine

1. Open the hood and secure it in its fully opened position (vertical). The hood may be removed if more clearance and working room is desired.

2. Obtain the radio security code, then disconnect the negative, then the positive cables.

3. Remove the battery and the battery tray.

4. Remove the engine ground cables and ignition coil wire.

5. Remove the battery cables from the under-hood fuse/relay box.

6. Disconnect the engine harness connectors on the right side of the engine compartment.

7. Unbolt the battery cable from the Antilock Brake (ABS) System fuse/relay box.

8. Remove the intake air cleaner duct and the air cleaner housing.

9. Loosen the component adjusting and mounting bolts, then remove the power steering pump and air conditioning compressor belts.

10. Without disconnecting the hoses, remove the power steering pump and the air conditioner compressor and secure them out of the way.

➡**Do not loosen or disconnect the air conditioning refrigerant lines.**

11. Remove the throttle cable by loosening the locknut, then slip the cable end out of the throttle bracket and accelerator linkage. Do not bend the cable when removing it. Unbolt the throttle cable clamp and move the cable aside.

12. Label and disconnect the engine wiring harness connectors on the left side of the engine compartment.

13. Properly relieve the residual fuel system pressure by loosening the service bolt on the fuel filter. Remove the banjo bolt to remove the fuel feed hose from the fuel filter. Remove the fuel return hose from the pressure regulator.

14. Disconnect the charcoal canister hoses, fuel return hose, brake booster hose and the emission control vacuum hoses.

15. Disconnect the transaxle wiring connector that is located near the firewall.

16. The distributor may be removed for extra access to the upper transaxle case bolts. Disconnect the wiring and remove the two bolts to remove the distributor. Do not lose the collar that fits on the distributor shaft.

17. Remove the torque converter cover and remove the drive plate bolts.

18. Remove the upper transaxle bolts and the 26mm differential shim. Note the location of the shim for installation.

19. Remove the power steering speed sensor from the differential case without disconnecting the hydraulic hoses. Disconnect the wiring and secure the sensor out of the way.

20. Remove the two upper brackets and lift the radiator and cooling fan assembly from the engine compartment.

21. Raise and support the vehicle safely.

22. Remove the splash shield and front tires.

23. Drain the engine, differential and transaxle fluids into sealable containers.

24. Disconnect the lower strut fork and ball joint.

25. To disconnect the halfshafts, carefully pry the inner CV–joint away from the transaxle and the intermediate shaft.

➡**Do not pull on the halfshaft; the CV–joint may come apart. Use care when prying out the assembly and pull it straight to avoid damaging the intermediate shaft seals.**

26. Support the halfshafts from the body with wire. Do not let them hang from the outer CV–joints or it will be damaged.

27. Disconnect the Oxygen (O_2S) sensor connector from the exhaust system and remove the front exhaust pipe and its brackets.

28. Remove the transaxle mount and bracket.

29. Be sure the transaxle is in **P** park. Remove the 33 mm extension shaft sealing cap on the lower left side of transaxle housing.

30. Use a suitable extension shaft puller tool, to remove the extension shaft from the differential.

31. Lower the vehicle and install a chain hoist onto the engine lifting hooks.

32. Disconnect the heater hoses.

33. Disconnect the transaxle cooler hoses from the radiator tank. Disconnect the upper and lower radiator hoses and the fan wiring.

34. Remove the radiator assembly.

35. Raise the engine hoist just enough to take up the weight of the engine.

36. Remove the mid–mounts along with the spacers.

37. Support the transaxle with a jack and remove the transaxle case bolts.

38. Install the transaxle mid–mounts and spacer to hold the transaxle in the vehicle. Be sure the engine will separate from the transaxle, and that the transaxle will be supported by the mounts after the engine has been removed.

39. Unbolt the front engine mounts.

40. Slowly raise the engine slightly to separate it from the transaxle. Verify that all wiring harnesses, fuel and coolant lines, and vacuum hoses are disconnected.

41. Lift the engine out of the vehicle. Be sure the engine clears the mounts, the transaxle case, and the differential extension shaft.

To install:

➡**Use new mounting bolts when installing the transaxle side mount and bracket.**

42. Install the front engine mounts into the engine compartment.

43. Install the engine in the vehicle. Keep the lifting chain attached to hold the weight of the engine. Install the mounting nuts to hold the engine in place. Do not tighten the nuts and bolts at this time. Be sure the differential lines up with the extension shaft. Be sure the mainshaft is aligned in the clutch pressure plate, or the torque converter is flush against the drive plate and mounted on the mainshaft.

44. Raise the vehicle.

45. Install new snap and set rings onto the extension shaft. Apply high temperature molybdenum grease to its splines and the shaft mating surface in the differential.

46. Support the transaxle with a jack and remove the mid–mounts. Carefully fit the engine into position and start the upper engine bolts. Slowly tighten two bolts on opposite sides just enough to draw the engine and transaxle together. Install all the remaining bolts except for the differential bolt and its shim. Do not fully tighten the bolts yet.

47. If either the engine, transaxle or differential is being replaced, the space between the differential and transaxle housings must be measured and the correct shim installed. Shims are available in increments of 0.004 in. (0.1mm). Measure the space between the housings with a feeler gauge. Install the largest shim possible that does not exceed the measurement. If the wrong shim is installed, the differential or transaxle housing will be out of alignment and could develop cracks.

48. Install the shim and tighten the bolts to 54 ft. lbs. (75 Nm). Tighten the transaxle case bolts to 54 ft. lbs. (75 Nm).

49. Install the mid–mount and spacer. Loosely install the nuts and bolts for all the mounts and set the engine into place. Remove the engine lifting equipment.

50. Tighten the mounting nuts and bolts to the correct torque in the proper sequence. This step is important to preload the engine and transaxle mounts. Following the proper sequence will minimize engine vibration and premature mount failure. Be sure the rubber strut mounting surface is not contaminated with oil. Tighten the nuts and bolts as follows:
- Left and right front mount nut: 54 ft. lbs. (75 Nm)
- Left front strut bolt: 28 ft. lbs. (39 Nm)
- Left front strut bracket bolt: 40 ft. lbs. (55 Nm)
- 2.5TL front mount–to–subframe bolts: 28 ft. lbs. (38 Nm)
- Mid–mount nuts: 32 ft. lbs. (43 Nm)
- Mid–mount bolts: 28 ft. lbs. (38 Nm)

51. After the engine and transaxle have been bolted together, install the extension shaft. Be sure the set ring snaps firmly into place. Coat the threads of the 33mm sealing cap with a sealing compound, install the cap and tighten it to 58 ft. lbs. (80 Nm).

52. On vehicles with automatic transaxles, install the torque converter bolts and tighten them to 9 ft. lbs. (12 Nm). Do not over tighten these bolts or the drive plate will warp. Install the torque converter cover.

53. Install the transaxle side mount and bracket. Tighten the bracket bolts to 40 ft. lbs. (54 Nm). Tighten the mount bolts to 47 ft. lbs. (64 Nm).

54. The balance of the installation is the reverse of the removal procedure.

55. Fill the engine with fresh oil. Refill the differential and transaxle. Fill the cooling system with the correct coolant mixture.

56. Connect the positive and negative battery cables.

57. Bleed the cooling system. Check fluid levels. Run the engine and check its operation.

58. Check for any fluid leaks and recheck the fluid levels.

59. Enter the radio security code.

3.2L Engine

1996–98 MODELS

➡**The engine and transaxle are removed as an assembly.**

1. Move the front passenger's seat forward.

2. Do not remove the hood. Disconnect the hood support strut and reconnect it to hold the hood in a vertical position.

➡**The radio may contain a coded theft protection circuit. Always obtain the code number before disconnecting the battery.**

3. Disconnect the negative battery cable, then the positive battery cable. Remove the battery and the battery box.

4. Remove the engine cover.

5. Remove the air cleaner assembly and intake duct.

6. Remove the throttle cable cover. Without turning the adjusting nut, loosen the locknut, which is closer to the throttle, and disconnect the throttle cable and cruise control cable from the throttle and bracket.

7. Detach the engine wiring harness connector on the left side of the engine compartment.

8. Remove the engine ground cable and engine wiring harness clamps.

9. Disconnect the vacuum hoses, then remove the clamp from the under-hood fuse/relay box.

10. Label, then disconnect the battery cables from the under-hood fuse/relay box, then remove the under-hood fuse/relay box.

11. Detach the engine wiring harness connector, located by the under-hood fuse/relay box.

12. Raise the power steering fluid reservoir, then disconnect the vacuum hoses and remove the vacuum pipe and vacuum tank.

➡**Do not disconnect the power steering hoses.**

13. Disconnect the ignition control module (igniter) located on the right shock tower and remove the wiring harness clamp. Disconnect the engine ground cable.

14. Disconnect the engine wiring harness connectors on the right side of the engine compartment.

15. Remove the ground cable and wiring harness clamp.

16. Disconnect the wiring harness from the control box and solenoid valve, then remove the control box.

17. Disconnect the brake booster vacuum hose.

18. Remove the two bolts mounting the heater valve.

19. Properly relieve the fuel pressure, as outlined in Section 5.

20. Disconnect the engine fuel feed hose from the fuel filter and disconnect the fuel return hose from the fuel regulator.

21. Disconnect the Evaporative Emissions (EVAP) control canister hose and the vacuum hose.

22. Detach the transaxle sub–harness connector, and remove the wiring harness clamp.

23. Loosen the alternator mounting bolt, lockbolt and adjusting rod, then remove the drive belt.

24. Loosen the A/C idler pulley center nut and adjusting bolt, then remove the drive belt.

25. Detach the power steering pressure switch connector.

26. Remove the power steering pump adjusting bolt, locknut and mounting bolt, then remove the drive belt and pump.

27. Pull the carpet back under the passenger seat to expose the secondary Heated Oxygen (HO$_2$S) sensor connector, then unplug the connector.

28. Remove the radiator cap.

29. Raise and safely support the vehicle.

30. Remove the front wheels and the splash guard.

31. Drain the engine coolant into a sealable container.

32. Drain the transaxle fluid into a proper container, then install the drain plug with a new washer.

33. Drain the oil from the differential, then install the drain plug with a new washer.

34. Drain the engine oil into a proper container, then install the drain plug with a new washer.

35. Remove the front suspension strut forks.

36. Disconnect the lower ball joints from the steering knuckles.

37. Disconnect the halfshafts from the differential and the intermediate shaft. Support the halfshafts with wire out of the way and cover the inner CV–joints with plastic bags.

38. Detach the A/C compressor clutch connector. Remove the compressor, without disconnecting the hoses.

39. Unplug the Vehicle Speed Sensor (VSS) connector, then remove the VSS/power steering sensor. Do not disconnect the fluid hoses.

40. Remove the heat shields from the front exhaust pipe.

41. Remove the nuts attaching the front exhaust pipe to the exhaust manifolds and the catalytic converter. Remove the front exhaust pipe.

42. Remove the O$_2$S sensor wiring harness cover and grommet, then remove the catalytic converter. Discard the nuts and gasket.

43. Remove the exhaust heat shield from the floor of the vehicle.

44. Disconnect the transaxle cooler hoses, then plug the hoses and pipes.

45. Remove the shift cable cover mounting bolts and remove the wiring harness clamps from the cover. Remove the shift cable cover from the transaxle.

46. Remove the shift cable holder from the holder base, do not lose the washers.

47. Remove the locknut attaching the shift cable to the control lever, then remove the shift cable.

48. Lower the vehicle.

49. Remove the upper and lower radiator hoses.

50. Remove the radiator assembly.

51. Disconnect the heater hoses.

52. Attach a suitable hoist to the engine lifting points.

53. Remove the center bracket from the front engine mounts.

54. Remove the center mount from the front beam.

55. Remove the nuts and bolts attaching the left and right engine mount brackets to the left and right brackets.

56. Working underneath the vehicle, remove the shift cable guide bracket.

57. Remove the bolts attaching the transaxle beam to the body, and loosen the three bolts on the transaxle beam.

58. Remove the stop holder, the mid mount stops and the mid mounts.

59. Verify that the engine and transaxle assembly is completely free of vacuum hoses, fuel and coolant lines and electrical wiring.

60. Slowly raise the engine and transaxle. Remove the left end right brackets from the front engine mounts.

61. Raise the engine all of the way and remove it from the vehicle.

To install:

62. Carefully install the engine and transaxle into the engine compartment, taking care to not hit the rear beam.

➡**Check carefully to be sure that the rubber mounts are not twisted or offset. Start all of the mount nuts and bolts before tightening them. This is important to help minimize engine vibrations.**

63. Install the center mount to the front beam and tighten the bolts to 40 ft. lbs. (54 Nm).

64. Install the left bracket to the left front mount and the engine mount bracket. Do not tighten the nuts and bolts at this time.

65. Install the right bracket to the right front mount and the engine mount bracket. Do not tighten the nuts and bolts at this time.

66. Install the center bracket. Tighten the bolts attaching the brackets to 40 ft. lbs. (54 Nm), then tighten the mount through bolt to 40 ft. lbs. (54 Nm).

67. Install the transaxle beam mounting bolts, do not tighten the bolts at this time. Loosen the bolts attaching the mount to the beam and the mount through bolt.

68. Install the mid mounts, then the mid mount stops. Tighten the 8mm bolts loosely, then install the stop holder.

69. Tighten the mid mount 10mm bolts to 28 ft. lbs. (38 Nm) and tighten the 8mm bolts to 16 ft. lbs. (22 Nm). Tighten the new nuts attaching the mid–mounts to 35 ft. lbs. (48 Nm) and tighten the nuts attaching the stop holder to 40 ft. lbs. (54 Nm).

70. Tighten the nut and bolt attaching the left bracket and the left engine mount bracket to 28 ft. lbs. (38 Nm). Tighten the left bracket through bolt to 40 ft. lbs. (54 Nm).

71. Tighten the nut and bolt attaching the right bracket and the right engine mount bracket to 28 ft. lbs. (38 Nm). Tighten the right bracket through bolt to 40 ft. lbs. (54 Nm).

72. Tighten the bolts attaching the transaxle beam to the vehicle to 28 ft. lbs. (38 Nm), then tighten the bolts attaching the mount to the beam to 40 ft. lbs. (54 Nm). Tighten the three bolts attaching the bracket to the transaxle to 28 ft. lbs. (38 Nm), then tighten the mount through bolt to 40 ft. lbs. (54 Nm).

73. Remove the engine hoist.

74. Connect the heater hoses to the heater core at the bulkhead.

75. Install the radiator assembly.

76. Install the upper and lower radiator hoses.

77. Raise and safely support the vehicle.

78. Connect the shift cable control lever to the control shaft, then install the washer and nut. Tighten the nut to 104 inch lbs. (12 Nm).

79. Install the shift cable holder to the shift cable holder base with the mounting washers. Install the attaching bolts and tighten the bolts to 104 inch lbs. (12 Nm).

80. Install the shift cable cover and tighten the mounting bolts to 104 inch lbs. (12 Nm).

81. The balance of installation is the reverse of the removal procedure.

82. Fill the engine and transaxle with the recommended type and amount of lubricant.

83. Fill the cooling system and bleed the air from the cooling system.

84. Connect the positive, then the negative battery cables and enter the radio security code.

85. Switch the ignition **ON** but do not engage the starter. The fuel pump should run for approximately 2 seconds, building pressure within the lines. Switch the ignition **OFF** , then **ON** 2 or 3 more times to build full system pressure. Check for fuel leaks.

86. Run the engine and check for leaks, check the transaxle oil level and add if necessary.

87. Enter the radio security code.

1999–00 MODELS

➡**The engine and transaxle are removed as an assembly.**

1. Do not remove the hood. Disconnect the hood support strut and reconnect it to hold the hood in a vertical position.

➡**The radio may contain a coded theft protection circuit. Always obtain the code number before disconnecting the battery.**

2. Disconnect the negative battery cable, then the positive battery cable. Remove the battery and battery support tray.

3. Remove the air cleaner intake duct.

4. Disconnect the throttle cable and cruise control cable from the throttle and bracket.

5. Detach the engine wiring harness connector on the left side of the engine compartment.

6. Properly relieve the fuel pressure, as outlined in Section 5.

7. Disconnect the engine fuel feed hose from the fuel filter and disconnect the fuel return hose from the fuel regulator.

8. Disconnect the brake booster vacuum hose.

9. Label, then disconnect the battery cables from the under-hood fuse/relay box, then remove the under-hood fuse/relay box.

10. Disconnect the Powertrain Control (PCM) Module wiring harness connector from the PCM.

11. Remove the alternator drive belt.

12. Remove the power steering pump belt and pump assembly leaving the hoses attached.

➡**Do not disconnect the power steering hoses.**

13. Detach the Vehicle Speed Sensor (VSS) connector, then remove the VSS/power steering sensor leaving the fluid hoses attached.

14. Remove the radiator cap.

15. Raise and safely support the vehicle.

16. Remove the front wheels and the lower splash guard.

17. Drain the engine coolant into a sealable container.

18. Drain the transaxle fluid into a proper container, then install the drain plug with a new washer.

19. Drain the oil from the differential, then install the drain plug with a new washer.

20. Drain the engine oil into a proper container, then install the drain plug with a new washer.

21. Detach the Heated Oxygen (HO$_2$S) sensor connector and remove the front pipe assembly.

22. Remove the front suspension strut forks.

23. Disconnect the lower ball joints from the steering knuckles.

24. Disconnect the halfshafts from the differential and the intermediate shaft by prying them outward using a suitable prytool. Support the halfshafts with wire, move out of the way and cover the inner CV–joints with plastic bags.

25. Remove the shift cable cover mounting bolts and remove the shift cable cover and cable from the transaxle.

26. Disconnect the power steering hose clamps and the engine mount control vacuum hose.

27. Carefully lower the vehicle.

28. Remove the upper and lower radiator hoses and the heater hoses.

29. Disconnect and plug the transaxle cooler hoses.

30. Remove the ground cable.

31. Remove the power steering hose clamp from the rear beam assembly.

32. Attach a suitable chain hoist to the engine lifting hooks and support the engine.

➡**The engine and transaxle assembly are removed by lowering it from the vehicle. Be sure the vehicle is in a position that will allow the engine and transaxle assembly enough clearance to be moved from the vehicle once it is lowered away from the vehicle.**

33. Remove the side, rear and front engine mount support fasteners.

34. Remove the front suspension radius rod support flange bolts.

35. Make alignment marks on the front beam and remove the front beam.

36. Remove the A/C compressor leaving the hoses attached.

37. Remove the rear mounts from the engine and transaxle.

38. Check that all hoses, cables and wires have been properly disconnected and slowly lower the engine about 6 inches (150 mm). Recheck that all hoses, cables and wires have been properly disconnected.

39. Carefully lower the engine/transaxle assembly from the vehicle.

To install:

40. Attach a suitable engine hoist and carefully raise the engine/transaxle assembly into the vehicle.

41. Install the rear mounts to the engine and transaxle.

42. Install the A/C compressor assembly.

43. Align the alignment marks on the front beam and install the front beam.

44. Install the front suspension radius rod support flange bolts.

45. Install the side, rear and front engine mount support fasteners.

46. Remove the engine lifting hoist from the engine.

47. Install the power steering hose clamp to the rear beam assembly.

48. Install the ground cable.

49. Connect and the transaxle cooler hoses.

50. Install the upper and lower radiator hoses and the heater hoses.

51. Raise and safely support the vehicle.

52. Connect the power steering hose clamps and the engine mount control vacuum hose.

53. Install the shift cable and the converter to the transaxle.

54. Connect the halfshafts to the differential and the intermediate shaft.

55. Connect the lower ball joints to the steering knuckles.

56. Install the front suspension strut forks.

57. Install the front pipe assembly and connect the heated O$_2$S sensor connector.

58. Install the front wheels and the splash guard.

59. Install the radiator cap.

60. Install the VSS/power steering sensor and attach the VSS sensor connector.

61. Install the power steering pump.

62. Install the alternator and power steering drive belts.

63. Install the PCM wiring harness connector to the PCM.

64. Install the under-hood fuse/relay box and connect the battery cables to the under-hood fuse/relay box.

65. Attach the brake booster vacuum hose.

66. Connect the engine fuel feed hose to the fuel filter and connect the fuel return hose to the fuel regulator.

67. Attach the engine wiring harness connector on the left side of the engine compartment.

68. Connect the throttle cable and cruise control cable to the throttle and bracket assemblies.

69. Install the air cleaner intake duct.

70. Install the battery support tray and the battery.

71. Fill the engine coolant, the transaxle, the differential, and the engine oil with the recommended type and amount of fluid.

72. Check that all hoses, cables and wires have been properly connected.

73. Connect the positive battery cable, then the negative cable.

74. Start the engine and check for any fluid leaks. Check and top off all fluid levels as necessary.

75. Enter the radio security code.

3.5L Engine

▸ **See Figures 3 and 4**

➡**The engine and transaxle are removed as an assembly.**

1. Before servicing the vehicle, refer to the precautions in the beginning of this section.

2. Move the front passenger's seat forward.

3. On 1996–98 models, do not remove the hood. Disconnect the hood support strut and reconnect it to hold the hood in a vertical position.

4. On 1999–00 models, make alignment marks between the hood and the hood hinges and remove the hood.

➡**The radio may contain a coded theft protection circuit. Always obtain the code number before disconnecting the battery.**

5. Disconnect the negative battery cable, then the positive battery cable.

6. Remove the strut brace.

7. Remove the engine cover.

8. Remove the air cleaner assembly and intake duct.

9. Remove the throttle cable cover. Without turning the adjusting nut, loosen the locknut, which is closer to the throttle, and disconnect the throttle cable and cruise control cable from the throttle and bracket assembly.

10. Raise the coolant reservoir, then remove the battery and tray.

11. Remove the relay box, ground cable and wiring harness clips from the firewall.

12. Disconnect the vacuum hose, the alternator and battery cables and the clamp from the under-hood fuse/relay box and remove the box.

13. Detach the engine wiring harness connector on the left side of the engine compartment.

14. Properly relieve the fuel system pressure, as outlined in Section 5.

15. Remove the fuel feed hose from the fuel filter and disconnect the fuel return hose.

16. Remove the canister and brake booster hoses.

17. Detach the transaxle sub-harness connector.

18. Detach the connector and remove the control box.
19. Detach the wiring harness connectors on the right side of the engine compartment.
20. Disconnect the spark plug voltage detection module and remove the engine ground cables.
21. Remove the alternator and A/C drive belts.
22. Detach the Power Steering Pressure (PSP) switch connector, remove the power steering pump drive belt and the power steering pump leaving the hoses attached.
23. Pull the carpet back under the front passengers seat and detach the secondary Heated Oxygen (HO$_2$S) sensor connector.
24. Remove the radiator cap.

25. Raise and safely support the vehicle.
26. Remove the front tires and lower splash shield.
27. Drain the engine coolant, transaxle fluid, differential and engine oils and reinstall the drain plugs using new sealing washers.
28. Remove the front suspension damper forks.
29. Disconnect the lower ball joints from the steering knuckles and carefully remove the halfshafts by prying them outward using a suitable prytool. Cover the machined ends of the inner CV–joints with a plastic bag.
30. Detach the A/C compressor clutch connector, then remove the compressor without disconnecting the hoses.
31. Disconnect and remove the Vehicle Speed Sensor (VSS) leaving the hoses attached.

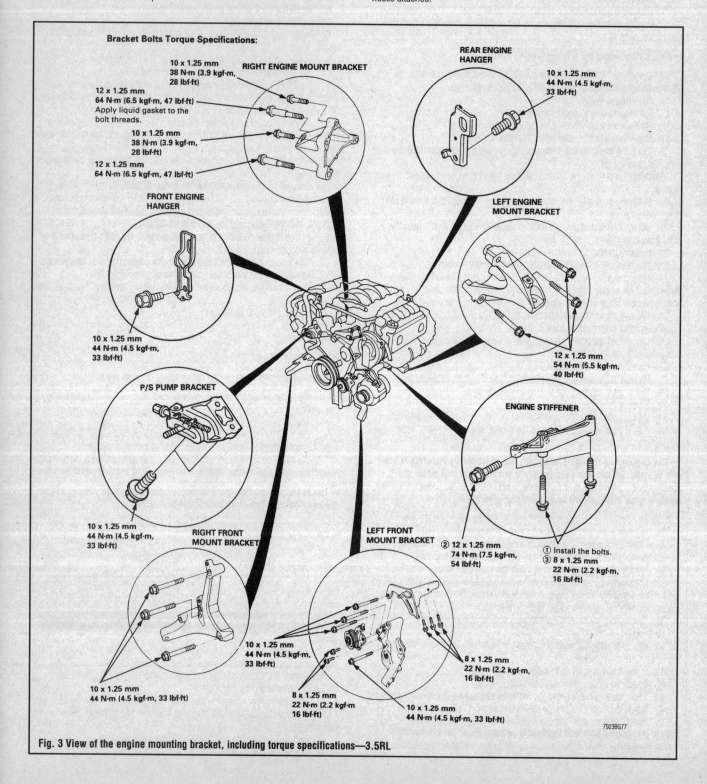

Fig. 3 View of the engine mounting bracket, including torque specifications—3.5RL

32. Remove the transaxle stop collars.

33. Remove the nuts attaching the front A pipe to the exhaust manifolds and the catalytic converter. Remove the front A pipe assembly.

34. Remove the O₂S sensor grommet and wire from the floor pan and the nuts attaching the catalytic converter and remove the converter.

35. Remove the converter heat shield.

36. Disconnect and plug the transaxle cooler lines.

37. Remove the shift cable cover, shift control solenoid valve/linear solenoid harness connector from the shift cable cover.

38. Disconnect the shift cable from the transaxles.

39. Remove the control lever from the control shaft.

40. Lower the vehicle to the floor.

41. Remove the radiator hoses and the radiator.

42. Disconnect the heater hoses.

43. Loosen the locknut on the fuel pressure regulator and rotate it 180 degrees.

44. Attach a chain hoist to the engine lifting eyelets.

45. Raise and safely support the vehicle.

46. Remove the shift cable guide and the transaxle beam.

47. Remove the transaxle mount and bracket.

48. Lower the vehicle.

49. Separate the left and right front mount brackets from the mounts and disconnect the vacuum line.

50. Remove the nuts from the right and left engine mounts.

51. Raise the engine slightly, be sure all connections have be removed.

52. Remove the engine/transaxle from the vehicle.

To install:

53. Position the engine/transaxle in the vehicle.

54. Install the transaxle mount bracket. Tighten the bolts to 28 ft. lbs. (38 Nm).

55. Install the vacuum hose on the right mount and install the nuts on the right and left engine mounts and tighten them to 47 ft. lbs. (64 Nm).

56. Install the transaxle beam. Tighten the bolts in the sequence shown to the correct specification.

57. Install the bolts in the left and right front mounts. Tighten them to 52 ft. lbs. (74 Nm).

58. Install the shift control solenoid valve/linear solenoid harness connector, the shift cable and cover to the transaxle.

59. Install the control lever to the control shaft.

60. Install the radiator and radiator hoses.

61. Attach the heater hoses.

62. Connect the transaxle cooler lines.

63. Remove the chain hoist from the engine lifting eyelets.

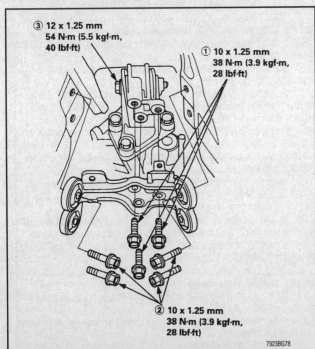

Fig. 4 Transaxle beam bolt tightening sequence and torque specifications—3.5RL

③ 12 x 1.25 mm
54 N·m (5.5 kgf·m, 40 lbf·ft)

① 10 x 1.25 mm
38 N·m (3.9 kgf·m, 28 lbf·ft)

② 10 x 1.25 mm
38 N·m (3.9 kgf·m, 28 lbf·ft)

7923BG78

64. Rotate the fuel pressure regulator 180 degrees, then tighten it.

65. Raise and safely support the vehicle.

66. Install the converter heat shield.

67. Install the catalytic converter and the O₂S sensor wire through the floor pan and install the grommet.

68. Attach the front A pipe to the exhaust manifolds and the catalytic converter.

69. Install the transaxle stop collars.

70. Install the CV–joints. Be sure the inner joint snapring seats completely.

71. Connect the lower ball joints to the steering knuckles.

72. Install the front suspension damper forks.

73. Connect the A/C compressor clutch connector and install the compressor.

74. Install and connect the Vehicle Speed Sensor (VSS).

75. Install the front tires and lower splash shield.

76. Carefully lower the vehicle.

77. Pull the carpet back under the front passengers seat and attach the HO₂S sensor connector.

78. Move the front passenger's seat back to its original position.

79. Install the radiator cap.

80. Attach the Power Steering Pressure (PSP) switch connector, install the power steering pump and drive belt.

81. Install the alternator and A/C drive belts.

82. Connect the spark plug voltage detection module and install the engine ground cables.

83. Attach the wiring harness connectors on the right side of the engine compartment.

84. Attach the transaxle sub–harness connector.

85. Install the control box and attach the connector.

86. Install the relay box, ground cable and wiring harness clips to the firewall.

87. Install the relay box and connect the vacuum hose, the alternator and battery cables and the clamp to the under-hood fuse/relay box.

88. Connect the engine wiring harness connector on the left side of the engine compartment.

89. Install the fuel feed hose to the fuel filter and connect the fuel return hose.

90. Install the canister and brake booster hoses.

91. Raise the coolant reservoir, then install the battery and tray.

92. Connect the throttle cable and cruise control cable to the throttle and install the throttle cable cover..

93. Install the air cleaner assembly and intake duct.

94. Install the engine cover.

95. Install the strut brace.

96. Refill the engine, differential, and transaxle fluids with the recommended type and amount of lubricant.

97. Fill the cooling system with the correct mixture of coolant and bleed the cooling system as necessary.

98. Connect the positive battery cable, then the negative battery cable.

99. Start the engine and check for leaks. Recheck the fluid levels and top off as necessary.

100. On 1999–00 models, reinstall the hood.

➡**Once the battery has been disconnected the PCM module must be programmed.**

101. Reprogram the PCM as follows:
  a. Set the parking brake.
  b. Shift the transaxle to Park or Neutral.
  c. Allow the engine to run at 3,000 RPM until the cooling fan cycles.
  d. Check that all electrical consumers (headlights, radio, air conditioner, etc.) are turned off.
  e. Allow the engine to idle at normal operating temperature for five minutes.

102. Enter the radio security code.

Rocker Arm (Valve) Cover

REMOVAL & INSTALLATION

1.8L, 2.2L, and 2.3L Engines

▶ **See Figures 5, 6, 7 and 8**

1. Disconnect the negative battery cable.

2. Label and disconnect any wires or hoses that interfere with valve cover removal.

Fig. 5 Remove all of the valve cover bolts

Fig. 6 You may need to tap the side of the valve cover lightly with a plastic or rubber mallet to break it free

Fig. 7 Carefully remove the valve cover and gasket from the engine

Fig. 8 Most Acura gaskets are made of a thin silicone rubber compound such as the one shown here

3. Remove the spark plug wire cover on 1.8L, 2.2L and 2.3L engines.
4. Tag and disconnect the spark plug wires.
5. Unfasten all necessary retainers, then remove the rocker arm (valve) cover. If the cover sticks to the cylinder head, tap it lightly with a rubber mallet or the palm of your hand.
6. Thoroughly clean the gasket mating surfaces.
7. Installation is the reverse of the removal procedure. During installation, be sure the valve cover gasket is seated properly in the corners with no visible gap.

Rocker Arms/Shafts

REMOVAL & INSTALLATION

→The radio may have a coded theft protection circuit. Make sure you have the code before disconnecting the battery, removing the radio fuse, or removing the radio.

1.8L (B18B1) Engine

▶ See Figure 9

1. Disconnect the negative battery cable.
2. Tag and disconnect the spark plug wires.
3. Remove the cylinder head/valve cover and timing belt cover.
4. Rotate the crankshaft to TDC, the compression stroke of the No. 1 piston, then remove the timing belt.
5. Remove the distributor from the cylinder head.
6. Install 5.0mm pin punches to the No.1 camshaft holders, then remove the camshaft sprockets.
7. Loosen the valve adjusters to remove as much spring tension as possible.
8. Remove the pin punches from the camshaft holders.
9. To check camshaft end play, perform the following:

a. Loosen the end bearing cap bolts 1 turn.
b. Install a dial indicator.
c. Push the camshaft fully towards the back of the head, zero the dial indicator and push the camshaft fully the other way to read end play.
d. End play on a new camshaft should be 0.002–0.006 in. (0.05–0.15mm), 0.020 in. (0.5mm) is the service limit.

10. To remove the camshaft bearing caps, loosen each bolt 2 turns at a time in a crisscross pattern to avoid damage to the valves or rockers. Mark the caps so they can be replaced in their original position.
11. Lift the camshafts from the cylinder head, wipe them clean and inspect the lift ramps. Replace the camshafts and rockers if the lobes are pitted, scored or excessively worn.
12. Tag or label the rocker arms before removing to install them to their original locations.
13. Use Plastigage® to check bearing clearance. The standard clearance is 0.0012–0.0027 in. (0.030–0.069mm), and absolute service limit is 0.006 in. (0.15mm).

To install:
14. Check the following before installing the camshafts:

a. Be certain the keyways on the camshafts are facing UP (No. 1 cylinder at TDC).
b. The valve adjuster lock nuts should be loosened and the adjusting screws backed off before installation.

15. Lubricate the rocker arms and camshafts with clean oil.
16. Place the rocker arms on the pivot bolts and the valve stems, making sure that the rocker arms are in their original positions.
17. Install the camshaft seals with the open side (spring) facing in. Lubricate the lip of the seal.
18. Be sure the keyways on the camshafts are facing up and install the camshafts to the cylinder head.
19. Apply liquid gasket to the head mating surfaces of the No. 1 and No. 6 camshaft holders, then install them along with Nos. 2, 3, 4 and 5 camshaft holders. The arrows stamped on the holders should point toward the timing belt. Do not apply oil to the holder mating surface where the camshaft seals are housed.
20. Tighten the camshaft holders temporarily and be sure that the rocker arms are properly positioned.
21. Press the oil seals into the No.1 camshaft holders with a seal driver.
22. Tighten the bolts in a crisscross pattern to 7 ft. lbs. (10 Nm). Check that the rockers do not bind on the valves.
23. Install the cylinder head plug to the end of the cylinder head. If the plug has alignment marks, align the marks with the cylinder head upper surface.
24. If equipped with a timing belt back cover, install the cover and tighten the bolts to 7.2 ft. lbs. (9.8 Nm).
25. Install 5.0mm pin punches to the No.1 camshaft holders, then install the camshaft pulley keys onto the grooves in the camshafts.
26. Push the camshaft pulleys onto the camshafts, then tighten the retaining bolts to 27 ft. lbs. (38 Nm).
27. Install the timing belt and timing belt covers. Remove the pin punches from the camshaft holders.
28. Adjust the valves and pour oil over the camshafts and rocker arms.
29. Apply liquid gasket to the rubber seal at the eight corners of the recesses. Do not install the parts if 20 minutes or more have elapsed since

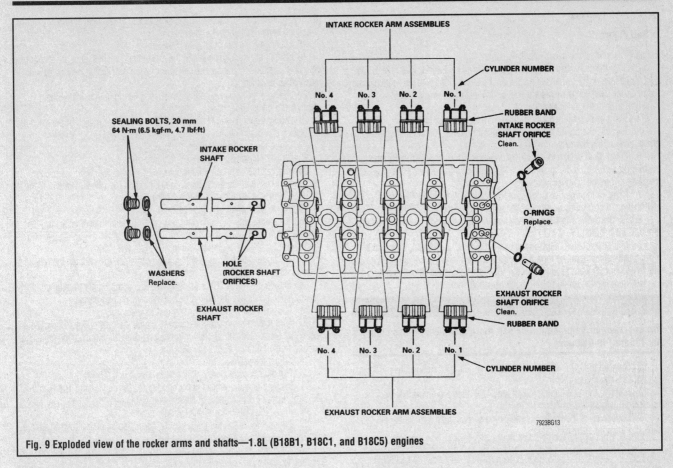

Fig. 9 Exploded view of the rocker arms and shafts—1.8L (B18B1, B18C1, and B18C5) engines

applying the liquid gasket. Instead, reapply liquid gasket after removing old residue.

30. Install the cylinder head cover and engine ground cable. Be sure the contact surfaces are clean and do not touch surfaces where liquid gasket has been applied.

31. Tighten the cylinder head cover nuts in 2–3 steps. In the final step, tighten all nuts in sequence, to 7 ft. lbs. (10 Nm).

32. Install the distributor to the cylinder head and reconnect the spark plug wires to the spark plugs.

33. Connect the negative battery cable and enter the radio security code.

34. Change the engine oil. Wait at least 20 minutes for the sealant to cure before filling the engine with oil.

1.8L (B18C1, B18C5) Engine

▶ See Figures 9 and 10

1. Remove the cylinder head from the vehicle, as outlined later in this section.

2. Hold each rocker arm assembly together with a rubber band to prevent them from separating.

3. Remove the intake and exhaust rocker shaft orifices from the cylinder head. The rocker shaft orifices are different and should be identified when removed. Discard the O-rings on the orifices.

4. Remove the Variable Valve Timing and Electronic Lift Control (VTEC) solenoid from the cylinder head and discard the filter.

5. Remove the rocker arm shaft sealing bolts, discard the washers.

6. Insert 12mm bolts into the rocker arm shafts. Remove each rocker arm set while slowly pulling out the rocker arm shaft.

➡**Tag each rocker arm set to assure installation in their original locations.**

7. Inspect the rocker arm pistons. If they do not move smoothly, replace the rocker arm assembly.

8. Remove the lost motion assembly from the cylinder head. Inspect the lost motion assembly by pushing the plunger with your finger. Replace the lost motion assembly if it does not move smoothly.

To install:

9. Install the lost motion assembly to the cylinder head.

10. Apply engine oil to the rocker arm pistons, then bundle the rocker arms with a rubber band. Apply a light coat of clean engine oil to the rocker arms.

11. Position the rocker arms in their original locations, if they are being reused. If new assembles are being used place them in the cylinder head. Don't forget to remove the rubber bands!

12. Lightly coat the rocker arm shafts with clean engine oil, then install the rocker arm shafts into the cylinder head. A 12mm bolt can be installed into the end of the rocker arm shafts to aid in their installation. Be sure to install the shafts in the proper positions. Remove the 12mm bolts from the rocker arm shafts, if used.

13. Clean and install the rocker arm shaft orifices with new O-rings. If the holes in the rocker arm shafts are not aligned screw a 12mm bolt into the end of the shaft to position the shaft.

14. Install the sealing bolts with new washers, tighten the bolts to 47 ft. lbs. (64 Nm).

15. Install the cylinder head into the vehicle, as outlined later in this section.

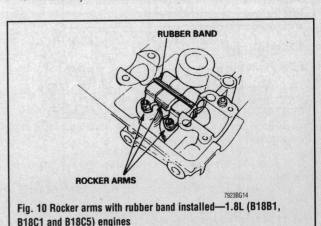

Fig. 10 Rocker arms with rubber band installed—1.8L (B18B1, B18C1 and B18C5) engines

2.2L, 2.3L Engines

♦ See Figure 11

1. Disconnect the negative battery cable.
2. Turn the crankshaft so the No. 1 piston is at Top Dead Center (TDC). The No. 1 piston is at TDC when the pointer on the block aligns with the white painted mark on the flywheel (manual transaxle) or driveplate (automatic transaxle).
3. Remove the air intake duct.
4. Remove the engine ground cable from the cylinder head cover.
5. Remove the connector and the terminal from the alternator, then remove the engine wiring harness from the valve cover.
6. Label, then detach the electrical connectors from the distributor and the spark plug wires from the spark plugs. Mark the position of the distributor and remove it from the cylinder head.
7. Remove the Positive Crankcase Ventilation (PCV) hose, then remove the cylinder head cover. Replace the rubber seals if damaged or deteriorated.
8. Ensure the words **UP** embossed on the camshaft pulley are aligned in the upward position.
9. Mark the rotation of the timing belt if it is to be used again. Loosen the timing belt adjusting nut ½ turn, then release the tension on the timing belt. Push the tensioner to release tension from the belt, then tighten the adjusting nut.
10. Remove the timing belt from the camshaft sprocket.

✳✳ WARNING

Do not crimp or bend the timing belt more than 90°, or less than 1 in. (25mm) in diameter.

11. Remove the camshaft sprocket attaching bolt, then remove the sprocket. Do not lose the sprocket key.
12. Remove the side engine mount bracket B, then the timing belt back cover from behind the camshaft sprockets.
13. Loosen all of the rocker arm adjusting screws, then remove the pin punches from the camshaft caps.
14. Remove the camshaft holders, note the holders locations for ease of installation. Loosen the bolts in the reverse order of the holder bolts torque sequence.
15. Remove the camshaft from the cylinder head, then discard the camshaft seals.
16. Remove the rocker arms from the cylinder head. Note the locations of the rocker arms.

➡The rocker arms have to be installed to their original locations if being reused.

To install:

17. Lubricate the rocker arms with clean oil, then install the rocker arms on the pivot bolts and the valve stems. If the rocker arms are being reused, install them to their original locations. The lock nuts and adjustment screws should be loosened before installing the rocker arms.
18. Lubricate the camshaft with clean oil.
19. Install the camshaft seals to the end of the camshafts that the timing belt sprocket attaches to. The open side (spring) should be facing into the cylinder head when installed.
20. Be sure the keyways on the camshaft is facing up and install the camshaft to the cylinder head.
21. Apply liquid gasket to the cylinder head mating surfaces of the No. 1 and No. 5 camshaft holders, then install them along with No. 2, 3 and 4.
22. Snug the camshaft holders in place.
23. Press the camshaft seals securely into place.
24. Tighten the camshaft holder bolts in two steps, following the proper sequence, to ensure that the rockers do not bind on the valves. Tighten all the 6mm bolts to 104 inch lbs. (12 Nm) and the 8mm bolts to 16 ft. lbs. (22 Nm).
25. Install the timing belt back cover.
26. Install the side engine mount bracket B. Tighten the bolt attaching the bracket to the cylinder head to 33 ft. lbs. (45 Nm). Tighten the bolts attaching the bracket to the side engine mount to 16 ft. lbs. (22 Nm).
27. Push the camshaft sprocket onto the camshaft, then tighten the retaining bolts to 43 ft. lbs. (59 Nm).
28. Ensure the words **UP** embossed on the camshaft pulley is aligned in the upward position. Install the timing belt to the camshaft sprockets.
29. Loosen, then tighten the timing belt adjuster nut.
30. Turn the crankshaft counterclockwise until the cam pulley has moved 3 teeth; this creates tension on the timing belt. Loosen, then tighten the adjusting nut and tighten it to 33 ft. lbs. (45 Nm).
31. Adjust the valves.
32. Tighten the crankshaft pulley bolt to 181 ft. lbs. (250 Nm).
33. Install the cylinder head cover and tighten the cap nuts to 104 inch lbs. (12 Nm). Install the PCV hose to the cylinder head cover.
34. Install the distributor to the cylinder head.
35. Connect the spark plug wires to the correct spark plugs, then attach the distributor electrical connectors.
36. Install the alternator wiring harness to the cylinder head cover, then connect the terminal and connector to the alternator.
37. Connect the engine ground cable to the cylinder head cover.
38. Install the air intake duct.
39. Drain the oil from the engine into a sealable container. Install the drain plug and refill the engine with clean oil.
40. Connect the negative battery cable and enter the radio security code.
41. Start the engine, checking carefully for any leaks.
42. Recode the radio.

2.5L, 3.2L and 3.5L Engines

♦ See Figures 12, 13, 14 and 15

1. Disconnect the negative battery cable. Remove the timing belt covers and cylinder head covers.
2. Rotate the crankshaft to Top Dead Center (TDC) compression of No.1 piston and remove the timing belt.

➡For 2.5L engines, the springs between the rocker arms are not all the same length. Carefully note their positions during disassembly.

3. Remove the camshaft sprocket.
4. Remove the cylinder head from the vehicle.
5. Loosen the rocker shaft holder bolts 1 turn at a time in the opposite of the installation sequence. Following this procedure will prevent the camshafts and rocker assemblies from warping.
6. After all bolts are loose, remove the rocker arm shafts as an assembly with the bolts still in the holders.
7. If the rocker shafts are to be disassembled, note that each rocker arm has a letter **A** or **B** stamped into the side. Before disassembling the rocker arms, make a note of the position of each letter so the arms can be reassembled the same way.
8. For 3.2L (C32A6) and 3.5L engines, do not remove the hydraulic tappets from the rocker arms unless they are to be replaced. Handle the rocker arms carefully so the oil does not drain out of the tappets.
9. Lift the camshafts from the cylinder head, wipe them clean and inspect the lift ramps. Replace the camshafts and rockers if the lobes are pitted, scored, or excessively worn.

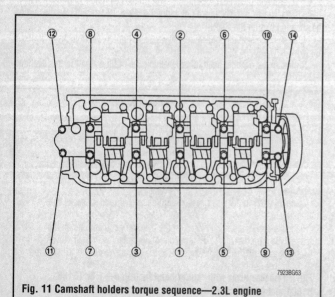

Fig. 11 Camshaft holders torque sequence—2.3L engine

7923BG63

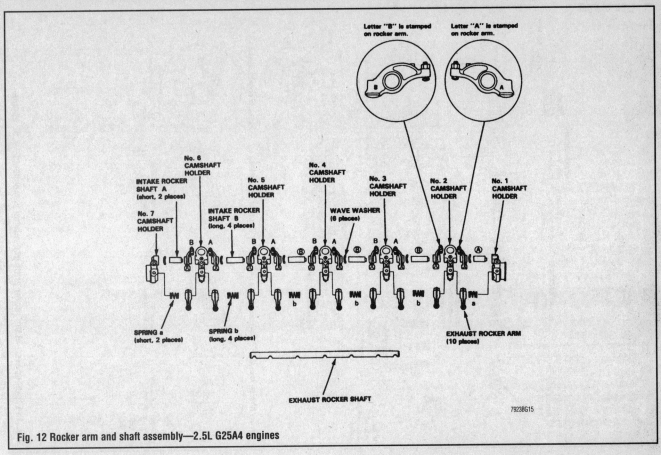

Fig. 12 Rocker arm and shaft assembly—2.5L G25A4 engines

To install:

10. Lubricate the camshaft and its journals with fresh engine oil.

11. Place a new camshaft seal on the end of the camshaft. The spring side of the seal must face in. Lubricate the journals and set the camshaft in place on the head.

12. Install the camshaft onto the cylinder head with the keyway pointed up.

13. Apply liquid gasket to the mounting surfaces of the camshaft end holders.

14. Set the rocker arm assemblies in place and start all the cam holder bolts. Be sure the rocker arms are properly positioned and turn each bolt

in sequence two turns at a time until the holders are seated on the head. Follow this procedure to avoid damaging the camshaft and rocker assemblies.

15. When all the camshaft and rocker holders are seated, tighten the bolts in the same sequence. Tighten the 8mm bolts to 16 ft. lbs. (22 Nm) and the 6mm bolts to 104 inch lbs. (12 Nm).

16. Install the cylinder head.

17. Install the camshaft sprocket. Tighten the bolts to 51 ft. lbs. (70 Nm) for 2.5L engines to 51 ft. lbs. (70 Nm) and to 23 ft. lbs. (32 Nm) for the 3.2L (C32A6) engine.

18. Install the timing belt, adjust the valves and oil the camshaft before completing the assembly.

19. Install the cylinder head cover and timing cover.

20. On 2.5L engines, install the distributor.

21. Reconnect the negative battery cable.

22. Check for proper engine and valve train operation.

3.0L Engine

▶ **See Figures 16 and 17**

1. Remove the cylinder head cover.

2. Loosen the jam nuts on the adjusters, then back out the screws.

3. Loosen the rocker arm shaft bolts two turns at a time in the sequence shown.

4. Lift the rocker arm assembly from the cylinder head. Leave the bolts in the shafts to retain the rocker arms and springs.

To install:

5. Clean all parts in solvent, dry with compressed air and lubricate with clean engine oil.

6. Place the rocker arm assemblies on the cylinder head and install the bolts loosely. Be sure that all rocker arms are in alignment with their valves.

7. Tighten each bolt two turns at a time in the correct sequence. Tighten the bolts to 17 ft. lbs. (24 Nm).

8. Adjust the valves and install the cylinder head covers.

Specified torque:
8 mm bolts: 22 N·m (2.2 kg-m, 16 lb-ft)
6 mm bolts: 12 N·m (1.2 kg-m, 9 lb-ft)

6 mm BOLTS

8 mm BOLTS

Fig. 13 Rocker arm assembly holder bolt torque sequence—2.5L G25A4 engines

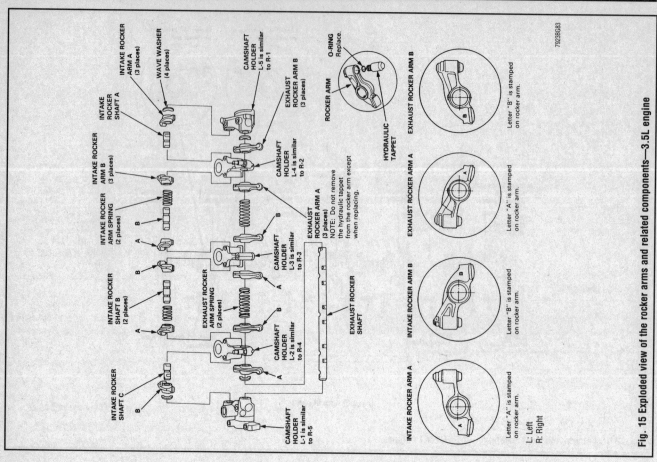

Fig. 15 Exploded view of the rocker arms and related components—3.5L engine

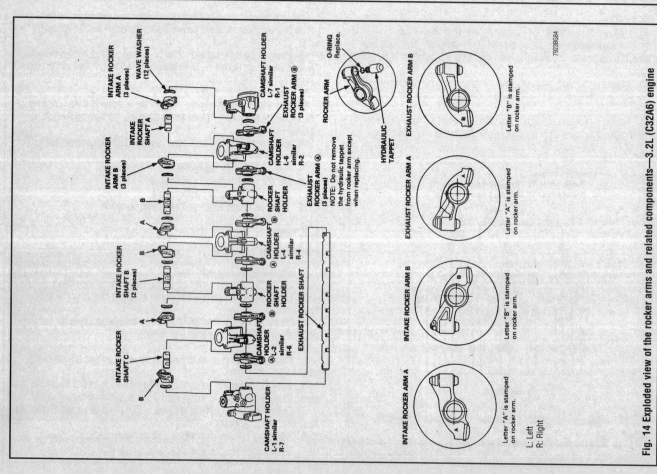

Fig. 14 Exploded view of the rocker arms and related components—3.2L (C32A6) engine

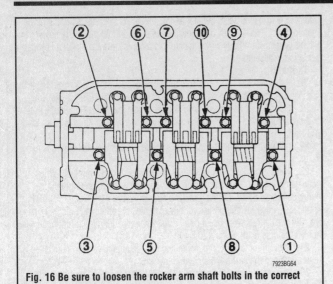

Fig. 16 Be sure to loosen the rocker arm shaft bolts in the correct order as shown—3.0L engine

Thermostat

REMOVAL & INSTALLATION

▶ See Figures 18, 19, 20, 21 and 22

1. Disconnect the negative battery cable.
2. Drain the cooling system into a suitable container.
3. Locate the thermostat housing by following the upper radiator hose to the engine.

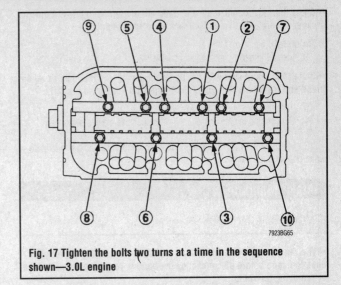

Fig. 17 Tighten the bolts two turns at a time in the sequence shown—3.0L engine

4. Loosen the hose clamps then carefully detach the hose from the fitting.

➡ If the hose is stuck, carefully use a pick to break the seal between the radiator hose and the housing. If the hose is deteriorated, replace it with a new one.

5. Disconnect any sensors or switches that may interfere with the removal of the thermostat from the housing.
6. Unfasten the retainers, then remove the thermostat housing.

➡ Some coolant may leak out of the housing as the seal is broken.

7. Remove the thermostat carefully noting how it's installed.
8. Clean the mating surfaces of the thermostat housing.

Fig. 18 Remove the thermostat housing bolts

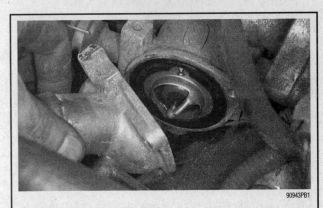

Fig. 19 Pull the water outlet neck away from the housing

Fig. 20 Note the installed position of the thermostat, then remove it

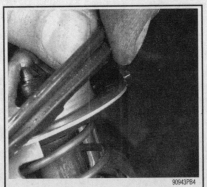

Fig. 21 A new gasket must be installed before installation

Fig. 22 Install the thermostat with the air bleed valve at the top

➡**Many thermostat housing's are made out of aluminum alloy. A plastic scraper is very effective and will not harm such metals.**

To install:

9. Install the new thermostat and gasket.

➡**Install the thermostat with the jiggle pin facing up. This acts as an air bleed and must be at the top of the thermostat to operate properly.**

10. Install the thermostat housing, then tighten the bolts securely.
11. Connect the radiator hose and tighten the hose clamps securely.
12. Install any remaining components, then refill the cooling system.
13. Start and run the engine until it reaches normal operating temperature while checking for leaks.

Intake Manifold

REMOVAL & INSTALLATION

➡**The radio may have a coded theft protection circuit. Make sure you have the code before disconnecting the battery, removing the radio fuse, or removing the radio.**

1.8L (B18B1, B18C1 and B18C5) Engines

♦ **See Figures 23, 24 and 25**

1. Disconnect the negative battery cable.
2. Drain the cooling system into a sealable container.
3. If equipped, remove the strut brace.
4. Remove the air intake duct.
5. Properly relieve the fuel pressure, as outlined in Section 5.
6. Disconnect the fuel feed hose.
7. Remove the breather hose, the water bypass hose and the control canister hose from the throttle body.
8. Remove the fuel return hose.
9. Disconnect the Positive Crankcase Ventilation (PCV) hose.
10. Remove the brake booster vacuum hose, the water bypass hose and the vacuum hose from the manifold.
11. Remove the throttle cable from the throttle body. Take great care not to kink or damage the cable.
12. If necessary, remove the throttle body.
13. Label and disconnect all the emission vacuum hoses from the intake manifold.
14. Label and detach the wiring connected to the intake manifold. Disconnect sensors as needed; release wiring retainers and clips.
15. Disconnect the water bypass hoses from the manifold.
16. Remove the bolts attaching the intake manifold to the support bracket.
17. Remove the nuts attaching the intake manifold to the cylinder head. Remove the nuts in a crisscross pattern, beginning from the center and moving out to both ends.
18. Remove the manifold and the old gasket.
19. Clean the intake manifold mating surfaces. Inspect the manifold for cracks, flatness and/or damage; replace the parts, if necessary. If the intake

manifold is to be replaced, transfer all the necessary components to the new manifold. On B18C1, B18C5 engines, the intake manifold may be removed from the air bypass valve body. If the manifold is removed, always install a new gasket before reassembly.

To install:

20. If the manifold was removed from the air bypass valve body, reassemble the components before installation. Tighten the through bolts to 17 ft. lbs. (24 Nm).
21. Use new gaskets when installing the intake manifold. Tighten the nuts, in a crisscross pattern, in 2–3 steps, starting with the inner nuts, to 17 ft. lbs. (23 Nm).
22. Install the bolts to the manifold support bracket. Tighten the bolts to 17 ft. lbs. (24 Nm).
23. The remainder of the procedure is the reverse of the removal. When connecting the fuel feed hose to the filter, use new washers and tighten the banjo bolt to 25 ft. lbs. (33 Nm) and the service bolt to 11 ft. lbs. (15 Nm). If applicable, when installing the strut brace, tighten the attaching nuts to 17 ft. lbs. (24 Nm). If removed, use a new gasket when installing the throttle body and tighten the nuts to 14 ft. lbs. (20 Nm).
24. After all removed components and connections have been reinstalled, refill and bleed the air from the cooling system.
25. Connect the negative battery cable and enter the radio security code. Start the engine and allow it to reach normal operating temperature.
26. Check for leaks and proper engine operation. Top off the engine coolant as necessary.

2.2L, 2.3L Engines

♦ **See Figure 26**

1. Disconnect the negative battery cable.
2. Drain the engine coolant into a sealable container.
3. Disconnect the cooling hoses from the intake manifold.
4. Label and unplug the vacuum hoses and electrical connectors on the manifold and throttle body. Unplug the connector from the Exhaust Gas Recirculation (EGR) valve. Position the wiring harnesses out of the way.
5. Disconnect the throttle cable from the throttle body.
6. Properly relieve the fuel pressure, as outlined in Section 5.
7. Remove the fuel rail and fuel injectors.
8. Remove the thermostat housing mounting bolts. Remove the thermostat housing from the intake manifold and the connecting pipe, by pulling and twisting the housing. Discard the O-rings.
9. It may be necessary to remove the upper intake manifold plenum and throttle body assembly in order to access the nuts securing the manifold to the head.
10. Remove the intake manifold support bracket bolts and the bracket. It may be necessary to access it from under the vehicle; raise and support the vehicle safely.
11. While supporting the intake manifold, remove the nuts attaching the intake manifold to the cylinder head, then remove the manifold. Remove the old gasket from the cylinder head.
12. Clean any old gasket material from the cylinder head and the intake manifold. check and clean the FIA chamber on the cylinder head.

To install:

13. Using a new gasket, place the manifold into position and support.

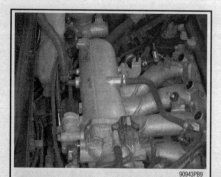

Fig. 23 As shown, space may be limited when trying to get to the bolts on the under side of the intake manifold

Fig. 24 Remove all of the intake manifold bolts as shown

Fig. 25 There may be bolts hidden on the under side of the manifold

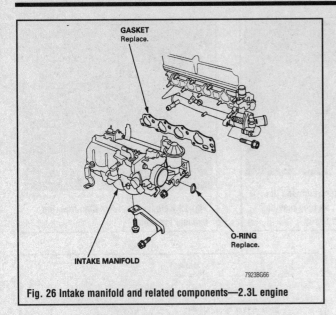

Fig. 26 Intake manifold and related components—2.3L engine

14. Install the support bracket to the manifold. Tighten the bolt holding the bracket to the manifold to 16 ft. lbs. (22 Nm).

15. Starting with the inner or center nuts, tighten the nuts, in a crisscross pattern, to the correct torque. The tension must be even across the entire face of the manifold if leaks are to be prevented. Correct torque is 16 ft. lbs. (22 Nm).

16. Using a new gasket, install the upper intake manifold and throttle body assembly, if removed as a separate unit. Tighten the nuts and bolts holding the chamber to 16 ft. lbs. (22 Nm).

17. Install a new O-ring to the coolant connecting pipe, and to the thermostat housing. Install the housing to the coolant pipe and the intake manifold. Tighten the mounting bolts to 16 ft. lbs. (22 Nm).

18. Connect and adjust the throttle cable.

19. Install the fuel rail/injector assembly. Connect the fuel lines.

20. Properly position the wiring harnesses and attach the electrical connectors.

21. Connect the vacuum hoses.

22. Fill and bleed the air from the cooling system.

23. Connect the negative battery cable and enter the radio security code.

24. Start the engine, checking carefully for any leaks of fuel, coolant or vacuum. Check the manifold gasket areas carefully for any leakage of vacuum.

2.5L Engine

1. Disconnect the negative battery cable.

2. Properly relieve the fuel system pressure, by removing the fuel filler cap and loosening the service bolt on the fuel filter. Remove the banjo bolt to remove the fuel feed hose from the fuel filter. Remove the fuel return hose from the pressure regulator.

3. Remove the throttle cable by loosening the locknut, then slip the cable end out of the throttle bracket and throttle linkage. Take care not to bend the cable when removing it. Move the cable aside.

4. Remove the engine harness cover. Label and disconnect the vacuum hoses and all wiring from the intake manifold.

5. To avoid having to drain the cooling system, remove the fast idle valve and the Idle Air Control (IAC) valve without disconnecting the coolant hoses. Move these components out of the work area so that they will not be damaged.

6. Remove the Exhaust Gas Recirculation (EGR) pipe and the vacuum pipe.

7. Remove the fuel rail. Remove the fuel injectors from the manifold. Handle the injectors and fuel rail carefully to avoid damaging them or contaminating them with dirt.

8. Unbolt the top bolts on the intake manifold brackets.

9. Remove the nuts that secure the manifold to the head. Remove the intake manifold from the engine.

To install:

➡Use new O-rings when installing the IAC and fast idle valves.

10. Inspect the manifold and its components for any signs of damage.

11. Fit the manifold to the engine with a new gasket and tighten the nuts to 16 ft. lbs. (22 Nm). Tighten the manifold bracket bolts to 16 ft. lbs. (22 Nm).

12. Install the fuel injectors into the rail and install the assembly onto the manifold with new sealing rings and cushion rings to prevent noise and leakage.

13. Connect the fuel injector harnesses and install the harness cover.

14. Install the IAC, fast idle, EGR, and EVAP valves. Use new O-rings.

15. Connect the wiring, vacuum hoses, and fuel lines. Use new sealing washers when connecting the fuel lines.

16. Install the throttle cable into its bracket and linkage. The throttle cable deflection is the measured by pressing down on the cable between the rubber boot and the linkage. The deflection must be 0.39–0.47 in. (10–12mm). Adjust the throttle cable as required.

17. Verify that all wiring and vacuum hoses are installed correctly.

18. Connect the negative battery cable. Run the engine and check for leaks.

3.2L and 3.5L Engines

1. Disconnect the negative battery cable.

2. Drain the cooling system into a suitable container.

3. Remove the air intake duct from the throttle body.

4. On GS models, remove the TCS control valve assembly and its brackets from the throttle body.

5. Properly relieve the fuel system pressure by loosening the service bolt on the fuel filter about 1 turn, then disconnect the fuel supply and return lines from the manifold.

6. Remove the engine harness covers, tag and disconnect the wiring harnesses from the fuel injectors.

7. Remove the vacuum pipe harness, air inlet pipe, and Exhaust Gas Recirculation (EGR) pipe.

8. Remove the pulsed air injection pipe and valve.

9. Remove the intake manifold nuts and bolts in a crisscross pattern, beginning from the center and moving out to both ends of the manifold.

10. Verify that all vacuum lines are disconnected and remove the intake manifold and throttle body as a unit.

11. Remove the water passage and clean the gasket mounting surfaces.

12. Inspect the manifold for cracks, flatness, or other damage; replace any damaged parts. If the intake manifold is to be replaced, transfer all the necessary components to the new manifold.

To install:

➡Always use new gaskets and O-rings during installation.

13. Install the water passage.

14. Install the intake manifold and tighten the nuts/bolts, in a crisscross pattern in 2–3 steps, starting with the inner nuts. Tighten the 8mm bolts to 16 ft. lbs. (22 Nm) and the 6mm bolts to 9 ft. lbs. (12 Nm).

15. Reconnect the vacuum lines and the air inlet, and the EGR pipes.

16. Reconnect the fuel supply and return lines to the manifold. Tighten the fuel system service bolt.

17. Reconnect all intake manifold wiring connectors.

18. Install the TCS control valve assembly and brackets.

19. Install the air duct to the throttle body. Refill the cooling system.

20. Reconnect the negative battery cable. Start the engine, allow it to reach normal operating temperature and check for leaks and proper engine operation.

Exhaust Manifold

REMOVAL & INSTALLATION

➡The radio may have a coded theft protection circuit. Make sure you have the code before disconnecting the battery, removing the radio fuse, or removing the radio.

1.8L Engines

▶ See Figures 27 thru 32

✳✳ WARNING

This procedure should only be performed on a cold engine.

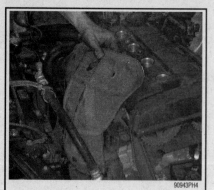

Fig. 27 Removal of the heat shield from the exhaust manifold —Integra 1.8L

Fig. 28 Use caution when removing the exhaust manifold bolts, as they may be rusted and will snap off easily

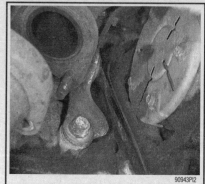

Fig. 29 Remove the down pipe from the exhaust manifold

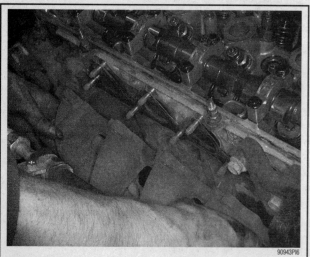

Fig. 30 Using both hands, pull the exhaust manifold away from the cylinder head

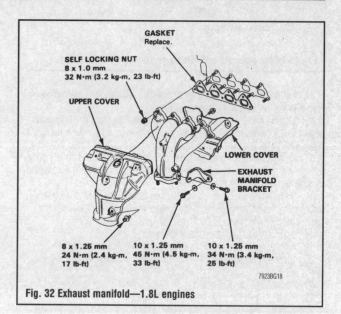

Fig. 32 Exhaust manifold—1.8L engines

Fig. 31 The lower support bracket may also have to be removed from the exhaust manifold

1. Disconnect the negative battery cable.
2. Remove the exhaust manifold cover.
3. Raise and safely support the vehicle.
4. Remove the three nuts attaching the front exhaust pipe to the exhaust manifold. Discard the nuts. Separate the exhaust pipe from the manifold and discard the gaskets.
5. Lower the vehicle.
6. Disconnect the bracket attaching the exhaust manifold to the engine.
7. Remove the exhaust manifold attaching nuts and discard the nuts.

8. Remove the exhaust manifold from the engine. Clean any old gasket material from the engine and the exhaust manifold mating surfaces.
9. Remove the rear cover from the exhaust manifold.

To install:
10. Install the rear cover to the exhaust manifold and tighten the mounting bolts to 17 ft. lbs. (24 Nm).
11. Install a new exhaust manifold gasket to the cylinder head.
12. Install the exhaust manifold to the engine and install new attaching nuts. Tighten the nuts to 23 ft. lbs. (31 Nm).
13. Install the bracket to the exhaust manifold and the engine. Tighten the bolts to 33 ft. lbs. (44 Nm).
14. Raise and safely support the vehicle.
15. Install new gaskets to the front exhaust pipe where it connects to the exhaust manifold.
16. Connect the front exhaust pipe to the exhaust manifold. Install new nuts and tighten the nuts to 40 ft. lbs. (54 Nm).
17. Lower the vehicle.
18. Install the exhaust manifold cover and tighten the bolts to 17 ft. lbs. (24 Nm).
19. Connect the negative battery cable and enter the radio security code.
20. Run the engine and check for exhaust leaks.

2.2L, 2.3L Engines

1. Disconnect the negative battery cable.
2. Safely raise and support the vehicle.
3. If the Oxygen (O2S) sensor is located in the exhaust manifold, detach the O2S sensor connector.

4. Remove the exhaust manifold upper cover.

5. If equipped with air conditioning, remove the heat insulator from the manifold.

6. Remove the nuts attaching the exhaust manifold to the front exhaust pipe. Separate the pipe from the manifold and discard the gasket. Support the pipe with wire; do not allow it to hang by itself.

7. Remove the exhaust manifold bracket(s) bolts and remove the bracket(s).

8. Using a crisscross pattern (starting from the center), remove the exhaust manifold attaching nuts.

9. Remove the manifold and discard the gasket. Clean the manifold and cylinder head mating surfaces.

10. If equipped, remove the lower manifold cover from the manifold.

To install:

11. If equipped, install the lower manifold cover, tighten the attaching bolts to 16 ft. lbs. (22 Nm).

12. Using a new gasket and nuts, place the manifold into position and support it. Install the nuts snug on the studs.

13. Install the support bracket(s) below the manifold. Tighten the bracket(s) mounting bolts to 33 ft. lbs. (44 Nm).

14. Starting with the manifold inner or center nuts, tighten the nuts in a crisscross pattern to the correct torque. The tension must be even across the entire face of the manifold if leaks are to be prevented. Tighten the nuts to 23 ft. lbs. (31 Nm).

15. Install the upper manifold cover, tighten the bolts to 16 ft. lbs. (22 Nm).

16. If disconnected, attach the O2S connector.

17. Connect the front exhaust pipe, using new gaskets and nuts. Tighten the exhaust pipe attaching nuts to 40 ft. lbs. (55 Nm).

18. Connect the negative battery cable and enter the radio security code.

19. Start the engine and check for exhaust leaks.

2.5L Engine

1. Disconnect the negative battery cable.

2. Remove the outer manifold heat shields.

3. Disconnect the wire and remove the Oxygen (O2S) sensor from the manifold.

4. Disconnect the manifold from exhaust pipe.

5. Remove the mounting bracket and remove the nuts to remove the manifold.

To install:

6. Be sure the gasket mating surfaces are clean. Install the bracket loosely and install the manifold with new gaskets and self–locking nuts. Tighten the nuts to 23 ft. lbs. (31–32 Nm), then tighten the bracket bolts. Be sure not to bend or damage the contact surface of the metal gasket.

7. Coat the threads of the O2S sensor with an anti–seize compound. Be careful not to get any on the head of the sensor. Install the sensor and carefully tighten to 33 ft. lbs. (44–45 Nm). Connect the sensor wire.

8. Install a new gasket and connect the manifold to the exhaust pipe. Tighten the nuts to 40 ft. lbs. (54–55 Nm). Install the outer manifold heat shields and tighten the bolts to 22 ft. lbs. (29 Nm).

9. Connect the negative battery cable. Start the engine and check for exhaust leaks.

3.0L Engine

▶ **See Figure 33**

1. Raise and safely support the vehicle.

2. Remove the engine undercover.

3. Disconnect the exhaust pipe from the manifold to be removed.

4. Lower the vehicle.

5. Remove the exhaust manifold heat shield.

6. Remove the mounting nuts and the exhaust manifold.

To install:

7. Clean the mounting surfaces.

8. Position a new gasket on the cylinder head.

9. Install the exhaust manifold. Tighten the nuts to 23 ft. lbs. (31 Nm).

10. Install the heat shield. Tighten the bolts to 16 ft. lbs. (22 Nm).

11. Raise the vehicle and connect the exhaust pipe to the manifold using a new gasket. Tighten the nuts to 40 ft. lbs. (54 Nm).

3.2L and 3.5L Engines

➡ **This operation should be performed with the engine and exhaust cold.**

1. Disconnect the negative battery cable. Be sure the engine is not hot or warm before performing this operation. Remove the exhaust manifold shrouds.

2. If applicable, remove the two small heat shields from the cylinder heads.

3. Remove the exhaust pipe nuts.

4. Remove the Oxygen (O2S) sensors.

5. Remove the air suction tube.

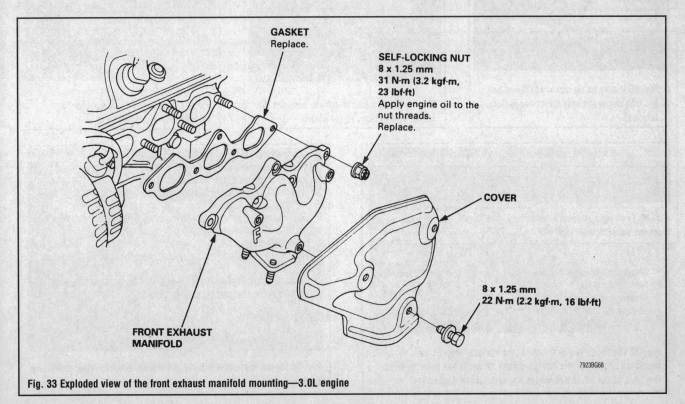

GASKET Replace.

SELF-LOCKING NUT
8 x 1.25 mm
31 N·m (3.2 kgf·m, 23 lbf·ft)
Apply engine oil to the nut threads. Replace.

COVER

8 x 1.25 mm
22 N·m (2.2 kgf·m, 16 lbf·ft)

FRONT EXHAUST MANIFOLD

7923BG68

Fig. 33 Exploded view of the front exhaust manifold mounting—3.0L engine

6. Remove the exhaust attaching nuts in a crisscross pattern starting from the center of the manifold.

7. Clean the gasket mounting surfaces. Inspect the manifold for cracks, flatness and/or damage; replace the parts, if necessary.

To install:

8. To install, use new gaskets and self–locking nuts. Be sure all mating surfaces are clean before installing exhaust manifold. Tighten the manifold nuts in a crisscross pattern starting from the center, for 3.2TL, tighten the manifold nuts to 22 ft. lbs. (30 Nm).

9. If applicable, install the two small heat shields and tighten the attaching bolts to 16 ft. lbs. (22 Nm).

10. Use new gaskets when installing the exhaust pipe to the manifold and tighten the nuts to 40 ft. lbs. (55 Nm).

11. Install the air suction tube, then install the O_2S sensors. Tighten the O_2S sensors to 33 ft. lbs. (45 Nm).

12. Install the manifold shrouds, tightening the bolts to 16 ft. lbs. (22 Nm).

13. Verify that all vacuum lines and wiring are properly connected.

14. Reconnect the negative battery cable, then start the engine and check for leaks.

Radiator

REMOVAL & INSTALLATION

▶ **See Figures 34 thru 39**

1. Disconnect the negative battery cable.

✳✳ CAUTION

Do not open the radiator draincock or remove the radiator cap when the cooling system is hot and under pressure. This can cause serious burns from hot, pressurized coolant. Allow a sufficient amount of time for the cooling system to cool down before opening up the system.

2. Loosen the radiator drain plug and, using a large capacity container, drain the cooling system.

3. Remove the radiator cap.

4. Disconnect the upper radiator hose.

➡**It is recommended that each clamp be matchmarked to the hose. Observe the marks and reinstall the clamps in exactly the same position when reinstalling the radiator.**

5. Remove the radiator hoses.

6. Label and disengage the wiring from the thermosensors and the electric fan assemblies.

Fig. 34 View of the upper radiator hold-down bracket and bolt

Fig. 35 It may be necessary to move an A/C line out of the way for easier radiator removal

Fig. 36 Using a pair of pliers, squeeze the spring clip to remove the clamp

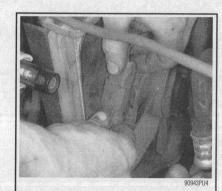
Fig. 37 Disengage the connector to release the wiring harness

Fig. 38 The lower radiator hose at the radiator may be hard to reach, as shown on this Integra model. If this is the case, remove the hose at the other end where it may be more accessible

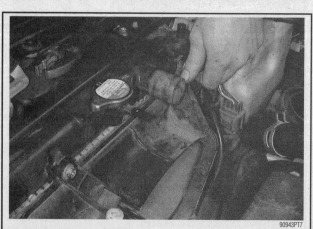
Fig. 39 Thread the radiator bolts in by hand to avoid cross-threading them

7. For vehicles with automatic transaxles, disconnect the oil cooler lines at the radiator. Plug the transaxle ports and the hose ends to contain the fluid and prevent contamination.

8. Remove the radiator. Be careful not to damage the radiators cooling fins while removing the unit. While the radiator is not heavy, it may be awkward. Use both hands to steady it during removal and installation

9. Installation is the reverse of the removal procedure. Refill the cooling system with the proper type and amount of coolant.

➡**You may need to bleed the air out of the system to avoid the possibility of a trapped air pocket that may cause engine overheating.**

Electric Cooling Fan

REMOVAL & INSTALLATION

▶ **See Figures 40, 41, 42 and 43**

❄❄ CAUTION

Do not open the radiator draincock or remove the radiator cap when the cooling system is hot and under pressure. This can cause serious burns from hot, pressurized coolant. Allow a sufficient amount of time for the cooling system to cool down before opening up the system.

1. Disconnect the negative battery cable.
2. Drain the engine coolant.
3. Remove any radiator hoses that interfere with the removal of the fans.
4. Detach the fan motor connectors.
5. Remove the fan shroud assemblies.
6. Installation is the reverse of the removal procedure.

Fig. 40 Use a suitable ratchet and socket to break the radiator fan housing bolts loose

TESTING

1. Detach the fan motor electrical connector.
2. Check to be sure that the radiator fan rotates when battery voltage is applied between the connector terminals.
3. Check that abnormal noises are not produced while the fan motor is turning.
4. If the fan runs normally, the motor is functioning properly.
5. If not, replace the fan module using the procedure earlier in this section.

➡**If the motor is noticeably overheated, the system voltage may be too high.**

Water Pump

REMOVAL & INSTALLATION

➡**The radio may have a coded theft protection circuit. Make sure you have the code before disconnecting the battery, removing the radio fuse, or removing the radio.**

1.8L Engines

1. Disconnect the negative battery cable.
2. If applicable, remove the front under panel.
3. Gradually release the system pressure by slowly and carefully removing the radiator cap. Be sure to protect your hands with gloves or a shop rag.
4. Drain the engine coolant into a sealable container.
5. Remove the timing belt from the engine.
6. Remove the camshaft pulleys and remove the back cover.
7. Unfasten the five water pump mounting bolts, then remove the water pump.
8. Remove and discard the old O-ring.
9. Remove the dowel pins from the oil water pump.
10. Clean the O-ring groove and the water pump mounting surface on the engine.
    To install:
11. Install the dowel pins to the new water pump.
12. Position a new O-ring to the new water pump, Apply a small amount of sealant to the O-ring to hold it in position.
13. Place the new water pump on the engine and install the mounting bolts. Tighten the mounting bolts to 104 inch lbs. (12 Nm).
14. Install the back cover and the camshaft pulleys.
15. Install the timing belt.
16. Fill the engine with coolant and bleed the air from the cooling system.
17. Connect the negative battery cable and enter the radio security code.
18. Run the engine and check for cooling system leaks.

2.2L, 2.3L, 2.5L, 3.0L, 3.2L and 3.5L Engines

▶ **See Figure 44**

➡**Perform this service operation with the engine cold.**

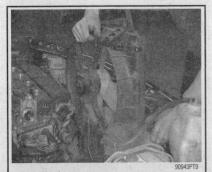

Fig. 41 After all fasteners have been removed, pull the fan housing free from the radiator

Fig. 42 Note how the bottom of the fan housing connects to the radiator

Fig. 43 Location of radiator fan shroud mounting tab on the radiator

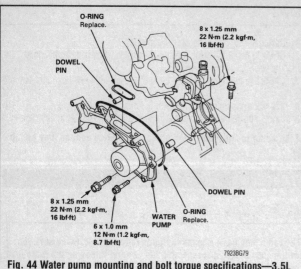

O-RING
Replace.

DOWEL
PIN

8 x 1.25 mm
22 N·m (2.2 kgf·m,
16 lbf·ft)

DOWEL PIN

8 x 1.25 mm
22 N·m (2.2 kgf·m,
16 lbf·ft)

WATER
PUMP

O-RING
Replace.

6 x 1.0 mm
12 N·m (1.2 kgf·m,
8.7 lbf·ft)

7923BG79

Fig. 44 Water pump mounting and bolt torque specifications—3.5L engine shown

1. Disconnect the negative battery cable.
2. Remove the front splash panel and release the system pressure by slowly removing the radiator cap.
3. Drain the cooling system.
4. Remove the timing belt. Inspect the timing belt for any signs of damage or oil and coolant contamination. Replace the timing belt if there is any doubt about its condition.
5. On 1996–97 3.2 TL and 1996–00 3.5 RL models, remove the left camshaft pulley and back cover.
6. On 1997–00 3.0 CL models and 1999–00 3.2 TL models, remove the timing belt tensioner.

7. Remove the water pump bolts. Then, remove the water pump and sprocket assembly from the engine block. Remove the O-rings from the water passage.

To install:

8. Before installation, be sure all gasket and O-ring groove surfaces are clean.
9. Install the water pump with a new O-ring. Use new bolts and tighten the 6mm mounting bolts evenly to 104 inch lbs. (12 Nm) and the 8mm bolts to 16 ft. lbs. (22 Nm).
10. If removed, install the timing belt rear cover and camshaft pulley.
11. If removed, install the timing belt tensioner.
12. Install the timing belt and timing belt covers.
13. Install and adjust the tension of the accessory drive belts.
14. Close the cooling system drain plug. Refill and bleed the cooling system.
15. Connect the negative battery cable.
16. Start the engine, allow it to reach normal operating temperature, check for leaks, and top off as necessary.
17. Enter the radio security code.

Cylinder Head

REMOVAL & INSTALLATION

➡The radio may have a coded theft protection circuit. Make sure you have the code before disconnecting the battery, removing the radio fuse, or removing the radio.

1.8L (B18B1) Engines

◆ See Figures 45 thru 59

1. Before removing the cylinder head, be sure the engine temperature is below 100° F. (38° C.); a fully cooled engine is best.
2. Disconnect the negative battery cable.

90943PG9

Fig. 45 Always align the timing marks before removing the timing belt.

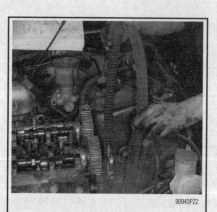

90943PZ2

Fig. 46 Removal of the timing belt

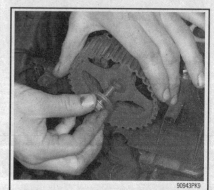

90943PK9

Fig. 47 Removing the camshaft sprocket bolt . . .

90943PL1

Fig. 48 . . . then remove the camshaft sprocket

90943PL2

Fig. 49 The woodruff keeps the camshaft pulley from spinning on the camshaft

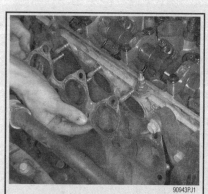

90943PJ1

Fig. 50 The exhaust manifold gasket may be stuck to the head

3. Be sure the crankshaft is at TDC on No. 1 cylinder by aligning the white mark on the crankshaft pulley with the pointer on the lower timing belt cover.

4. Drain the engine coolant. Remove the radiator cap to speed draining.

5. Remove the intake air duct.

6. Properly relieve the fuel system pressure, as outlined in Section 5.

7. Disconnect the fuel feed hose. Be sure to mark all connectors and vacuum hoses before disconnecting them.

8. Disconnect the breather hose, water bypass hose and the evaporative emission control canister hose.

9. Remove the Positive Crankcase Ventilation (PCV) hose and the fuel return hose.

Fig. 51 Remove the camshaft holder bolts. Notice that the caps are marked (E1) for exhaust camshaft cap #1 and (I1) for intake camshaft #1

10. Remove the brake booster vacuum hose, water bypass and EVAP (Evaporative emissions) purge control solenoid vacuum hose.

11. Remove the throttle cable. Remove the throttle control cable (automatic transaxle only). Be careful not to bend the cables when removing them.

12. Remove the wiring harness clamps, then label and detach the following:
- Four fuel injector connectors
- Intake Air Temperature (IAT) sensor connector
- Engine Coolant Temperature (ECT) sensor connector
- Ignition coil connector
- Throttle Position (TP) sensor connector
- Manifold Absolute Pressure (MAP) sensor connector
- Idle Air Control (IAC) valve connector
- Purge control solenoid valve connector

13. Disconnect the upper radiator hose, heater hose and water bypass hose.

14. Remove the splash shield.

15. Remove the power steering adjusting and mounting bolts, then remove the power steering pump and belt. Do not disconnect the power steering hoses.

16. Remove the air conditioning belts and the compressor, then remove the cruise control actuator.

17. Remove the engine side mount.

18. Remove the cylinder head cover, timing belt cover, and timing belt.

19. Remove the camshaft pulleys and back cover.

20. Remove the exhaust manifold cover, bracket, and exhaust manifold.

21. Remove the bolts attaching the intake manifold to the support bracket.

22. Remove the nuts attaching the intake manifold to the cylinder head. Remove the nuts in a crisscross pattern, beginning from the center and moving out to both ends.

➡️**It may be more timely to remove the head and then the intake manifold. This method will provide easier access to any hidden intake manifold bolts.**

23. Remove the manifold and the old gasket.

24. Loosen the lock nuts and adjusting screws, then remove the camshaft holder bolts. Remove the camshaft holders, camshafts and rocker arms.

25. Remove the cylinder head bolts, then remove the cylinder head. To pre-

Fig. 52 Lift the camshaft cap away from the camshaft as shown

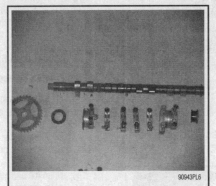

Fig. 53 Make sure to keep the caps, and all components in order at all times

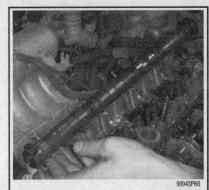

Fig. 54 Evenly lift the camshaft from the head

Fig. 55 Note the location of the camshaft oil seal

Fig. 56 Remove the valve adjusters—Integra

Fig. 57 To ensure they are installed in the proper position on the head, place each valve adjuster in the correct slot of the cardboard keeper as shown

vent warpage, unscrew the bolts in the reverse of the torque sequence, ⅓ turn at a time. Repeat the sequence until all bolts are loosened. Remember that cylinder head bolts are under great stress, exercise caution whenever you apply extreme force to these bolts.

26. Remove and discard the gasket, thoroughly clean the gasket mating surfaces.

To install:

27. Install the cylinder head onto the engine block, after making sure the mating surface was cleaned and a new gasket was installed. Be sure to pay attention to the following points:
- Be sure the No. 1 cylinder is at top dead center and the camshaft pulley UP mark is on the top before positioning the head in place.
- The cylinder head dowel pins and oil control orifice must be cleaned and aligned.
- Replace the washer when damaged or deteriorated.
- Apply engine oil to the cylinder head bolts and the washers.
- Use the longer cylinder head bolts at the No. 1 and No. 2 positions.

28. Tighten the cylinder head bolts in two steps. In the first step tighten all bolts in sequence to 22 ft. lbs. (29 Nm), then in the second step tighten all bolts in the same sequence to 63 ft. lbs. (85 Nm).

29. Use new gaskets and install the intake manifold onto the cylinder head. Tighten the nuts in a crisscross pattern in 2–3 steps, beginning in the middle to 17 ft. lbs. (23 Nm).

30. Install and tighten the intake manifold bracket bolts to 17 ft. lbs. (24 Nm).

31. Install the exhaust manifold and tighten the new self–locking nuts in a crisscross pattern in 2–3 steps, beginning with the inner nuts. Tighten the nuts to 23 ft. lbs. (31 Nm). Install a new exhaust pipe gasket and tighten the new nuts to 40 ft. lbs. (54 Nm).

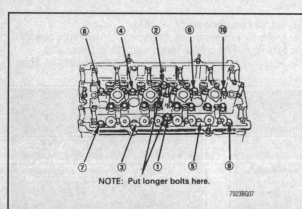

NOTE: Put longer bolts here.

7923BG07

Fig. 58 Cylinder head bolt torque sequence—1.8L (B18B1) engines

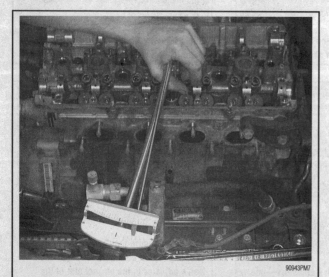

90943PM7

Fig. 59 Properly torque all of the head bolts in the correct order

32. Be sure that the keyways on the camshafts are facing up and that the rocker arms are in their original position. The valve lock nuts should be loosened and the adjusting screw backed off before installation.

33. Place the rocker arms on the pivot bolts and the valve stems.

34. Install the camshafts, then install the camshaft seals with the open side facing in. Install the rubber cap with liquid gasket applied. If the rubber cap has two horizontal marks, align the marks with the cylinder head upper surface.

35. Apply liquid gasket to the cylinder head mating surfaces of the No. 1 and No. 6 intake and exhaust camshaft holders and install them, along with No. 2, 3, 4 and 5. Be sure to pay attention to the following points:
- "I" or "E" marks are stamped on the camshaft holders.
- Do not apply oil to the holder mating surface of camshaft seals.
- The arrows marked on the camshaft holders should point to the timing belt.

36. Tighten the camshaft holders temporarily. Be sure that the rocker arms are properly positioned on the valve stems.

37. Tighten each bolt in 2 steps to ensure that the rockers do not bind on the valves. Tighten the 6mm bolts to 86 inch lbs. (9.8 Nm) working from the middle outward.

38. Install the keys into the camshaft grooves. To set the No. 1 piston at TDC, align the holes on the camshaft with the holes in the No. 1 camshaft holders and insert 5.0mm pin punches into the holes.

39. Install the back cover and push the camshaft pulleys onto the camshafts, then tighten the retaining bolts to 27 ft. lbs. (37 Nm). Install the timing belt and adjust the tension, then install the timing belt covers.

40. Adjust the valve clearance.

41. Apply sealant to the corners of the outer camshaft journal gasket surfaces, install the cylinder head cover, and torque the fasteners to 86 inch lbs. (9.8 Nm).

42. Install the engine side mount, tighten the two new nuts and new bolt to the engine to 38 ft. lbs. (52 Nm) and tighten the bolt attaching the mount to the vehicle to 54 ft. lbs. (74 Nm).

43. The balance of installation is the reverse of the removal procedure.

44. Connect the negative battery cable and enter the radio security code.

45. After installation, check to see that all hoses and wires are installed correctly.

46. Fill and bleed the air from the cooling system.

47. Attach the negative battery cable.

48. Enter the radio security code.

1.8L (B18C1, B18C5) engines

▶ See Figures 60 and 61

1. Before removing the cylinder head, be sure the engine temperature is below 100° F degrees; a fully cooled engine is best.

2. Disconnect the negative battery cable.

3. Be sure the crankshaft is at TDC/compression on No. 1 cylinder. Align the white mark on the crankshaft pulley with the pointer on the lower timing belt cover.

4. Drain the engine coolant into a sealable container. Remove the radiator cap to speed draining.

5. Remove the strut brace.

6. Remove the intake air duct.

7. Properly relieve the fuel pressure.

8. Disconnect the fuel feed hose.

9. Be sure to mark all connectors and vacuum hoses before disconnecting them. Disconnect the Evaporative Emissions (EVAP) purge control solenoid vacuum hose and the EVAP control canister hose.

10. Remove the Positive Crankcase Ventilation (PCV) hose and the water bypass hose.

11. Remove the brake booster vacuum hose, and the fuel return hose.

12. Remove the throttle cable. Remove the throttle control cable (automatic transaxle only). Be careful not to bend the cables when removing them.

13. Remove the wiring harness clamps, then tag and detach the following:
- Four fuel injector connectors
- Intake Air Temperature (IAT) sensor connector
- Engine Coolant Temperature (ECT) sensor connector
- Top Dead Center (TDC) Crank Position (CKP) sensor and Camshaft Position (CYP) sensor connector
- Ignition coil connector
- Engine Coolant Temperature (ECT) gauge sending unit connector

- Throttle Position (TP) sensor connector
- Variable Valve Timing and Electronic Lift Control (VTEC) solenoid connector
- VTEC pressure switch connector
- Manifold Absolute Pressure (MAP) sensor connector
- Idle Air Control (IAC) valve connector
- Purge control solenoid valve connector
- Intake Air Bypass (IAB) control solenoid valve connector
- Crankshaft Speed Fluctuation (CKF) sensor connector

14. Remove the spark plug wires and distributor from the cylinder head.

15. Disconnect the upper radiator hose, heater hose and water bypass hose.

16. Remove the splash shield.

17. Remove the engine ground cable.

18. Remove the power steering adjusting and mounting bolts, then remove the power steering pump and belt. Do not disconnect the power steering hoses.

19. Remove the heat shield from the power steering bracket.

20. Remove the air conditioning compressor and alternator belts.

21. Remove the cruise control actuator.

22. Remove the engine side mount.

23. Remove the cylinder head cover, timing belt cover, and timing belt.

24. Remove the camshaft sprockets and back cover.

25. Remove the exhaust manifold cover, bracket, and exhaust manifold.

26. Remove the bolts attaching the intake manifold to the support bracket.

27. Remove the nuts attaching the intake manifold to the cylinder head. Remove the nuts in a crisscross pattern, beginning from the center and moving out to both ends.

28. Remove the manifold and the old gasket.

29. Remove the VTEC solenoid from the cylinder head.

30. Loosen the rocker arm lock nuts and adjusting screws.

31. Remove the camshaft holder bolts, then remove the camshaft holder plates, the camshaft holders, and camshafts.

32. Remove the cylinder head bolts, then remove the cylinder head. To prevent warpage, loosen the bolts in the reverse of the torque sequence 1/3 turn at a time. Repeat this sequence until all bolts are loosened.

To install:

33. Install the cylinder head onto the engine block, after making sure the mating surface was cleaned and a new gasket was installed. Be sure to pay attention to the following points:

- Be sure the No. 1 cylinder is at top dead center and the camshaft pulley UP mark is on the top before positioning the head in place.
- The cylinder head dowel pins and oil control orifice must be cleaned and aligned.
- Replace the washer when damaged or deteriorated.
- Apply engine oil to the cylinder head bolts and the washers.
- Use the longer cylinder head bolts at the No. 1 and No. 2 positions.

34. Tighten the cylinder head bolts in two steps. In the first step tighten all bolts in sequence to 22 ft. lbs. (29 Nm). In the second step tighten all the bolts in the same sequence to 63 ft. lbs. (85 Nm).

35. Use new gaskets and install the intake manifold onto the cylinder head; tighten the nuts in a crisscross pattern in 2–3 steps, beginning in the middle. Tighten the nuts to 17 ft. lbs. (23 Nm).

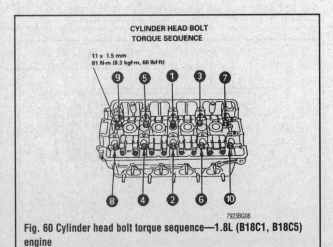

Fig. 60 Cylinder head bolt torque sequence—1.8L (B18C1, B18C5) engine

36. Install and tighten the intake manifold bracket bolts to 17 ft. lbs. (24 Nm).

37. Install the VTEC solenoid with a new filter, tighten the attaching bolts to 17 ft. lbs. (24 Nm).

38. Install the exhaust manifold and tighten the new self–locking nuts in a crisscross pattern in 2–3 steps, beginning with the inner nuts. Tighten the nuts to 23 ft. lbs. (31 Nm). Install a new exhaust pipe gasket and tighten the new nuts to 40 ft. lbs. (54 Nm).

39. Install the exhaust manifold bracket and cover. Tighten the bracket attaching bolts to 33 ft. lbs. (44 Nm) and the cover bolts to 17 ft. lbs. (24 Nm).

40. Be sure that the keyways on the camshafts are facing up and that the rocker arms are in their original position. The valve lock nuts should be loosened and the adjusting screw backed off.

41. Install the camshafts, then install the camshaft seals with the open side facing in. Install the rubber cap with liquid gasket applied. If the rubber cap has two horizontal marks, align the marks with the cylinder head upper surface.

42. Install a new O-ring and the dowel pin to the oil passage of the No. 3 camshaft holder.

43. Apply liquid gasket to the cylinder head mating surfaces of the No. 1 and No. 5 intake and exhaust camshaft holders, then install them, along with No. 2, 3, and 4. Be sure to pay attention to the following points:

- Do not apply oil to the holder mating surface of camshaft seals.
- The arrows marked on the camshaft holders should point to the timing belt.

44. Tighten the camshaft holders temporarily. Be sure that the rocker arms are properly positioned on the valve stems.

45. Tighten each bolt in 2 steps to ensure that the rockers do not bind on the valves. Tighten the 8x1.25mm bolts to 20 ft. lbs. (27 Nm), and the 6 x 1.0mm bolts to 7.2 ft. lbs. (9.8 Nm).

46. Install the back cover and tighten the attaching bolt to 86 inch lbs. (9.8 Nm). Install the keys into the camshaft grooves, then push the camshaft pulleys onto the camshafts, and then tighten the retaining bolts to 41 ft. lbs. (56 Nm).

47. Install the timing belt and adjust the tension, then install the timing belt covers.

48. Adjust the valve clearance.

49. Install the rubber seal in the groove of the cylinder head cover. Be sure that the seal and groove are thoroughly clean first.

50. Apply liquid gasket to the rubber seal at the eight corners of the recesses. Do not install the parts if 20 minutes or more have elapsed since applying the liquid gasket. Instead, reapply liquid gasket after removing old residue.

51. Install the cylinder head cover and engine ground cable. Be sure the contact surfaces are clean and do not touch surfaces where liquid gasket has been applied.

52. Tighten the cylinder head cover nuts in 2–3 steps. In the final step, tighten all nuts in sequence, to 86 inch lbs. (10 Nm).

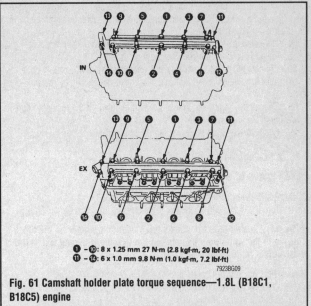

❶ – ⑩: 8 x 1.25 mm 27 N·m (2.8 kgf·m, 20 lbf·ft)
⑪ – ⑬: 6 x 1.0 mm 9.8 N·m (1.0 kgf·m, 7.2 lbf·ft)

7923BG09

Fig. 61 Camshaft holder plate torque sequence—1.8L (B18C1, B18C5) engine

53. Install the engine side mount, tighten the two new nuts and new bolt to the engine to 38 ft. lbs. (52 Nm) and tighten the bolt attaching the mount to the vehicle to 54 ft. lbs. (74 Nm).

54. The balance of installation is the reverse of the removal procedure.

55. Fill and bleed the air from the cooling system.

56. Connect the negative battery cable and enter the radio security code.

57. After installation, check to see that all hoses and wires are installed correctly.

58. Change the engine oil. Wait at least 20 minutes for the sealant to cure before filling the engine with oil.

59. Check for any fluid leaks and top off as necessary.

2.2L, 2.3L Engines

♦ **See Figures 62 and 63**

1. Disconnect the negative battery cable.
2. Turn the crankshaft so the No. 1 piston is at Top Dead Center (TDC).

➡**The No. 1 piston is at top dead center when the pointer on the block aligns with the white painted mark on the flywheel (manual transaxle) or driveplate (automatic transaxle).**

3. Drain the engine coolant into a sealable container.
4. Properly relieve the fuel system pressure, as outlined in Section 5.
5. Remove the air intake duct.
6. Remove the evaporative emissions (EVAP) control canister hose from the intake manifold.
7. Remove the throttle cable from the throttle body.

➡**Be careful not to bend the cable when removing. Always replace a kinked cable with a new one.**

8. Disconnect the fuel feed and return hose.
9. Remove the brake booster vacuum hose from the intake manifold.
10. Tag and detach the following engine wiring harness connectors:
    - Fuel injector connectors
    - Variable Valve Timing and Electronic Lift Control (VTEC) solenoid connector
    - Intake Air Temperature (IAT) sensor connector
    - Idle Air Control (IAC) valve connector
    - Throttle Position (TP) sensor connector
    - Exhaust Gas Recirculation (EGR) valve lift sensor
    - Ground cable terminals
    - Engine Coolant Temperature (ECT) switch B connector
    - Heated Oxygen (HO$_2$S) sensor connector
    - ECT sensor
    - ECT gauge sending unit connector
    - Ignition Control Module (ICM) connector
    - Top Dead Center (TDC) Crank Position (CKP) sensor and Camshaft Position (CYP) sensor connector
    - Vehicle Speed Sensor (VSS) connector
    - Ignition coil connector
    - Intake Air Bypass (IAB) solenoid valve connector
    - ECT switch A connector
    - Knock sensor connector
11. Remove the engine ground cable from the cylinder head cover.
12. Remove the distributor and ignition wires.
13. Remove the connector and the terminal from the alternator, then remove the engine wiring harness from the valve cover.
14. Remove the mounting bolts and drive belt from the power steering pump. Pull the pump away from the mounting bracket, without disconnecting the hoses. Support the pump out of the way.
15. Remove the ignition coil.
16. Tag, then disconnect the emissions vacuum hoses from the intake manifold assembly.
17. Remove the bypass hose from the intake manifold.
18. Remove the upper radiator hose and the heater hose from the cylinder head.
19. Remove the lower radiator hose and bypass hose.
20. Support the engine with a jack and remove the side engine mount.
21. Remove the cylinder head cover.
22. Remove the timing belt.
23. Remove the camshaft pulley and the back cover.
24. Remove the lower splash shield.

25. Remove the intake manifold bracket bolts.
26. Remove the intake manifold.
27. Disconnect the exhaust pipe from the exhaust manifold.
28. Remove the exhaust manifold and the exhaust manifold heat insulator.
29. Remove the cylinder head bolts in the reverse order of the tightening sequence.

➡**To prevent warpage, unscrew the bolts in sequence ⅓ turn at a time. Repeat the sequence until all bolts are loosened.**

30. Separate the cylinder head from the engine block with a suitable flat bladed prytool.

To install:

31. Be sure all cylinder head and block gasket surfaces are clean. Check the cylinder head for warpage. If warpage is less than 0.002 in. (0.05mm), cylinder head resurfacing is not required. Maximum resurface limit is 0.008 in. (0.2mm) based on a cylinder head height of 5.20 in. (132.0mm).

32. Always use a new head gasket.

33. Be sure the No. 1 cylinder is at TDC.

34. Clean the oil control orifice and install a new O-ring. The cylinder head dowel pins and oil control jet must be aligned.

35. Install the bolts that secure the intake manifold to its bracket but do not tighten them.

36. Install the cylinder head, then tighten the cylinder head bolts sequentially in the following steps:
    - Step 1: 22 ft. lbs. (29 Nm).
    - Step 2: 90 degrees
    - Step 3: 90 degrees
    - Step 4 (Only if using new bolts): 90 degrees

➡**A beam type torque wrench is recommended. If a bolt makes any noise while being tightened, loosen the bolt and retighten it.**

37. Install the intake manifold with a new gasket.
38. Install the exhaust manifold with a new gasket.
39. Install the exhaust manifold bracket, then install the exhaust pipe, bracket and upper shroud.

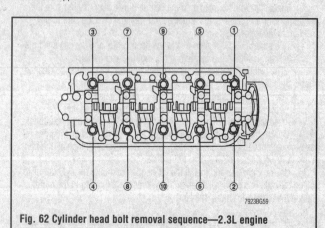

Fig. 62 Cylinder head bolt removal sequence—2.3L engine

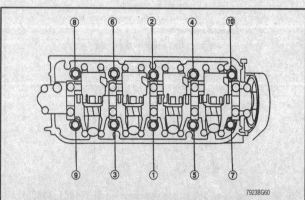

Fig. 63 Cylinder head bolt torque sequence—2.3L engine

40. Install the camshafts and rocker arms.
41. Install the timing belt back cover.
42. Install the side engine mount bracket B. Tighten the bolt attaching the bracket to the cylinder head to 33 ft. lbs. (45 Nm). Tighten the bolts attaching the bracket to the side engine mount to 16 ft. lbs. (22 Nm).
43. Install the camshaft sprockets onto the camshafts.
44. Install the timing belt.
45. Adjust the valves.
46. Tighten the crankshaft pulley bolt to 181 ft. lbs. (250 Nm).
47. Install the splash shield.
48. Install the remaining components in the reverse order of removal.
49. Drain the oil from the engine into a sealable container. Install the drain plug and refill the engine with clean oil.
50. Fill and bleed the air from the cooling system.
51. Connect the negative battery cable and enter the radio security code.
52. Start the engine, checking carefully for any leaks.

2.5L Engine

▶ See Figures 64 and 65

1. Disconnect the negative battery cable and drain the coolant into a suitable container.
2. Disconnect the wiring from the ignition coil and the ground wire.
3. Properly relieve the fuel system pressure, as outlined in Section 5.
4. Remove the fuel filler cap and loosen the service bolt on the fuel filter banjo bolt to relieve the fuel system pressure. Remove the banjo bolt to disconnect the fuel feed hose from the fuel filter. Disconnect the fuel return hose from the pressure regulator.
5. Remove the intake air duct and air cleaner assembly.
6. Loosen the air conditioner compressor and alternator adjustment bolts. Remove the drive belts.
7. Remove the throttle cable by loosening the locknut, then slip the cable end out of the throttle bracket and accelerator linkage. Do not bend the cable when removing it. Unbolt the throttle cable clamp and move the cable aside.
8. Label and disconnect the fuel and vacuum hoses from the intake manifold. Be sure to mark all electrical connectors and vacuum hoses before disconnecting them.
9. Disconnect the upper radiator hose, the heater hoses, and the water bypass hoses and unbolt the wiring harness clips.
10. Disconnect the brake booster hose, canister hose, and the two vacuum hoses from the rear of the cylinder head.
11. Remove the two distributor mounting bolts. Remove the distributor, ignition wires, and ground cables from the cylinder head.
12. Disconnect the wiring harness holder that is routed across the front of the cylinder head.
13. Tag and detach the following:
   • Five fuel injector connectors
   • Intake Air Temperature (IAT) sensor connector
   • Engine Coolant Temperature (ECT) sensor connector
   • Top Dead Center (TDC) Crank Position (CKP) sensor and Camshaft Position (CMP) sensor connector
   • Engine Coolant Temperature (ECT) gauge sending unit connector
   • Throttle Position (TP) sensor connector

   • Purge control solenoid valve connector
   • Intake Air Bypass (IAB) control solenoid valve connector
14. Unbolt the intake manifold support brackets. The manifold may be removed after removing the cylinder head.
15. Detach the Oxygen (O2S) sensor connector.
16. Remove the exhaust manifold heat shields and disconnect the exhaust pipe from the manifold.
17. Remove the support bracket and remove the exhaust manifold.
18. Remove the cylinder head cover and upper timing belt cover.
19. Remove the timing belt. Replace the belt if it shows any signs of stress or damage.
20. Remove the camshaft position sensor and the camshaft sprocket.
21. Remove the back cover and unbolt the TDC/CKP sensor.
22. Loosen each cylinder head bolt about 1/3 turn at a time. Follow the reverse of the installation sequence to prevent warping the head. Repeat until all bolts are loose and can be removed.
23. If the cylinder head is stuck to the block, there are pry points at each end of the cylinder head. Do not pry against the gasket surfaces.
24. Carefully remove the cylinder head from the vehicle.

To install:

25. Be sure the cylinder head and the engine block sealing surfaces are flat and clean. Resurface the head if it is warped. Clean all gasket surfaces and run a tap through the bolt holes in the block to clean the threads. Be sure the bolt holes are clean and dry so the head can be tightened properly.
26. Install a new O-ring onto the oil control orifice and install the orifice and dowel pins onto the block. Lay the new head gasket in place.
27. Verify that the crankshaft and camshaft are both at TDC for number one piston.
28. Carefully fit the cylinder head to the block. Be sure the oil control orifice is properly aligned.
29. Lightly oil the threads and washer surfaces of the cylinder head bolts and install them. Tighten the bolts in sequence as follows:
   • Step 1: 29 ft. lbs.(39 Nm)
   • Step 2: 51 ft. lbs. (69 Nm)
   • Step 3: 72 ft. lbs. (97 Nm)
30. Install the intake manifold onto the cylinder head with a new gasket. Tighten the nuts in a crisscross pattern in 2 steps to 16 ft. lbs. (22 Nm).
31. Install the intake manifold brackets.
32. Loosely install the exhaust manifold bracket onto the manifold. Install the exhaust manifold with a new gasket and new self–locking nuts and tighten the nuts to 23 ft. lbs. (32 Nm).
33. Connect the exhaust pipe and install the manifold shields.
34. Reconnect the O2S sensor.
35. Install the timing belt and covers.
36. Adjust the valves.
37. Apply sealant to the ends of the cylinder head near the camshaft holders. Install the cylinder head cover with new rubber seals as required.

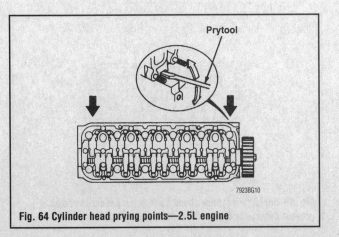

Fig. 64 Cylinder head prying points—2.5L engine

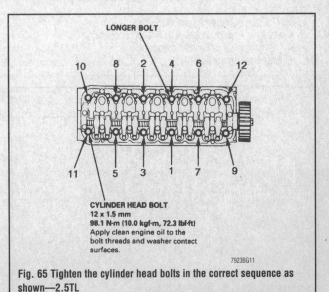

LONGER BOLT

CYLINDER HEAD BOLT
12 x 1.5 mm
98.1 N·m (10.0 kgf·m, 72.3 lbf·ft)
Apply clean engine oil to the bolt threads and washer contact surfaces.

7923BG11

Fig. 65 Tighten the cylinder head bolts in the correct sequence as shown—2.5TL

38. The balance of installation is the reverse of the removal procedure.

39. Replace the engine oil and filter.

40. Verify that all wiring, grounds, hoses, and cables are properly connected.

41. Connect the battery cable. Run the engine to bleed the cooling system and check for leaks. Check for proper cooling system and engine operation. Top off all fluid levels as necessary.

42. Enter the radio security code.

3.0L, 3.2 and 3.5L Engines

▶ **See Figures 66, 67, 68, 69 and 70**

1. Obtain the security code for the radio.
2. Disconnect the negative battery cable.
3. On 3.5L engines, remove the strut brace.
4. Drain the coolant into a sealable container.
5. Remove the canister hose from the throttle body.
6. Remove the air intake duct.
7. Remove the upper engine covers.
8. Disconnect the accelerator and cruise control cables from the throttle body.
9. Remove the spark plug wire holder, cover and intake manifold covers.
10. Properly relieve the fuel system pressure, as outlined in Section 5.
11. Disconnect the fuel hoses from the supply rail.
12. Remove the upper and lower radiator hoses.
13. Disconnect the heater hoses.
14. Tag and disconnect the following hoses and lines:
    - Brake booster vacuum hose
    - Positive Crankcase Ventilation (PCV) hose
    - Breather hose
    - Water bypass hose
    - Vacuum hose from the throttle body
15. Remove the ground cable from the engine.
16. Remove the A/C, alternator and power steering belts.
17. On 3.0L engines, perform the following:
    a. Support the engine with a jack and a block of wood and remove the side engine mounting bracket.
    b. Remove the power steering pump without disconnecting the hoses.
    c. Remove the alternator.
18. Tag and detach the following engine wiring harness connectors:
    - Intake Air Temperature (IAT) sensor connector
    - Engine Coolant Temperature (ECT) sensor connector
    - Top Dead Center (TDC) Crank Position (CKP) sensor and Camshaft Position (CYP) sensor connector
    - Ignition coil connector
    - Engine Coolant Temperature (ECT) gauge sending unit connector
    - Throttle Position (TP) sensor connector
    - Variable Valve Timing and Electronic Lift Control (VTEC) solenoid connector
    - VTEC pressure switch connector
    - Manifold Absolute Pressure (MAP) sensor connector
    - Idle Air Control (IAC) valve connector
    - Engine oil pressure switch

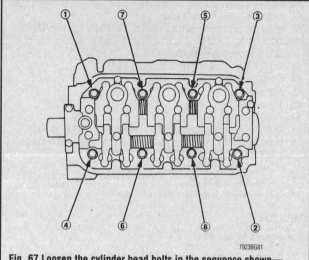

Fig. 67 Loosen the cylinder head bolts in the sequence shown—3.5L engine

19. On 3.0L engines, remove the distributor and spark plug wires.
20. On 3.2 and 3.5L engines disconnect the battery cables from the underhood fuse/relay box and remove the box, then disconnect and remove the six ignition coils.
21. On 3.2L engines remove the Exhaust Gas Recirculation (EGR) pipe.
22. Remove the intake manifold.
23. On 3.0L engines, detach the connectors from the fuel injectors, remove the fuel supply rails and remove the vacuum hoses from the fuel control valve.
24. Set the engine to TDC by aligning the marks on the crankshaft and camshaft pulleys.
25. Remove the timing belt.
26. Remove both exhaust manifolds.
27. Remove the water passage assembly.
28. Remove the camshaft pulleys and rear timing belt covers.
29. Loosen each cylinder head bolt ⅓ turn at a time in the reverse order of the tightening sequence.
30. Remove the cylinder heads.

To install:

31. Clean the cylinder head and the surface of the cylinder block.
32. Install the oil control orifices and using new O-rings.
33. If removed, install the dowel pins.
34. Position new cylinder head gaskets on the cylinder block.
35. If moved, set the crankshaft and camshaft pulleys to TDC by aligning the marks on the pulley and oil pump.
36. Carefully position the cylinder heads on the engine.
37. Lubricate the cylinder head bolts with clean engine oil.

➡**If any cylinder head bolt makes noise while being tightened, loosen the bolts and begin the tightening sequence again.**

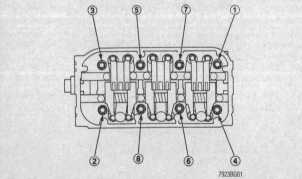

Fig. 66 Loosen the cylinder head bolts in the sequence shown to prevent damage to the head—3.0L engine

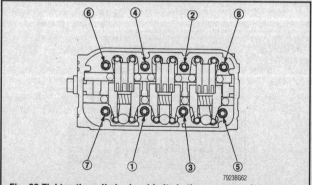

Fig. 68 Tighten the cylinder head bolts in the sequence shown to prevent damage to the head—3.0L engine

38. On the 3.0L engine tighten the cylinder head bolts in three steps. Be sure to follow the proper torque sequence:
- Step 1: 29 ft. lbs. (39 Nm)
- Step 2: 51 ft. lbs. (69 Nm)
- Step 3: 72 ft. lbs. (98 Nm).

39. On the 3.2L and 3.5L engines tighten the cylinder head bolts in two steps. Be sure to follow the proper torque sequence:
- Step 1: 29 ft. lbs. (39 Nm)
- Step 2: 56 ft. lbs. (76 Nm)

40. Install the exhaust manifolds.

41. Install the back covers.

42. Install the camshaft pulleys and torque to the following specifications:
- 3.0L engines: 67 ft. lbs. (90 Nm)
- 3.2L and 3.5L engines: 23 ft. lbs. (31 Nm)

43. Install the timing belt.

44. Check and adjust the valve clearance if necessary.

45. Install the cylinder head cover. Tighten the bolts to 104 inch lbs. (12 Nm).

46. Install the intake manifold. Be sure to use new gaskets and O-rings. Tighten the bolts to 16 ft. lbs. (22 Nm).

47. Install all of the remaining hoses, tubes and connectors in reverse order of disassembly.

48. Change the engine oil and filter.

49. Top off the cooling system with the correct mixture of coolant and bleed as necessary.

50. Connect the negative battery cable.

51. Bring the engine to operating temperature and inspect for any fluid leaks. Top off all fluid levels as necessary.

52. Enter the security code for the radio.

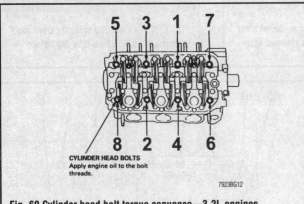

CYLINDER HEAD BOLTS
Apply engine oil to the bolt threads.

7923BG12

Fig. 69 Cylinder head bolt torque sequence—3.2L engines

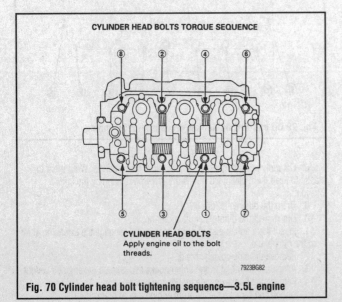

CYLINDER HEAD BOLTS TORQUE SEQUENCE

CYLINDER HEAD BOLTS
Apply engine oil to the bolt threads.

7923BG82

Fig. 70 Cylinder head bolt tightening sequence—3.5L engine

➡The PCM idle memory must be reset after reconnecting the battery. Start the engine and hold it at 3000 rpm until the cooling fan comes on. Then allow the engine to idle for about five minutes with all accessories OFF and with the transaxle in Park or Neutral.

Oil Pan

REMOVAL & INSTALLATION

➡The radio may have a coded theft protection circuit. Make sure you have the code before disconnecting the battery, removing the radio fuse, or removing the radio.

1.8L, 2.2L and 2.3L Engines

▶ See Figures 71 thru 79

1. Disconnect negative cable at the battery.

2. Raise and safely support the vehicle. Drain the oil and remove the lower splash panel.

3. Detach the Heated Oxygen (HO2S) sensor connector.

4. Remove the nuts and bolts connecting exhaust pipe A to the catalytic converter. Discard the gasket and the lock nuts.

5. Remove and discard the nuts attaching exhaust pipe A to the exhaust hanger.

6. If applicable, remove the mounting bolts from the center beam. Remove the center beam from the subframe.

7. Remove and discard the lock nuts attaching exhaust pipe A to the exhaust manifold, then remove exhaust pipe A from the vehicle. discard the exhaust gaskets.

8. Loosen the oil pan bolts in a crisscross pattern. To remove the oil pan, lightly tap the corners of the oil pan with a rubber or plastic faced mallet. Clean off all the old gasket material.

To install:

9. Apply liquid gasket to the oil pan mating surface where the oil pump and the right side cover meet the engine block.

10. Install the oil pan gasket to the oil pan.

11. Install the oil pan, then finger tighten the center and end mounting nuts and bolts in the proper sequence.

12. Tighten the oil pan mounting nuts and bolts starting from the center bolt next to the oil drain plug (bolt No. 1) and work clockwise, tightening the bolts in three steps. Tighten the bolts to 10 ft. lbs. (14 Nm).

➡Excessive tightening can cause distortion of the oil pan gasket and oil leakage.

13. Install the oil drain plug with a new gasket, tighten the plug to 33 ft. lbs. (44 Nm).

14. Install exhaust pipe A using new gaskets and lock nuts. Tighten the nuts attaching the exhaust pipe to the exhaust manifold to 40 ft. lbs. (54 Nm). Tighten the nuts attaching the exhaust pipe to the catalytic converter and the exhaust pipe hanger to 16 ft. lbs. (22 Nm).

15. Attach the heated O2S sensor connector.

16. Install the lower splash panel, then lower the vehicle.

90943P71

Fig. 71 The exhaust downpipe will have to be removed—Integra shown

Fig. 72 The rear engine stiffener may have to be removed to gain access to the engine's oil pan

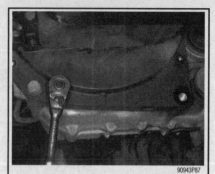

Fig. 73 The flywheel cover may have to be removed to allow access to all of the oil pan bolts

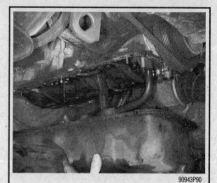

Fig. 74 Removing the oil pan on the Integra

Fig. 75 Once the oil pan has been removed, wipe it clean with a shop towel.

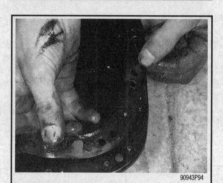

Fig. 76 The gasket must be removed from the oil pan and the surface cleaned thoroughly

Fig. 77 If any cleaning solvents were used to clean the pan, allow it to dry before reinstallation.

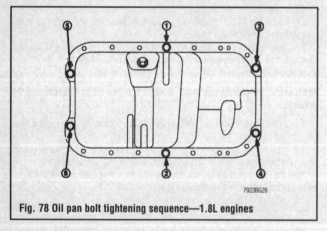

Fig. 78 Oil pan bolt tightening sequence—1.8L engines

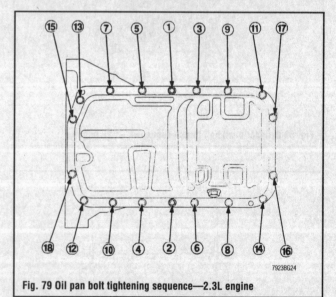

Fig. 79 Oil pan bolt tightening sequence—2.3L engine

17. Fill the engine with oil.
18. Connect the negative battery cable and enter the radio security code.
19. Run the engine and check for leaks.
20. Turn off engine and check the oil level. Top off the oil level if necessary.

2.5L Engine

◆ See Figure 80

1. Shift the manual transaxle to 1st gear or automatic transaxle to the **P** position.
2. Disconnect the negative battery cable.
3. Remove the air cleaner housing.
4. Raise and safely support the vehicle and remove the front wheels.
5. Drain the engine oil and coolant.
6. Remove the strut forks.
7. Remove the lower ball joint nut. Use a ball joint remover to disconnect the ball joint from the control arm.

8. Carefully pry the inner CV–joints out of their sockets. Wrap them in plastic to keep them clean. Do not let the driveshafts hang by the outer CV–joint.
9. Drain the differential oil.
10. Disconnect the differential oil cooler hoses.
11. Install the a suitable shaft puller tool, and disengage the extension shaft from the differential.
12. Remove the side splash shield.
13. Attach a chain hoist to the lifting hooks and take up the engine's weight.
14. Remove the transaxle side mount and bracket.
15. Unbolt and remove the left front engine mount bracket.

16. Remove the power steering speed sensor from the differential. Do not disconnect the hoses.

17. Remove the differential mounting bolts and the 26mm shim. Remove the differential from the vehicle.

18. Unbolt the intermediate shaft bearing housing from the oil pan and pull the intermediate shaft assembly from the oil pan pipe.

19. Remove the A/C compressor, then its mounting bracket. Leave the A/C lines connected to the compressor. Support the compressor with a piece of wire to move it out of the work area and take the weight off the A/C lines.

20. Remove the set plate that holds the oil pan inner pipe from the right side of the engine.

21. Unbolt the oil pan and remove it from the vehicle.

To install:

22. Clean the oil pan and engine block mating surfaces. Apply an even bead of liquid gasket to the engine block sealing surface. Apply some liquid gasket to the inner threads of the bolt holes.

23. Install the oil pan and tighten the bolts in the correct sequence to 16–17 ft. lbs. (22–24 Nm), as shown in the accompanying figure.

24. Install new O-rings on the oil pan inner pipe. Install the pipe and tighten the set plate bolts to 9 ft. lbs. (12 Nm).

25. Install the differential, making sure the original shim is in the proper position. Tighten the bolts to 54 ft. lbs. (75 Nm). Connect the cooling hoses.

26. Install new set and snaprings on the extension shaft. Coat the splines and their mating surfaces with high temperature grease. Thread the special installation tool into the transaxle case to install the extension shaft.

27. Pack the extension shaft cavity with high temperature grease and install the 33mm sealing bolt. Tighten the bolt to 58 ft. lbs. (80 Nm) and install the secondary cover.

28. Install the intermediate shaft, tighten the bolts to 16 ft. lbs. (22 Nm).

29. Install the left front engine mount bracket and tighten the bolts to 40 ft. lbs. (54 Nm). Tighten the mounting bolt to 54 ft. lbs. (74 Nm).

30. Install the transaxle side bracket and mount. Tighten the bracket mounting bolts and through bolt to 40 ft. lbs. (54 Nm). Install new mount bolts and tighten them to 47 ft. lbs. (64 Nm).

31. Install the A/C compressor mount. Tighten the mounting bolts on the oil pan, then the mounting bolts on the engine block, 36 ft. lbs. (49 Nm). Install the A/C compressor onto the mount and tighten the bolts to 16 ft. lbs. (22 Nm).

32. Install the speed sensor and tighten the mounting bolt to 7 ft. lbs. (10 Nm).

33. Install new set rings on the CV–joints and press them into their sockets.

34. Refill the differential.

35. Connect the lower ball joints to the control arms and install the nuts, tighten them to 36–43 ft. lbs. (49–59 Nm) and install a new cotter pin. Tighten the strut fork bolts to 47 ft. lbs. (64 Nm). Install the front wheels.

36. Carefully lower the vehicle.

37. Remove the chain hoist.

38. Refill the engine oil and cooling system.

39. Install the air cleaner and intake duct.

40. Bleed the cooling system by opening the bleeder on the upper radiator hose inlet when filling the system.

41. Connect the negative battery cable.

3.0L Engine

▶ **See Figure 81**

1. Raise and safely support the vehicle.

2. Drain the engine oil into a suitable container.

3. Remove the exhaust pipe if necessary.

4. Unfasten the oil pan mounting bolts, then remove the oil pan.

To install:

5. Clean the sealing surface on the engine and oil pan flange.

6. Apply a bead of sealant to the oil pan flange and install the oil pan. Tighten the bolts, in the sequence shown, to 104 inch lbs. (12 Nm).

7. If removed, install the exhaust pipe.

✳✳ WARNING

Operating the engine without the proper amount and type of engine oil will result in severe engine damage.

8. Add the correct amount of engine oil to the crankcase.

9. Start the engine and check for leaks.

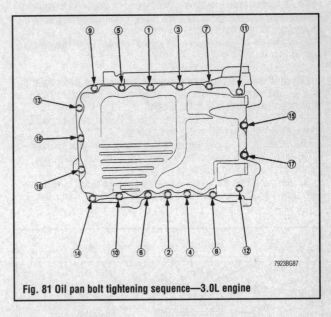

Fig. 81 Oil pan bolt tightening sequence—3.0L engine

3.2L and 3.5L Engines

▶ **See Figure 82**

1. Disconnect the negative, then the positive battery cables.

2. Remove the air conditioning compressor drive belt.

3. Raise and safely support the vehicle.

4. Remove the front wheels and splash shield.

5. Remove the strut forks. Remove the lower ball joint nut and use a ball joint press tool to disconnect the ball joint from the control arm.

6. Remove the halfshafts from the differential and the intermediate shaft.

7. Remove the intermediate shaft from the oil pan.

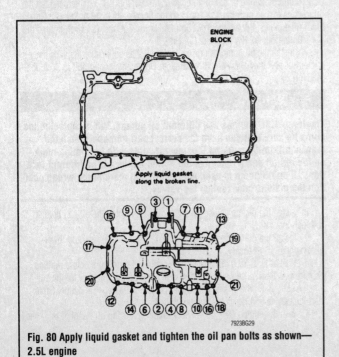

Fig. 80 Apply liquid gasket and tighten the oil pan bolts as shown—2.5L engine

8. Drain the oil from the differential into a sealable container the install the drain plug with a new washer.

9. Drain the engine oil into a sealable container.

10. If equipped, disconnect the Vehicle Speed Sensor (VSS) harness, then remove the VSS/power steering speed sensor. Do not disconnect the fluid hoses, support the sensor out of the way.

11. Remove the right front beam bridge.

12. Remove the lower plate from the rack and pinion, install the two rack and pinion mounting bolts that were removed.

13. Remove the 36mm sealing bolt on the transaxle. Ensure that the transaxle is in 1st gear (manual) or **P** (automatic).

14. Disconnect the extension shaft from the differential with the extension shaft puller part number 07LAC–PW50101 or its equivalent.

15. Remove the differential mounting bolts and the 26mm shim, then remove the differential.

16. Detach the A/C compressor clutch connector, then remove the compressor. Do not disconnect the A/C hoses from the compressor and do not let the compressor hang by the hoses.

17. Remove the rear engine stiffener.

18. Remove the flywheel cover or the torque converter covers.

19. Remove the oil pan. Do not lose the dowel pins from the oil pan.

To install:

20. Clean the oil pan and cylinder block mating surfaces, then apply liquid gasket to the cylinder block. Be sure that the mating surfaces are clean and dry before installing the liquid gasket. Do not apply liquid gasket to the O-ring grooves.

21. Install the dowel pins to the oil pan and new O-rings coated with clean oil. Install the oil pan to the cylinder block. Coat the oil pan bolts with liquid gasket, then install them. Tighten the bolts, in the proper sequence, to 16 ft. lbs. (22 Nm).

22. For manual transaxle, install the flywheel cover and engine stiffener.

23. For automatic transaxle, install the torque converter covers and tighten the mounting bolts to 104 inch lbs. (12 Nm).

24. Install the rear engine stiffener. Tighten the bolt attaching the engine stiffener to the transaxle first, to 47 ft. lbs. (64 Nm), then tighten the bolts to the engine block to 16 ft. lbs. (22 Nm).

25. Install the A/C compressor to the engine block and tighten the mounting bolts to 16 ft. lbs. (22 Nm).

26. Attach the A/C clutch connector.

27. Install the dowel pins to the differential, then install the differential to the engine. Install the mounting bolts loosely and install the 26mm shim. Tighten all of the mounting bolts to 47 ft. lbs. (64 Nm).

28. Install a new set ring to the extension shaft. Using a suitable extension shaft installer tool, install the shaft to the differential.

29. Fill the secondary gear with super high temperature grease part number 08798–9002. Applying sealer to the threads of the 36mm sealing bolt, then install the bolt and tighten to 58 ft. lbs.(78 Nm).

30. Remove the two bolts from the rack and pinion necessary to install the lower plate, then install the lower plate and the attaching bolts. Tighten the lower plate attaching bolt to 28 ft. lbs. (38 Nm) and tighten the rack and pinion bolts to 43 ft. lbs. (59 Nm).

31. When installing the lower ball joint nuts, tighten them to 51–58 ft. lbs. (70–80 Nm) and install a new cotter pin. Tighten the strut fork bolts to 51 ft. lbs. (70 Nm).

32. Install the right beam bridge and tighten the attaching bolts to 28 ft. lbs. (38 Nm).

33. Install the VSS and tighten the attaching bolt to 104 inch lbs. (12 Nm). Connect the VSS harness to the VSS sensor.

34. Install the intermediate shaft and the halfshafts.

35. Fill the differential with oil.

36. Install the engine splash shield and tighten the bolts to 7.2 ft. lbs. (9.8 Nm).

37. Install the front wheels.

38. Lower the vehicle.

39. Install the A/C compressor drive belt.

40. Fill the engine with oil.

41. Connect the positive, then the negative battery cables and enter the radio security code.

42. Run the engine and check for leaks.

43. Check the front wheel alignment.

Oil Pump

REMOVAL & INSTALLATION

▶ **See Figures 83 thru 88**

➡ **The radio may have a coded theft protection circuit. Make sure you have the code before disconnecting the battery, removing the radio fuse, or removing the radio.**

1. Disconnect the negative battery cable. Raise and safely support the vehicle. Drain the oil and remove the lower splash panel, if necessary.

2. Be sure the crankshaft is at Top Dead Center (TDC) on No. 1 cylinder and remove the timing belt cover, timing belt, and the gear off the crankshaft.

3. Remove the oil pan. Remove the pickup screen.

4. Remove the oil filter assembly, if necessary.

5. Remove the oil pump from the front of the engine. Any time the oil pump is removed, the front oil seal should be replaced.

To install:

6. Install the oil pump, using new O-rings and liquid gasket applied to a clean pump mounting face. For all engines, except the 1.8L engines, tighten the 6mm bolts to 104 inch lbs. (12 Nm) and the 8mm bolts to 16 ft. lbs. (22 Nm). For 1.8L engines, tighten the 8x1.25mm bolts to 17 ft. lbs. (24 Nm), tighten the 6 x 1.0mm bolts to 104 inch lbs. (12 Nm).

7. Install the oil pump cap or oil cooler unit, as applicable. Replace the cooler hoses if they show signs of damage. Tighten the center bolt to 30 ft. lbs. (42 Nm).

❉❉ WARNING

The three 1.8L engines use different oil pumps. When replacing the pump be sure that you have the correct part number. Match the crankshaft timing mark on the new oil pump with the timing mark on the old oil pump, because the timing marks are in different locations. If an oil pump is used with the timing mark in the wrong position the pistons may contact the valves.

8. Install the pickup screen, then the oil pan. Tighten the oil pan bolts to 104 inch lbs. (12 Nm).

9. Install the oil filter assembly, exhaust pipe, center beam, and lower splash panel, if necessary.

10. Wait at least 30 minutes after completion of procedure before refilling the engine with oil. The waiting period is to allow a curing period for the silicone sealant. Refill the engine with oil and connect the negative battery cable. Start the engine and check the engine for leaks.

11. Turn the engine **OFF**, then check the oil level. Top off the oil level if necessary.

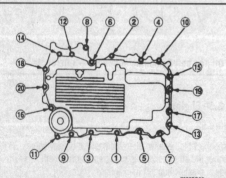

7923BG30

Fig. 82 Be sure to tighten the oil pan bolts in the sequence shown—3.2L engines

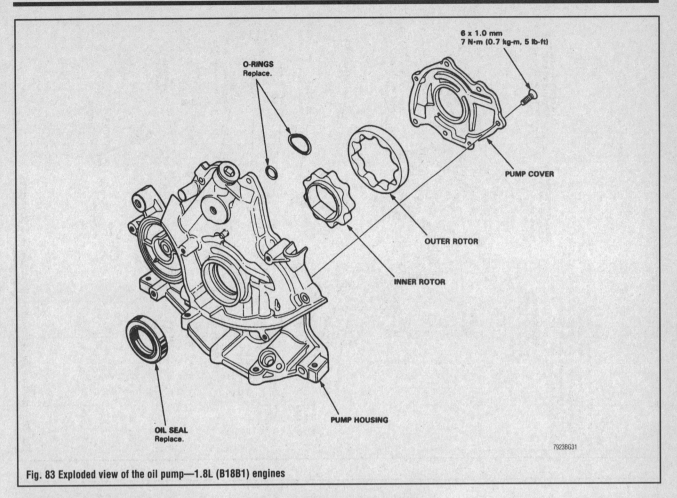

**6 x 1.0 mm
7 N·m (0.7 kg-m, 5 lb-ft)**

O-RINGS
Replace.

PUMP COVER

OUTER ROTOR

INNER ROTOR

PUMP HOUSING

OIL SEAL
Replace.

7923BG31

Fig. 83 Exploded view of the oil pump—1.8L (B18B1) engines

90943P95

Fig. 84 Oil pump screen mounting position—Integra shown

90943P96

Fig. 85 Always check the condition of the screen while the oil pan is removed

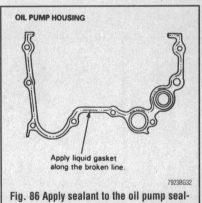

OIL PUMP HOUSING

Apply liquid gasket along the broken line.

7923BG32

Fig. 86 Apply sealant to the oil pump sealing surface as shown—2.5L engine

Front Crankshaft Seal

REMOVAL & INSTALLATION

▶ See Figure 89

➡The radio may have a coded theft protection circuit. Make sure you have the code before disconnecting the battery, removing the radio fuse, or removing the radio.

1. Disconnect negative cable at the battery.
2. Raise and safely support the vehicle. Drain the engine oil and properly dispose of it.
3. Be sure the crankshaft is at Top Dead Center (TDC) on No. 1 cylinder by aligning the white mark on the crankshaft pulley with the pointer on the lower timing belt cover.
4. Remove the crankshaft pulley.
5. Remove the cylinder head cover, timing belt cover and timing belt.
6. If equipped with a Crankshaft Speed Fluctuation (CKF) sensor, remove the sensor.
7. Remove the timing belt and the drive gear from the crankshaft.
8. Using a suitable prytool, carefully remove the seal.

To install:
9. Apply a light coat of oil to the seal lip.
10. Position the seal, then using a seal driver, install the seal into the housing.
11. Install the timing belt pulley , the timing belt, and engine covers. If equipped with a CKF sensor, install the sensor tighten the attaching bolts to 96 inch lbs. (11 Nm).

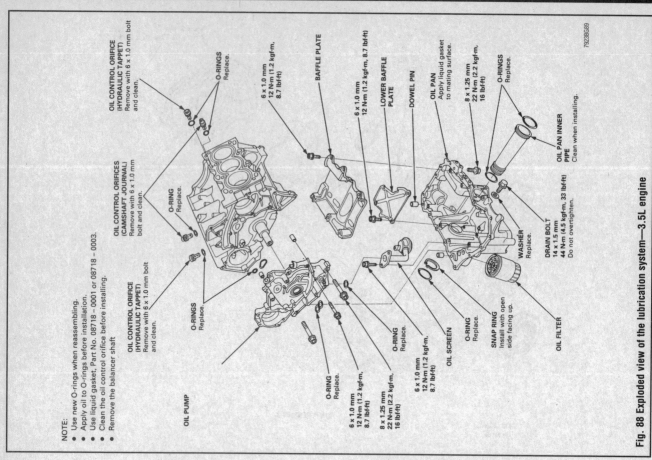

Fig. 88 Exploded view of the lubrication system—3.5L engine

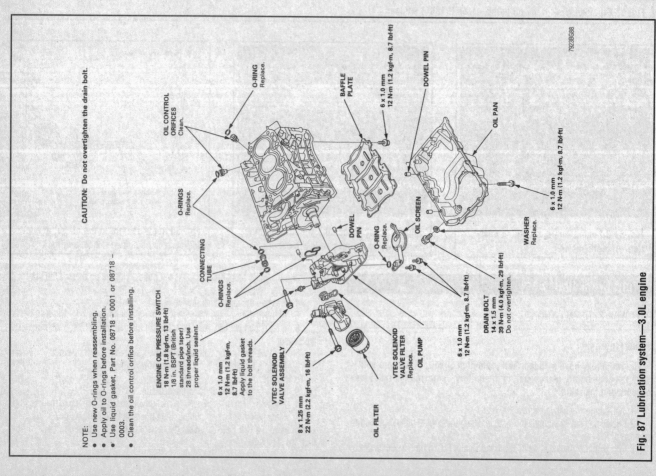

Fig. 87 Lubrication system—3.0L engine

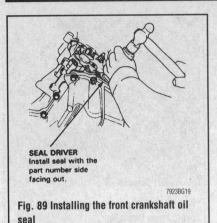

Fig. 89 Installing the front crankshaft oil seal

Fig. 90 Observe how the tool interlocks with the dampener

Fig. 91 Side a socket through the opening in the tool and ensure that it engages with the dampener bolt

Fig. 92 Removal of the bolt from the crankshaft—Integra

Fig. 93 Remove the woodruff key from the crankshaft

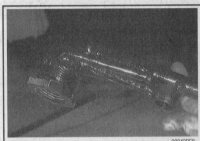

Fig. 94 A simple design consisting of a plumbing fitting welded to a pipe, saved this technician from purchasing the factory tool otherwise needed to hold the crankshaft

12. Install the crankshaft pulley and cylinder head cover.
13. Lower the vehicle and check and fill the engine with oil as necessary .
14. Connect the negative battery cable and enter the radio security code.
15. Run the engine and check for leaks.
16. Turn off engine and check the oil level. Top off the oil level if necessary.

Crankshaft Damper

REMOVAL & INSTALLATION

▶ **See Figures 90, 91, 92, 93 and 94**

1. Remove the negative battery cable.
2. Remove the splash shield from the wheel well.
3. Remove the adjusting and mounting bolts.
4. Remove the power steering pump belt.
5. Remove the adjusting bolt and idler pulley bracket bolt.
6. Remove the air conditioning compressor belt.
7. Remove the alternator belt.
8. To hold the crankshaft pulley still while you are removing the damper bolt, a Honda factory tool (#07MAB-PY3010A) or equivalent is required. However, it is also possible to construct your own tool by attaching a length of pipe to a 2 inch plumbing fitting as shown in the accompanying figure.
9. Remove the crankshaft damper.
To install:
10. Install the damper the reverse order of removal.
11. Lubricate the damper bolt with engine oil before installation.
12. Torque the damper pulley bolt to 130 ft. lbs. (177 Nm) on 1.8L engines, or to 181 ft. lbs. (245 Nm) on all other engines.
13. Connect the negative battery cable.

Timing Belt Covers

REMOVAL & INSTALLATION

1.8L engine

▶ See Figures 95, 96 and 97

➡**To inspect the belt from the top you can gain access by removing only the valve cover.**

1. Remove the negative battery cable.
2. Remove the splash shield from the wheel well.
3. Remove the power steering pump by loosening the adjusting bolts and removing the mounting bolts.
4. Loosen the adjusting and idler pulley bracket bolt to free the belt.
5. Loosen the adjusting nut and then the mounting nuts to allow the alternator belt to be removed.
6. If equipped, remove the cruise control actuator.
7. Remove the side engine mount bolts, then remove the mount.
8. Remove the valve cover (this is the upper timing belt cover).
9. Remove the crankshaft dampener bolt.
10. Remove the crankshaft dampener; this will allow access to the lower timing belt cover.
11. Remove the fasteners and remove the lower timing belt cover.

➡**Be careful when removing the crankshaft damper bolt. Excessive force may snap or strip the bolt.**

12. The middle timing cover can be removed by unbolting the two fasteners.
To install:
13. Install the components in the reverse order of the removal procedure.
14. Connect the negative battery cable.

Fig. 95 Loosening the timing belt cover bolts—Integra shown

Fig. 96 Remove the middle cover spacer

Fig. 97 Install the cover bolts by hand to avoid cross threading

Timing Belt and Sprockets

➡For recommended timing belt replacement intervals, refer to Section 1.

REMOVAL & INSTALLATION

➡Replace the timing and balancer shaft belts at no more that 105,000 miles (168,000km). Acura also specifies that under extreme conditions

the timing and balancer shaft belts should be replaced more frequently, at 60,000 miles (100,000 km). These abnormal conditions include very high temperatures over 110°F (43°C) or very low ambient temperatures of minus 20°F (-29°C).

1.8L Engines

▸ See Figures 98, 99, 100, 101 and 102

1. Remove the negative battery cable.
2. Remove the splash shield from the wheel well.

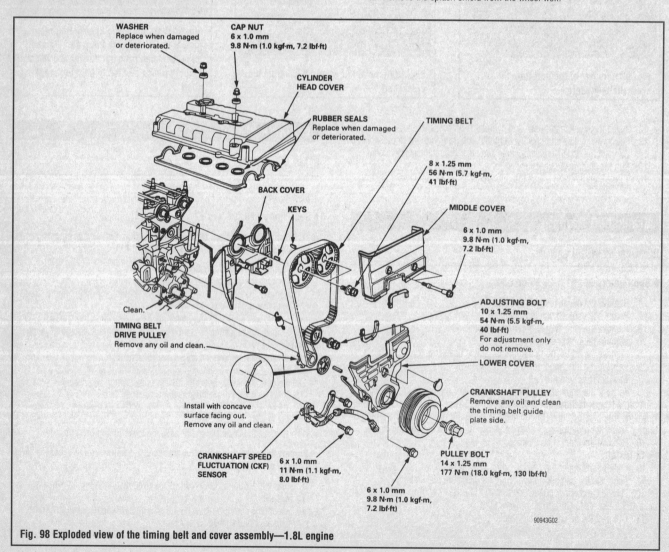

Fig. 98 Exploded view of the timing belt and cover assembly—1.8L engine

Fig. 99 View of the timing belt tensioner

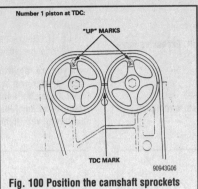

Fig. 100 Position the camshaft sprockets with the arrows in the "UP" position— 1.8L engine

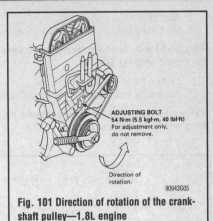

Fig. 101 Direction of rotation of the crankshaft pulley—1.8L engine

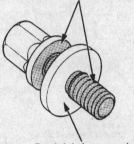

Fig. 102 Lubricate the crankshaft pulley bolt with engine oil—1.8L engine

3. Remove the power steering pump by loosening the adjusting bolts and removing the mounting bolts.

4. Loosen the adjusting and idler pulley bracket bolt on the (A/C) to free the belt.

5. Loosen the adjusting nut and then the mounting nuts to allow the alternator belt to be removed.

6. Remove the cruise control actuator if equipped.

7. Remove the side engine mount bolts and then mount.

8. Remove the valve cover.

9. Remove the crankshaft bolt.

➡Be careful when removing the crankshaft damper bolt. Excessive force may snap or strip the bolt.

10. The middle timing cover can be removed by unbolting the two fasteners.

11. Remove the lower timing belt cover.

12. The timing belt tensioner adjusting bolt must now be loosened no more than180°.

13. The tension on the belt can be released by pushing against it.

14. After the tension is released retighten the adjusting bolt.

15. Remove the timing belt from the pulleys.

➡If oil leakage is detected around the camshaft or crankshaft seals, replace them.

16. Remove the camshaft pulley(s) by removing the bolt(s) from the pulley(s).

17. The camshaft pulleys do not need to be match marked to the location of the camshafts. They are machined to only go on in one direction via the use of a woodruff key. It is a good idea to mark the pulleys left and right respectively.

To install:

18. Install the camshaft pulleys.

➡Clean the covers before installation. The smallest piece of dirt may cause premature belt failure.

19. Set the crankshaft and camshaft pulleys as in the illustration before installing the timing belt.

20. Set the crankshaft so that the No. 1 position is at top dead center (TDC). Position the groove on the teeth side of the belt to the pointer of the oil pump.

21. Install the timing belt, its components, and covers.

22. Align the TDC marks located on the intake and exhaust pulleys.

23. Install the belt in the following sequence:

   a. Timing belt drive pulley.
   b. Adjusting pulley.
   c. Water pump pulley.
   d. Exhaust camshaft pulley.
   e. Intake camshaft pulley.

✳✳ WARNING

Turning the crankshaft in the clockwise direction may cause the timing belt to not seat properly causing component damage.

24. Turn the crankshaft about four to six turns counterclockwise to ensure that the belt properly seats on the pulleys.

25. Set the number one piston at top dead center (TDC).

26. Loosen the adjusting bolt (180°only)

27. Rotate the crankshaft counterclockwise 3 teeth on the camshaft pulley, then tighten he adjusting bolt to 40 ft. lbs. (54 Nm).

28. Check that the crankshaft and camshaft pulleys are at TDC.

➡If the camshaft pulley is not positioned at TDC, remove the timing belt and repeat the above procedures.

29. Install the valve cover.

30. Install the engine mount(s).

31. If equipped, install the cruise control actuator.

➡Lubricate the crankshaft pulley bolt with engine oil.

32. Install the crankshaft damper and damper mounting bolt. Tighten the mounting bolt to 130 ft. lbs. (177 Nm).

33. Install the alternator, A/C, and power steering accessories.

34. Install the splash shield into the wheel well.

35. Connect the negative battery cable.

2.2L, 2.3L engines

▶ See Figures 103 thru 112

1. Remove the negative battery cable.

2. Remove the splash shield from the wheel well.

3. Remove the power steering pump by loosening the adjusting bolts and removing the mounting bolts.

4. Loosen the adjusting nut and then the mounting nuts to allow the alternator belt to be removed.

5. Remove the alternator terminal and connector by pulling up on the lock.

6. If equipped, remove the cruise control actuator.

➡Use a jack to support the engine before removing the engine mount. Use a block of wood to cushion the oil pan from being damaged.

7. Remove the side engine mount bolts and then mount.

8. Remove the dipstick from the tube and then remove the tube.

9. Remove the valve cover.
10. Remove the crankshaft pulley bolt and then the pulley.

➥**Be careful when removing the crankshaft damper bolt. Excessive force may snap or strip the bolt.**

11. Remove the adjusting nuts rubber seal.
12. Remove the timing belt and balancer shaft covers.

➥**To prevent damage to the cover do not use them to store removed items such as fasteners or brackets.**

13. The timing belt tensioner adjusting bolt must now be loosened no more than180°.
14. The tension on the belt can be released by pushing against it.
15. After the tension is released, retighten the adjusting bolt.

➥**If you are removing only the balancer belt, you can lock the timing belt adjuster arm by threading a 6 x 1.0 mm bolt in to hold the tension. Next loosen the adjusting nut about one turn. Push the tensioner to remove the any tension from the balancer belt. After the tension has been removed, tighten the adjusting bolt.**

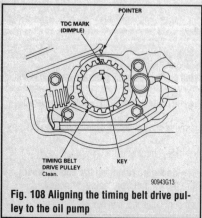

Fig. 103 Power steering adjusting and mounting bolt locations

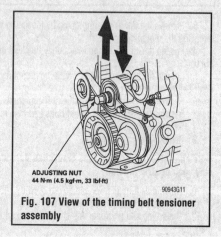

Fig. 104 Alternator mounting bolt location

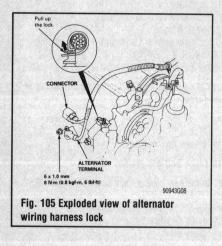

Fig. 105 Exploded view of alternator wiring harness lock

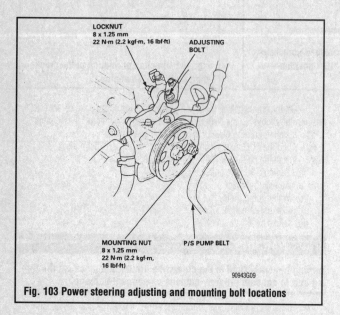

Fig. 106 Installing the 6.0 x 1.0mm bolt

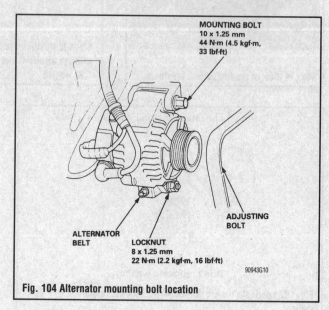

Fig. 107 View of the timing belt tensioner assembly

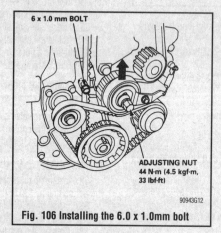

Fig. 108 Aligning the timing belt drive pulley to the oil pump

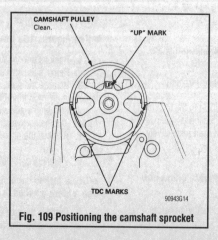

Fig. 109 Positioning the camshaft sprocket

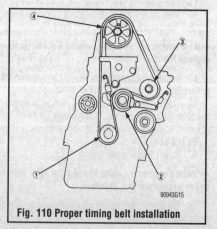

Fig. 110 Proper timing belt installation

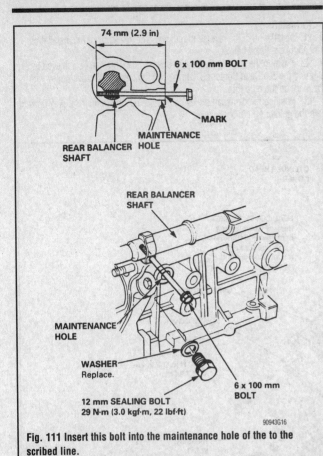

Fig. 111 Insert this bolt into the maintenance hole of the to the scribed line.

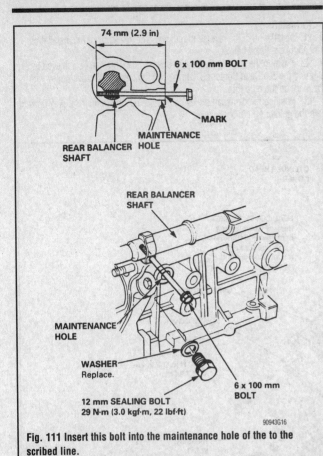

Fig. 112 Align the pointer and the groove

16. Remove the balancer and timing belts from the pulleys.

➡️**If oil leakage is detected around the camshaft or crankshaft seals, replace them.**

17. Remove the camshaft pulley(s) by removing the bolt(s) from the pulley(s).
18. The camshaft pulleys do not need to be match marked to the location of the camshafts. They are machined to only go on in one direction via the use of a woodruff key. It is a good idea to mark the pulleys left and right respectively.

To install:

19. Installation of the timing belt is the reverse of the removal procedure.

➡️**Follow the below steps to ensure that the timing and balancer belts are installed with the engine properly timed.**

20. Remove the balancer drive pulley.
21. Position No. 1 piston at top dead center.
22. Position the dimple on the tooth of the timing belt drive pulley to the pointer on the oil pump.
23. Position the camshaft pulley with the stamping facing up.
24. Install the timing belt by routing it as follows:
    a. Crankshaft pulley
    b. Adjusting pulley
    c. Water pump pulley
    d. Camshaft pulley.
25. Loosen the adjusting nut to tension the timing belt, then retighten the nut.
26. Install the lower timing belt cover and the balancer belt drive pulley.
27. Install and tighten the crankshaft pulley and bolt.
28. Turn the crankshaft six turns to seat it on the pulley.
29. Adjust the timing belt tension.
30. Make sure that the crankshaft pulley and the camshaft pulleys are both positioned at top dead center.

➡️**If the camshaft or crankshaft is not positioned at top dead center (TDC), you must remove the timing belt and readjust the position.**

31. Remove the lower timing cover by removing the crankshaft pulley.
32. Set the number one piston at top dead center.
33. Install one of the 6.0 x 1.0mm bolts to lock the timing belt adjuster.
34. To verify that the balancer belt moves freely, loosen the adjusting nut ⅔ turn.
35. To remove tension from the belt, push on the adjuster mechanism.

➡️**To align the rear balancer shaft, use a 6.0x1.0mm bolt, scribe a line 74mm (2.9 in) from the end of the bolt. Insert this bolt into the maintenance hole of the to the scribed line.**

36. Align the front balancer groove and the pointer which is located on the oil pump housing.
37. Install the balancer belt.
38. Tension the balancer belt.
39. Remove the 6.0x1.0mm bolt, then install the sealing bolt.
40. Install the crankshaft pulley and then torque the pulley bolt to the correct specification.
41. Spin the crankshaft pulley approximately one turn then tighten the adjusting nut.
42. Remove the 6.0x1.0 mm bolt from the timing belt adjuster arm.
43. To install the lower timing cover you must remove the timing cover.
44. Do not loosen the adjusting nut while installing the rubber seal.
45. Install the crankshaft pulley then tighten the bolt to proper torque specs.
46. Install all other components.
47. Connect the negative battery cable.
48. Enter the anti-theft code for the radio, if applicable.

2.5L Engines

▶ **See Figures 113 thru 122**

➡️**Position the No. 1 piston at top dead center.**

1. Remove the power steering pump by loosening the adjusting nut and removing the mounting bolts.
2. Remove the air conditioning compressor by loosening the adjusting nut and removing the mounting bolts.
3. Remove the alternator belt by loosening the adjusting nut and mounting bolt.

4. Remove the 6 x 1.0 mm bolt from the dipstick filler tube.
5. Remove the dipstick and tube.
6. Remove the valve cover.
7. Remove the crankshaft pulley.
8. Remove the upper and lower timing belt covers.
9. Relieve the tension from the timing belt by loosening the adjusting bolt no more than 180°.
10. Remove the timing belt from the pulleys.

To install:

11. Installation is the reverse of removal. The key steps of the installation procedure are listed below.
12. Position the No. 1 piston at top dead center. This can be achieved by aligning the Top Dead Center (TDC) mark on the timing belt drive pulley with the mark on the oil pump.
13. Position the camshaft pulley so that the TDC mark on the pulley lines up with the pointer on the back cover.

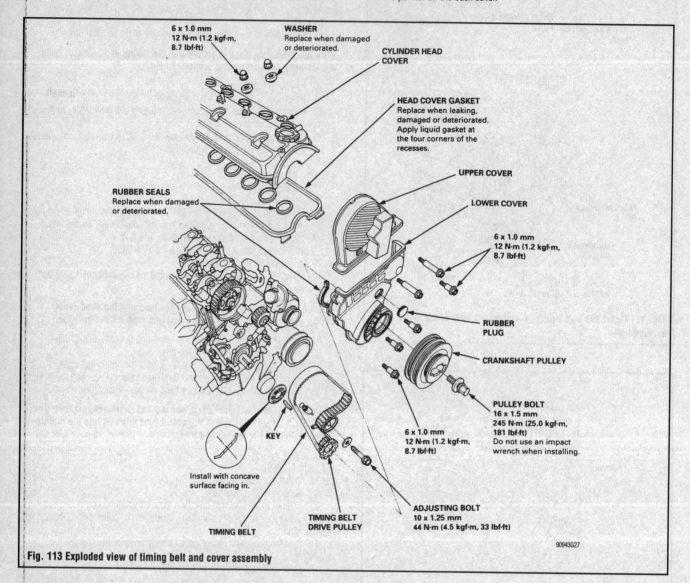

Fig. 113 Exploded view of timing belt and cover assembly

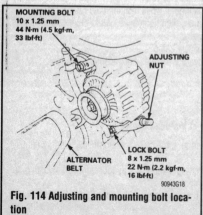

Fig. 114 Adjusting and mounting bolt location

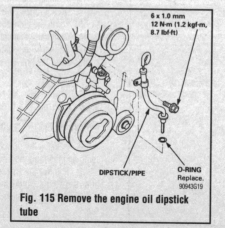

Fig. 115 Remove the engine oil dipstick tube

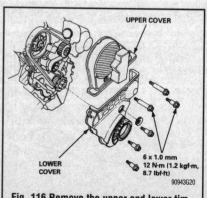

Fig. 116 Remove the upper and lower timing belt covers

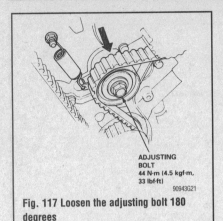

Fig. 117 Loosen the adjusting bolt 180 degrees

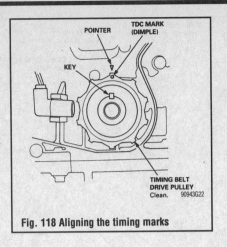

Fig. 118 Aligning the timing marks

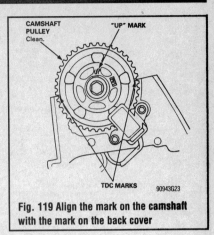

Fig. 119 Align the mark on the camshaft with the mark on the back cover

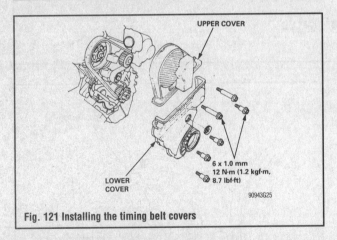

Fig. 120 Proper timing belt routing

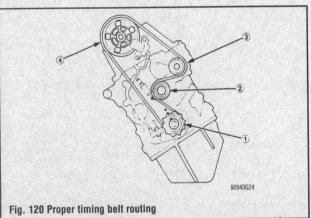

Fig. 121 Installing the timing belt covers

14. Install the timing belt on the crankshaft drive pulley.
15. Next position the belt around the adjusting pulley.
16. Position the belt around the water pump pulley.
17. Apply light tension to the timing belt as you loop it over the camshaft pulley.
18. To tension the timing belt, loosen the adjusting nut.
19. Once the adjuster spring has applied tension to the timing belt, retighten the adjusting nut.
20. Install the lower and upper timing belt covers.
21. After installing the crankshaft pulley, tighten the bolt to the proper specifications.
22. To check that the timing belt has positioned itself on the pulley by rotating the crankshaft pulley about five to six turns.
23. Adjust the timing belt tension and check that the crankshaft and camshaft pulleys are at Top Dead Center (TDC).
24. Install the remaining components in the reverse of the removal procedure.
25. Connect the negative battery cable.

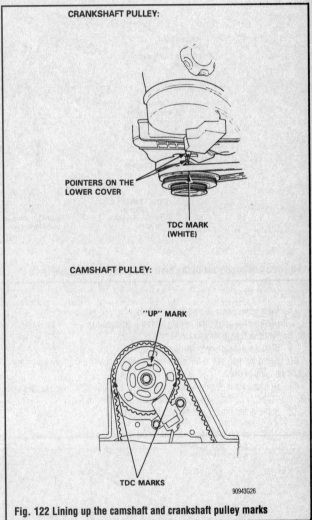

Fig. 122 Lining up the camshaft and crankshaft pulley marks

3.0L Engines

▶ See Figures 123 thru 129

1. Remove the splash shield from the wheel well.
2. Release the tension from the automatic tensioner and then remove the alternator belt.
3. Remove the power steering pump.
4. Remove the dipstick tube and the sealing O-ring.
5. Support the engine using a jack. Place a block of wood between the jack and the oil pan to prevent damage to the pan.

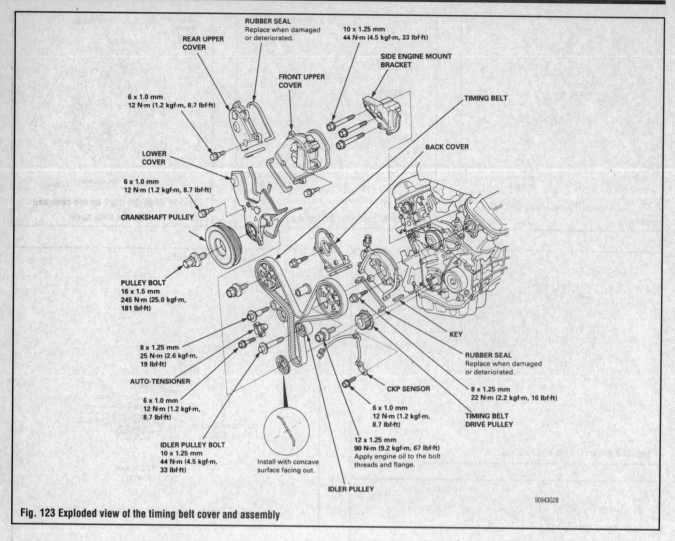

Fig. 123 Exploded view of the timing belt cover and assembly

6. Remove the side engine motor mount.
7. Remove the crankshaft pulley from the crankshaft.
8. Remove the upper and lower timing covers.
9. Remove the battery hold-down clamp.
10. Grind the end of the threaded rod to aid reinstallation, as shown in the accompanying figure.
11. Hold the timing belt adjuster in its current position by threading the battery clamp bolt into the guide just below the camshaft sprocket.
12. Remove the timing belt by backing the idler pulley bolt six turns.

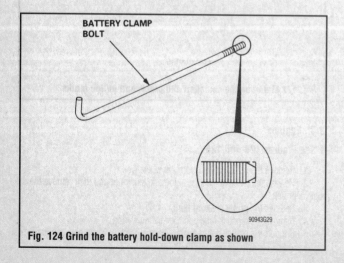

Fig. 124 Grind the battery hold-down clamp as shown

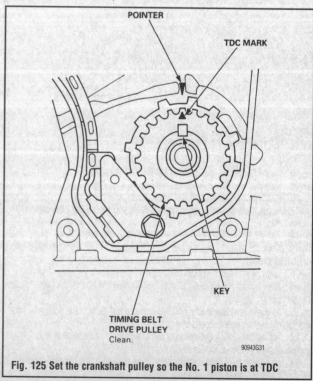

Fig. 125 Set the crankshaft pulley so the No. 1 piston is at TDC

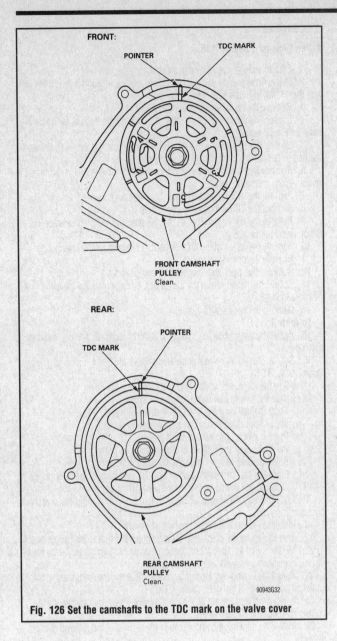

Fig. 126 Set the camshafts to the TDC mark on the valve cover

To install:

13. Install the timing belt in the reverse order of removal. The key steps are listed below.

14. Set the crankshaft drive belt pulley to where the No. 1 piston is at Top Dead Center (TDC).

15. Set the camshafts to the TDC mark on the valve cover.

16. Remove the battery clamp, that is holding the auto tensioner, from the back cover.

17. Remove the auto tensioner.

18. Remove the maintenance bolt from the tensioner.

➡️**If the oil drains out of the tensioner, refill it with no more than 0.22 fl. oz. (6.5ml).**

19. Clamp the auto tensioner in a vise.

✳✳ WARNING

Do not clamp the tensioner by the body.

20. Use a flat head screw driver to turn the tensioner, then slip the special stopper tool or equivalent over the assembly to hold it in place.

21. Install the maintenance bolt.

22. Install the auto tensioner.

23. Install the timing belt in the following order:
   a. Loop the belt over the timing belt drive pulley.
   b. Install the timing belt around the adjusting pulley.
   c. Place it around the left camshaft pulley.
   d. Install it under the bottom of the water pump pulley.
   e. Route the belt around the right camshaft pulley.
   f. Place the last part of the belt around the back side of the idler pulley.
24. Tighten the idler pulley bolt.
25. Remove the stopper tool.
26. Install the timing covers.
27. Install the crankshaft pulley.
28. To position the pulleys, turn the crankshaft pulley about five to six turns.
29. The crankshaft and camshaft pulleys should be at TDC.
30. If the camshafts are not at TDC, remove the timing belt and adjust the pulleys by repeating the above procedure.
31. Install all other components.
32. Connect the negative battery cable.

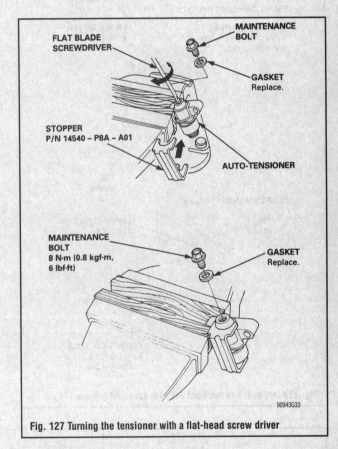

Fig. 127 Turning the tensioner with a flat-head screw driver

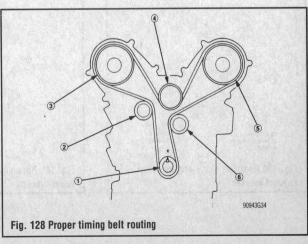

Fig. 128 Proper timing belt routing

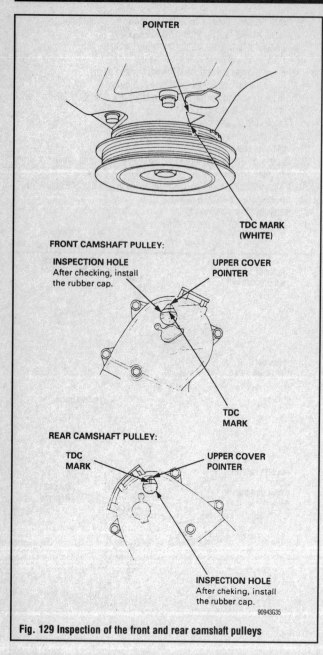

Fig. 129 Inspection of the front and rear camshaft pulleys

3.2L Engines

♦ **See Figures 130 thru 138**

1. Disconnect the negative battery cable.
2. Support the engine using a jack. Place a block of wood between the jack and the oil pan to prevent damage to the pan.
3. Remove the center engine support bracket.
4. Loosen the adjusting nut and then the mounting nuts to allow the alternator belt to be removed.
5. Loosen the adjusting and idler pulley bracket bolt on the (A/C) to free the belt.
6. Remove the power steering pump by loosening the adjusting bolts and removing the mounting bolts.
7. Remove the TCS upper and lower bracket assemblies.
8. Remove the TCS control valve assembly.
9. Remove the wiring harness and the oil pressure switch connector from the oil pressure switch.
10. Remove the idler pulley dipstick which is located by the idler pulley,
11. Remove the crankshaft pulley.
12. Remove the upper and lower timing belt covers.
13. Relieve the tension from the timing belt by loosening the adjusting bolt no more than 180°.
14. Remove the engine timing belt.

To install:

15. Install the timing belt in the reverse order of removal. The key steps are listed below.
16. Set the crankshaft drive belt pulley to where the No. 1 piston is at Top Dead Center (TDC).
17. Align the camshafts to the TDC mark on the valve cover.
18. Install the timing belt in the following order:
    a. Loop the belt over the timing belt drive pulley.
    b. Install the timing belt around the adjusting pulley.
    c. Place it around the left camshaft pulley.
    d. Install it under the bottom of the water pump pulley.
    e. Route the belt around the right camshaft pulley.
    f. Place the last part of the belt around the back side of the idler pulley.
19. To tension the timing belt, loosen the adjusting nut.
20. Once the adjuster spring has applied tension to the timing belt, retighten the adjusting nut.
21. Install the lower and upper timing belt covers.
22. After installing the crankshaft pulley, tighten the bolt to the proper specs.
23. To check that the timing belt has positioned itself on the pulley by rotating the crankshaft pulley about five to six turns.
24. Adjust the timing belt tension and check that the crankshaft and camshaft pulleys are at top dead center (TDC).
25. If the camshafts are not at TDC, remove the timing belt and adjust the pulleys by repeating the above procedure.
26. Install the remaining components in the reverse of the removal procedure.
27. Connect the negative battery cable.

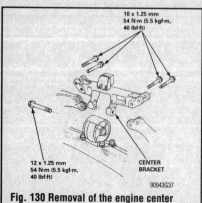

Fig. 130 Removal of the engine center support bracket

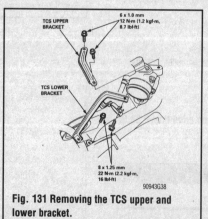

Fig. 131 Removing the TCS upper and lower bracket.

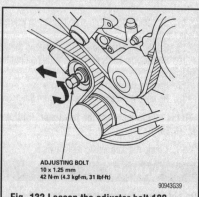

Fig. 132 Loosen the adjuster bolt 180 degrees

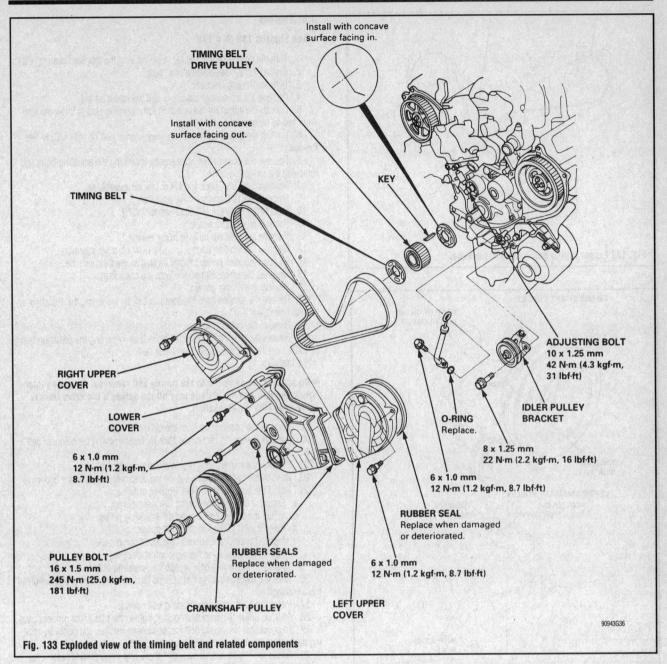

Fig. 133 Exploded view of the timing belt and related components

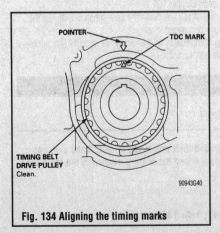

Fig. 134 Aligning the timing marks

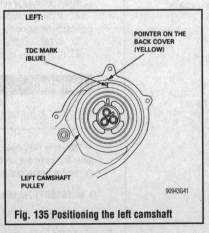

Fig. 135 Positioning the left camshaft

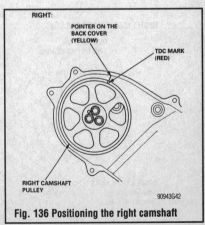

Fig. 136 Positioning the right camshaft

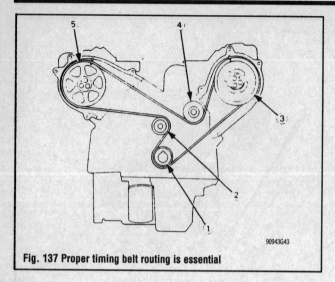

Fig. 137 Proper timing belt routing is essential

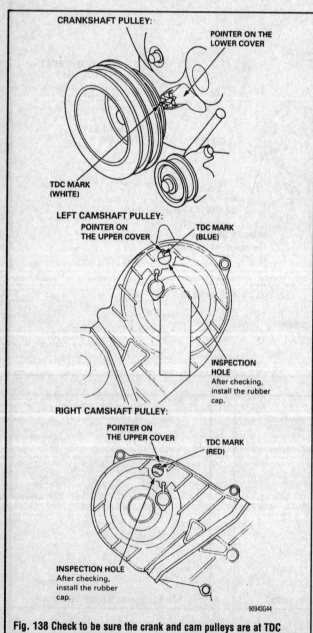

Fig. 138 Check to be sure the crank and cam pulleys are at TDC

3.5L Engines

♦ **See Figures 139 thru 146**

1. Turn the engine so that the No. 1 piston is at the top dead center (TDC).
2. Disconnect the negative battery cable.
3. Remove the engine cover.
4. Remove the air cleaner assembly and the intake tubing.
5. Loosen the adjusting nut and then the mounting nuts to allow the alternator belt to be removed.
6. Loosen the adjusting and idler pulley bracket bolt on the (A/C) to free the belt.
7. Remove the power steering pump by loosening the adjusting bolts and removing the mounting bolts.
8. Remove the TCS upper and lower bracket assemblies.
9. Remove the TCS control valve assembly.
10. Disconnect the Vehicle Speed Sensor (VSS).
11. Remove all vacuum hoses.
12. Remove the breather hose from the engine.
13. Remove the ignition control module (ICM) bracket assembly.
14. Remove the idler pulley bracket as well as the dipstick tube.
15. Separate the crankshaft pulley from the crankshaft.
16. Remove the timing covers.
17. Relieve the tension from the balancer belt by loosening the adjusting bolt no more than 180°.
18. Remove the balancer belt.
19. Relieve the tension from the timing belt by loosening the adjusting bolt no more than 180°, then remove the timing belt.

To install:

➡**Do not turn the engine with the timing belt removed. This is an interference engine and the pistons may hit the valves if the valve train is out of sync with the crankshaft.**

20. Remove the spark plugs from the cylinder head.
21. Remove the timing belt guide plate by first removing the balancer belt drive.
22. Position the number one piston at top dead center.
23. Position the camshaft pulleys at the top dead center mark on the back cover.
24. Install the timing belt in the following order:
    a. Loop the belt over the timing belt drive pulley.
    b. Install the timing belt around the adjusting pulley.
    c. Place it around the left camshaft pulley.
    d. Install it under the bottom of the water pump pulley.
    e. Route the belt around the right camshaft pulley.
25. To tension the timing belt, loosen the adjusting nut.
26. Once the adjuster spring has applied tension to the timing belt, retighten the adjusting nut.
27. Install the lower and upper timing belt covers.
28. After installing the crankshaft pulley, tighten the bolt to the proper specs.
29. To check that the timing belt has positioned itself on the pulley by rotating the crankshaft pulley about five to six turns.
30. Adjust the timing belt tension and check that the crankshaft and camshaft pulleys are at top dead center (TDC).
31. If the camshafts are not at TDC, remove the timing belt and adjust the pulleys by repeating the above procedure.
32. Install the remaining components in the reverse of removal procedure.
33. Connect the negative battery cable.

Camshaft

REMOVAL & INSTALLATION

➡**The radio may have a coded theft protection circuit. Make sure you have the code before disconnecting the battery, removing the radio fuse, or removing the radio.**

1.8L (B18B1) Engines

♦ **See Figures 56, 57, 147, 148, 149 and 150**

1. Disconnect the negative battery cable.
2. Tag and disconnect the spark plug wires.

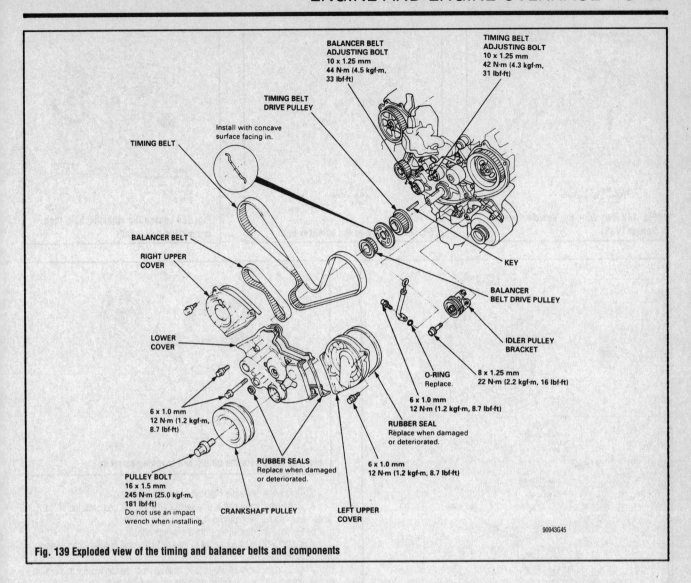

BALANCER BELT
ADJUSTING BOLT
10 x 1.25 mm
44 N·m (4.5 kgf·m,
33 lbf·ft)

TIMING BELT
ADJUSTING BOLT
10 x 1.25 mm
42 N·m (4.3 kgf·m,
31 lbf·ft)

TIMING BELT
DRIVE PULLEY

Install with concave
surface facing in.

TIMING BELT

BALANCER BELT

RIGHT UPPER
COVER

KEY

BALANCER
BELT DRIVE PULLEY

LOWER
COVER

IDLER PULLEY
BRACKET

8 x 1.25 mm
22 N·m (2.2 kgf·m, 16 lbf·ft)

O-RING
Replace.

6 x 1.0 mm
12 N·m (1.2 kgf·m,
8.7 lbf·ft)

6 x 1.0 mm
12 N·m (1.2 kgf·m, 8.7 lbf·ft)

RUBBER SEAL
Replace when damaged
or deteriorated.

RUBBER SEALS
Replace when damaged
or deteriorated.

6 x 1.0 mm
12 N·m (1.2 kgf·m, 8.7 lbf·ft)

PULLEY BOLT
16 x 1.5 mm
245 N·m (25.0 kgf·m,
181 lbf·ft)
Do not use an impact
wrench when installing.

CRANKSHAFT PULLEY

LEFT UPPER
COVER

90943G45

Fig. 139 Exploded view of the timing and balancer belts and components

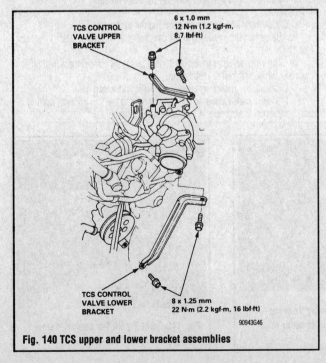

TCS CONTROL
VALVE UPPER
BRACKET

6 x 1.0 mm
12 N·m (1.2 kgf·m,
8.7 lbf·ft)

TCS CONTROL
VALVE LOWER
BRACKET

8 x 1.25 mm
22 N·m (2.2 kgf·m, 16 lbf·ft)

90943G46

Fig. 140 TCS upper and lower bracket assemblies

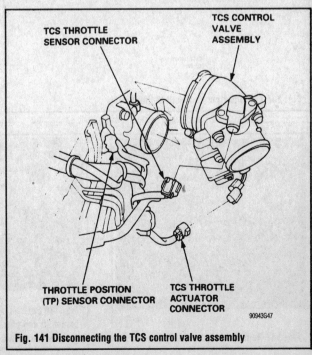

TCS THROTTLE
SENSOR CONNECTOR

TCS CONTROL
VALVE
ASSEMBLY

THROTTLE POSITION
(TP) SENSOR CONNECTOR

TCS THROTTLE
ACTUATOR
CONNECTOR

90943G47

Fig. 141 Disconnecting the TCS control valve assembly

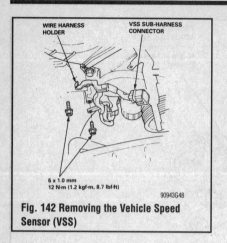

Fig. 142 Removing the Vehicle Speed Sensor (VSS)

Fig. 143 Removing the balancer belt

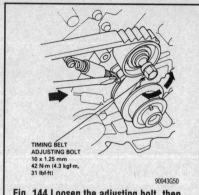

Fig. 144 Loosen the adjusting bolt, then remove the timing belt

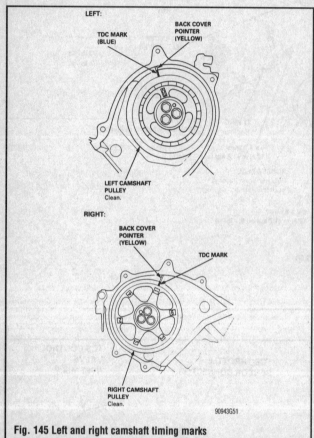

Fig. 145 Left and right camshaft timing marks

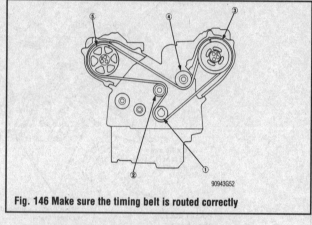

Fig. 146 Make sure the timing belt is routed correctly

3. Remove the cylinder head cover and timing belt cover.

4. Rotate the crankshaft to Top Dead Center (TDC), compression of No. 1 piston and remove the timing belt.

5. Remove the distributor from the cylinder head.

6. Install 5.0mm pin punches to the No.1 camshaft holders, then remove the camshaft sprockets.

7. Loosen the valve adjusters to remove as much spring tension as possible.

8. Remove the pin punches from the camshaft holders.

To install:

9. Check the following before installing the camshafts:

   a. Be certain the keyways on the camshafts are facing UP (No. 1 cylinder at TDC).

   b. The valve adjuster lock nuts should be loosened and the adjusting screws backed off before installation.

10. Lubricate the rocker arms and camshafts with clean oil.

11. Place the rocker arms on the pivot bolts and the valve stems, making sure that the rocker arms are in their original positions.

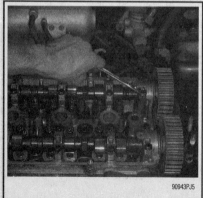

Fig. 147 Remove the camshaft cap bolts

Fig. 148 Pull the caps away from the camshaft and place them in order on a piece of cardboard

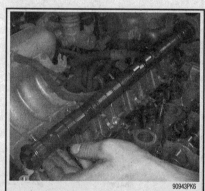

Fig. 149 Carefully lift the camshaft from the cylinder head

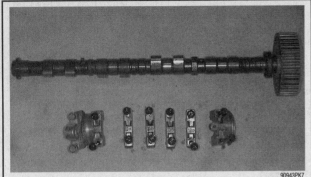

Fig. 150 Keep the correct camshaft with the appropriate caps at all times

12. Install the camshaft seals with the open side (spring) facing in. Lubricate the lip of the seal.

13. Be sure the keyways on the camshafts are facing up and install the camshafts to the cylinder head.

14. Apply liquid gasket to the head mating surfaces of the No. 1 and No. 6 camshaft holders, then install them along with No. 2, 3, 4 and 5 camshaft holders. The arrows stamped on the holders should point toward the timing belt. Do not apply oil to the holder mating surface where the camshaft seals are housed.

15. Tighten the camshaft holders temporarily and be sure that the rocker arms are properly positioned.

16. Press the oil seals into the No.1 camshaft holders with a seal driver.

17. Tighten the bolts in a crisscross pattern to 7 ft. lbs. (10 Nm). Check that the rockers do not bind on the valves.

18. Install the cylinder head plug to the end of the cylinder head. If the plug has alignment marks, align the marks with the cylinder head upper surface.

19. If equipped with a timing belt back cover, install the cover and tighten the bolts to 7.2 ft. lbs. (9.8 Nm).

20. Install 5.0mm pin punches to the No.1 camshaft holders, then install the camshaft pulley keys onto the grooves in the camshafts.

21. Push the camshaft pulleys onto the camshafts, then tighten the retaining bolts to 27 ft. lbs. (38 Nm).

22. Install the timing belt and timing belt covers. Remove the pin punches from the camshaft holders.

23. Adjust the valves and pour oil over the camshafts and rocker arms.

24. Install the cylinder head cover and engine ground cable.

25. Install the distributor to the cylinder head and reconnect the spark plug wires to the spark plugs.

26. Connect the negative battery cable and enter the radio security code.

27. Change the engine oil. Wait at least 20 minutes for the sealant to cure before filling the engine with oil.

1.8L (B18C1, B18C5) Engines

▶ **See Figure 151**

1. Disconnect the negative battery cable.
2. Be sure the crankshaft is at Top Dead Center (TDC), compression on No. 1 cylinder, by aligning the white mark on the crankshaft pulley with the pointer on the lower timing belt cover.
3. Remove the strut brace.
4. Remove the cylinder head cover, timing belt cover, and timing belt.
5. Remove the camshaft pulleys and back cover.
6. Loosen the rocker arm lock nuts and adjusting screws.
7. Remove the camshaft holder bolts, then remove the camshaft holder plates, the camshaft holders, and camshafts.

To install:

8. Be sure that the keyways on the camshafts are facing up and that the rocker arms are in their original position. The valve lock nuts should be loosened and the adjusting screw backed off before installation

9. Install the camshafts, then install the camshaft seals with the open side facing in. Install the rubber cap with liquid gasket applied.

10. Install a new O-ring and the dowel pin to the oil passage of the No. 3 camshaft holder.

11. Apply liquid gasket to the head of the mating surfaces of the No. 1 and

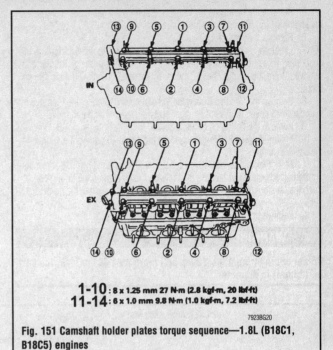

1-10 : 8 x 1.25 mm 27 N·m (2.8 kgf·m, 20 lbf·ft)
11-14 : 6 x 1.0 mm 9.8 N·m (1.0 kgf·m, 7.2 lbf·ft)

Fig. 151 Camshaft holder plates torque sequence—1.8L (B18C1, B18C5) engines

No. 5 camshaft holders, then install them, along with No. 2, 3, and 4. Be sure to pay attention to the following points:

- Do not apply oil to the holder mating surface of camshaft seals.
- The arrows marked on the camshaft holders should point to the timing belt.

12. Tighten the camshaft holders temporarily. Be sure that the rocker arms are properly positioned on the valve stems.

13. Tighten the camshaft holder bolts in two steps, following the proper sequence, to ensure that the rockers do not bind on the valves. Tighten the 8x1.25mm bolts to 20 ft. lbs. (27 Nm). Tighten the 6 x 1.0mm bolts to 84 inch lbs. (10 Nm).

14. Install the keys into the camshaft grooves. To set the No. 1 piston at TDC, align the holes on the camshaft with the holes in the No. 1 camshaft holders and insert 5.0mm pin punches into the holes.

15. Install the back cover and push the camshaft pulleys onto the camshafts, then tighten the retaining bolts to 27 ft. lbs. (37 Nm). Install the timing belt and adjust the tension, then install the timing belt covers.

16. Adjust the valve clearance.

17. Install the cylinder head cover. Be sure that the seal and groove are thoroughly clean first.

18. Install the engine side mount, tighten the two new nuts and new bolt to the engine to 38 ft. lbs. (52 Nm) and tighten the bolt attaching the mount to the vehicle to 54 ft. lbs. (74 Nm).

19. Install the distributor to the cylinder head and reconnect the spark plug wires to the spark plugs.

20. Install the intake air duct.

21. Install the strut brace, tighten the nuts to 17 ft. lbs. (24 Nm).

22. Connect the negative battery cable and enter the radio security code.

23. Drain the engine oil. Wait at least 20 minutes before filling the engine with oil; the time delay allows the sealant to cure.

2.2L, 2.3L Engines

▶ **See Figures 152, 153 and 154**

1. Disconnect the negative battery cable.
2. Turn the crankshaft so the No. 1 piston is at Top Dead Center (TDC).

➡**The No. 1 piston is at top dead center when the pointer on the block aligns with the white painted mark on the flywheel (manual transaxle) or driveplate (automatic transaxle).**

3. Remove the air intake duct.
4. Remove the engine ground cable from the cylinder head cover.

5. Remove the connector and the terminal from the alternator, then remove the engine wiring harness from the valve cover.

6. Remove the ignition coil.

7. Label, then detach the electrical connectors from the distributor and the spark plug wires from the spark plugs. Mark the position of the distributor and remove it from the cylinder head. Disconnect the ignition coil wire from the distributor.

8. Remove the Positive Crankcase Ventilation (PCV) hose, then remove the cylinder head cover. Replace the rubber seals if damaged or deteriorated.

9. Remove the timing belt middle cover.

10. Ensure the words **UP** embossed on the camshaft pulleys are aligned in the upward position.

11. Mark the rotation of the timing belt if it is to be used again. Loosen the timing belt adjusting nut ½ turn, then release the tension on the timing belt. Push the tensioner to release tension from the belt, then tighten the adjusting nut.

12. Remove the timing belt from the camshaft sprockets.

❊❊ WARNING

Do not crimp or bend the timing belt more than 90° or less, then 1 in. (25mm) in diameter

13. Remove the side engine mount bracket, then the timing belt back cover from behind the camshaft sprockets.

14. Loosen all of the rocker arm adjusting screws, then remove the pin punches from the camshaft caps.

15. Remove the camshaft holders, note the holders locations for ease of installation. Loosen the bolts in the reverse order of the installation.

16. Remove the camshafts from the cylinder head, then discard the camshaft seals.

17. Remove the rubber cap from the head, located at the end of the intake camshaft.

18. Remove the rocker arms from the cylinder head. Note the locations of the rocker arms.

➡ The rocker arms have to be installed to their original locations if being reused.

To install:

19. Lubricate the rocker arms with clean oil, then install the rocker arms on the pivot bolts and the valve stems. If the rocker arms are being reused, install them to their original locations. The lock nuts and adjustment screws should be loosened before installing the rocker arms.

20. Lubricate the camshafts with clean oil.

21. Install the camshaft seals to the end of the camshafts that the timing belt

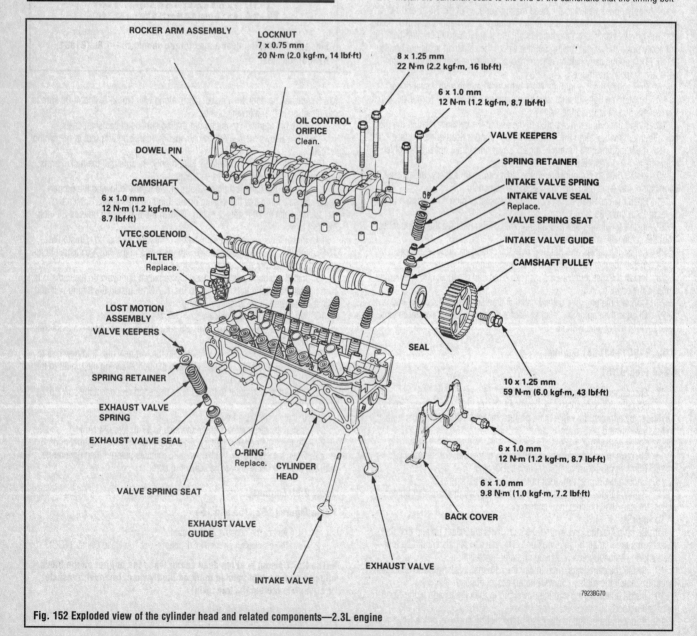

Fig. 152 Exploded view of the cylinder head and related components—2.3L engine

7923BG70

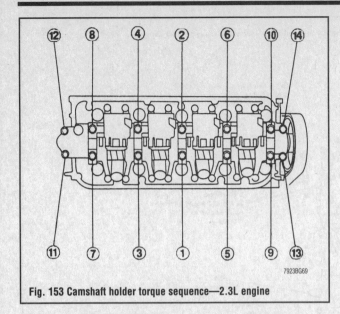

Fig. 153 Camshaft holder torque sequence—2.3L engine

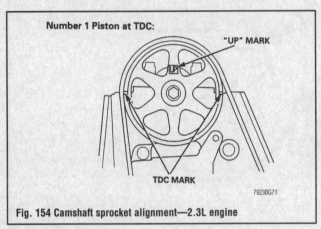

Fig. 154 Camshaft sprocket alignment—2.3L engine

sprockets attach to. The open side (spring) should be facing into the cylinder head when installed.

22. Be sure the keyways on the camshaft is facing up and install the camshaft to the cylinder head.

23. Apply liquid gasket to the head mating surfaces of the No. 1 and No. 5 camshaft holders, then install them along with No. 2, 3 and 4.

24. Snug the camshaft holders in place.

25. Press the camshaft seals securely into place.

26. Tighten the camshaft holder bolts in two steps, following the proper sequence, to ensure that the rockers do not bind on the valves. Tighten all the 6 mm bolts to 104 inch lbs. (12 Nm). Tighten the 8 mm bolts to 16 ft. lbs. (22 Nm).

27. Install the timing belt back cover.

28. Install the side engine mount bracket B. Tighten the bolt attaching the bracket to the cylinder head to 33 ft. lbs. (45 Nm). Tighten the bolts attaching the bracket to the side engine mount to 16 ft. lbs. (22 Nm).

29. Push the camshaft sprocket onto the camshaft, then tighten the retaining bolt to 43 ft. lbs. (59 Nm).

30. Ensure the words **UP** embossed on the camshaft pulley is aligned in the upward position. Install the timing belt to the camshaft sprocket.

31. Loosen, then tighten the timing belt adjuster nut.

32. Turn the crankshaft counterclockwise until the cam pulley has moved 3 teeth; this creates tension on the timing belt. Loosen, then tighten the adjusting nut and tighten it to 33 ft. lbs. (45 Nm).

33. Adjust the valves.

34. Tighten the crankshaft pulley bolt to 181 ft. lbs. (250 Nm).

35. Install the middle timing belt cover and tighten the attaching bolts to 104 inch lbs. (12 Nm).

36. Install the cylinder head cover and tighten the cap nuts to 104 inch lbs. (12 Nm). Install the PCV hose to the cylinder head cover.

37. Install the distributor to the cylinder head.

38. Connect the spark plug wires to the correct spark plugs, then attach the distributor electrical connectors. Install the ignition coil wire to the distributor.

39. Install the ignition coil.

40. Install the alternator wiring harness to the cylinder head cover, then attach the terminal and connector to the alternator.

41. Connect the engine ground cable to the cylinder head cover.

42. Install the air intake duct.

43. Drain the oil from the engine into a sealable container. Install the drain plug and refill the engine with clean oil.

44. Connect the negative battery cable and enter the radio security code.

45. Start the engine, checking carefully for any leaks.

46. Enter the radio security code.

2.5L Engine

▶ See Figure 155

1. Disconnect the negative battery cable. Remove the timing belt covers and cylinder head covers.

2. Rotate the crankshaft to Top Dead Center (TDC) compression of No. 1 piston and remove the timing belt.

3. Remove the camshaft sprocket.

4. Remove the cylinder head from the vehicle.

5. Loosen the rocker shaft holder bolts 1 turn at a time in the opposite of the installation sequence. Following this procedure will prevent the camshafts and rocker assemblies from warping.

6. After all bolts are loose, remove the rocker arm shafts as an assembly with the bolts still in the holders.

7. If the rocker shafts are to be disassembled, note that each rocker arm has a letter **A** or **B** stamped into the side. Before disassembling the rocker arms, make a note of the position of each letter so the arms can be reassembled the same way. The springs between the rocker arms are not all the same length. Carefully note their positions during disassembly.

To install:

8. Lubricate the camshaft and its journals with fresh engine oil.

9. Place a new camshaft seal on the end of the camshaft. The spring side of the seal must face in. Lubricate the journals and set the camshaft in place on the head.

10. Install the camshaft onto the cylinder head with the keyway pointed up.

11. Apply liquid gasket to the mounting surfaces of the camshaft end holders.

12. Set the rocker arm assemblies in place and start all the cam holder bolts. Be sure the rocker arms are properly positioned and turn each bolt in sequence two turns at a time until the holders are seated on the head. Follow this procedure to avoid damaging the camshaft and rocker assemblies.

13. When all of the camshaft and rocker holders are seated, tighten the bolts in the same sequence. Tighten the 8mm bolts to 16 ft. lbs. (22 Nm) and the 6mm bolts to 104 inch lbs. (12 Nm).

14. Install the cylinder head.

15. Install the camshaft sprocket and tighten the bolts to 51 ft. lbs. (70 Nm).

16. Install the timing belt, adjust the valves and oil the camshaft before completing the assembly.

17. Install the cylinder head cover and timing cover.

18. Install the distributor.

19. Reconnect the negative battery cable.

20. Check for proper engine and valve train operation.

3.0L Engine

▶ See Figure 156

1. Disconnect the negative battery cable.

2. Remove the timing belt and cylinder head as outlined earlier in this section.

3. Remove the camshaft sprocket and rear cover.

4. Remove the rocker arm/shaft assembly.

5. Remove the camshaft thrust cover and O-ring.

6. Carefully pull out the camshaft.

To install:

7. Lubricate the camshaft with clean engine oil.

8. Carefully slide the camshaft into position.

9. Install the thrust plate using a new O-ring. Tighten the bolts to 16 ft. lbs. (22 Nm).

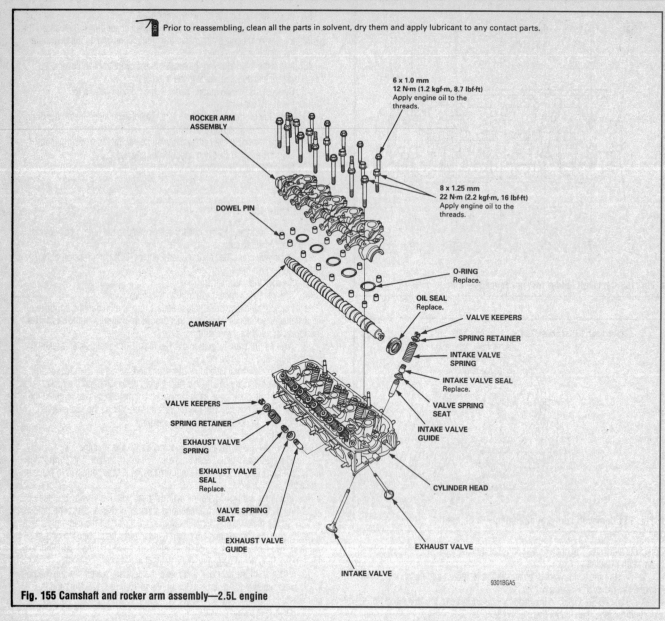

Prior to reassembling, clean all the parts in solvent, dry them and apply lubricant to any contact parts.

6 x 1.0 mm
12 N·m (1.2 kgf·m, 8.7 lbf·ft)
Apply engine oil to the
threads.

8 x 1.25 mm
22 N·m (2.2 kgf·m, 16 lbf·ft)
Apply engine oil to the
threads.

ROCKER ARM
ASSEMBLY

DOWEL PIN

CAMSHAFT

O-RING
Replace.

OIL SEAL
Replace.

VALVE KEEPERS

SPRING RETAINER

INTAKE VALVE
SPRING

INTAKE VALVE SEAL
Replace.

VALVE SPRING
SEAT

INTAKE VALVE
GUIDE

VALVE KEEPERS

SPRING RETAINER

EXHAUST VALVE
SPRING

EXHAUST VALVE
SEAL
Replace.

VALVE SPRING
SEAT

EXHAUST VALVE
GUIDE

CYLINDER HEAD

EXHAUST VALVE

INTAKE VALVE

9301BGA5

Fig. 155 Camshaft and rocker arm assembly—2.5L engine

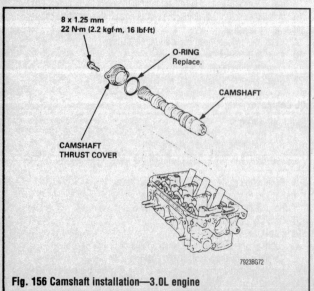

8 x 1.25 mm
22 N·m (2.2 kgf·m, 16 lbf·ft)

O-RING
Replace.

CAMSHAFT

CAMSHAFT
THRUST COVER

7923BG72

Fig. 156 Camshaft installation—3.0L engine

10. Install the rocker arm/shaft assembly.
11. Install the cylinder head.
12. Install the rear cover and camshaft sprocket. Tighten the bolt to 67 ft. lbs. (90 Nm).
13. Install the timing belt.
14. Adjust the valves.

3.2L and 3.5L Engines

▶ See Figures 157, 158, 159 and 160

1. Disconnect the negative battery cable.
2. Remove the timing belt covers and cylinder head covers.
3. Rotate the crankshaft to Top Dead Center (TDC) for the No. 1 piston and remove the timing belt.
4. Remove the camshaft sprockets.
5. Loosen the rocker shaft holder bolts one turn at a time in the reverse of the torque sequence to avoid damaging the valves, camshafts, or rocker assemblies.
6. After all bolts are loose, remove the rocker arm shafts as an assembly with the bolts still in the holders.
7. If the rocker shafts are to be disassembled, note that each rocker arm has a letter **A** or

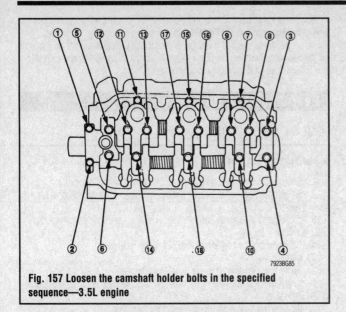

Fig. 157 Loosen the camshaft holder bolts in the specified sequence—3.5L engine

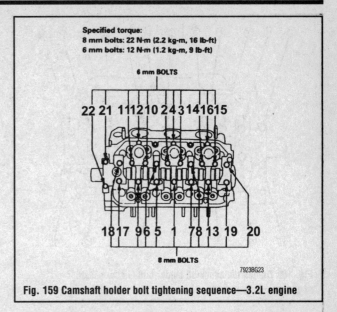

Fig. 159 Camshaft holder bolt tightening sequence—3.2L engine

B stamped into the side. Before disassembling the rocker arms, make a note of the position of each letter so that the arms can be reassembled in the same position.

8. Do not remove the hydraulic tappets from the rocker arms unless they are to be replaced. Handle the rocker arms carefully so the oil does not drain out of the tappets.

9. Lift the camshafts from the cylinder head, wipe them clean and inspect the lift ramps. Replace the camshafts and rockers if the lobes are pitted, scored, or excessively worn.

To install:

10. Place a new seal on the end of the camshaft, lubricate the journals and set the camshaft in place on the head.

➡ The pin hole in the front of the camshaft designates the top position.

11. Apply liquid gasket to the mounting surfaces of the camshaft end holders.

12. Set the rocker arm assemblies in place and start all of the camshaft holder bolts. Be sure the rocker arms are properly positioned and turn each bolt in sequence two turns at a time until the holders are seated on the head to avoid damaging the valves or rocker assemblies.

13. When all the camshaft and rocker holders are seated, tighten the bolts in the same sequence. Tighten the 8mm bolts to 16 ft. lbs. (22 Nm) and the 6mm bolts to 104 inch lbs. (12 Nm).

14. Install the camshaft pulleys and tighten the bolts to 23 ft. lbs. (32 Nm).

15. Install the timing belt and pour oil over the camshafts.

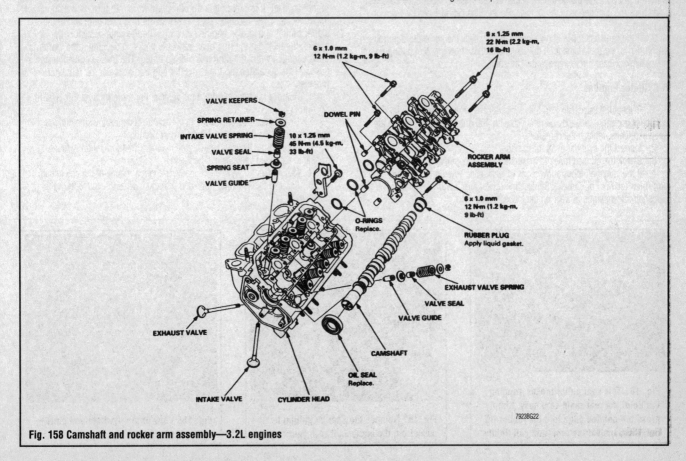

Fig. 158 Camshaft and rocker arm assembly—3.2L engines

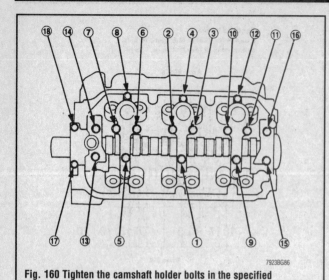

Fig. 160 Tighten the camshaft holder bolts in the specified sequence—3.5L engine

7923BG86

16. Install the cylinder head cover and reassemble accessory components.
17. Verify that all electrical connections and vacuum lines are connected.
18. Reconnect the negative battery cable.
19. Run the engine and check for leaks and proper operation.

INSPECTION

4-Cylinder Engines

1. Thoroughly clean all parts. Inspect the camshaft journals for scoring. Check the oil feed holes in the cylinder head for blockage. Check the camshaft bearing journals for scoring. If light scratches are present, they may be removed with 400 grit abrasive paper. If deep scratches are present, replace the camshaft and check the cylinder head for damage. Replace the cylinder head if worn or damaged.

2. If the camshaft lobes show signs of wear, check the corresponding rocker arm roller for wear or damage. If the camshaft lobes show signs of pitting on the nose, flank or base circle, replace the camshaft.

6-Cylinder Engines

1. Inspect the camshafts carefully for scratches or worn areas. If light scratches are seen, they may be removed with 400 grit sandpaper. If there are deep scratches, replace the camshaft.

2. Inspect the cylinder head for damage.

3. Check the oil feed holes to make sure they are open and free of debris.

4. If the camshaft lobes show signs of wear, check the corresponding rocker arm roller for wear or damage. Replace the rocker arm if worn or damaged. If the camshaft shows signs of wear on the lobes, replace it.

5. Check camshaft end-play. Oil the camshaft journals with clean engine oil and install the camshaft **WITHOUT** the rocker arm assemblies. Move the camshaft as far rearward as it will go. Mount a dial indicator to bear on the front of the camshaft. Zero the indicator. Move the camshaft as far forward as it will go. Check to see if the endplay is with in specs.

Rear Crankshaft Oil Seal

REMOVAL & INSTALLATION

▶ **See Figures 161 and 162**

1. Remove the transaxle, as outlined in Section 7 of this manual.
2. If equipped with an automatic transaxle vehicles, remove the driveplate from the crankshaft.
3. If equipped with a manual transaxle vehicles, remove the flywheel from the crankshaft.
4. Carefully pry the crankshaft seal out of the retainer.
To install:
5. Apply clean engine oil to the lip of the new seal.
6. Install the seal onto the crankshaft and into the retainer using the appropriate seal driver.
7. Install the flywheel or driveplate and the transaxle.

Flywheel/Flexplate

REMOVAL & INSTALLATION

▶ **See Figures 163 thru 164**

The flywheel on manual transaxle cars serves as the forward clutch engagement surface. It also serves as the ring gear with which the starter pinion engages to crank the engine. The most common reason to replace the flywheel is broken teeth on the starter ring gear.

On automatic transaxle cars, the torque converter actually forms part of the flywheel. It is bolted to a thin flexplate which, in turn, is bolted to the crankshaft. The flexplate also serves as the ring gear with which the starter pinion engages in engine cranking. The flexplate occasionally cracks; the teeth on the ring gear may also break, especially if the starter is often engaged while the pinion is still spinning. The torque converter and flexplate are separated, so the converter and transaxle can be removed together.

1. Remove the transaxle from the vehicle. For more information, refer to Section 7.
2. On vehicles equipped with a manual transaxle, remove the clutch assembly from the flywheel, as described in Section 7.
3. Support the flywheel in a secure manner (the flywheel on manual transaxle-equipped vehicles can be heavy).
4. Matchmark the flywheel/flexplate to the rear flange of the crankshaft.
5. Remove the attaching bolts and pull the flywheel/flexplate from the crankshaft.

Fig. 161 This seal puller makes gripping the lip of the rear main seal easy. Simply press the pointed edge into the rubber lip of the seal, pivot the arm, and pull lightly

90947P51

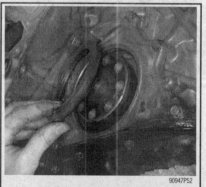

Fig. 162 Remove the seal by pulling it away from the crankshaft with your fingers

90947P52

Fig. 163 View of the flywheel and bolts—manual transaxle shown

90947P44

Fig. 164 Removing the flywheel from an Integra with a manual transaxle

To install:

6. Clean the flywheel/flexplate attaching bolts, the flywheel/flexplate and the rear crankshaft mounting flange.

7. Position the flywheel/flexplate onto the crankshaft flange so that the matchmarks align.

8. Coat the threads of the attaching bolts with Loctite® Thread Locker 271, or equivalent, to help ensure that the attaching bolts will not work loose. Install the bolts finger-tight.

9. Tighten the attaching bolts in a crisscross fashion in 3 even steps to 68–70 ft. lbs. (92–95 Nm).

10. For manual transaxle-equipped vehicles, install the clutch assembly. For more information, refer to Section 7.

11. Install the transaxle, as described in Section 7.

EXHAUST SYSTEM

Inspection

◆ See Figures 165 thru 171

➡Safety glasses should be worn at all times when working on or near the exhaust system. Older exhaust systems will almost always be covered with loose rust particles which will shower you when disturbed. These particles are more than a nuisance and could injure your eye.

✻✻ CAUTION

DO NOT perform exhaust repairs or inspection with the engine or exhaust hot. Allow the system to cool completely before attempting any work. Exhaust systems are noted for sharp edges, flaking metal and rusted bolts. Gloves and eye protection are required. A healthy supply of penetrating oil and rags is highly recommended.

Your vehicle must be raised and supported safely to inspect the exhaust system properly. By placing 4 safety stands under the vehicle for support should provide enough room for you to slide under the vehicle and inspect the system completely. Start the inspection at the exhaust manifold or turbocharger pipe where the header pipe is attached and work your way to the back of the vehicle. On dual exhaust systems, remember to inspect both sides of the vehicle. Check the complete exhaust system for open seams, holes loose connections, or other deterioration which could permit exhaust fumes to seep into the passenger compartment. Inspect all mounting brackets and hangers for deterioration, some models may have rubber O-rings that can be overstretched and non-supportive. These components will need to be replaced if found. It has always been a practice to use a pointed tool to poke up into the exhaust system where the deterioration spots are to see whether or not they crumble. Some models may have heat shield covering certain parts of the exhaust system, it will be necessary to remove these shields to have the exhaust visible for inspection also.

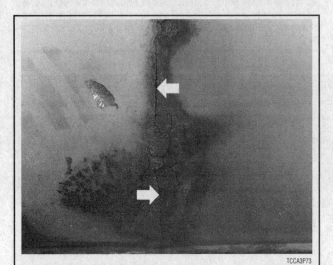

Fig. 165 Cracks in the muffler are guaranteed to cause a leak

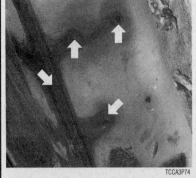

Fig. 166 Check the muffler for rotted spot welds and seams

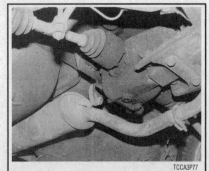

Fig. 167 Make sure the exhaust components are not contacting the body or suspension

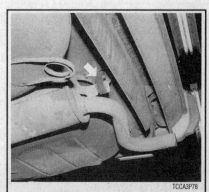

Fig. 168 Check for overstretched or torn exhaust hangers

Fig. 169 Example of a badly deteriorated exhaust pipe

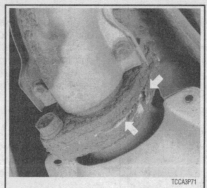
Fig. 170 Inspect flanges for gaskets that have deteriorated and need replacement

Fig. 171 Some systems, like this one, use large O-rings (donuts) in between the flanges

REPLACEMENT

▶ See Figures 172, 173, 174, 175 and 176

There are basically two types of exhaust systems. One is the flange type where the component ends are attached with bolts and a gasket in-between. The other exhaust system is the slip joint type. These components slip into one another using clamps to retain them together.

✴✴ CAUTION

Allow the exhaust system to cool sufficiently before spraying a solvent exhaust fasteners. Some solvents are highly flammable and could ignite when sprayed on hot exhaust components.

Before removing any component of the exhaust system, ALWAYS squirt a liquid rust dissolving agent onto the fasteners for ease of removal. A lot of knuckle skin will be saved by following this rule. It may even be wise to spray the fasteners and allow them to sit overnight.

Flange Type

▶ See Figure 177

✴✴ CAUTION

Do NOT perform exhaust repairs or inspection with the engine or exhaust hot. Allow the system to cool completely before attempting any work. Exhaust systems are noted for sharp edges, flaking metal and rusted bolts. Gloves and eye protection are required. A healthy supply of penetrating oil and rags is highly recommended. Never spray liquid rust dissolving agent onto a hot exhaust component.

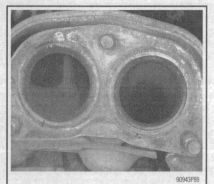
Fig. 172 Top view of the manifold down pipe on an Integra

Fig. 173 Use a pick tool to remove the gasket from the exhaust manifold down pipe

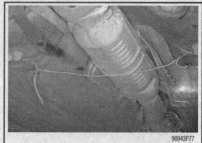
Fig. 174 Use rope to tie the exhaust to the vehicle when removing the mounting hangers. This will prevent any accidental injury due to falling components. As always, never work on a hot exhaust

Fig. 175 Always use two hands when removing the lower half of an exhaust manifold. Many are made out of cast iron an can be cumbersome

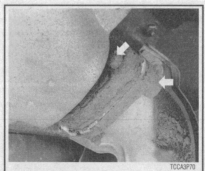
Fig. 176 Nuts and bolts will be extremely difficult to remove when deteriorated with rust

Fig. 177 Example of a flange type exhaust system joint

Before removing any component on a flange type system, ALWAYS squirt a liquid rust dissolving agent onto the fasteners for ease of removal. Start by unbolting the exhaust piece at both ends (if required). When unbolting the headpipe from the manifold, make sure that the bolts are free before trying to remove them. if you snap a stud in the exhaust manifold, the stud will have to be removed with a bolt extractor, which often means removal of the manifold itself. Next, disconnect the component from the mounting; slight twisting and turning may be required to remove the component completely from the vehicle. You may need to tap on the component with a rubber mallet to loosen the component. If all else fails, use a hacksaw to separate the parts. An oxy-acetylene cutting torch may be faster but the sparks are DANGEROUS near the fuel tank, and at the very least, accidents could happen, resulting in damage to the under-car parts, not to mention yourself.

Slip Joint Type

▶ See Figure 178

Before removing any component on the slip joint type exhaust system, ALWAYS squirt a liquid rust dissolving agent onto the fasteners for ease of removal. Start by unbolting the exhaust piece at both ends (if required). When unbolting the headpipe from the manifold, make sure that the bolts are free before trying to remove them. if you snap a stud in the exhaust manifold, the stud will have to be removed with a bolt extractor, which often means removal of

TCCA3P79

Fig. 178 Example of a common slip joint type system

the manifold itself. Next, remove the mounting U-bolts from around the exhaust pipe you are extracting from the vehicle. Don't be surprised if the U-bolts break while removing the nuts. Loosen the exhaust pipe from any mounting brackets retaining it to the floor pan and separate the components.

ENGINE RECONDITIONING

Determining Engine Condition

Anything that generates heat and/or friction will eventually burn or wear out (i.e. a light bulb generates heat, therefore its life span is limited). With this in mind, a running engine generates tremendous amounts of both; friction is encountered by the moving and rotating parts inside the engine and heat is created by friction and combustion of the fuel. However, the engine has systems designed to help reduce the effects of heat and friction and provide added longevity. The oiling system reduces the amount of friction encountered by the moving parts inside the engine, while the cooling system reduces heat created by friction and combustion. If either system is not maintained, a break-down will be inevitable. Therefore, you can see how regular maintenance can affect the service life of your vehicle. If you do not drain, flush and refill your cooling system at the proper intervals, deposits will begin to accumulate in the radiator, thereby reducing the amount of heat it can extract from the coolant. The same applies to your oil and filter; if it is not changed often enough it becomes laden with contaminates and is unable to properly lubricate the engine. This increases friction and wear.

There are a number of methods for evaluating the condition of your engine. A compression test can reveal the condition of your pistons, piston rings, cylinder bores, head gasket(s), valves and valve seats. An oil pressure test can warn you of possible engine bearing, or oil pump failures. Excessive oil consumption, evidence of oil in the engine air intake area and/or bluish smoke from the tail pipe may indicate worn piston rings, worn valve guides and/or valve seals. As a general rule, an engine that uses no more than one quart of oil every 1000 miles is in good condition. Engines that use one quart of oil or more in less than 1000 miles should first be checked for oil leaks. If any oil leaks are present, have them fixed before determining how much oil is consumed by the engine, especially if blue smoke is not visible at the tail pipe.

COMPRESSION TEST

▶ See Figure 179

A noticeable lack of engine power, excessive oil consumption and/or poor fuel mileage measured over an extended period are all indicators of internal engine wear. Worn piston rings, scored or worn cylinder bores, blown head gaskets, sticking or burnt valves, and worn valve seats are all possible culprits. A check of each cylinder's compression will help locate the problem.

➡A screw-in type compression gauge is more accurate than the type you simply hold against the spark plug hole. Although it takes slightly longer to use, it's worth the effort to obtain a more accurate reading.

1. Make sure that the proper amount and viscosity of engine oil is in the crankcase, then ensure the battery is fully charged.

2. Warm-up the engine to normal operating temperature, then shut the engine **OFF**.

3. Disable the ignition system.

4. Label and disconnect all of the spark plug wires from the plugs.

5. Thoroughly clean the cylinder head area around the spark plug ports, then remove the spark plugs.

6. Set the throttle plate to the fully open (wide-open throttle) position. You can block the accelerator linkage open for this, or you can have an assistant fully depress the accelerator pedal.

7. Install a screw-in type compression gauge into the No. 1 spark plug hole until the fitting is snug.

❊❊ WARNING

Be careful not to crossthread the spark plug hole.

8. According to the tool manufacturer's instructions, connect a remote starting switch to the starting circuit.

9. With the ignition switch in the **OFF** position, use the remote starting switch to crank the engine through at least five compression strokes (approximately 5 seconds of cranking) and record the highest reading on the gauge.

10. Repeat the test on each cylinder, cranking the engine approximately the same number of compression strokes and/or time as the first.

11. Compare the highest readings from each cylinder to that of the others. The indicated compression pressures are considered within specifications if the lowest reading cylinder is within 75 percent of the pressure recorded for the highest reading cylinder. For example, if your highest reading cylinder pressure

TCCS3801

Fig. 179 A screw-in type compression gauge is more accurate and easier to use without an assistant

was 150 psi (1034 kPa), then 75 percent of that would be 113 psi (779 kPa). So the lowest reading cylinder should be no less than 113 psi (779 kPa).

12. If a cylinder exhibits an unusually low compression reading, pour a tablespoon of clean engine oil into the cylinder through the spark plug hole and repeat the compression test. If the compression rises after adding oil, it means that the cylinder's piston rings and/or cylinder bore are damaged or worn. If the pressure remains low, the valves may not be seating properly (a valve job is needed), or the head gasket may be blown near that cylinder. If compression in any two adjacent cylinders is low, and if the addition of oil doesn't help raise compression, there is leakage past the head gasket. Oil and coolant in the combustion chamber, combined with blue or constant white smoke from the tail pipe, are symptoms of this problem. However, don't be alarmed by the normal white smoke emitted from the tail pipe during engine warm-up or from cold weather driving. There may be evidence of water droplets on the engine dipstick and/or oil droplets in the cooling system if a head gasket is blown.

OIL PRESSURE TEST

Check for proper oil pressure at the sending unit passage with an externally mounted mechanical oil pressure gauge (as opposed to relying on a factory installed dash-mounted gauge). A tachometer may also be needed, as some specifications may require running the engine at a specific rpm.

1. With the engine cold, locate and remove the oil pressure sending unit.
2. Following the manufacturer's instructions, connect a mechanical oil pressure gauge and, if necessary, a tachometer to the engine.
3. Start the engine and allow it to idle.
4. Check the oil pressure reading when cold and record the number. You may need to run the engine at a specified rpm, so check the specifications chart located earlier in this section.
5. Run the engine until normal operating temperature is reached (upper radiator hose will feel warm).
6. Check the oil pressure reading again with the engine hot and record the number. Turn the engine **OFF**.
7. Compare your hot oil pressure reading to that given in the chart. If the reading is low, check the cold pressure reading against the chart. If the cold pressure is well above the specification, and the hot reading was lower than the specification, you may have the wrong viscosity oil in the engine. Change the oil, making sure to use the proper grade and quantity, then repeat the test.

Low oil pressure readings could be attributed to internal component wear, pump related problems, a low oil level, or oil viscosity that is too low. High oil pressure readings could be caused by an overfilled crankcase, too high of an oil viscosity or a faulty pressure relief valve.

Buy or Rebuild?

Now that you have determined that your engine is worn out, you must make some decisions. The question of whether or not an engine is worth rebuilding is largely a subjective matter and one of personal worth. Is the engine a popular one, or is it an obsolete model? Are parts available? Will it get acceptable gas mileage once it is rebuilt? Is the car it's being put into worth keeping? Would it be less expensive to buy a new engine, have your engine rebuilt by a pro, rebuild it yourself or buy a used engine from a salvage yard? Or would it be simpler and less expensive to buy another car? If you have considered all these matters and more, and have still decided to rebuild the engine, then it is time to decide how you will rebuild it.

➡The editors at Chilton feel that most engine machining should be performed by a professional machine shop. Don't think of it as wasting money, rather, as an assurance that the job has been done right the first time. There are many expensive and specialized tools required to perform such tasks as boring and honing an engine block or having a valve job done on a cylinder head. Even inspecting the parts requires expensive micrometers and gauges to properly measure wear and clearances. Also, a machine shop can deliver to you clean, and ready to assemble parts, saving you time and aggravation. Your maximum savings will come from performing the removal, disassembly, assembly and installation of the engine and purchasing or renting only the tools required to perform the above tasks. Depending on the particular circumstances, you may save 40 to 60 percent of the cost doing these yourself.

A complete rebuild or overhaul of an engine involves replacing all of the moving parts (pistons, rods, crankshaft, camshaft, etc.) with new ones and machining the non-moving wearing surfaces of the block and heads. Unfortunately, this may not be cost effective. For instance, your crankshaft may have been damaged or worn, but it can be machined undersize for a minimal fee.

So, as you can see, you can replace everything inside the engine, but, it is wiser to replace only those parts which are really needed, and, if possible, repair the more expensive ones. Later in this section, we will break the engine down into its two main components: the cylinder head and the engine block. We will discuss each component, and the recommended parts to replace during a rebuild on each.

Engine Overhaul Tips

Most engine overhaul procedures are fairly standard. In addition to specific parts replacement procedures and specifications for your individual engine, this section is also a guide to acceptable rebuilding procedures. Examples of standard rebuilding practice are given and should be used along with specific details concerning your particular engine.

Competent and accurate machine shop services will ensure maximum performance, reliability and engine life. In most instances it is more profitable for the do-it-yourself mechanic to remove, clean and inspect the component, buy the necessary parts and deliver these to a shop for actual machine work.

Much of the assembly work (crankshaft, bearings, piston rods, and other components) is well within the scope of the do-it-yourself mechanic's tools and abilities. You will have to decide for yourself the depth of involvement you desire in an engine repair or rebuild.

TOOLS

The tools required for an engine overhaul or parts replacement will depend on the depth of your involvement. With a few exceptions, they will be the tools found in a mechanic's tool kit (see Section 1 of this manual). More in-depth work will require some or all of the following:

- A dial indicator (reading in thousandths) mounted on a universal base
- Micrometers and telescope gauges
- Jaw and screw-type pullers
- Scraper
- Valve spring compressor
- Ring groove cleaner
- Piston ring expander and compressor
- Ridge reamer
- Cylinder hone or glaze breaker
- Plastigage®
- Engine stand

The use of most of these tools is illustrated in this section. Many can be rented for a one-time use from a local parts jobber or tool supply house specializing in automotive work.

Occasionally, the use of special tools is called for. See the information on Special Tools and the Safety Notice in the front of this book before substituting another tool.

OVERHAUL TIPS

Aluminum has become extremely popular for use in engines, due to its low weight. Observe the following precautions when handling aluminum parts:

• Never hot tank aluminum parts (the caustic hot tank solution will eat the aluminum.

• Remove all aluminum parts (identification tag, etc.) from engine parts prior to the tanking.

• Always coat threads lightly with engine oil or anti-seize compounds before installation, to prevent seizure.

• Never over tighten bolts or spark plugs especially in aluminum threads.

When assembling the engine, any parts that will be exposed to frictional contact must be prelubed to provide lubrication at initial start-up. Any product specifically formulated for this purpose can be used, but engine oil is not recommended as a prelube in most cases.

When semi-permanent (locked, but removable) installation of bolts or nuts is desired, threads should be cleaned and coated with Loctite• or another similar, commercial non-hardening sealant.

CLEANING

▶ **See Figures 180, 181, 182 and 183**

Before the engine and its components are inspected, they must be thoroughly cleaned. You will need to remove any engine varnish, oil sludge and/or carbon deposits from all of the components to insure an accurate inspection. A crack in the engine block or cylinder head can easily become overlooked if hidden by a layer of sludge or carbon.

Most of the cleaning process can be carried out with common hand tools and readily available solvents or solutions. Carbon deposits can be chipped away using a hammer and a hard wooden chisel. Old gasket material and varnish or sludge can usually be removed using a scraper and/or cleaning solvent. Extremely stubborn deposits may require the use of a power drill with a wire brush. If using a wire brush, use extreme care around any critical machined surfaces (such as the gasket surfaces, bearing saddles, cylinder bores, etc.). USE OF A WIRE BRUSH IS NOT RECOMMENDED ON ANY ALUMINUM COMPONENTS. Always follow any safety recommendations given by the manufacturer of the tool and/or solvent. You should always wear eye protection during any cleaning process involving scraping, chipping or spraying of solvents.

An alternative to the mess and hassle of cleaning the parts yourself is to drop them off at a local garage or machine shop. They will, more than likely, have the necessary equipment to properly clean all of the parts for a nominal fee.

✷✷ CAUTION

Always wear eye protection during any cleaning process involving scraping, chipping or spraying of solvents.

Remove any oil galley plugs, freeze plugs and/or pressed-in bearings and carefully wash and degrease all of the engine components including the fasteners and bolts. Small parts such as the valves, springs, etc., should be placed in a metal basket and allowed to soak. Use pipe cleaner type brushes, and clean all passageways in the components. Use a ring expander and remove the rings from the pistons. Clean the piston ring grooves with a special tool or a piece of broken ring. Scrape the carbon off of the top of the piston. You should never use a wire brush on the pistons. After preparing all of the piston assemblies in this manner, wash and degrease them again.

✷✷ WARNING

Use extreme care when cleaning around the cylinder head valve seats. A mistake or slip may cost you a new seat.

When cleaning the cylinder head, remove carbon from the combustion chamber with the valves installed. This will avoid damaging the valve seats.

REPAIRING DAMAGED THREADS

▶ **See Figures 184, 185, 186, 187 and 188**

Several methods of repairing damaged threads are available. Heli-Coil® (shown here), Keenserts® and Microdot® are among the most widely used. All involve basically the same principle—drilling out stripped threads, tapping the hole and installing a prewound insert—making welding, plugging and oversize fasteners unnecessary.

Two types of thread repair inserts are usually supplied: a standard type for most inch coarse, inch fine, metric course and metric fine thread sizes and a spark lug type to fit most spark plug port sizes. Consult the individual tool manufacturer's catalog to determine exact applications. Typical thread repair kits will contain a selection of prewound threaded inserts, a tap (corresponding to the outside diameter threads of the insert) and an installation tool. Spark plug inserts usually differ because they require a tap equipped with pilot threads and a combined reamer/tap section. Most manufacturers also supply blister-packed thread repair inserts separately in addition to a master kit containing a variety of taps and inserts plus installation tools.

Before attempting to repair a threaded hole, remove any snapped, broken or damaged bolts or studs. Penetrating oil can be used to free frozen threads. The offending item can usually be removed with locking pliers or using a screw/stud extractor. After the hole is clear, the thread can be repaired, as shown in the series of accompanying illustrations and in the kit manufacturer's instructions.

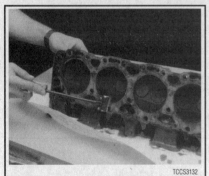

TCCS3132

Fig. 180 Use a gasket scraper to remove the old gasket material from the mating surfaces

TCCS3211

Fig. 181 Use a ring expander tool to remove the piston rings

TCCS3208

Fig. 182 Clean the piston ring grooves using a ring groove cleaner tool, or . . .

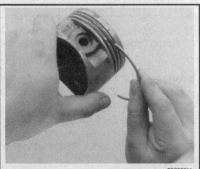

TCCS3911

Fig. 183 . . . use a piece of an old ring to clean the grooves. Be careful, the ring can be quite sharp

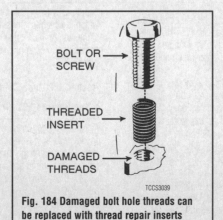

TCCS3039

Fig. 184 Damaged bolt hole threads can be replaced with thread repair inserts

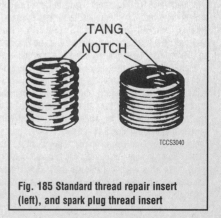

TCCS3040

Fig. 185 Standard thread repair insert (left), and spark plug thread insert

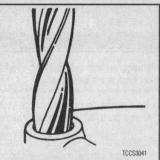

Fig. 186 Drill out the damaged threads with the specified size bit. Be sure to drill completely through the hole or to the bottom of a blind hole

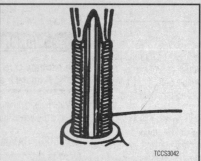

Fig. 187 Using the kit, tap the hole in order to receive the thread insert. Keep the tap well oiled and back it out frequently to avoid clogging the threads

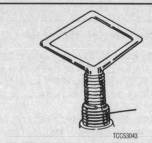

Fig. 188 Screw the insert onto the installer tool until the tang engages the slot. Thread the insert into the hole until it is ¼–½ turn below the top surface, then remove the tool and break off the tang using a punch

Engine Preparation

To properly rebuild an engine, you must first remove it from the vehicle, then disassemble and diagnose it. Ideally you should place your engine on an engine stand. This affords you the best access to the engine components. Follow the manufacturer's directions for using the stand with your particular engine. Remove the flywheel or flexplate before installing the engine to the stand.

Now that you have the engine on a stand, and assuming that you have drained the oil and coolant from the engine, it's time to strip it of all but the necessary components. Before you start disassembling the engine, you may want to take a moment to draw some pictures, or fabricate some labels or containers to mark the locations of various components and the bolts and/or studs which fasten them. Modern day engines use a lot of little brackets and clips which hold wiring harnesses and such, and these holders are often mounted on studs and/or bolts that can be easily mixed up. The manufacturer spent a lot of time and money designing your vehicle, and they wouldn't have wasted any of it by haphazardly placing brackets, clips or fasteners on the vehicle. If it's present when you disassemble it, put it back when you assemble, you will regret not remembering that little bracket which holds a wire harness out of the path of a rotating part.

You should begin by unbolting any accessories still attached to the engine, such as the water pump, power steering pump, alternator, etc. Then, unfasten any manifolds (intake or exhaust) which were not removed during the engine removal procedure. Finally, remove any covers remaining on the engine such as the rocker arm, front or timing cover and oil pan. Some front covers may require the vibration damper and/or crank pulley to be removed beforehand. The idea is to reduce the engine to the bare necessities (cylinder head(s), valve train, engine block, crankshaft, pistons and connecting rods), plus any other `in block' components such as oil pumps, balance shafts and auxiliary shafts.

Finally, remove the cylinder head(s) from the engine block and carefully place on a bench. Disassembly instructions for each component follow later in this section.

Cylinder Head

There are two basic types of cylinder heads used on today's automobiles: the Overhead Valve (OHV) and the Overhead Camshaft (OHC). The latter can also be broken down into two subgroups: the Single Overhead Camshaft (SOHC) and the Dual Overhead Camshaft (DOHC). Generally, if there is only a single camshaft on a head, it is just referred to as an OHC head. Also, an engine with an OHV cylinder head is also known as a pushrod engine.

Most cylinder heads these days are made of an aluminum alloy due to its light weight, durability and heat transfer qualities. However, cast iron was the material of choice in the past, and is still used on many vehicles today. Whether made from aluminum or iron, all cylinder heads have valves and seats. Some use two valves per cylinder, while the more hi-tech engines will utilize a multi-valve configuration using 3, 4 and even 5 valves per cylinder. When the valve contacts the seat, it does so on precision machined surfaces, which seals the combustion chamber. All cylinder heads have a valve guide for each valve. The guide centers the valve to the seat and allows it to move up and down within it. The clearance between the valve and guide can be critical. Too much clearance and the engine may consume oil, lose vacuum and/or damage the seat. Too

little, and the valve can stick in the guide causing the engine to run poorly if at all, and possibly causing severe damage. The last component all cylinder heads have are valve springs. The spring holds the valve against its seat. It also returns the valve to this position when the valve has been opened by the valve train or camshaft. The spring is fastened to the valve by a retainer and valve locks (sometimes called keepers). Aluminum heads will also have a valve spring shim to keep the spring from wearing away the aluminum.

An ideal method of rebuilding the cylinder head would involve replacing all of the valves, guides, seats, springs, etc. with new ones. However, depending on how the engine was maintained, often this is not necessary. A major cause of valve, guide and seat wear is an improperly tuned engine. An engine that is running too rich, will often wash the lubricating oil out of the guide with gasoline, causing it to wear rapidly. Conversely, an engine which is running too lean will place higher combustion temperatures on the valves and seats allowing them to wear or even burn. Springs fall victim to the driving habits of the individual. A driver who often runs the engine rpm to the redline will wear out or break the springs faster then one that stays well below it. Unfortunately, mileage takes it toll on all of the parts. Generally, the valves, guides, springs and seats in a cylinder head can be machined and re-used, saving you money. However, if a valve is burnt, it may be wise to replace all of the valves, since they were all operating in the same environment. The same goes for any other component on the cylinder head. Think of it as an insurance policy against future problems related to that component.

Unfortunately, the only way to find out which components need replacing, is to disassemble and carefully check each piece. After the cylinder head(s) are disassembled, thoroughly clean all of the components.

DISASSEMBLY

▶ **See Figures 189 and 190**

Whether it is a single or dual overhead camshaft cylinder head, the disassembly procedure is relatively unchanged. One aspect to pay attention to is careful labeling of the parts on the dual camshaft cylinder head. There will be an intake camshaft and followers as well as an exhaust camshaft and followers and they must be labeled as such. In some cases, the components are identical and could easily be installed incorrectly. DO NOT MIX THEM UP! Determining which is which is very simple; the intake camshaft and components are on the same side of the head as was the intake manifold. Conversely, the exhaust camshaft and components are on the same side of the head as was the exhaust manifold.

Rocker Arm Type Camshaft Followers

▶ **See Figures 191 thru 199**

Most cylinder heads with rocker arm-type camshaft followers are easily disassembled using a standard valve spring compressor. However, certain models may not have enough open space around the spring for the standard tool and may require you to use a C-clamp style compressor tool instead.

1. If not already removed, remove the rocker arms and/or shafts and the camshaft. If applicable, also remove the hydraulic lash adjusters. Mark their positions for assembly.
2. Position the cylinder head to allow access to the valve spring.

Fig. 189 Exploded view of a valve, seal, spring, retainer and locks from an OHC cylinder head

Fig. 190 Example of a multi-valve cylinder head. Note how it has 2 intake and 2 exhaust valve ports

Fig. 191 Example of the shaft mounted rocker arms on some OHC heads

Fig. 192 Another example of the rocker arm type OHC head. This model uses a follower under the camshaft

Fig. 193 Before the camshaft can be removed, all of the followers must first be removed . . .

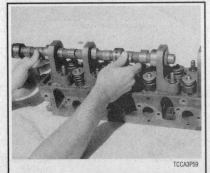
Fig. 194 . . . then the camshaft can be removed by sliding it out (shown), or unbolting a bearing cap (not shown)

Fig. 195 Compress the valve spring . . .

Fig. 196 . . . then remove the valve locks from the valve stem and spring retainer

Fig. 197 Remove the valve spring and retainer from the cylinder head

Fig. 198 Remove the valve seal from the guide. Some gentle prying or pliers may help to remove stubborn ones

Fig. 199 All aluminum and some cast iron heads will have these valve spring shims. Remove all of them as well

3. Use a valve spring compressor tool to relieve the spring tension from the retainer.

➡Due to engine varnish, the retainer may stick to the valve locks. A gentle tap with a hammer may help to break it loose.

4. Remove the valve locks from the valve tip and/or retainer. A small magnet may help in removing the small locks.
5. Lift the valve spring, tool and all, off of the valve stem.
6. If equipped, remove the valve seal. If the seal is difficult to remove with the valve in place, try removing the valve first, then the seal. Follow the steps below for valve removal.
7. Position the head to allow access for withdrawing the valve.

➡Cylinder heads that have seen a lot of miles and/or abuse may have mushroomed the valve lock grove and/or tip, causing difficulty in removal of the valve. If this has happened, use a metal file to carefully remove the high spots around the lock grooves and/or tip. Only file it enough to allow removal.

8. Remove the valve from the cylinder head.
9. If equipped, remove the valve spring shim. A small magnetic tool or screwdriver will aid in removal.
10. Repeat Steps 3 though 9 until all of the valves have been removed.

INSPECTION

Now that all of the cylinder head components are clean, it's time to inspect them for wear and/or damage. To accurately inspect them, you will need some specialized tools:
- A 0–1 in. micrometer for the valves
- A dial indicator or inside diameter gauge for the valve guides
- A spring pressure test gauge

If you do not have access to the proper tools, you may want to bring the components to a shop that does.

Valves

▶ See Figures 200 and 201

The first thing to inspect are the valve heads. Look closely at the head, margin and face for any cracks, excessive wear or burning. The margin is the best place to look for burning. It should have a squared edge with an even width all around the diameter. When a valve burns, the margin will look melted and the edges rounded. Also inspect the valve head for any signs of tulipping. This will show as a lifting of the edges or dishing in the center of the head and will usually not occur to all of the valves. All of the heads should look the same, any that seem dished more than others are probably bad. Next, inspect the valve lock grooves and valve tips. Check for any burrs around the lock grooves, especially if you had to file them to remove the valve. Valve tips should appear flat, although slight rounding with high mileage engines is normal. Slightly worn valve tips will need to be machined flat. Last, measure the valve stem diameter with the micrometer. Measure the area that rides within the guide, especially towards the tip where most of the wear occurs. Take several measurements along its length and compare them to each other. Wear should be even along the length with little to no taper. If no minimum diameter is given in the specifications, then the stem should not read more than 0.001 in. (0.025mm) below the specification. Any valves that fail these inspections should be replaced.

Springs, Retainers and Valve Locks

▶ See Figures 202 and 203

The first thing to check is the most obvious, broken springs. Next check the free length and squareness of each spring. If applicable, insure to distinguish between intake and exhaust springs. Use a ruler and/or carpenters square to measure the length. A carpenters square should be used to check the springs for squareness. If a spring pressure test gauge is available, check each springs rating and compare to the specifications chart. Check the readings against the specifications given. Any springs that fail these inspections should be replaced.

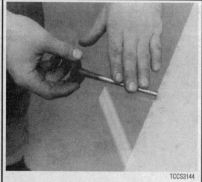

Fig. 200 Valve stems may be rolled on a flat surface to check for bends

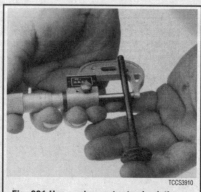

Fig. 201 Use a micrometer to check the valve stem diameter

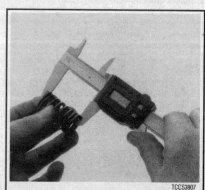

Fig. 202 Use a caliper to check the valve spring free-length

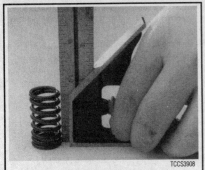

Fig. 203 Check the valve spring for squareness on a flat surface; a carpenter's square can be used

Fig. 204 A dial gauge may be used to check valve stem-to-guide clearance; read the gauge while moving the valve stem

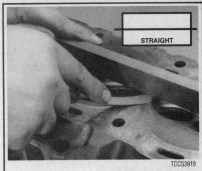

Fig. 205 Check the head for flatness across the center of the head surface using a straightedge and feeler gauge

The spring retainers rarely need replacing, however they should still be checked as a precaution. Inspect the spring mating surface and the valve lock retention area for any signs of excessive wear. Also check for any signs of cracking. Replace any retainers that are questionable.

Valve locks should be inspected for excessive wear on the outside contact area as well as on the inner notched surface. Any locks which appear worn or broken and its respective valve should be replaced.

Cylinder Head

There are several things to check on the cylinder head: valve guides, seats, cylinder head surface flatness, cracks and physical damage.

VALVE GUIDES

♦ See Figure 204

Now that you know the valves are good, you can use them to check the guides, although a new valve, if available, is preferred. Before you measure anything, look at the guides carefully and inspect them for any cracks, chips or breakage. Also if the guide is a removable style (as in most aluminum heads), check them for any looseness or evidence of movement. All of the guides should appear to be at the same height from the spring seat. If any seem lower (or higher) from another, the guide has moved. Mount a dial indicator onto the spring side of the cylinder head. Lightly oil the valve stem and insert it into the cylinder head. Position the dial indicator against the valve stem near the tip and zero the gauge. Grasp the valve stem and wiggle towards and away from the dial indicator and observe the readings. Mount the dial indicator 90 degrees from the initial point and zero the gauge and again take a reading. Compare the two readings for a out of round condition. Check the readings against the specifications given. An Inside Diameter (I.D.) gauge designed for valve guides will give you an accurate valve guide bore measurement. If the I.D. gauge is used, compare the readings with the specifications given. Any guides that fail these inspections should be replaced or machined.

VALVE SEATS

A visual inspection of the valve seats should show a slightly worn and pitted surface where the valve face contacts the seat. Inspect the seat carefully for severe pitting or cracks. Also, a seat that is badly worn will be recessed into the cylinder head. A severely worn or recessed seat may need to be replaced. All cracked seats must be replaced. A seat concentricity gauge, if available, should be used to check the seat run-out. If run-out exceeds specifications the seat must be machined (if no specification is given use 0.002 in. or 0.051mm).

CYLINDER HEAD SURFACE FLATNESS

♦ See Figures 205 and 206

After you have cleaned the gasket surface of the cylinder head of any old gasket material, check the head for flatness.

Place a straightedge across the gasket surface. Using feeler gauges, determine the clearance at the center of the straightedge and across the cylinder head at several points. Check along the centerline and diagonally on the head surface. If the warpage exceeds 0.003 in. (0.076mm) within a 6.0 in. (15.2cm) span, or 0.006 in. (0.152mm) over the total length of the head, the cylinder

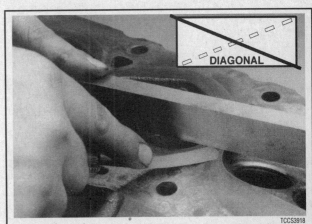

Fig. 206 Checks should also be made along both diagonals of the head surface

head must be resurfaced. After resurfacing the heads of a V-type engine, the intake manifold flange surface should be checked, and if necessary, milled proportionally to allow for the change in its mounting position.

CRACKS AND PHYSICAL DAMAGE

Generally, cracks are limited to the combustion chamber, however, it is not uncommon for the head to crack in a spark plug hole, port, outside of the head or in the valve spring/rocker arm area. The first area to inspect is always the hottest: the exhaust seat/port area.

A visual inspection should be performed, but just because you don't see a crack does not mean it is not there. Some more reliable methods for inspecting for cracks include Magnaflux®, a magnetic process or Zyglo®, a dye penetrant. Magnaflux® is used only on ferrous metal (cast iron) heads. Zyglo® uses a spray on fluorescent mixture along with a black light to reveal the cracks. It is strongly recommended to have your cylinder head checked professionally for cracks, especially if the engine was known to have overheated and/or leaked or consumed coolant. Contact a local shop for availability and pricing of these services.

Physical damage is usually very evident. For example, a broken mounting ear from dropping the head or a bent or broken stud and/or bolt. All of these defects should be fixed or, if unrepairable, the head should be replaced.

Camshaft and Followers

Inspect the camshaft(s) and followers as described earlier in this section.

REFINISHING & REPAIRING

Many of the procedures given for refinishing and repairing the cylinder head components must be performed by a machine shop. Certain steps, if the inspected part is not worn, can be performed yourself inexpensively. However, you spent a lot of time and effort so far, why risk trying to save a couple bucks if you might have to do it all over again?

Valves

Any valves that were not replaced should be refaced and the tips ground flat. Unless you have access to a valve grinding machine, this should be done by a machine shop. If the valves are in extremely good condition, as well as the valve seats and guides, they may be lapped in without performing machine work.

It is a recommended practice to lap the valves even after machine work has been performed and/or new valves have been purchased. This insures a positive seal between the valve and seat.

LAPPING THE VALVES

➡Before lapping the valves to the seats, read the rest of the cylinder head section to insure that any related parts are in acceptable enough condition to continue.

➡Before any valve seat machining and/or lapping can be performed, the guides must be within factory recommended specifications.

1. Invert the cylinder head.
2. Lightly lubricate the valve stems and insert them into the cylinder head in their numbered order.
3. Raise the valve from the seat and apply a small amount of fine lapping compound to the seat.
4. Moisten the suction head of a hand-lapping tool and attach it to the head of the valve.
5. Rotate the tool between the palms of both hands, changing the position of the valve on the valve seat and lifting the tool often to prevent grooving.
6. Lap the valve until a smooth, polished circle is evident on the valve and seat.
7. Remove the tool and the valve. Wipe away all traces of the grinding compound and store the valve to maintain its lapped location.

✳✳ WARNING

Do not get the valves out of order after they have been lapped. They must be put back with the same valve seat with which they were lapped.

Springs, Retainers and Valve Locks

There is no repair or refinishing possible with the springs, retainers and valve locks. If they are found to be worn or defective, they must be replaced with new (or known good) parts.

Cylinder Head

Most refinishing procedures dealing with the cylinder head must be performed by a machine shop. Read the sections below and review your inspection data to determine whether or not machining is necessary.

VALVE GUIDES

➡If any machining or replacements are made to the valve guides, the seats must be machined.

Unless the valve guides need machining or replacing, the only service to perform is to thoroughly clean them of any dirt or oil residue.

There are only two types of valve guides used on automobile engines: the replaceable-type (all aluminum heads) and the cast-in integral-type (most cast iron heads). There are four recommended methods for repairing worn guides.
- Knurling
- Inserts
- Reaming oversize
- Replacing

Knurling is a process in which metal is displaced and raised, thereby reducing clearance, giving a true center, and providing oil control. It is the least expensive way of repairing the valve guides. However, it is not necessarily the best, and in some cases, a knurled valve guide will not stand up for more than a short time. It requires a special knurlizer and precision reaming tools to obtain proper clearances. It would not be cost effective to purchase these tools, unless you plan on rebuilding several of the same cylinder head.

Installing a guide insert involves machining the guide to accept a bronze insert. One style is the coil-type which is installed into a threaded guide. Another is the thin-walled insert where the guide is reamed oversize to accept a split-sleeve insert. After the insert is installed, a special tool is then run through the guide to expand the insert, locking it to the guide. The insert is then reamed to the standard size for proper valve clearance.

Reaming for oversize valves restores normal clearances and provides a true valve seat. Most cast-in type guides can be reamed to accept an valve with an oversize stem. The cost factor for this can become quite high as you will need to purchase the reamer and new, oversize stem valves for all guides which were reamed. Oversizes are generally 0.003 to 0.030 in. (0.076 to 0.762mm), with 0.015 in. (0.381mm) being the most common.

To replace cast-in type valve guides, they must be drilled out, then reamed to accept replacement guides. This must be done on a fixture which will allow centering and leveling off of the original valve seat or guide, otherwise a serious guide-to-seat misalignment may occur making it impossible to properly machine the seat.

Replaceable-type guides are pressed into the cylinder head. A hammer and a stepped drift or punch may be used to install and remove the guides. Before removing the guides, measure the protrusion on the spring side of the head and record it for installation. Use the stepped drift to hammer out the old guide from the combustion chamber side of the head. When installing, determine whether or not the guide also seals a water jacket in the head, and if it does, use the recommended sealing agent. If there is no water jacket, grease the valve guide and its bore. Use the stepped drift, and hammer the new guide into the cylinder head from the spring side of the cylinder head. A stack of washers the same thickness as the measured protrusion may help the installation process.

VALVE SEATS

➡Before any valve seat machining can be performed, the guides must be within factory recommended specifications.

➡If any machining or replacements were made to the valve guides, the seats must be machined.

If the seats are in good condition, the valves can be lapped to the seats, and the cylinder head assembled. See the valves section for instructions on lapping.

If the valve seats are worn, cracked or damaged, they must be serviced by a machine shop. The valve seat must be perfectly centered to the valve guide, which requires very accurate machining.

CYLINDER HEAD SURFACE

If the cylinder head is warped, it must be machined flat. If the warpage is extremely severe, the head may need to be replaced. In some instances, it may be possible to straighten a warped head enough to allow machining. In either case, contact a professional machine shop for service.

➡Any OHC cylinder head that shows excessive warpage should have the camshaft bearing journals align bored after the cylinder head has been resurfaced.

✳✳ WARNING

Failure to align bore the camshaft bearing journals could result in severe engine damage including but not limited to: valve and piston damage, connecting rod damage, camshaft and/or crankshaft breakage.

CRACKS AND PHYSICAL DAMAGE

Certain cracks can be repaired in both cast iron and aluminum heads. For cast iron, a tapered threaded insert is installed along the length of the crack. Aluminum can also use the tapered inserts, however welding is the preferred method. Some physical damage can be repaired through brazing or welding. Contact a machine shop to get expert advice for your particular dilemma.

ASSEMBLY

The first step for any assembly job is to have a clean area in which to work. Next, thoroughly clean all of the parts and components that are to be assembled. Finally, place all of the components onto a suitable work space and, if necessary, arrange the parts to their respective positions.

1. Lightly lubricate the valve stems and insert all of the valves into the cylinder head. If possible, maintain their original locations.
2. If equipped, install any valve spring shims which were removed.

3. If equipped, install the new valve seals, keeping the following in mind:
  • If the valve seal presses over the guide, lightly lubricate the outer guide surfaces.
  • If the seal is an O-ring type, it is installed just after compressing the spring but before the valve locks.

4. Place the valve spring and retainer over the stem.

5. Position the spring compressor tool and compress the spring.

6. Assemble the valve locks to the stem.

7. Relieve the spring pressure slowly and insure that neither valve lock becomes dislodged by the retainer.

8. Remove the spring compressor tool.

9. Repeat Steps 2 through 8 until all of the springs have been installed.

10. Install the camshaft(s), rockers, shafts and any other components that were removed for disassembly.

Engine Block

GENERAL INFORMATION

A thorough overhaul or rebuild of an engine block would include replacing the pistons, rings, bearings, timing belt/chain assembly and oil pump. For OHV engines also include a new camshaft and lifters. The block would then have the cylinders bored and honed oversize (or if using removable cylinder sleeves, new sleeves installed) and the crankshaft would be cut undersize to provide new wearing surfaces and perfect clearances. However, your particular engine may not have everything worn out. What if only the piston rings have worn out and the clearances on everything else are still within factory specifications? Well, you could just replace the rings and put it back together, but this would be a very rare example. Chances are, if one component in your engine is worn, other components are sure to follow, and soon. At the very least, you should always replace the rings, bearings and oil pump. This is what is commonly called a "freshen up".

Cylinder Ridge Removal

Because the top piston ring does not travel to the very top of the cylinder, a ridge is built up between the end of the travel and the top of the cylinder bore.

Pushing the piston and connecting rod assembly past the ridge can be difficult, and damage to the piston ring lands could occur. If the ridge is not removed before installing a new piston or not removed at all, piston ring breakage and piston damage may occur.

➡**It is always recommended that you remove any cylinder ridges before removing the piston and connecting rod assemblies. If you know that new pistons are going to be installed and the engine block will be bored oversize, you may be able to forego this step. However, some ridges may actually prevent the assemblies from being removed, necessitating its removal.**

There are several different types of ridge reamers on the market, none of which are inexpensive. Unless a great deal of engine rebuilding is anticipated, borrow or rent a reamer.

1. Turn the crankshaft until the piston is at the bottom of its travel.

2. Cover the head of the piston with a rag.

3. Follow the tool manufacturers instructions and cut away the ridge, exercising extreme care to avoid cutting too deeply.

4. Remove the ridge reamer, the rag and as many of the cuttings as possible. Continue until all of the cylinder ridges have been removed.

DISASSEMBLY

♦ **See Figures 207 and 208**

The engine disassembly instructions following assume that you have the engine mounted on an engine stand. If not, it is easiest to disassemble the engine on a bench or the floor with it resting on the bellhousing or transaxle mounting surface. You must be able to access the connecting rod fasteners and turn the crankshaft during disassembly. Also, all engine covers (timing, front, side, oil pan, whatever) should have already been removed. Engines which are seized or locked up may not be able to be completely disassembled, and a core (salvage yard) engine should be purchased.

If not done during the cylinder head removal, remove the timing belt and/or gear/sprocket assembly. Remove the oil pick-up and pump assembly and, if necessary, the pump drive. If equipped, remove any balance or auxiliary shafts. If necessary, remove the cylinder ridge from the top of the bore. See the cylinder ridge removal procedure earlier in this section.

Rotate the engine over so that the crankshaft is exposed. Use a number punch or scribe and mark each connecting rod with its respective cylinder number. The cylinder closest to the front of the engine is always number 1. However, depending on the engine placement, the front of the engine could either be the flywheel or damper/pulley end. Generally the front of the engine faces the front of the vehicle. Use a number punch or scribe and also mark the main bearing caps from front to rear with the front most cap being number 1 (if there are five caps, mark them 1 through 5, front to rear).

TCCS3803

Fig. 207 Place rubber hose over the connecting rod studs to protect the crankshaft and cylinder bores from damage

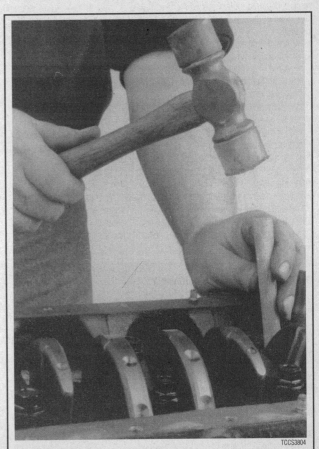

TCCS3804

Fig. 208 Carefully tap the piston out of the bore using a wooden dowel

✳✳ WARNING

Take special care when pushing the connecting rod up from the crankshaft because the sharp threads of the rod bolts/studs will score the crankshaft journal. Insure that special plastic caps are installed over them, or cut two pieces of rubber hose to do the same.

Again, rotate the engine, this time to position the number one cylinder bore (head surface) up. Turn the crankshaft until the number one piston is at the bottom of its travel, this should allow the maximum access to its connecting rod. Remove the number one connecting rods fasteners and cap and place two lengths of rubber hose over the rod bolts/studs to protect the crankshaft from damage. Using a sturdy wooden dowel and a hammer, push the connecting rod up about 1 in. (25mm) from the crankshaft and remove the upper bearing insert. Continue pushing or tapping the connecting rod up until the piston rings are out of the cylinder bore. Remove the piston and rod by hand, put the upper half of the bearing insert back into the rod, install the cap with its bearing insert installed, and hand-tighten the cap fasteners. If the parts are kept in order in this manner, they will not get lost and you will be able to tell which bearings came form what cylinder if any problems are discovered and diagnosis is necessary. Remove all the other piston assemblies in the same manner. On V-style engines, remove all of the pistons from one bank, then reposition the engine with the other cylinder bank head surface up, and remove that banks piston assemblies.

The only remaining component in the engine block should now be the crankshaft. Loosen the main bearing caps evenly until the fasteners can be turned by hand, then remove them and the caps. Remove the crankshaft from the engine block. Thoroughly clean all of the components.

INSPECTION

Now that the engine block and all of its components are clean, it's time to inspect them for wear and/or damage. To accurately inspect them, you will need some specialized tools:

- Two or three separate micrometers to measure the pistons and crankshaft journals
- A dial indicator
- Telescoping gauges for the cylinder bores
- A rod alignment fixture to check for bent connecting rods

If you do not have access to the proper tools, you may want to bring the components to a shop that does.

Generally, you shouldn't expect cracks in the engine block or its components unless it was known to leak, consume or mix engine fluids, it was severely overheated, or there was evidence of bad bearings and/or crankshaft damage. A visual inspection should be performed on all of the components, but just because you don't see a crack does not mean it is not there. Some more reliable methods for inspecting for cracks include Magnaflux®, a magnetic process or Zyglo®, a dye penetrant. Magnaflux® is used only on ferrous metal (cast iron). Zyglo® uses a spray on fluorescent mixture along with a black light to reveal the cracks. It is strongly recommended to have your engine block checked professionally for cracks, especially if the engine was known to have overheated and/or leaked or consumed coolant. Contact a local shop for availability and pricing of these services.

Engine Block

ENGINE BLOCK BEARING ALIGNMENT

Remove the main bearing caps and, if still installed, the main bearing inserts. Inspect all of the main bearing saddles and caps for damage, burrs or high spots. If damage is found, and it is caused from a spun main bearing, the block will need to be align-bored or, if severe enough, replacement. Any burrs or high spots should be carefully removed with a metal file.

Place a straightedge on the bearing saddles, in the engine block, along the centerline of the crankshaft. If any clearance exists between the straightedge and the saddles, the block must be align-bored.

Align-boring consists of machining the main bearing saddles and caps by means of a flycutter that runs through the bearing saddles.

DECK FLATNESS

The top of the engine block where the cylinder head mounts is called the deck. Insure that the deck surface is clean of dirt, carbon deposits and old gasket material. Place a straightedge across the surface of the deck along its center-line and, using feeler gauges, check the clearance along several points. Repeat the checking procedure with the straightedge placed along both diagonals of the deck surface. If the reading exceeds 0.003 in. (0.076mm) within a 6.0 in. (15.2cm) span, or 0.006 in. (0.152mm) over the total length of the deck, it must be machined.

CYLINDER BORES

◆ See Figure 209

The cylinder bores house the pistons and are slightly larger than the pistons themselves. A common piston-to-bore clearance is 0.0015–0.0025 in. (0.0381mm–0.0635mm). Inspect and measure the cylinder bores. The bore should be checked for out-of-roundness, taper and size. The results of this inspection will determine whether the cylinder can be used in its existing size and condition, or a rebore to the next oversize is required (or in the case of removable sleeves, have replacements installed).

The amount of cylinder wall wear is always greater at the top of the cylinder than at the bottom. This wear is known as taper. Any cylinder that has a taper of 0.0012 in. (0.305mm) or more, must be rebored. Measurements are taken at a number of positions in each cylinder: at the top, middle and bottom and at two points at each position; that is, at a point 90 degrees from the crankshaft centerline, as well as a point parallel to the crankshaft centerline. The measurements are made with either a special dial indicator or a telescopic gauge and micrometer. If the necessary precision tools to check the bore are not available, take the block to a machine shop and have them mike it. Also if you don't have the tools to check the cylinder bores, chances are you will not have the necessary devices to check the pistons, connecting rods and crankshaft. Take these components with you and save yourself an extra trip.

For our procedures, we will use a telescopic gauge and a micrometer. You will need one of each, with a measuring range which covers your cylinder bore size.

1. Position the telescopic gauge in the cylinder bore, loosen the gauges lock and allow it to expand.

➡ **Your first two readings will be at the top of the cylinder bore, then proceed to the middle and finally the bottom, making a total of six measurements.**

2. Hold the gauge square in the bore, 90 degrees from the crankshaft centerline, and gently tighten the lock. Tilt the gauge back to remove it from the bore.
3. Measure the gauge with the micrometer and record the reading.
4. Again, hold the gauge square in the bore, this time parallel to the crankshaft centerline, and gently tighten the lock. Again, you will tilt the gauge back to remove it from the bore.
5. Measure the gauge with the micrometer and record this reading. The difference between these two readings is the out-of-round measurement of the cylinder.
6. Repeat steps 1 through 5, each time going to the next lower position, until you reach the bottom of the cylinder. Then go to the next cylinder, and continue until all of the cylinders have been measured.

The difference between these measurements will tell you all about the wear in your cylinders. The measurements which were taken 90 degrees from the crankshaft centerline will always reflect the most wear. That is because at this position is where the engine power presses the piston against the cylinder bore the hard-

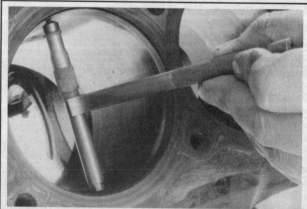

TCCS3209

Fig. 209 Use a telescoping gauge to measure the cylinder bore diameter—take several readings within the same bore

est. This is known as thrust wear. Take your top, 90 degree measurement and compare it to your bottom, 90 degree measurement. The difference between them is the taper. When you measure your pistons, you will compare these readings to your piston sizes and determine piston-to-wall clearance.

Crankshaft

Inspect the crankshaft for visible signs of wear or damage. All of the journals should be perfectly round and smooth. Slight scores are normal for a used crankshaft, but you should hardly feel them with your fingernail. When measuring the crankshaft with a micrometer, you will take readings at the front and rear of each journal, then turn the micrometer 90 degrees and take two more readings, front and rear. The difference between the front-to-rear readings is the journal taper and the first-to-90 degree reading is the out-of-round measurement. Generally, there should be no taper or out-of-roundness found, however, up to 0.0005 in. (0.0127mm) for either can be overlooked. Also, the readings should fall within the factory specifications for journal diameters.

If the crankshaft journals fall within specifications, it is recommended that it be polished before being returned to service. Polishing the crankshaft insures that any minor burrs or high spots are smoothed, thereby reducing the chance of scoring the new bearings.

Pistons and Connecting Rods

PISTONS

♦ See Figure 210

The piston should be visually inspected for any signs of cracking or burning (caused by hot spots or detonation), and scuffing or excessive wear on the skirts. The wristpin attaches the piston to the connecting rod. The piston should move freely on the wrist pin, both sliding and pivoting. Grasp the connecting rod securely, or mount it in a vise, and try to rock the piston back and forth along the centerline of the wristpin. There should not be any excessive play evident between the piston and the pin. If there are C-clips retaining the pin in the piston then you have wrist pin bushings in the rods. There should not be any excessive play between the wrist pin and the rod bushing. Normal clearance for the wrist pin is approx. 0.001–0.002 in. (0.025mm–0.051mm).

Use a micrometer and measure the diameter of the piston, perpendicular to the wrist pin, on the skirt. Compare the reading to its original cylinder measurement obtained earlier. The difference between the two readings is the piston-to-wall clearance. If the clearance is within specifications, the piston may be used as is. If the piston is out of specification, but the bore is not, you will need a new piston. If both are out of specification, you will need the cylinder rebored and oversize pistons installed. Generally if two or more pistons/bores are out of specification, it is best to rebore the entire block and purchase a complete set of oversize pistons.

CONNECTING ROD

You should have the connecting rod checked for straightness at a machine shop. If the connecting rod is bent, it will unevenly wear the bearing and piston, as well as place greater stress on these components. Any bent or twisted connecting rods must be replaced. If the rods are straight and the wrist pin clearance is within specifications, then only the bearing end of the rod need be checked. Place the connecting rod into a vice, with the bearing inserts in place,

install the cap to the rod and tighten the fasteners to specifications. Use a telescoping gauge and carefully measure the inside diameter of the bearings. Compare this reading to the rods original crankshaft journal diameter measurement. The difference is the oil clearance. If the oil clearance is not within specifications, install new bearings in the rod and take another measurement. If the clearance is still out of specifications, and the crankshaft is not, the rod will need to be reconditioned by a machine shop.

➡**You can also use Plastigage® to check the bearing clearances. The assembling section has complete instructions on its use.**

Camshaft

Inspect the camshaft and lifters/followers as described earlier in this section.

Bearings

All of the engine bearings should be visually inspected for wear and/or damage. The bearing should look evenly worn all around with no deep scores or pits. If the bearing is severely worn, scored, pitted or heat blued, then the bearing, and the components that use it, should be brought to a machine shop for inspection. Full-circle bearings (used on most camshafts, auxiliary shafts, balance shafts, etc.) require specialized tools for removal and installation, and should be brought to a machine shop for service.

Oil Pump

➡**The oil pump is responsible for providing constant lubrication to the whole engine and so it is recommended that a new oil pump be installed when rebuilding the engine.**

Completely disassemble the oil pump and thoroughly clean all of the components. Inspect the oil pump gears and housing for wear and/or damage. Insure that the pressure relief valve operates properly and there is no binding or sticking due to varnish or debris. If all of the parts are in proper working condition, lubricate the gears and relief valve, and assemble the pump.

REFINISHING

♦ See Figure 211

Almost all engine block refinishing must be performed by a machine shop. If the cylinders are not to be rebored, then the cylinder glaze can be removed with a ball hone. When removing cylinder glaze with a ball hone, use a light or penetrating type oil to lubricate the hone. Do not allow the hone to run dry as this may cause excessive scoring of the cylinder bores and wear on the hone. If new pistons are required, they will need to be installed to the connecting rods. This should be performed by a machine shop as the pistons must be installed in the correct relationship to the rod or engine damage can occur.

Pistons and Connecting Rods

♦ See Figure 212

Only pistons with the wrist pin retained by C-clips are serviceable by the home-mechanic. Press fit pistons require special presses and/or heaters to

Fig. 210 Measure the piston's outer diameter, perpendicular to the wrist pin, with a micrometer

Fig. 211 Use a ball type cylinder hone to remove any glaze and provide a new surface for seating the piston rings

Fig. 212 Most pistons are marked to indicate positioning in the engine (usually a mark means the side facing the front)

remove/install the connecting rod and should only be performed by a machine shop.

All pistons will have a mark indicating the direction to the front of the engine and the must be installed into the engine in that manner. Usually it is a notch or arrow on the top of the piston, or it may be the letter F cast or stamped into the piston.

ASSEMBLY

Before you begin assembling the engine, first give yourself a clean, dirt free work area. Next, clean every engine component again. The key to a good assembly is cleanliness.

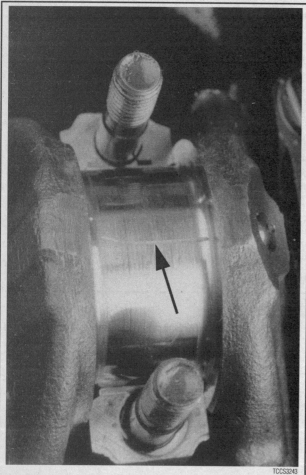

TCCS3243

Fig. 213 Apply a strip of gauging material to the bearing journal, then install and tighten the cap

Mount the engine block into the engine stand and wash it one last time using water and detergent (dishwashing detergent works well). While washing it, scrub the cylinder bores with a soft bristle brush and thoroughly clean all of the oil passages. Completely dry the engine and spray the entire assembly down with an anti-rust solution such as WD-40® or similar product. Take a clean lint-free rag and wipe up any excess anti-rust solution from the bores, bearing saddles, etc. Repeat the final cleaning process on the crankshaft. Replace any freeze or oil galley plugs which were removed during disassembly.

Crankshaft

◆ See Figures 213, 214, 215 and 216

1. Remove the main bearing inserts from the block and bearing caps.
2. If the crankshaft main bearing journals have been refinished to a definite undersize, install the correct undersize bearing. Be sure that the bearing inserts and bearing bores are clean. Foreign material under inserts will distort bearing and cause failure.
3. Place the upper main bearing inserts in bores with tang in slot.

➡**The oil holes in the bearing inserts must be aligned with the oil holes in the cylinder block.**

4. Install the lower main bearing inserts in bearing caps.
5. Clean the mating surfaces of block and rear main bearing cap.
6. Carefully lower the crankshaft into place. Be careful not to damage bearing surfaces.
7. Check the clearance of each main bearing by using the following procedure:

   a. Place a piece of Plastigage® or its equivalent, on bearing surface across full width of bearing cap and about ¼ in. off center.

   b. Install cap and tighten bolts to specifications. Do not turn crankshaft while Plastigage® is in place.

   c. Remove the cap. Using the supplied Plastigage® scale, check width of Plastigage® at widest point to get maximum clearance. Difference between readings is taper of journal.

   d. If clearance exceeds specified limits, try a 0.001 in. or 0.002 in. undersize bearing in combination with the standard bearing. Bearing clearance must be within specified limits. If standard and 0.002 in. undersize bearing does not bring clearance within desired limits, refinish crankshaft journal, then install undersize bearings.

8. After the bearings have been fitted, apply a light coat of engine oil to the journals and bearings. Install the rear main bearing cap. Install all bearing caps except the thrust bearing cap. Be sure that main bearing caps are installed in original locations. Tighten the bearing cap bolts to specifications.

9. Install the thrust bearing cap with bolts finger-tight.

10. Pry the crankshaft forward against the thrust surface of upper half of bearing.

11. Hold the crankshaft forward and pry the thrust bearing cap to the rear. This aligns the thrust surfaces of both halves of the bearing.

12. Retain the forward pressure on the crankshaft. Tighten the cap bolts to specifications.

13. Measure the crankshaft end-play as follows:

   a. Mount a dial gauge to the engine block and position the tip of the gauge to read from the crankshaft end.

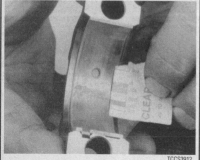

TCCS3912

Fig. 214 After the cap is removed again, use the scale supplied with the gauging material to check the clearance

TCCS3805

Fig. 215 A dial gauge may be used to check crankshaft end-play

TCCS3806

Fig. 216 Carefully pry the crankshaft back and forth while reading the dial gauge for end-play

b. Carefully pry the crankshaft toward the rear of the engine and hold it there while you zero the gauge.

c. Carefully pry the crankshaft toward the front of the engine and read the gauge.

d. Confirm that the reading is within specifications. If not, install a new thrust bearing and repeat the procedure. If the reading is still out of specifications with a new bearing, have a machine shop inspect the thrust surfaces of the crankshaft, and if possible, repair it.

14. Rotate the crankshaft so as to position the first rod journal to the bottom of its stroke.

15. Install the rear main seal.

Pistons and Connecting Rods

▶ See Figures 217, 218, 219 and 220

1. Before installing the piston/connecting rod assembly, oil the pistons, piston rings and the cylinder walls with light engine oil. Install connecting rod bolt protectors or rubber hose onto the connecting rod bolts/studs. Also perform the following:

a. Select the proper ring set for the size cylinder bore.

b. Position the ring in the bore in which it is going to be used.

c. Push the ring down into the bore area where normal ring wear is not encountered.

d. Use the head of the piston to position the ring in the bore so that the ring is square with the cylinder wall. Use caution to avoid damage to the ring or cylinder bore.

e. Measure the gap between the ends of the ring with a feeler gauge. Ring gap in a worn cylinder is normally greater than specification. If the ring gap is greater than the specified limits, try an oversize ring set.

f. Check the ring side clearance of the compression rings with a feeler gauge inserted between the ring and its lower land according to specification. The gauge should slide freely around the entire ring circumference without binding. Any wear that occurs will form a step at the inner portion of the lower land. If the lower lands have high steps, the piston should be replaced.

2. Unless new pistons are installed, be sure to install the pistons in the

cylinders from which they were removed. The numbers on the connecting rod and bearing cap must be on the same side when installed in the cylinder bore. If a connecting rod is ever transposed from one engine or cylinder to another, new bearings should be fitted and the connecting rod should be numbered to correspond with the new cylinder number. The notch on the piston head goes toward the front of the engine.

3. Install all of the rod bearing inserts into the rods and caps.

4. Install the rings to the pistons. Install the oil control ring first, then the second compression ring and finally the top compression ring. Use a piston ring expander tool to aid in installation and to help reduce the chance of breakage.

5. Make sure the ring gaps are properly spaced around the circumference of the piston. Fit a piston ring compressor around the piston and slide the piston and connecting rod assembly down into the cylinder bore, pushing it in with the wooden hammer handle. Push the piston down until it is only slightly below the top of the cylinder bore. Guide the connecting rod onto the crankshaft bearing journal carefully, to avoid damaging the crankshaft.

6. Check the bearing clearance of all the rod bearings, fitting them to the crankshaft bearing journals. Follow the procedure in the crankshaft installation above.

7. After the bearings have been fitted, apply a light coating of assembly oil to the journals and bearings.

8. Turn the crankshaft until the appropriate bearing journal is at the bottom of its stroke, then push the piston assembly all the way down until the connecting rod bearing seats on the crankshaft journal. Be careful not to allow the bearing cap screws to strike the crankshaft bearing journals and damage them.

9. After the piston and connecting rod assemblies have been installed, check the connecting rod side clearance on each crankshaft journal.

10. Prime and install the oil pump and the oil pump intake tube.

Cylinder Head(s)

1. Install the cylinder head(s) using new gaskets.
2. Install the timing sprockets/gears and the belt/chain assemblies.

Engine Covers and Components

1. If equipped, install the auxiliary/balance shaft assembly.
2. Install the timing cover(s) and oil pan. Refer to your notes and drawings made prior to disassembly and install all of the components that were removed. Install the engine into the vehicle.

Engine Start-up and Break-in

STARTING THE ENGINE

Now that the engine is installed and every wire and hose is properly connected, go back and double check that all coolant and vacuum hoses are connected. Check that you oil drain plug is installed and properly tightened. If not already done, install a new oil filter onto the engine. Fill the crankcase with the proper amount and grade of engine oil. Fill the cooling system with a 50/50 mixture of coolant/water.

Fig. 217 Checking the piston ring-to-ring groove side clearance using the ring and a feeler gauge

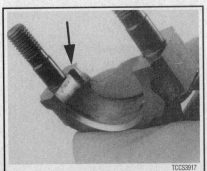
Fig. 218 The notch on the side of the bearing cap matches the tang on the bearing insert

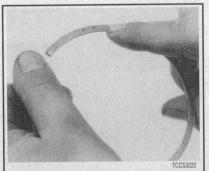
Fig. 219 Most rings are marked to show which side of the ring should face up when installed to the piston

Fig. 220 Install the piston and rod assembly into the block using a ring compressor and the handle of a hammer

1. Connect the vehicle battery.
2. Start the engine. Keep your eye on your oil pressure indicator; if it does not indicate oil pressure within 10 seconds of starting, turn the vehicle off.

✳✳ WARNING

Damage to the engine can result if it is allowed to run with no oil pressure. Check the engine oil level to make sure that it is full. Check for any leaks and if found, repair the leaks before continuing. If there is still no indication of oil pressure, you may need to prime the system.

3. Confirm that there are no fluid leaks (oil or other).
4. Allow the engine to reach normal operating temperature (the upper radiator hose will be hot to the touch).
5. If necessary, set the ignition timing.
6. Install any remaining components such as the air cleaner (if removed for ignition timing) or body panels which were removed.

BREAKING IT IN

Make the first miles on the new engine, easy ones. Vary the speed but do not accelerate hard. Most importantly, do not lug the engine, and avoid sustained high speeds until at least 100 miles. Check the engine oil and coolant levels frequently. Expect the engine to use a little oil until the rings seat. Change the oil and filter at 500 miles, 1500 miles, then every 3000 miles past that.

KEEP IT MAINTAINED

Now that you have just gone through all of that hard work, keep yourself from doing it all over again by thoroughly maintaining it. Not that you may not have maintained it before, heck you could have had one to two hundred thousand miles on it before doing this. However, you may have bought the vehicle used, and the previous owner did not keep up on maintenance. Which is why you just went through all of that hard work. See?

1.8L (B18B1) ENGINE MECHANICAL SPECIFICATIONS

Description	English	Metric
General information		
Engine type	Double Overhead Camshaft (DOHC) in-line 4 cylinder	
Compression ratio	9.2:1	
Firing order	1-3-4-2	
Displacement	112 cid	1.8L
Bore	3.19 in.	81.0mm
Stroke	3.50 in.	89.0mm
Cylinder Head		
Compression	199 psi	1,370kPa
Minimum	140 psi	930kPa
Maximum deviation	28.0 psi	200kPa
Warpage	0.002 in.	0.05mm
Height	5.195-5.199 in.	131.95-132.05mm
Camshaft		
End-play	0.002-0.006 in.	0.050-0.150mm
Camshaft to holder clearance	0.0012-0.0027 in.	0.030-0.069mm
Run-out	0.001 in.	0.030mm
Camshaft lobe height		
Intake	1.3274 in.	33.716mm
Exhaust	1.32 in.	33.528mm
Valve and Valve Seats		
Valve clearance (cold)		
Intake	0-003-0.005 in.	0.08-0.12mm
Exhaust	0-006-0.008 in.	0.16-0.20mm
Valve stem		
Outer diameter		
Intake	0-2591-0.2594 in.	6.580-6.590mm
Exhaust	0-2579-0.2583 in.	6.550-6.560mm
Valve stem-to-guide clearance		
Intake	0.001-0.002 in.	0.02-0.05mm
Exhaust	0-002-0.003 in.	0.05-0.08mm
Valve seat width		
Intake	0.049-0.061 in.	1.25-1.55mm
Exhaust	0.049-0.061 in.	1.25-1.55mm
Valve stem installed height		
Intake	1.6049-1.6234 in.	40.765-41.235mm
Exhaust	1.6837-1.7022 in.	42.765-43.235mm
Valve Spring and Guide		
Valve spring free length		
Intake	1.668 in.	42.36mm
Exhaust	1.854 in.	47.09mm
Valve guide		
Inner dimension		
Intake	0.260-0.261 in.	6.61-6.63mm
Exhaust	0.260-0.261 in.	6.61-6.63mm
Valve guide installed height		
Intake	0.541-0.561 in.	13.75-14.25mm
Exhaust	0.620-0.640 in.	15.75-16.25mm

90943C01

1.8L (B18B1) ENGINE MECHANICAL SPECIFICATIONS

Description	English	Metric
Engine Block		
Deck surface warpage	0.003 in. (max.)	0.07mm (max.)
Cylinder bore diameter	3.189-3.190 in.	81.00-81.02mm
Cylinder bore taper	NA	0.05mm
Cylinder re-boring limit	NA	0.25mm
Piston, Ring and Pin		
Piston ring-to-groove clearance		
Top	0.0018-0.0028 in.	0.045-0.070mm
2nd		
Riken	0.0016-0.0026 in.	0.040-0.065mm
Teikoku	0.0018-0.0028 in.	0.045-0.070mm
Piston ring end gap		
Top		
Riken	0.008-0.014 in.	0.20-0.35mm
Teikoku	0.008-0.012 in.	0.20-0.30mm
2nd	0.016-0.022 in.	0.40-0.55mm
Oil		
Riken	0.008-0.020 in.	0.20-0.50mm
Teikoku	0.008-0.018 in.	0.20-0.45mm
Ring groove width		
Top	0.0406-0.0409 in.	1.030-1.040mm
2nd	0.0484-0.0488 in.	1.230-1.240mm
Oil	0.1104-0.1110 in.	2.805-2.820mm
Piston-to-cylinder wall clearance	0.0004-0.0016 in.	0.010-0.040mm
Piston skirt outer diameter measured 15mm from the bottom of the skirt	3.188-3.189 in.	80.98-80.99mm
Piston pin		
Outer diameter	0.8265-0.8268 in.	20.994-21.00mm
Pin-to-piston clearance	0.0004-0.0009 in.	0.010-0.022mm
Connecting Rod		
End-play		
Installed on the crankshaft	0.008-0.018 in.	0.20-0.45mm
Bore diameter		
Crankshaft end	0.8265-0.8268 in.	20.994-21.000mm
Piston pin end	0.0004-0.0009 in.	0.010-0.022mm
Pin-to-rod clearance	0.0005-0.0013 in.	0.013-0.032mm
Crankshaft		
Main journal diameter		
No. 1, 2, 4, 5 journals	2.1644-2.1654 in.	54.976-55.00mm
No. 3 journal	2.1642-2.1651 in.	54.970-54.994mm
Connecting rod journal diameter	1.7707-1.7717 in.	44.976-45.00mm
Taper	0.0002 in. (max.)	0.005mm (max.)
Out-of-round	0.0002 in. (max.)	0.005mm (max.)
End-play	0.004-0.014 in.	0.100-0.350mm
Run-out	0.001 in. (max.)	0.030mm (max.)
Bearing		
Main bearing to journal oil clearance		
No. 1, 2, 4, 5 journals	0.0009-0.0017 in.	0.024-0.042mm
No. 3 journal	0.0012-0.0019 in.	0.030-0.048mm
Rod bearing-to-journal oil clearance	0.0008-0.0015 in.	0.020-0.038mm

NA: Not Available

90943C02

1.8L (B18C1) ENGINE MECHANICAL SPECIFICATIONS

Description	English	Metric
General Information		
Engine type	Double Overhead Camshaft (DOHC) in-line 4 cylinder	
Compression ratio	10.0:1	
Firing order	1-3-4-2	
Displacement	110 cid	1.797L
Bore	3.19 in.	81.0mm
Stroke	3.43 in.	87.2mm
Cylinder Head		
Compression	270 psi	1,860 kPa
Minimum	140 psi	930 kPa
Maximum deviation	28.0 psi	200kPa
Warpage	0.002 in.	0.05mm
Height	5.589-5.593 in.	141.95-142.05mm
Camshaft		
End-play	0.002-0.006 in.	0.050-0.15mm
Camshaft to holder clearance	0.0020-0.0035 in.	0.050-0.089mm
Run-out	0.0006 in.	0.015mm
Camshaft lobe height		
Intake		
Primary	1.3154 in.	33.411mm
Middle	1.4322 in.	36.377mm
Secondary	1.3601 in.	34.547mm
Exhaust		
Primary	1.3036 in.	33.111mm
Middle	1.4063 in.	35.720mm
Secondary	1.3536 in.	34.381mm
Valve and Valve Seats		
Valve clearance (cold)		
Intake	0.006-0.007 in.	0.15-0.19mm
Exhaust	0.007-0.008 in.	0.17-0.21mm
Valve stem		
Outer diameter		
Intake	0.2156-0.2159 in.	5.475-5.485mm
Exhaust	0.2146-0.2150 in.	5.450-5.460mm
Valve stem-to-guide clearance		
Intake	0.0010-0.0022 in.	0.025-0.055mm
Exhaust	0.0020-0.0031 in.	0.050-0.080mm
Valve seat width		
Intake	0.049-0.061 in.	1.25-1.55mm
Exhaust	0.049-0.061 in.	1.25-1.55mm
Valve stem installed height		
Intake	1.4750-1.4935 in.	37.465-37.935mm
Exhaust	1.4632-1.4817 in.	37.165-37.635mm
Valve Spring and Guide		
Valve spring free length		
Intake		
Outer	1.616 in.	41.05mm
Inner	1.424 in.	36.16mm
Exhaust		
Outer	1.652-1.612 in.	41.96-40.95mm
Inner	1.651-1.612 in.	41.94-40.95mm

90943C03

1.8L (B18C1) ENGINE MECHANICAL SPECIFICATIONS

Description	English	Metric
Valve Spring and Guide (cont.)		
Valve guide		
Inner dimension		
Intake	0.217–0.218 in.	5.51–5.53mm
Exhaust	0.217–0.218 in.	5.51–5.53mm
Valve guide installed height		
Intake	0.494–0.514 in.	12.55–13.05mm
Exhaust	0.494–0.514 in.	12.55–13.05mm
Engine Block		
Deck surface warpage	0.002–0.003 in.	0.05–0.08mm
Cylinder bore diameter	3.189–3.192 in.	81.00–81.07mm
Cylinder bore taper	0.002 in.	0.05mm
Cylinder re-boring limit	0.010 in.	0.25mm
Piston, Ring and Pin		
Piston ring-to-groove clearance		
Top	0.0018–0.0028 in.	0.045–0.070mm
2nd	0.0016–0.0026 in.	0.040–0.065mm
Piston ring end gap		
Top	0.008–0.014 in.	0.20–0.35mm
2nd	0.016–0.022 in.	0.40–0.55mm
Oil	0.008–0.020 in.	0.20–0.50mm
Ring groove width		
Top	0.0406–0.0409 in.	1.030–1.040mm
2nd	0.0484–0.0488 in.	1.230–1.240mm
Oil	0.1104–0.1110 in.	2.805–2.820mm
Piston-to-cylinder wall clearance	0.0004–0.0016 in.	0.01–0.04mm
Piston skirt outer diameter measured 15mm from the bottom of the skirt	3.188–3.189 in.	80.98–80.99mm
Piston pin		
Outer diameter	0.8265–0.8268 in.	20.994–21.000mm
Pin-to-piston clearance	0.0004–0.0009 in.	0.010–0.022mm
Connecting Rod		
End-play		
Installed on the crankshaft	0.006–0.012 in.	0.15–0.30mm
Bore diameter		
Crankshaft end	1.89 in.	48.0mm
Piston pin end	0.8254–0.8267 in.	20.964–20.997mm
Pin-to-rod clearance	0.0007–0.0014 in.	0.017–0.036mm
Crankshaft		
Main journal diameter		
No. 1, 2, 4, 5 journals	2.1644–2.1654 in.	54.976–55.000mm
No. 3 journal	2.1643–2.1653 in.	54.974–54.998mm
Connecting rod journal diameter	1.7707–1.7717 in.	44.976–45.000mm
Taper	0.0002 in.	0.005mm
Out-of-round	0.0002 in.	0.004mm
End-play	0.004–0.014 in.	0.10–0.35mm
Run-out	0.0008 in.	0.02mm
Bearing		
Main bearing to journal oil clearance		
No. 1, 2, 4, 5 journals	120.0 in.	0.024–0.042mm
No. 3 journal	0.0012–0.0019 in.	0.030–0.048mm
Rod bearing-to-journal oil clearance	0.0013–0.0020 in.	0.032–0.050mm

90943C04

1.8L (B18C5) ENGINE MECHANICAL SPECIFICATIONS

Description	English	Metric
General Information		
Engine type	Double Overhead Camshaft (DOHC) in-line 4 cylinder	
Compression ratio	9.2:1	
Firing order	1-3-4-2	
Displacement	112 cid	1.8L
Bore	3.19 in.	81.0mm
Stroke	3.50 in.	89.0mm
Cylinder Head		
Compression	270 psi	1860kPa
Minimum	135 psi	930kPa
Maximum deviation	28 psi	200kPa
Warpage	0.002 in.	0.05mm
Height	5.589–5.593 in.	141.95–142.05mm
Camshaft		
End-play	0.002–0.006 in.	0.05–0.15mm
Camshaft to holder clearance	0.0020–0.0035 in.	0.050–0.089mm
Run-out	0.001 in.	0.03mm
Camshaft lobe height		
Intake		
Primary	1.3154 in.	33.411mm
Middle	1.4322 in.	36.377mm
Secondary	1.3601 in.	34.547mm
Exhaust		
Primary	1.3036 in.	33.111mm
Middle	1.4063 in.	35.720mm
Secondary	1.3536 in.	34.381mm
Valve and Valve Seats		
Valve clearance (cold)		
Intake	0.006–0.007 in.	0.15–0.19mm
Exhaust	0.007–0.008 in.	0.17–0.21mm
Valve stem		
Outer diameter		
Intake	0.2156–0.2159 in.	5.475–5.485mm
Exhaust	0.2146–0.2150 in.	5.450–5.460mm
Valve stem-to-guide clearance		
Intake	0.0010–0.0022 in.	0.025–0.055mm
Exhaust	0.0020–0.0031 in.	0.050–0.080mm
Valve seat width		
Intake	0.033–0.045 in.	0.85–1.15mm
Exhaust	0.033–0.045 in.	0.85–1.15mm
Valve stem installed height		
Intake	1.4750–1.4935 in.	37.465–37.935mm
Exhaust	1.4632–1.4817 in.	37.165–37.635mm
Valve Spring and Guide		
Valve spring free length		
Intake		
Outer	1.700 in.	43.19mm
Inner	1.450 in.	36.84mm
Exhaust		
Outer	1.616 in.	41.05mm
Inner	1.424 in.	36.16mm

90943C05

1.8L (B18C5) ENGINE MECHANICAL SPECIFICATIONS

Description	English	Metric
Valve Spring and Guide (cont.)		
Valve guide		
Inner dimension		
Intake	0.217-0.0218 in.	5.51-5.53mm
Exhaust	0.217-0.218 in.	5.51-5.53mm
Valve guide installed height		
Intake	0.494-0.514 in.	12.55-13.05mm
Exhaust	0.494-0.514 in.	12.55-13.05mm
Engine Block		
Deck surface warpage	0.002-0.003 in.	0.05-0.08mm
Cylinder bore diameter	3.189-3.190 in.	81.00-81.02mm
Cylinder bore taper	0.002 in.	0.05mm
Cylinder re-boring limit	0.010 in.	0.25mm
Piston, Ring and Pin		
Piston ring-to-groove clearance		
Top	0.0018-0.0028 in.	0.045-0.070mm
2nd	0.0016-0.0026 in.	0.040-0.065mm
Piston ring end gap		
Top	0.008-0.014 in.	0.20-0.35mm
2nd	0.016-0.022 in.	0.40-0.55mm
Oil	0.008-0.020 in.	0.20-0.50mm
Ring groove width		
Top	0.0406-0.0409 in.	1.030-1.040mm
2nd	0.0484-0.0488 in.	1.230-1.240mm
Oil	0.1104-0.1110 in.	2.805-2.820mm
Piston-to-cylinder wall clearance	0.0004-0.0016 in.	0.01-0.04mm
Piston skirt outer diameter measured 15mm from the bottom of the skirt	3.188-3.189 in.	80.98-80.99mm
Piston pin		
Outer diameter	0.8265-0.8268 in.	20.994-21.00mm
Pin-to-piston clearance	0.0004-0.0009 in.	0.010-0.022mm
Connecting Rod		
End-play	0.006-0.012 in.	0.15-0.30mm
Installed on the crankshaft		
Bore diameter		
Crankshaft end	1.89 in.	48.0mm
Piston pin end	0.8254-0.8267 in.	20.964-20.997mm
Pin-to-rod clearance	0.0007-0.0014 in.	0.017-0.036mm
Crankshaft		
Main journal diameter		
No. 1, 2, 4, 5 journals	2.1644-2.1654 in.	54.976-55.000mm
No. 3 journal	2.1643-2.1653 in.	54.974-54.998mm
Connecting rod journal diameter	1.7707-1.7717 in.	44.976-45.000mm
Taper	0.0002 in.	0.005mm
Out-of-round	0.0002 in.	0.005mm
End-play	0.004-0.014 in.	0.10-0.35mm
Run-out	0.0008 in.	0.02mm
Bearing		
Main bearing to journal oil clearance		
No. 1, 2, 4, 5 journals	0.0012-0.0019 in.	0.024-0.042mm
No. 3 journal	0.0013-0.0020 in.	0.030-0.048mm
Rod bearing-to-journal oil clearance		0.032-0.050mm

90943C06

2.2L (F22B1) ENGINE MECHANICAL SPECIFICATIONS

Description	English	Metric
General Information		
Engine type	Overhead Camshaft (OHC) in-line 4 cylinder	
Compression ratio	8.8:1	
Firing order	1-3-4-2	
Displacement	132 in.	2.2L
Bore	3.35 in.	85.09mm
Stroke	3.74 in.	94.99mm
Cylinder Head		
Compression		
Minimum	178 psi	1230kPa
Maximum deviation	135 psi	930kPa
Warpage	28 psi	200kPa
Height	0.002 in.	0.05mm
	3.935-3.939 in.	99.95-100.05mm
Camshaft		
End-play	0.002-0.006 in.	0.05-0.15 mm
Camshaft to holder clearance	0.0020-0.0035 in.	0.050-0.089mm
Run-out	0.001 in.	0.03mm
Camshaft lobe height		
Intake		
Primary	1.3154 in.	37.775mm
Middle	1.4322 in.	39.725mm
Secondary	1.3601 in.	34.481mm
Exhaust	1.3036 in.	38.366mm
Valve and Valve Seats		
Valve clearance (cold)		
Intake	0.009-0.011 in.	0.24-0.28mm
Exhaust	0.011-0.013 in.	0.28-0.32mm
Valve stem		
Outer diameter		
Intake	0.2159-0.2163 in.	5.485-5.495mm
Exhaust	0.2146-0.2150 in.	5.450-5.460mm
Valve stem-to-guide clearance		
Intake	0.0008-0.0018 in.	0.020-0.045mm
Exhaust	0.0022-0.0031 in.	0.055-0.080mm
Valve seat width		
Intake	0.049-0.061 in.	1.25-1.55mm
Exhaust	0.049-0.061 in.	1.25-1.55mm
Valve stem installed height		
Intake	1.841-1.872 in.	46.75-47.55mm
Exhaust	1.838-1.869 in.	46.68-47.48mm
Valve Spring and Guide		
Valve spring free length		
Intake	2.011 in.	51.08mm
Exhaust	2.188 in.	55.58mm
Valve guide		
Inner dimension		
Intake	0.2171-0.2177 in.	5.515-5.530mm
Exhaust	0.2171-0.2177 in.	5.515-5.530mm
Valve guide installed height		
Intake	0.835-0.874 in.	21.20-22.20mm
Exhaust	0.812-0.852 in.	20.63-21.63mm

90943C07

2.2L (F22B1) ENGINE MECHANICAL SPECIFICATIONS

Description	English	Metric
Engine Block		
Deck surface warpage	0.003 in.	0.07mm
Cylinder bore diameter	3.3468-3.3472 in.	85.010-85.020mm
Cylinder bore taper	0.002 in.	0.05mm
Cylinder re-boring limit	0.02 in.	0.5mm
Piston, Ring and Pin		
Piston ring-to-groove clearance		
Top	0.0014-0.0024 in.	0.035-0.060mm
2nd	0.0012-0.0022 in.	0.030-0.055mm
Piston ring end gap		
Top	0.008-0.014 in.	0.20-0.35mm
2nd	0.016-0.022 in.	0.40-0.55mm
Oil	0.008-0.028 in.	0.20-0.70mm
Ring groove width		
Top	0.0480-0.0484 in.	1.220-1.230mm
2nd	0.0480-0.0484 in.	1.220-1.230mm
Oil	0.1104-0.1112 in.	2.805-2.825mm
Piston-to-cylinder wall clearance	0.0008-0.0016 in.	0.020-0.040mm
Piston skirt outer diameter measured 15mm from the bottom of the skirt	3.3457-3.3461 in.	84.980-84.990mm
Piston pin		
Outer diameter	0.8659-0.8661 in.	21.994-22.000mm
Pin-to-piston clearance	0.0004-0.0009 in.	0.010-0.022mm
Connecting Rod		
End-play		
Installed on the crankshaft	0.006-0.012 in.	0.15-0.30mm
Bore diameter		
Crankshaft end	2.01 in.	51.0mm
Piston pin end	0.8649-0.8654 in.	21.968-21.981mm
Pin-to-rod clearance	0.0005-0.0013 in.	0.013-0.032mm
Crankshaft		
Main journal diameter		
No. 1 and 4 journals	1.9679-1.9688 in.	49.984-50.008mm
No. 2	1.9676-1.9685 in.	49.976-50.000mm
No. 3 journal	1.9674-1.9683 in.	49.972-49.996mm
No. 5 journal	1.9680-1.9690 in.	49.988-50.012mm
Connecting rod journal diameter	1.888-1.8898 in.	47.976-48.000mm
Taper	0.0002 in.	0.005mm
Out-of-round	0.0002 in.	0.005mm
End-play	0.004-0.014 in.	0.10-0.35mm
Run-out	0.001 in.	0.03mm
Bearing		
Main bearing to journal oil clearance		
No. 1 and 4 journals	0.0005-0.0015 in.	0.013-0.037mm
No. 2	0.0008-0.0018 in.	0.021-0.045mm
No. 3 journal	0.0010-0.0019 in.	0.025-0.049mm
No. 5 journal	0.0004-0.0013 in.	0.009-0.033mm
Rod bearing-to-journal oil clearance	0.0008-0.0019 in.	0.021-0.049mm

90943C08

2.3L (F23A1) ENGINE MECHANICAL SPECIFICATIONS

Description	English	Metric
General information		
Engine type	Overhead Camshaft (OHC) in-line 4 cylinder	
Compression ratio	9.3:1	
Firing order	1-3-4-2	
Displacement	138 in.	2.3L
Bore	3.39	86.106
Stroke	3.82	97.028
Cylinder Head		
Compression	242 psi	1670kPa
Minimum	135 psi	930kPa
Maximum deviation	28 psi	200kPa
Warpage	0.002 in.	0.05mm
Height	3.935-3.939 in.	99.95-100.05mm
Camshaft		
End-play	0.002-0.006 in.	0.05-0.15 mm
Camshaft to holder clearance	0.0020-0.0035 in.	0.050-0.089mm
Run-out	0.001 in.	0.03mm
Camshaft lobe height		
Intake		
Primary	1.3154 in.	37.775mm
Middle	1.4322 in.	39.725mm
Secondary	1.3601 in.	34.481mm
Exhaust	1.3036 in.	38.366mm
Valve and Valve Seats		
Valve clearance (cold)		
Intake	0.009-0.011 in.	0.24-0.28mm
Exhaust	0.011-0.013 in.	0.28-0.32mm
Valve stem		
Outer diameter		
Intake	0.2159-0.2163 in.	5.485-5.495mm
Exhaust	0.2146-0.2150 in.	5.450-5.460mm
Valve stem-to-guide clearance		
Intake	0.0008-0.0018 in.	0.020-0.045mm
Exhaust	0.0022-0.0031 in.	0.055-0.080mm
Valve seat width		
Intake	0.049-0.061 in.	1.25-1.55mm
Exhaust	0.049-0.061 in.	1.25-1.55mm
Valve stem installed height		
Intake	1.841-1.872 in.	46.75-47.55mm
Exhaust	1.838-1.869 in.	46.68-47.48mm
Valve Spring and Guide		
Valve spring free length		
Intake	2.011 in.	51.08mm
Exhaust	2.188 in.	55.58mm
Valve guide		
Inner dimension		
Intake	0.2171-0.2177 in.	5.515-5.530mm
Exhaust	0.2171-0.2177 in.	5.515-5.530mm
Valve guide installed height		
Intake	0.835-0.874 in.	21.20-22.20mm
Exhaust	0.812-0.852 in.	20.63-21.63mm

90943C09

2.3L (F23A1) ENGINE MECHANICAL SPECIFICATIONS

Description	English	Metric
Engine Block		
Deck surface warpage	0.003 in.	0.07mm
Cylinder bore diameter	3.3468-3.3472 in.	85.010-85.020mm
Cylinder bore taper	0.002 in.	0.05mm
Cylinder re-boring limit	0.02 in.	0.5mm
Piston, Ring and Pin		
Piston ring-to-groove clearance		
Top	0.0014-0.0024 in.	0.035-0.060mm
2nd	0.0012-0.0022 in.	0.030-0.055mm
Piston ring end gap		
Top	0.008-0.014 in.	0.20-0.35mm
2nd	0.016-0.022 in.	0.40-0.55mm
Oil	0.008-0.028 in.	0.20-0.70mm
Ring groove width		
Top	0.0480-0.0484 in.	1.220-1.230mm
2nd	0.0480-0.0484 in.	1.220-1.230mm
Oil	0.1104-0.1112 in.	2.805-2.825mm
Piston-to-cylinder wall clearance	0.0008-0.0016 in.	0.020-0.040mm
Piston skirt outer diameter measured 15mm from the bottom of the skirt	3.3457-3.3461 in.	84.980-84.990mm
Piston pin		
Outer diameter	0.8659-0.8661 in.	21.994-22.000mm
Pin-to-piston clearance	0.0002-0.0006 in.	0.005-0.015mm
Connecting Rod		
End-play	0.006-0.012 in.	0.15-0.30mm
Installed on the crankshaft	1.90 in.	48.0mm
Bore diameter		
Crankshaft end	0.8650-0.8654 in.	21.968-21.981mm
Pin end		
Pin-to-rod clearance	0.0005-0.0013 in.	0.013-0.032mm
Crankshaft		
Main journal diameter		
No. 1 and 4 journals	1.9679-1.9688 in.	49.984-50.008mm
No. 2	1.9676-1.9685 in.	49.976-50.000mm
No. 3 journal	1.9674-1.9683 in.	49.972-49.996mm
No. 5 journal	1.9680-1.9690 in.	49.988-50.012mm
Connecting rod journal diameter	1.888-1.8898 in.	47.976-48.000mm
Taper	0.0002 in.	0.005mm
Out-of-round	0.0002 in.	0.005mm
End-play	0.004-0.014 in.	0.10-0.35mm
Run-out	0.001 in.	0.03mm
Bearing		
Main bearing to journal oil clearance		
No. 1 and 4 journals	0.0005-0.0015 in.	0.013-0.037mm
No. 2	0.0008-0.0018 in.	0.021-0.045mm
No. 3 journal	0.0010-0.0019 in.	0.025-0.049mm
No. 5 journal	0.0004-0.0013 in.	0.009-0.033mm
Rod bearing-to-journal oil clearance	0.0008-0.0019 in.	0.021-0.049mm

90943C10

2.5L (G25A1) ENGINE MECHANICAL SPECIFICATIONS

Description	English	Metric
General Information		
Engine type	Overhead Cam in-line 5 cylinder	
Compression ratio	9.0:1	
Firing order	1-2-4-5-3	
Displacement	150 cid	2.5L
Bore	3.35 in.	85.09mm
Stroke	3.40 in.	86.36mm
Cylinder Head		
Compression		
Minimum	206 psi	1450kPa
	135 psi	950kPa
Maximum deviation	28 psi	200kPa
Warpage	0.002 in.	0.05mm
Height	3.935-3.939 in.	99.95-100.05mm
Camshaft		
End-play	0.002-0.006 in.	0.05 - 0.15mm
Camshaft to holder clearance	0.0020-0.0035 in.	0.050-0.089mm
Run-out	0.001 in.	0.03mm
Camshaft lobe height		
Intake	1.5434 in.	39.203mm
Exhaust	1.5305 in.	38.875mm
Valve and Valve Seats		
Valve clearance (cold)		
Intake	0.009-0.011 in.	0.24-0.28mm
Exhaust	0.011-0.013 in.	0.28-0.32mm
Valve stem		
Outer diameter		
Intake	0.2156-0.2159 in.	5.475-5.485mm
Exhaust	0.2146-0.2150 in.	5.450-5.460mm
Valve stem-to-guide clearance		
Intake	0.0008-0.0018 in.	0.020-0.045mm
Exhaust	0.0022-0.0031 in.	0.055-0.080mm
Valve seat width		
Intake	0.049-0.061 in.	1.25-1.55mm
Exhaust	0.049-0.061 in.	1.25-1.55mm
Valve stem installed height		
Intake	1.9191-1.9376 in.	48.745-49.215mm
Exhaust	2.0203-2.0388 in.	51.315-51.785mm
Valve Spring and Guide		
Valve spring free length		
Intake		
Nihon Hatsujo	2.011 in.	52.13mm
Chuo Hatsujo	2.188 in.	52.12mm
Exhaust		
Nihon Hatsujo	2.209 in.	56.10mm
Chuo Hatsujo	2.208 in.	56.08mm
Valve guide		
Inner dimension		
Intake	0.2167-0.2173 in.	5.505-5.520mm
Exhaust	0.2170-0.2180 in.	5.510-5.530mm

90943C11

2.5L (G25A1) ENGINE MECHANICAL SPECIFICATIONS

Description	English	Metric
Valve Spring and Guide (cont.)		
Valve guide installed height		
Intake	0.974-0.994 in.	24.75-25.25mm
Exhaust	0.632-0.652 in.	16.05-16.55mm
Engine Block		
Deck surface warpage	0.003 in.	0.07mm
Cylinder bore diameter	3.3468-3.3472 in.	85.010-85.020mm
Cylinder bore taper	0.002 in.	0.05mm
Cylinder re-boring limit	0.02 in.	0.5mm
Piston, Ring and Pin		
Piston ring-to-groove clearance		
Top	0.0014-0.0024 in.	0.035-0.060mm
2nd	0.0012-0.0022 in.	0.030-0.055mm
Piston ring end gap		
Top	0.008-0.014 in.	0.20-0.35mm
2nd	0.016-0.022 in.	0.40-0.55mm
Oil	0.008-0.028 in.	0.20-0.70mm
Ring groove width		
Top	0.0480-0.0484 in.	1.220-1.230mm
2nd	0.0480-0.0484 in.	1.220-1.230mm
Oil	0.1104-0.1112 in.	2.805-2.825mm
Piston-to-cylinder wall clearance	0.0008-0.0016 in.	0.020-0.040mm
Piston skirt outer diameter measured 15mm from the bottom of the skirt	3.3453-3.3461 in.	84.970-84.990mm
Piston pin		
Outer diameter	0.8659-0.8661 in.	21.994-22.000mm
Pin-to-piston clearance	0.0005-0.0009 in.	0.012-0.024mm
Connecting Rod		
End-play	0.006-0.012 in.	0.15-0.30mm
Bore diameter		
Installed on the crankshaft	1.90 in.	48.0mm
Crankshaft end	0.8649-0.8654 in.	21.968-21.981mm
Piston pin end		
Pin-to-rod clearance	0.0005-0.0013 in.	0.013-0.032mm
Crankshaft		
Main journal diameter	1.9679-1.9688 in.	49.984-50.008mm
Connecting rod journal diameter	1.7707-1.7717 in.	44.976-45.000mm
Taper	0.0004 in.	0.010mm
Out-of-round	0.0004 in.	0.010mm
End-play	0.004-0.014 in.	0.10-0.35mm
Run-out	0.001 in.	0.03mm
Bearing		
Main bearing to journal oil clearance	0.0007-0.0019 in.	0.018-0.048mm
Rod bearing-to-journal oil clearance	0.0006-0.0017 in.	0.015-0.043mm

90943C12

2.5L (G25A4) ENGINE MECHANICAL SPECIFICATIONS

Description	English	Metric
General Information		
Engine type	Overhead Cam in-line 5 cylinder	
Compression ratio	9.0:1	
Firing order	1-2-4-5-3	
Displacement	150 cid	2.5L
Bore	3.35 in.	85.09mm
Stroke	3.40 in.	86.36mm
Cylinder Head		
Compression	228	1570kPa
Minimum	135	930kPa
Maximum deviation	28	200kPa
Warpage	0.002 in.	0.05mm
Height	3.935-3.939 in.	99.95-100.05mm
Camshaft		
End-play	0.002-0.006 in.	0.05 - 0.15 mm
Camshaft to holder clearance	0.0020-0.0035 in.	0.050-0.089mm
Run-out	0.001 in.	0.03mm
Camshaft lobe height		
Intake	1.5434 in.	39.203mm
Exhaust	1.5305 in.	38.875mm
Valve and Valve Seats		
Valve clearance (cold)		
Intake	0.009-0.011 in.	0.24-0.28mm
Exhaust	0.011-0.013 in.	0.28-0.32mm
Valve stem		
Outer diameter		
Intake	0.2156-0.2159 in.	5.475-5.485mm
Exhaust	0.2146-0.2150 in.	5.450-5.460mm
Valve stem-to-guide clearance		
Intake	0.0008-0.0018 in.	0.020-0.045mm
Exhaust	0.0022-0.0031 in.	0.055-0.080mm
Valve seat width		
Intake	0.049-0.061 in.	1.25-1.55mm
Exhaust	0.049-0.061 in.	1.25-1.55mm
Valve stem installed height		
Intake	1.9191-1.9376 in.	48.745-49.215mm
Exhaust	2.0203-2.0388 in.	51.315-51.785mm
Valve Spring and Guide		
Valve spring free length		
Intake		
Nihon Hatsujo	2.011 in.	52.13mm
Chuo Hatsujo	2.188 in.	52.12mm
Exhaust		
Nihon Hatsujo	2.209 in.	56.10mm
Chuo Hatsujo	2.208 in.	56.08mm
Valve guide		
Inner dimension		
Intake	0.2167-0.2173 in.	5.505-5.520mm
Exhaust	0.2170-0.2180 in.	5.510-5.530mm

90943C13

2.5L (G25A4) ENGINE MECHANICAL SPECIFICATIONS

Description	English	Metric
Valve Spring and Guide (cont.)		
Valve guide installed height		
Intake	0.974-0.994 in.	24.75-25.25mm
Exhaust	0.632-0.652 in.	16.05-16.55mm
Engine Block		
Deck surface warpage	0.003 in.	0.07mm
Cylinder bore diameter	3.3468-3.3472 in.	85.010-85.020mm
Cylinder bore taper	0.002 in.	0.05mm
Cylinder re-boring limit	0.02 in.	0.5mm
Piston, Ring and Pin		
Piston ring-to-groove clearance		
Top	0.0018-0.0028 in.	0.045-0.070mm
2nd	0.0012-0.0022 in.	0.030-0.055mm
Piston ring end gap		
Top	0.008-0.014 in.	0.20-0.35mm
2nd	0.016-0.022 in.	0.40-0.55mm
Oil	0.008-0.028 in.	0.20-0.70mm
Ring groove width		
Top	0.0480-0.0484 in.	1.220-1.230mm
2nd	0.0480-0.0484 in.	1.220-1.230mm
Oil	0.1104-0.1112 in.	2.805-2.825mm
Piston-to-cylinder wall clearance	0.0008-0.0016 in.	0.020-0.040mm
Piston skirt outer diameter measured 15mm from the bottom of the skirt	3.3453-3.3461 in.	84.970-84.990mm
Piston pin		
Outer diameter	0.8659-0.8661 in.	21.994-22.000mm
Pin-to-piston clearance	0.0005-0.0009 in.	0.0012-0.024mm
Connecting Rod		
End-play	0.006-0.012 in.	0.15-0.30mm
Installed on the crankshaft	1.90 in.	48.0mm
Bore diameter		
Crankshaft end	0.8649-0.8654 in.	21.968-21.981mm
Piston pin end		
Pin-to-rod clearance	0.0005-0.0013 in.	0.013-0.032mm
Crankshaft		
Main journal diameter	2.1644-2.1654 in.	54.976-55.000mm
Connecting rod journal diameter	1.7707-1.7717 in.	44.976-45.000mm
Taper	0.0002 in.	0.005mm
Out-of-round	0.0002 in.	0.005mm
End-play	0.004-0.014 in.	0.10-0.35mm
Run-out	0.001 in.	0.03mm
Bearing		
Main bearing to journal oil clearance	0.0007-0.0019 in.	0.018-0.048mm
Rod bearing-to-journal oil clearance	0.0006-0.0017 in.	0.015-0.043mm

90943C14

3.0L (J30A1) ENGINE MECHANICAL SPECIFICATIONS

Description	English	Metric
General Information		
Engine type	V-6 cylinder	
Compression ratio	9.4:1	
Firing order	1-4-2-5-3-6	
Displacement	183	3.0L (2997)
Bore	3.39 in.	86.106mm
Stroke	3.39 in.	86.106mm
Cylinder Head		
Compression	178 psi	1230 kPa
Minimum	135 psi	930kPa
Maximum deviation	28 psi	200kPa
Warpage	0.002 in.	0.05mm
Height	4.762-4.766 in.	120.95-121.05mm
Camshaft		
End-play	0.002-0.006 in.	0.05 - 0.15 mm
Camshaft to holder clearance	0.0020-0.0035 in.	0.050-0.089mm
Run-out	0.001 in.	0.03mm
Camshaft lobe height		
Intake		
Primary	1.3628 in.	34.615mm
Middle	1.4256 in.	36.210mm
Secondary	1.2279 in.	31.188mm
Exhaust	1.4203 in.	36.076mm
Valve and Valve Seats		
Valve clearance (cold)		
Intake	0.011-0.013 in.	0.20-0.24mm
Exhaust		0.28-0.32mm
Valve stem		
Outer diameter		
Intake	0.2159-0.2163 in.	5.485-5.495mm
Exhaust	0.2146-0.2150 in.	5.450-5.460mm
Valve stem-to-guide clearance		
Intake	0.0008-0.0018 in.	0.020-0.045mm
Exhaust	0.0022-0.0031 in.	0.055-0.080mm
Valve seat width		
Intake	0.049-0.061 in.	1.25-1.55mm
Exhaust	0.049-0.061 in.	1.25-1.55mm
Valve stem installed height		
Intake	1.841-1.872 in.	46.75-47.55mm
Exhaust	1.839-1.869 in.	46.68-47.48mm
Valve Spring and Guide		
Valve spring free length		
Intake	2.011 in.	51.08mm
Exhaust	2.106 in.	53.48mm
Valve guide		
Inner dimension		
Intake	0.2171-0.2177 in.	5.515-5.530mm
Exhaust	0.2171-0.2177 in.	5.515-5.530mm

90943C15

3.0L (J30A1) ENGINE MECHANICAL SPECIFICATIONS

Description	English	Metric
Valve Spring and Guide (cont.)		
Valve guide installed height		
Intake	0.835-0.874 in.	21.20-22.20mm
Exhaust	0.812-0.852 in.	20.63-21.63mm
Engine Block		
Deck surface warpage	0.003 in.	0.07mm
Cylinder bore diameter	3.3858-3.3864 in.	86.000-86.015mm
Cylinder bore taper	0.002 in.	0.05mm
Cylinder re-boring limit	0.02 in.	0.5mm
Piston, Ring and Pin		
Piston ring-to-groove clearance		
Top	0.0014-0.0024 in.	0.035-0.060mm
2nd	0.0012-0.0022 in.	0.030-0.055mm
Piston ring end gap		
Top	0.008-0.014 in.	0.20-0.35mm
2nd	0.016-0.022 in.	0.40-0.55mm
Oil	0.008-0.028 in.	0.20-0.70mm
Ring groove width		
Top	0.0480-0.0484 in.	1.220-1.230mm
2nd	0.0480-0.0484 in.	1.220-1.230mm
Oil	0.1104-0.1112 in.	2.805-2.825mm
Piston-to-cylinder wall clearance	0.0006-0.0016 in.	0.015-0.040mm
Piston skirt outer diameter measured 15mm from the bottom of the skirt	3.3848-3.3852 in.	85.975-85.985mm
Piston pin		
Outer diameter	0.8646-0.8648 in.	21.962-21.965mm
Pin-to-piston clearance	-0.0002minus(+0.0004) in.	0.0050(+0.0010)mm
Connecting Rod		
End-play	0.006-0.014 in.	0.15-0.35mm
Installed on the crankshaft		
Bore diameter	2.20 in.	56.0mm
Crankshaft end	0.8650-0.8652 in.	21.970-21.976mm
Piston pin end	0.0002-0.0006 in.	0.005-0.015mm
Pin-to-rod clearance		
Crankshaft		
Main journal diameter	2.8337-2.8346 in.	71.976-72.000mm
Connecting rod journal diameter	2.0857-2.0866 in.	52.976-53.000mm
Taper	0.0002 in.	0.005mm
Out-of-round	0.0002 in.	0.005mm
End-play	0.004-0.014 in.	0.10-0.35mm
Run-out	0.0008 in.	0.020mm
Bearing		
Main bearing to journal oil clearance	0.0008-0.0017 in.	0.020-0.044mm
Rod bearing-to-journal oil clearance	0.0008-0.0017 in.	0.020-0.044mm

9094C16

3.2L (C32A1) ENGINE MECHANICAL SPECIFICATIONS

Description	English	Metric
General information		
Engine type	V-6 cylinder	
Compression ratio	9.4:1	
Firing order	1-4-2-5-3-6	
Displacement	196	3.2L
Bore	3.54 in.	89.92mm
Stroke	3.31 in.	84.07mm
Cylinder Head		
Compression	199	1400
Minimum	142	1000
Maximum deviation	28	200
Warpage	0.002 in.	0.05mm
Height	3.935-3.939 in.	99.95-100.05mm
Camshaft		
End-play	0.002-0.006 in.	0.05-0.15mm
Camshaft to holder clearance	0.0020-0.0035 in.	0.050-0.089mm
Run-out	0.001 in.	0.03mm
Camshaft lobe height		
Intake		
Primary	1.5750 in.	40.005mm
Middle	1.4868 in.	37.766mm
Secondary	1.5884 in.	40.345mm
Exhaust	1.4935 in.	37.934mm
Valve and Valve Seats		
Valve clearance (cold)		
Intake	Hydrolic Tappets, Auto-adjusting	
Exhaust	Hydrolic Tappets, Auto-adjusting	
Valve stem		
Outer diameter		
Intake	0.2159-0.2163 in.	5.485-5.495mm
Exhaust	0.2146-0.2150 in.	5.450-5.460mm
Valve stem-to-guide clearance		
Intake	0.001-0.002 in.	0.02-0.05mm
Exhaust	0.002-0.003 in.	0.05-0.08mm
Valve seat width		
Intake	0.049-0.061 in.	1.25-1.55mm
Exhaust	0.049-0.061 in.	1.25-1.55mm
Valve stem installed height		
Intake	1.8478-1.8652 in.	46.935-47.375mm
Exhaust	1.8852-1.9045 in.	47.885-48.375mm
Valve Spring and Guide		
Valve spring free length		
L andLS models		
Intake		
-Nihon Hatsujo	2.011 in.	50.16mm
-Chuo Hatsujo	2.106 in.	50.17mm
Exhaust	1.9827 in.	50.36mm
GS model		
Intake		
-Nihon Hatsujo	1.935 in.	49.15mm
-Chuo Hatsujo	1.933 in.	49.10mm
Exhaust		
-Nihon Hatsujo	1.975 in.	50.16mm
-Chuo Hatsujo	1.975 in.	50.17mm

9094C17

3.2L (C32A1) ENGINE MECHANICAL SPECIFICATIONS

Description	English	Metric
Valve Spring and Guide (cont.)		
Valve guide		
Inner dimension		
Intake	0.2171-0.2177 in.	5.515-5.530mm
Exhaust	0.2171-0.2177 in.	5.515-5.530mm
Valve guide installed height		
Intake	0.620-0.640 in.	15.75-16.25mm
Exhaust	0.620-0.640 in.	15.75-16.25mm
Engine Block		
Deck surface warpage	0.003 in.	0.07mm
Cylinder bore diameter	3.543-3.544 in.	90.00-90.02mm
Cylinder bore taper	0.002 in.	0.05mm
Cylinder re-boring limit	0.02 in.	0.5mm
Piston, Ring and Pin		
Piston ring-to-groove clearance		
Top	0.0014-0.0024 in.	0.035-0.060mm
2nd	0.0012-0.0022 in.	0.030-0.055mm
Piston ring end gap		
Top	0.010-0.016 in.	0.25-0.40mm
2nd	0.016-0.022 in.	0.40-0.55mm
Oil	0.008-0.028 in.	0.20-0.70mm
	0.008-0.020 in.	0.20-0.50mm
Ring groove width		
Top	0.0480-0.0484 in.	1.220-1.230mm
2nd	0.0480-0.0484 in.	1.220-1.230mm
Oil	0.1104-0.1112 in.	2.805-2.825mm
Piston-to-cylinder wall clearance	0.001-0.002 in.	0.020-0.040mm
Piston skirt outer diameter measured 15mm from the bottom of the skirt		
-Nihon Hatsujo	3.5425-3.5429 in.	89.980-89.990mm
-Chuo Hatsujio	3.5421-3.5425 in.	89.970-89.980mm
Piston pin		
Outer diameter	0.8659-0.8661 in.	21.994-22.000mm
Pin-to-piston clearance	0.0005-0.0009 in.	0.012-0.024mm
Connecting Rod		
End-play	0.006-0.012 in.	0.15-0.30mm
Bore diameter		
Crankshaft end	2.24 in.	57.0mm
Piston pin end	0.8649-0.8654 in.	21.968-21.981mm
Pin-to-rod clearance	0.0005-0.0013 in.	0.013-0.032mm
Crankshaft		
Main journal diameter	2.6762-2.6772 in.	67.976-68.000mm
Connecting rod journal diameter	2.1248-2.1257 in.	53.970-53.994mm
Taper	0.0002 in.	0.005mm
Out-of-round	0.0002 in.	0.004mm
End-play	0.004-0.011 in.	0.10-0.29mm
Run-out	0.0008 in.	0.020mm
Bearing		
Main bearing to journal oil clearance	0.0008-0.0017 in.	0.020-0.044mm
Rod bearing-to-journal oil clearance	0.0009-0.0018 in.	0.022-0.046mm

90943C18

3.2L (C32A6) ENGINE MECHANICAL SPECIFICATIONS

Description	English	Metric
General Information		
Engine type	V-6 cylinder	
Compression ratio	9.6:1	
Firing order	1-2-3-4-5-6	
Displacement	196	3.2L
Bore	3.54 in.	90.0mm
Stroke	3.31 in.	84.0mm
Cylinder Head		
Compression	199	1370
Minimum	142	980
Maximum deviation	28	200
Warpage	0.002 in.	0.05mm
Height	3.935-3.939 in.	99.95-100.05mm
Camshaft		
End-play	0.002-0.006 in.	0.05-0.15mm
Camshaft to holder clearance	0.0020-0.0035 in.	0.050-0.089mm
Run-out	0.001 in.	0.03mm
Camshaft lobe height		
Intake	1.5750 in.	40.005mm
Exhaust	1.4868 in.	37.766mm
Valve and Valve Seats		
Valve clearance (cold)		
Intake	Hydrolic Tappets, Auto-adjusting	
Exhaust	Hydrolic Tappets, Auto-adjusting	
Valve stem		
Outer diameter		
Intake	0.2159-0.2163 in.	5.485-5.495mm
Exhaust	0.2146-0.2150 in.	5.450-5.460mm
Valve stem-to-guide clearance		
Intake	0.001-0.002 in.	0.02-0.05mm
Exhaust	0.002-0.003 in.	0.05-0.08mm
Valve seat width		
Intake	0.049-0.061 in.	1.25-1.55mm
Exhaust	0.049-0.061 in.	1.25-1.55mm
Valve stem installed height		
Intake	1.8478-1.8652 in.	46.935-47.375mm
Exhaust	1.8852-1.9045 in.	47.885-48.375mm
Valve Spring and Guide		
Valve spring free length		
Intake		
-Nihon Hatsujo	2.011 in.	50.16mm
-Chuo Hatsujio	2.106 in.	50.17mm
Exhaust	1.9827 in.	50.36mm
Valve guide		
Inner dimension		
Intake	0.2171-0.2177 in.	5.515-5.530mm
Exhaust	0.2171-0.2177 in.	5.515-5.530mm

90943C19

3.2L (C32A6) ENGINE MECHANICAL SPECIFICATIONS

Description	English	Metric
Valve Spring and Guide (cont.)		
Valve guide installed height		
Intake	0.620-0.640 in.	15.75-16.25mm
Exhaust	0.620-0.640 in.	15.75-16.25mm
Engine Block		
Deck surface warpage	0.003 in.	0.07mm
Cylinder bore diameter	3.5437-3.5441 in.	90.010-90.020mm
Cylinder bore taper	0.002 in.	0.05mm
Cylinder re-boring limit	0.02 in.	0.5mm
Piston, Ring and Pin		
Piston ring-to-groove clearance		
Top	0.0022-0.0031 in.	0.055-0.080mm
2nd	0.0012-0.0022 in.	0.030-0.055mm
Piston ring end gap		
Top	0.010-0.016 in.	0.25-0.40mm
2nd	0.016-0.022 in.	0.40-0.55mm
Oil		
-Nihon Hatsujo	0.008-0.028 in.	0.20-0.70mm
-Chuo Hatsujo	0.008-0.020 in.	0.20-0.50mm
Ring groove width		
Top	0.0488-0.0492 in.	1.240-1.250mm
2nd	0.0480-0.0484 in.	1.220-1.230mm
Oil	0.1104-0.1112 in.	2.805-2.825mm
Piston-to-cylinder wall clearance	0.001-0.002 in.	0.020-0.040mm
Piston skirt outer diameter measured 15mm from the bottom of the skirt		
-Nihon Hatsujo	3.5425-3.5429 in.	89.980-89.990mm
-Chuo Hatsujo	3.5421-3.5425 in.	89.970-89.980mm
Piston pin		
Outer diameter	0.8659-0.8661 in.	21.994-22.000mm
Pin-to-piston clearance	0.0004-0.0007 in.	0.010-0.019mm
Connecting Rod		
End-play		
Installed on the crankshaft	0.006-0.012 in.	0.15-0.30mm
Bore diameter		
Crankshaft end	2.24 in.	57.0mm
Piston pin end	0.8649-0.8654 in.	21.968-21.981mm
Pin-to-rod clearance	0.0005-0.0013 in.	0.013-0.032mm
Crankshaft		
Main journal diameter	2.6762-2.6772 in.	67.976-68.000mm
Connecting rod journal diameter	2.1248-2.1257 in.	53.970-53.994mm
Taper	0.0002 in.	0.005mm
Out-of-round	0.0002 in.	0.004mm
End-play	0.004-0.011 in.	0.10-0.29mm
Run-out	0.0008 in.	0.020mm
Bearing		
Main bearing to journal oil clearance	0.0008-0.0017 in.	0.020-0.044mm
Rod bearing-to-journal oil clearance	0.0009-0.0018 in.	0.022-0.046mm

90943C20

3.2L (J32A1) ENGINE MECHANICAL SPECIFICATIONS

Description	English	Metric
General Information		
Engine type	V-6 cylinder	
Compression ratio	9.8:1	
Firing order	1-2-3-4-5-6	
Displacement	196	3.2L
Bore	3.50 in.	88.9mm
Stroke	3.39 in.	86.1mm
Cylinder Head		
Compression	199	1370
Minimum	142	980
Maximum deviation	28	200
Warpage	0.002 in.	0.05mm
Height	3.935-3.939 in.	99.95-100.05mm
Camshaft		
End-play	0.002-0.006 in.	0.05-0.15mm
Camshaft to holder clearance	0.0020-0.0035 in.	0.050-0.089mm
Run-out	0.001 in.	0.03mm
Camshaft lobe height		
Intake	1.5750 in.	40.005mm
Exhaust	1.4868 in.	37.766mm
Valve and Valve Seats		
Valve clearance (cold)		
Intake	Hydraulic Tappets, Auto-adjusting	
Exhaust	Hydraulic Tappets, Auto-adjusting	
Valve stem		
Outer diameter		
Intake	0.2159-0.2163 in.	5.485-5.495mm
Exhaust	0.2146-0.2150 in.	5.450-5.460mm
Valve stem-to-guide clearance		
Intake	0.001-0.002 in.	0.02-0.05mm
Exhaust	0.002-0.003 in.	0.05-0.08mm
Valve seat width		
Intake	0.049-0.061 in.	1.25-1.55mm
Exhaust	0.049-0.061 in.	1.25-1.55mm
Valve stem installed height		
Intake	1.8478-1.8652 in.	46.935-47.375mm
Exhaust	1.8852-1.9045 in.	47.885-48.375mm
Valve Spring and Guide		
Valve spring free length		
Intake		
-Nihon Hatsujo	2.011 in.	50.16mm
-Chuo Hatsujo	2.106 in.	50.17mm
Exhaust	1.9827 in.	50.36mm
Valve guide		
Inner dimension		
Intake	0.2171-0.2177 in.	5.515-5.530mm
Exhaust	0.2171-0.2177 in.	5.515-5.530mm

90943C21

3.2L (J32A1) ENGINE MECHANICAL SPECIFICATIONS

Description	English	Metric
Valve Spring and Guide (cont.)		
Valve guide installed height		
Intake	0.620-0.640 in.	15.75-16.25mm
Exhaust	0.620-0.640 in.	15.75-16.25mm
Engine Block		
Deck surface warpage	0.003 in.	0.07mm
Cylinder bore diameter	3.5437-3.5441 in.	90.010-90.020mm
Cylinder bore taper	0.002 in.	0.05mm
Cylinder re-boring limit	0.02 in.	0.5mm
Piston, Ring and Pin		
Piston ring-to-groove clearance		
Top	0.0022-0.0031 in.	0.055-0.080mm
2nd	0.0012-0.0022 in.	0.030-0.055mm
Piston ring end gap		
Top	0.010-0.016 in.	0.25-0.40mm
2nd	0.016-0.022 in.	0.40-0.55mm
Oil		
-Nihon Hatsujo	0.008-0.028 in.	0.20-0.70mm
-Chuo Hatsujo	0.008-0.020 in.	0.20-0.50mm
Ring groove width		
Top	0.0488-0.0492 in.	1.240-1.250mm
2nd	0.0480-0.0484 in.	1.220-1.230mm
Oil	0.1104-0.1112 in.	2.805-2.825mm
Piston-to-cylinder wall clearance	0.001-0.002 in.	0.020-0.040mm
Piston skirt outer diameter measured 15mm from the bottom of the skirt		
-Nihon Hatsujo	3.5425-3.5429 in.	89.980-89.990mm
-Chuo Hatsujo	3.5421-3.5425 in.	89.970-89.980mm
Piston pin		
Outer diameter	0.8659-0.8661 in.	21.994-22.000mm
Pin-to-piston clearance	0.0004-0.0007 in.	0.010-0.019mm
Connecting Rod		
End-play	0.006-0.012 in.	0.15-0.30mm
Installed on the crankshaft		
Bore diameter		
Crankshaft end	2.24 in.	57.0mm
Piston pin end	0.8649-0.8654 in.	21.968-21.981mm
Pin-to-rod clearance	0.0005-0.0013 in.	0.013-0.032mm
Crankshaft		
Main journal diameter	2.6762-2.6772 in.	67.976-68.000mm
Connecting rod journal diameter	2.1248-2.1257 in.	53.970-53.994mm
Taper	0.0002 in.	0.005mm
Out-of-round	0.0002 in.	0.004mm
End-play	0.004-0.011 in.	0.10-0.29mm
Run-out	0.0008 in.	0.020mm
Bearing		
Main bearing to journal oil clearance	0.0008-0.0017 in.	0.020-0.044mm
Rod bearing-to-journal oil clearance	0.0009-0.0018 in.	0.022-0.046mm

90943C22

3.2L (J32A1) ENGINE MECHANICAL SPECIFICATIONS

Description	English	Metric
General Information		
Engine type	V-6 cylinder	
Compression ratio	9.8:1	
Firing order	1-2-3-4-5-6	
Displacement	196	3.2L
Bore	3.50 in.	88.9mm
Stroke	3.39 in.	86.1mm
Cylinder Head		
Compression	199	1370
Minimum	142	980
Maximum deviation	28	200
Warpage	0.002 in.	0.05mm
Height	3.935-3.939 in.	99.95-100.05mm
Camshaft		
End-play	0.002-0.006 in.	0.05-0.15mm
Camshaft to holder clearance	0.0020-0.0035 in.	0.050-0.089mm
Run-out	0.001 in.	0.03mm
Camshaft lobe height		
Intake	1.5750 in.	40.005mm
Exhaust	1.4868 in.	37.766mm
Valve and Valve Seats		
Valve clearance (cold)		
Intake	Hydrolic Tappets, Auto-adjusting	
Exhaust	Hydrolic Tappets, Auto-adjusting	
Valve stem		
Outer diameter		
Intake	0.2159-0.2163 in.	5.485-5.495mm
Exhaust	0.2146-0.2150 in.	5.450-5.460mm
Valve stem-to-guide clearance		
Intake	0.001-0.002 in.	0.02-0.05mm
Exhaust	0.002-0.003 in.	0.05-0.08mm
Valve seat width		
Intake	0.049-0.061 in.	1.25-1.55mm
Exhaust	0.049-0.061 in.	1.25-1.55mm
Valve stem installed height		
Intake	1.8478-1.8652 in.	46.935-47.375mm
Exhaust	1.8852-1.9045 in.	47.885-48.375mm
Valve Spring and Guide		
Valve spring free length		
Intake		
-Nihon Hatsujo	2.011 in.	50.16mm
-Chuo Hatsujo	2.106 in.	50.17mm
Exhaust	1.9827 in.	50.36mm
Valve guide		
Inner dimension		
Intake	0.2171-0.2177 in.	5.515-5.530mm
Exhaust	0.2171-0.2177 in.	5.515-5.530mm

90943C23

3.2L (J32A1) ENGINE MECHANICAL SPECIFICATIONS

Description	English	Metric
Valve Spring and Guide (cont.)		
Valve guide installed height		
Intake	0.620-0.640 in.	15.75-16.25mm
Exhaust	0.620-0.640 in.	15.75-16.25mm
Engine Block		
Deck surface warpage	0.003 in.	0.07mm
Cylinder bore diameter	3.5437-3.5441 in.	90.010-90.020mm
Cylinder bore taper	0.002 in.	0.05mm
Cylinder re-boring limit	0.02 in.	0.5mm
Piston, Ring and Pin		
Piston ring-to-groove clearance		
Top	0.0022-0.0031 in.	0.055-0.080mm
2nd	0.0012-0.0022 in.	0.030-0.055mm
Piston ring end gap		
Top	0.010-0.016 in.	0.25-0.40mm
2nd	0.016-0.022 in.	0.40-0.55mm
Oil	0.008-0.028 in.	0.20-0.70mm
-Nihon Hatsujo	0.008-0.020 in.	0.20-0.50mm
-Chuo Hatsujo		
Ring groove width		
Top	0.0488-0.0492 in.	1.240-1.250mm
2nd	0.0480-0.0484 in.	1.220-1.230mm
Oil	0.1104-0.1112 in.	2.805-2.825mm
Piston-to-cylinder wall clearance	0.001-0.002 in.	0.020-0.040mm
Piston skirt outer diameter measured 15mm from the bottom of the skirt		
-Nihon Hatsujo	3.5425-3.5429 in.	89.980-89.990mm
-Chuo Hatsujo	3.5421-3.5425 in.	89.970-89.980mm
Piston pin		
Outer diameter	0.8659-0.8661 in.	21.994-22.000mm
Pin-to-piston clearance	0.0004-0.0007 in.	0.010-0.019mm
Connecting Rod		
End-play		
Installed on the crankshaft	0.006-0.012 in.	0.15-0.30mm
Bore diameter		
Crankshaft end	2.24 in.	57.0mm
Piston pin end	0.8649-0.8654 in.	21.968-21.981mm
Pin-to-rod clearance	0.0005-0.0013 in.	0.013-0.032mm
Crankshaft		
Main journal diameter	2.6762-2.6772 in.	67.976-68.000mm
Connecting rod journal diameter	2.1248-2.1257 in.	53.970-53.994mm
Taper	0.0002 in.	0.005mm
Out-of-round	0.0002 in.	0.004mm
End-play	0.004-0.011 in.	0.10-0.29mm
Run-out	0.0008 in.	0.020mm
Bearing		
Main bearing to journal oil clearance	0.0008-0.0017 in.	0.020-0.044mm
Rod bearing-to-journal oil clearance	0.0009-0.0018 in.	0.022-0.046mm

90943C24

3.5L (C35A1) ENGINE MECHANICAL SPECIFICATIONS

Description	English	Metric
General Information		
Engine type	V-6 cylinder	
Compression ratio	9.6:1	
Firing order	1-2-3-4-5-6	
Displacement	211	3.5L
Bore	3.54 in.	89.92mm
Stroke	3.58 in.	90.93mm
Cylinder Head		
Compression		
Minimum	199 psi	1400kPa
	142 psi	980kPa
Maximum deviation	28 psi	200kPa
Warpage	0.002 in.	0.05mm
Height	3.935-3.939 in.	99.95-100.05mm
Camshaft		
End-play	0.002-0.006 in.	0.05-0.15mm
Camshaft to holder clearance	0.0020-0.0035 in.	0.050-0.089mm
Run-out	0.001 in.	0.03mm
Camshaft lobe height		
Intake	1.5817 in.	40.175mm
Exhaust	1.4913 in.	37.878mm
Valve and Valve Seats		
Valve clearance (cold)		
Intake	Hydraulic Tappets, Auto-adjusting	
Exhaust	Hydraulic Tappets, Auto-adjusting	
Valve stem		
Outer diameter		
Intake	0.2157-0.2161 in.	5.48-5.49mm
Exhaust	0.2146-0.2150 in.	5.45-5.46mm
Valve stem-to-guide clearance		
Intake	0.001-0.002 in.	0.02-0.05mm
Exhaust	0.002-0.003 in.	0.05-0.08mm
Valve seat width		
Intake	0.031-0.039 in.	0.80-1.00mm
Exhaust	0.049-0.061 in.	1.25-1.55mm
Valve stem installed height		
Intake	1.8478-1.8652 in.	46.935-47.375mm
Exhaust	1.8852-1.9045 in.	47.885-48.375mm
Valve Spring and Guide		
Valve spring free length		
Intake		
-Nihon Hatsujo	2.018 in.	51.25mm
-Chuo Hatsujo	2.022 in.	51.35mm
Exhaust		
-Nihon Hatsujo	2.210 in.	56.13mm
-Chuo Hatsujo	2.208 in.	56.09mm
Valve guide		
Inner dimension		
Intake	0.2171-0.2177 in.	5.515-5.530mm
Exhaust	0.2171-0.2177 in.	5.515-5.530mm

90943C25

3.5L (C35A1) ENGINE MECHANICAL SPECIFICATIONS

Description	English	Metric
Valve Spring and Guide (cont.)		
Valve guide installed height		
Intake	0.620-0.640 in.	15.75-16.25mm
Exhaust	0.620-0.640 in.	15.75-16.25mm
Engine Block		
Deck surface warpage	0.003 in.	0.07mm
Cylinder bore diameter	3.5437-3.5441 in.	90.010-90.020mm
Cylinder bore taper	0.002 in.	0.05mm
Cylinder re-boring limit	0.02 in.	0.5mm
Piston, Ring and Pin		
Piston ring-to-groove clearance		
Top	0.0022-0.0031 in.	0.055-0.080mm
2nd	0.0012-0.0022 in.	0.030-0.055mm
Piston ring end gap		
Top	0.010-0.016 in.	0.25-0.40mm
2nd	0.016-0.022 in.	0.40-0.55mm
Oil	0.008-0.028 in.	0.20-0.70mm
-Nihon Hatsujo	0.008-0.020 in.	0.20-0.50mm
-Chuo Hatsujo		
Ring groove width		
Top	0.0602-0.0606 in.	1.530-1.540mm
2nd	0.0480-0.0484 in.	1.220-1.230mm
Oil	0.1104-0.1112 in.	2.805-2.825mm
Piston-to-cylinder wall clearance	0.001-0.002 in.	0.020-0.040mm
Piston skirt outer diameter measured 15mm from the bottom of the skirt		
-Nihon Hatsujo	3.5425-3.5429 in.	89.980-89.990mm
-Chuo Hatsujo	3.5421-3.5425 in.	89.970-89.980mm
Piston pin	0.8646-0.8648 in.	21.961-21.965mm
Pin-to-piston clearance	-0.0002-(-0.0001) in.	-0.005-(-0.002)mm
Connecting Rod		
End-play	0.006-0.012 in.	0.15-0.30mm
Bore diameter		
Installed on the crankshaft		
Crankshaft end	2.24 in.	57.0mm
Piston pin end	0.8649-0.8654 in.	21.968-21.981mm
Pin-to-rod clearance	0.0002-0.0006 in.	0.005-0.015mm
Crankshaft		
Main journal diameter	2.6762-2.6772 in.	67.976-68.000mm
Connecting rod journal diameter	2.1248-2.1257 in.	53.970-53.994mm
Taper	0.0002 in.	0.005mm
Out-of-round	0.0002 in.	0.004mm
End-play	0.004-0.011 in.	0.10-0.29mm
Run-out	0.0008 in.	0.020mm
Bearing		
Main bearing to journal oil clearance	0.0008-0.0017 in.	0.020-0.044mm
Rod bearing-to-journal oil clearance	0.0009-0.0018 in.	0.022-0.046mm

90943C26

TORQUE SPECIFICATIONS

Components	Ft. Lbs.	Nm
Transaxle housing mounting bolts		
Manual	42-47	57-64
Automatic	40-43	54-59
Torque converter to drive plate	100-104 inch lbs.	11.0-12.0
Rear engine stiffener		
Stiffner to transaxle	15-17	20-24
Manual	40-42	54-57
Automatic	29-32	39-43
Engine mounting brackets		
2.2, 2.3L	37-40	50-54
3.0L	24-28	32-38
Valve/Rocker Arm Cover		
Cover retainers	6.9-7.2	9.3-9.8
Cylinder Head		
Camshaft Caps	6.7-7.2	9.0-9.8
Camshaft Pulley	23-27	31-37
Rocker arm locknut	14-18	19-25
Cylinder head bolts		
Step 1	19-22	25-29
Step 2	59-63	80-85
Ignition System		
Distributor attaching bolt	13-17	17-24
Thermostat		
Mounting bolts	72-96 inch lbs.	7-11
Intake Manifold		
Throttle body	13-16	17-22
Manifold bolts	15-17	20-23
Idle air control valve	13-16	17-22
Idle air temperature sensor	3.9-4.0	5.2-6.0
Evap purge control solenoid	7.3-8.0	9.9-11.0
Throttle body	14.6-17.0	19.7-22.0
Exhaust Manifold		
Manifold-to-block	21-23	28-31
Self-locking nut	16-17	21-24
Manifold heat shield	40.0	54.0
Manifold down-pipe to manifold	33.0	44.0
Oxygen sensor		
Catalytic converter		
Mounting bolts	11.0-12.0	15-16
Heat-shield/cover	7.2	9.8
Radiator		
Radiator mounting nuts	60-84 inch lbs.	7-9
Electrical Cooling Fan		
Fan motor-to-fan shroud nuts	44-66 inch lbs.	5-8
Fan assembly		
Nuts	35-41 inch lbs.	4-5
Screws	23-33 inch lbs.	3-4
Water Pump		
Water pump bolts	15-22	20-30
Oil Pan		
Oil pan bolts	8.5-8.7	12.0

90943C27

TORQUE SPECIFICATIONS

Components	Ft. Lbs.	Nm
Oil Pump		
Gasoline engines		
Pick-up tube and screen assembly bolts	72-108 inch lbs.	8-12
Oil pump bolts	60-84 inch lbs.	7-10
Crankshaft Damper		
Pulley bolt	74-90	100-122
Timing Belt and Sprockets		
Belt tensioner adjusting bolt	35-40	54.0
Middle cover bolt	7.0-7.2	9.4-9.8
Lower cover bolt	7.0-7.2	9.4-9.8
Camshaft		
Camshaft thrust plate bolts	84-132 inch lbs.	10-15
Connecting Rods		
Rod cap-to-rod retainers	19-25	26-34
Flywheel/Flexplate		
Flywheel/Flexplate bolts	54-64	73-87

90943C28

USING A VACUUM GAUGE

White needle = steady needle   Dark needle = drifting needle

The vacuum gauge is one of the most useful and easy-to-use diagnostic tools. It is inexpensive, easy to hook up, and provides valuable information about the condition of your engine.

Indication: Normal engine in good condition

Gauge reading: Steady, from 17–22 in./Hg.

Indication: Sticking valve or ignition miss

Gauge reading: Needle fluctuates from 15–20 in./Hg. at idle

Indication: Late ignition or valve timing, low compression, stuck throttle valve, leaking carburetor or manifold gasket.

Gauge reading: Low (15–20 in./Hg.) but steady

Indication: Improper carburetor adjustment, or minor intake leak at carburetor or manifold

NOTE: Bad fuel injector O-rings may also cause this reading.

Gauge reading: Drifting needle

Indication: Weak valve springs, worn valve stem guides, or leaky cylinder head gasket (vibrating excessively at all speeds).

NOTE: A plugged catalytic converter may also cause this reading.

Gauge reading: Needle fluctuates as engine speed increases

Indication: Burnt valve or improper valve clearance. The needle will drop when the defective valve operates.

Gauge reading: Steady needle, but drops regularly

Indication: Choked muffler or obstruction in system. Speed up the engine. Choked muffler will exhibit a slow drop of vacuum to zero.

Gauge reading: Gradual drop in reading at idle

Indication: Worn valve guides

Gauge reading: Needle vibrates excessively at idle, but steadies as engine speed increases

TCCS3D01

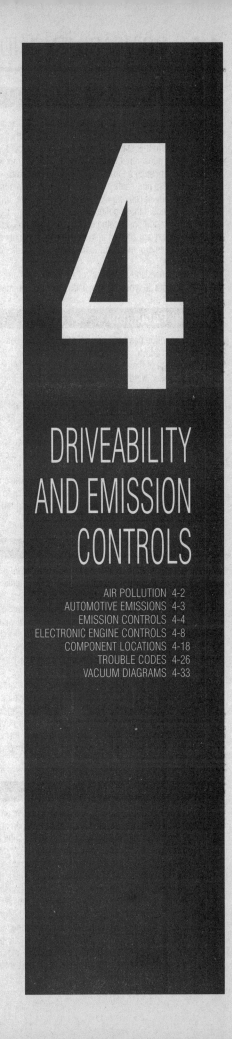

4

DRIVEABILITY AND EMISSION CONTROLS

AIR POLLUTION

The earth's atmosphere, at or near sea level, consists approximately of 78 percent nitrogen, 21 percent oxygen and 1 percent other gases. If it were possible to remain in this state, 100 percent clean air would result. However, many varied sources allow other gases and particulates to mix with the clean air, causing our atmosphere to become unclean or polluted.

Some of these pollutants are visible while others are invisible, with each having the capability of causing distress to the eyes, ears, throat, skin and respiratory system. Should these pollutants become concentrated in a specific area and under certain conditions, death could result due to the displacement or chemical change of the oxygen content in the air. These pollutants can also cause great damage to the environment and to the many man made objects that are exposed to the elements.

To better understand the causes of air pollution, the pollutants can be categorized into 3 separate types, natural, industrial and automotive.

Natural Pollutants

Natural pollution has been present on earth since before man appeared and continues to be a factor when discussing air pollution, although it causes only a small percentage of the overall pollution problem. It is the direct result of decaying organic matter, wind born smoke and particulates from such natural events as plain and forest fires (ignited by heat or lightning), volcanic ash, sand and dust which can spread over a large area of the countryside.

Such a phenomenon of natural pollution has been seen in the form of volcanic eruptions, with the resulting plume of smoke, steam and volcanic ash blotting out the sun's rays as it spreads and rises higher into the atmosphere. As it travels into the atmosphere the upper air currents catch and carry the smoke and ash, while condensing the steam back into water vapor. As the water vapor, smoke and ash travel on their journey, the smoke dissipates into the atmosphere while the ash and moisture settle back to earth in a trail hundreds of miles long. In some cases, lives are lost and millions of dollars of property damage result.

Industrial Pollutants

Industrial pollution is caused primarily by industrial processes, the burning of coal, oil and natural gas, which in turn produce smoke and fumes. Because the burning fuels contain large amounts of sulfur, the principal ingredients of smoke and fumes are sulfur dioxide and particulate matter. This type of pollutant occurs most severely during still, damp and cool weather, such as at night. Even in its less severe form, this pollutant is not confined to just cities. Because of air movements, the pollutants move for miles over the surrounding countryside, leaving in its path a barren and unhealthy environment for all living things.

Working with Federal, State and Local mandated regulations and by carefully monitoring emissions, big business has greatly reduced the amount of pollutant introduced from its industrial sources, striving to obtain an acceptable level. Because of the mandated industrial emission clean up, many land areas and streams in and around the cities that were formerly barren of vegetation and life, have now begun to move back in the direction of nature's intended balance.

Automotive Pollutants

The third major source of air pollution is automotive emissions. The emissions from the internal combustion engines were not an appreciable problem years ago because of the small number of registered vehicles and the nation's small highway system. However, during the early 1950's, the trend of the American people was to move from the cities to the surrounding suburbs. This caused an immediate problem in transportation because the majority of suburbs were not afforded mass transit conveniences. This lack of transportation created an attractive market for the automobile manufacturers, which resulted in a dramatic increase in the number of vehicles produced and sold, along with a marked increase in highway construction between cities and the suburbs. Multi-vehicle families emerged with a growing emphasis placed on an individual vehicle per family member. As the increase in vehicle ownership and usage occurred, so did pollutant levels in and around the cities, as suburbanites drove daily to their

businesses and employment, returning at the end of the day to their homes in the suburbs.

It was noted that a smoke and fog type haze was being formed and at times, remained in suspension over the cities, taking time to dissipate. At first this "smog," derived from the words "smoke" and "fog," was thought to result from industrial pollution but it was determined that automobile emissions shared the blame. It was discovered that when normal automobile emissions were exposed to sunlight for a period of time, complex chemical reactions would take place.

It is now known that smog is a photo chemical layer which develops when certain oxides of nitrogen (NOx) and unburned hydrocarbons (HC) from automobile emissions are exposed to sunlight. Pollution was more severe when smog would become stagnant over an area in which a warm layer of air settled over the top of the cooler air mass, trapping and holding the cooler mass at ground level. The trapped cooler air would keep the emissions from being dispersed and diluted through normal air flows. This type of air stagnation was given the name "Temperature Inversion."

TEMPERATURE INVERSION

In normal weather situations, surface air is warmed by heat radiating from the earth's surface and the sun's rays. This causes it to rise upward, into the atmosphere. Upon rising it will cool through a convection type heat exchange with the cooler upper air. As warm air rises, the surface pollutants are carried upward and dissipated into the atmosphere.

When a temperature inversion occurs, we find the higher air is no longer cooler, but is warmer than the surface air, causing the cooler surface air to become trapped. This warm air blanket can extend from above ground level to a few hundred or even a few thousand feet into the air. As the surface air is trapped, so are the pollutants, causing a severe smog condition. Should this stagnant air mass extend to a few thousand feet high, enough air movement with the inversion takes place to allow the smog layer to rise above ground level but the pollutants still cannot dissipate. This inversion can remain for days over an area, with the smog level only rising or lowering from ground level to a few hundred feet high. Meanwhile, the pollutant levels increase, causing eye irritation, respiratory problems, reduced visibility, plant damage and in some cases, even disease.

This inversion phenomenon was first noted in the Los Angeles, California area. The city lies in terrain resembling a basin and with certain weather conditions, a cold air mass is held in the basin while a warmer air mass covers it like a lid.

Because this type of condition was first documented as prevalent in the Los Angeles area, this type of trapped pollution was named Los Angeles Smog, although it occurs in other areas where a large concentration of automobiles are used and the air remains stagnant for any length of time.

HEAT TRANSFER

Consider the internal combustion engine as a machine in which raw materials must be placed so a finished product comes out. As in any machine operation, a certain amount of wasted material is formed. When we relate this to the internal combustion engine, we find that through the input of air and fuel, we obtain power during the combustion process to drive the vehicle. The by-product or waste of this power is, in part, heat and exhaust gases with which we must dispose.

The heat from the combustion process can rise to over 4000°F (2204°C). The dissipation of this heat is controlled by a ram air effect, the use of cooling fans to cause air flow and a liquid coolant solution surrounding the combustion area to transfer the heat of combustion through the cylinder walls and into the coolant. The coolant is then directed to a thin-finned, multi-tubed radiator, from which the excess heat is transferred to the atmosphere by 1 of the 3 heat transfer methods, conduction, convection or radiation.

The cooling of the combustion area is an important part in the control of exhaust emissions. To understand the behavior of the combustion and transfer of its heat, consider the air/fuel charge. It is ignited and the flame front burns progressively across the combustion chamber until the burning charge reaches the cylinder walls. Some of the fuel in contact with the walls is not hot enough to burn, thereby snuffing out or quenching the combustion process. This leaves unburned fuel in the combustion chamber. This unburned fuel is then forced out of the cylinder and into the exhaust system, along with the exhaust gases.

Many attempts have been made to minimize the amount of unburned fuel in the combustion chambers due to quenching, by increasing the coolant tempera-

ture and lessening the contact area of the coolant around the combustion area. However, design limitations within the combustion chambers prevent the complete burning of the air/fuel charge, so a certain amount of the unburned fuel is still expelled into the exhaust system, regardless of modifications to the engine.

AUTOMOTIVE EMISSIONS

Before emission controls were mandated on internal combustion engines, other sources of engine pollutants were discovered along with the exhaust emissions. It was determined that engine combustion exhaust produced approximately 60 percent of the total emission pollutants, fuel evaporation from the fuel tank and carburetor vents produced 20 percent, with the final 20 percent being produced through the crankcase as a by-product of the combustion process.

Exhaust Gases

The exhaust gases emitted into the atmosphere are a combination of burned and unburned fuel. To understand the exhaust emission and its composition, we must review some basic chemistry.

When the air/fuel mixture is introduced into the engine, we are mixing air, composed of nitrogen (78 percent), oxygen (21 percent) and other gases (1 percent) with the fuel, which is 100 percent hydrocarbons (HC), in a semi-controlled ratio. As the combustion process is accomplished, power is produced to move the vehicle while the heat of combustion is transferred to the cooling system. The exhaust gases are then composed of nitrogen, a diatomic gas (N_2), the same as was introduced in the engine, carbon dioxide (CO_2), the same gas that is used in beverage carbonation, and water vapor (H_2O). The nitrogen (N_2), for the most part, passes through the engine unchanged, while the oxygen (O_2) reacts (burns) with the hydrocarbons (HC) and produces the carbon dioxide (CO_2) and the water vapors (H_2O). If this chemical process would be the only process to take place, the exhaust emissions would be harmless. However, during the combustion process, other compounds are formed which are considered dangerous. These pollutants are hydrocarbons (HC), carbon monoxide (CO), oxides of nitrogen (NOx) oxides of sulfur (SOx) and engine particulates.

HYDROCARBONS

Hydrocarbons (HC) are essentially fuel which was not burned during the combustion process or which has escaped into the atmosphere through fuel evaporation. The main sources of incomplete combustion are rich air/fuel mixtures, low engine temperatures and improper spark timing. The main sources of hydrocarbon emission through fuel evaporation on most vehicles used to be the vehicle's fuel tank and carburetor float bowl.

To reduce combustion hydrocarbon emission, engine modifications were made to minimize dead space and surface area in the combustion chamber. In addition, the air/fuel mixture was made more lean through the improved control which feedback carburetion and fuel injection offers and by the addition of external controls to aid in further combustion of the hydrocarbons outside the engine. Two such methods were the addition of air injection systems, to inject fresh air into the exhaust manifolds and the installation of catalytic converters, units that are able to burn traces of hydrocarbons without affecting the internal combustion process or fuel economy.

To control hydrocarbon emissions through fuel evaporation, modifications were made to the fuel tank to allow storage of the fuel vapors during periods of engine shut-down. Modifications were also made to the air intake system so that at specific times during engine operation, these vapors may be purged and burned by blending them with the air/fuel mixture.

CARBON MONOXIDE

Carbon monoxide is formed when not enough oxygen is present during the combustion process to convert carbon (C) to carbon dioxide (CO_2). An increase in the carbon monoxide (CO) emission is normally accompanied by an increase in the hydrocarbon (HC) emission because of the lack of oxygen to completely burn all of the fuel mixture.

Carbon monoxide (CO) also increases the rate at which the photo chemical smog is formed by speeding up the conversion of nitric oxide (NO) to nitrogen dioxide (NO_2). To accomplish this, carbon monoxide (CO) combines with oxy-

gen (O_2) and nitric oxide (NO) to produce carbon dioxide (CO_2) and nitrogen dioxide (NO_2). ($CO + O_2 + NO = CO_2 + NO_2$).

The dangers of carbon monoxide, which is an odorless and colorless toxic gas are many. When carbon monoxide is inhaled into the lungs and passed into the blood stream, oxygen is replaced by the carbon monoxide in the red blood cells, causing a reduction in the amount of oxygen supplied to the many parts of the body. This lack of oxygen causes headaches, lack of coordination, reduced mental alertness and, should the carbon monoxide concentration be high enough, death could result.

NITROGEN

Normally, nitrogen is an inert gas. When heated to approximately 2500°F (1371°C) through the combustion process, this gas becomes active and causes an increase in the nitric oxide (NO) emission.

Oxides of nitrogen (NOx) are composed of approximately 97–98 percent nitric oxide (NO). Nitric oxide is a colorless gas but when it is passed into the atmosphere, it combines with oxygen and forms nitrogen dioxide (NO_2). The nitrogen dioxide then combines with chemically active hydrocarbons (HC) and when in the presence of sunlight, causes the formation of photo-chemical smog.

Ozone

To further complicate matters, some of the nitrogen dioxide (NO_2) is broken apart by the sunlight to form nitric oxide and oxygen. (NO_2 + sunlight = NO + O). This single atom of oxygen then combines with diatomic (meaning 2 atoms) oxygen (O_2) to form ozone (O_3). Ozone is one of the smells associated with smog. It has a pungent and offensive odor, irritates the eyes and lung tissues, affects the growth of plant life and causes rapid deterioration of rubber products. Ozone can be formed by sunlight as well as electrical discharge into the air.

The most common discharge area on the automobile engine is the secondary ignition electrical system, especially when inferior quality spark plug cables are used. As the surge of high voltage is routed through the secondary cable, the circuit builds up an electrical field around the wire, which acts upon the oxygen in the surrounding air to form the ozone. The faint glow along the cable with the engine running that may be visible on a dark night, is called the "corona discharge." It is the result of the electrical field passing from a high along the cable, to a low in the surrounding air, which forms the ozone gas. The combination of corona and ozone has been a major cause of cable deterioration. Recently, different and better quality insulating materials have lengthened the life of the electrical cables.

Although ozone at ground level can be harmful, ozone is beneficial to the earth's inhabitants. By having a concentrated ozone layer called the "ozonosphere," between 10 and 20 miles (16–32 km) up in the atmosphere, much of the ultra violet radiation from the sun's rays are absorbed and screened. If this ozone layer were not present, much of the earth's surface would be burned, dried and unfit for human life.

OXIDES OF SULFUR

Oxides of sulfur (SOx) were initially ignored in the exhaust system emissions, since the sulfur content of gasoline as a fuel is less than 1/10 of 1 percent. Because of this small amount, it was felt that it contributed very little to the overall pollution problem. However, because of the difficulty in solving the sulfur emissions in industrial pollution and the introduction of catalytic converters to automobile exhaust systems, a change was mandated. The automobile exhaust system, when equipped with a catalytic converter, changes the sulfur dioxide (SO_2) into sulfur trioxide (SO_3).

When this combines with water vapors (H_2O), a sulfuric acid mist (H_2SO_4) is formed and is a very difficult pollutant to handle since it is extremely corrosive. This sulfuric acid mist that is formed, is the same mist that rises from the vents of an automobile battery when an active chemical reaction takes place within the battery cells.

When a large concentration of vehicles equipped with catalytic converters are operating in an area, this acid mist may rise and be distributed over a large ground area causing land, plant, crop, paint and building damage.

PARTICULATE MATTER

A certain amount of particulate matter is present in the burning of any fuel, with carbon constituting the largest percentage of the particulates. In gasoline, the remaining particulates are the burned remains of the various other compounds used in its manufacture. When a gasoline engine is in good internal condition, the particulate emissions are low but as the engine wears internally, the particulate emissions increase. By visually inspecting the tail pipe emissions, a determination can be made as to where an engine defect may exist. An engine with light gray or blue smoke emitting from the tail pipe normally indicates an increase in the oil consumption through burning due to internal engine wear. Black smoke would indicate a defective fuel delivery system, causing the engine to operate in a rich mode. Regardless of the color of the smoke, the internal part of the engine or the fuel delivery system should be repaired to prevent excess particulate emissions.

Diesel and turbine engines emit a darkened plume of smoke from the exhaust system because of the type of fuel used. Emission control regulations are mandated for this type of emission and more stringent measures are being used to prevent excess emission of the particulate matter. Electronic components are being introduced to control the injection of the fuel at precisely the proper time of piston travel, to achieve the optimum in fuel ignition and fuel usage. Other particulate after-burning components are being tested to achieve a cleaner emission.

Good grades of engine lubricating oils should be used, which meet the manufacturer's specification. Cut-rate oils can contribute to the particulate emission problem because of their low flash or ignition temperature point. Such oils burn prematurely during the combustion process causing emission of particulate matter.

The cooling system is an important factor in the reduction of particulate matter. The optimum combustion will occur, with the cooling system operating at a temperature specified by the manufacturer. The cooling system must be maintained in the same manner as the engine oiling system, as each system is required to perform properly in order for the engine to operate efficiently for a long time.

Crankcase Emissions

Crankcase emissions are made up of water, acids, unburned fuel, oil fumes and particulates. These emissions are classified as hydrocarbons (HC) and are formed by the small amount of unburned, compressed air/fuel mixture entering the crankcase from the combustion area (between the cylinder walls and piston rings) during the compression and power strokes. The head of the compression and combustion help to form the remaining crankcase emissions.

Since the first engines, crankcase emissions were allowed into the atmosphere through a road draft tube, mounted on the lower side of the engine block. Fresh air came in through an open oil filler cap or breather. The air passed through the crankcase mixing with blow-by gases. The motion of the vehicle and the air blowing past the open end of the road draft tube caused a low pressure area (vacuum) at the end of the tube. Crankcase emissions were simply drawn out of the road draft tube into the air.

To control the crankcase emission, the road draft tube was deleted. A hose and/or tubing was routed from the crankcase to the intake manifold so the blow-by emission could be burned with the air/fuel mixture. However, it was found that intake manifold vacuum, used to draw the crankcase emissions into the manifold, would vary in strength at the wrong time and not allow the proper emission flow. A regulating valve was needed to control the flow of air through the crankcase.

Testing, showed the removal of the blow-by gases from the crankcase as quickly as possible, was most important to the longevity of the engine. Should large accumulations of blow-by gases remain and condense, dilution of the engine oil would occur to form water, soots, resins, acids and lead salts, resulting in the formation of sludge and varnishes. This condensation of the blow-by gases occurs more frequently on vehicles used in numerous starting and stopping conditions, excessive idling and when the engine is not allowed to attain normal operating temperature through short runs.

Evaporative Emissions

Gasoline fuel is a major source of pollution, before and after it is burned in the automobile engine. From the time the fuel is refined, stored, pumped and transported, again stored until it is pumped into the fuel tank of the vehicle, the gasoline gives off unburned hydrocarbons (HC) into the atmosphere. Through the redesign of storage areas and venting systems, the pollution factor was diminished, but not eliminated, from the refinery standpoint. However, the automobile still remained the primary source of vaporized, unburned hydrocarbon (HC) emissions.

Fuel pumped from an underground storage tank is cool but when exposed to a warmer ambient temperature, will expand. Before controls were mandated, an owner might fill the fuel tank with fuel from an underground storage tank and park the vehicle for some time in warm area, such as a parking lot. As the fuel would warm, it would expand and should no provisions or area be provided for the expansion, the fuel would spill out of the filler neck and onto the ground, causing hydrocarbon (HC) pollution and creating a severe fire hazard. To correct this condition, the vehicle manufacturers added overflow plumbing and/or gasoline tanks with built in expansion areas or domes.

However, this did not control the fuel vapor emission from the fuel tank. It was determined that most of the fuel evaporation occurred when the vehicle was stationary and the engine not operating. Most vehicles carry 5–25 gallons (19–95 liters) of gasoline. Should a large concentration of vehicles be parked in one area, such as a large parking lot, excessive fuel vapor emissions would take place, increasing as the temperature increases.

To prevent the vapor emission from escaping into the atmosphere, the fuel systems were designed to trap the vapors while the vehicle is stationary, by sealing the system from the atmosphere. A storage system is used to collect and hold the fuel vapors from the carburetor (if equipped) and the fuel tank when the engine is not operating. When the engine is started, the storage system is then purged of the fuel vapors, which are drawn into the engine and burned with the air/fuel mixture.

EMISSION CONTROLS

Crankcase Ventilation System

OPERATION

The Positive Crankcase Ventilation (PCV) system is used to control crankcase blow-by vapors. The gases are recycled in the following way:

As the engine is running, clean, filtered air is drawn through the air filter and into the crankcase. As the air passes through the crankcase, it picks up the combustion gases and carries them out of the crankcase, through the PCV valve, and into the induction system. As they enter the intake manifold, they are drawn into the combustion chamber where they are reburned.

The most critical component in the system is the PCV valve. This valve controls the amount of gases which are recycled into the combustion chamber. At low engine speeds, the valve is partially closed, limiting the flow of gases into the intake manifold. As engine speed increases, the valve opens to admit greater quantities of gases into the intake manifold. If the PCV valve becomes clogged, the system is designed to allow excessive amounts of blow-by gases to back flow through the crankcase tube into the air cleaner to be consumed by normal combustion.

The Positive Crankcase Ventilation (PCV) system must be operating correctly to provide complete removal of the crankcase vapors. Fresh air is supplied to the crankcase from the air filter, mixed with the internal exhaust gases, passed through the PCV valve and into the intake manifold.

The PCV valve meters the flow at a rate depending upon the manifold vacuum. If the manifold vacuum is high, the PCV restricts the flow to the intake manifold. If abnormal operating conditions occur, excessive amounts of internal exhaust gases back flow through the crankcase vent tube into the air filter to be burned by normal combustion.

TESTING

➡**Never operate an engine without a PCV valve or a ventilation system, except as directed by testing procedures, for it can become damaged.**

Incorrect operation of the PCV system can cause multiple driveability symptoms.

A plugged valve or hose may cause:
- Rough idle
- Stalling or slow idle speed
- Oil leaks
- Sludge in engine

A leaking valve or hose would cause:
- Rough idle
- Stalling
- High idle speed

PCV Valve

▶ See Figure 1

1. Remove the PCV valve from the intake manifold or valve cover.
2. Run the engine at idle.
3. Place your thumb over the end of the valve. Check for vacuum. If there is no vacuum at the valve, check for plugged valve or vacuum lines.
4. Shut off the engine. Shake the valve and listen for the rattle. If valve doesn't rattle, replace it.

System Functional Check

1. Check the crankcase ventilation valve for correct application.
2. Run engine until normal operating temperature is obtained.
3. Block off crankcase ventilation system fresh air intake passage.
4. Remove the engine oil dipstick and install a vacuum gauge on the dipstick tube.
5. Run the engine at 1500 rpm for 30 seconds, then read the vacuum gage while at 1500 rpm. If vacuum is present, the crankcase ventilation system is functioning properly. No vacuum indicates the engine may not be sealed and/or is drawing in outside air. Check valve cover and oil pan gaskets for leaks and repair, as required. If the vacuum gage registers a pressure or the vacuum gage is pushed out of the dipstick tube, check for the correct crankcase ventilation valve, a plugged hose or excessive engine blow-by.

REMOVAL & INSTALLATION

Refer to Section 1 for removal and installation of the PCV valve. The PCV nipple should be replaced and inspected every 60,000 miles (96,000 km).

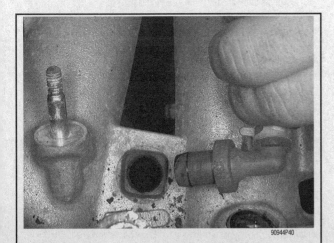

Fig. 1 Pulling the PCV valve from the intake manifold

Evaporative Emission Controls

OPERATION

▶ See Figure 2

Changes in atmospheric temperature cause fuel tanks to breathe, that is, the air within the tank expands and contracts with outside temperature changes. If an unsealed system was used, when the temperature rises, air would escape through the tank vent tube or the vent in the tank cap. The air which escapes contains gasoline vapors.

The Evaporative Emission Control System provides a sealed fuel system with the capability to store and condense fuel vapors. When the fuel evaporates in the fuel tank, the vapor passes through the EVAP emission valve, through vent hoses or tubes to a carbon filled evaporative canister. When the engine is operating the vapors are drawn into the intake manifold and burned during combustion..

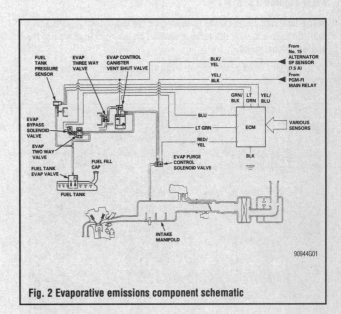

Fig. 2 Evaporative emissions component schematic

A sealed, maintenance free evaporative canister is used. The canister is filled with granules of an activated carbon mixture. Fuel vapors entering the canister are absorbed by the charcoal granules. A vent cap is located on the top of the canister to provide fresh air to the canister when it is being purged. The vent cap opens to provide fresh air into the canister, which circulates through the charcoal, releasing trapped vapors and carrying them to the engine to be burned.

Fuel tank pressure vents fuel vapors into the canister. They are held in the canister until they can be drawn into the intake manifold. The canister purge valve allows the canister to be purged at a pre-determined time and engine operating conditions.

Vacuum to the canister is controlled by the canister purge valve. The valve is operated by the PCM. The PCM regulates the valve by switching the ground circuit on and off based on engine operating conditions. When energized, the valve prevents vacuum from reaching the canister. When not energized the valve allows vacuum to purge the vapors from the canister.

During warm up and for a specified time after hot starts, the PCM energizes (grounds) the valve preventing vacuum from reaching the canister. When the engine temperature reaches the operating level of about 120°F (49°C), the PCM removes the ground from the valve allowing vacuum to flow through the canister and purges vapors through the throttle body. During certain idle conditions, the purge valve may be grounded to control fuel mixture calibrations.

The fuel tank is sealed with a pressure-vacuum relief filler cap. The relief valve in the cap is a safety feature, preventing excessive pressure or vacuum in the fuel tank. If the cap is malfunctioning, and needs to be replaced, ensure that the replacement is the identical cap to ensure correct system operation.

COMPONENT TESTING

Evaporative Emissions (EVAP) Control Canister

This canister is used as a storage facility for fuel vapors which have escaped from components such as the fuel tank. This canister prevents these vapors from entering into the atmosphere.

Generally, the only testing done to the canister is a visual inspection. Look the canister over and replace it with a new one if there is any evidence of cracks or other damage.

Evaporative Hoses and Tubes

Inspect all system hoses and tubes for signs of damage or cracks. Any damage or leakage must be repaired.

Evaporative Emissions Control Shunt Valve/Solenoid Valve

▶ **See Figures 3 and 4**

➡ **The Integra's control valve is located on the top of the intake manifold. On 2.5L engines, the valve is located on the right front side of the engine compartment.**

The evaporative emissions control shunt valve is located at the top of the charcoal canister.

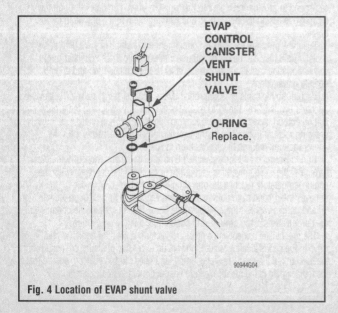

Fig. 3 Typical emissions control shunt valve

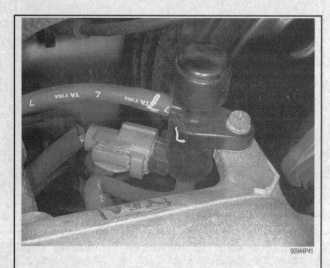

Fig. 4 Location of EVAP shunt valve

1. Disconnect the vacuum hose from the valve.
2. Remove the canister vent shunt valve from the canister.
3. Turn the ignition switch **ON**.
4. Apply vacuum to the hose.
5. If it holds vacuum, check for a short in the wire.
6. When finished testing, attach all disconnected hoses, connectors, and wires.

REMOVAL & INSTALLATION

Evaporative Emissions Canister

▶ **See Figure 5**

1. Raise and support the vehicle.
2. Remove the bolts retaining the Evaporative Emissions (EVAP) canister and bracket assembly.
3. Label and disconnect the vapor hoses from the canister.
4. Remove the canister from the bracket.
5. Installation is the reverse of the removal procedure.

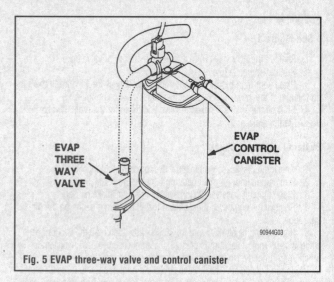

Fig. 5 EVAP three-way valve and control canister

Evaporative Emissions Control Shunt Valve

▶ **See Figure 4**

1. Disconnect the vacuum hose from the EVAP shunt valve.
2. Remove the fasteners which hold the EVAP shunt valve to the canister.
3. Remove the EVAP control shunt valve from the canister.
To install:
4. Install the EVAP control shunt valve and fasteners.
5. Connect all vacuum hoses.

Canister Purge Valve (Two-Way Valve)

▶ **See Figure 6**

1. Raise and support the vehicle.
2. Disconnect the electrical harness from the valve.
3. Disconnect the fuel vapor hoses and remove the valve.
4. Installation is the reverse of the removal procedure.

Exhaust Gas Recirculation System

OPERATION

The Exhaust Gas Recirculation (EGR) system is designed to reintroduce exhaust gas into the combustion chambers, thereby lowering combustion temperatures and reducing the formation of Oxides of Nitrogen (NO_x).

The amount of exhaust gas that is reintroduced into the combustion cycle is determined by several factors, such as: engine speed, engine vacuum, exhaust

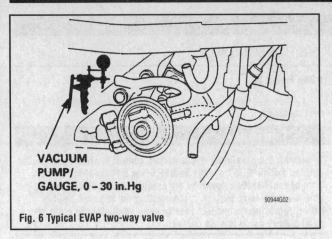

**VACUUM
PUMP/
GAUGE, 0 – 30 in.Hg**

90944G02

Fig. 6 Typical EVAP two-way valve

system backpressure, coolant temperature, throttle position. All EGR valves are vacuum operated. The EGR vacuum diagram for your particular vehicle is displayed on the Vehicle Emission Control Information (VECI) label.

The EGR system is Differential Pressure Feedback EGR (DPFE) system is controlled by the Powertrain Control Module (PCM).

COMPONENT TESTING

EGR Valve

1. Install a tachometer on the engine, following the manufacturer's instructions.
2. Detach the engine wiring harness connector from the Idle Air Control (IAC) solenoid.
3. Disconnect and plug the vacuum supply hose from the EGR valve.
4. Start the engine, then apply the parking brake, block the rear wheels and position the transaxle in Neutral.
5. Observe and note the idle speed.

➡**If the engine will not idle with the IAC solenoid disconnected, provide an air bypass to the engine by slightly opening the throttle plate or by creating an intake vacuum leak. Do not allow the idle speed to exceed typical idle rpm.**

6. Using a hand-held vacuum pump, slowly apply 5–10 in. Hg (17–34 kPa) of vacuum to the EGR valve nipple, and compare the results with the following:
   a. If the idle speed drops more than 100 rpm with the vacuum applied and returns to normal after the vacuum is removed, the EGR valve is OK.
   b. If the idle speed does not drop more than 100 rpm with the vacuum applied and return to normal after the vacuum is removed, inspect the EGR valve for a blockage; clean it if a blockage is found. Replace the EGR valve if no blockage is found, or if cleaning the valve does not remedy the malfunction.

REMOVAL & INSTALLATION

EGR Valve

1. Disconnect the negative battery cable.
2. On Legend, remove the EGR lift sensor electrical connector.
3. Disconnect the vacuum hose from the EGR valve.
4. Remove the EGR valve mounting fasteners, then separate the valve from the intake manifold.
5. Remove and discard the old EGR valve gasket, and clean the gasket mating surfaces on the valve and the intake manifold.

To install:

6. Install the EGR valve, along with a new gasket, on the upper intake manifold, then install and tighten the mounting bolts
7. Attach the vacuum hose to the EGR valve.
8. Connect the negative battery cable.

EGR Valve Solenoid

1. Locate the EGR solenoid.
2. Remove the vacuum lines and wiring connectors.
3. Unfasten the mounting screws, then remove the solenoid by lifting it off.

To install:

4. Install the solenoid and secure with the mounting screws.
5. Attach all disconnected vacuum lines and wiring connectors.

Emission Service Light

RESETTING

1996 2.5TL, CL, and 3.2TL models

◆ **See Figure 7**

The Maintenance Reminder Indicator informs you when it is time for scheduled maintenance. When it is near 7500 miles (12,000 km) since the last maintenance, the indicator will turn yellow. If you exceed 7500 miles (12,000 km), the indicator will turn red. The indicator can be reset by inserting the ignition key or other similar object into the slot below the indicator. This will extinguish the indicator for the next 7500 miles (12,000 km).

1996–97 Integra and 1996–97 3.5 RL

◆ **See Figure 8**

The Maintenance Reminder Indicator reminds you that it is time for scheduled maintenance. For the first 6000 miles (9600 km) after the Maintenance Required Indicator is reset, it will come on for 2 seconds when you turn the ignition **ON**. Between 6000 miles (9600 km) and 7500 miles (12,000 km), this indicator will light for 2 seconds when you first turn the ignition **ON**, then flash for 10 seconds. If you exceed 7500 miles (12,000 km) without having the scheduled maintenance performed, this indicator will remain on as a constant reminder. Reset the indicator by pressing the reset button. This button is located on the bottom of the dashboard to the right of the steering column.

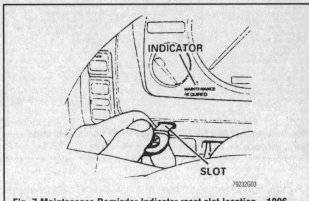

INDICATOR

MAINTE-NANCE
REQUIRED

SLOT

79232G03

Fig. 7 Maintenance Reminder Indicator reset slot location—1996 Acura TL series shown

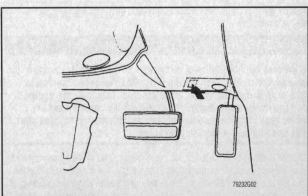

79232G02

Fig. 8 Location of the reset button for the Maintenance Reminder Indicator—1996 Acura Integra

ELECTRONIC ENGINE CONTROLS

Engine Control Module (ECM)

OPERATION

▶ See Figure 9

➡Whenever the term Electronic Control Module (ECM) is used in this manual, it will refer to the engine control computer, whether it is a Powertrain Control Module (PCM) or Electronic Control Module (ECM).

The heart of the electronic control system, which is found on the vehicles covered by this manual, is a computer control module. The module gathers information from various sensors, then controls fuel supply and engine emission systems. Most early model vehicles are equipped with an Engine Control Module (ECM) which, as its name implies, controls the engine and related emissions systems. Later model vehicles may be equipped with a Powertrain Control Module (PCM). This is similar to the original ECMs, but is designed to control additional systems as well. The PCM may control the manual transaxle shift lamp or the shift functions of the electronically controlled automatic transaxle.

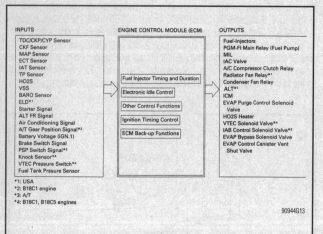

Fig. 9 Example of how the ECM receives inputs from various sensors, accesses the information, then issues outputs

Regardless of the name, all computer control modules are serviced in a similar manner. Care must be taken when handling these expensive components in order to protect them from damage. Carefully follow all instructions included with the replacement part. Avoid touching pins or connectors to prevent damage from static electricity.

All of these computer control modules contain a Programmable Read Only Memory (PROM) chips that contains calibration information specific to the vehicle application.

✴✴ WARNING

To prevent the possibility of permanent control module damage, the ignition switch MUST always be OFF when disconnecting power from or reconnecting power to the module. This includes unplugging the module connector, disconnecting the negative battery cable, removing the module fuse or even attempting to jump start your dead battery using jumper cables.

In the event of an ECM failure, the system will default to a pre-programmed set of values. These are compromise values which allow the engine to operate, although at a reduced efficiency. This is variously known as the default, limp-in or back-up mode. Driveability is almost always affected when the ECM enters this mode.

REMOVAL & INSTALLATION

▶ See Figure 10

1. Make sure the ignition switch is turned **OFF**, then disconnect the negative battery cable.

✴✴ CAUTION

To prevent the possibility of permanent control module damage, the ignition switch MUST always be OFF when disconnecting power from or reconnecting power to the module. This includes unplugging the module connector, disconnecting the negative battery cable, removing the module fuse or even attempting to jump your dead battery using jumper cables.

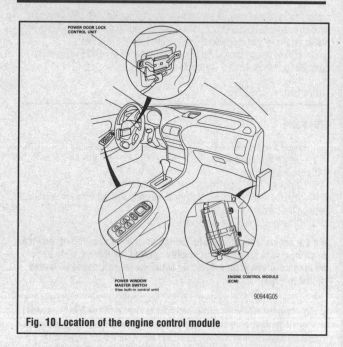

Fig. 10 Location of the engine control module

2. Locate the computer control module. It is usually located in the passenger compartment, under the right hand (passenger's) side of the instrument panel.
3. Remove the right side kick/hush panel.
4. Remove the computer control module mounting hardware.
5. If equipped, remove the electrical connector cover.
6. Detach the electrical connectors from the control module.
7. Remove the computer control module from the passenger or engine compartment.

To install:
8. Attach the electrical connectors to the computer control module.
9. Position the control module in its mounting location and secure with the mounting hardware.
10. Install the right side kick-hush panel and secure with the retainers.
11. Check that the ignition switch is **OFF**, then connect the negative battery cable.

Oxygen Sensor

OPERATION

▶ See Figures 11 and 12

An Oxygen (O_2) sensor is an input device used by the engine control computer to monitor the amount of oxygen in the exhaust gas stream. The information is used by the computer, along with other inputs, to fine-tune the air/fuel mixture so that the engine can run with the greatest efficiency in all conditions. The O_2sensor sends this information to the computer in the form of a 100–900 millivolt (mV) reference signal. The signal is actually created by the O_2sensor itself through chemical interactions between the sensor tip material (zirconium dioxide in almost all cases) and the oxygen levels in the exhaust gas stream and ambient atmosphere gas. At operating temperatures, approximately 1100°F (600°C), the element becomes a semiconductor. Essentially, through the differing levels of oxygen in the exhaust gas stream and in the surrounding atmosphere, the sensor creates a voltage signal that is directly and consistently related to the concentration of oxygen in the exhaust stream. Typically, a higher than normal amount of oxygen in the exhaust stream indicates that not all of the available oxygen was used in the combustion process, because there was not enough fuel (lean condition) present. Inversely, a lower than normal concentration of oxygen in the exhaust stream indicates that a large amount was used in the combustion process, because a larger than necessary amount of fuel was present (rich condition). Thus, the engine control computer can correct the amount of fuel introduced into the combustion chambers.

Since the control computer uses the O_2sensor output voltage as an indication of the oxygen concentration, and the oxygen concentration directly affects O_2sensor output, the signal voltage from the sensor to the computer fluctuates constantly. This fluctuation is caused by the nature of the interaction between the computer and the O_2sensor, which follows a general pattern: detect, compare, compensate, detect, compare, compensate, etc. This means that when the computer detects a lean signal from the O_2sensor, it compares the reading with known parameters stored within its memory. It calculates that there is too much oxygen present in the exhaust gases, so it compensates by adding more fuel to the air/fuel mixture. This, in turn, causes the O_2sensor to send a rich signal to the computer, which, then compares this new signal, and adjusts the air/fuel mixture again. This pattern constantly repeats itself: detect rich, compare, compensate lean, detect lean, compare, compensate rich, etc. Since the O_2sensor fluctuates between rich and lean, and because the lean limit for sensor output is 100 mV

and the rich limit is 900 mV, the proper voltage signal from a normally functioning O_2sensor consistently fluctuates between 100–300 and 700–900 mV.

➡**The sensor voltage may never quite reach 100 or 900 mV, but it should fluctuate from at least below 300 mV to above 700 mV, and the mid-point of the fluctuations should be centered around 500 mV.**

To improve O_2sensor efficiency, newer O_2sensors were designed with a built-in heating element, and are called Heated O_2(HO_2) sensors. This heating element was incorporated into the sensor so that the sensor would reach optimal operating temperature quicker, meaning that the O_2sensor output signal could be used by the engine control computer sooner. Because the sensor reaches optimal temperature quicker, modern vehicles enjoy improved driveability and fuel economy even before the engine reaches normal operating temperature.

On-Board Diagnostics second generation (OBD-II), an updated system based on the former OBD-I, calls for additional O_2sensors to be used after the catalytic converter, so that catalytic converter efficiency can be measured by the vehicle's engine control computer. The O_2sensors mounted in the exhaust system after the catalytic converters are not used to affect air/fuel mixture; they are used solely to monitor catalytic converter efficiency.

TESTING

▸ **See Figure 13**

The best, and most accurate method to test the operation of an O_2sensor is with the use of either an oscilloscope or a Diagnostic Scan Tool (DST), following their specific instructions for testing. It is possible, however, to test whether the O_2sensor is functioning properly within general parameters using a Digital Volt-Ohmmeter (DVOM), also referred to as a Digital Multi-Meter (DMM). Newer DMM's are often designed to perform many advanced diagnostic functions. Some are constructed to be used as an oscilloscope. Two in-vehicle testing procedures, and 1 bench test procedure, will be provided for the common zirconium dioxide oxygen sensor. The first in-vehicle test makes use of a standard DVOM with a 10 megohms impedance, whereas the second in-vehicle test presented necessitates the usage of an advanced DMM with MIN/MAX/Average functions. Both of these in-vehicle test procedures are likely to set Diagnostic Trouble Codes (DTC's) in the engine control computer. Therefore, after testing, be sure to clear all DTC's before retesting the sensor, if necessary.

These are some of the common DTC's which may be set during testing:
- Open in the O_2sensor circuit
- Constant low voltage in the O_2sensor circuit
- Constant high voltage in the O_2sensor circuit
- Other fuel system problems could set a O_2sensor code

➡**Because an improperly functioning fuel delivery and/or control system can adversely affect the O_2sensor voltage output signal, testing only the O_2sensor is an inaccurate method for diagnosing an engine driveability problem.**

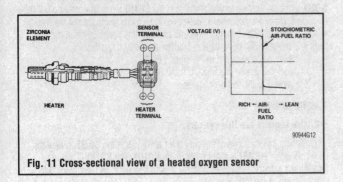

Fig. 11 Cross-sectional view of a heated oxygen sensor

Fig. 12 A cut-away view of a heated oxygen sensor

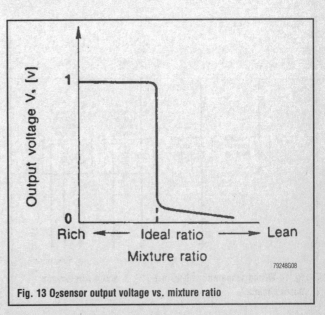

Fig. 13 O_2sensor output voltage vs. mixture ratio

If after testing the sensor, the sensor is thought to be defective because of high or low readings, be sure to check that the fuel delivery and engine management system is working properly before condemning the O_2sensor. Otherwise, the new O_2sensor may continue to register the same high or low readings.

Often, by testing the O_2sensor, another problem in the engine control management system can be diagnosed. If the sensor appears to be defective while installed in the vehicle, perform the bench test. If the sensor functions properly during the bench test, chances are that there may be a larger problem in the vehicle's fuel delivery and/or control system.

Many things can cause an O_2sensor to fail, including old age, antifreeze contamination, physical damage, prolonged exposure to overly-rich exhaust gases, and exposure to silicone sealant fumes. Be sure to remedy any such condition prior to installing a new sensor, otherwise the new sensor may be damaged as well.

➡**Perform a visual inspection of the sensor. Black sooty deposits may indicate a rich air/fuel mixture, brown deposits may indicate an oil consumption problem, and white gritty deposits may indicate an internal coolant leak. All of these conditions can destroy a new sensor if not corrected before installation.**

O_2Sensor Terminal Identification

▶ **See Figure 14**

The easiest method for determining sensor terminal identification is to use a wiring diagram for the vehicle and engine in question. However, if a wiring diagram is not available there is a method for determining terminal identification. Throughout the testing procedures, the following terms will be used for clarity:
- Vehicle harness connector—this refers to the connector on the wires which are attached to the vehicle, NOT the connector at the end of the sensor pigtail.
- Sensor pigtail connector—this refers to the connector attached to the sensor itself.
- O_2circuit—this refers to the circuit in a Heated O_2(HO_2) sensor which corresponds to the oxygen-sensing function of the sensor; NOT the heating element circuit.
- Heating circuit—this refers to the circuit in a HO_2sensor which is designed to warm the HO_2sensor quickly to improve driveability.
- Sensor Output (**SOUT**) terminal—this is the terminal which corresponds to the O_2circuit output. This is the terminal that will register the millivolt signals created by the sensor based upon the amount of oxygen in the exhaust gas stream.
- Sensor Ground (**SGND**) terminal—when a sensor is so equipped, this refers to the O_2circuit ground terminal. Many O_2sensors are not equipped with a ground wire, rather they utilize the exhaust system for the ground circuit.
- Heating Power (**HPWR**) terminal—this terminal corresponds to the circuit which provides the O_2sensor heating circuit with power when the ignition key is turned to the **ON** or **RUN** positions.

- Heating Ground (**HGND**) terminal—this is the terminal connected to the heating circuit ground wire.

1-WIRE SENSOR

1-wire sensors are by far the easiest to determine sensor terminal identification, but this is self-evident. On 1-wire O_2sensors, the single wire terminal is the **SOUT** and the exhaust system is used to provide the sensor ground pathway. Proceed to the test procedures.

2-WIRE SENSOR

On 2-wire sensors, one of the connector terminals is the **SOUT** and the other is the **SGND**. To determine which one is which, perform the following:
  1. Locate the O_2sensor and its pigtail connector. It may be necessary to raise and safely support the vehicle to gain access to the connector.
  2. Start the engine and allow it to warm up to normal operating temperature, then turn the engine **OFF**.
  3. Using a DVOM set to read 100–900 mV (millivolts) DC, backprobe the positive DVOM lead to one of the unidentified terminals and attach the negative lead to a good engine ground.

✳✳ CAUTION

While the engine is running, keep clear of all moving and hot components. Do not wear loose clothing. Otherwise severe personal injury or death may occur.

---

  4. Have an assistant restart the engine and allow it to idle.
  5. Check the DVOM for voltage.
  6. If no voltage is evident, check your DVOM leads to ensure that they are properly connected to the terminal and engine ground. If still no voltage is evident at the first terminal, move the positive meter lead to backprobe the second terminal.
  7. If voltage is now present, the positive meter lead is attached to the **SOUT** terminal. The remaining terminal is the **SGND** terminal. If still no voltage is evident, either the O_2sensor is defective or the meter leads are not making adequate contact with the engine ground and terminal contacts; clean the contacts and retest. If still no voltage is evident, the sensor is defective.
  8. Have your assistant turn the engine **OFF**.
  9. Label the sensor pigtail **SOUT** and **SGND** terminals.
  10. Proceed to the test procedures.

3-WIRE SENSOR

➡**3-wire sensors are HO_2 sensors.**

On 3-wire sensors, one of the connector terminals is the **SOUT**, one of the terminals is the **HPWR** and the other is the **HGND**. The **SGND** is achieved through the exhaust system, as with the 1-wire O_2sensor. To identify the 3 terminals, perform the following:
  1. Locate the O_2sensor and its pigtail connector. It may be necessary to raise and safely support the vehicle to gain access to the connector.
  2. Disengage the sensor pigtail connector from the vehicle harness connector.
  3. Using a DVOM set to read 12 volts, attach the DVOM ground lead to a good engine ground.
  4. Have an assistant turn the ignition switch **ON** without actually starting the engine.
  5. Probe all 3 terminals in the vehicle harness connector. One of the terminals should exhibit 12 volts of power with the ignition key **ON**; this is the **HPWR** terminal.
   a. If the **HPWR** terminal was identified, note which of the sensor harness connector terminals is the **HPWR**, then match the vehicle harness connector to the sensor pigtail connector. Label the corresponding sensor pigtail connector terminal with **HPWR**.
   b. If none of the terminals showed 12 volts of power, locate and test the heater relay or fuse. Then, perform Steps 3–6 again.
  6. Start the engine and allow it to warm up to normal operating temperature, then turn the engine **OFF**.
  7. Have your assistant turn the ignition **OFF**.
  8. Using the DVOM set to measure resistance (ohms), attach one of the leads to the **HPWR** terminal of the sensor pigtail connector. Use the other lead to probe the 2 remaining terminals of the sensor pigtail connector, one at a time.

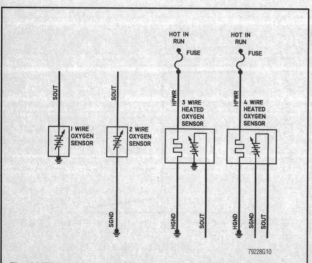

Fig. 14 Wiring schematic of typical 1-, 2-, 3- and 4-wire oxygen sensor circuits

79228G10

The DVOM should show continuity with only one of the remaining unidentified terminals; this is the **HGND** terminal. The remaining terminal is the **SOUT**.

  a. If continuity was found with only one of the 2 unidentified terminals, label the **HGND** and **SOUT** terminals on the sensor pigtail connector.

  b. If no continuity was evident, or if continuity was evident from both unidentified terminals, the O$_2$sensor is defective.

  9. All 3-wire terminals should now be labeled on the sensor pigtail connector. Proceed with the test procedures.

4-WIRE SENSOR

➡4-wire sensors are HO$_2$ sensors.

On 4-wire sensors, one of the connector terminals is the **SOUT**, one of the terminals is the **SGND**, one of the terminals is the **HPWR** and the other is the **HGND**. To identify the 4 terminals, perform the following:

  1. Locate the O$_2$sensor and its pigtail connector. It may be necessary to raise and safely support the vehicle to gain access to the connector.

  2. Disengage the sensor pigtail connector from the vehicle harness connector.

  3. Using a DVOM set to read 12 volts, attach the DVOM ground lead to a good engine ground.

  4. Have an assistant turn the ignition switch **ON** without actually starting the engine.

  5. Probe all 4 terminals in the vehicle harness connector. One of the terminals should exhibit 12 volts of power with the ignition key **ON**; this is the **HPWR** terminal.

  a. If the **HPWR** terminal was identified, note which of the sensor harness connector terminals is the **HPWR**, then match the vehicle harness connector to the sensor pigtail connector. Label the corresponding sensor pigtail connector terminal with **HPWR**.

  b. If none of the terminals showed 12 volts of power, locate and test the heater relay or fuse. Then, perform Steps 2–6 again.

  6. Have your assistant turn the ignition **OFF**.

  7. Using the DVOM set to measure resistance (ohms), attach one of the leads to the **HPWR** terminal of the sensor pigtail connector. Use the other lead to probe the 3 remaining terminals of the sensor pigtail connector, one at a time. The DVOM should show continuity with only one of the remaining unidentified terminals; this is the **HGND** terminal.

  a. If continuity was found with only 1 of the 2 unidentified terminals, label the **HGND** terminal on the sensor pigtail connector.

  b. If no continuity was evident, or if continuity was evident from all unidentified terminals, the O$_2$sensor is defective.

  c. If continuity was found at 2 of the other terminals, the sensor is probably defective. However, the sensor may not necessarily be defective, because it may have been designed with the 2 ground wires joined inside the sensor in case one of the ground wires is damaged; the other circuit could still function properly. Though, this is highly unlikely. A wiring diagram is necessary in this particular case to know whether the sensor was so designed.

  8. Reattach the sensor pigtail connector to the vehicle harness connector.

  9. Start the engine and allow it to warm up to normal operating temperature, then turn the engine **OFF**.

  10. Using a DVOM set to read 100–900 mV (millivolts) DC, backprobe the negative DVOM lead to one of the unidentified terminals and the positive lead to the other unidentified terminal.

✳✳ CAUTION

While the engine is running, keep clear of all moving and hot components. Do not wear loose clothing. Otherwise severe personal injury or death may occur.

  11. Have an assistant restart the engine and allow it to idle.

  12. Check the DVOM for voltage.

  a. If no voltage is evident, check your DVOM leads to ensure that they are properly connected to the terminals. If still no voltage is evident at either of the terminals, either the terminals were accidentally marked incorrectly or the sensor is defective.

  b. If voltage is present, but the polarity is reversed (the DVOM will show a negative voltage amount), turn the engine **OFF** and swap the 2 DVOM leads on the terminals. Start the engine and ensure that the voltage now shows the proper polarity.

  c. If voltage is evident and is the proper polarity, the positive DVOM lead is attached to the **SOUT** and the negative lead to the **SGND** terminals.

  13. Have your assistant turn the engine **OFF**.

  14. Label the sensor pigtail **SOUT** and **SGND** terminals.

REMOVAL & INSTALLATION

▶ **See Figures 15, 16, 17 and 18**

✳✳ WARNING

The sensors use a pigtail and connector. This pigtail should not be removed from the sensor. Damage or removal of the pigtail or connector could affect proper operation of the oxygen sensor. Keep the electrical connector and louvered end of the sensor clean and free of grease. NEVER use cleaning solvents of any type on the sensor! The sensor may be difficult to remove when the engine temperature is below 120°F (48°C). Excessive removal force may damage the threads in the exhaust manifold or pipe; follow the removal procedure carefully.

  1. Make sure the ignition is **OFF**, then disconnect the negative battery cable.

Fig. 15 Loosen the oxygen sensor using a wrench as shown, or use a sensor socket made especially for that purpose

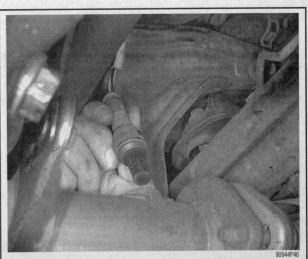

Fig. 16 Remove the oxygen sensor by hand once it has been loosened

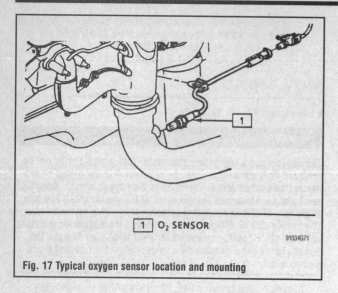

1 O₂ SENSOR

91034G71

Fig. 17 Typical oxygen sensor location and mounting

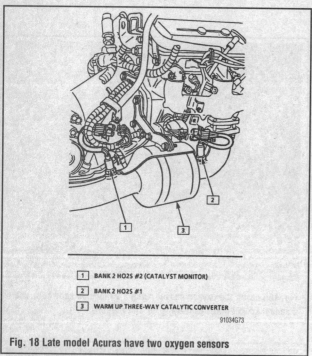

1 BANK 2 HO2S #2 (CATALYST MONITOR)

2 BANK 2 HO2S #1

3 WARM UP THREE-WAY CATALYTIC CONVERTER

91034G73

Fig. 18 Late model Acuras have two oxygen sensors

2. Locate the oxygen sensor. It protrudes from the exhaust manifold or exhaust pipe (it looks somewhat like a spark plug). It may be necessary to raise and safely support the vehicle to access the sensor.

3. Unplug the sensor electrical connector.

➡There are special wrenches, either socket or open-end available from reputable retail outlets for removing the oxygen sensor. These tools make the job much easier and often prevent unnecessary damage.

4. Carefully unscrew the sensor, then remove the oxygen sensor from the manifold or pipe.

To install:

5. During and after the removal, be very careful to protect the tip of the sensor if it is to be reused. Do not let it to come in contact with fluids or dirt. Do not clean it or wash it.

6. Apply a coat of anti-seize compound to the bolt threads but DO NOT allow any to get on the tip of the sensor.

7. Install the sensor in the manifold or exhaust pipe.

8. Attach the electrical connector and ensure a clean, tight connection.

9. If raised, carefully lower the vehicle.

10. Connect the negative battery cable.

Idle Air Control Valve

OPERATION

▶ **See Figures 19, 20 and 21**

Engine idle speeds are controlled by the PCM through the Idle Air Control (IAC) valve mounted on the throttle body. The PCM sends voltage pulses to the IAC motor windings causing the IAC motor shaft and pintle to move in or out a given distance (number of steps) for each pulse (called counts). The movement of the pintle controls the airflow around the throttle plate, which in turn, controls engine idle speed. IAC valve pintle position counts can be observed using a scan tool. Zero counts correspond to a fully closed passage, while 140 counts or more corresponds to full flow.

Idle speed can be categorized in 2 ways: actual (controlled) idle speed and minimum idle speed. Controlled idle speed is obtained by the PCM positioning the IAC valve pintle. Resulting idle speed is determined by total air flow (IAC/passage + PCV + throttle valve + calibrated vacuum leaks). Controlled idle speed is specified at normal operating conditions, which consists of engine coolant at normal operating temperature, air conditioning compressor OFF, manual transaxle in neutral or automatic transaxle in **D**.

Minimum idle air speed is set at the factory with a stop screw. This setting allows a certain amount of air to bypass the throttle valves regardless of IAC valve pintle positioning. A combination of this air flow and IAC pintle positioning allows the PCM to control engine idle speed. During normal engine idle operation, the IAC valve pintle is positioned a calibrated number of steps (counts) from the seat. No adjustment is required during routine maintenance. Tampering with the minimum idle speed adjustment may result in premature failure of the IAC valve or improperly controlled engine idle operation.

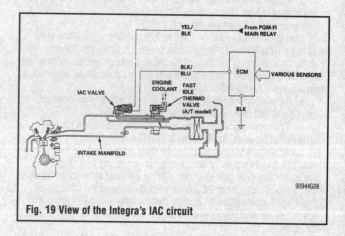

90944G08

Fig. 19 View of the Integra's IAC circuit

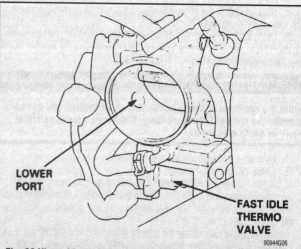

LOWER PORT

FAST IDLE THERMO VALVE

90944G06

Fig. 20 View of lower port of a typical IAC control system air bypass port

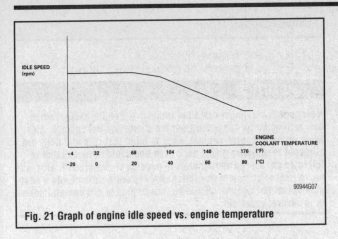

Fig. 21 Graph of engine idle speed vs. engine temperature

TESTING

▶ **See Figure 22**

1. Start the vehicle's engine.
2. Allow to run until it reaches normal operating temperature which is indicated by one complete fan cycle.
3. Disconnect the IAC valve.

➡**With the IAC valve disconnected, there should be a noticeable drop in engine speed. If a drop in idle speed was noted but an intermittent idle still persists, check the wiring harness for high resistance connections**

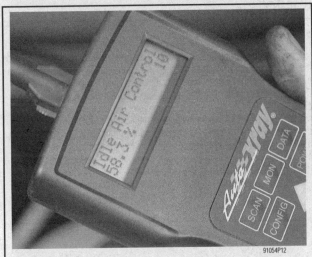

Fig. 22 The IAC can be monitored with an appropriate and Data-stream capable scan tool

or exposed wires.

REMOVAL & INSTALLATION

1. Disconnect the negative battery cable.
2. Disconnect the wiring harness from the IAC valve.
3. Remove the two retaining bolts.
4. Remove the IAC valve and discard the old gasket.
To install:
5. Clean the gasket mating surfaces thoroughly.
6. Using a new gasket, position the IAC valve on the throttle body.
7. Install and tighten the retaining bolts.
8. Connect the wiring harness to the IAC valve.
9. If raised, lower the vehicle.
10. Connect the negative battery cable.

Engine Coolant Temperature Sensor

OPERATION

▶ **See Figure 23**

The Engine Coolant Temperature (ECT) sensor is a thermistor, a sensor whose resistance changes in response to engine coolant temperature. The sensor resistance decreases as the coolant temperature increases, and increases as the coolant temperature decreases. This provides a reference signal to the PCM, which indicates engine coolant temperature. The signal sent to the PCM by the ECT sensor helps the PCM to determine spark advance, EGR flow rate, air/fuel ratio, and engine temperature. The ECT also is used for temperature gauge

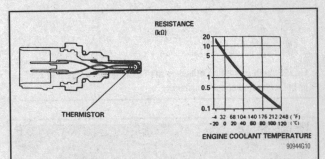

Fig. 23 Resistance vs. engine temperature for a typical coolant temperature sensor

operation by sending it's signal to the instrument cluster. The ECT sensor is a two wire sensor, a 5-volt reference signal is sent to the sensor and the signal return is based upon the change in the measured resistance due to temperature.

TESTING

▶ **See Figures 24, 25, 26 and 27**

1. Disconnect the engine wiring harness from the ECT sensor.
2. Connect an ohmmeter between the ECT sensor terminals.
3. With the engine cold and the ignition switch in the **OFF** position, measure and note the ECT sensor resistance.
4. Connect the engine wiring harness to the sensor.
5. Start the engine and allow the engine to reach normal operating temperature.
6. Once the engine has reached normal operating temperature, turn the engine **OFF**.

Fig. 24 Unplug the ECT sensor to access the sensor

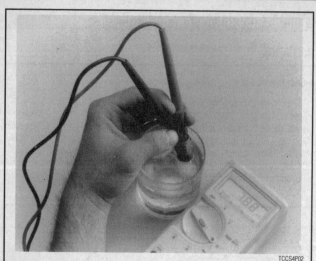

Fig. 25 Another method of testing the ECT is to submerge it in cold or hot water and check resistance

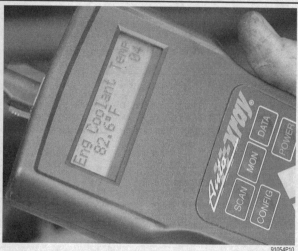

Fig. 26 The ECT can be monitored with an appropriate and Datastream capable scan tool

Temperature		Engine Coolant/Intake Air Temperature Sensor Values
°F	°C	Resistance (K ohms)
248	120	1.18
230	110	1.55
212	100	2.07
194	90	2.80
176	80	3.84
158	70	5.37
140	60	7.70
122	50	10.97
104	40	16.15
86	30	24.27
68	20	37.30
50	10	58.75

89694G23

Fig. 27 ECT and IAT resistance-to-temperature specifications

7. Once again, disconnect the engine wiring harness from the ECT sensor.

8. Measure and note the ECT sensor resistance with the engine hot.

9. Compare the cold and hot ECT sensor resistance measurements with the accompanying chart.

10. If readings do not approximate those in the chart, the sensor may be faulty.

REMOVAL & INSTALLATION

1. Disconnect the negative battery cable.
2. Drain and recycle the engine coolant to a level below the sensor.

❊❊ CAUTION

Never open, service or drain the radiator or cooling system when hot; serious burns can occur from the steam and hot coolant. Also, when draining engine coolant, keep in mind that cats and dogs are attracted to ethylene glycol antifreeze and could drink any that is left in an uncovered container or in puddles on the ground. This will prove fatal in sufficient quantities. Always drain coolant into a sealable container. Coolant should be reused unless it is contaminated or is several years old.

3. Detach the ECT sensor connector.
4. Remove the ECT sensor from the thermostat housing

To install:

5. Coat the sensor threads with Teflon® sealant.
6. Thread the sensor into position and tighten.
7. Attach the ECT sensor connector.
8. Connect the negative battery cable.
9. Refill the engine cooling system.
10. Start the engine and check for coolant leaks.
11. Bleed the cooling system.

Intake Air Temperature Sensor

OPERATION

▶ **See Figure 28**

The Intake Air Temperature (IAT) sensor determines the air temperature inside the intake manifold. Resistance changes in response to the ambient air temperature. The sensor has a negative temperature coefficient. As the temperature of the sensor rises the resistance across the sensor decreases. This provides a signal to the PCM indicating the temperature of the incoming air charge. This sensor helps the PCM to determine spark timing and air/fuel ratio. Information from this sensor is added to the pressure sensor information to calculate the air mass being sent to the cylinders. The IAT is a two wire sensor, a 5-volt reference signal is sent to the sensor and the signal return is based upon the change in the measured resistance due to temperature.

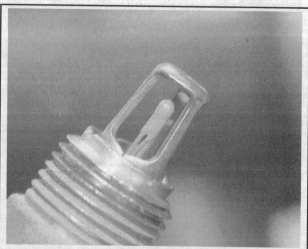

Fig. 28 The tip of the IAT sensor has an exposed thermistor that changes the resistance of the sensor based upon the force of the air rushing past it

TESTING

▶ **See Figures 27, 29 and 30**

1. Turn the ignition switch **OFF**.
2. Disconnect the wiring harness from the IAT sensor.
3. Measure the resistance between the sensor terminals.
4. Compare the resistance reading with the accompanying chart.
5. If the resistance is not within specification, the IAT may be faulty.
6. Connect the wiring harness to the sensor.

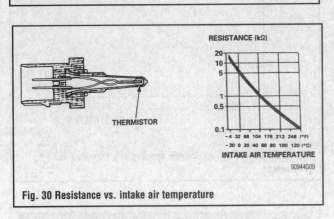

Fig. 29 The IAT sensor can be monitored with an appropriate and Data-stream capable scan tool

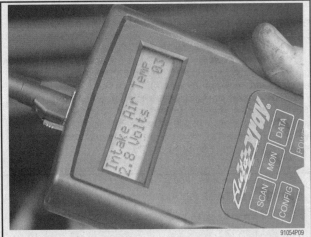

Fig. 30 Resistance vs. intake air temperature

REMOVAL & INSTALLATION

1. Disconnect the negative battery cable.
2. Detach the IAT sensor electrical connector.
3. Remove the retaining screws from the sensor (some models may unscrew from the manifold).
4. Remove the IAT sensor from the intake manifold.
To install:
5. Coat the sensor threads with Teflon® sealant.
6. Install the sensor into the intake manifold.
7. Attach the connectors on the IAT.
8. Connect the negative battery cable.

Mass Air Flow Sensor

OPERATION

The Mass Air Flow (MAF) sensor directly measures the mass of air being drawn into the engine. The sensor output is used to calculate injector pulse width. The MAF sensor is what is referred to as a "hot-wire sensor". The sensor uses a thin platinum wire filament, wound on a ceramic bobbin and coated with glass, that is heated to 200°C (417°F) above the ambient air temperature and subjected to the intake airflow stream. A "cold-wire" is used inside the MAF sensor to determine the ambient air temperature.

Battery voltage, a reference signal and a ground signal from the PCM are supplied to the MAF sensor. The sensor returns a signal proportionate to the current flow required to keep the "hot-wire" at the required temperature. The increased airflow across the "hot-wire" acts as a cooling fan, lowering the resistance and requiring more current to maintain the temperature of the wire. The increased current is measured by the voltage in the circuit, as current increases, voltage increases. As the airflow increases the signal return voltage of a normally operating MAF sensor will increase.

TESTING

1. Using a multimeter, check for voltage by backprobing the MAF sensor connector.
2. With the key **ON**, and the engine **OFF**, verify that there is at least 10.5 volts between the terminals of the MAF sensor connector. If voltage is not within specification, check power and ground circuits and repair as necessary.
3. With the key **ON**, and the engine **ON**, verify that there is at least 4.5 volts between the SIG and GND terminals of the MAF sensor connector. If voltage is not within specification, check power and ground circuits and repair as necessary.
4. With the key **ON**, and the engine **ON**, check voltage between GND and SIG RTN terminals. Voltage should be approximately 0.34–1.96 volts. If voltage is not within specification, the sensor may be faulty.

REMOVAL & INSTALLATION

1. Disconnect the negative battery cable.
2. Unplug the MAF sensor wiring connectors.
3. Loosen the retaining clamps.
4. Carefully remove the MAF.
5. Install the sensor in the reverse order of removal.

Manifold Absolute Pressure Sensor

OPERATION

▶ **See Figure 31**

The Manifold Absolute Pressure (MAP) sensor measures manifold vacuum using a frequency. This gives the ECU information on engine load. It is used as a barometric sensor for altitude adjustment of the air/fuel ratio.

TESTING

▶ **See Figure 31**

1. Check the MAP sensor connection.
2. Inspect the terminals within the connector for corrosion or points of high resistance.
3. Repair or replace as necessary.

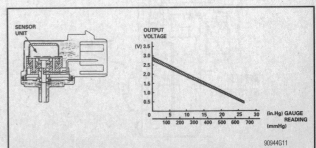

Fig. 31 Typical Manifold Absolute Pressure (MAP) sensor and voltage reading specifications

4. If code three is detected, an electrical problem in the system may be present.

5. Remove the electrical connector from the map sensor.

6. Turn the ignition key to the **ON** position.

7. On the Integra, connect the positive lead of a voltmeter to the yellow/red wire

8. On the Legend, connect the positive lead of the voltmeter to the yellow/white wire.

9. Connect the negative probe to the green/white wire in the harness. Do not probe the MAP sensor side.

10. With the voltmeter connected properly, you should see a voltage of five volts.

11. On the Integra, probe the white wire; a five volt signal should be seen.

12. On the Legend, probe the red wire for a five volt reference signal.

13. If no voltage is detected, and all of the wiring is also OK, the Powertrain Control Module (PCM) may be faulty.

14. If the connector does have five volts going to it, reconnect it to the MAP sensor.

15. Backprobe the weather pack connector. There should be about three volts to the sensor.

16. If there are three volts, the PCM may be at fault.

17. If the sensor voltage is high or low, the sensor is the cause.

18. Turn the ignition to the **OFF** position and perform the repair.

REMOVAL & INSTALLATION

1. Disconnect the negative battery cable.
2. Disconnect the MAP sensor vacuum lines.
3. Remove the mounting screws from the MAP sensor.
4. Remove the MAP sensor.
5. Installation is the reverse of the removal procedure.

Throttle Position Sensor

OPERATION

▶ See Figure 32

The Throttle Position (TP) sensor is a potentiometer that provides a signal to the PCM that is directly proportional to the throttle plate position. The TP sensor is mounted on the side of the throttle body and is connected to the throttle plate shaft. The TP sensor monitors throttle plate movement and position, and transmits an appropriate electrical signal to the PCM. These signals are used by the PCM to adjust the air/fuel mixture, spark timing and EGR operation according to engine load at idle, part throttle, or full throttle. The TP sensor is not adjustable.

The TP sensor receives a 5 volt reference signal and a ground circuit from the PCM. A return signal circuit is connected to wiper that runs on a resistor internally on the sensor. The further the throttle is opened, the wiper moves along the resistor, at wide open throttle, the wiper essentially creates a loop between the reference signal and the signal return returning the full or nearly full 5 volt signal back to the PCM. At idle the signal return should be approximately 0.9 volts.

TESTING

▶ See Figures 33 and 34

1. With the engine **OFF** and the ignition **ON**, check the voltage at the signal return circuit of the TP sensor by carefully backprobing the connector using a DVOM.

2. It idle, voltage should be between 0.2–1.4 volts.

3. Slowly move the throttle pulley to the Wide Open Throttle (WOT) position and watch the voltage on the DVOM. The voltage should slowly rise to slightly less than 4.8v at Wide Open Throttle (WOT).

4. If no voltage is present, check the wiring harness for supply voltage (5.0v) and ground (0.3v or less), by referring to your corresponding wiring guide. If supply voltage and ground are present, but no output voltage from TP, replace the TP sensor. If supply voltage and ground do not meet specifications, make necessary repairs to the harness or PCM.

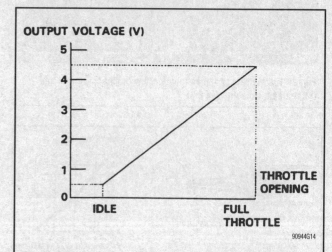

Fig. 33 Output voltage vs. throttle opening of a Throttle Position (TP) sensor

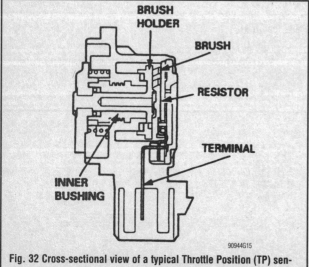

Fig. 32 Cross-sectional view of a typical Throttle Position (TP) sensor

Fig. 34 The TP sensor can be monitored with an appropriate and Data-stream capable scan tool

REMOVAL & INSTALLATION

1. Disconnect the negative battery cable.
2. Detach the wiring harness from the TP sensor.
3. Remove the two sensor mounting screws.
4. Pull the TP sensor off of the throttle shaft.

To install:

5. Install the TP sensor onto the shaft.
6. Install and tighten the sensor mounting screws.
7. Connect the wiring harness to the sensor.
8. Connect the negative battery cable.

Crankshaft Position Sensor

OPERATION

The Crankshaft Fluctuation (CKF) sensor, a.k.a. the Crankshaft Position (CKP) sensor, measures speed fluctuations in each revolution of the crankshaft. Any time there is a significant fluctuation in the speed of the crankshaft a misfire of one or more cylinders has occurred.

TESTING

1. With the ignition switch **OFF**, detach the Crankshaft Fluctuation sensor (CKF) connector.
2. Measure the resistance between the two terminals.
3. The resistance should measure 1.6–3.2 kohms.
4. If the resistance is not in the above specified range, replace the sensor.

REMOVAL & INSTALLATION

1. Remove the negative battery cable.
2. Locate the sensor. It may be located on the crankshaft timing cover by the flywheel or on some Integra models it is located inside the distributor.
3. Detach the connector from the sensor.
4. Remove the fasteners, then remove the sensor from the vehicle.
5. Installation is the reverse of the removal procedure.

Knock Sensor

OPERATION

The operation of the Knock Sensor (KS) is to monitor preignition or "engine knock" and send the signal to the PCM. The PCM responds by adjusting ignition timing until the "knocks" stop. The sensor works by generating a signal produced by the frequency of the knock as recorded by the piezoelectric ceramic disc inside the KS. The disc absorbs the shock waves from the knocks and exerts a pressure on the metal diaphragm inside the KS. This compresses the crystals inside the disc and the disc generates a voltage signal proportional to the frequency of the knocks ranging from zero to 1 volt.

TESTING

There is real no test for this sensor, the sensor produces it's own signal based on information gathered while the engine is running. The sensors also are usually inaccessible without major component removal. The sensors can be monitored with an appropriate scan tool using a data display or other data stream information. Follow the instructions included with the scan tool for information on accessing the data. The only test available is to test the continuity of the harness from the PCM to the sensor.

REMOVAL & INSTALLATION

➡**On Integra models, the sensor is most easily accessed from underneath the vehicle.**

1. Disconnect the negative battery cable.
2. Drain the engine coolant into a suitable container.

3. If working on an Integra, raise and safely support the vehicle securely on jackstands .
4. Unplug the sensor connector.
5. Using the proper size socket, loosen and remove the knock sensor.

To install:

6. Carefully thread the sensor into the engine block.
7. Tighten the sensor.
8. Attach the sensor connector.
9. Lower the vehicle.
10. Refill the engine coolant.
11. Connect the negative battery cable.

Vehicle Speed Sensor

OPERATION

♦ **See Figure 35**

The Vehicle Speed Sensor (VSS) is a magnetic pick-up sensor that sends a signal to the Powertrain Control Module (PCM) and the speedometer. The sensor measures the rotation of the output shaft on the transaxle and sends an AC voltage signal to the PCM which determines the corresponding vehicle speed.

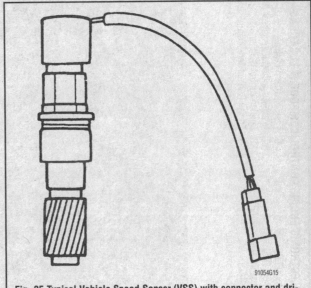

Fig. 35 Typical Vehicle Speed Sensor (VSS) with connector and driven gear

TESTING

1. Disconnect the negative battery cable.
2. Disengage the wiring harness connector from the VSS.
3. Using a Digital Volt-Ohmmeter (DVOM), measure the resistance (ohmmeter function) between the sensor terminals. If the resistance is 190–250 ohms, the sensor is okay.

REMOVAL & INSTALLATION

1. Disconnect the negative battery cable.
2. Detach the three-prong connector from the Vehicle Speed Sensor (VSS).
3. Unfasten the two mounting bolts, then remove the VSS.

To install:

4. Install the VSS and secure with the mounting bolts.
5. Attach the three prong connector to the sensor.
6. Connect the negative battery cable.

COMPONENT LOCATIONS

♦ See Figures 36 thru 47

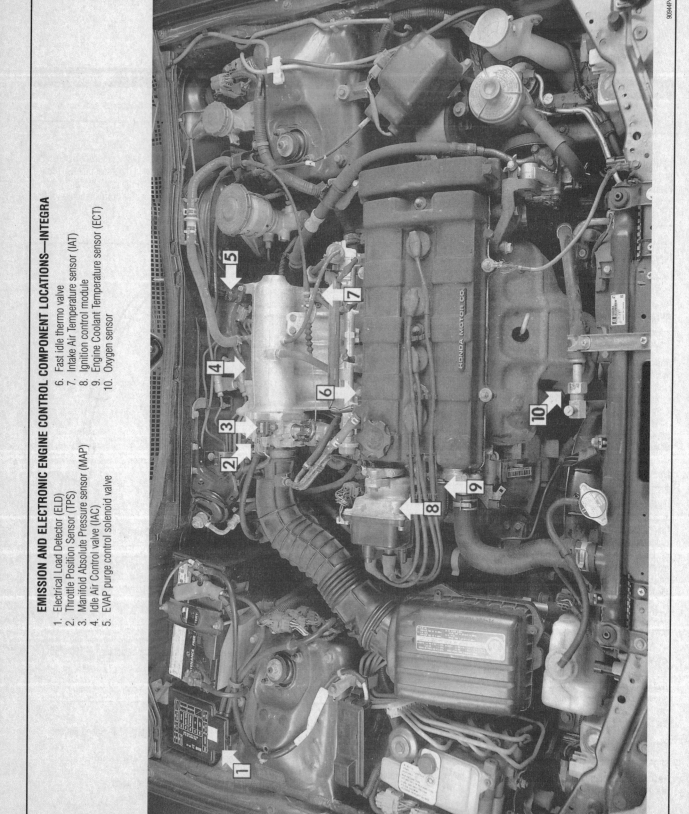

EMISSION AND ELECTRONIC ENGINE CONTROL COMPONENT LOCATIONS—INTEGRA

1. Electrical Load Detector (ELD)
2. Throttle Position Sensor (TPS)
3. Manifold Absolute Pressure sensor (MAP)
4. Idle Air Control valve (IAC)
5. EVAP purge control solenoid valve
6. Fast idle thermo valve
7. Intake Air Temperature sensor (IAT)
8. Ignition control module
9. Engine Coolant Temperature sensor (ECT)
10. Oxygen sensor

EMISSION AND ELECTRONIC ENGINE CONTROL COMPONENT LOCATIONS—3.2TL

1. EVAP Control canister check valve
2. Manifold Absolute Pressure sensor (MAP)
3. EVAP purge control solenoid valve
4. Positive crankcase ventilation system
5. Fuel pressure regulator
6. Oxygen sensor
7. Coolant temperature sensor

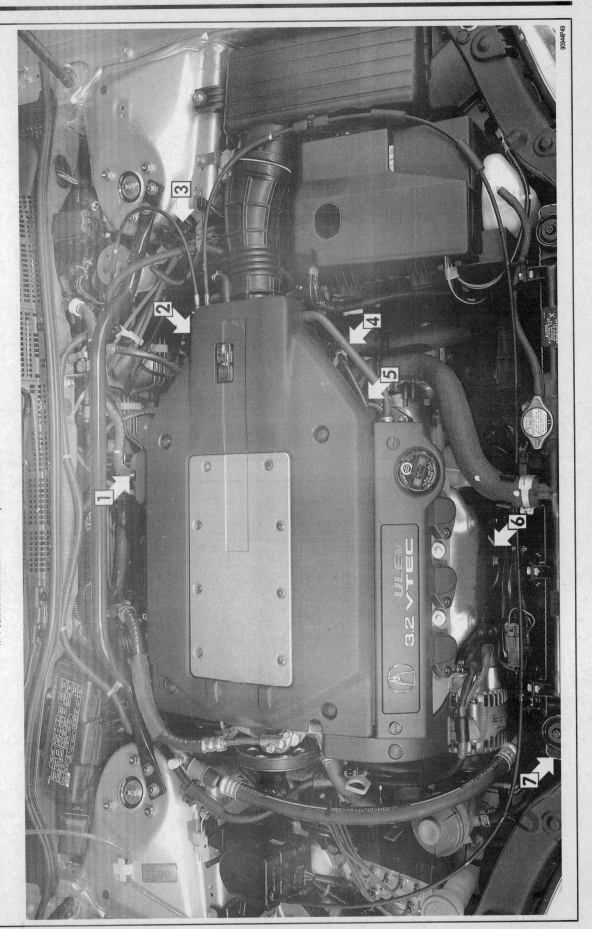

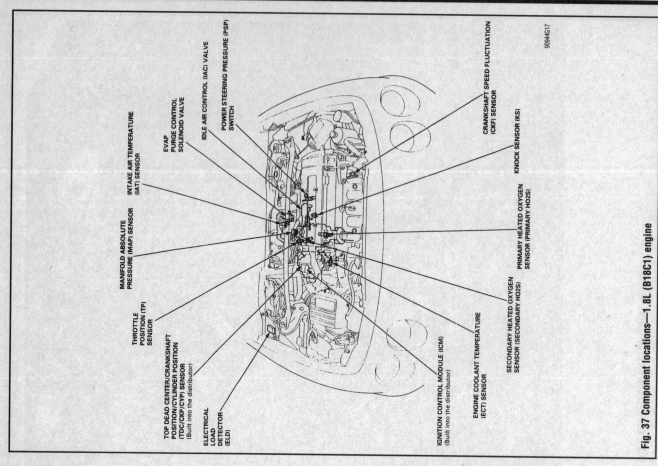

Fig. 37 Component locations—1.8L (B18C1) engine

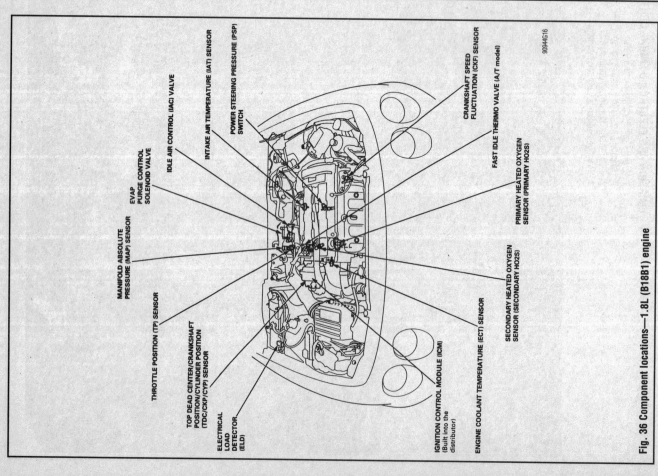

Fig. 36 Component locations—1.8L (B18B1) engine

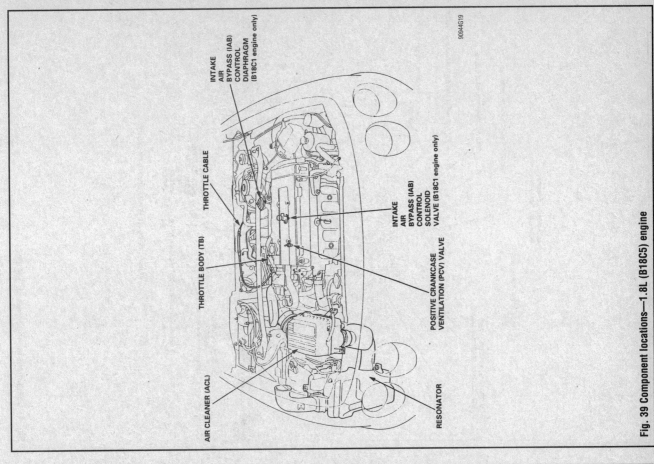

Fig. 39 Component locations—1.8L (B18C5) engine

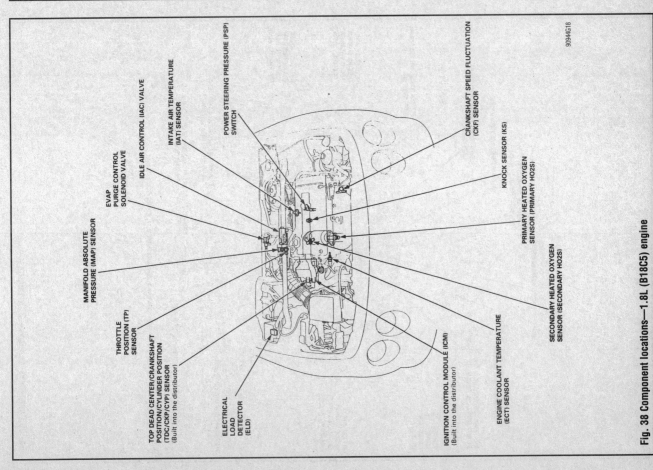

Fig. 38 Component locations—1.8L (B18C5) engine

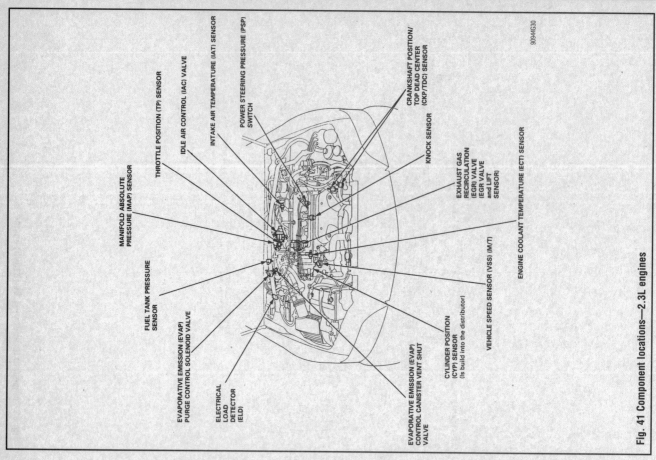

Fig. 41 Component locations—2.3L engines

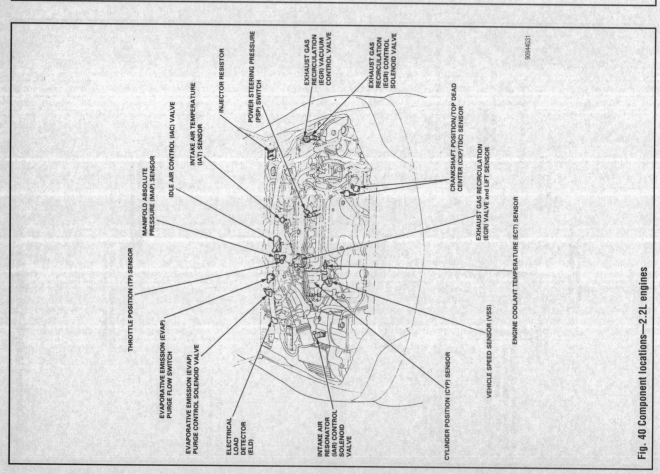

Fig. 40 Component locations—2.2L engines

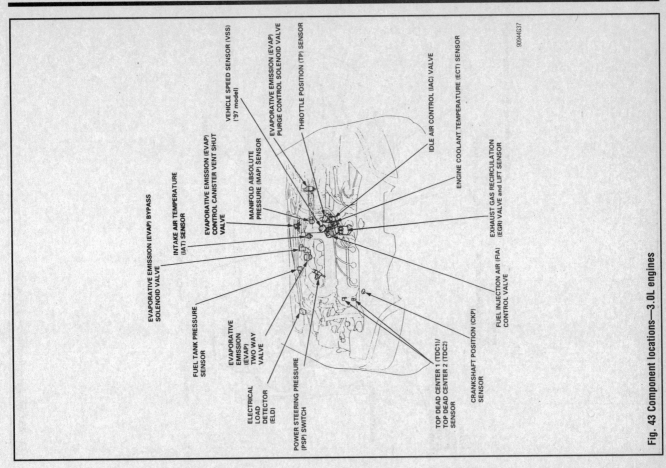

Fig. 43 Component locations—3.0L engines

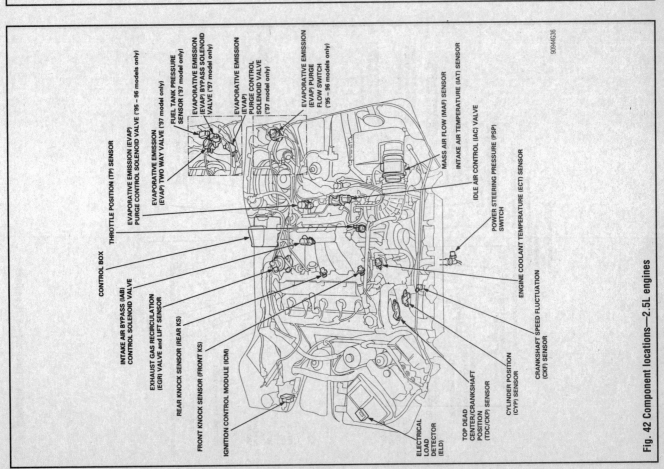

Fig. 42 Component locations—2.5L engines

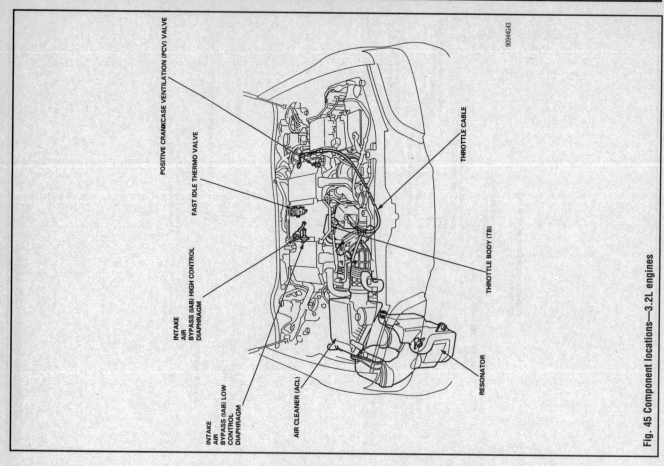

Fig. 45 Component locations—3.2L engines

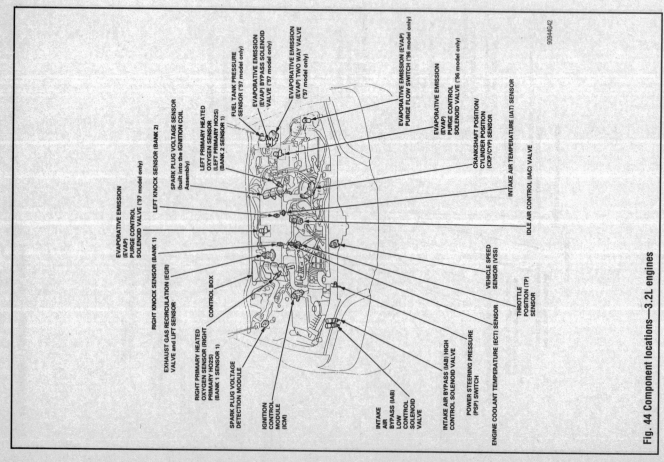

Fig. 44 Component locations—3.2L engines

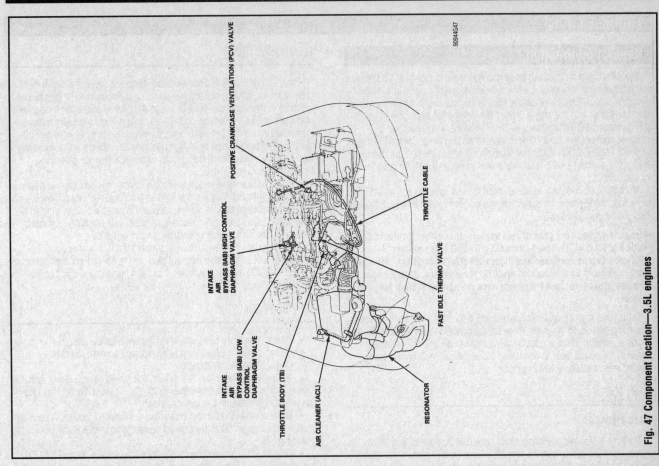

Fig. 47 Component location—3.5L engines

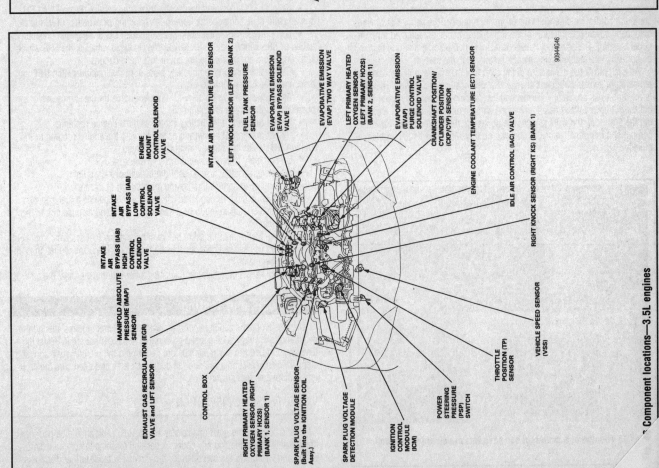

Component locations—3.5L engines

TROUBLE CODES

General Information

Since the computer control module is programmed to recognize the presence and value of electrical inputs, it will also note the lack of a signal or a radical change in values. It will, for example, react to the loss of signal from the vehicle speed sensor or note that engine coolant temperature has risen beyond acceptable (programmed) limits. Once a fault is recognized, a numeric code is assigned and held in memory. The dashboard warning lamp: CHECK ENGINE or SERVICE ENGINE SOON (SES), will illuminate to advise the operator that the system has detected a fault. This lamp is also known as the Malfunction Indicator Lamp (MIL).

More than one code may be stored. Keep in mind not every engine uses every code. Additionally, the same code may carry different meanings relative to each engine or engine family.

➥**Depending upon the year of your vehicle, it is either On-Board Diagnostic I (OBD I) of On-Board Diagnostic II (OBD II) compliant. All 1994–95 Integras, Legends and Vigors are OBD I compliant. All other models covered by this manual are OBD II compliant. Before beginning any procedure, make sure you have the correct system for your vehicle.**

In the event of an computer control module failure, the system will default to a pre-programmed set of values. These are compromise values which allow the engine to operate, although possibly at reduced efficiency. This is variously known as the default, limp-in or back-up mode. Driveability is almost always affected when the ECM enters this mode.

SCAN TOOLS

▶ **See Figure 48**

The scan tool allows any stored codes to be read from the ECM or PCM memory. The tool also allows the operator to view the data being sent to the computer control module while the engine is running. This ability has obvious diagnostic advantages; the use of the scan tool is frequently required for component testing. The scan tool makes collecting information easier; the data must be correctly interpreted by an operator familiar with the system.

An example of the usefulness of the scan tool may be seen in the case of a temperature sensor which has changed its electrical characteristics. The ECM is reacting to an apparently warmer engine (causing a driveability problem), but the sensor's voltage has not changed enough to set a fault code. Connecting the scan tool, the voltage signal being sent to the ECM may be viewed; comparison to normal values or a known good vehicle reveals the problem quickly.

90942P93
Fig. 48 The use of a scan tool can save lots of valuable diagnostic time

ELECTRICAL TOOLS

The most commonly required electrical diagnostic tool is the digital multimeter, allowing voltage, ohmage (resistance) and amperage to be read by one instrument. The multimeter must be a high-impedance unit, with 10 megohms of impedance in the voltmeter. This type of meter will not place an additional load on the circuit it is testing; this is extremely important in low voltage circuits. The multimeter must be of high quality in all respects. It should be handled carefully and protected from impact or damage. Replace batteries frequently in the unit.

A digital storage oscilloscope is become increasingly necessary to diagnose today's cars. Although they are expensive to purchase, you may be able to rent one from an auto parts store. The oscilloscope is capable of displaying an electrical pattern rather then just measuring its value. This enables you to catch intermittent problems which a digital multimeter will miss.

Other necessary tools include an unpowered test light and a quality tachometer with an inductive (clip-on) pick up. The Micro-Pack connectors are used at the ECM electrical connector. A vacuum pump/gauge may also be required for checking sensors, solenoids and valves.

SERVICE PRECAUTIONS

- Do not operate the fuel pump when the fuel lines are empty.
- Do not operate the fuel pump when removed from the fuel tank.
- Do not reuse fuel hose clamps.
- The washer(s) below any fuel system bolt (banjo fittings, service bolt, fuel filter, etc.) must be replaced whenever the bolt is loosened. Do not reuse the washers; a high-pressure fuel leak may result.
- Make sure all ECU harness connectors are fastened securely. A poor connection can cause an extremely high voltage surge and result in damage to integrated circuits.
- Keep all ECU parts and harnesses dry during service. Protect the ECU and all solid-state components from rough handling or extremes of temperature.
- Use extreme care when working around the ECU or other components; the airbag or SRS wiring may be in the vicinity. On these vehicles, the SRS wiring and connectors are yellow; do not cut or test these circuits.
- Before attempting to remove any parts, turn the ignition switch **OFF** and disconnect the battery ground cable.
- Always use a 12 volt battery as a power source for the engine, never a booster or high-voltage charging unit.
- Do not disconnect the battery cables with the engine running.
- Do not disconnect any wiring connector with the engine running or the ignition **ON** unless specifically instructed to do so.
- Do not apply battery power directly to injectors.
- Whenever possible, use a flashlight instead of a drop light.
- Keep all open flame and smoking material out of the area.
- Use a shop cloth or similar to catch fuel when opening a fuel system. Consider the fuel-soaked rag to be a flammable solid and dispose of it in the proper manner.
- Relieve fuel system pressure before servicing any fuel system component.
- Always use eye or full-face protection when working around fuel lines, fittings or components.
- Always keep a dry chemical (class B-C) fire extinguisher near the area.

Diagnosis and Testing

Diagnosis of a driveability and/or emissions problems requires attention to detail and following the diagnostic procedures in the correct order. Resist the temptation to perform any repairs before performing the preliminary diagnostic steps. In many cases this will shorten diagnostic time and often cure the problem without electronic testing.

VISUAL/PHYSICAL INSPECTION

This is possibly the most critical step of diagnosis and should be performed immediately after retrieving any codes. A detailed examination of connectors, wiring and vacuum hoses can often lead to a repair without further diagnosis.

Performance of this step relies on the skill of the technician performing it; a careful inspector will check the undersides of hoses as well as the integrity of hard-to-reach hoses blocked by the air cleaner or other component. Wiring should be checked carefully for any sign of strain, burning, crimping, or terminal pull-out from a connector. Checking connectors at components or in harnesses is required; usually, pushing them together will reveal a loose fit.

INTERMITTENTS

If a fault occurs intermittently, such as a loose connector pin breaking contact as the vehicle hits a bump, the ECM will note the fault as it occurs and energize the dash warning lamp. If the problem self-corrects, as with the terminal pin again making contact, the dash lamp will extinguish after 15 seconds but a code will remain stored in the computer control module's memory.

When an unexpected code appears during diagnostics, it may have been set during an intermittent failure that self-corrected; the codes are still useful in diagnosis and should not be discounted.

CIRCUIT/COMPONENT REPAIR

The fault codes and the scan tool data will lead to diagnosis and checking of a particular circuit. It is important to note that the fault code indicates a fault or loss of signal in an ECM-controlled system, not necessarily in the specific component.

Refer to the appropriate Diagnostic Code chart to determine the codes meaning. The component may then be tested following the appropriate component test procedures found in this section. If the component is OK, check the wiring for shorts or opens. Further diagnoses should be left to an experienced driveability technician.

If a code indicates the ECM to be faulty and the ECM is replaced, but does not correct the problem, one of the following may be the reason:

- There is a problem with the ECM terminal connections: The terminals may have to be removed from the connector in order to check them properly.
- The ECM or PROM is not correct for the application: The incorrect ECM or PROM may cause a malfunction and may or may not set a code.
- The problem is intermittent: This means that the problem is not present at the time the system is being checked. In this case, make a careful physical inspection of all portions of the system involved.
- Shorted solenoid, relay coil or harness: Solenoids and relays are turned on and off by the ECM using internal electronic switches called drivers. A shorted solenoid, relay coil or harness may cause an ECM to fail, and a replacement ECM to fail when it is installed.
- The Programmable Read Only Memory (PROM) may be faulty: Although the PROM rarely fails, it operates as part of the ECM. Therefore, it could be the cause of the problem. Substitute a known good PROM.
- The replacement ECM may be faulty: After the ECM is replaced, the system should be rechecked for proper operation. If the diagnostic code again indicates the ECM is the problem, substitute a known good ECM. Although this is a very rare condition, it could happen.

Reading Codes

Listings of the trouble codes for the various engine control systems covered in this manual are located in this section. Remember that a code only points to the faulty circuit NOT necessarily to a faulty component. Loose, damaged or corroded connections may contribute to a fault code on a circuit when the sensor or component is operating properly. Be sure that the components are faulty before replacing them, especially the expensive ones. Depending upon the year of your vehicle, it is either On-Board Diagnostic I (OBD I) of On-Board Diagnostic II (OBD II) compliant. All 1994–95 Integras, Legends and Vigors are OBD I compliant. All other models covered by this manual are OBD II compliant. Before beginning any procedure, make sure you have the correct system for your vehicle.

OBD I VEHICLES

♦ See Figures 49 and 50

When a fault is noted, the ECU (otherwise known as the ECM) stores an identifying code and illuminates the CHECK ENGINE light. The code will remain in memory until cleared; the dashboard warning lamp may not illuminate during the next ignition cycle if the fault is no longer present. Not all faults noted by the

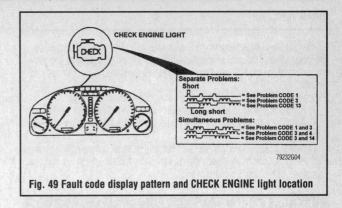

Fig. 49 Fault code display pattern and CHECK ENGINE light location

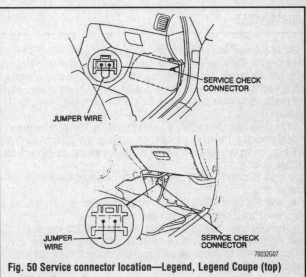

Fig. 50 Service connector location—Legend, Legend Coupe (top) and Vigor (bottom)

ECU will trigger the dashboard warning lamp although the fault code will be set in memory. For this reason, troubleshooting should be based on the presence of stored codes, not the illumination of the warning lamp while the car is operating.

All models are equipped with a service connector in side the cabin of the vehicle. If the service connector is jumped, the CHECK ENGINE lamp will display the stored codes in the same fashion.

The 2-pin service connector is located under the extreme right dashboard on Integra, Legend & 2.5TL; on Vigor models, it is found behind the right side of the center console well under the dashboard.

Codes 1–9 are indicated by a series of short flashes; two-digit codes use a number of long flashes for the first digit followed by the appropriate number of short flashes. For example, Code 43 would be indicated by 4 long flashes followed by 3 short flashes. Codes are separated by a longer pause between transaxles. The position of the codes during output can be helpful in diagnostic work. Multiple codes transmitted in isolated order indicate unique occurrences; a display of showing 1-1-1-pause-9-9-9 indicates two problems or problems occurring at different times. An alternating display, such as 1-9-1-9-1, indicates simultaneous occurrences of the faults.

When counting flashes to determine codes, a code not valid for the vehicle may be found. In this case, first recount the flashes to confirm an accurate count. If necessary, turn the ignition switch OFF, then recycle the system and begin the count again. If the Code is not valid for the vehicle, the ECU must be replaced.

➡On vehicles with automatic transaxles, the S, D or D4 lamp may flash with the CHECK ENGINE lamp if certain codes are stored. For Legend this may occur with Codes 6, 7 or 17. On Vigor and Integra it may occur with codes 6, 7 or 13. In addition, the TCS lamp on NSX may flash with codes 3, 5, 6,13,15,16,17, 35 or 36. In all cases, proceed with the diagnosis based on the engine code shown. After repairs, recheck the lamp. If the additional warning lamp is still lit, proceed with diagnosis for that system.

OBD II VEHICLES

Reading the control module memory is one of the first steps in OBD II system diagnostics. This step should be initially performed to determine the general nature of the fault. Subsequent readings will determine if the fault has been cleared.

Reading codes can be performed by either of the methods below:
- Read the control module memory with the Generic Scan Tool (GST).
- Read the control module memory with the vehicle manufacturer's specific tester.

To read the fault codes, connect the scan tool or tester according to the manufacturer's instructions. Always make sure to follow the manufacturer's specified procedure for reading the codes explicitly.

Clearing Codes

OBD I VEHICLES

Stored codes are removed from memory by removing power to the ECU. Disconnecting the power may also clear the memories used for other solid-state equipment such as the clock and radio. For this reason, always make note of the radio presets before clearing the system. Additionally, some radios contain anti-theft programming; make sure you have the code number before clearing the codes.

While disconnecting the battery will clear the memory, this is not the recommended procedure. The memory should be cleared after the ignition is switched **OFF** by removing the appropriate fuse for at least 10 seconds. The correct fuses and their locations are:
- 1994–95 Integra—BACK UP, located in the underhood fuse and relay panel.
- 1994-95 Legend—ACG, located in the dashboard fuse panel. Removing this fuse will cancel memories for the power seat.
- 1994-95 Vigor—BACK UP, located in the underhood fuse and relay panel. Removing this fuse will cancel memories for the clock and radio.

Codes may also be cleared using the a suitable scan tool, following the tool manufacturer's directions.

OBD II VEHICLES

➡**It is not recommended that the negative battery cable be disconnected to clear DTC's. Doing so will clear all settings from the vehicle's computer system, resulting in lost radio presets, seat memories, anti-theft codes, driveability parameters, etc., and there are better ways of spending your afternoon than resetting all of these.**

Control module reset procedures are a very important part of OBD II system diagnostics. This step should be done at the end of any fault code repair and at the end of any driveability repair.

Clearing codes can be performed by either of the methods below:
- Clear the control module memory with the Generic Scan Tool (GST)
- Clear the control module memory with the vehicle manufacturer's specific tester
- Turn the ignition **OFF** and remove the negative battery cable for at least 1 minute.

Removing the negative battery cable may cause other systems in the vehicle to loose their memory. Prior to removing the cable, ensure you have the proper reset codes for radios and alarms.

➡**The MIL may also be de-activated for some codes if the vehicle completes three consecutive trips without a fault detected with vehicle conditions similar to those present during the fault.**

Diagnostic Trouble Codes

➡**Depending upon the year of your vehicle, it is either On-Board Diagnostic I (OBD I) of On-Board Diagnostic II (OBD II) compliant. All 1994–95 Integras, Legends and Vigors are OBD I compliant. All other models covered by this manual are OBD II compliant.**

OBD I VEHICLES

1994–95 1.8L (B18B1 and B18C1) Engines

Code 0 Electronic Control Unit
Code 1 Oxygen Content
Code 3 Manifold Absolute Pressure
Code 4 Crank Angle sensor
Code 5 Manifold Absolute Pressure
Code 6 Coolant Temperature
Code 7 Throttle Angle
Code 8 TDC Position
Code 9 No. 1 Cylinder Position
Code 10 Intake Air Temperature
Code 12 EGR system
Code 13 Atmospheric Pressure
Code 14 Electronic Air Control
Code 15 Ignition output signal
Code 16 Fuel injector
Code 17 Vehicle speed sensor
Code 20 Electric Load Detector
Code 21 VTEC Solenoid Valve (1.8L GS-R)
Code 22 VTEC Oil Pressure Switch (1.8L GS-R)
Code 30 TCM Signal A
Code 31 TCM Signal B
Code 41 HO25 Heater
Code 43 Fuel supply system

1994 2.5L (G25A1) Engine

Code 0 Electronic Control Unit
Code 1 HO25 circuit
Code 3 Manifold Absolute Pressure
Code 4 Crank Angle Sensor
Code 5 Manifold Absolute Pressure
Code 6 Coolant Temperature
Code 7 Throttle Angle
Code 8 TDC and or Crankshaft Position sensors
Code 9 No. 1 Cylinder Position
Code 10 Intake Air Temperature
Code 12 EGR system
Code 13 Atmospheric Pressure
Code 14 Electronic Air Control
Code 15 Ignition output signal
Code 16 Fuel injector
Code 17 Vehicle speed sensor
Code 18 Ignition Timing Adjuster
Code 20 Electric Load Detector
Code 30 NT FI Signal
Code 31 NT FI Signal
Code 41 HO25 Heater
Code 43 Fuel supply system
Code 45 Fuel Supply Metering
Code 50 Mass Air Flow (MAF) circuit—2.5TL
Code 53 Rear Knock Sensor
Code 54 Crankshaft Speed Fluctuation sensor—2.5TL
Code 61 HO25 sensor heater—2.5TL
Code 65 Secondary HO25 sensor—2.5TL
Code 67 Catalytic Converter System—2.5TL
Code 70 Automatic transaxle or NT FI Data line—2.5TL
Code 71 Misfire detected; cylinder No. 1 or random misfire
Code 72 Misfire detected; cylinder No. 2 or random misfire
Code 73 Misfire detected; cylinder No. 3 or random misfire
Code 74 Misfire detected; cylinder No. 4 or random misfire
Code 75 Misfire detected; cylinder No. 5 or random misfire
Code 76 Random misfire detected—2.5TL
Code 80 EGR system—2.5TL
Code 86 Coolant Temperature circuit—2.5TL
Code 92 Evaporative Emission Control System—2.5TL

1994–95 3.0L (C30A1) Engine

Code 0 CU
Code 1 Front Oxygen Sensor
Code 2 Rear Oxygen Sensor
Code 3 Manifold Absolute Pressure (MAP)
Code 4 Crank angle A
Code 5 Manifold Absolute Pressure (MAP)
Code 6 Coolant Temperature
Code 7 Throttle angle
Code 9 Crank Angle-Number 1 Cylinder/Position A
Code 10 Intake Air temperature
Code 12 Exhaust Gas Recirculation (EGR) system
Code 13 Atmospheric pressure
Code 14 Electronic Air Control (EACV)
Code 15 Ignition output signal
Code 16 Fuel Injector
Code 17 Vehicle speed pulser
Code 18 Ignition timing adjustment
Code 22 VTEC System; front, bank 2
Code 23 Front Knock Sensor
Code 30 A/T FI Signal A
Code 31 NT FI Signal B
Code 35 TC STB signal
Code 36 TCFC signal
Code 37 Accelerator Position; Sensors 1, 2 or 1 and 2 circuits
Code 40 Throttle Position or Throttle Valve Control Motor Circuits 1 or 2
Code 41 Front Oxygen Sensor Heater; (circuit malfunction; bank 2 sensor 1)
Code 42 Rear Primary Heated Oxygen Sensor Heater (circuit malfunction)
Code 43 Front Fuel Supply System
Code 44 Rear Fuel Supply System
Code 45 Front Fuel Supply Metering; front bank 2
Code 46 Rear Fuel Supply Metering; rear bank 1
Code 47 Fuel Pump
Code 51 Rear Spool Solenoid Valve
Code 52 VTEC System; rear, bank 1
Code 53 Rear Knock Sensor
Code 54 Crank Angle B
Code 59 No. 1 Cylinder Position B (Cylinder Sensor)
Code 61 Front Heated Oxygen Sensor (slow response; bank 2 sensor 1)
Code 62 Rear Primary Heated Oxygen Sensor (slow response; bank 1 sensor 1)
Code 63 Front Secondary Oxygen Sensor (slow response or circuit voltage high or low)
Code 65 Front Secondary Heated Oxygen Sensor (circuit malfunction; bank 2 sensor 2)
Code 64 Rear Secondary Oxygen Sensor (slow response or circuit voltage high or low)
Code 66 Rear Secondary Heated Oxygen Sensor (circuit malfunction; bank 1 sensor 2)
Code 67 Front Catalytic Converter System
Code 68 Rear Catalytic Converter System
Code 80 Exhaust Gas Recirculation (EGR) system
Code 86 Coolant temperature
Code 70 Automatic Transaxle; the D indicator light and MIL may come on simultaneously.
Code 71 Misfire detected; cylinder No. 1 or random misfire
Code 72 Misfire detected; cylinder No. 2 or random misfire
Code 73 Misfire detected; cylinder No. 3 or random misfire
Code 74 Misfire detected; cylinder No. 4 or random misfire
Code 75 Misfire detected; cylinder No. 5 or random misfire
Code 76 Misfire detected; cylinder No. 6 or random misfire
Code 79 Spark Plug Voltage Detection; circuit malfunction; (Front Bank (Bank 2) or (Rear Bank (Bank 1))
Code 79 Spark Plug Voltage Detection; circuit malfunction; (Front Bank (Bank 2) or (Rear Bank (Bank 1))
Code 79 Spark Plug Voltage Detection Module; reset circuit malfunction; (Front Bank (Bank 2)) or (Rear Bank (Bank 1))
Code 92 Evaporative Emission Control System

1994–95 3.2L (C32A1) Engine

Code 0 Electronic Control Unit (ECU)
Code 1 Left Oxygen Sensor
Code 2 Right Oxygen Sensor
Code 3 Manifold Absolute Pressure (MAP)
Code 4 Crank angle 1
Code 5 Manifold Absolute Pressure (MAP)
Code 6 Coolant Temperature
Code 7 Throttle angle
Code 9 Crank Angle-Number 1 Cylinder
Code 10 Intake Air temperature
Code 12 Exhaust Gas Recirculation (EGR) system
Code 13 Atmospheric pressure
Code 14 Electronic Air Control (EACV)
Code 15 Ignition output signal
Code 17 Vehicle speed pulser
Code 18 Ignition timing adjustment
Code 23 Left Knock Sensor
Code 30 A/T FI Signal A
Code 35 Traction Control System Circuit
Code 36 Traction Control System Circuit
Code 41 Left Oxygen Sensor Heater
Code 42 Right Oxygen Sensor Heater
Code 43 Left Fuel Supply System
Code 44 Right Fuel Supply System
Code 45 Left Fuel Supply Metering
Code 46 Right Fuel Supply Metering
Code 53 Right Knock Sensor
Code 54 Crank angle 2
Code 59 No. 1 Cylinder Position 2 (Cylinder Sensor)

OBD II VEHICLES

P0000 No Failures
P0100 Mass or Volume Air Flow Circuit Malfunction
P0101 Mass or Volume Air Flow Circuit Range/Performance Problem
P0102 Mass or Volume Air Flow Circuit Low Input
P0103 Mass or Volume Air Flow Circuit High Input
P0104 Mass or Volume Air Flow Circuit Intermittent
P0105 Manifold Absolute Pressure/Barometric Pressure Circuit Malfunction
P0106 Manifold Absolute Pressure/Barometric Pressure Circuit Range/Performance Problem
P0107 Manifold Absolute Pressure/Barometric Pressure Circuit Low Input
P0108 Manifold Absolute Pressure/Barometric Pressure Circuit High Input
P0109 Manifold Absolute Pressure/Barometric Pressure Circuit Intermittent
P0110 Intake Air Temperature Circuit Malfunction
P0111 Intake Air Temperature Circuit Range/Performance Problem
P0112 Intake Air Temperature Circuit Low Input
P0113 Intake Air Temperature Circuit High Input
P0114 Intake Air Temperature Circuit Intermittent
P0115 Engine Coolant Temperature Circuit Malfunction
P0116 Engine Coolant Temperature Circuit Range/Performance Problem
P0117 Engine Coolant Temperature Circuit Low Input
P0118 Engine Coolant Temperature Circuit High Input
P0119 Engine Coolant Temperature Circuit Intermittent
P0120 Throttle/Pedal Position Sensor/Switch "A" Circuit Malfunction
P0121 Throttle/Pedal Position Sensor/Switch "A" Circuit Range/Performance Problem
P0122 Throttle/Pedal Position Sensor/Switch "A" Circuit Low Input
P0123 Throttle/Pedal Position Sensor/Switch "A" Circuit High Input
P0124 Throttle/Pedal Position Sensor/Switch "A" Circuit Intermittent
P0125 Insufficient Coolant Temperature For Closed Loop Fuel Control
P0126 Insufficient Coolant Temperature For Stable Operation
P0130 O2 Circuit Malfunction (Bank no. 1 Sensor no. 1)
P0131 O2 Sensor Circuit Low Voltage (Bank no. 1 Sensor no. 1)
P0132 O2 Sensor Circuit High Voltage (Bank no. 1 Sensor no. 1)
P0133 O2 Sensor Circuit Slow Response (Bank no. 1 Sensor no. 1)
P0134 O2 Sensor Circuit No Activity Detected (Bank no. 1 Sensor no. 1)
P0135 O2 Sensor Heater Circuit Malfunction (Bank no. 1 Sensor no. 1)

P0136 O2 Sensor Circuit Malfunction (Bank no. 1 Sensor no. 2)
P0137 O2 Sensor Circuit Low Voltage (Bank no. 1 Sensor no. 2)
P0138 O2 Sensor Circuit High Voltage (Bank no. 1 Sensor no. 2)
P0139 O2 Sensor Circuit Slow Response (Bank no. 1 Sensor no. 2)
P0140 O2 Sensor Circuit No Activity Detected (Bank no. 1 Sensor no. 2)
P0141 O2 Sensor Heater Circuit Malfunction (Bank no. 1 Sensor no. 2)
P0142 O2 Sensor Circuit Malfunction (Bank no. 1 Sensor no. 3)
P0143 O2 Sensor Circuit Low Voltage (Bank no. 1 Sensor no. 3)
P0144 O2 Sensor Circuit High Voltage (Bank no. 1 Sensor no. 3)
P0145 O2 Sensor Circuit Slow Response (Bank no. 1 Sensor no. 3)
P0146 O2 Sensor Circuit No Activity Detected (Bank no. 1 Sensor no. 3)
P0147 O2 Sensor Heater Circuit Malfunction (Bank no. 1 Sensor no. 3)
P0150 O2 Sensor Circuit Malfunction (Bank no. 2 Sensor no. 1)
P0151 O2 Sensor Circuit Low Voltage (Bank no. 2 Sensor no. 1)
P0152 O2 Sensor Circuit High Voltage (Bank no. 2 Sensor no. 1)
P0153 O2 Sensor Circuit Slow Response (Bank no. 2 Sensor no. 1)
P0154 O2 Sensor Circuit No Activity Detected (Bank no. 2 Sensor no. 1)
P0155 O2 Sensor Heater Circuit Malfunction (Bank no. 2 Sensor no. 1)
P0156 O2 Sensor Circuit Malfunction (Bank no. 2 Sensor no. 2)
P0157 O2 Sensor Circuit Low Voltage (Bank no. 2 Sensor no. 2)
P0158 O2 Sensor Circuit High Voltage (Bank no. 2 Sensor no. 2)
P0159 O2 Sensor Circuit Slow Response (Bank no. 2 Sensor no. 2)
P0160 O2 Sensor Circuit No Activity Detected (Bank no. 2 Sensor no. 2)
P0161 O2 Sensor Heater Circuit Malfunction (Bank no. 2 Sensor no. 2)
P0162 O2 Sensor Circuit Malfunction (Bank no. 2 Sensor no. 3)
P0163 O2 Sensor Circuit Low Voltage (Bank no. 2 Sensor no. 3)
P0164 O2 Sensor Circuit High Voltage (Bank no. 2 Sensor no. 3)
P0165 O2 Sensor Circuit Slow Response (Bank no. 2 Sensor no. 3)
P0166 O2 Sensor Circuit No Activity Detected (Bank no. 2 Sensor no. 3)
P0167 O2 Sensor Heater Circuit Malfunction (Bank no. 2 Sensor no. 3)
P0170 Fuel Trim Malfunction (Bank no. 1)
P0171 System Too Lean (Bank no. 1)
P0172 System Too Rich (Bank no. 1)
P0173 Fuel Trim Malfunction (Bank no. 2)
P0174 System Too Lean (Bank no. 2)
P0175 System Too Rich (Bank no. 2)
P0176 Fuel Composition Sensor Circuit Malfunction
P0177 Fuel Composition Sensor Circuit Range/Performance
P0178 Fuel Composition Sensor Circuit Low Input
P0179 Fuel Composition Sensor Circuit High Input
P0180 Fuel Temperature Sensor "A" Circuit Malfunction
P0181 Fuel Temperature Sensor "A" Circuit Range/Performance
P0182 Fuel Temperature Sensor "A" Circuit Low Input
P0183 Fuel Temperature Sensor "A" Circuit High Input
P0184 Fuel Temperature Sensor "A" Circuit Intermittent
P0185 Fuel Temperature Sensor "B" Circuit Malfunction
P0186 Fuel Temperature Sensor "B" Circuit Range/Performance
P0187 Fuel Temperature Sensor "B" Circuit Low Input
P0188 Fuel Temperature Sensor "B" Circuit High Input
P0189 Fuel Temperature Sensor "B" Circuit Intermittent
P0190 Fuel Rail Pressure Sensor Circuit Malfunction
P0191 Fuel Rail Pressure Sensor Circuit Range/Performance
P0192 Fuel Rail Pressure Sensor Circuit Low Input
P0193 Fuel Rail Pressure Sensor Circuit High Input
P0194 Fuel Rail Pressure Sensor Circuit Intermittent
P0195 Engine Oil Temperature Sensor Malfunction
P0196 Engine Oil Temperature Sensor Range/Performance
P0197 Engine Oil Temperature Sensor Low
P0198 Engine Oil Temperature Sensor High
P0199 Engine Oil Temperature Sensor Intermittent
P0200 Injector Circuit Malfunction
P0201 Injector Circuit Malfunction—Cylinder no. 1
P0202 Injector Circuit Malfunction—Cylinder no. 2
P0203 Injector Circuit Malfunction—Cylinder no. 3
P0204 Injector Circuit Malfunction—Cylinder no. 4
P0205 Injector Circuit Malfunction—Cylinder no. 5
P0206 Injector Circuit Malfunction—Cylinder no. 6
P0207 Injector Circuit Malfunction—Cylinder no. 7
P0208 Injector Circuit Malfunction—Cylinder no. 8
P0209 Injector Circuit Malfunction—Cylinder no. 9
P0210 Injector Circuit Malfunction—Cylinder no. 10

P0211 Injector Circuit Malfunction—Cylinder no. 11
P0212 Injector Circuit Malfunction—Cylinder no. 12
P0213 Cold Start Injector no. 1 Malfunction
P0214 Cold Start Injector no. 2 Malfunction
P0215 Engine Shutoff Solenoid Malfunction
P0216 Injection Timing Control Circuit Malfunction
P0217 Engine Over Temperature Condition
P0218 Transmission Over Temperature Condition
P0219 Engine Over Speed Condition
P0220 Throttle/Pedal Position Sensor/Switch "B" Circuit Malfunction
P0221 Throttle/Pedal Position Sensor/Switch "B" Circuit Range/Performance Problem
P0222 Throttle/Pedal Position Sensor/Switch "B" Circuit Low Input
P0223 Throttle/Pedal Position Sensor/Switch "B" Circuit High Input
P0224 Throttle/Pedal Position Sensor/Switch "B" Circuit Intermittent
P0225 Throttle/Pedal Position Sensor/Switch "C" Circuit Malfunction
P0226 Throttle/Pedal Position Sensor/Switch "C" Circuit Range/Performance Problem
P0227 Throttle/Pedal Position Sensor/Switch "C" Circuit Low Input
P0228 Throttle/Pedal Position Sensor/Switch "C" Circuit High Input
P0229 Throttle/Pedal Position Sensor/Switch "C" Circuit Intermittent
P0230 Fuel Pump Primary Circuit Malfunction
P0231 Fuel Pump Secondary Circuit Low
P0232 Fuel Pump Secondary Circuit High
P0233 Fuel Pump Secondary Circuit Intermittent
P0234 Engine Over Boost Condition
P0261 Cylinder no. 1 Injector Circuit Low
P0262 Cylinder no. 1 Injector Circuit High
P0263 Cylinder no. 1 Contribution/Balance Fault
P0264 Cylinder no. 2 Injector Circuit Low
P0265 Cylinder no. 2 Injector Circuit High
P0266 Cylinder no. 2 Contribution/Balance Fault
P0267 Cylinder no. 3 Injector Circuit Low
P0268 Cylinder no. 3 Injector Circuit High
P0269 Cylinder no. 3 Contribution/Balance Fault
P0270 Cylinder no. 4 Injector Circuit Low
P0271 Cylinder no. 4 Injector Circuit High
P0272 Cylinder no. 4 Contribution/Balance Fault
P0273 Cylinder no. 5 Injector Circuit Low
P0274 Cylinder no. 5 Injector Circuit High
P0275 Cylinder no. 5 Contribution/Balance Fault
P0276 Cylinder no. 6 Injector Circuit Low
P0277 Cylinder no. 6 Injector Circuit High
P0278 Cylinder no. 6 Contribution/Balance Fault
P0279 Cylinder no. 7 Injector Circuit Low
P0280 Cylinder no. 7 Injector Circuit High
P0281 Cylinder no. 7 Contribution/Balance Fault
P0282 Cylinder no. 8 Injector Circuit Low
P0283 Cylinder no. 8 Injector Circuit High
P0284 Cylinder no. 8 Contribution/Balance Fault
P0285 Cylinder no. 9 Injector Circuit Low
P0286 Cylinder no. 9 Injector Circuit High
P0287 Cylinder no. 9 Contribution/Balance Fault
P0288 Cylinder no. 10 Injector Circuit Low
P0289 Cylinder no. 10 Injector Circuit High
P0290 Cylinder no. 10 Contribution/Balance Fault
P0291 Cylinder no. 11 Injector Circuit Low
P0292 Cylinder no. 11 Injector Circuit High
P0293 Cylinder no. 11 Contribution/Balance Fault
P0294 Cylinder no. 12 Injector Circuit Low
P0295 Cylinder no. 12 Injector Circuit High
P0296 Cylinder no. 12 Contribution/Balance Fault
P0300 Random/Multiple Cylinder Misfire Detected
P0301 Cylinder no. 1—Misfire Detected
P0302 Cylinder no. 2—Misfire Detected
P0303 Cylinder no. 3—Misfire Detected
P0304 Cylinder no. 4—Misfire Detected
P0305 Cylinder no. 5—Misfire Detected
P0306 Cylinder no. 6—Misfire Detected
P0307 Cylinder no. 7—Misfire Detected
P0308 Cylinder no. 8—Misfire Detected

P0309 Cylinder no. 9—Misfire Detected
P0310 Cylinder no. 10—Misfire Detected
P0311 Cylinder no. 11—Misfire Detected
P0312 Cylinder no. 12—Misfire Detected
P0320 Ignition/Distributor Engine Speed Input Circuit Malfunction
P0321 Ignition/Distributor Engine Speed Input Circuit Range/Performance
P0322 Ignition/Distributor Engine Speed Input Circuit No Signal
P0323 Ignition/Distributor Engine Speed Input Circuit Intermittent
P0325 Knock Sensor no. 1—Circuit Malfunction (Bank no. 1 or Single Sensor)
P0326 Knock Sensor no. 1—Circuit Range/Performance (Bank no. 1 or Single Sensor)
P0327 Knock Sensor no. 1—Circuit Low Input (Bank no. 1 or Single Sensor)
P0328 Knock Sensor no. 1—Circuit High Input (Bank no. 1 or Single Sensor)
P0329 Knock Sensor no. 1—Circuit Input Intermittent (Bank no. 1 or Single Sensor)
P0330 Knock Sensor no. 2—Circuit Malfunction (Bank no. 2)
P0331 Knock Sensor no. 2—Circuit Range/Performance (Bank no. 2)
P0332 Knock Sensor no. 2—Circuit Low Input (Bank no. 2)
P0333 Knock Sensor no. 2—Circuit High Input (Bank no. 2)
P0334 Knock Sensor no. 2—Circuit Input Intermittent (Bank no. 2)
P0335 Crankshaft Position Sensor "A" Circuit Malfunction
P0336 Crankshaft Position Sensor "A" Circuit Range/Performance
P0337 Crankshaft Position Sensor "A" Circuit Low Input
P0338 Crankshaft Position Sensor "A" Circuit High Input
P0339 Crankshaft Position Sensor "A" Circuit Intermittent
P0340 Camshaft Position Sensor Circuit Malfunction
P0341 Camshaft Position Sensor Circuit Range/Performance
P0342 Camshaft Position Sensor Circuit Low Input
P0343 Camshaft Position Sensor Circuit High Input
P0344 Camshaft Position Sensor Circuit Intermittent
P0350 Ignition Coil Primary/Secondary Circuit Malfunction
P0351 Ignition Coil "A" Primary/Secondary Circuit Malfunction
P0352 Ignition Coil "B" Primary/Secondary Circuit Malfunction
P0353 Ignition Coil "C" Primary/Secondary Circuit Malfunction
P0354 Ignition Coil "D" Primary/Secondary Circuit Malfunction
P0355 Ignition Coil "E" Primary/Secondary Circuit Malfunction
P0356 Ignition Coil "F" Primary/Secondary Circuit Malfunction
P0357 Ignition Coil "G" Primary/Secondary Circuit Malfunction
P0358 Ignition Coil "H" Primary/Secondary Circuit Malfunction
P0359 Ignition Coil "I" Primary/Secondary Circuit Malfunction
P0360 Ignition Coil "J" Primary/Secondary Circuit Malfunction
P0361 Ignition Coil "K" Primary/Secondary Circuit Malfunction
P0362 Ignition Coil "L" Primary/Secondary Circuit Malfunction
P0370 Timing Reference High Resolution Signal "A" Malfunction
P0371 Timing Reference High Resolution Signal "A" Too Many Pulses
P0372 Timing Reference High Resolution Signal "A" Too Few Pulses
P0373 Timing Reference High Resolution Signal "A" Intermittent/Erratic Pulses
P0374 Timing Reference High Resolution Signal "A" No Pulses
P0375 Timing Reference High Resolution Signal "B" Malfunction
P0376 Timing Reference High Resolution Signal "B" Too Many Pulses
P0377 Timing Reference High Resolution Signal "B" Too Few Pulses
P0378 Timing Reference High Resolution Signal "B" Intermittent/Erratic Pulses
P0379 Timing Reference High Resolution Signal "B" No Pulses
P0380 Glow Plug/Heater Circuit "A" Malfunction
P0381 Glow Plug/Heater Indicator Circuit Malfunction
P0382 Glow Plug/Heater Circuit "B" Malfunction
P0385 Crankshaft Position Sensor "B" Circuit Malfunction
P0386 Crankshaft Position Sensor "B" Circuit Range/Performance
P0387 Crankshaft Position Sensor "B" Circuit Low Input
P0388 Crankshaft Position Sensor "B" Circuit High Input
P0389 Crankshaft Position Sensor "B" Circuit Intermittent
P0400 Exhaust Gas Recirculation Flow Malfunction
P0401 Exhaust Gas Recirculation Flow Insufficient Detected
P0402 Exhaust Gas Recirculation Flow Excessive Detected
P0403 Exhaust Gas Recirculation Circuit Malfunction

P0404 Exhaust Gas Recirculation Circuit Range/Performance
P0405 Exhaust Gas Recirculation Sensor "A" Circuit Low
P0406 Exhaust Gas Recirculation Sensor "A" Circuit High
P0407 Exhaust Gas Recirculation Sensor "B" Circuit Low
P0408 Exhaust Gas Recirculation Sensor "B" Circuit High
P0410 Secondary Air Injection System Malfunction
P0411 Secondary Air Injection System Incorrect Flow Detected
P0412 Secondary Air Injection System Switching Valve "A" Circuit Malfunction
P0413 Secondary Air Injection System Switching Valve "A" Circuit Open
P0414 Secondary Air Injection System Switching Valve "A" Circuit Shorted
P0415 Secondary Air Injection System Switching Valve "B" Circuit Malfunction
P0416 Secondary Air Injection System Switching Valve "B" Circuit Open
P0417 Secondary Air Injection System Switching Valve "B" Circuit Shorted
P0418 Secondary Air Injection System Relay "A" Circuit Malfunction
P0419 Secondary Air Injection System Relay "B" Circuit Malfunction
P0420 Catalyst System Efficiency Below Threshold (Bank no. 1)
P0421 Warm Up Catalyst Efficiency Below Threshold (Bank no. 1)
P0422 Main Catalyst Efficiency Below Threshold (Bank no. 1)
P0423 Heated Catalyst Efficiency Below Threshold (Bank no. 1)
P0424 Heated Catalyst Temperature Below Threshold (Bank no. 1)
P0430 Catalyst System Efficiency Below Threshold (Bank no. 2)
P0431 Warm Up Catalyst Efficiency Below Threshold (Bank no. 2)
P0432 Main Catalyst Efficiency Below Threshold (Bank no. 2)
P0433 Heated Catalyst Efficiency Below Threshold (Bank no. 2)
P0434 Heated Catalyst Temperature Below Threshold (Bank no. 2)
P0440 Evaporative Emission Control System Malfunction
P0441 Evaporative Emission Control System Incorrect Purge Flow
P0442 Evaporative Emission Control System Leak Detected (Small Leak)
P0443 Evaporative Emission Control System Purge Control Valve Circuit Malfunction
P0444 Evaporative Emission Control System Purge Control Valve Circuit Open
P0445 Evaporative Emission Control System Purge Control Valve Circuit Shorted
P0446 Evaporative Emission Control System Vent Control Circuit Malfunction
P0447 Evaporative Emission Control System Vent Control Circuit Open
P0448 Evaporative Emission Control System Vent Control Circuit Shorted
P0449 Evaporative Emission Control System Vent Valve/Solenoid Circuit Malfunction
P0450 Evaporative Emission Control System Pressure Sensor Malfunction
P0451 Evaporative Emission Control System Pressure Sensor Range/Performance
P0452 Evaporative Emission Control System Pressure Sensor Low Input
P0453 Evaporative Emission Control System Pressure Sensor High Input
P0454 Evaporative Emission Control System Pressure Sensor Intermittent
P0455 Evaporative Emission Control System Leak Detected (Gross Leak)
P0460 Fuel Level Sensor Circuit Malfunction
P0461 Fuel Level Sensor Circuit Range/Performance
P0462 Fuel Level Sensor Circuit Low Input
P0463 Fuel Level Sensor Circuit High Input
P0464 Fuel Level Sensor Circuit Intermittent
P0465 Purge Flow Sensor Circuit Malfunction
P0466 Purge Flow Sensor Circuit Range/Performance
P0467 Purge Flow Sensor Circuit Low Input
P0468 Purge Flow Sensor Circuit High Input
P0469 Purge Flow Sensor Circuit Intermittent
P0470 Exhaust Pressure Sensor Malfunction
P0471 Exhaust Pressure Sensor Range/Performance
P0472 Exhaust Pressure Sensor Low
P0473 Exhaust Pressure Sensor High
P0474 Exhaust Pressure Sensor Intermittent
P0475 Exhaust Pressure Control Valve Malfunction
P0476 Exhaust Pressure Control Valve Range/Performance
P0477 Exhaust Pressure Control Valve Low
P0478 Exhaust Pressure Control Valve High
P0479 Exhaust Pressure Control Valve Intermittent
P0480 Cooling Fan no. 1 Control Circuit Malfunction
P0481 Cooling Fan no. 2 Control Circuit Malfunction

P0482 Cooling Fan no. 3 Control Circuit Malfunction
P0483 Cooling Fan Rationality Check Malfunction
P0484 Cooling Fan Circuit Over Current
P0485 Cooling Fan Power/Ground Circuit Malfunction
P0500 Vehicle Speed Sensor Malfunction
P0501 Vehicle Speed Sensor Range/Performance
P0502 Vehicle Speed Sensor Circuit Low Input
P0503 Vehicle Speed Sensor Intermittent/Erratic/High
P0505 Idle Control System Malfunction
P0506 Idle Control System RPM Lower Than Expected
P0507 Idle Control System RPM Higher Than Expected
P0510 Closed Throttle Position Switch Malfunction
P0520 Engine Oil Pressure Sensor/Switch Circuit Malfunction
P0521 Engine Oil Pressure Sensor/Switch Range/Performance
P0522 Engine Oil Pressure Sensor/Switch Low Voltage
P0523 Engine Oil Pressure Sensor/Switch High Voltage
P0530 A/C Refrigerant Pressure Sensor Circuit Malfunction
P0531 A/C Refrigerant Pressure Sensor Circuit Range/Performance
P0532 A/C Refrigerant Pressure Sensor Circuit Low Input
P0533 A/C Refrigerant Pressure Sensor Circuit High Input
P0534 A/C Refrigerant Charge Loss
P0550 Power Steering Pressure Sensor Circuit Malfunction
P0551 Power Steering Pressure Sensor Circuit Range/Performance
P0552 Power Steering Pressure Sensor Circuit Low Input
P0553 Power Steering Pressure Sensor Circuit High Input
P0554 Power Steering Pressure Sensor Circuit Intermittent
P0560 System Voltage Malfunction
P0561 System Voltage Unstable
P0562 System Voltage Low
P0563 System Voltage High
P0565 Cruise Control On Signal Malfunction
P0566 Cruise Control Off Signal Malfunction
P0567 Cruise Control Resume Signal Malfunction
P0568 Cruise Control Set Signal Malfunction
P0569 Cruise Control Coast Signal Malfunction
P0570 Cruise Control Accel Signal Malfunction
P0571 Cruise Control/Brake Switch "A" Circuit Malfunction
P0572 Cruise Control/Brake Switch "A" Circuit Low
P0573 Cruise Control/Brake Switch "A" Circuit High
P0574 Through P0580 Reserved for Cruise Codes
P0600 Serial Communication Link Malfunction
P0601 Internal Control Module Memory Check Sum Error
P0602 Control Module Programming Error
P0603 Internal Control Module Keep Alive Memory (KAM) Error
P0604 Internal Control Module Random Access Memory (RAM) Error
P0605 Internal Control Module Read Only Memory (ROM) Error
P0606 PCM Processor Fault
P0608 Control Module VSS Output "A" Malfunction
P0609 Control Module VSS Output "B" Malfunction
P0620 Generator Control Circuit Malfunction
P0621 Generator Lamp "L" Control Circuit Malfunction
P0622 Generator Field "F" Control Circuit Malfunction
P0650 Malfunction Indicator Lamp (MIL) Control Circuit Malfunction
P0654 Engine RPM Output Circuit Malfunction
P0655 Engine Hot Lamp Output Control Circuit Malfunction
P0656 Fuel Level Output Circuit Malfunction
P0700 Transmission Control System Malfunction
P0701 Transmission Control System Range/Performance
P0702 Transmission Control System Electrical
P0703 Torque Converter/Brake Switch "B" Circuit Malfunction
P0704 Clutch Switch Input Circuit Malfunction
P0705 Transmission Range Sensor Circuit Malfunction (PRNDL Input)
P0706 Transmission Range Sensor Circuit Range/Performance
P0707 Transmission Range Sensor Circuit Low Input
P0708 Transmission Range Sensor Circuit High Input
P0709 Transmission Range Sensor Circuit Intermittent
P0710 Transmission Fluid Temperature Sensor Circuit Malfunction
P0711 Transmission Fluid Temperature Sensor Circuit Range/Performance
P0712 Transmission Fluid Temperature Sensor Circuit Low Input
P0713 Transmission Fluid Temperature Sensor Circuit High Input
P0714 Transmission Fluid Temperature Sensor Circuit Intermittent

P0715 Input/Turbine Speed Sensor Circuit Malfunction
P0716 Input/Turbine Speed Sensor Circuit Range/Performance
P0717 Input/Turbine Speed Sensor Circuit No Signal
P0718 Input/Turbine Speed Sensor Circuit Intermittent
P0719 Torque Converter/Brake Switch "B" Circuit Low
P0720 Output Speed Sensor Circuit Malfunction
P0721 Output Speed Sensor Circuit Range/Performance
P0722 Output Speed Sensor Circuit No Signal
P0723 Output Speed Sensor Circuit Intermittent
P0724 Torque Converter/Brake Switch "B" Circuit High
P0725 Engine Speed Input Circuit Malfunction
P0726 Engine Speed Input Circuit Range/Performance
P0727 Engine Speed Input Circuit No Signal
P0728 Engine Speed Input Circuit Intermittent
P0730 Incorrect Gear Ratio
P0731 Gear no. 1 Incorrect Ratio
P0732 Gear no. 2 Incorrect Ratio
P0733 Gear no. 3 Incorrect Ratio
P0734 Gear no. 4 Incorrect Ratio
P0735 Gear no. 5 Incorrect Ratio
P0736 Reverse Incorrect Ratio
P0740 Torque Converter Clutch Circuit Malfunction
P0741 Torque Converter Clutch Circuit Performance or Stuck Off
P0742 Torque Converter Clutch Circuit Stuck On
P0743 Torque Converter Clutch Circuit Electrical
P0744 Torque Converter Clutch Circuit Intermittent
P0745 Pressure Control Solenoid Malfunction
P0746 Pressure Control Solenoid Performance or Stuck Off
P0747 Pressure Control Solenoid Stuck On
P0748 Pressure Control Solenoid Electrical
P0749 Pressure Control Solenoid Intermittent
P0750 Shift Solenoid "A" Malfunction
P0751 Shift Solenoid "A" Performance or Stuck Off
P0752 Shift Solenoid "A" Stuck On
P0753 Shift Solenoid "A" Electrical
P0754 Shift Solenoid "A" Intermittent
P0755 Shift Solenoid "B" Malfunction
P0756 Shift Solenoid "B" Performance or Stuck Off
P0757 Shift Solenoid "B" Stuck On
P0758 Shift Solenoid "B" Electrical
P0759 Shift Solenoid "B" Intermittent
P0760 Shift Solenoid "C" Malfunction
P0761 Shift Solenoid "C" Performance Or Stuck Off
P0762 Shift Solenoid "C" Stuck On
P0763 Shift Solenoid "C" Electrical
P0764 Shift Solenoid "C" Intermittent
P0765 Shift Solenoid "D" Malfunction
P0766 Shift Solenoid "D" Performance Or Stuck Off
P0767 Shift Solenoid "D" Stuck On
P0768 Shift Solenoid "D" Electrical
P0769 Shift Solenoid "D" Intermittent
P0770 Shift Solenoid "E" Malfunction
P0771 Shift Solenoid "E" Performance Or Stuck Off
P0772 Shift Solenoid "E" Stuck On
P0773 Shift Solenoid "E" Electrical
P0774 Shift Solenoid "E" Intermittent
P0780 Shift Malfunction
P0781 1–2 Shift Malfunction
P0782 2–3 Shift Malfunction
P0783 3–4 Shift Malfunction
P0784 4–5 Shift Malfunction
P0785 Shift/Timing Solenoid Malfunction
P0786 Shift/Timing Solenoid Range/Performance
P0787 Shift/Timing Solenoid Low
P0788 Shift/Timing Solenoid High
P0789 Shift/Timing Solenoid Intermittent
P0790 Normal/Performance Switch Circuit Malfunction
P0801 Reverse Inhibit Control Circuit Malfunction
P0803 1–4 Upshift (Skip Shift) Solenoid Control Circuit Malfunction
P0804 1–4 Upshift (Skip Shift) Lamp Control Circuit Malfunction
P1106 Map Sensor Circuit Intermittent High Voltage

P1107 MAP Sensor Circuit Intermittent Low Voltage
P1111 IAT Sensor Circuit Intermittent High Voltage
P1112 IAT Sensor Circuit Intermittent Low Voltage
P1114 ECT Sensor Circuit Intermittent Low Voltage
P1115 ECT Sensor Circuit Intermittent High Voltage
P1121 TP Sensor Circuit Intermittent High Voltage
P1122 TP Sensor Circuit Intermittent Low Voltage
P1133 HO2S-11 Insufficient Switching (Bank 1 Sensor 1)
P1134 HO2S-11 Transition Time Ratio (Bank 1 Sensor 1)
P1153 HO2S-21 Insufficient Switching (Bank 2 Sensor I)
P1154 HO2S-21 Transition Time Ratio (Bank 2 Sensor 1)
P1171 Fuel System Lean During Acceleration
P1391 G-Acceleration Sensor Intermittent Low Voltage
P1390 G-Acceleration (Low G) Sensor Performance
P1392 Rough Road G-Sensor Circuit Low Voltage

P1393 Rough Road G-Sensor Circuit High Voltage **P1394** G-Acceleration Sensor Intermittent High Voltage
P1406 EGR Valve Pintle Position Sensor Circuit Fault
P1441 EVAP System Flow During Non-Purge
P1442 EVAP System Flow During Non-Purge **P1508** Idle Speed Control System-Low
P1509 Idle Speed Control System-High
P1618 Serial Peripheral Interface Communication Error
P1640 Output Driver Module `A' Fault
P1790 PCM ROM (Transmission Side) Check Sum Error
P1792 PCM EEPROM (Transmission Side) Check Sum Error
P1835 Kick Down Switch Always On
P1850 Brake Band Apply Solenoid Electrical Fault
P1860 TCC PWM Solenoid Electrical Fault
P1870 Transmission Component Slipping

VACUUM DIAGRAMS

▶ **See Figures 51 thru 64**

Following are vacuum diagrams for most of the engine and emissions package combinations covered by this manual. Because vacuum circuits will vary based on various engine and vehicle options, always refer first to the vehicle emission control information label, if present. Should the label be missing, or should vehicle be equipped with a different engine from the vehicle's original equipment, refer to the diagrams below for the same or similar configuration.

If you wish to obtain a replacement emissions label, most manufacturers make the labels available for purchase. The labels can usually be ordered from a local dealer.

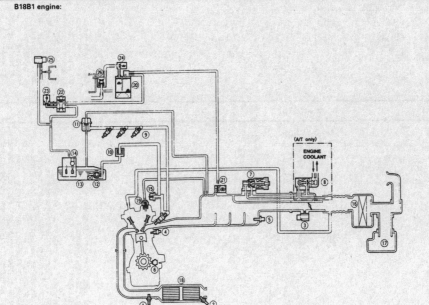

B18B1 engine:

① PRIMARY HEATED OXYGEN SENSOR (PRIMARY HO2S) (SENSOR 1)
② SECONDARY HEATED OXYGEN SENSOR (SECONDARY HO2S) (SENSOR 2)
③ MANIFOLD ABSOLUTE PRESSURE (MAP) SENSOR
④ ENGINE COOLANT TEMPERATURE (ECT) SENSOR
⑤ INTAKE AIR TEMPERATURE (IAT) SENSOR
⑥ CRANKSHAFT SPEED FLUCTUATION (CKF) SENSOR
⑦ IDLE AIR CONTROL (IAC) VALVE
⑧ FAST IDLE THERMO VALVE
⑨ FUEL INJECTOR
⑩ FUEL FILTER
⑪ FUEL PRESSURE REGULATOR
⑫ FUEL PUMP (FP)
⑬ FUEL TANK
⑭ FUEL TANK EVAPORATIVE EMISSION (EVAP) VALVE
⑮ FUEL PULSATION DAMPER
⑯ AIR CLEANER
⑰ RESONATOR
⑱ THREE WAY CATALYTIC CONVERTER (TWC)
⑲ POSITIVE CRANKCASE VENTILATION (PCV) VALVE
⑳ EVAPORATIVE EMISSION (EVAP) CONTROL CANISTER
㉑ EVAPORATIVE EMISSION (EVAP) PURGE CONTROL SOLENOID VALVE
㉒ EVAPORATIVE EMISSION (EVAP) TWO WAY VALVE
㉓ EVAPORATIVE EMISSION (EVAP) BYPASS SOLENOID VALVE
㉔ EVAPORATIVE EMISSION (EVAP) CONTROL CANISTER VENT SHUT VALVE
㉕ FUEL TANK PRESSURE SENSOR
㉖ EVAPORATIVE EMISSION (EVAP) THREE WAY VALVE

90944G20

Fig. 51 Vacuum hose routing—1.8L (B18B1) engine

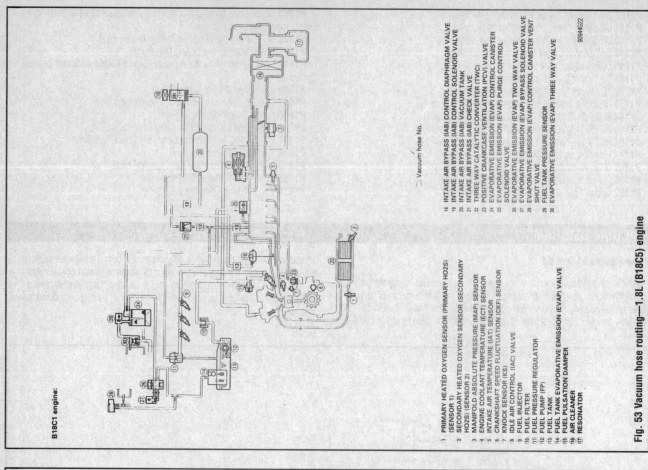

B18C1 engine:

90944G22

☷ Vacuum hose No.

① PRIMARY HEATED OXYGEN SENSOR (PRIMARY HO2S) (SENSOR 1)
② SECONDARY HEATED OXYGEN SENSOR (SECONDARY HO2S) (SENSOR 2)
③ MANIFOLD ABSOLUTE PRESSURE (MAP) SENSOR
④ ENGINE COOLANT TEMPERATURE (ECT) SENSOR
⑤ INTAKE AIR TEMPERATURE (IAT) SENSOR
⑥ CRANKSHAFT SPEED FLUCTUATION (CKF) SENSOR
⑦ KNOCK SENSOR (KS)
⑧ IDLE AIR CONTROL (IAC) VALVE
⑨ FUEL FILTER
⑩ FUEL PRESSURE REGULATOR
⑪ FUEL PUMP (FP)
⑫ FUEL TANK
⑬ FUEL INJECTOR
⑭ FUEL TANK EVAPORATIVE EMISSION (EVAP) VALVE
⑮ FUEL PULSATION DAMPER
⑯ AIR CLEANER
⑰ RESONATOR

18 INTAKE AIR BYPASS (IAB) CONTROL DIAPHRAGM VALVE
19 INTAKE AIR BYPASS (IAB) CONTROL SOLENOID VALVE
20 INTAKE AIR BYPASS (IAB) VACUUM TANK
21 INTAKE AIR BYPASS (IAB) CHECK VALVE
22 THREE WAY CATALYTIC CONVERTER (TWC)
23 POSITIVE CRANKCASE VENTILATION (PCV) VALVE
24 EVAPORATIVE EMISSION (EVAP) CONTROL CANISTER
25 EVAPORATIVE EMISSION (EVAP) PURGE CONTROL SOLENOID VALVE
26 EVAPORATIVE EMISSION (EVAP) TWO WAY VALVE
27 EVAPORATIVE EMISSION (EVAP) BYPASS SOLENOID VALVE
28 EVAPORATIVE EMISSION (EVAP) CONTROL CANISTER VENT SHUT VALVE
29 FUEL TANK PRESSURE SENSOR
30 EVAPORATIVE EMISSION (EVAP) THREE WAY VALVE

Fig. 53 Vacuum hose routing—1.8L (B18C5) engine

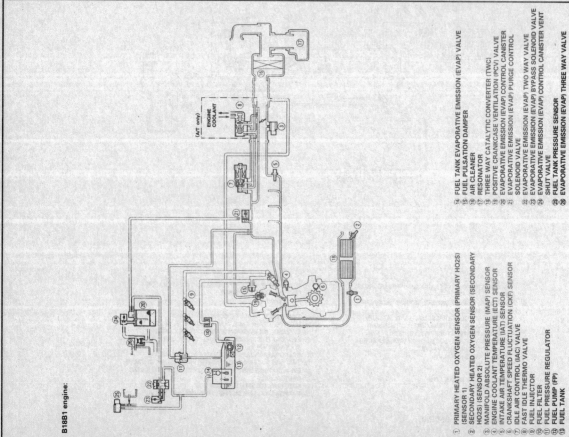

B18B1 engine:

90944G21

① PRIMARY HEATED OXYGEN SENSOR (PRIMARY HO2S) (SENSOR 1)
② SECONDARY HEATED OXYGEN SENSOR (SECONDARY HO2S) (SENSOR 2)
③ MANIFOLD ABSOLUTE PRESSURE (MAP) SENSOR
④ ENGINE COOLANT TEMPERATURE (ECT) SENSOR
⑤ INTAKE AIR TEMPERATURE (IAT) SENSOR
⑥ CRANKSHAFT SPEED FLUCTUATION (CKF) SENSOR
⑦ IDLE AIR CONTROL (IAC) VALVE
⑧ FAST IDLE THERMO VALVE
⑨ FUEL INJECTOR
⑩ FUEL FILTER
⑪ FUEL PRESSURE REGULATOR
⑫ FUEL PUMP (FP)
⑬ FUEL TANK

⑭ FUEL TANK EVAPORATIVE EMISSION (EVAP) VALVE
⑮ FUEL PULSATION DAMPER
⑯ AIR CLEANER
⑰ RESONATOR
⑱ THREE WAY CATALYTIC CONVERTER (TWC)
⑲ POSITIVE CRANKCASE VENTILATION (PCV) VALVE
⑳ EVAPORATIVE EMISSION (EVAP) CONTROL CANISTER
㉑ EVAPORATIVE EMISSION (EVAP) PURGE CONTROL SOLENOID VALVE
㉒ EVAPORATIVE EMISSION (EVAP) TWO WAY VALVE
㉓ EVAPORATIVE EMISSION (EVAP) BYPASS SOLENOID VALVE
㉔ EVAPORATIVE EMISSION (EVAP) CONTROL CANISTER VENT SHUT VALVE
㉕ FUEL TANK PRESSURE SENSOR
㉖ EVAPORATIVE EMISSION (EVAP) THREE WAY VALVE

Fig. 52 Vacuum hose routing—1.8L (B18C1) engine

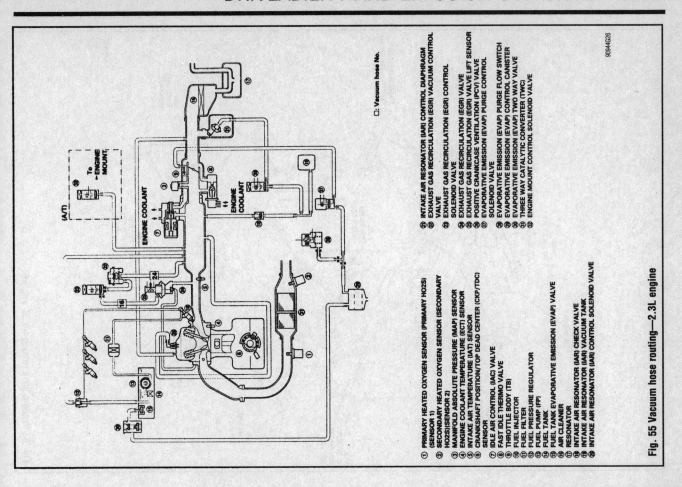

90944G26

☐: Vacuum hose No.

① PRIMARY HEATED OXYGEN SENSOR (PRIMARY HO2S) (SENSOR 1)
② SECONDARY HEATED OXYGEN SENSOR (SECONDARY HO2S) (SENSOR 2)
③ MANIFOLD ABSOLUTE PRESSURE (MAP) SENSOR
④ ENGINE COOLANT TEMPERATURE (ECT) SENSOR
⑤ INTAKE AIR TEMPERATURE (IAT) SENSOR
⑥ CRANKSHAFT POSITION/TOP DEAD CENTER (CKP/TDC) SENSOR
⑦ IDLE AIR CONTROL (IAC) VALVE
⑧ FAST IDLE THERMO VALVE
⑨ THROTTLE BODY (TB)
⑩ FUEL INJECTOR
⑪ FUEL FILTER
⑫ FUEL PRESSURE REGULATOR
⑬ FUEL PUMP (FP)
⑭ FUEL TANK
⑮ FUEL TANK EVAPORATIVE EMISSION (EVAP) VALVE
⑯ AIR CLEANER
⑰ RESONATOR
⑱ INTAKE AIR RESONATOR (IAR) CHECK VALVE
⑲ INTAKE AIR RESONATOR (IAR) VACUUM TANK
⑳ INTAKE AIR RESONATOR (IAR) CONTROL SOLENOID VALVE

㉑ INTAKE AIR RESONATOR (IAR) CONTROL DIAPHRAGM
㉒ EXHAUST GAS RECIRCULATION (EGR) VACUUM CONTROL VALVE
㉓ EXHAUST GAS RECIRCULATION (EGR) CONTROL SOLENOID VALVE
㉔ EXHAUST GAS RECIRCULATION (EGR) VALVE
㉕ EXHAUST GAS RECIRCULATION (EGR) VALVE LIFT SENSOR
㉖ POSITIVE CRANKCASE VENTILATION (PCV) VALVE
㉗ EVAPORATIVE EMISSION (EVAP) PURGE CONTROL SOLENOID VALVE
㉘ EVAPORATIVE EMISSION (EVAP) PURGE FLOW SWITCH
㉙ EVAPORATIVE EMISSION (EVAP) CONTROL CANISTER
㉚ EVAPORATIVE EMISSION (EVAP) TWO WAY VALVE
㉛ THREE WAY CATALYTIC CONVERTER (TWC)
㉜ ENGINE MOUNT CONTROL SOLENOID VALVE

Fig. 55 Vacuum hose routing—2.3L engine

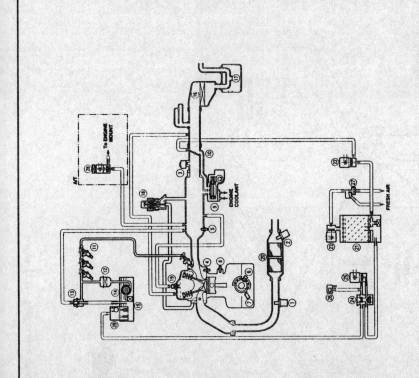

90944G25

① PRIMARY HEATED OXYGEN SENSOR (PRIMARY HO2S) (SENSOR 1)
② SECONDARY HEATED OXYGEN SENSOR (SECONDARY HO2S) (SENSOR 2)
③ MANIFOLD ABSOLUTE PRESSURE (MAP) SENSOR
④ ENGINE COOLANT TEMPERATURE (ECT) SENSOR
⑤ INTAKE AIR TEMPERATURE (IAT) SENSOR
⑥ CRANKSHAFT POSITION (CKP) SENSOR
⑦ TOP DEAD CENTER (TDC) SENSOR
⑧ KNOCK SENSOR (KS)
⑨ IDLE AIR CONTROL (IAC) VALVE
⑩ THROTTLE BODY (TB)
⑪ FUEL INJECTOR
⑫ FUEL FILTER
⑬ FUEL PRESSURE REGULATOR
⑭ FUEL PUMP (FP)
⑮ FUEL TANK
⑯ AIR CLEANER
⑰ RESONATOR
⑱ EXHAUST GAS RECIRCULATION (EGR) VALVE and LIFT SENSOR
⑲ POSITIVE CRANKCASE VENTILATION (PCV) VALVE
⑳ THREE WAY CATALYTIC CONVERTER
㉑ EVAPORATIVE EMISSION (EVAP) CONTROL CANISTER
㉒ EVAPORATIVE EMISSION (EVAP) PURGE CONTROL SOLENOID VALVE
㉓ VENT SHUT VALVE
㉔ EVAPORATIVE EMISSION (EVAP) TWO WAY VALVE
㉕ EVAPORATIVE EMISSION (EVAP) CONTROL CANISTER
㉖ FUEL TANK PRESSURE SENSOR
㉗ EVAPORATIVE EMISSION (EVAP) THREE WAY VALVE
㉘ ENGINE MOUNT CONTROL SOLENOID VALVE
㉙ EVAPORATIVE EMISSION (EVAP) BYPASS SOLENOID VALVE
㉚ FUEL TANK EVAPORATIVE EMISSION (EVAP) VALVE

Fig. 54 Vacuum hose routing—2.2L engine

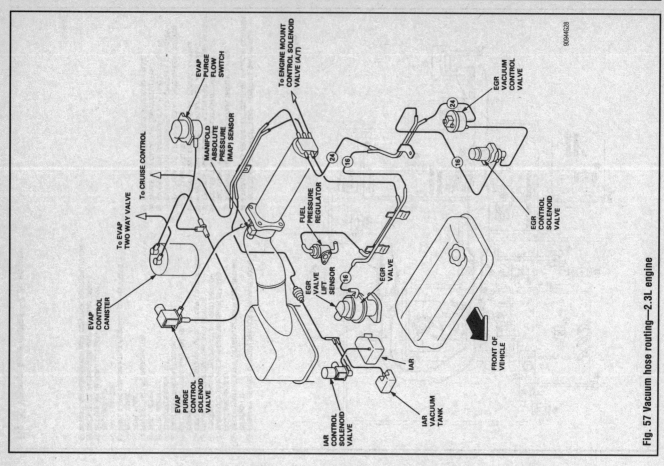

Fig. 57 Vacuum hose routing—2.3L engine

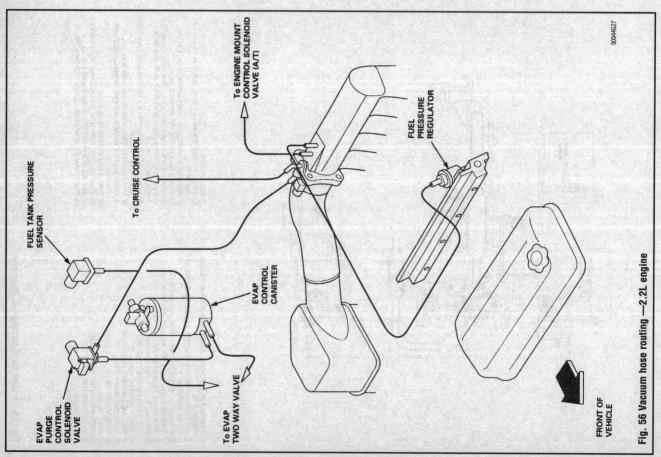

Fig. 56 Vacuum hose routing —2.2L engine

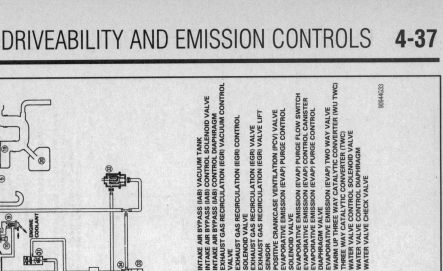

'95 – 96 models:

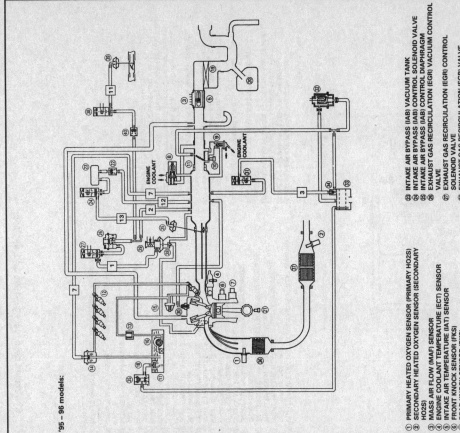

① PRIMARY HEATED OXYGEN SENSOR (PRIMARY HO2S)
② SECONDARY HEATED OXYGEN SENSOR (SECONDARY HO2S)
③ MASS AIR FLOW (MAF) SENSOR
④ ENGINE COOLANT TEMPERATURE (ECT) SENSOR
⑤ INTAKE AIR TEMPERATURE (IAT) SENSOR
⑥ FRONT KNOCK SENSOR (FKS)
⑦ REAR KNOCK SENSOR (RKS)
⑧ IDLE AIR CONTROL (IAC) VALVE
⑨ FAST IDLE THERMO VALVE
⑩ IDLE ADJUSTING SCREW
⑪ THROTTLE BODY (TB)
⑫ FUEL INJECTOR
⑬ FUEL FILTER
⑭ FUEL PRESSURE REGULATOR
⑮ FUEL PULSATION DAMPER
⑯ FUEL PUMP (FP)
⑰ FUEL TANK
⑱ FUEL TANK EVAPORATIVE EMISSION (EVAP) VALVE
⑲ AIR CLEANER
⑳ RESONATOR
㉑ CRANKSHAFT SPEED FLUCTUATION (CKF) SENSOR
㉒ INTAKE AIR BYPASS (IAB) CHECK VALVE
㉓ INTAKE AIR BYPASS (IAB) VACUUM TANK
㉔ INTAKE AIR BYPASS (IAB) CONTROL SOLENOID VALVE
㉕ INTAKE AIR BYPASS (IAB) CONTROL DIAPHRAGM
㉖ EXHAUST GAS RECIRCULATION (EGRI) VACUUM CONTROL VALVE
㉗ EXHAUST GAS RECIRCULATION (EGRI) CONTROL SOLENOID VALVE
㉘ EXHAUST GAS RECIRCULATION (EGRI) VALVE
㉙ EXHAUST GAS RECIRCULATION (EGRI) VALVE LIFT SENSOR
㉚ POSITIVE CRANKCASE VENTILATION (PCV) VALVE
㉛ EVAPORATIVE EMISSION (EVAP) PURGE CONTROL SOLENOID VALVE
㉜ EVAPORATIVE EMISSION (EVAP) PURGE FLOW SWITCH
㉝ EVAPORATIVE EMISSION (EVAP) CONTROL CANISTER
㉞ EVAPORATIVE EMISSION (EVAP) PURGE CONTROL DIAPHRAGM VALVE
㉟ EVAPORATIVE EMISSION (EVAP) TWO WAY VALVE
㊱ WARM UP THREE WAY CATALYTIC CONVERTER (WU TWC)
㊲ THREE WAY CATALYTIC CONVERTER (TWC)
㊳ WATER VALVE CONTROL SOLENOID VALVE
㊴ WATER VALVE CONTROL DIAPHRAGM
㊵ WATER VALVE CHECK VALVE

90944G33

Fig. 59 Vacuum hose routing—1997 2.5L engines

'95 – 96 models:

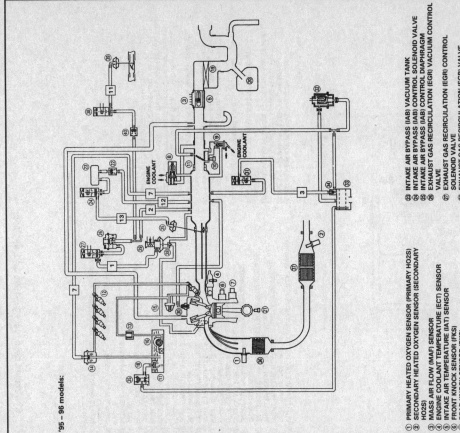

① PRIMARY HEATED OXYGEN SENSOR (PRIMARY HO2S)
② SECONDARY HEATED OXYGEN SENSOR (SECONDARY HO2S)
③ MASS AIR FLOW (MAF) SENSOR
④ ENGINE COOLANT TEMPERATURE (ECT) SENSOR
⑤ INTAKE AIR TEMPERATURE (IAT) SENSOR
⑥ FRONT KNOCK SENSOR (FKS)
⑦ REAR KNOCK SENSOR (RKS)
⑧ IDLE AIR CONTROL (IAC) VALVE
⑨ FAST IDLE THERMO VALVE
⑩ IDLE ADJUSTING SCREW
⑪ THROTTLE BODY (TB)
⑫ FUEL INJECTOR
⑬ FUEL FILTER
⑭ FUEL PRESSURE REGULATOR
⑮ FUEL PULSATION DAMPER
⑯ FUEL PUMP (FP)
⑰ FUEL TANK
⑱ FUEL TANK EVAPORATIVE EMISSION (EVAP) VALVE
⑲ AIR CLEANER
⑳ RESONATOR
㉑ CRANKSHAFT SPEED FLUCTUATION (CKF) SENSOR
㉒ INTAKE AIR BYPASS (IAB) CHECK VALVE
㉓ INTAKE AIR BYPASS (IAB) VACUUM TANK
㉔ INTAKE AIR BYPASS (IAB) CONTROL SOLENOID VALVE
㉕ INTAKE AIR BYPASS (IAB) CONTROL DIAPHRAGM
㉖ EXHAUST GAS RECIRCULATION (EGRI) VACUUM CONTROL VALVE
㉗ EXHAUST GAS RECIRCULATION (EGRI) CONTROL SOLENOID VALVE
㉘ EXHAUST GAS RECIRCULATION (EGRI) VALVE
㉙ EXHAUST GAS RECIRCULATION (EGRI) VALVE LIFT SENSOR
㉚ POSITIVE CRANKCASE VENTILATION (PCV) VALVE
㉛ EVAPORATIVE EMISSION (EVAP) PURGE CONTROL SOLENOID VALVE
㉜ EVAPORATIVE EMISSION (EVAP) PURGE FLOW SWITCH
㉝ EVAPORATIVE EMISSION (EVAP) CONTROL CANISTER
㉞ EVAPORATIVE EMISSION (EVAP) PURGE CONTROL DIAPHRAGM VALVE
㉟ EVAPORATIVE EMISSION (EVAP) TWO WAY VALVE
㊱ WARM UP THREE WAY CATALYTIC CONVERTER (WU TWC)
㊲ THREE WAY CATALYTIC CONVERTER (TWC)
㊳ WATER VALVE CONTROL SOLENOID VALVE
㊴ WATER VALVE CONTROL DIAPHRAGM
㊵ WATER VALVE CHECK VALVE

90944G32

Fig. 58 Vacuum hose routing—1995-96 2.5L engines

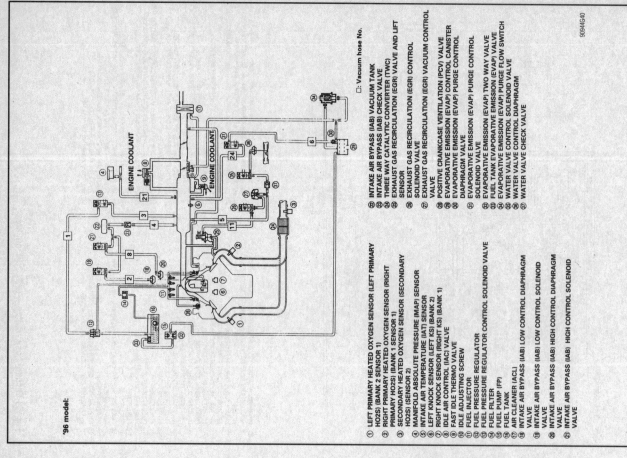

'96 model:

☐: Vacuum hose No.

① LEFT PRIMARY HEATED OXYGEN SENSOR (LEFT PRIMARY HO2S) (BANK 2 SENSOR 1)
② RIGHT PRIMARY HEATED OXYGEN SENSOR (RIGHT PRIMARY HO2S) (BANK 1 SENSOR 1)
③ SECONDARY HEATED OXYGEN SENSOR (SECONDARY HO2S) (SENSOR 2)
④ MANIFOLD ABSOLUTE PRESSURE (MAP) SENSOR
⑤ INTAKE AIR TEMPERATURE (IAT) SENSOR
⑥ LEFT KNOCK SENSOR (LEFT KS) (BANK 2)
⑦ RIGHT KNOCK SENSOR (RIGHT KS) (BANK 1)
⑧ IDLE AIR CONTROL (IAC) VALVE
⑨ FAST IDLE THERMO VALVE
⑩ IDLE ADJUSTING SCREW
⑪ FUEL INJECTOR
⑫ FUEL PRESSURE REGULATOR
⑬ FUEL PRESSURE REGULATOR CONTROL SOLENOID VALVE
⑭ FUEL FILTER
⑮ FUEL PUMP (FP)
⑯ FUEL TANK
⑰ AIR CLEANER (ACL)
⑱ INTAKE AIR BYPASS (IAB) LOW CONTROL DIAPHRAGM VALVE
⑲ INTAKE AIR BYPASS (IAB) LOW CONTROL SOLENOID VALVE
⑳ INTAKE AIR BYPASS (IAB) HIGH CONTROL DIAPHRAGM VALVE
㉑ INTAKE AIR BYPASS (IAB) HIGH CONTROL SOLENOID VALVE

㉒ INTAKE AIR BYPASS (IAB) VACUUM TANK
㉓ INTAKE AIR BYPASS (IAB) CHECK VALVE
㉔ THREE WAY CATALYTIC CONVERTER (TWC)
㉕ EXHAUST GAS RECIRCULATION (EGR) VALVE AND LIFT SENSOR
㉖ EXHAUST GAS RECIRCULATION (EGR) CONTROL SOLENOID VALVE
㉗ EXHAUST GAS RECIRCULATION (EGR) VACUUM CONTROL VALVE
㉘ POSITIVE CRANKCASE VENTILATION (PCV) VALVE
㉙ EVAPORATIVE EMISSION (EVAP) CONTROL CANISTER
㉚ EVAPORATIVE EMISSION (EVAP) PURGE CONTROL DIAPHRAGM VALVE
㉛ EVAPORATIVE EMISSION (EVAP) PURGE CONTROL SOLENOID VALVE
㉜ FUEL TANK EVAPORATIVE EMISSION (EVAP) TWO WAY VALVE
㉝ EVAPORATIVE EMISSION (EVAP) PURGE FLOW SWITCH
㉞ WATER VALVE CONTROL SOLENOID VALVE
㉟ WATER VALVE CONTROL DIAPHRAGM
㊱ WATER VALVE CHECK VALVE

90944G40

Fig. 61 Vacuum hose routing—1996 3.2L engines

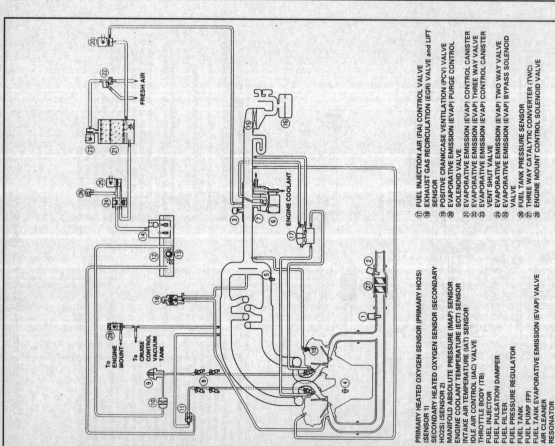

① PRIMARY HEATED OXYGEN SENSOR (PRIMARY HO2S) (SENSOR 1)
② SECONDARY HEATED OXYGEN SENSOR (SECONDARY HO2S) (SENSOR 2)
③ MANIFOLD ABSOLUTE PRESSURE (MAP) SENSOR
④ ENGINE COOLANT TEMPERATURE (ECT) SENSOR
⑤ INTAKE AIR TEMPERATURE (IAT) SENSOR
⑥ IDLE AIR CONTROL (IAC) VALVE
⑦ THROTTLE BODY (TB)
⑧ FUEL INJECTOR
⑨ FUEL PULSATION DAMPER
⑩ FUEL FILTER
⑪ FUEL PRESSURE REGULATOR
⑫ FUEL TANK
⑬ FUEL PUMP (FP)
⑭ FUEL TANK EVAPORATIVE EMISSION (EVAP) VALVE
⑮ AIR CLEANER
⑯ RESONATOR

⑰ FUEL INJECTION AIR (FIA) CONTROL VALVE
⑱ EXHAUST GAS RECIRCULATION (EGR) VALVE and LIFT SENSOR
⑲ POSITIVE CRANKCASE VENTILATION (PCV) VALVE
⑳ EVAPORATIVE EMISSION (EVAP) PURGE CONTROL SOLENOID VALVE
㉑ EVAPORATIVE EMISSION (EVAP) CONTROL CANISTER
㉒ EVAPORATIVE EMISSION (EVAP) THREE WAY VALVE
㉓ EVAPORATIVE EMISSION (EVAP) CONTROL CANISTER VENT SHUT VALVE
㉔ EVAPORATIVE EMISSION (EVAP) TWO WAY VALVE
㉕ EVAPORATIVE EMISSION (EVAP) BYPASS SOLENOID VALVE
㉖ FUEL TANK PRESSURE SENSOR
㉗ THREE WAY CATALYTIC CONVERTER (TWC)
㉘ ENGINE MOUNT CONTROL SOLENOID VALVE

90944G39

Fig. 60 Vacuum hose routing—3.0L engines

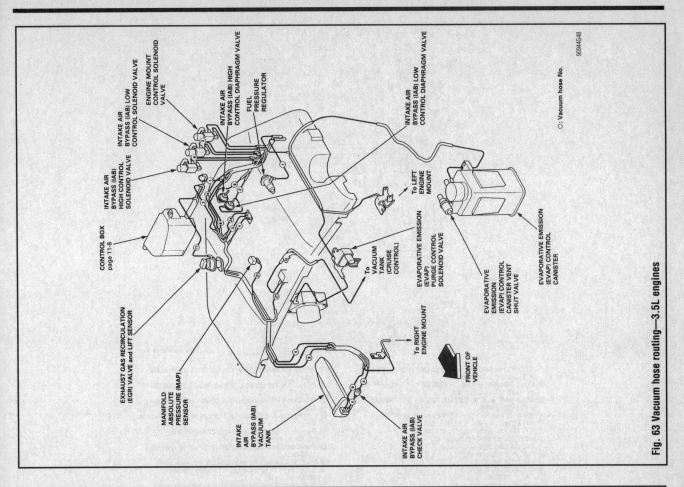

Fig. 63 Vacuum hose routing—3.5L engines

90944G48

O: Vacuum hose No.

INTAKE AIR BYPASS (IAB) LOW CONTROL SOLENOID VALVE

ENGINE MOUNT CONTROL SOLENOID VALVE

INTAKE AIR BYPASS (IAB) HIGH CONTROL DIAPHRAGM VALVE

FUEL PRESSURE REGULATOR

INTAKE AIR BYPASS (IAB) LOW CONTROL DIAPHRAGM VALVE

INTAKE AIR BYPASS (IAB) HIGH CONTROL SOLENOID VALVE

CONTROL BOX page 11-8

To LEFT ENGINE MOUNT

EVAPORATIVE EMISSION (EVAP) PURGE CONTROL SOLENOID VALVE

EVAPORATIVE EMISSION (EVAP) CONTROL CANISTER VENT SHUT VALVE

EVAPORATIVE EMISSION (EVAP) CONTROL CANISTER

EXHAUST GAS RECIRCULATION (EGR) VALVE and LIFT SENSOR

MANIFOLD ABSOLUTE PRESSURE (MAP) SENSOR

INTAKE AIR BYPASS (IAB) VACUUM TANK

INTAKE AIR BYPASS (IAB) CHECK VALVE

To VACUUM TANK (CRUISE CONTROL)

To RIGHT ENGINE MOUNT

FRONT OF VEHICLE

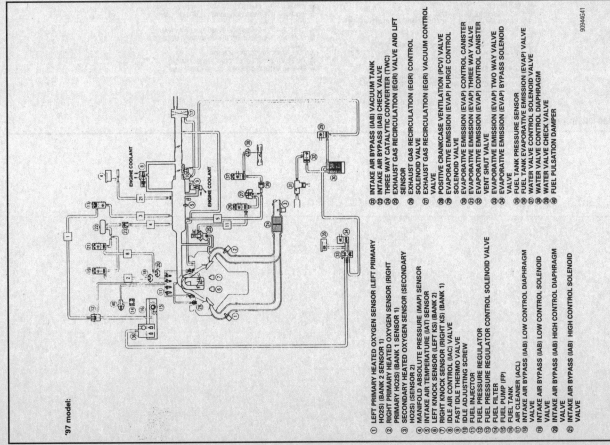

Fig. 62 Vacuum hose routing—1997 3.2L engines

90944G41

'97 model:

① LEFT PRIMARY HEATED OXYGEN SENSOR (LEFT PRIMARY HO2S) (BANK 2 SENSOR 1)
② RIGHT PRIMARY HEATED OXYGEN SENSOR (RIGHT PRIMARY HO2S) (BANK 1 SENSOR 1)
③ SECONDARY HEATED OXYGEN SENSOR (SECONDARY HO2S) (SENSOR 2)
④ MANIFOLD ABSOLUTE PRESSURE (MAP) SENSOR
⑤ INTAKE AIR TEMPERATURE (IAT) SENSOR
⑥ LEFT KNOCK SENSOR (LEFT KS) (BANK 2)
⑦ RIGHT KNOCK SENSOR (RIGHT KS) (BANK 1)
⑧ IDLE AIR CONTROL (IAC) VALVE
⑨ FAST IDLE THERMO VALVE
⑩ IDLE ADJUSTING SCREW
⑪ FUEL INJECTOR
⑫ FUEL PRESSURE REGULATOR
⑬ FUEL PRESSURE REGULATOR CONTROL SOLENOID VALVE
⑭ FUEL FILTER
⑮ FUEL PUMP (FP)
⑯ FUEL TANK
⑰ AIR CLEANER (ACL)
⑱ INTAKE AIR BYPASS (IAB) LOW CONTROL DIAPHRAGM VALVE
⑲ INTAKE AIR BYPASS (IAB) LOW CONTROL SOLENOID VALVE
⑳ INTAKE AIR BYPASS (IAB) HIGH CONTROL DIAPHRAGM VALVE
㉑ INTAKE AIR BYPASS (IAB) HIGH CONTROL SOLENOID VALVE

㉒ INTAKE AIR BYPASS (IAB) VACUUM TANK
㉓ INTAKE AIR BYPASS (IAB) CHECK VALVE
㉔ THREE WAY CATALYTIC CONVERTER (TWC)
㉕ EXHAUST GAS RECIRCULATION (EGR) VALVE AND LIFT SENSOR
㉖ EXHAUST GAS RECIRCULATION (EGR) CONTROL SOLENOID VALVE
㉗ EXHAUST GAS RECIRCULATION (EGR) VACUUM CONTROL VALVE
㉘ POSITIVE CRANKCASE VENTILATION (PCV) VALVE
㉙ EVAPORATIVE EMISSION (EVAP) PURGE CONTROL SOLENOID VALVE
㉚ EVAPORATIVE EMISSION (EVAP) CONTROL CANISTER
㉛ EVAPORATIVE EMISSION (EVAP) THREE WAY VALVE
㉜ EVAPORATIVE EMISSION (EVAP) CONTROL CANISTER VENT SHUT VALVE
㉝ EVAPORATIVE EMISSION (EVAP) TWO WAY VALVE
㉞ EVAPORATIVE EMISSION (EVAP) BYPASS SOLENOID VALVE
㉟ FUEL TANK PRESSURE SENSOR
㊱ FUEL TANK EVAPORATIVE EMISSION (EVAP) VALVE
㊲ WATER VALVE CONTROL SOLENOID VALVE
㊳ WATER VALVE CONTROL DIAPHRAGM
㊴ WATER VALVE CHECK VALVE
㊵ FUEL PULSATION DAMPER

ENGINE COOLANT

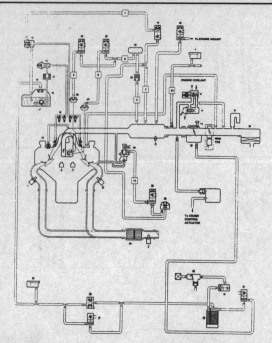

□: Vacuum hose No.

① LEFT PRIMARY HEATED OXYGEN SENSOR (LEFT PRIMARY HO2S) (BANK 2, SENSOR 1)
② RIGHT PRIMARY HEATED OXYGEN SENSOR (RIGHT PRIMARY HO2S) (BANK 1, SENSOR 1)
③ SECONDARY HEATED OXYGEN SENSOR (SECONDARY HO2S) (SENSOR 2)
④ MANIFOLD ABSOLUTE PRESSURE (MAP) SENSOR
⑤ INTAKE AIR TEMPERATURE (IAT) SENSOR
⑥ LEFT KNOCK SENSOR (LEFT KS) (BANK 2)
⑦ RIGHT KNOCK SENSOR (RIGHT KS) (BANK 1)
⑧ IDLE AIR CONTROL (IAC) VALVE
⑨ FAST IDLE THERMO VALVE
⑩ THROTTLE BODY (TB)
⑪ IDLE ADJUSTING SCREW
⑫ FUEL INJECTOR
⑬ FUEL PULSATION DAMPER
⑭ FUEL FILTER
⑮ FUEL PRESSURE REGULATOR
⑯ FUEL PRESSURE REGULATOR CONTROL SOLENOID VALVE
⑰ FUEL PUMP (FP)
⑱ FUEL TANK
⑲ FUEL TANK EVAPORATIVE EMISSION (EVAP) VALVE
⑳ AIR CLEANER
㉑ RESONATOR
㉒ INTAKE AIR BYPASS (IAB) CHECK VALVE
㉓ INTAKE AIR BYPASS (IAB) VACUUM TANK
㉔ INTAKE AIR BYPASS (IAB) LOW CONTROL SOLENOID VALVE

㉕ INTAKE AIR BYPASS (IAB) LOW CONTROL DIAPHRAGM VALVE
㉖ INTAKE AIR BYPASS (IAB) HIGH CONTROL SOLENOID VALVE
㉗ INTAKE AIR BYPASS (IAB) HIGH CONTROL DIAPHRAGM VALVE
㉘ EXHAUST GAS RECIRCULATION (EGR) VACUUM CONTROL VALVE
㉙ EXHAUST GAS RECIRCULATION (EGR) CONTROL SOLENOID VALVE
㉚ EXHAUST GAS RECIRCULATION (EGR) VALVE and LIFT SENSOR
㉛ POSITIVE CRANKCASE VENTILATION (PCV) VALVE
㉜ EVAPORATIVE EMISSION (EVAP) PURGE CONTROL SOLENOID VALVE
㉝ EVAPORATIVE EMISSION (EVAP) CONTROL CANISTER
㉞ EVAPORATIVE EMISSION (EVAP) THREE WAY VALVE
㉟ EVAPORATIVE EMISSION (EVAP) CONTROL CANISTER VENT SHUT VALVE
㊱ EVAPORATIVE EMISSION (EVAP) TWO WAY VALVE
㊲ EVAPORATIVE EMISSION (EVAP) BYPASS SOLENOID VALVE
㊳ FUEL TANK PRESSURE SENSOR
㊴ THREE WAY CATALYTIC CONVERTER (TWC)
㊵ ENGINE MOUNT CONTROL SOLENOID VALVE

90944G49

Fig. 64 Vacuum hose routing—3.5L engines

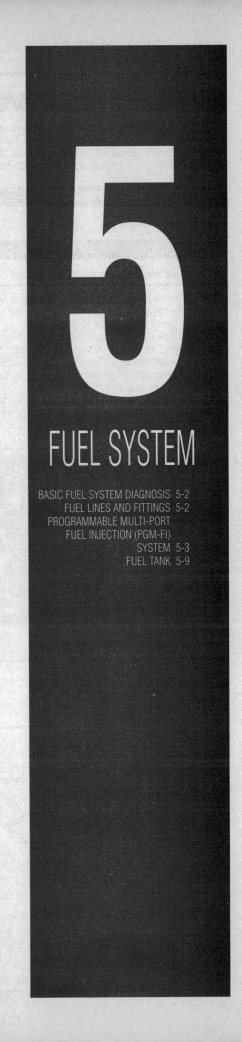

5

FUEL SYSTEM

BASIC FUEL SYSTEM DIAGNOSIS

When there is a problem starting or driving a vehicle, two of the most important checks involve the ignition and the fuel systems. The questions most mechanics attempt to answer first, "is there spark?" and "is there fuel?" will often lead to solving most basic problems. For ignition system diagnosis and testing, please refer to the information on engine electrical components and ignition systems found earlier in this manual. If the ignition system checks out (there is spark), then you must determine if the fuel system is operating properly (is there fuel?).

FUEL LINES AND FITTINGS

♦ See Figures 1 and 2

✳✳ CAUTION

Do not smoke while working on the fuel system!

The fuel system is inter-connected using a network of lines and connectors. At times these connectors must be disconnected in order to properly repair the system. Pay careful attention to the following.

The fuel tubing connectors are not heat resistant, therefore be careful when doing a welding. Due to the construction of the fuel lines, acid may damage the integrity of the line. Replace the fuel tubing if there is any suspect of an acid or electrolyte contamination. When disconnecting the lines, be cautious not to twist the connectors. As always, replace if damaged.

A disconnected quick disconnect fitting can be re-attached. The retainer on the mating pipe should not be used once disconnected. It should be replaced when:

- Replacing the fuel pump.
- Replacing the fuel feed pipe.
- It has been removed from the pipe.
- It is damaged.

Quick-Connect Fittings

REMOVAL & INSTALLATION

♦ See Figures 3, 4 and 5

1. Properly relieve the fuel system pressure, as outlined later in this section..
2. Clean all dirt off of the fuel system connectors before removal of the fitting.

Fig. 1 View of fuel filter line and banjo fitting

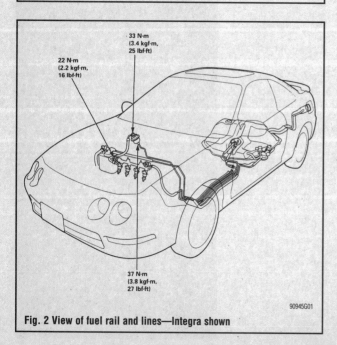

Fig. 2 View of fuel rail and lines—Integra shown

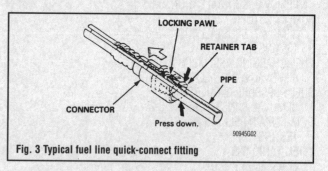

Fig. 3 Typical fuel line quick-connect fitting

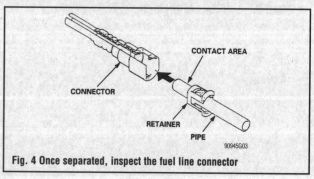

Fig. 4 Once separated, inspect the fuel line connector

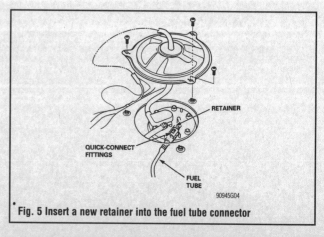

Fig. 5 Insert a new retainer into the fuel tube connector

3. Hold the connector with one hand, then pull the connector off with your other hand by pressing down on the retainer tabs.

4. Inspect the contact area of the connector for dirt and grime. If the surface is dirty, clean it. If the surface area is rusty or damaged, replace it.

5. To keep foreign material out of the fitting, cover the end of the line/fitting assembly with a plastic bag such as a sandwich style or locking freezer bag.

To install:

6. Insert a new retainer into the connector.

7. Attach the connector.

PROGRAMMABLE MULTI-PORT FUEL INJECTION (PGM-FI) SYSTEM

General Information

The fuel system includes such components as a fuel tank, lines, in-tank high pressure fuel pump, PGM-FI main relay, filter, pressure regulator, injectors, and fuel pulsation dampener. This style fuel injection system delivers pressurized fuel to the injectors with the engine **ON** and cuts that fuel delivery when the engine is turned **OFF**.

Acura prides itself in being a technologically advanced automobile manufacturer. This is seen in various aspects of the company's design philosophy, and the fuel injection system was not an area to be left out. For example, on the Integra GS—R models, the fuel injectors were altered by a mere eight degrees from their previous design. This was done to position the injectors directly at the center of the intake valves to further enhance the vaporization of the sprayed fuel with the incoming air. This reduced fuel condensation on the intake walls and improved driveability as well as throttle response. As you can see, the fuel injection system was carefully designed and tested. Therefore use caution and common sense when disconnecting and reinstalling fuel system components. Precision and accuracy count!

FUEL SYSTEM SERVICE PRECAUTIONS

Safety is an important factor when servicing the fuel system. Failure to conduct maintenance and repairs in a safe manner may result in serious personal injury. Maintenance and testing of the vehicle's fuel system components can be accomplished safely and effectively by adhering to the following rules and guidelines.

• To avoid the possibility of fire and personal injury, always disconnect the negative battery cable unless the repair or test procedure requires that battery voltage be applied.

• Always relieve the fuel system pressure prior to disconnecting any fuel system component (injector, fuel rail, pressure regulator, etc.), fitting or fuel line connection. Exercise extreme caution whenever relieving fuel system pressure to avoid exposing skin, face and eyes to fuel spray. Please be advised that fuel under pressure may penetrate the skin or any part of the body that it contacts.

• Always place a shop towel or cloth around the fitting or connection prior to loosening to absorb any excess fuel due to spillage. Ensure that all fuel spillage is quickly removed from engine surfaces. Ensure that all fuel soaked cloths or towels are deposited into a suitable waste container.

• Always keep a dry chemical (Class B) fire extinguisher near the work area.

• Do not allow fuel spray or fuel vapors to come into contact with a spark or open flame.

• Always use a backup wrench when loosening and tightening fuel line connection fittings. This will prevent unnecessary stress and torsion to fuel line piping. Always follow the proper torque specifications.

• Always replace worn fuel fitting O-rings. Do not substitute fuel hose where fuel pipe is installed.

Relieving Fuel System Pressure

✳ CAUTION

Be sure that the ignition switch is OFF before relieving the fuel system. Never smoke while working on the fuel system!

1.8L, 3.0L & 3.2L ENGINES

▶ See Figure 6

1. Disconnect the negative battery cable.
2. Remove the fuel filler cap.

Fig. 6 Slowly turn the banjo bolt on the fuel filter to relieve the fuel system pressure

3. Using a 12mm box-end wrench, loosen the banjo bolt from the top of the fuel filter. Be sure to hold the fuel filter with another wrench.

4. Place a shop towel over the banjo bolt to absorb any fuel that may leak out as the bolt is loosened.

5. Slowly unscrew the banjo bolt one turn.

6. Always replace the washers whenever the bolt is loosened.

7. After the fuel system pressure is relieved, Tighten the service port bolt, install the fuel filler cap, then connect the negative battery cable.

2.2L, 2.3L & 2.5L ENGINES

▶ See Figure 7

1. Disconnect the negative battery cable.
2. Remove the fuel filler cap.
3. Use a 6mm box-end wrench to loosen the fuel rail service bolt.
4. Place a shop towel over the banjo bolt to absorb any fuel that may leak out as the bolt is loosened.
5. Slowly unscrew the banjo bolt one turn.
6. Always replace the washers whenever the bolt is loosened.
7. After the fuel system pressure is relieved, Tighten the service port bolt, install the fuel filler cap, then connect the negative battery cable.

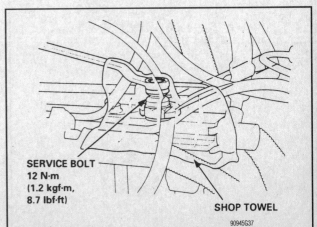

SERVICE BOLT
12 N·m
(1.2 kgf·m,
8.7 lbf·ft)

SHOP TOWEL

Fig. 7 Loosening the service bolt from the fuel rail—2.2L and 2.3L engines

3.5L ENGINE

1. Disconnect the negative battery cable.
2. Remove the fuel filler cap.
3. Using a box end wrench, loosen the banjo bolt from the top of the fuel filter. Be sure to hold the fuel filter with another wrench.
4. Place a shop towel over the banjo bolt to absorb any fuel that may leak out as the bolt is loosened.
5. Slowly unscrew the banjo bolt one turn.
6. Always replace the washers whenever the bolt is loosened.
7. After the fuel system pressure is relieved, Tighten the service port bolt, install the fuel filler cap, then connect the negative battery cable.

Fuel Pump

REMOVAL & INSTALLATION

♦ **See Figure 8**

✳✳ CAUTION

Observe all applicable safety precautions when working around fuel. Whenever servicing the fuel system, always work in a well ventilated area. Do not allow fuel spray or vapors to come in contact with a spark or open flame. Keep a dry chemical fire extinguisher near the work area. Always keep fuel in a container specifically designed for fuel storage; also, always properly seal fuel containers to avoid the possibility of fire or explosion.

✳✳ CAUTION

The fuel injection system remains under pressure, even after the engine has been turned OFF. The fuel system pressure MUST BE relieved before disconnecting any fuel lines. Failure to do so may result in fire and/or personal injury.

Integra and Legend Coupe

1. Disconnect the negative battery cable.
2. Relieve the fuel pressure, as outlined earlier in this section.

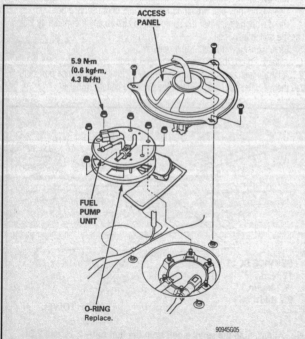

**5.9 N·m
(0.6 kgf·m,
4.3 lbf·ft)**

ACCESS
PANEL

FUEL
PUMP
UNIT

O-RING
Replace.

90945G05

Fig. 8 Exploded view of an Acura fuel pump assembly

3. Open the fuel tank filler cap to vent off pressure in the tank.
4. Remove the rear seat.
5. Remove the access panel.
6. Unplug the electrical connector from the fuel pump.

✳✳ WARNING

Ensure that the battery is disconnected before any wires are removed.

7. Remove the fuel pump mounting nuts, then remove the fuel pump from the tank.
8. Installation is the reverse of the removal procedure.

CL, TL, and Vigor

1. Disconnect the negative battery cable.
2. Relieve the fuel pressure, as outlined earlier in this section.
3. Open the fuel tank filler cap to vent off pressure in the tank.
4. Remove the fuel tank, as outlined later in this section.
5. Detach the electrical connector from the fuel pump.

✳✳ WARNING

Ensure that the battery is disconnected before any wires are removed.

6. Remove the fuel pump mounting nuts, then remove the fuel pump from the tank.
7. Installation is the reverse of the removal procedure.

RL

1. Disconnect the negative battery cable.
2. Relieve the fuel pressure, as outlined earlier in this section.
3. Open the fuel tank filler cap to vent off pressure in the tank.
4. Remove the rear seat cushion.
5. Remove the rear access panel from the floor.
6. Detach the connector from the fuel pump.

✳✳ WARNING

Ensure that the battery is disconnected before any wires are removed.

7. Remove the fuel pump mounting nuts, then remove the fuel pump from the tank.
8. Installation is the reverse of the removal procedure.

TESTING THE FUEL PUMP

If you suspect a problem with the fuel pump, listen to the pump during the first five seconds after the ignition key is turned to the "ON" position. You should hear the fuel pump motor running.

Integra

1. Remove the rear seat.
2. Remove the access panel.
3. Detach the fuel pump 2-prong connector.

✳✳ WARNING

Be sure the ignition switch is OFF before removing the wires.

4. Connect the No. 4 terminal and No. 5 terminal, using a jumper wire.
5. Battery voltage must be present at terminal number two when the ignition is **ON**.
6. If the battery voltage is present, check the fuel pump's ground.
7. If the ground is "OK", check the fuel pump.
8. If battery voltage is not present, check the wiring harness.
9. If all wiring checks out, you must next test the fuel pressure, as outlined later in this section.

2.2L, 2.3L 3.0CL & 2.5TL

1. Remove the trunk floor.
2. Remove the access panel.
3. Unplug the fuel pump 3-prong connector.

✳✳ WARNING

Be sure the ignition switch is OFF before removing the wires.

4. Connect the No. 4 terminal and No.5 terminal using a jumper wire.
5. For the 2.2L, 2.3L & 3.0CL, battery voltage must be present at terminal number one when the ignition is **ON**.
6. For the 2.2L, 2.3L & 3.0CL, battery voltage must be present at terminal number three when the ignition is **ON**.
7. If the battery voltage is present, check the fuel pumps ground. .
8. If the ground is "OK", check the fuel pump.
9. If battery voltage is not present, check the wiring harness.
10. If all wiring checks out, you must next test the fuel pressure, as outlined later in this section.

3.2TL & 3.5RL

1. On the 3.2TL, remove the trunk floor.
2. On the 3.5RL, remove the rear seat.
3. Remove the access panel.

✳✳ WARNING

Be sure the ignition switch is OFF before removing the wires.

4. Remove the wires from the PGM-FI main relay connector.
5. Connect the No. 2 terminal and No. 5 terminal using a jumper wire.
6. On the 3.2TL, battery voltage must be present at terminal number three when the ignition is **ON**.
7. On the 3.5RL, battery voltage must be present at terminal number seven when the ignition is **ON**.
8. If the battery voltage is present, check the fuel pump ground.
9. If the ground is "OK", check the fuel pump.
10. If battery voltage is not present, check the wiring harness.
11. If all wiring checks out, you must next test the fuel pressure, as outlined later in this section.

Legend & Vigor

1. On the Legend, remove the rear seat.
2. On the Vigor, remove the trunk floor.
3. Remove the access panel.

➡**Be sure the ignition switch is OFF before removing the wires.**

4. Remove the wires from the PGM-FI main relay connector.
5. Connect the No. 5 terminal and No. 7 terminal using a jumper wire.
6. Battery voltage must be present at the fuel pump connector, when the ignition is "ON".
7. If the battery voltage is present, check the fuel pumps ground.
8. If the ground is "OK", check the fuel pump.
9. If battery voltage is not present, check the wiring harness.
10. If all wiring checks out, you must next test the fuel pressure, as outlined later in this section.

FUEL PRESSURE TESTING

◆ **See Figures 9, 10 and 11**

1. Relieve the fuel filler cap.
2. Remove the service bolt from the fuel filter.
3. Install a fuel pressure gauge.
4. Start the engine and measure the fuel pressure with the engine idling and the fuel pressure regulator vacuum line pinched off.
5. If the engine wont start, turn on the ignition switch **ON**, wait two seconds, then turn off the ignition switch **OFF**. Turn the ignition switch back **ON** again and read the fuel pressure.
6. The acceptable fuel pressure is 43.4–50.5 psi (299–348 kPa).

7. Reconnect the vacuum hose to the pressure regulator.
8. The fuel pressure should be 34.8–41.9 psi (240–289 kPa).
9. If the fuel pressure is higher than normal, inspect the fuel return hose for a clog or pinched area. Also check for a faulty fuel pressure regulator.
10. If the fuel pressure is lower than normal, inspect the system for a clogged fuel filter, faulty pressure regulator, or fuel line leakage.
11. Once the test is complete, perform the following:
    a. Remove the fuel pressure gauge.
    b. Install the service port bolt and tighten to 25 ft. lbs. (33 Nm).
    c. Install the fuel filler cap.

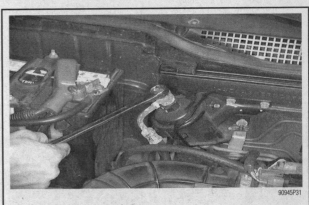

Fig. 9 Loosen the service bolt . . .

Fig. 10 . . . then remove the service bolt from the fuel filter

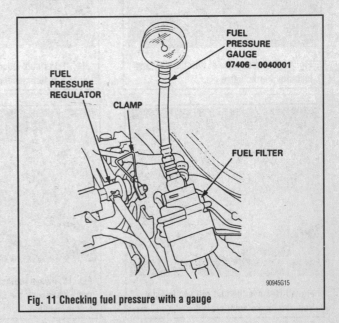

Fig. 11 Checking fuel pressure with a gauge

Throttle Body

REMOVAL & INSTALLATION

♦ **See Figures 12, 13, 14 and 15**

1. Remove the negative battery cable.
2. Remove the air duct from the throttle body.
3. If working on a Legend model with traction control, remove the Traction Control Solenoid (TCS) assembly.
4. Remove the wiring harness connector from the throttle body.
5. Label and detach all vacuum hoses from the throttle body.
6. Detach the accelerator cable.
7. Detach the coolant hoses from the throttle body.
8. Remove the mounting nuts and/or bolts.
9. Remove the throttle body gasket.

10. Using a plastic scraper, remove any gasket material from the throttle body and air intake plenum.
11. Installation is the reverse of the removal procedure.

Fuel Injector(s)

REMOVAL & INSTALLATION

♦ **See Figures 16 thru 22**

❋❋ CAUTION

Fuel injection systems remain under pressure, even after the engine has been turned OFF. The fuel system pressure must be relieved before disconnecting any fuel lines. Failure to do so may result in fire and/or personal injury.

Fig. 12 View of typical Acura throttle body

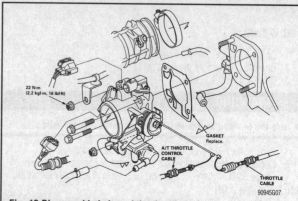

Fig. 13 Disassembled view of the throttle body

Fig. 14 Exploded view of throttle body and fast idle thermo valve

Fig. 15 Periodic cleaning of the throttle body is recommended

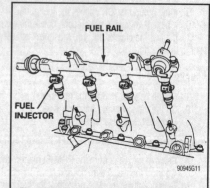

Fig. 16 View of a typical Acura fuel rail and injectors

Fig. 17 Remove the fuel rail and injectors from the intake manifold

Fig. 18 Always replace the fuel injector O-rings when ever the injectors are removed and reinstalled

Fig. 19 Remove the injector from the fuel rail

Fig. 20 Use a pick tool to remove the injector O-ring

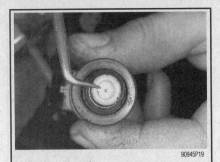

Fig. 21 Check needle and seat of the injector for carbon deposits that may inhibit the injector from closing all of the way

Fig. 22 The fuel injectors on the Integra have a spacer and a O-ring gasket. Both must be replaced whenever the injectors have been removed

※ CAUTION

Observe all applicable safety precautions when working around fuel. Whenever servicing the fuel system, always work in a well ventilated area. Do not allow fuel spray or vapors to come in contact with a spark or open flame. Keep a dry chemical fire extinguisher near the work area. Always keep fuel in a container specifically designed for fuel storage; also, always properly seal fuel containers to avoid the possibility of fire or explosion.

1. Disconnect the negative battery cable.
2. Relieve the fuel system pressure.
3. Remove the connectors from the fuel rail.
4. Disconnect the vacuum hose and fuel return from the fuel pressure regulator.
5. Loosen the retainer nuts on the fuel rail.
6. Remove the fuel rail.
7. Grasp the fuel injectors body and pull up while gently rocking the fuel injector from side to side.
8. Once removed, inspect the fuel injector cap and body for signs of deterioration. Replace as required.
9. Remove the O-rings and discard. If an O-ring or end cap is missing, look in the intake manifold for the missing part.

To install:

10. Install new O-rings onto each injector and apply a small amount of clean engine oil to the O-rings.
11. Install the injectors using a slight twisting downward motion.
12. Install the injector retaining clips.
13. Install the fuel injection supply manifold (fuel rail).
14. Connect the negative battery cable.
15. Run the engine at idle for 2 minutes, then turn the engine **OFF** and check for fuel leaks and proper operation.

TESTING

The easiest way to test the operation of the fuel injectors is to listen for a clicking sound coming from the injectors while the engine is running. This is accomplished using a mechanic's stethoscope, or a long screwdriver. Place the end of the stethoscope or the screwdriver (tip end, not handle) onto the body of the injector. Place the ear pieces of the stethoscope in your ears, or if using a screwdriver, place your ear on top of the handle. An audible clicking noise should be heard; this is the solenoid operating. If the injector makes this noise, the injector driver circuit and computer are operating as designed. Continue testing all the injectors this way.

※ CAUTION

Be extremely careful while working on an operating engine, make sure you have no dangling jewelry, extremely loose clothes, power tool cords or other items that might get caught in a moving part of the engine.

All Injectors Clicking

If all the injectors are clicking, but you have determined that the fuel system is the cause of your driveability problem, continue diagnostics. Make sure that you have checked fuel pump pressure as outlined earlier in this section. An easy way to determine a weak or unproductive cylinder is a cylinder drop test. This is accomplished by removing one spark plug wire at a time, and seeing which cylinder causes the least difference in the idle. The one that causes the least change is the weak cylinder.

If the injectors were all clicking and the ignition system is functioning properly, remove the injector of the suspect cylinder and bench test it. This is accomplished by checking for a spray pattern from the injector itself. Install a fuel supply line to the injector (or rail if the injector is left attached to the rail) and momentarily apply 12 volts DC and a ground to the injector itself; a visible fuel spray should appear. If no spray is achieved, replace the injector and check the running condition of the engine.

One or More Injectors Are Not Clicking

▶ See Figures 23, 24, 25 and 26

If one or more injectors are found to be not operating, testing the injector driver circuit and computer can be accomplished using a "noid" light. First, with the engine not running and the ignition key in the **OFF** position, remove the connector from the injector you plan to test, then plug the "noid" light tool into the injector connector. Start the engine and the "noid" light should flash, signaling that the injector driver circuit is working. If the "noid" light flashes, but the injector does not click when plugged in, test the injector's resistance. resistance should be between 11–18 ohms.

If the "noid" light does not flash, the injector driver circuit is faulty. Disconnect the negative battery cable. Unplug the "noid" light from the injector connector and also unplug the PCM. Check the harness between the appropriate pins on the harness side of the PCM connector and the injector connector. Resistance should be less than 5.0 ohms; if not, repair the circuit. If resistance is within specifications, the injector driver inside the PCM is faulty and replacement of the PCM will be necessary.

Fig. 23 Unplug the fuel injector connector

Fig. 24 Probe the two terminals of a fuel injector to check it's resistance

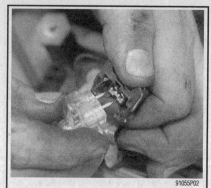

Fig. 25 Plug the correct "noid" light directly into the injector harness connector

Fig. 26 If the correct "noid" light flashes while the engine is running, the injector driver circuit inside the PCM is working

Fuel Charging Assembly

REMOVAL & INSTALLATION

1. Disconnect the negative battery cable.
2. Relieve the fuel system pressure, as outlined earlier in this section.
3. Detach the electrical harness connectors.
4. Remove the vacuum hose and fuel return hose from the fuel pressure regulator.
5. Remove the fuel line from the fuel rail.
6. Unfasten the fuel rail retaining nuts, then remove the fuel rail.

To install:

7. Install the fuel rail and secure with the retaining nuts.
8. Connect the fuel line to the fuel rail.
9. Install the vacuum hose and fuel return hose to the fuel pressure regulator.
10. Attach the electrical harness connectors.
11. Connect the negative battery cable.
12. Pressurize the fuel system by turning the ignition switch to the **ON** position.
13. Check for leaks, if none are found, start the engine and recheck for any leaks.

Fuel Pressure Regulator

REMOVAL & INSTALLATION

◆ See Figure 27

The fuel pressure regulator keeps a constant fuel pressure to the fuel injectors. When the manifold pressure and fuel pressure vary more than 43 psi (294 kPa) the diaphragm is pushed upward causing the excess fuel to be fed back into the fuel tank through a return line.

✳✳ CAUTION

Observe all applicable safety precautions when working around fuel. Whenever servicing the fuel system, always work in a well ventilated area. Do not allow fuel spray or vapors to come in contact with a spark or open flame. Keep a dry chemical fire extinguisher near the work area. Always keep fuel in a container specifically designed for fuel storage; also, always properly seal fuel containers to avoid the possibility of fire or explosion.

1. Properly relieve the fuel system pressure.
2. Disconnect the negative battery cable.
3. Detach the vacuum hose from the fuel pressure regulator.
4. Unfasten the two fuel pressure regulator retaining bolts.
5. Remove the fuel pressure regulator and the O-rings. Discard the O-rings.

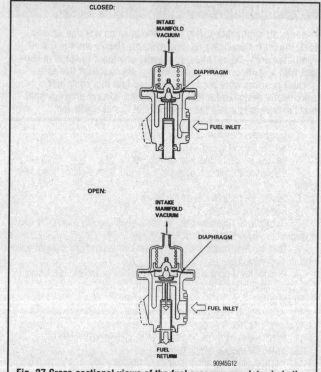

Fig. 27 Cross-sectional views of the fuel pressure regulator in both the open and closed positions

To install:

6. Lubricate the new O-rings with a light engine oil.
7. Position a new O-rings onto the fuel pressure regulator.
8. Place the fuel pressure regulator into position and install the retainers.
9. Attach the vacuum line to the fuel pressure regulator.
10. Connect the negative battery cable.
11. Run the engine at idle for 2 minutes, then turn the engine **OFF** and check for fuel leaks and proper operation.

PGM-FI Main Relay

◆ See Figure 28

This relay is located behind the dashboard's lower cover. It consists of two individual relays. One is energized whenever the ignition is **ON**, thus supplying battery voltage to the Powertrain Control Module (PCM). This relay also supplies voltage to the fuel injectors, and power to the second relay. The second relay is energized for two seconds, when the engine is turned **ON**, to power the fuel pump.

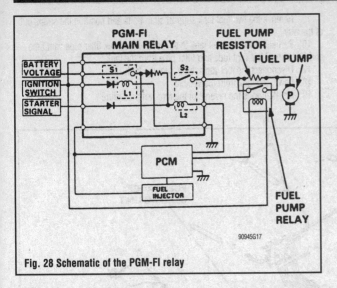

Fig. 28 Schematic of the PGM-FI relay

TESTING

▶ See Figure 29

➡If the engine starts and continues to run, the PGM—FI relay is working and does not need to be replaced.

1. Remove the relay.
2. Apply battery voltage to the number three terminal.
3. Ground the number two terminal.
4. Check for continuity between terminals five and two.
5. If continuity is detected, proceed to the step 7.
6. If there is no continuity, replace the relay.
7. Connect the number four terminal to the positive side of the battery.

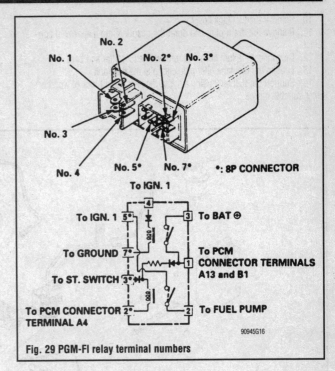

Fig. 29 PGM-FI relay terminal numbers

8. Ground the number two terminal of the relay.
9. Check for continuity between the number five terminal and the number two terminal of the relay.
10. If there is continuity, the relay checks out "OK". If the fuel pump still does not work, test the harness.
11. If there is no continuity, replace the relay and retest.

FUEL TANK

Tank Assembly

REMOVAL & INSTALLATION

▶ See Figures 30 and 31

❈ CAUTION

Observe all applicable safety precautions when working around fuel. Whenever servicing the fuel system, always work in a well ventilated area. Do not allow fuel spray or vapors to come in contact with a spark or open flame. Keep a dry chemical fire extinguisher near the work area. Always keep fuel in a container specifically designed for fuel storage; also, always properly seal fuel containers to avoid the possibility of fire or explosion.

1. Disconnect the negative battery cable.
2. Relieve the fuel pressure, as outlined earlier in this section.
3. Remove the rear seat cushion.
4. Remove the plastic grommet from the floor pan.
5. Detach the fuel pump electrical harness.
6. Disconnect the fuel lines from the fuel pump by compressing the tabs on both sides of each nylon push connect fitting and easing the fuel line off of the fuel pump.
7. Raise and safely support the vehicle securely on jackstands.
8. Remove the muffler mount.
9. Remove the heat shields.

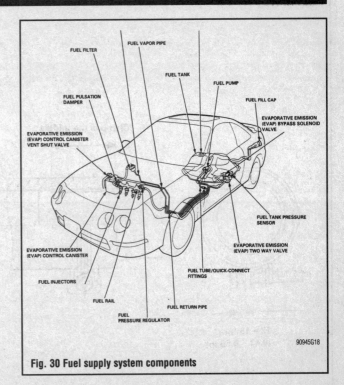

Fig. 30 Fuel supply system components

10. Remove the fuel tank cover.
11. Remove the drain plug and drain the gasoline into a approved container.
12. Disconnect the fuel lines and remove the fuel filter and base.
13. Loosen the fuel tank filler pipe clamp at the fuel tank.
14. Support the fuel tank using a hydraulic jack and a block of wood or other suitable device.

15. Remove the two fuel tank support strap bolts and position the straps out of the way.
16. Partially lower the fuel tank to access the fuel tank filler pipe vent tube and disconnect the vent tube and filler pipe from the tank.
17. Disconnect the fuel vapor tube from the tank.
18. Lower the tank from the vehicle.
19. Installation is the reverse of the removal procedure.

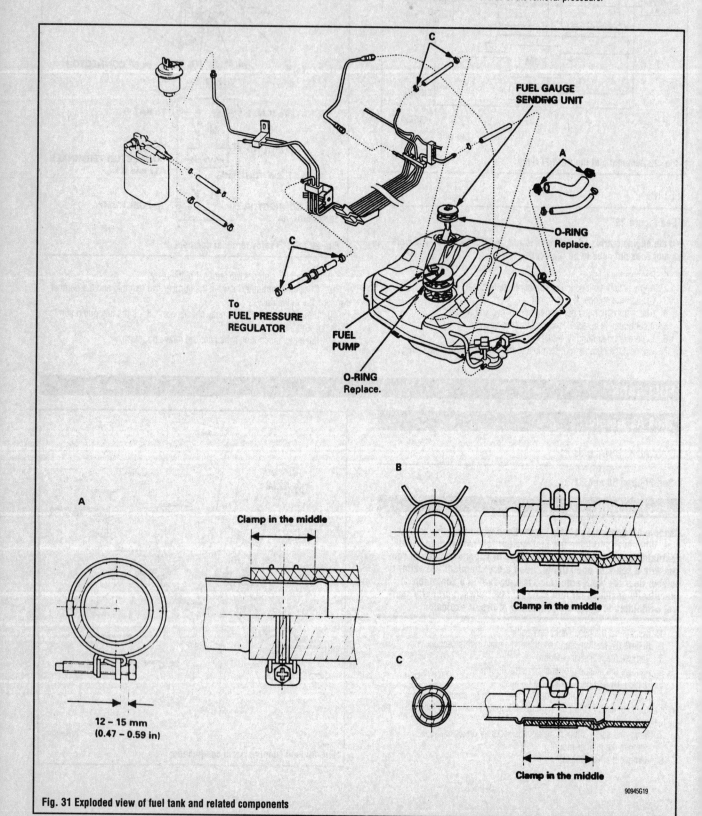

Fig. 31 Exploded view of fuel tank and related components

90945G19

6

CHASSIS ELECTRICAL

UNDERSTANDING AND TROUBLESHOOTING ELECTRICAL SYSTEMS

Basic Electrical Theory

♦ **See Figure 1**

For any 12 volt, negative ground, electrical system to operate, the electricity must travel in a complete circuit. This simply means that current (power) from the positive (+) terminal of the battery must eventually return to the negative (–) terminal of the battery. Along the way, this current will travel through wires, fuses, switches and components. If, for any reason, the flow of current through the circuit is interrupted, the component fed by that circuit will cease to function properly.

Perhaps the easiest way to visualize a circuit is to think of connecting a light bulb (with two wires attached to it) to the battery—one wire attached to the negative (–) terminal of the battery and the other wire to the positive (+) terminal. With the two wires touching the battery terminals, the circuit would be complete and the light bulb would illuminate. Electricity would follow a path from the battery to the bulb and back to the battery. It's easy to see that with longer wires on our light bulb, it could be mounted anywhere. Further, one wire could be fitted with a switch so that the light could be turned on and off.

The normal automotive circuit differs from this simple example in two ways. First, instead of having a return wire from the bulb to the battery, the current travels through the frame of the vehicle. Since the negative (–) battery cable is attached to the frame (made of electrically conductive metal), the frame of the vehicle can serve as a ground wire to complete the circuit. Secondly, most automotive circuits contain multiple components which receive power from a single circuit. This lessens the amount of wire needed to power components on the vehicle.

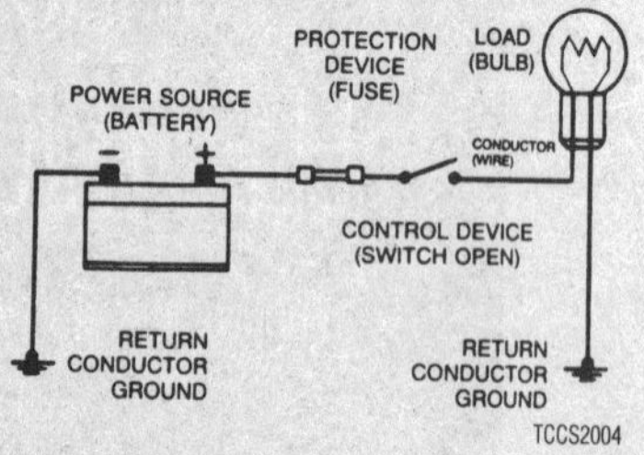

Fig. 1 This example illustrates a simple circuit. When the switch is closed, power from the positive (+) battery terminal flows through the fuse and the switch, and then to the light bulb. The light illuminates and the circuit is completed through the ground wire back to the negative (–) battery terminal. In reality, the two ground points shown in the illustration are attached to the metal frame of the vehicle, which completes the circuit back to the battery

HOW DOES ELECTRICITY WORK: THE WATER ANALOGY

Electricity is the flow of electrons—the subatomic particles that constitute the outer shell of an atom. Electrons spin in an orbit around the center core of an atom. The center core is comprised of protons (positive charge) and neutrons (neutral charge). Electrons have a negative charge and balance out the positive charge of the protons. When an outside force causes the number of electrons to unbalance the charge of the protons, the electrons will split off the atom and look for another atom to balance out. If this imbalance is kept up, electrons will continue to move and an electrical flow will exist.

Many people have been taught electrical theory using an analogy with water. In a comparison with water flowing through a pipe, the electrons would be the water and the wire is the pipe.

The flow of electricity can be measured much like the flow of water through a pipe. The unit of measurement used is amperes, frequently abbreviated as amps (a). You can compare amperage to the volume of water flowing through a pipe. When connected to a circuit, an ammeter will measure the actual amount of current flowing through the circuit. When relatively few electrons flow through a circuit, the amperage is low. When many electrons flow, the amperage is high.

Water pressure is measured in units such as pounds per square inch (psi); The electrical pressure is measured in units called volts (v). When a voltmeter is connected to a circuit, it is measuring the electrical pressure.

The actual flow of electricity depends not only on voltage and amperage, but also on the resistance of the circuit. The higher the resistance, the higher the force necessary to push the current through the circuit. The standard unit for measuring resistance is an ohm. Resistance in a circuit varies depending on the amount and type of components used in the circuit. The main factors which determine resistance are:

• Material—some materials have more resistance than others. Those with high resistance are said to be insulators. Rubber materials (or rubber-like plastics) are some of the most common insulators used in vehicles as they have a very high resistance to electricity. Very low resistance materials are said to be conductors. Copper wire is among the best conductors. Silver is actually a superior conductor to copper and is used in some relay contacts, but its high cost prohibits its use as common wiring. Most automotive wiring is made of copper.

• Size—the larger the wire size being used, the less resistance the wire will have. This is why components which use large amounts of electricity usually have large wires supplying current to them.

• Length—for a given thickness of wire, the longer the wire, the greater the resistance. The shorter the wire, the less the resistance. When determining the proper wire for a circuit, both size and length must be considered to design a circuit that can handle the current needs of the component.

• Temperature—with many materials, the higher the temperature, the greater the resistance (positive temperature coefficient). Some materials exhibit the opposite trait of lower resistance with higher temperatures (negative temperature coefficient). These principles are used in many of the sensors on the engine.

OHM'S LAW

There is a direct relationship between current, voltage and resistance. The relationship between current, voltage and resistance can be summed up by a statement known as Ohm's law.

Voltage (E) is equal to amperage (I) times resistance (R): $E = I \times R$

Other forms of the formula are $R = E/I$ and $I = E/R$

In each of these formulas, E is the voltage in volts, I is the current in amps and R is the resistance in ohms. The basic point to remember is that as the resistance of a circuit goes up, the amount of current that flows in the circuit will go down, if voltage remains the same.

The amount of work that the electricity can perform is expressed as power. The unit of power is the watt (w). The relationship between power, voltage and current is expressed as:

Power (w) is equal to amperage (I) times voltage (E): $W = I \times E$

This is only true for direct current (DC) circuits; The alternating current formula is a tad different, but since the electrical circuits in most vehicles are DC type, we need not get into AC circuit theory.

Electrical Components

POWER SOURCE

Power is supplied to the vehicle by two devices: The battery and the alternator. The battery supplies electrical power during starting or during periods when the current demand of the vehicle's electrical system exceeds the output capacity of the alternator. The alternator supplies electrical current when the engine is running. Just not does the alternator supply the current needs of the vehicle, but it recharges the battery.

The Battery

In most modern vehicles, the battery is a lead/acid electrochemical device consisting of six 2 volt subsections (cells) connected in series, so that the unit is capable of producing approximately 12 volts of electrical pressure. Each subsection consists of a series of positive and negative plates held a short distance apart in a solution of sulfuric acid and water.

The two types of plates are of dissimilar metals. This sets up a chemical reaction, and it is this reaction which produces current flow from the battery when its positive and negative terminals are connected to an electrical load . The power removed from the battery is replaced by the alternator, restoring the battery to its original chemical state.

The Alternator

On some vehicles there isn't an alternator, but a generator. The difference is that an alternator supplies alternating current which is then changed to direct current for use on the vehicle, while a generator produces direct current. Alternators tend to be more efficient and that is why they are used.

Alternators and generators are devices that consist of coils of wires wound together making big electromagnets. One group of coils spins within another set and the interaction of the magnetic fields causes a current to flow. This current is then drawn off the coils and fed into the vehicles electrical system.

GROUND

Two types of grounds are used in automotive electric circuits. Direct ground components are grounded to the frame through their mounting points. All other components use some sort of ground wire which is attached to the frame or chassis of the vehicle. The electrical current runs through the chassis of the vehicle and returns to the battery through the ground (−) cable; if you look, you'll see that the battery ground cable connects between the battery and the frame or chassis of the vehicle.

➡️It should be noted that a good percentage of electrical problems can be traced to bad grounds.

PROTECTIVE DEVICES

▸ See Figure 2

It is possible for large surges of current to pass through the electrical system of your vehicle. If this surge of current were to reach the load in the circuit, the surge could burn it out or severely damage it. It can also overload the wiring, causing the harness to get hot and melt the insulation. To prevent this, fuses, circuit breakers and/or fusible links are connected into the supply wires of the electrical system. These items are nothing more than a built-in weak spot in the system. When an abnormal amount of current flows through the system, these protective devices work as follows to protect the circuit:

• Fuse—when an excessive electrical current passes through a fuse, the fuse "blows" (the conductor melts) and opens the circuit, preventing the passage of current.

• Circuit Breaker—a circuit breaker is basically a self-repairing fuse. It will open the circuit in the same fashion as a fuse, but when the surge subsides, the circuit breaker can be reset and does not need replacement.

• Fusible Link—a fusible link (fuse link or main link) is a short length of special, high temperature insulated wire that acts as a fuse. When an excessive electrical current passes through a fusible link, the thin gauge wire inside the link melts, creating an intentional open to protect the circuit. To repair the circuit, the link must be replaced. Some newer type fusible links are housed in plug-in modules, which are simply replaced like a fuse, while older type fusible links must be cut and spliced if they melt. Since this link is very early in the electrical path, it's the first place to look if nothing on the vehicle works, yet the battery seems to be charged and is properly connected.

Always replace fuses, circuit breakers and fusible links with identically rated components. Under no circumstances should a component of higher or lower amperage rating be substituted.

SWITCHES & RELAYS

▸ See Figures 3 and 4

Switches are used in electrical circuits to control the passage of current. The most common use is to open and close circuits between the battery and the various electric devices in the system. Switches are rated according to the amount of amperage they can handle. If a sufficient amperage rated switch is not used in a circuit, the switch could overload and cause damage.

Some electrical components which require a large amount of current to operate use a special switch called a relay. Since these circuits carry a large amount of current, the thickness of the wire in the circuit is also greater. If this large wire were connected from the load to the control switch, the switch would have to carry the high amperage load and the fairing or dash would be twice as large to accommodate the increased size of the wiring harness. To prevent these problems, a relay is used.

Relays are composed of a coil and a set of contacts. When the coil has a current passed though it, a magnetic field is formed and this field causes the contacts to move together, completing the circuit. Most relays are normally open, preventing current from passing through the circuit, but they can take any electrical form depending on the job they are intended to do. Relays can be considered "remote control switches." They allow a smaller current to operate devices that require higher amperages. When a small current operates the coil, a larger current is allowed to pass by the contacts. Some common circuits which may use relays are the horn, headlights, starter, electric fuel pump and other high draw circuits.

LOAD

Every electrical circuit must include a "load" (something to use the electricity coming from the source). Without this load, the battery would attempt to deliver its entire power supply from one pole to another. This is called a "short circuit." All this electricity would take a short cut to ground and cause a great amount of damage to other components in the circuit by developing a tremendous amount of heat. This condition could develop sufficient heat to melt the insulation on all the surrounding wires and reduce a multiple wire cable to a lump of plastic and copper.

WIRING & HARNESSES

The average vehicle contains meters and meters of wiring, with hundreds of individual connections. To protect the many wires from damage and to keep them from becoming a confusing tangle, they are organized into bundles, enclosed in plastic or taped together and called wiring harnesses. Different harnesses serve different parts of the vehicle. Individual wires are color coded to help trace them through a harness where sections are hidden from view.

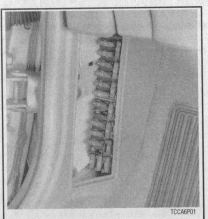

Fig. 2 Most vehicles use one or more fuse panels. This one is located on the driver's side kick panel

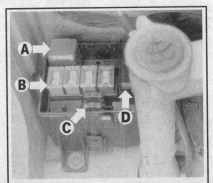

A. Relay   C. Fuse
B. Fusible link   D. Flasher

Fig. 3 The underhood fuse and relay panel usually contains fuses, relays, flashers and fusible links

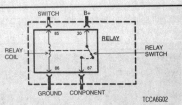

Fig. 4 Relays are composed of a coil and a switch. These two components are linked together so that when one operates, the other operates at the same time. The large wires in the circuit are connected from the battery to one side of the relay switch (B+) and from the opposite side of the relay switch to the load (component). Smaller wires are connected from the relay coil to the control switch for the circuit and from the opposite side of the relay coil to ground

Automotive wiring or circuit conductors can be either single strand wire, multi-strand wire or printed circuitry. Single strand wire has a solid metal core and is usually used inside such components as alternators, motors, relays and other devices. Multi-strand wire has a core made of many small strands of wire twisted together into a single conductor. Most of the wiring in an automotive electrical system is made up of multi-strand wire, either as a single conductor or grouped together in a harness. All wiring is color coded on the insulator, either as a solid color or as a colored wire with an identification stripe. A printed circuit is a thin film of copper or other conductor that is printed on an insulator backing. Occasionally, a printed circuit is sandwiched between two sheets of plastic for more protection and flexibility. A complete printed circuit, consisting of conductors, insulating material and connectors for lamps or other components is called a printed circuit board. Printed circuitry is used in place of individual wires or harnesses in places where space is limited, such as behind instrument panels.

Since automotive electrical systems are very sensitive to changes in resistance, the selection of properly sized wires is critical when systems are repaired. A loose or corroded connection or a replacement wire that is too small for the circuit will add extra resistance and an additional voltage drop to the circuit.

The wire gauge number is an expression of the cross-section area of the conductor. Vehicles from countries that use the metric system will typically describe the wire size as its cross-sectional area in square millimeters. In this method, the larger the wire, the greater the number. Another common system for expressing wire size is the American Wire Gauge (AWG) system. As gauge number increases, area decreases and the wire becomes smaller. An 18 gauge wire is smaller than a 4 gauge wire. A wire with a higher gauge number will carry less current than a wire with a lower gauge number. Gauge wire size refers to the size of the strands of the conductor, not the size of the complete wire with insulator. It is possible, therefore, to have two wires of the same gauge with different diameters because one may have thicker insulation than the other.

It is essential to understand how a circuit works before trying to figure out why it doesn't. An electrical schematic shows the electrical current paths when a circuit is operating properly. Schematics break the entire electrical system down into individual circuits. In a schematic, usually no attempt is made to represent wiring and components as they physically appear on the vehicle; switches and other components are shown as simply as possible. Face views of harness connectors show the cavity or terminal locations in all multi-pin connectors to help locate test points.

CONNECTORS

▶ See Figures 5 and 6

Three types of connectors are commonly used in automotive applications—weatherproof, molded and hard shell.

• Weatherproof—these connectors are most commonly used where the connector is exposed to the elements. Terminals are protected against moisture and dirt by sealing rings which provide a weathertight seal. All repairs require the use of a special terminal and the tool required to service it. Unlike standard blade type terminals, these weatherproof terminals cannot be straightened once they are bent. Make certain that the connectors are properly seated and all of the sealing rings are in place when connecting leads.

• Molded—these connectors require complete replacement of the connector if found to be defective. This means splicing a new connector assembly into the harness. All splices should be soldered to insure proper contact. Use care when prob-

ing the connections or replacing terminals in them, as it is possible to create a short circuit between opposite terminals. If this happens to the wrong terminal pair, it is possible to damage certain components. Always use jumper wires between connectors for circuit checking and NEVER probe through weatherproof seals.

• Hard Shell—unlike molded connectors, the terminal contacts in hard-shell connectors can be replaced. Replacement usually involves the use of a special terminal removal tool that depresses the locking tangs (barbs) on the connector terminal and allows the connector to be removed from the rear of the shell. The connector shell should be replaced if it shows any evidence of burning, melting, cracks, or breaks. Replace individual terminals that are burnt, corroded, distorted or loose.

Test Equipment

Pinpointing the exact cause of trouble in an electrical circuit is most times accomplished by the use of special test equipment. The following describes different types of commonly used test equipment and briefly explains how to use them in diagnosis. In addition to the information covered below, the tool manufacturer's instructions booklet (provided with the tester) should be read and clearly understood before attempting any test procedures.

JUMPER WIRES

▶ See Figure 7

❊❊ CAUTION

Never use jumper wires made from a thinner gauge wire than the circuit being tested. If the jumper wire is of too small a gauge, it may overheat and possibly melt. Never use jumpers to bypass high resistance loads in a circuit. Bypassing resistances, in effect, creates a short circuit. This may, in turn, cause damage and fire. Jumper wires should only be used to bypass lengths of wire or to simulate switches.

Jumper wires are simple, yet extremely valuable, pieces of test equipment. They are basically test wires which are used to bypass sections of a circuit. Although jumper wires can be purchased, they are usually fabricated from lengths of standard automotive wire and whatever type of connector (alligator clip, spade connector or pin connector) that is required for the particular application being tested. In cramped, hard-to-reach areas, it is advisable to have insulated boots over the jumper wire terminals in order to prevent accidental grounding. It is also advisable to include a standard automotive fuse in any jumper wire. This is commonly referred to as a "fused jumper". By inserting an in-line fuse holder between a set of test leads, a fused jumper wire can be used for bypassing open circuits. Use a 5 amp fuse to provide protection against voltage spikes.

Jumper wires are used primarily to locate open electrical circuits, on either the ground (–) side of the circuit or on the power (+) side. If an electrical component fails to operate, connect the jumper wire between the component and a good ground. If the component operates only with the jumper installed, the ground circuit is open. If the ground circuit is good, but the component does not operate, the circuit between the power feed and component may be open. By moving the jumper wire successively back from the component toward the power source, you can isolate the area of the circuit where the open is located.

TCCA6P03

Fig. 5 Hard shell (left) and weatherproof (right) connectors have replaceable terminals

TCCA6P04

Fig. 6 Weatherproof connectors are most commonly used in the engine compartment or where the connector is exposed to the elements

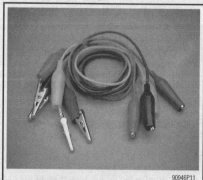

90946P11

Fig. 7 Jumper wire set with alligator clips attached

When the component stops functioning, or the power is cut off, the open is in the segment of wire between the jumper and the point previously tested.

You can sometimes connect the jumper wire directly from the battery to the "hot" terminal of the component, but first make sure the component uses 12 volts in operation. Some electrical components, such as fuel injectors or sensors, are designed to operate on about 4 to 5 volts, and running 12 volts directly to these components will cause damage.

TEST LIGHTS

▶ **See Figure 8**

The test light is used to check circuits and components while electrical current is flowing through them. It is used for voltage and ground tests. To use a 12 volt test light, connect the ground clip to a good ground and probe wherever necessary with the pick. The test light will illuminate when voltage is detected. This does not necessarily mean that 12 volts (or any particular amount of voltage) is present; it only means that some voltage is present. It is advisable before using the test light to touch its ground clip and probe across the battery posts or terminals to make sure the light is operating properly.

✳✳ WARNING

Do not use a test light to probe electronic ignition, spark plug or coil wires. Never use a pick-type test light to probe wiring on computer controlled systems unless specifically instructed to do so. Any wire insulation that is pierced by the test light probe should be taped and sealed with silicone after testing.

Like the jumper wire, the 12 volt test light is used to isolate opens in circuits. But, whereas the jumper wire is used to bypass the open to operate the load, the 12 volt test light is used to locate the presence of voltage in a circuit. If the test light illuminates, there is power up to that point in the circuit; if the test light does not illuminate, there is an open circuit (no power). Move the test light in successive steps back toward the power source until the light in the handle illuminates. The open is between the probe and a point which was previously probed.

The self-powered test light is similar in design to the 12 volt test light, but contains a 1.5 volt penlight battery in the handle. It is most often used in place of a multimeter to check for open or short circuits when power is isolated from the circuit (continuity test).

The battery in a self-powered test light does not provide much current. A weak battery may not provide enough power to illuminate the test light even when a complete circuit is made (especially if there is high resistance in the circuit). Always make sure that the test battery is strong. To check the battery, briefly touch the ground clip to the probe; if the light glows brightly, the battery is strong enough for testing.

➡**A self-powered test light should not be used on any computer controlled system or component. The small amount of electricity transmitted by the test light is enough to damage many electronic automotive components.**

MULTIMETERS

▶ **See Figure 9**

Multimeters are an extremely useful tool for troubleshooting electrical problems. They can be purchased in either analog or digital form and have a price range to suit any budget. A multimeter is a voltmeter, ammeter and ohmmeter (along with other features) combined into one instrument. It is often used when testing solid state circuits because of its high input impedance (usually 10 megaohms or more). A brief description of the multimeter main test functions follows:

• Voltmeter—the voltmeter is used to measure voltage at any point in a circuit, or to measure the voltage drop across any part of a circuit. Voltmeters usually have various scales and a selector switch to allow the reading of different voltage ranges. The voltmeter has a positive and a negative lead. To avoid damage to the meter, always connect the negative lead to the negative (–) side of the circuit (to ground or nearest the ground side of the circuit) and connect the positive lead to the positive (+) side of the circuit (to the power source or the nearest power source). Note that the negative voltmeter lead will always be black and that the positive voltmeter will always be some color other than black (usually red).

• Ohmmeter—the ohmmeter is designed to read resistance (measured in ohms) in a circuit or component. Most ohmmeters will have a selector switch which permits the measurement of different ranges of resistance (usually the selector switch allows the multiplication of the meter reading by 10, 100, 1,000 and 10,000). Some ohmmeters are "auto-ranging" which means the meter itself will determine which scale to use. Since the meters are powered by an internal battery, the ohmmeter can be used like a self-powered test light. When the ohmmeter is connected, current from the ohmmeter flows through the circuit or component being tested. Since the ohmmeter's internal resistance and voltage are known values, the amount of current flow through the meter depends on the resistance of the circuit or component being tested. The ohmmeter can also be used to perform a continuity test for suspected open circuits. In using the meter for making continuity checks, do not be concerned with the actual resistance readings. Zero resistance, or any ohm reading, indicates continuity in the circuit. Infinite resistance indicates an opening in the circuit. A high resistance reading where there should be none indicates a problem in the circuit. Checks for short circuits are made in the same manner as checks for open circuits, except that the circuit must be isolated from both power and normal ground. Infinite resistance indicates no continuity, while zero resistance indicates a dead short.

✳✳ WARNING

Never use an ohmmeter to check the resistance of a component or wire while there is voltage applied to the circuit.

• Ammeter—an ammeter measures the amount of current flowing through a circuit in units called amperes or amps. At normal operating voltage, most circuits have a characteristic amount of amperes, called "current draw" which can be measured using an ammeter. By referring to a specified current draw rating,

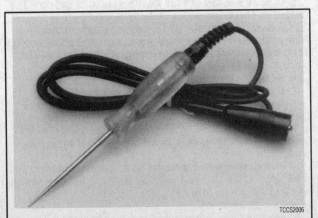

Fig. 8 A 12 volt test light is used to detect the presence of voltage in a circuit

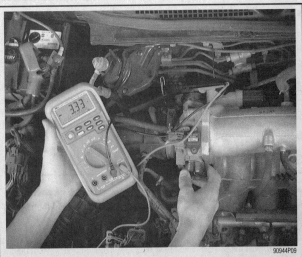

Fig. 9 A multimeter is a very useful tool that aids in troubleshooting electrical problems

then measuring the amperes and comparing the two values, one can determine what is happening within the circuit to aid in diagnosis. An open circuit, for example, will not allow any current to flow, so the ammeter reading will be zero. A damaged component or circuit will have an increased current draw, so the reading will be high. The ammeter is always connected in series with the circuit being tested. All of the current that normally flows through the circuit must also flow through the ammeter; if there is any other path for the current to follow, the ammeter reading will not be accurate. The ammeter itself has very little resistance to current flow and, therefore, will not affect the circuit, but it will measure current draw only when the circuit is closed and electricity is flowing. Excessive current draw can blow fuses and drain the battery, while a reduced current draw can cause motors to run slowly, lights to dim and other components to not operate properly.

Troubleshooting Electrical Systems

When diagnosing a specific problem, organized troubleshooting is a must. The complexity of a modern automotive vehicle demands that you approach any problem in a logical, organized manner. There are certain troubleshooting techniques, however, which are standard:

• Establish when the problem occurs. Does the problem appear only under certain conditions? Were there any noises, odors or other unusual symptoms? Isolate the problem area. To do this, make some simple tests and observations, then eliminate the systems that are working properly. Check for obvious problems, such as broken wires and loose or dirty connections. Always check the obvious before assuming something complicated is the cause.

• Test for problems systematically to determine the cause once the problem area is isolated. Are all the components functioning properly? Is there power going to electrical switches and motors. Performing careful, systematic checks will often turn up most causes on the first inspection, without wasting time checking components that have little or no relationship to the problem.

• Test all repairs after the work is done to make sure that the problem is fixed. Some causes can be traced to more than one component, so a careful verification of repair work is important in order to pick up additional malfunctions that may cause a problem to reappear or a different problem to arise. A blown fuse, for example, is a simple problem that may require more than another fuse to repair. If you don't look for a problem that caused a fuse to blow, a shorted wire (for example) may go undetected.

Experience has shown that most problems tend to be the result of a fairly simple and obvious cause, such as loose or corroded connectors, bad grounds or damaged wire insulation which causes a short. This makes careful visual inspection of components during testing essential to quick and accurate troubleshooting.

Testing

OPEN CIRCUITS

♦ **See Figure 10**

This test already assumes the existence of an open in the circuit and it is used to help locate the open portion.

1. Isolate the circuit from power and ground.
2. Connect the self-powered test light or ohmmeter ground clip to the ground side of the circuit and probe sections of the circuit sequentially.
3. If the light is out or there is infinite resistance, the open is between the probe and the circuit ground.
4. If the light is on or the meter shows continuity, the open is between the probe and the end of the circuit toward the power source.

SHORT CIRCUITS

➡**Never use a self-powered test light to perform checks for opens or shorts when power is applied to the circuit under test. The test light can be damaged by outside power.**

1. Isolate the circuit from power and ground.
2. Connect the self-powered test light or ohmmeter ground clip to a good ground and probe any easy-to-reach point in the circuit.
3. If the light comes on or there is continuity, there is a short somewhere in the circuit.

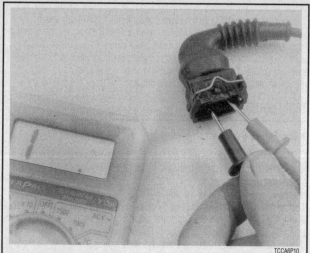

Fig. 10 The infinite reading on this multimeter indicates that the circuit is open

TCCA6P10

4. To isolate the short, probe a test point at either end of the isolated circuit (the light should be on or the meter should indicate continuity).
5. Leave the test light probe engaged and sequentially open connectors or switches, remove parts, etc. until the light goes out or continuity is broken.
6. When the light goes out, the short is between the last two circuit components which were opened.

VOLTAGE

This test determines voltage available from the battery and should be the first step in any electrical troubleshooting procedure after visual inspection. Many electrical problems, especially on computer controlled systems, can be caused by a low state of charge in the battery. Excessive corrosion at the battery cable terminals can cause poor contact that will prevent proper charging and full battery current flow.

1. Set the voltmeter selector switch to the 20V position.
2. Connect the multimeter negative lead to the battery's negative (–) post or terminal and the positive lead to the battery's positive (+) post or terminal.
3. Turn the ignition switch **ON** to provide a load.
4. A well charged battery should register over 12 volts. If the meter reads below 11.5 volts, the battery power may be insufficient to operate the electrical system properly.

VOLTAGE DROP

♦ **See Figure 11**

When current flows through a load, the voltage beyond the load drops. This voltage drop is due to the resistance created by the load and also by small resistances created by corrosion at the connectors and damaged insulation on the wires. The maximum allowable voltage drop under load is critical, especially if there is more than one load in the circuit, since all voltage drops are cumulative.

1. Set the voltmeter selector switch to the 20 volt position.
2. Connect the multimeter negative lead to a good ground.
3. Operate the circuit and check the voltage prior to the first component (load).
4. There should be little or no voltage drop in the circuit prior to the first component. If a voltage drop exists, the wire or connectors in the circuit are suspect.
5. While operating the first component in the circuit, probe the ground side of the component with the positive meter lead and observe the voltage readings. A small voltage drop should be noticed. This voltage drop is caused by the resistance of the component.
6. Repeat the test for each component (load) down the circuit.
7. If a large voltage drop is noticed, the preceding component, wire or connector is suspect.

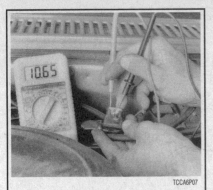

Fig. 11 This voltage drop test revealed high resistance (low voltage) in the circuit

TCCA6P07

Fig. 12 Checking the resistance of a coolant temperature sensor with an ohmmeter. Reading is 1.04 kilohms

TCCA6P08

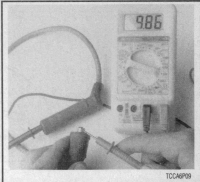

Fig. 13 Spark plug wires can be checked for excessive resistance using an ohmmeter

TCCA6P09

RESISTANCE

▶ See Figures 12 and 13

✳✳ WARNING

Never use an ohmmeter with power applied to the circuit. The ohmmeter is designed to operate on its own power supply. The normal 12 volt electrical system voltage could damage the meter!

1. Isolate the circuit from the vehicle's power source.
2. Ensure that the ignition key is **OFF** when disconnecting any components or the battery.
3. Where necessary, also isolate at least one side of the circuit to be checked, in order to avoid reading parallel resistances. Parallel circuit resistances will always give a lower reading than the actual resistance of either of the branches.
4. Connect the meter leads to both sides of the circuit (wire or component) and read the actual measured ohms on the meter scale. Make sure the selector switch is set to the proper ohm scale for the circuit being tested, to avoid misreading the ohmmeter test value.

Wire and Connector Repair

▶ See Figure 14

Almost anyone can replace damaged wires, as long as the proper tools and parts are available. Wire and terminals are available to fit almost any need. Even

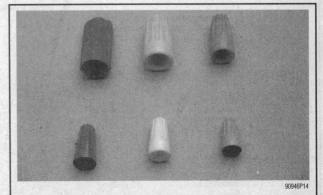

Fig. 14 Wire caps are used to quickly join two wires

90946P14

the specialized weatherproof, molded and hard shell connectors are now available from aftermarket suppliers.

Be sure the ends of all the wires are fitted with the proper terminal hardware and connectors. Wrapping a wire around a stud is never a permanent solution and will only cause trouble later. Replace wires one at a time to avoid confusion. Always route wires exactly the same as the factory.

➡If connector repair is necessary, only attempt it if you have the proper tools. Weatherproof and hard shell connectors require special tools to release the pins inside the connector. Attempting to repair these connectors with conventional hand tools will damage them.

BATTERY CABLES

Disconnecting the Cables

When working on any electrical component on the vehicle, it is always a good idea to disconnect the negative (–) battery cable. This will prevent potential damage to many sensitive electrical components such as the Powertrain Control Module (PCM), radio, alternator, etc.

➡Any time you disengage the battery cables, it is recommended that you disconnect the negative (–) battery cable first. This will prevent your accidentally grounding the positive (+) terminal to the body of the vehicle when disconnecting it, thereby preventing damage to the above mentioned components.

Before you disconnect the cable(s), first turn the ignition to the **OFF** position. This will prevent a draw on the battery which could cause arcing (electricity trying to ground itself to the body of a vehicle, just like a spark plug jumping the gap) and, of course, damaging some components such as the alternator diodes.

When the battery cable(s) are reconnected (negative cable last), be sure to check that your lights, windshield wipers and other electrically operated safety components are all working correctly. If your vehicle contains an Electronically Tuned Radio (ETR), don't forget to also reset your radio stations. Ditto for the clock.

AIR BAG (SUPPLEMENTAL RESTRAINT SYSTEM)

General Information

▶ See Figure 15

The Air Bag or Supplemental Restraint System (SRS) is designed to provide additional protection for front seat occupants when used in conjunction with a seat belt. The system is an electronically controlled, mechanically operated system. The system contains two basic sub-systems: the air bag module(s) (the actual air bag(s) themselves), and the electrical system. The system consists of:
• The crash sensors
• The safing sensor
• The air bag module(s)

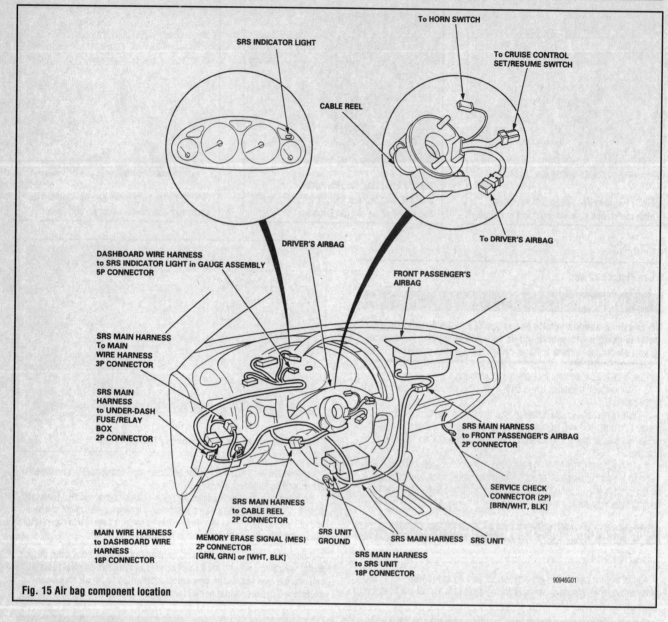

SRS INDICATOR LIGHT

To HORN SWITCH

To CRUISE CONTROL SET/RESUME SWITCH

CABLE REEL

DRIVER'S AIRBAG

To DRIVER'S AIRBAG

DASHBOARD WIRE HARNESS to SRS INDICATOR LIGHT in GAUGE ASSEMBLY 5P CONNECTOR

FRONT PASSENGER'S AIRBAG

SRS MAIN HARNESS To MAIN WIRE HARNESS 3P CONNECTOR

SRS MAIN HARNESS to UNDER-DASH FUSE/RELAY BOX 2P CONNECTOR

SRS MAIN HARNESS to FRONT PASSENGER'S AIRBAG 2P CONNECTOR

SERVICE CHECK CONNECTOR (2P) [BRN/WHT, BLK]

MAIN WIRE HARNESS to DASHBOARD WIRE HARNESS 16P CONNECTOR

SRS MAIN HARNESS to CABLE REEL 2P CONNECTOR

MEMORY ERASE SIGNAL (MES) 2P CONNECTOR [GRN, GRN] or [WHT, BLK]

SRS UNIT GROUND

SRS MAIN HARNESS

SRS UNIT

SRS MAIN HARNESS to SRS UNIT 18P CONNECTOR

Fig. 15 Air bag component location

90946G01

- The diagnostic monitor
- The instrument cluster indicator
- The sliding contacts (clock spring assembly)

The system is operates as follows: The system remains out of sight until activated in an accident that is determined to be the equivalent of hitting a parked car of the same size and weight at 28 mph (40 km/h) with the vehicle receiving severe front end damage. This determination is made by crash and safing sensors mounted on the vehicle which when an sufficient impact occurs, close their contacts completing the electrical circuit and inflating the air bags. When not activated the system is monitored by the air bag diagnostic monitor and system readiness is indicated by the lamp located on the instrument cluster. Any fault detected by the diagnostic monitor will illuminate the lamp and store a Diagnostic Trouble Code (DTC).

SERVICE PRECAUTIONS

When working on the SRS or any components which require the removal of the air bag, adhere to all of these precautions to minimize the risks of personal injury or component damage:

- Before attempting to diagnose, remove or install the air bag system components, you must first detach and isolate the negative (–) battery cable. Failure to do so could result in accidental deployment and possible personal injury.

- SRS components should not be subjected to heat over 200°F (93°C), so remove the SRS control unit, air bag modules and clock spring before drying or baking the vehicle after painting.

- When an undeployed air bag assembly is to be removed, after detaching the negative battery cable, allow the system capacitor to discharge for two minutes before commencing with the air bag system component removal.

- Replace the air bag system components only with factory specified replacement parts, or equivalent. Substitute parts may visually appear interchangeable, but internal differences may result in inferior occupant protection.

- Never use an analog ohmmeter to test SRS components.

- The fasteners, screws, and bolts originally used for the SRS have special coatings and are specifically designed for the SRS. They must never be replaced with any substitutes. Anytime a new fastener is needed, replace with the correct fasteners provided in the service package or fasteners listed in the parts books.

Handling a Live Air Bag Module

▶ See Figures 16 and 17

At no time should any source of electricity be permitted near the inflator on the back of the module. When carrying a live module, the trim cover should be pointed away from the body to minimize injury in the event of accidental deployment. In addition, if the module is placed on a bench or other surface, the

Fig. 16 Use extreme caution when removing an air bag

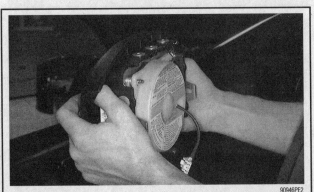

Fig. 17 Always carry an air bag with the trim side away from you

plastic trim cover should be face up to minimize movement in case of accidental deployment.

When handling a steering column with an air bag module attached, never place the column on the floor or other surface with the steering wheel or module face down.

Handling a Deployed Air Bag Module

The vehicle interior may contain a very small amount of sodium hydroxide powder, a by-product of air bag deployment. Since this powder can irritate the skin, eyes, nose or throat, be sure to wear safety glasses, rubber gloves and long sleeves during cleanup.

If you find that the cleanup is irritating your skin, run cool water over the affected area. Also, if you experience nasal or throat irritation, exit the vehicle for fresh air until the irritation ceases. If irritation continues, see a physician.

Begin the cleanup by putting tape over the two air bag exhaust vents so that no additional powder will find its way into the vehicle interior. Then, remove the air bag(s) and air bag module(s) from the vehicle.

Use a vacuum cleaner to remove any residual powder from the vehicle interior. Work from the outside in so that you avoid kneeling or sitting in an uncleaned area.

Be sure to vacuum the heater and A/C outlets as well. In fact, it's a good idea to run the blower on low and to vacuum up any powder expelled from the plenum. You may need to vacuum the interior of the car a second time to recover all of the powder.

Check with the local authorities before disposing of the deployed bag and module in your trash.

After an air bag has been deployed, the air bag module and clockspring must be replaced because they cannot be reused. Other air bag system components should be replaced with new ones if damaged.

DISARMING THE SYSTEM

1. Position the front wheels straight ahead.
2. Place the ignition switch in the **LOCK** position, then remove the ignition key.
3. Disconnect the negative battery cable. Isolate the battery cable by taping up any exposed metal areas of the cable. This will keep the cable from inadvertently contacting the battery and causing accidental deployment of the air bag.
4. Allow the system capacitor to discharge for at least 3 minutes, although 10 minutes is recommended to allow the complete dissipation of any residual energy.

ARMING THE SYSTEM

1. Turn the ignition switch to the **ON** position. The SRS indicator lamp should come on for about six seconds and then it will go off.
2. Test drive the vehicle and check for an illumination of the SRS indicator lamp.
3. Test the horn to ensure that it too works.

HEATING AND AIR CONDITIONING

Blower Motor

REMOVAL & INSTALLATION

→**Before attempting the removal of the blower motor assembly, we at Chilton® feel it should be noted that this procedure requires the removal of components for the air conditioning system. This requires the system to be discharged. If you attempt this procedure, have a MVAC-trained, EPA-certified, automotive technician discharge the A/C system before removing any components, and recharge the system upon completion of the installation.**

Integra

♦ **See Figures 18 thru 23**

1. Disconnect the negative battery cable.
2. Remove the front seats.
3. Remove the glove box.
4. Remove the four bolts, then the glove box frame.
5. Remove the dashboard.
6. On vehicles without air conditioning, remove the wiring harness away from the heater duct and then remove the fasteners and heater duct assembly.
7. On vehicles with air conditioning, remove the evaporator.

8. Detach the connectors from the blower motor resistor and also from the recirculation control motor.
9. Remove the wire harness clip from the recirculation control motor and from the blower motor.
10. Unfasten the mounting nuts, then remove the blower motor.
11. Installation is the reverse of the removal procedure.

2.2, 2.3 & 3.0CL

♦ **See Figure 24**

1. Disconnect the negative battery cable.
2. Remove the evaporator.
3. Detach the connectors from the recirculation control motor.
4. Remove the blower motor high relay.
5. Remove the blower motor unit.
6. Installation is the reverse of the removal procedure.

2.5 & 3.2TL

♦ **See Figure 25**

1. Disconnect the negative battery cable.
2. Remove the evaporator from the vehicle to gain access to the blower unit.
3. Remove the mounting nut from the blower unit.
4. Detach the connector from the recirculation control motor.
5. Remove the screw from the pipe clamp.

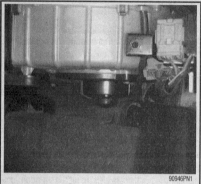

Fig. 18 Installed view of blower motor and housing

Fig. 19 Remove the front seats for easier access to the dashboard

GLOVE BOX FRAME

Fig. 20 Removing the glove box frame

Fig. 21 Heater core, duct work, evaporator and blower motor assembly

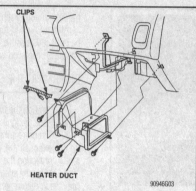

CLIPS

HEATER DUCT

Fig. 22 Removing the heater duct from vehicles without air conditioning

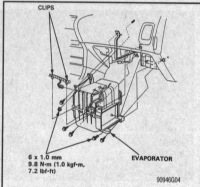

CLIPS

6 x 1.0 mm
9.8 N·m (1.0 kgf·m,
7.2 lbf·ft)

EVAPORATOR

Fig. 23 If equipped with A/C you must remove the evaporator

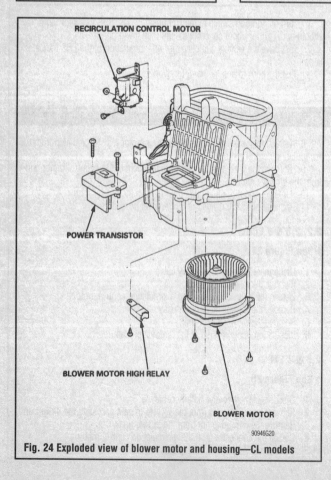

RECIRCULATION CONTROL MOTOR

POWER TRANSISTOR

BLOWER MOTOR HIGH RELAY

BLOWER MOTOR

Fig. 24 Exploded view of blower motor and housing—CL models

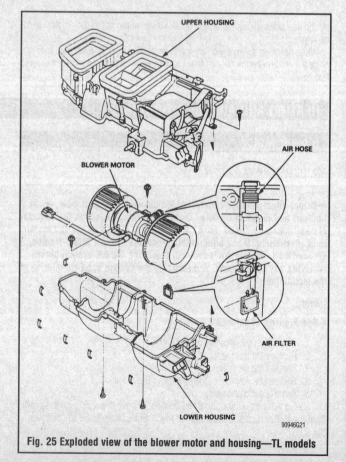

UPPER HOUSING

AIR HOSE

BLOWER MOTOR

AIR FILTER

LOWER HOUSING

Fig. 25 Exploded view of the blower motor and housing—TL models

6. Unfasten the mounting bolt, then remove the blower unit by pulling it back and to the right.

➡️**It may be necessary to remove the three self tapping screws that hold the recirculation control motor to the flange collar.**

7. Installation is the reverse of the removal procedure.

3.5RL

▶ **See Figure 26**

➡️**Air bag components are located in this area. Please read the SRS section before beginning any repairs.**

1. Take the vehicle to a reputable repair shop to have the A/C system discharged and recovered.
2. Disconnect the negative battery cable.
3. Remove the bolt and clamp from the evaporator.
4. Remove the bolt and then the capillary tube from the suction line.
5. Disconnect the suction and receiver lines from the evaporator.
6. Remove the mounting nut from the evaporator.
7. Turn the ignition switch **ON**.
8. Set the control switch to recirculate.
9. Remove the glove box.
10. Detach the connector from the trunk opener.
11. Remove the glove box back cover.
12. Unplug the service check connector.
13. Remove the blower under cover, together as an assembly with the glove box frame.
14. Detach the A/C wire harness connector from the main wiring harness.
15. Remove the clips from the wiring harness.
16. Tag and detach the connectors from the following components:
   - Recirculation control motor
   - Evaporator temperature sensor
   - Power transistor
   - Blower motor
17. Remove the blower motor relay and high motor relay, together with the bracket.
18. Remove the wiring harness connectors and the SRS harness clip from the mount on the body.
19. Remove the multi-plex control unit by removing the mounting bolts.
20. Remove the A/C filter assemblies.
21. Disconnect the drain hose.
22. Remove the evaporator/blower unit.
23. Installation is the reverse of the removal procedure.
24. After all of the components are installed, take the vehicle to a reputable repair shop to have the A/C system recharged.

Legend

▶ **See Figure 27**

1. Disconnect the negative battery cable.
2. Remove the glove box lower panel, then remove the glove box.
3. Remove the glove box side covers and dash board side cover.
4. Remove the glove box frame.
5. Remove the blower unit from the vehicle.
6. Installation is the reverse of the removal procedure.

Vigor

▶ **See Figure 28**

1. Remove the heater evaporator unit.
2. Remove the pipe cover by removing the mounting screws.
3. Remove the left side heater duct.
4. Disconnect the blower motor wiring harness.

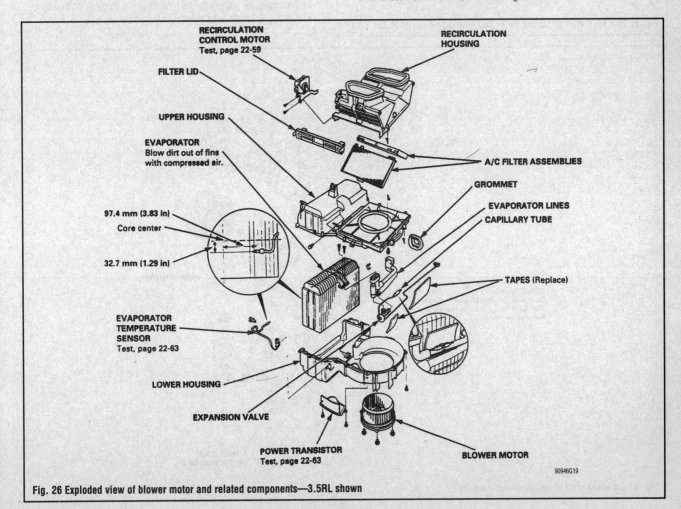

RECIRCULATION CONTROL MOTOR
Test, page 22-59

RECIRCULATION HOUSING

FILTER LID

UPPER HOUSING

EVAPORATOR
Blow dirt out of fins with compressed air.

A/C FILTER ASSEMBLIES

GROMMET

EVAPORATOR LINES
CAPILLARY TUBE

97.4 mm (3.83 in)
Core center

32.7 mm (1.29 in)

TAPES (Replace)

EVAPORATOR TEMPERATURE SENSOR
Test, page 22-63

LOWER HOUSING

EXPANSION VALVE

POWER TRANSISTOR
Test, page 22-63

BLOWER MOTOR

90946G19

Fig. 26 Exploded view of blower motor and related components—3.5RL shown

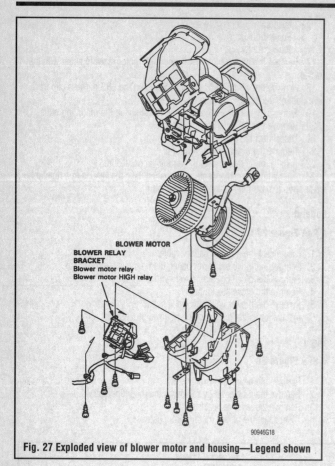

BLOWER MOTOR

BLOWER RELAY BRACKET
Blower motor relay
Blower motor HIGH relay

90946G18

Fig. 27 Exploded view of blower motor and housing—Legend shown

5. Remove the lower blower motor housing.
6. Remove the blower motor.
7. Installation is the reverse of the removal procedure.

Heater Core

REMOVAL & INSTALLATION

➡Before attempting the removal of the heater core assembly, we at Chilton® feel it should be noted that this procedure requires the removal of components for the air conditioning system. This requires the system to be discharged. If you attempt this procedure, have a MVAC-trained, EPA-certified, automotive technician discharge the A/C system before removing any components, and recharge the system upon completion of the installation.

✷✷ CAUTION

When draining the coolant, keep in mind that cats and dogs are attracted by ethylene glycol antifreeze, and are quite likely to drink any that is left in an uncovered container or in puddles on the ground. This will prove fatal in sufficient quantity. Always drain the coolant into a sealable container. Coolant should be reused unless it is contaminated or several years old.

Integra

▶ See Figures 29 thru 35

1. Disconnect the negative battery cable.
2. Drain the engine coolant into a suitable container.
3. Disconnect the heater valve from the valve arm by removing the clamp.
4. Remove all of the heater hoses from the unit.

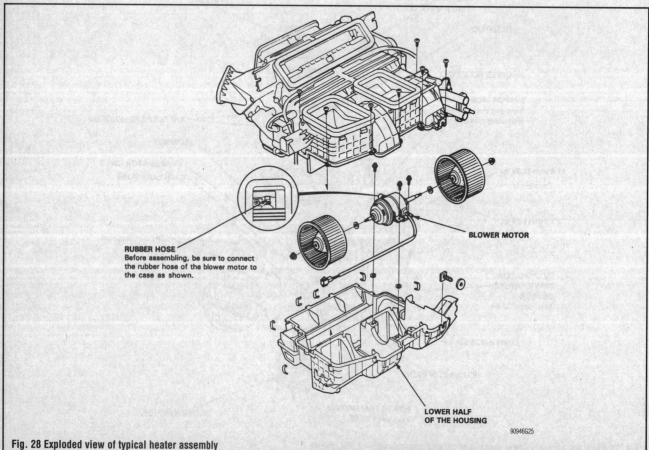

RUBBER HOSE
Before assembling, be sure to connect the rubber hose of the blower motor to the case as shown.

BLOWER MOTOR

LOWER HALF OF THE HOUSING

90946G25

Fig. 28 Exploded view of typical heater assembly

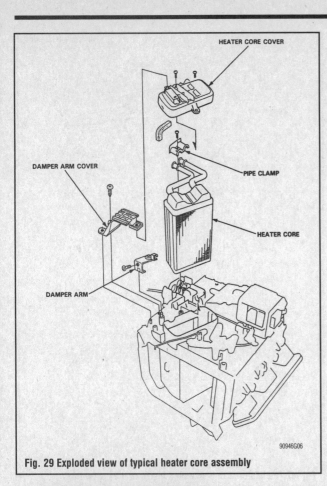

Fig. 29 Exploded view of typical heater core assembly

5. Remove the dashboard.

6. Remove the heater duct.

7. Remove the two bolts from the passengers SRS beam.

8. Detach the mode control connector from the heater control unit.

9. Remove the two mounting nuts and then remove the heater control unit.

10. Remove the heater core from the unit.

To install:

11. Installation is the reverse of the removal procedure. During installation pay careful attention to the following details:

    a. Be cautious as to not interchange inlet and outlet hoses.

    b. Always apply sealant to the grommets.

    c. Refill the radiator before starting the engine.

    d. Make sure all cables are connected and properly adjusted.

2.2, 2.3 & 3.0CL

▶ See Figures 36 and 37

1. Disconnect the negative battery cable.

2. Drain the engine coolant into a suitable container

3. Open the cable clamp, then disconnect the heater valve cable from the valve arm.

4. Position the heater valve arm to the fully open position.

5. Disconnect the heater hoses from the unit.

6. Remove the mounting nuts from the unit.

7. Remove the dashboard.

8. Remove the steering hanger beam.

9. Remove the evaporator.

10. Remove the air mixture control motor and the mode control motor by removing the harness clip.

11. Unfasten the heater box mounting bolts, then remove the heater core assembly.

To install:

12. Installation is the reverse of the removal procedure. During installation pay careful attention to the following details:

    a. Be cautious as to not interchange inlet and outlet hoses.

Fig. 30 Removing the heater valve cable

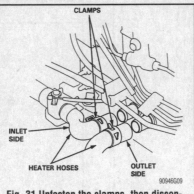

Fig. 31 Unfasten the clamps, then disconnect the heater hoses

Fig. 32 Remove the dashboard by pulling it up, then out of the vehicle

Fig. 33 On Integras, it may be necessary to remove the dashboard support bars

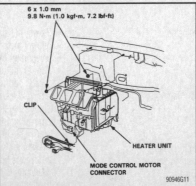

Fig. 34 Unplug the mode control motor connector

Fig. 35 Removing the heater core from the control box

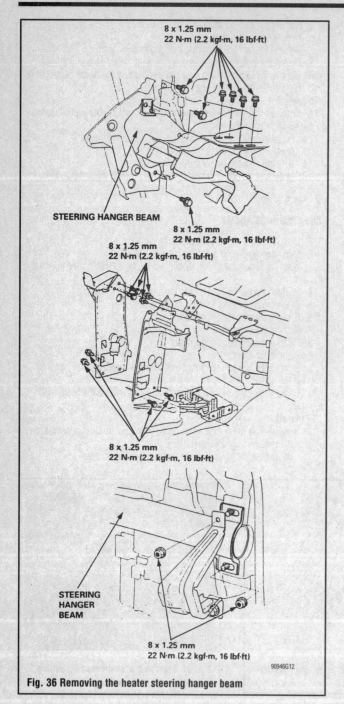

8 x 1.25 mm
22 N·m (2.2 kgf·m, 16 lbf·ft)

STEERING HANGER BEAM

8 x 1.25 mm
22 N·m (2.2 kgf·m, 16 lbf·ft)

8 x 1.25 mm
22 N·m (2.2 kgf·m, 16 lbf·ft)

8 x 1.25 mm
22 N·m (2.2 kgf·m, 16 lbf·ft)

**STEERING
HANGER
BEAM**

8 x 1.25 mm
22 N·m (2.2 kgf·m, 16 lbf·ft)

90946G12

Fig. 36 Removing the heater steering hanger beam

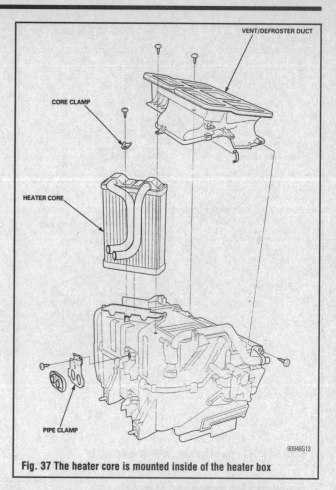

VENT/DEFROSTER DUCT

CORE CLAMP

HEATER CORE

PIPE CLAMP

90946G13

Fig. 37 The heater core is mounted inside of the heater box

HEATER CORE

HEATER CORE COVER

90946G15

Fig. 38 Exploded view of heater core and cover mounting—TL Models

b. Always apply sealant to the grommets.
c. Refill the radiator before starting the engine.
d. Make sure all cables are connected and properly adjusted.

2.5 & 3.2TL

▶ **See Figure 38**

1. Disconnect the negative battery cable.
2. Drain the engine coolant into a suitable container.
3. Remove the heater hoses from the heater core inlet.
4. Remove the dashboard.
5. Remove the seven mounting bolts and steering mounting beam.
6. Remove the wiring harness clips and the three self tapping screws.
7. Remove the pipe cover.
8. Detach the connector from the recirculation motor.
9. Unfasten the screws from the pipe clamp.
10. Detach the connectors from the following items:

- Power transistor
- blower motor high relay
- Evaporator temperature sensor
- Blower motor
- Heater sub-harness

11. Remove the sub-harness connector from the bracket.
12. Remove the clips from the heater ducts (left and right).
13. Remove the SRS main harness clips from the heater unit.
14. Remove the three self tapping screws from the assembly.
15. Unfasten the six mounting bolts, then remove the bracket.
16. Remove the heater unit.
17. Installation is the reverse of the removal procedure. During installation pay careful attention to the following details:

a. Be cautious as to not interchange inlet and outlet hoses.
b. Always apply sealant to the grommets.

c. Refill the radiator before starting the engine.

d. Make sure all cables are connected and properly adjusted.

3.5RL

▶ See Figure 39

1. Disconnect the negative battery cable.
2. Drain the engine coolant into a suitable container
3. Open the cable clamp, then disconnect the heater valve cable from the valve arm.
4. Position the heater valve arm to the fully open position.
5. Disconnect the heater hoses from the unit.
6. Remove the dashboard.
7. Unfasten the mounting nuts from the unit.
8. Remove the steering hanger beam.
9. Remove the evaporator/blower unit..
10. Remove the air mixture control motor and the mode control motor by removing the harness clip.
11. Unfasten the heater box mounting bolts, then remove the heater core assembly.
12. Installation is the reverse of the removal procedure. During installation pay careful attention to the following details:

   a. Be cautious as to not interchange inlet and outlet hoses.

   b. Always apply sealant to the grommets.

   c. Refill the radiator before starting the engine.

   d. Make sure all cables are connected and properly adjusted.

Legend

▶ See Figure 40

1. Take the vehicle to a reputable repair shop to have the A/C system discharged and recovered.
2. Disconnect the negative battery cable.
3. Remove the dashboard.
4. Remove the blower unit.
5. Drain the engine coolant into a suitable container.
6. Disconnect the heater hoses.

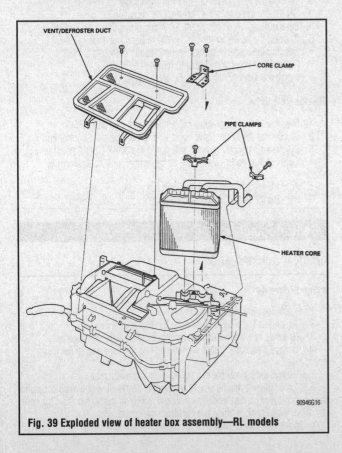

Fig. 39 Exploded view of heater box assembly—RL models

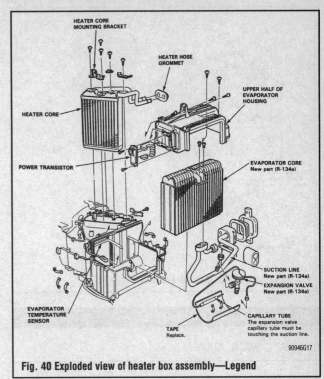

Fig. 40 Exploded view of heater box assembly—Legend

7. Remove the heater valve cable from the heater valve.
8. Unfasten the suction line and receiver line bolts, then disconnect the lines.
9. Cap off the lines to prevent dirt from entering.
10. Remove the evaporator seal plate.
11. Remove the ducts and remove the connectors.
12. Unfasten the heater-evaporator unit mounting nuts and bolts.
13. Detach the air mixture control motor connector.
14. If equipped with automatic climate control, detach the heater core temperature sensor connector.
15. Remove the heater-evaporator unit from the vehicle.
16. Installation is the reverse of the removal procedure. During installation pay careful attention to the following details:

   a. Be cautious as to not interchange inlet and outlet hoses.

   b. Always apply sealant to the grommets.

   c. Refill the radiator before starting the engine.

   d. Make sure all cables are connected and properly adjusted.

17. After all of the components are installed, take the vehicle to a reputable repair shop to have the A/C system recharged.

Vigor

▶ See Figure 41

1. Disconnect the negative battery cable.
2. Drain the engine coolant.
3. Remove the dashboard.
4. Remove the heater hoses from the unit.
5. Remove the refrigerant from the A/C system and remove the suction line and receiver line bolts, then disconnect the lines.
6. Cap off the lines to prevent dirt from entering.
7. Remove the evaporator seal plate.
8. Remove the ducts and remove the connectors.
9. Remove the heater-evaporator unit mounting nuts and bolts.
10. Remove the heating duct and remove the connector.
11. Unfasten the heater/evaporator unit mounting bolts, then remove the unit from the vehicle.
12. Installation is the reverse of the removal procedure. During installation pay careful attention to the following details:

   a. Be cautious as to not interchange inlet and outlet hoses.

   b. Always apply sealant to the grommets.

   c. Refill the radiator before starting the engine.

   d. Make sure all cables are connected and properly adjusted.

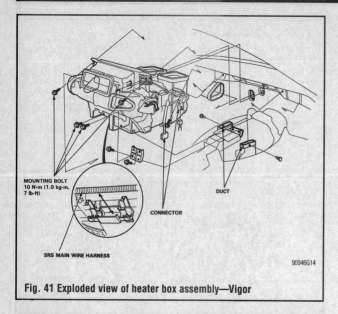

Fig. 41 Exploded view of heater box assembly—Vigor

Air Conditioning Components

REMOVAL & INSTALLATION

Repair or service of air conditioning components is not covered by this manual, because of the risk of personal injury or death, and because of the legal ramifications of servicing these components without the proper EPA certification and experience. Cost, personal injury or death, environmental damage, and legal considerations (such as the fact that it is a federal crime to vent refrigerant into the atmosphere), dictate that the A/C components on your vehicle should be serviced only by a Motor Vehicle Air Conditioning (MVAC) trained, and EPA certified automotive technician.

➡️ If your vehicle's A/C system uses R-12 refrigerant and is in need of recharging, the A/C system can be converted over to R-134a refrigerant (less environmentally harmful and expensive). Refer to Section 1 for additional information on R-12 to R-134a conversions, and for additional considerations dealing with your vehicle's A/C system.

Temperature Control Cable

REMOVAL & INSTALLATION

▶ See Figures 42 and 43

1. Disconnect the negative battery cable.
2. Remove the heater and A/C control head.

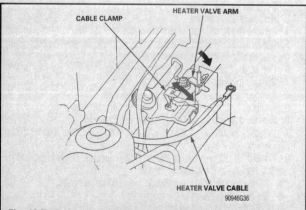

Fig. 42 Typical temperature control cable—heater valve side

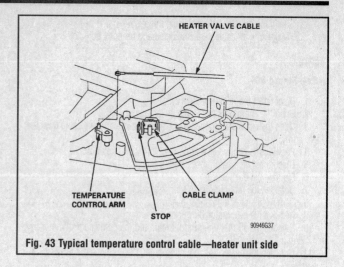

Fig. 43 Typical temperature control cable—heater unit side

3. Remove the trim panel, as necessary.
4. Unfasten the screw and/or retaining clip(s) securing the cable, then remove the temperature control cable from the vehicle.
   To install:
5. Properly route the temperature control cable to the control head.
6. Install the retaining clip(s) and/or screw.
7. Install the trim panel.
8. Install the control head.
9. Connect the negative battery cable.

ADJUSTMENT

Heater Valve Side

1. Open the cable clamp, then disconnect the heater valve cable from the heater valve arm.
2. Turn on the A/C but do not turn the engine **ON**.
3. Set the control dial to the "MAX COOL" position.
4. Set the heater valve arm to the fully closed position.
5. Connect the heater valve cable to the heater valve arm.
6. Position the heater valve arm in the closed position.
7. Pull on the heater valve cable to remove any slack.
8. Install the cable housing into the cable clamp.

Heater Unit Side

1. Disconnect the heater valve cable housing at the heater unit.
2. Disconnect the heater valve cable from the temperature control arm.
3. Set the air mix control motor selector to the "MAX COOL" position.
4. Connect the heater valve cable to the temperature control arm as shown.
5. Hold the heater valve cable housing to the stop.
6. Position the heater valve cable housing into the cable clamp.

Control Panel

REMOVAL & INSTALLATION

▶ See Figure 44

1. Disconnect the negative battery cable.
2. Disconnect the control cable from the heater unit.
3. Remove any switches or sensors that hinder the removal process.
4. Remove all fasteners that are holding the control panel to the dashboard.
5. Remove the control panel from the dashboard assembly.
6. Some vehicles require you to remove the center air vent to gain access to the control unit. This can be done by simply removing the screws from the central air vent and gently pulling the vent from the control unit.
7. Installation is the reverse of the removal procedure.

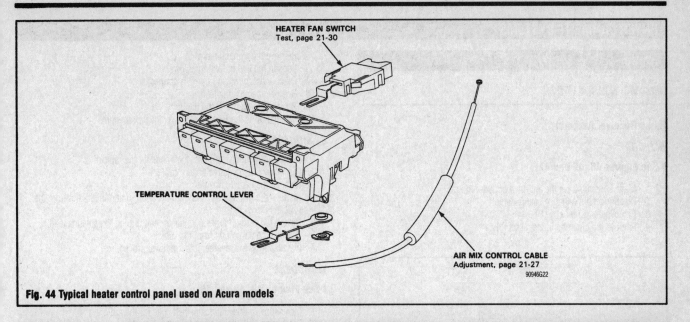

HEATER FAN SWITCH
Test, page 21-30

TEMPERATURE CONTROL LEVER

AIR MIX CONTROL CABLE
Adjustment, page 21-27

90946G22

Fig. 44 Typical heater control panel used on Acura models

CRUISE CONTROL

General Information

Cruise control is a speed control system that maintains a desired vehicle speed under normal driving conditions. However, steep grades up or down may cause variations in the selected speeds. The electronic cruise control system has the capability to cruise, coast, resume speed, accelerate, "tap-up" and "tap-down".

The main parts of the cruise control system are the functional control switches, cruise control module servo, vacuum tank, switch assembly, vacuum hoses, wiring and cruise control servo cable.

The cruise control system works a mechanical linkage to the throttle by way of a vacuum motor which is inside a server. This is a diaphragm moved by vacuum applied to one side. A solenoid driven valve connects the vacuum motor to a vacuum tank. Another solenoid vents the vacuum. The cruise control module controls the servo and the throttle by pulsing these solenoid valves on and off.

One input to the cruise control module is the vehicle speed, which is sent to the computer control module (ECM or PCM, as applicable) by the Vehicle Speed Sensor (VSS). The cruise control module contains a low speed limit which will prevent system engagement below 25 mph (40 km/h).

Other inputs to the module are the switches. The module is controlled by the functional switches in the turn signal/headlamp switch and windshield wiper lever. The release switches are mounted on the brake/clutch/accelerator pedal bracket. When the brake or clutch pedal is depressed, the cruise control system is electrically disengaged and the throttle is returned to the idle position.

CRUISE CONTROL TROUBLESHOOTING

Problem	Possible Cause
Will not hold proper speed	Incorrect cable adjustment
	Binding throttle linkage
	Leaking vacuum servo diaphragm
	Leaking vacuum tank
	Faulty vacuum or vent valve
	Faulty stepper motor
	Faulty transducer
	Faulty speed sensor
	Faulty cruise control module
Cruise intermittently cuts out	Clutch or brake switch adjustment too tight
	Short or open in the cruise control circuit
	Faulty transducer
	Faulty cruise control module
Vehicle surges	Kinked speedometer cable or casing
	Binding throttle linkage
	Faulty speed sensor
	Faulty cruise control module
Cruise control inoperative	Blown fuse
	Short or open in the cruise control circuit
	Faulty brake or clutch switch
	Leaking vacuum circuit
	Faulty cruise control switch
	Faulty stepper motor
	Faulty transducer
	Faulty speed sensor
	Faulty cruise control module

Note: Use this chart as a guide. Not all systems will use the components listed.

TCCA6C01

ENTERTAINMENT SYSTEMS

Radio

REMOVAL & INSTALLATION

Radio Receiver Assembly

INTEGRA

▶ See Figures 45, 46 and 47

1. Make sure you have the anti-theft code for the radio.
2. Disconnect the negative battery cable.
3. Remove the center console.
4. Remove the cigarette lighter assembly.

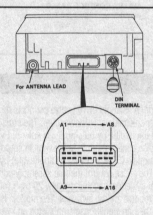

Terminal	Wire	Connects to
A1	RED/GRN	Front passenger's door speaker ⊕
A2	BLU/GRN	Driver's door speaker ⊕
A3	RED/BLK	Lights-on signal
A4	WHT/BLU	Constant power (Tuning memory)
A5	YEL/RED	ACC (Main stereo power supply)
A6	YEL/GRN	Radio switched power (To antenna)
A7	BLU/YEL	Left rear speaker ⊕
A8	RED/YEL	Right rear speaker ⊕
A9	BRN/BLK	Front passenger's door speaker ⊖
A10	GRY/BLK	Driver's door speaker ⊖
A11	——	(not used)
A12	——	(not used)
A13	——	(not used)
A14	BLK	Ground (G551)
A15	GRY/WHT	Left rear speaker ⊖
A16	BRN/WHT	Right rear speaker ⊖

90946G24

Fig. 45 Radio wiring chart—1998 Integra shown

5. Remove the front console.
6. Loosen the two mounting screws.
7. Disconnect the wiring harness connector.
8. Remove the antenna lead.
9. Pull the stereo out of the dash.
10. Installation is the reverse of the removal procedure.

CL MODELS

1. Make sure you have the anti-theft code for the radio.
2. Disconnect the negative battery cable.
3. Remove the center console.
4. Remove the two screws, then pull the audio unit partially out from the dash to access the wiring.
5. Detach the wiring harness connector and unplug the antenna lead.
6. Remove the audio unit from the vehicle.
7. Installation is the reverse of the removal procedure.

TL MODELS

▶ See Figures 48, 49 and 50

1. Make sure you have the anti-theft code for the radio.
2. Disconnect the negative battery cable.
3. Remove the center panel of the dashboard by lightly prying on it.
4. Detach the connectors from the climate control unit.
5. Unplug the radio panel and radio/cassette/CD player connectors.
6. Remove the radio/cassette/CD player from the radio panel.
7. Installation is the reverse of the removal procedure.

RL MODELS

▶ See Figures 51, 52 and 53

1. Make sure you have the anti-theft code for the radio.
2. Disconnect the negative battery cable.
3. On vehicles with navigation system, perform the following steps:
   a. Remove the navigation panel.
   b. Remove the audio panel assembly.
   c. Remove the navigation monitor by removing the four mounting screws.
   d. Loosen the audio mounting screws.
   e. Remove the pins from the navigation bracket.
   f. Remove the audio unit by removing the four screws.
4. On vehicles without the navigation system, perform the following:
   a. Unfasten the audio unit mounting screws, then remove the audio unit from the vehicle.
5. Installation is the reverse of the removal procedure.

LEGEND

▶ See Figures 54 and 55

1. Disconnect the negative battery cable.
2. Remove the center console.

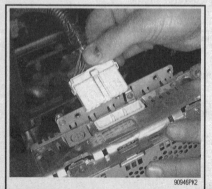

Fig. 46 Detach the wiring the wiring harness from the rear of the radio

90946PK2

Fig. 47 Pull the radio out of the dash as shown

90946PH9

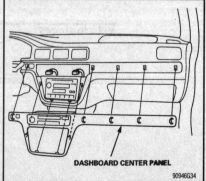

DASHBOARD CENTER PANEL

90946G34

Fig. 48 Exploded view of the center panel—TL

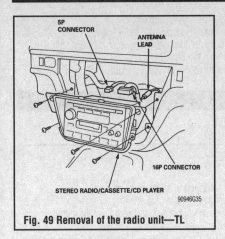

Fig. 49 Removal of the radio unit—TL

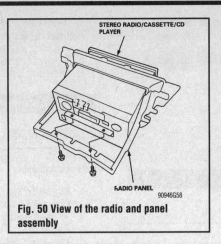

Fig. 50 View of the radio and panel assembly

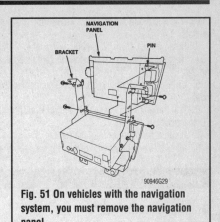

Fig. 51 On vehicles with the navigation system, you must remove the navigation panel

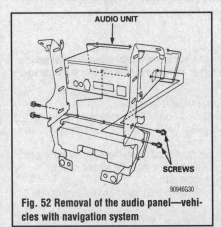

Fig. 52 Removal of the audio panel—vehicles with navigation system

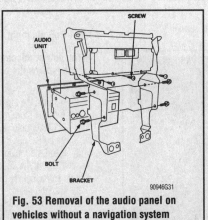

Fig. 53 Removal of the audio panel on vehicles without a navigation system

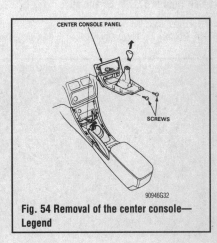

Fig. 54 Removal of the center console—Legend

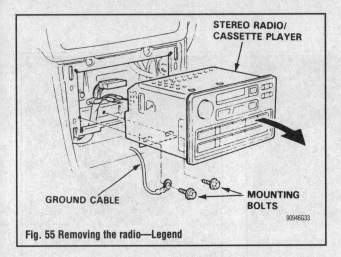

Fig. 55 Removing the radio—Legend

CD Changer

▶ See Figure 56

1. Disconnect the negative battery cable.
2. Obtain access to the CD changer. On most models, the CD

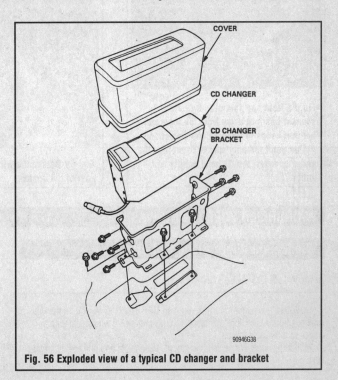

Fig. 56 Exploded view of a typical CD changer and bracket

3. Remove the two mounting bolts and then the ground cable.
4. Pull the radio receiver partially out for access to the wiring.
5. Detach the connectors and the antenna lead, then remove the radio from the vehicle.
6. Installation is the reverse of the removal procedure.

VIGOR

1. Disconnect the negative battery cable.
2. Remove the center control panel.
3. Remove the ashtray.
4. Disconnect the wiring and then remove the antenna.
5. Remove the radio panel assembly.
6. Remove the audio power amplifier by extracting the two screws.
7. Installation is the reverse of the removal procedure.

changer is located in such areas as the trunk, glove box, or the interior console.

3. Remove the CD magazine (the device which actually holds the CD's).

4. Remove all necessary components to gain access to the CD changer's mounts.

5. Unfasten the mounting bolts while supporting the changer with your hands.

6. Pull the unit from the vehicle and remove all wiring from the rear of the CD changer.

7. Remove the changer from the vehicle.

8. Installation is the reverse of the removal procedure.

Speakers

REMOVAL & INSTALLATION

▶ See Figures 57, 58, 59 and 60

1. Disconnect the negative battery cable.

2. Remove any necessary paneling to gain access to the speaker.

Fig. 57 Removing an Acura door mounted speaker

Fig. 58 Note how this old, dry rotted speaker has torn away from the foam rubber that keeps the paper cone suspended. At this point the only cure is to replace the entire speaker; if not sound quality will suffer

Fig. 59 Detach the wiring harness from the rear of the speaker

Fig. 60 Remove the plastic baffle from the speaker

3. Remove the protective mesh grill if applicable.

4. Unfasten the speaker mounting screws.

5. Pull the speaker partially up, then detach the electrical connector.

6. Remove the speaker from the vehicle.

7. Installation is the reverse of the removal procedure.

Power Antenna

REMOVAL & INSTALLATION

Antenna Assembly

1. Remove the trunk panel covering the antenna assembly.

2. Remove the top antenna nut, spacer and bushing.

3. Remove the antenna mounting nut or bolt. Disconnect the wiring.

4. Pull the antenna assembly out of the trunk.

5. Install the components in the reverse order of installation. Be sure to insert the drain tube and tighten the nut to 1.7 ft. lbs. (2.3 Nm).

Mast Replacement

➡The power antenna mast can be replaced if damaged. It is not necessary to replace the entire power antenna assembly if only the mast was damaged.

1. Remove the top antenna nut, spacer and bushing.

2. Turn the radio receiver to the ON position and gently pull the antenna mast out of the motor assembly. Note the direction the teeth were facing as the mast was pulled out.

3. Insert the replacement mast toothed cable into the motor assembly with the teeth facing the direction the old one was. Insert the toothed cable far enough so engagement is felt with the gear.

4. Turn the receiver to the OFF position and gently feed the antenna mast into the motor assembly.

5. Install the bushing, spacer and nut. Tighten the nut to 1.7 ft. lbs. (2.3 Nm).

6. Check the operation of the antenna.

WINDSHIELD WIPERS AND WASHERS

Windshield Wiper Blade and Arm

REMOVAL & INSTALLATION

1. With the wipers on, turn the ignition **OFF** when the wiper is at the mid-wipe position. At the tip of the blade assembly, mark the windshield with a crayon to aid in reassembly.

2. Lift the wiper arm assembly from the windshield and pull the retaining latch out.

3. Lift the wiper arm assembly from the transaxle driveshaft.

4. Disconnect the washer nozzle hose from the end of the wiper arm.

5. If necessary, remove the blade as outlined in Section 1 of this manual.

To install:

6. Connect the washer hose to the end of the wiper arm.

7. Position the wiper arm assembly on the transaxle driveshaft.

8. Push the retaining latch in to lock the wiper arm in position, then carefully lower the wiper arm and blade onto the windshield.

Windshield Wiper Motor

REMOVAL & INSTALLATION

Front

▶ **See Figures 61 thru 68**

1. Disconnect the negative battery cable.
2. Remove the cap nuts and wiper arms.
3. Remove the hood seal.
4. Remove the air scoop by prying it out of the trim clips.

5. Remove the connector from the wiper molding.
6. Remove the mounting bolts.
7. Disconnect and remove the wiper linkage assembly.
8. Remove the wiring harness from the linkage assembly.
9. Separate the wiper linkage and the crank arm at the joint.
10. Unfasten the three mounting bolts that hold the wiper motor to the mount, then remove the wiper motor.
11. Installation is the reverse of the removal procedure.

Rear

1. Disconnect the negative battery cable.
2. Remove the cover, mounting nut, and wiper.

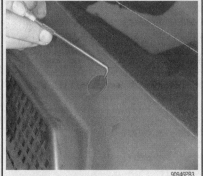

Fig. 61 Matchmark the wiper arm to the shaft. This will allow you to install the arm on the splined shaft in the correct position

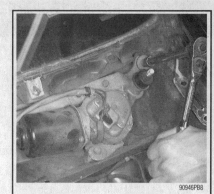

Fig. 62 Once the arm is matchmarked, you can pull of off the shaft

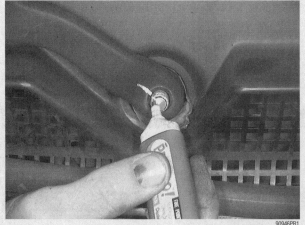

Fig. 63 Use a small prytool to pop up the plastic fasteners

Fig. 64 After removing all of the retainers, pull the air scoop away from the windshield

Fig. 65 Loosen and remove the wiper motor linkage mounting bolts . . .

Fig. 66 . . . then remove the wiper motor and linkage assembly from the vehicle

Fig. 67 Unfasten the wiper motor mounting nuts . . .

Fig. 68 . . . then remove the wiper motor from the linkage assembly

3. Remove the rubber seal.
4. Unfasten the special nut and remove the washer.
5. Remove any trim panels that hinder removal.
6. Detach the wiring connector from the wiper motor.
7. Remove the motor mounting bolts, then remove the motor assembly.
8. Installation is the reverse of the removal procedure.

Intermittent Wiper Relay

The intermittent wiper function is controlled by either a specialized control unit or the integrated control unit. The integrated control unit controls other timed functions as well as the wipers.

The wipers are controlled by a relay located at the top left of the under dash fuse panel. On the Integra, the function is controlled by the integrated control unit located in the fuse and relay panel at the left kick panel.The Legend uses a relay located in the center of the relay panel in the engine compartment. This relay is controlled by the integrated control unit located in the fuse and relay panel at the left kick panel. The Vigor is similar to the Legend, but the intermittent relay is located at the front of the engine compartment.

INSTRUMENTS AND SWITCHES

✳✳ WARNING

Many solid state electrical components utilized in these vehicles can be damaged by Electrostatic Discharge (ESD). Some of these vehicles will display a label informing you that they will be damaged by ESD and some will not have labels, but they may be damaged also. To avoid the possible damage to any of these components, follow the steps outlines in Handling Electrostatic Discharge (ESD) sensitive parts in this section.

Handling Electrostatic Discharge (ESD) Sensitive Parts

▶ See Figure 69

1. Body movement produces an electrostatic charge. To discharge personal static electricity, touch a ground point (metal) on the vehicle. This should be performed any time you:
   - Slide across the vehicle seat
   - Sit down or get up
   - Do any walking
2. Do not touch any exposed terminals on components or connectors with your fingers or any tools.
3. Never use jumper wires, ground a terminal on a component, use test equipment on any component or terminal unless instructed to in a diagnosis or testing procedure. When using test equipment, always connect the ground lead first.
4. If installing a new components, never remove the replacement component from its protective packaging until you are ready to install it.
5. Always touch the component package to ground before opening it.

NOTICE

CONTENTS SENSITIVE
TO
STATIC ELECTRICITY

91036G24

Fig. 69 Electrostatic Discharge (ESD) label

Windshield Washer Pump

REMOVAL & INSTALLATION

1. Disconnect the negative battery cable.
2. Locate and gain access to the water washer reservoir tank and pump.
3. Detach the water motor electrical connector.
4. Place a suitable drain pan under the vehicle. Drain the washer reservoir.
5. Remove the washer reservoir from the vehicle.
6. Remove the washer pump from the reservoir.
7. Disconnect the washer hose from the pump.

To install:

8. Connect the washer hose to the pump.
9. Place the washer pump into the reservoir using a pair of pliers. Make sure the pump is pushed in all the way into the reservoir seal.
10. Install the reservoir tank assembly.
11. Attach the washer motor electrical connector.
12. Refill the windshield washer reservoir.
13. Connect the negative battery cable, then check for proper washer motor operation.

6. Solid state components may also be damaged if they are dropped, bumped, laid near any components that operated electrically such as a TV, radio, or an oscilloscope.

Instrument Cluster

REMOVAL & INSTALLATION

▶ See Figures 70, 71 and 72

Integra

1. Disconnect the negative battery cable.
2. Lower the steering column.
3. Remove the screws.
4. Detach any necessary retaining clips.
5. Remove the instrument cluster as an assembly.
6. Installation is the reverse of the removal procedure.

CL

1. Disconnect the negative battery cable.
2. Lower the steering column.
3. Remove the cruise control master switch.
4. Remove the panel brightness controller.
5. Remove the retaining screws.
6. Detach any necessary clips.
7. Remove the instrument cluster as an assembly.
8. Installation is the reverse of the removal procedure.

RL

1. Disconnect the negative battery cable.
2. Remove the center air vent from the dash.
3. Remove the climate control unit and audio unit as a unit.
4. Remove the dashboard lower cover.
5. Remove the drivers switch trim.
6. Remove the screws and clips.
7. Carefully pull out the instrument panel in the numbered sequence seen in the included art.

Legend

1. Disconnect the negative battery cable.
2. Remove the dashboard lower cover.
3. Remove the instrument cluster.
4. Installation is the reverse of the removal procedure.

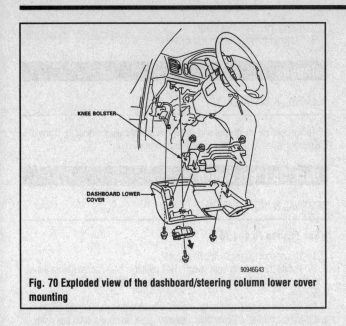

Fig. 70 Exploded view of the dashboard/steering column lower cover mounting

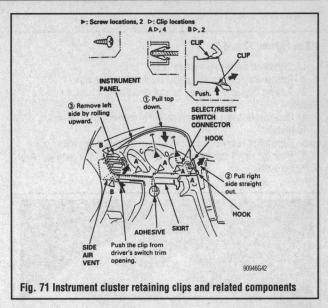

Fig. 71 Instrument cluster retaining clips and related components

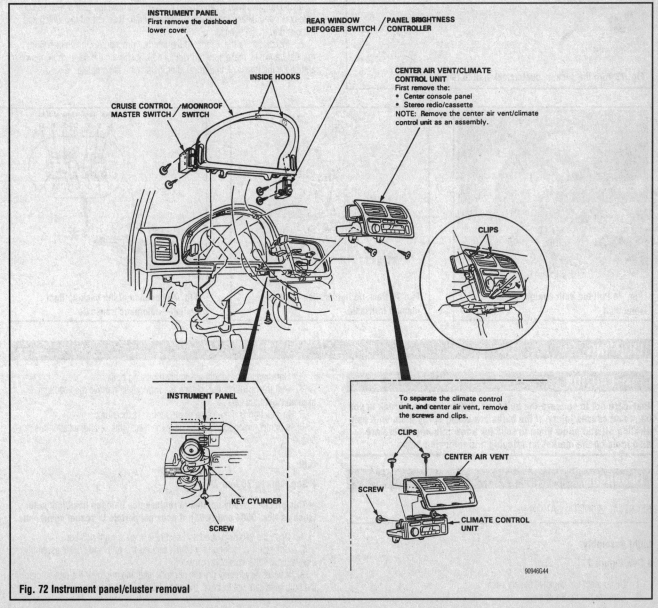

Fig. 72 Instrument panel/cluster removal

BULB REPLACEMENT

▶ **See Figures 73 and 74**

1. Disconnect the negative battery cable.
2. Remove the instrument cluster as outlined in this section.
3. Turn the desired bulb socket counter clockwise to remove it from the cluster.
4. Grasp the bulb and pull it straight out to remove it from the socket.

To install:

5. Place a new bulb into the socket and lightly press it into place.
6. Place the socket into the cluster and turn the socket clockwise to engage it into the cluster.

Fig. 73 Turn the socket counterclockwise to remove it

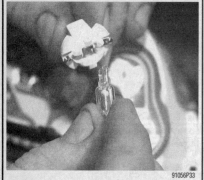

Fig. 74 Pull the bulb straight out to remove it

7. Install the instrument cluster.
8. Connect the negative battery cable.

Gauges

REMOVAL & INSTALLATION

The gauges are an integral part of the instrument cluster assembly. If one of the gauges is faulty, the entire cluster must be replaced.

Back-Up Light Switch

REMOVAL & INSTALLATION

▶ **See Figures 75 and 76**

1. Disconnect the negative battery cable.
2. Locate the back-up light switch. This switch is found screwed into the housing on manual transaxles and under the gear selector on automatic transaxles.
3. Remove the switch from the manual transaxle by detaching the wiring and then unscrewing it. Some fluid loss may occur, so have a drain pan ready.
4. If equipped with an automatic transaxle, remove the gear selector's console cover and detach the wiring from the switch. Then unbolt the switch and remove it from the vehicle.
5. Installation is the reverse of the removal procedure. On vehicles with manual transaxle, make sure to install a new washer on the back-up light switch and check the transaxle fluid level after installation is complete.

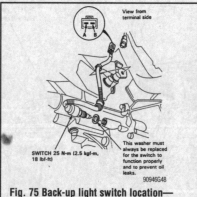

Fig. 75 Back-up light switch location—manual transaxle

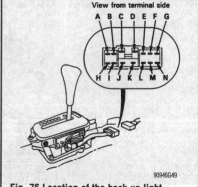

Fig. 76 Location of the back-up light switch—automatic transaxle

LIGHTING

❋❋ CAUTION

Take care not to squeeze the bulbs too tightly, they can break in you hand and causes injury. If the bulbs are stuck, spray them with penetrating oil and allow them to soak for a few minutes. There are also tools on the market for gripping and removing bulbs.

Headlights

REMOVAL & INSTALLATION

Light Assembly

▶ **See Figure 77**

1. Disconnect the negative battery cable.
2. Remove the front bumper.

3. Unfasten the headlight assembly mounting bolts.
4. Pull the headlight out, detach the wiring then remove the headlight assembly from the vehicle.
5. Installation is the reverse of the removal procedure.
6. It is recommended that you have the headlights re-aligned after this procedure.

Bulb

▶ **See Figures 78 and 79**

➡ **This procedure only applies to replaceable halogen headlight bulbs (such as Nos. 9004 and 9005); it does not pertain to sealed beam units.**

1. Open the vehicle's hood and secure it in an upright position.
2. Unfasten the locking ring which secures the bulb and socket assembly, then withdraw the assembly rearward.
3. If necessary, gently pry the socket's retaining clip over the projection on the bulb (use care not to break the clip.) Pull the bulb from the socket.

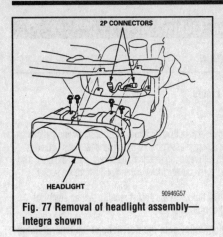

Fig. 77 Removal of headlight assembly—Integra shown

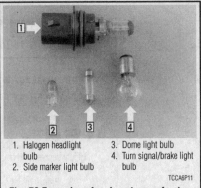

1. Halogen headlight bulb
2. Side marker light bulb
3. Dome light bulb
4. Turn signal/brake light bulb

Fig. 78 Examples of various types of automotive light bulbs

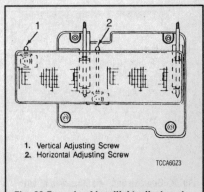

Fig. 79 Carefully pull the halogen headlight bulb from its socket. If applicable, release the retaining clip

To install:

4. Before installing a light bulb into the socket, ensure that all electrical contact surfaces are free of corrosion or dirt.

5. Line up the replacement headlight bulb with the socket. Firmly push the bulb onto the socket until the spring clip latches over the bulb's projection.

✳ WARNING

Do not touch the glass bulb with your fingers. Oil from your fingers can severely shorten the life of the bulb. If necessary, wipe off any dirt or oil from the bulb with rubbing alcohol before completing installation.

6. To ensure that the replacement bulb functions properly, activate the applicable switch to illuminate the bulb which was just replaced. (If this is a combination low and high beam bulb, be sure to check both intensities.) If the replacement light bulb does not illuminate, either it too is faulty or there is a problem in the bulb circuit or switch. Correct if necessary.

7. Position the headlight bulb and secure it with the locking ring.

8. Close the vehicle's hood.

9. If removal of the entire headlight assembly was necessary, it is advised that you have the headlights realigned.

AIMING THE HEADLIGHTS

▶ See Figures 80, 81, 82, 83 and 84

The headlights must be properly aimed to provide the best, safest road illumination. The lights should be checked for proper aim and adjusted as necessary. Certain state and local authorities have requirements for headlight aiming; these should be checked before adjustment is made.

✳ CAUTION

About once a year, when the headlights are replaced or any time front end work is performed on your vehicle, the headlight should

be accurately aimed by a reputable repair shop using the proper equipment. Headlights not properly aimed can make it virtually impossible to see and may blind other drivers on the road, possibly causing an accident. Note that the following procedure is a temporary fix, until you can take your vehicle to a repair shop for a proper adjustment.

Headlight adjustment may be temporarily made using a wall, as described below, or on the rear of another vehicle. When adjusted, the lights should not glare in oncoming car or truck windshields, nor should they illuminate the passenger compartment of vehicles driving in front of you. These adjustments are rough and should always be fine-tuned by a repair shop which is equipped with headlight aiming tools. Improper adjustments may be both dangerous and illegal.

For most of the vehicles covered by this manual, horizontal and vertical aiming of each sealed beam unit is provided by two adjusting screws which move the retaining ring and adjusting plate against the tension of a coil spring. There is no adjustment for focus; this is done during headlight manufacturing.

➡ **Because the composite headlight assembly is bolted into position, no adjustment should be necessary or possible. Some applications, however, may be bolted to an adjuster plate or may be retained by adjusting screws. If so, follow this procedure when adjusting the lights, BUT always have the adjustment checked by a reputable shop.**

Before removing the headlight bulb or disturbing the headlamp in any way, note the current settings in order to ease headlight adjustment upon reassembly. If the high or low beam setting of the old lamp still works, this can be done using the wall of a garage or a building:

1. Park the vehicle on a level surface, with the fuel tank about ½ full and with the vehicle empty of all extra cargo (unless normally carried). The vehicle should be facing a wall which is no less than 6 feet (1.8m) high and 12 feet (3.7m) wide. The front of the vehicle should be about 25 feet from the wall.

2. If aiming is to be performed outdoors, it is advisable to wait until dusk in order to properly see the headlight beams on the wall. If done in a garage, darken the area around the wall as much as possible by closing shades or hanging cloth over the windows.

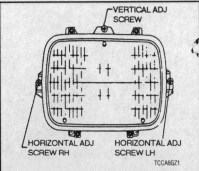

Fig. 80 Location of the aiming screws on most vehicles with sealed beam headlights

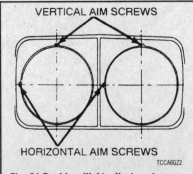

Fig. 81 Dual headlight adjustment screw locations—one side shown here (other side should be mirror image)

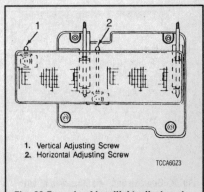

1. Vertical Adjusting Screw
2. Horizontal Adjusting Screw

Fig. 82 Example of headlight adjustment screw location for composite headlamps

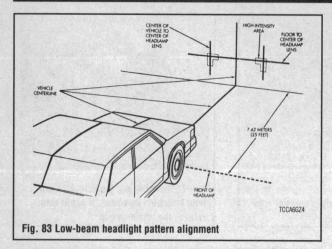

Fig. 83 Low-beam headlight pattern alignment

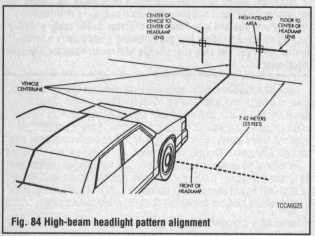

Fig. 84 High-beam headlight pattern alignment

3. Turn the headlights **ON** and mark the wall at the center of each light's low beam, then switch on the brights and mark the center of each light's high beam. A short length of masking tape which is visible from the front of the vehicle may be used. Although marking all four positions is advisable, marking one position from each light should be sufficient.

4. If neither beam on one side is working, and if another like-sized vehicle is available, park the second one in the exact spot where the vehicle was and mark the beams using the same-side light. Then switch the vehicles so the one to be aimed is back in the original spot. It must be parked no closer to or farther away from the wall than the second vehicle.

5. Perform any necessary repairs, but make sure the vehicle is not moved, or is returned to the exact spot from which the lights were marked. Turn the headlights **ON** and adjust the beams to match the marks on the wall.

6. Have the headlight adjustment checked as soon as possible by a reputable repair shop.

Signal and Marker Lights

REMOVAL & INSTALLATION

Turn Signal and Brake Lights

▶ **See Figure 85**

1. Depending on the vehicle and bulb application, either unscrew and remove the lens or disengage the bulb and socket assembly from the rear of the lens housing.

2. To remove a light bulb with retaining pins from its socket, grasp the bulb, then gently depress and twist it 1/8 turn counterclockwise, and pull it from the socket.

To install:

3. Before installing a light bulb into the socket, ensure that all electrical contact surfaces are free of corrosion or dirt.

➡**Before installing the light bulb, note the positions of the two retaining pins on the bulb. They will likely be at different heights on the bulb, to ensure that the bulb is installed correctly. If, when installing the bulb, it does not turn easily, do not force it. Remove the bulb and rotate it 180 degrees from its former position, then reinsert it into the bulb socket.**

4. Insert the light bulb into the socket and, while depressing the bulb, twist it 1/8 turn clockwise until the two pins on the light bulb are properly engaged in the socket.

5. To ensure that the replacement bulb functions properly, activate the applicable switch to illuminate the bulb which was just replaced. If the replacement light bulb does not illuminate, either it too is faulty or there is a problem in the bulb circuit or switch. Correct if necessary.

6. If applicable, install the socket and bulb assembly into the rear of the lens housing; otherwise, install the lens over the bulb.

Side Marker Light

▶ **See Figure 86**

1. Disengage the bulb and socket assembly from the lens housing.

2. Gently grasp the light bulb and pull it straight out of the socket.

To install:

3. Before installing the light bulb into the socket, ensure that all electrical contact surfaces are free of corrosion or dirt.

4. Line up the base of the light bulb with the socket, then insert the light bulb into the socket until it is fully seated.

5. To ensure that the replacement bulb functions properly, activate the applicable switch to illuminate the bulb which was just replaced. If the replacement light bulb does not illuminate, either it too is faulty or there is a problem in the bulb circuit or switch. Correct as necessary.

6. Install the socket and bulb assembly into the lens housing.

Dome Light

▶ **See Figure 87**

1. Using a small prytool, carefully remove the cover lens from the lamp assembly.

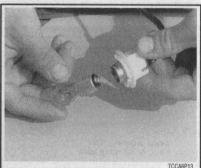

Fig. 85 Depress and twist this type of bulb counterclockwise, then pull the bulb straight from its socket

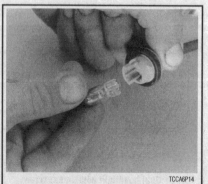

Fig. 86 Simply pull this side marker light bulb straight from its socket

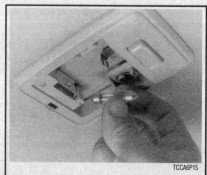

Fig. 87 Disengage the spring clip which retains one tapered end of this dome light bulb, then withdraw the bulb

2. Remove the bulb from its retaining clip contacts. If the bulb has tapered ends, gently depress the spring clip/metal contact and disengage the light bulb, then pull it free of the two metal contacts.

To install:

3. Before installing the light bulb into the metal contacts, ensure that all electrical conducting surfaces are free of corrosion or dirt.

4. Position the bulb between the two metal contacts. If the contacts have small holes, be sure that the tapered ends of the bulb are situated in them.

5. To ensure that the replacement bulb functions properly, activate the applicable switch to illuminate the bulb which was just replaced. If the replacement light bulb does not illuminate, either it is faulty or there is a problem in the bulb circuit or switch. Correct as necessary.

6. Install the cover lens until its retaining tabs are properly engaged.

High Mount Brake Light

TAILGATE SPOILER

▶ See Figure 88

1. Disconnect the negative battery cable.
2. Remove the four screws.
3. Pull the high mount brake light away from the spoiler.
4. Detach the wiring connectors, then remove the high mount brake light.
5. Installation is the reverse of the removal procedure.

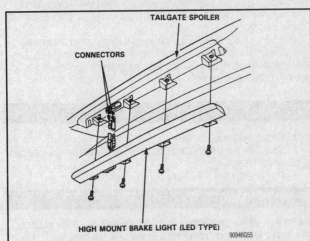

Fig. 88 Exploded view of the rear deck brake light—Light Emitting Diode (L.E.D.) style

DECK MOUNTED

▶ See Figure 89

1. Disconnect the negative battery cable.
2. Remove the two clips and the cover.
3. Unfasten the hold down nuts.
4. Remove the high mount brake light.
5. Detach the wiring connector.
6. Clean the window glass before installing.
7. Installation is the reverse of the removal procedure.

Cargo Area Light

1. Disconnect the negative battery cable.
2. Pry the lens out of its housing.
3. Carefully pry the light bulb out of its housing.
4. Clean the window glass before installing.
5. Installation is the reverse of the removal procedure.

License Plate Lights

1. Disconnect the negative battery cable.
2. Remove the attaching screws.
3. Pull out the license plate bulbs.

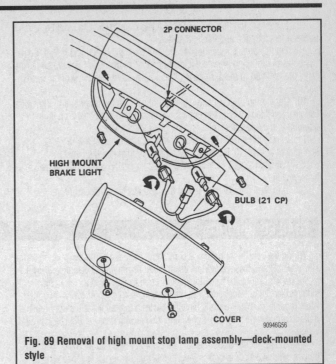

Fig. 89 Removal of high mount stop lamp assembly—deck-mounted style

4. Turn the bulb socket 45°to remove it from the housing.
5. Installation is the reverse of the removal procedure.

Fog/Driving Lights

REMOVAL & INSTALLATION

1. Disconnect the negative battery cable.
2. Remove the mounting bolts.
3. Remove the fog light assembly.
4. Remove the wiring connector.
5. Install the fog light in the reverse order of removal.
6. After replacing the fog light, adjust the lights to local requirements.

INSTALLING AFTERMARKET AUXILIARY LIGHTS

➡Before installing any aftermarket light, make sure it is legal for road use. Most acceptable lights will have a DOT approval number. Also check your local and regional inspection regulations. In certain areas, aftermarket lights must be installed in a particular manner or they may not be legal for inspection.

1. Disconnect the negative battery cable.
2. Unpack the contents of the light kit purchased. Place the contents in an open space where you can easily retrieve a piece if needed.
3. Choose a location for the lights. If you are installing fog lights, below the bumper and apart from each other is desirable. Most fog lights are mounted below or very close to the headlights. If you are installing driving lights, above the bumper and close together is desirable. Most driving lights are mounted between the headlights.
4. Drill the needed hole(s) to mount the light. Install the light, and secure using the supplied retainer nut and washer. Tighten the light mounting hardware, but not the light adjustment nut or bolt.
5. Install the relay that came with the light kit in the engine compartment, in a rigid area, such as a fender. Always install the relay with the terminals facing down. This will prevent water from entering the relay assembly.
6. Using the wire supplied, locate the ground terminal on the relay, and connect a length of wire from this terminal to a good ground source. You can drill a hole and screw this wire to an inside piece of metal; just scrape the paint away from the hole to ensure a good connection.
7. Locate the light terminal on the relay; and attach a length of wire between this terminal and the fog/driving lamps.

8. Locate the ignition terminal on the relay, and connect a length of wire between this terminal and the light switch.

9. Find a suitable mounting location for the light switch and install. Some examples of mounting areas are a location close to the main light switch, auxiliary light position in the dash panel, if equipped, or in the center of the dash panel.

10. Depending on local and regional regulations, the other end of the switch can be connected to a constant power source such as the battery, an ignition opening in the fuse panel, or a parking or headlight wire.

11. Locate the power terminal on the relay, and connect a wire with an in-line fuse of at least 10 amperes between the terminal and the battery.

12. With all the wires connected and tied up neatly, connect the negative battery cable.

13. Turn the lights ON and adjust the light pattern, if necessary.

AIMING

1. Park the vehicle on level ground, so it is perpendicular to and, facing a flat wall about 25 ft. (7.6m) away.

2. Remove any stone shields, if equipped, and switch ON the lights.

3. Loosen the mounting hardware of the lights so you can aim them as follows:

   a. The horizontal distance between the light beams on the wall should be the same as between the lights themselves.

   b. The vertical height of the light beams above the ground should be 4 in. (10cm) less than the distance between the ground and the center of the lamp lenses for fog lights. For driving lights, the vertical height should be even with the distance between the ground and the center of the lamp.

4. Tighten the mounting hardware.

5. Test to make sure the lights work correctly, and the light pattern is even.

TRAILER WIRING

Wiring the vehicle for towing is fairly easy. There are a number of good wiring kits available and these should be used, rather than trying to design your own.

All trailers will need brake lights and turn signals as well as tail lights and side marker lights. Most areas require extra marker lights for overwide trailers. Also, most areas have recently required back-up lights for trailers, and most trailer manufacturers have been building trailers with back-up lights for several years.

Additionally, some Class I, most Class II and just about all Class III and IV trailers will have electric brakes. Add to this number an accessories wire, to operate trailer internal equipment or to charge the trailer's battery, and you can have as many as seven wires in the harness.

Determine the equipment on your trailer and buy the wiring kit necessary. The kit will contain all the wires needed, plus a plug adapter set which includes the female plug, mounted on the bumper or hitch, and the male plug, wired into, or plugged into the trailer harness.

When installing the kit, follow the manufacturer's instructions. The color coding of the wires is usually standard throughout the industry. One point to note: some domestic vehicles, and most imported vehicles, have separate turn signals. On most domestic vehicles, the brake lights and rear turn signals operate with the same bulb. For those vehicles without separate turn signals, you can purchase an isolation unit so that the brake lights won't blink whenever the turn signals are operated.

One, final point, the best kits are those with a spring loaded cover on the vehicle mounted socket. This cover prevents dirt and moisture from corroding the terminals. Never let the vehicle socket hang loosely; always mount it securely to the bumper or hitch.

CIRCUIT PROTECTION

Fuses

REPLACEMENT

♦ **See Figures 90 thru 94**

Fuses are located either in the engine compartment or passenger compartment fuse and relay panels. If a fuse blows, a single component or single circuit will not function properly. Excessive current draw is what causes a fuse to blow. Observing the condition of the fuse will provide insight as to what caused this to occur.

A fuse with signs of burns, melting of the plastic shell, or little to no trace of the wire that once served as the conductor indicates that a direct short to ground exists.

1. Remove the fuse or relay box cover.
2. Inspect the fuses to determine which is faulty.

3. Unplug and discard the fuse.
4. Inspect the box terminals and clean if corroded. If any terminals are damaged, replace the terminals.
5. Plug in a new fuse of the same amperage rating.

✱✱ WARNING

Never exceed the amperage rating of a blown fuse. If the replacement fuse also blows, check for a problem in the circuit.

6. Check for proper operation of the affected component or circuit.

Maxi-Fuses (Fusible Links)

Maxi-fuses are located in the engine compartment relay box. If a maxi-fuse blows, an entire circuit or several circuits will not function properly.

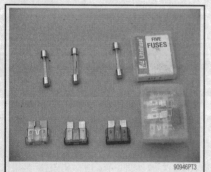

90946PT3

Fig. 90 You can purchase an inexpensive kit, such as this one, that includes a variety of fuses

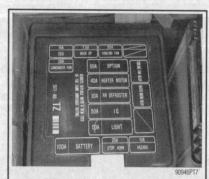

90946PT7

Fig. 91 The fuse box cover usually has a fuse identification label, so you can tell which fuses go to which components

90946PU9

Fig. 92 Push the fuse box cover retaining clip in to release it . . .

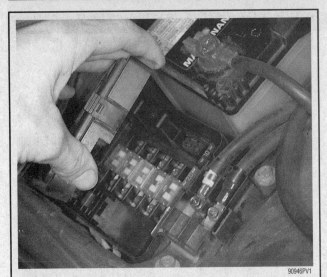

Fig. 93 . . . then lift the cover off for access to the fuses

Fig. 94 To replace a fuse, simply pull it straight out, and replace with a new one of the same amperage rating

REPLACEMENT

1. Remove the fuse and relay box cover.
2. Inspect the fusible links to determine which is faulty.
3. Unplug and discard the fusible link.
4. Inspect the box terminals and clean if corroded. If any terminals are damaged, replace the terminals.
5. Plug in a new fusible link of the same amperage rating.

✳✳ WARNING

Never exceed the amperage rating of a blown maxi-fuse. If the replacement fuse also blows, check for a problem in the circuit(s).

6. Check for proper operation of the affected circuit(s).

Circuit Breakers

RESETTING AND/OR REPLACEMENT

Circuit breakers are located inside the fuse panel. They are automatically reset when the problem corrects itself, is repaired, or the circuit cools down to allow operation again.

Fusible Link

▶ **See Figure 95**

The fuse link is a short length of wire, integral with the engine compartment wiring harness and should not be confused with standard wire. The fusible link wire gauge is smaller than the circuit which it protects. Under no circumstances should a fuse link replacement repair be made using a length of standard wire cut from bulk stock or from another wiring harness.

Fusible link wire is covered with a special thick, non-flammable insulation. An overload condition causes the insulation to blister. If the overall condition continues, the wire will melt. To check a fusible link, look for blistering insulation. If the insulation is okay, pull gently on the wire. If the fusible link stretches, the wire has melted.

Fusible links are often identified by the color coding of the insulation. Refer to the accompanying illustration for wire link size and color.

FUSIBLE LINK COLOR CODING	
WIRE LINK SIZE	**INSULATION COLOR**
20 GA	Blue
18 GA	Brown or Red
16 GA	Black or Orange
14 GA	Green
12 GA	Gray

Fig. 95 Common fusible link color coding

Flashers

REPLACEMENT

Turn Signal Flasher/Hazard Warning Relay

1. Disconnect the negative battery cable.
2. Grasp and pull the flasher from the connector located near the top of the steering column.
3. Inspect the socket for corrosion or any other signs of a bad contact.

To install:

4. Install a new flasher in the connector.
5. Install the knee bolster panel.
6. Connect the negative battery cable.

WIRING DIAGRAMS

INDEX OF WIRING DIAGRAMS

90946W01A

90946W01B

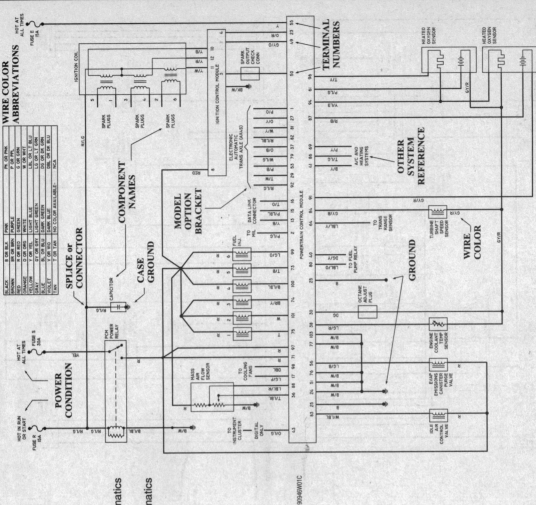

DIAGRAM 1

SAMPLE DIAGRAM: HOW TO READ & INTERPRET WIRING DIAGRAMS

DIAGRAM 58   1997-00 CL Parking/Marker Lights, Fuel Pump Chassis Schematics

DIAGRAM 59   1997-00 CL Turn/Hazard Lights Chassis Schematic

DIAGRAM 60   1997-00 CL Stop Lights, Back-up Lights Chassis Schematics

DIAGRAM 61   1997-00 CL Windsheild Wiper/Washer Chassis Schematics

DIAGRAM 62   1994 Vigor/1995-98 2.5TL Starting, Charging, Horns Chassis Schematics

DIAGRAM 63   1994 Vigor/1995-98 2.5TL Cooling Fans, Fuel Pump Chassis Schematics

DIAGRAM 64   1994 Vigor/1995-98 2.5TL Headlights Chassis Schematics

DIAGRAM 65   1994 Vigor Parking/Marker Lights Chassis Schematics

DIAGRAM 66   1995-98 2.5TL Parking/Marker Lights Chassis Schematic

DIAGRAM 67   1994 Vigor/1995-98 2.5TL Turn/Hazard Lights, Back-up Lights, Stop Lights Chassis Schematics

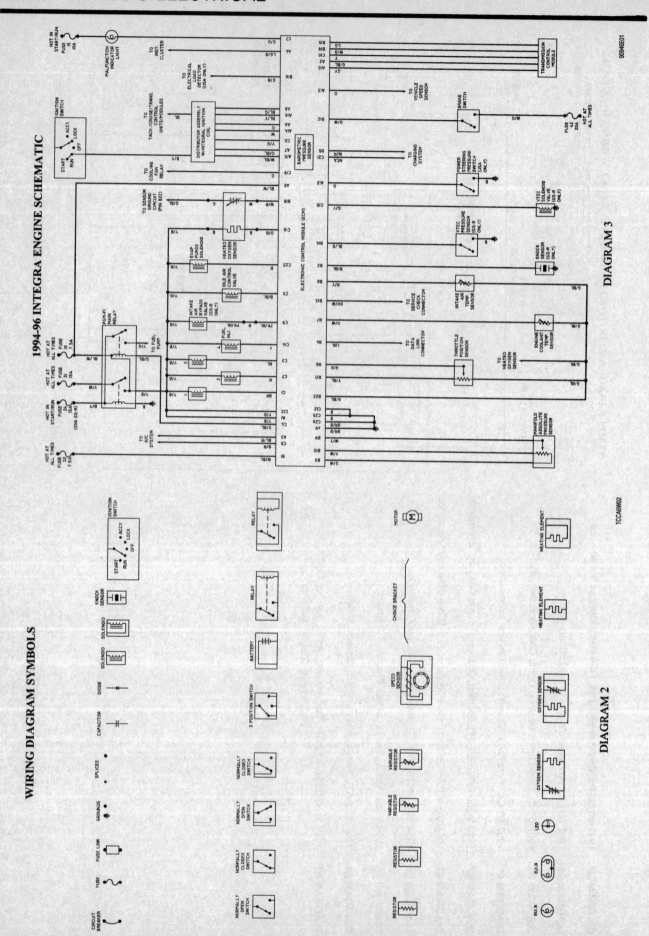

1994-96 INTEGRA ENGINE SCHEMATIC

DIAGRAM 3

DIAGRAM 2

WIRING DIAGRAM SYMBOLS

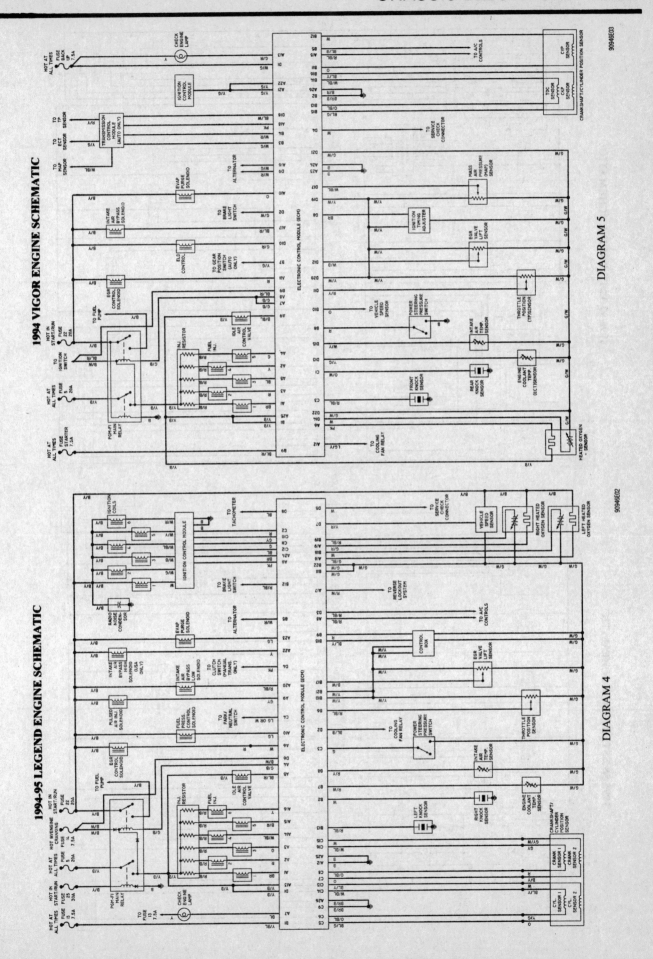

1994 VIGOR ENGINE SCHEMATIC

DIAGRAM 5

1994-95 LEGEND ENGINE SCHEMATIC

DIAGRAM 4

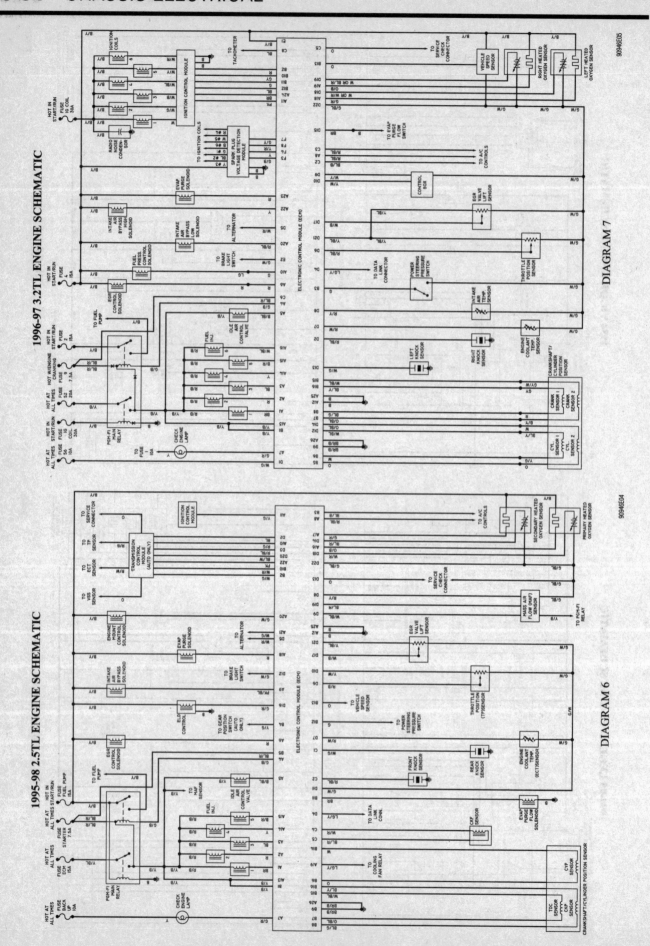

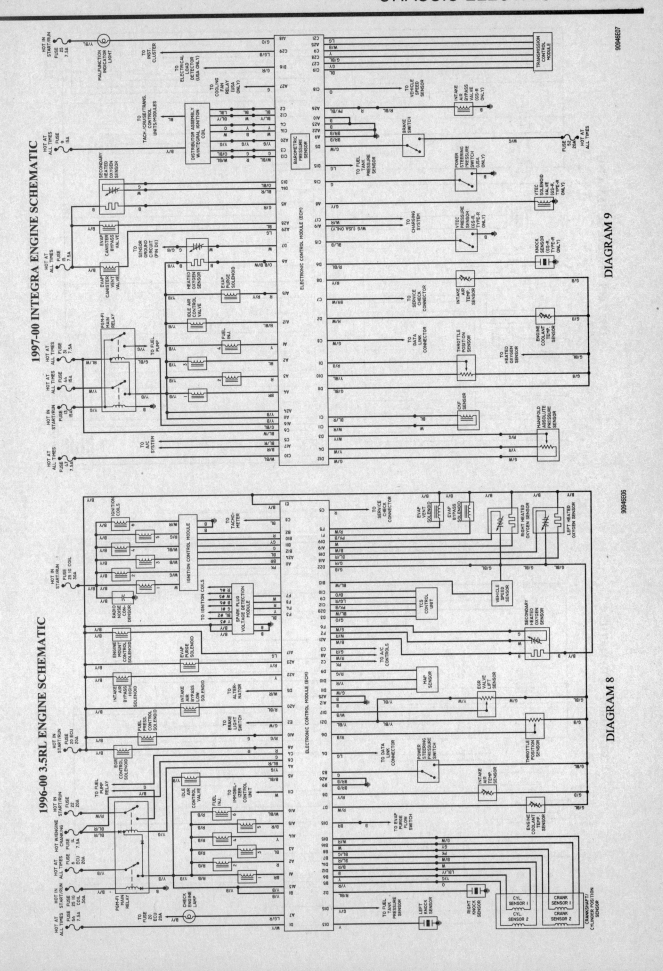

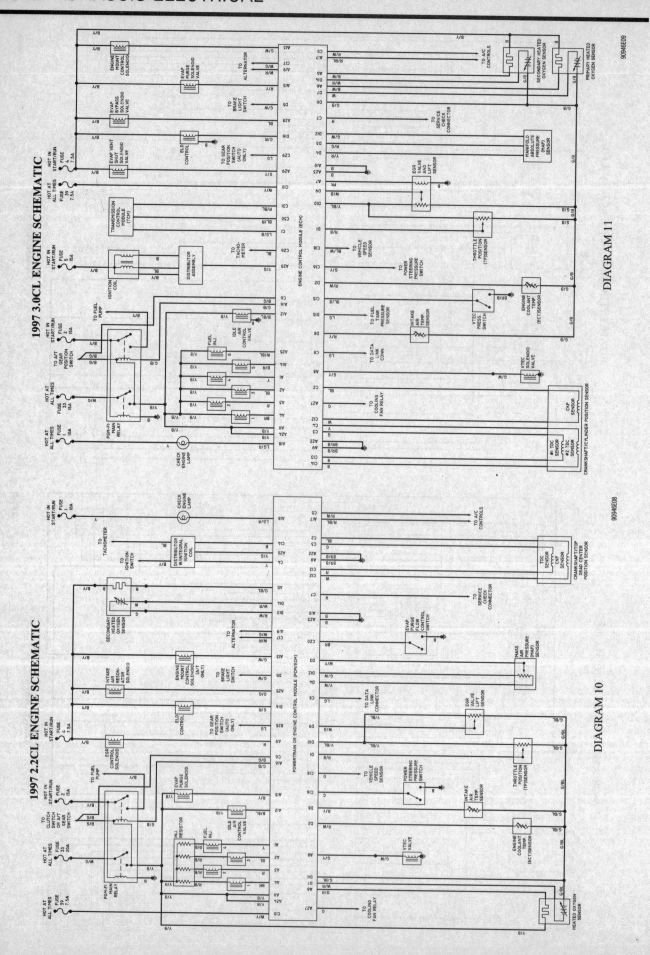

1997 3.0CL ENGINE SCHEMATIC

DIAGRAM 11

1997 2.2CL ENGINE SCHEMATIC

DIAGRAM 10

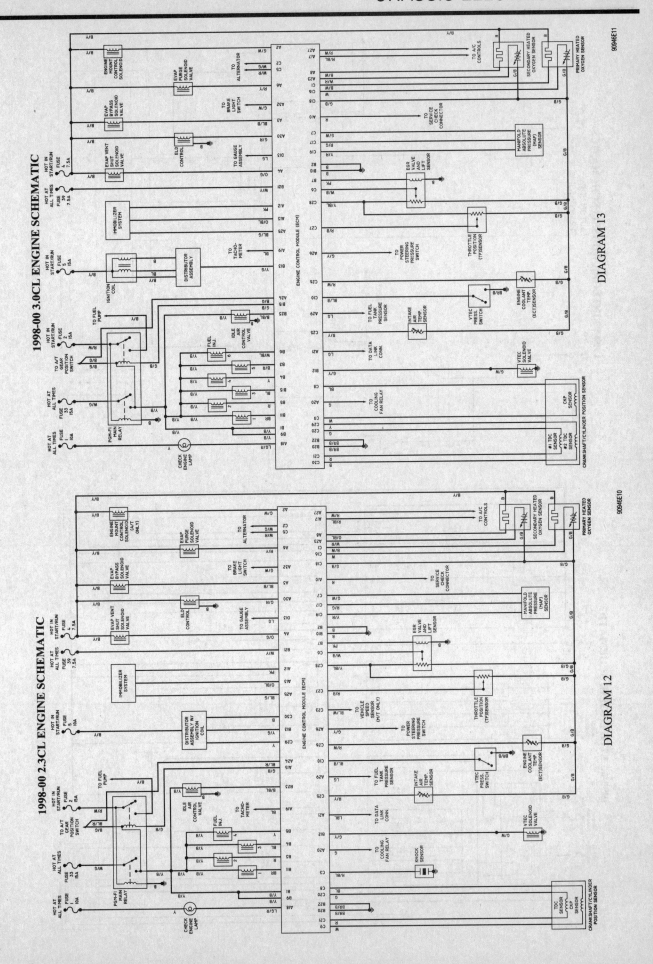

1998-00 3.0CL ENGINE SCHEMATIC

DIAGRAM 13

1998-00 2.3CL ENGINE SCHEMATIC

DIAGRAM 12

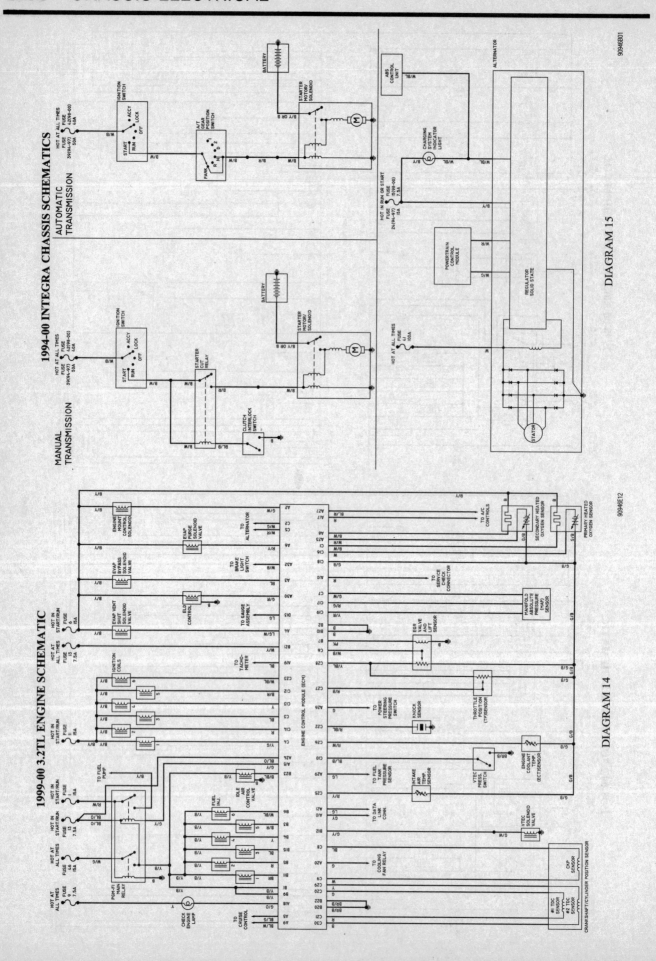

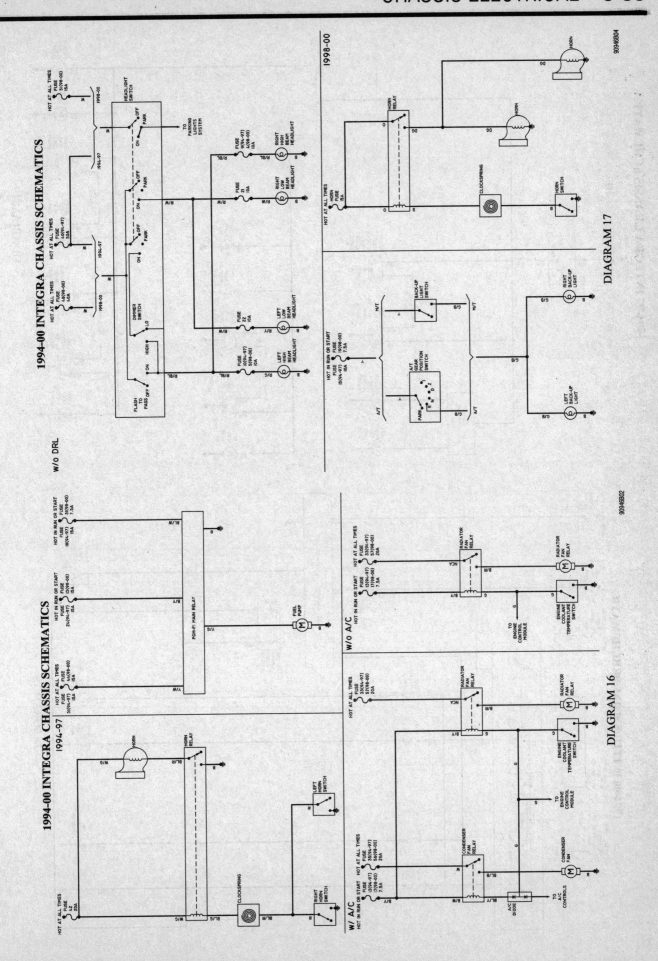

1994-00 INTEGRA CHASSIS SCHEMATICS

W/o DRL

1994-00 INTEGRA CHASSIS SCHEMATICS

1994-97

W/o A/C

W/ A/C

DIAGRAM 17

DIAGRAM 16

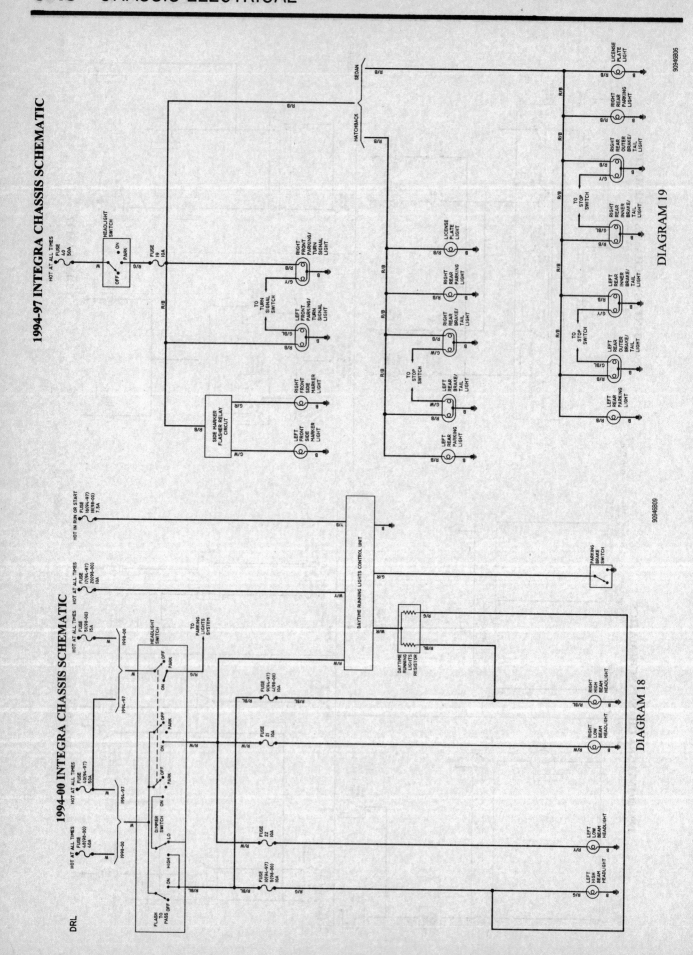

1994-97 INTEGRA CHASSIS SCHEMATIC

DIAGRAM 19

1994-00 INTEGRA CHASSIS SCHEMATIC

DIAGRAM 18

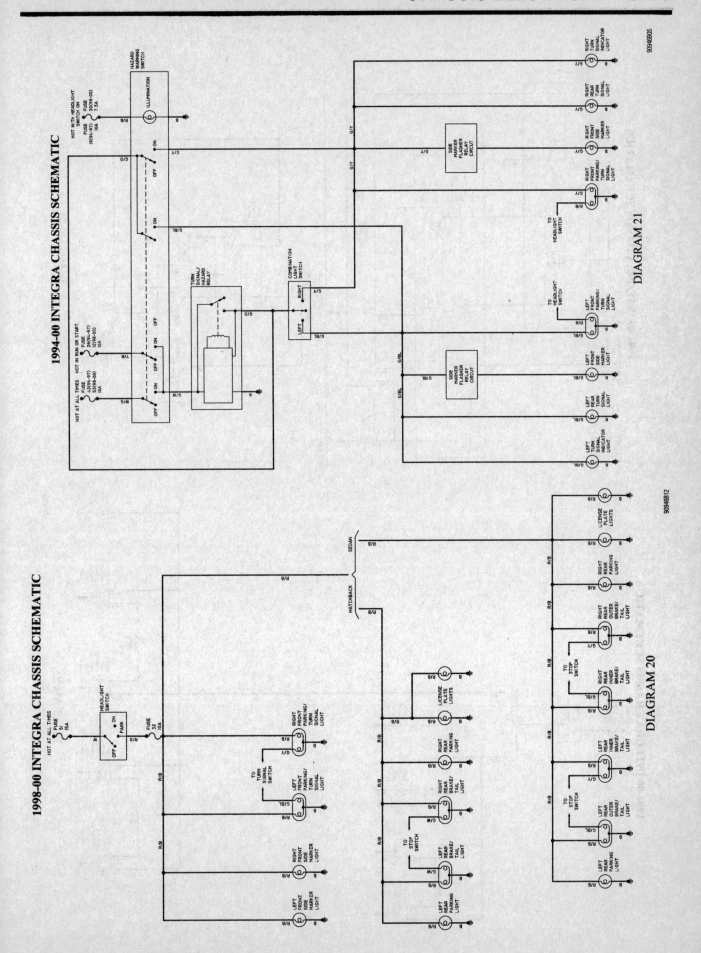

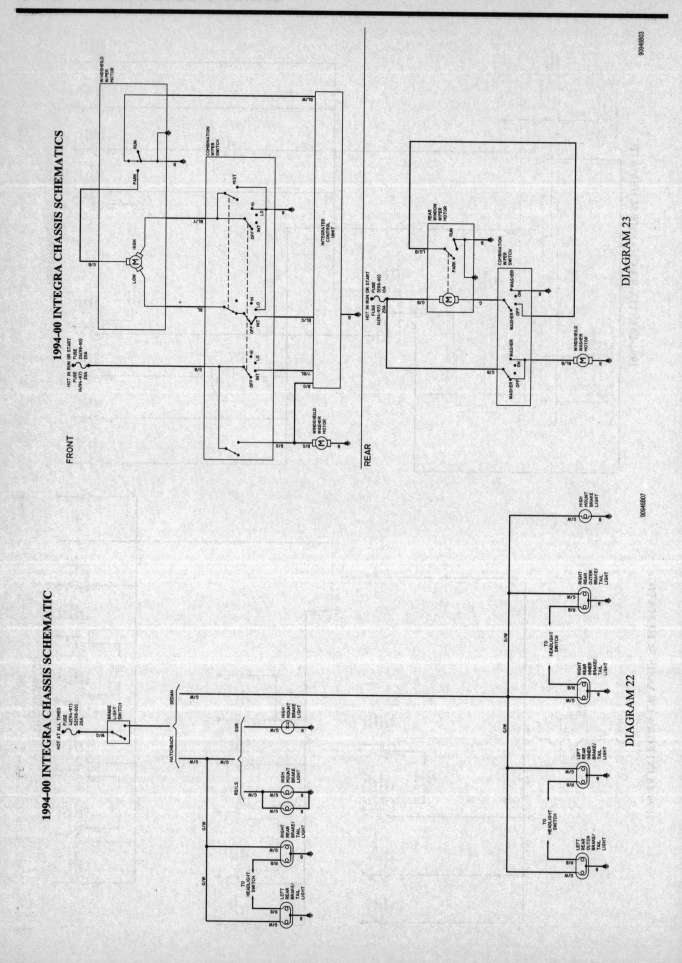

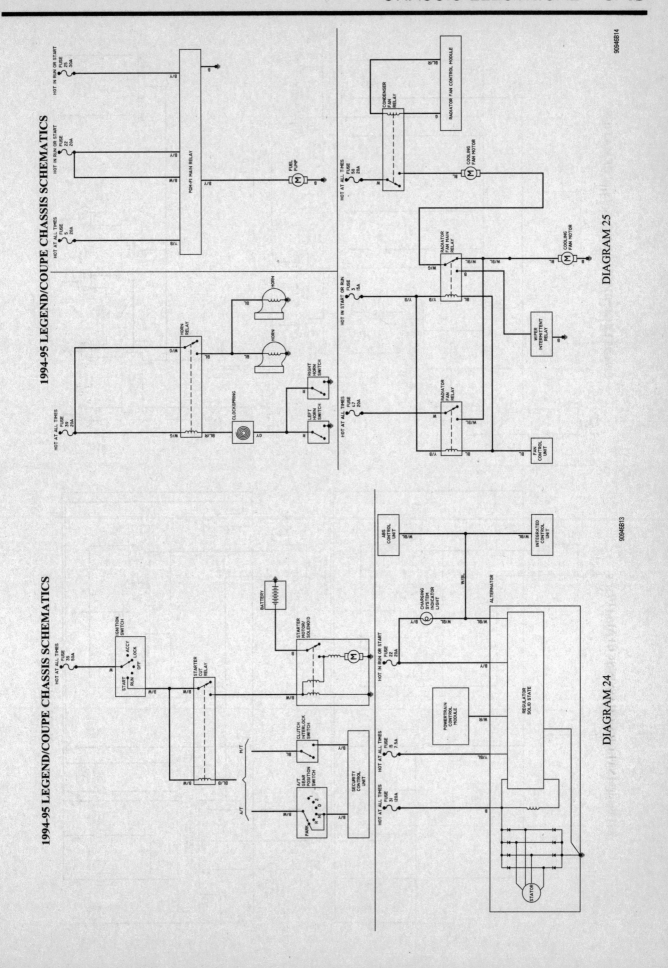

1994-95 LEGEND/COUPE CHASSIS SCHEMATICS

DIAGRAM 25

1994-95 LEGEND/COUPE CHASSIS SCHEMATICS

DIAGRAM 24

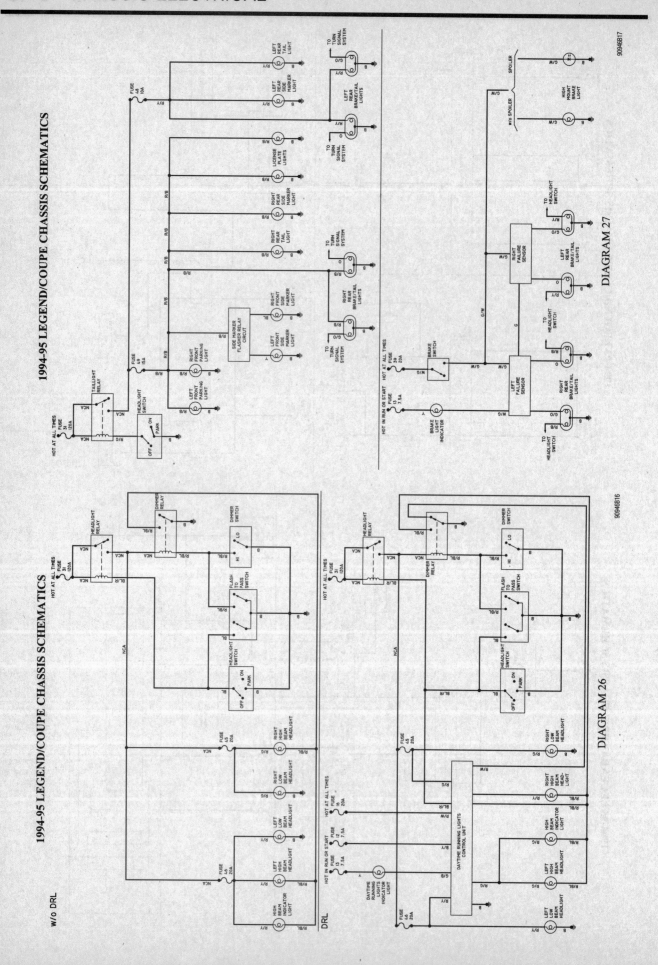

1994-95 LEGEND/COUPE CHASSIS SCHEMATICS

DIAGRAM 27

DIAGRAM 26

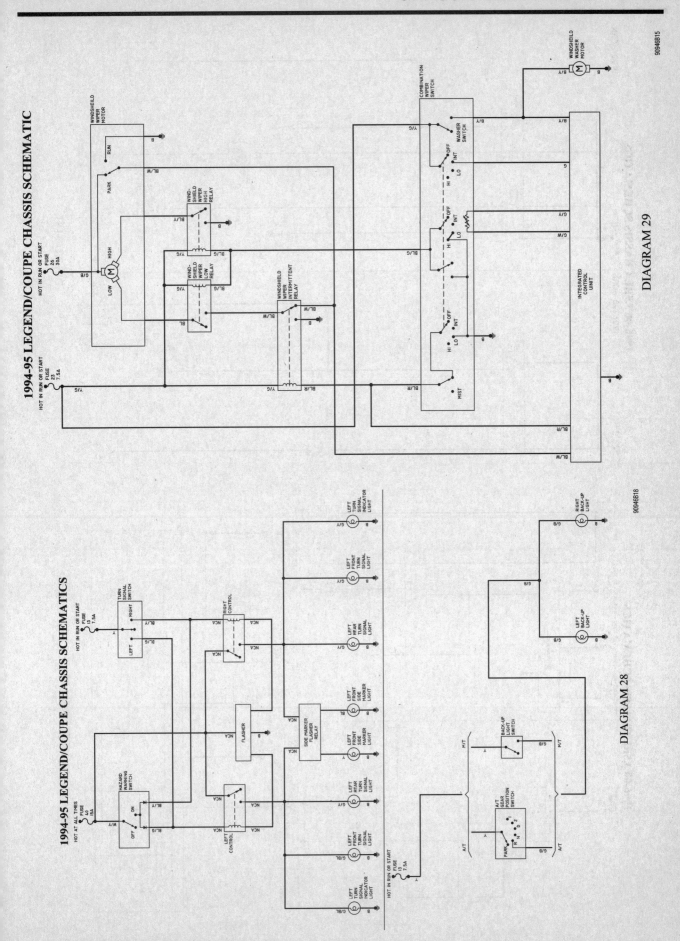

1994-95 LEGEND/COUPE CHASSIS SCHEMATIC

DIAGRAM 29

1994-95 LEGEND/COUPE CHASSIS SCHEMATICS

DIAGRAM 28

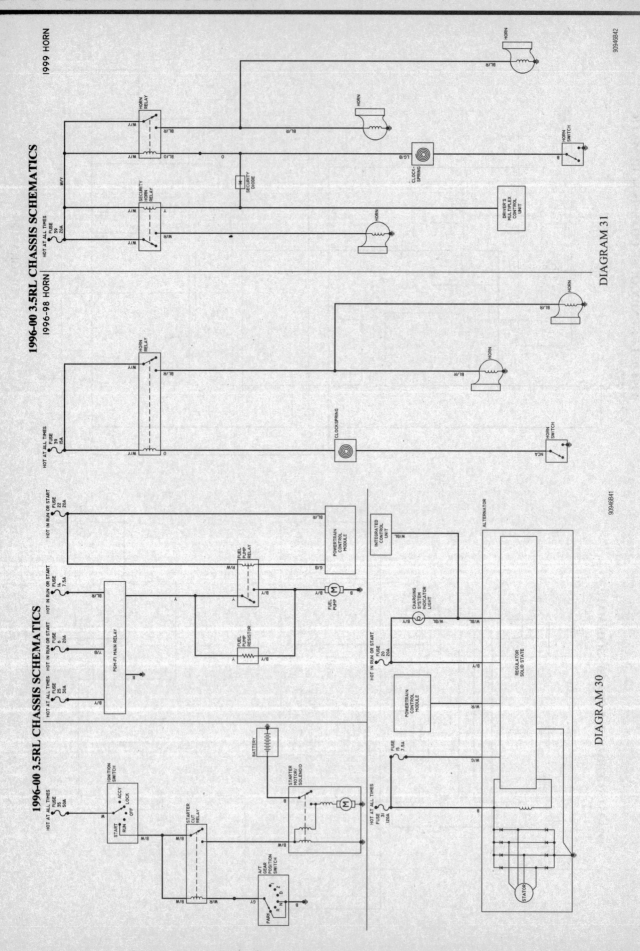

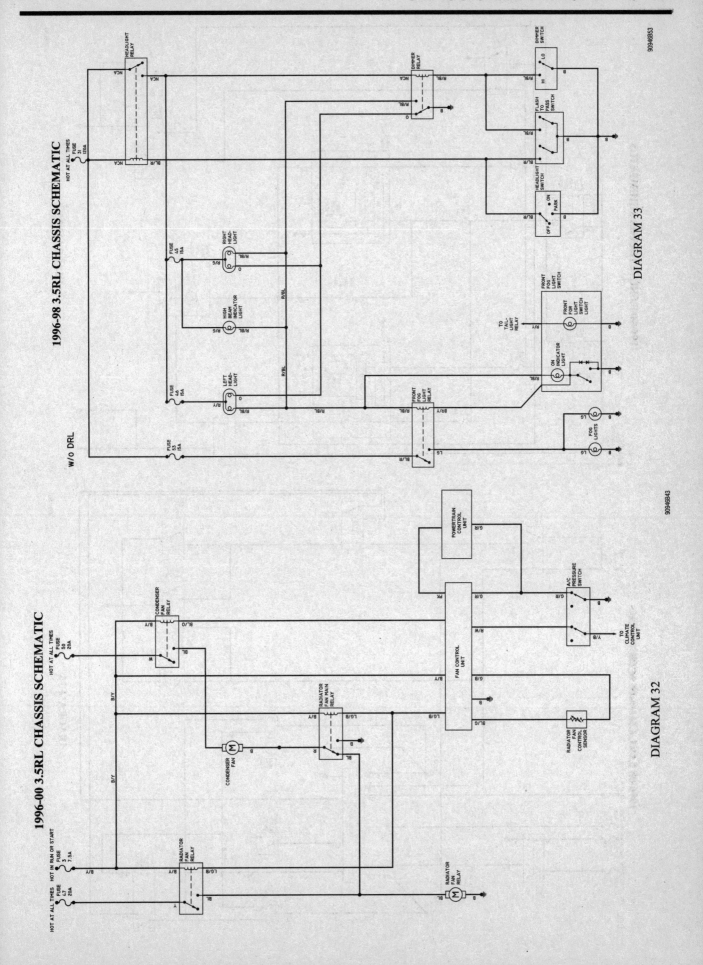

1996-98 3.5RL CHASSIS SCHEMATIC

DIAGRAM 33

1996-00 3.5RL CHASSIS SCHEMATIC

DIAGRAM 32

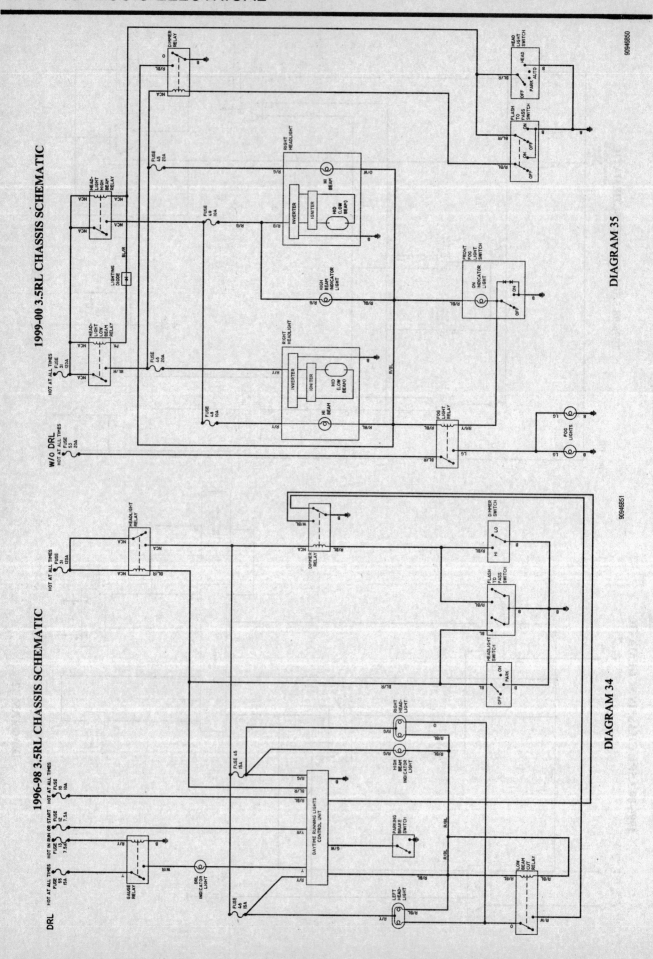

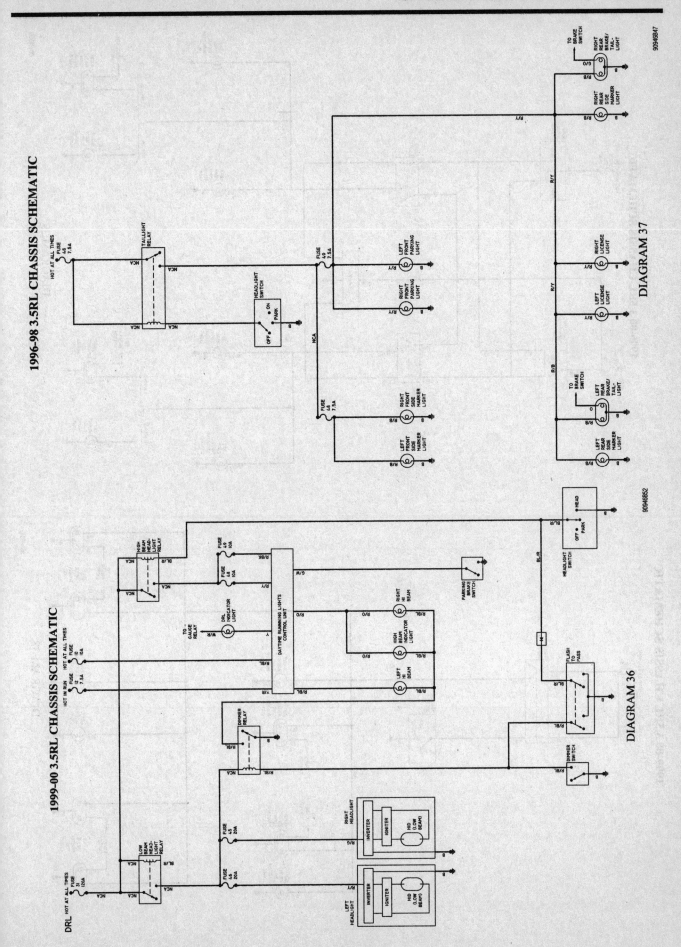

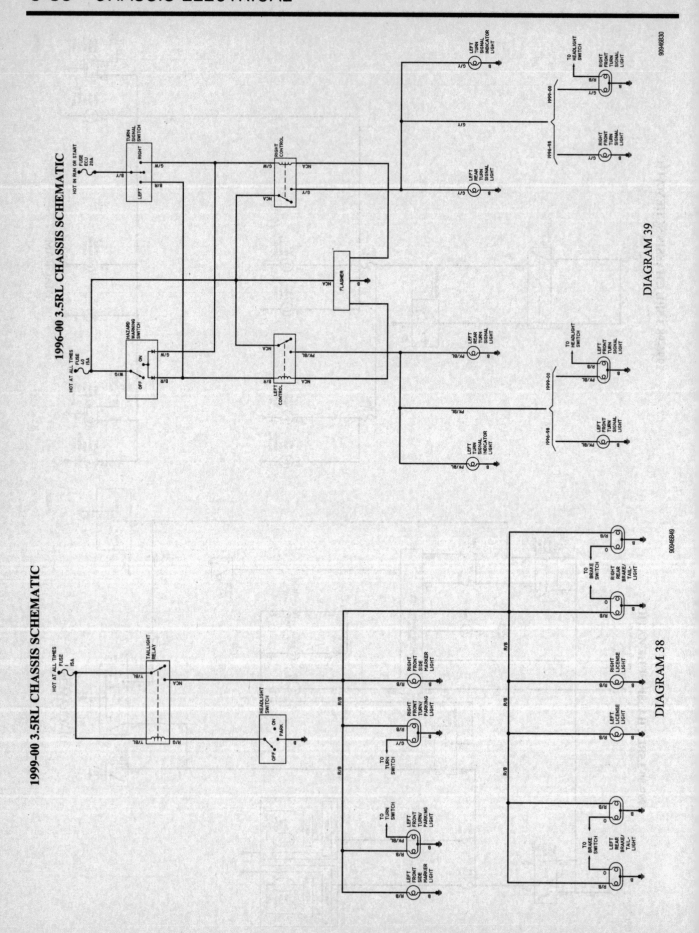

1996-00 3.5RL CHASSIS SCHEMATIC

DIAGRAM 39

1999-00 3.5RL CHASSIS SCHEMATIC

DIAGRAM 38

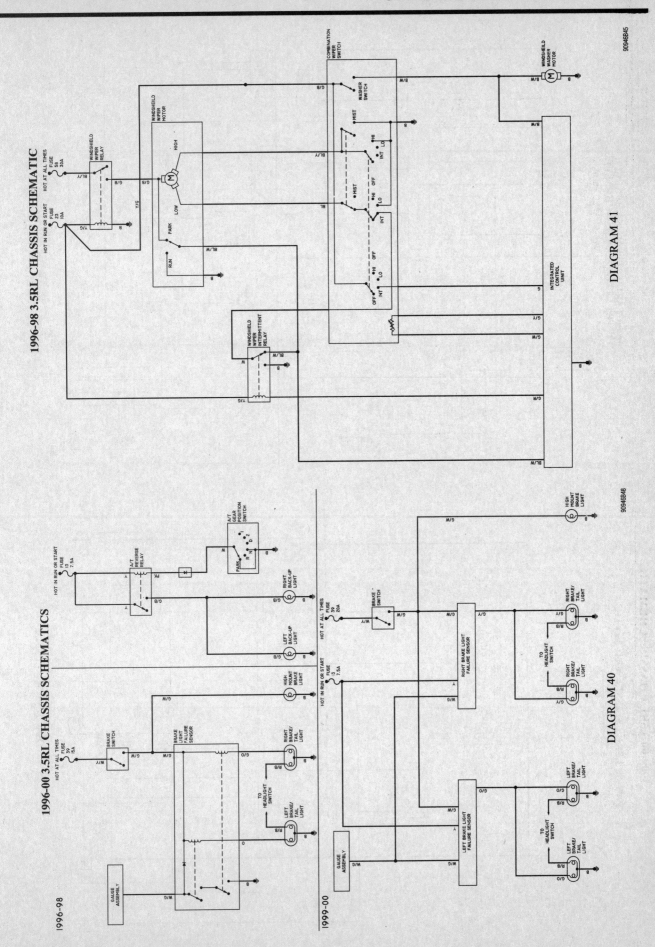

1996-98 3.5RL CHASSIS SCHEMATIC

DIAGRAM 41

1996-00 3.5RL CHASSIS SCHEMATICS

DIAGRAM 40

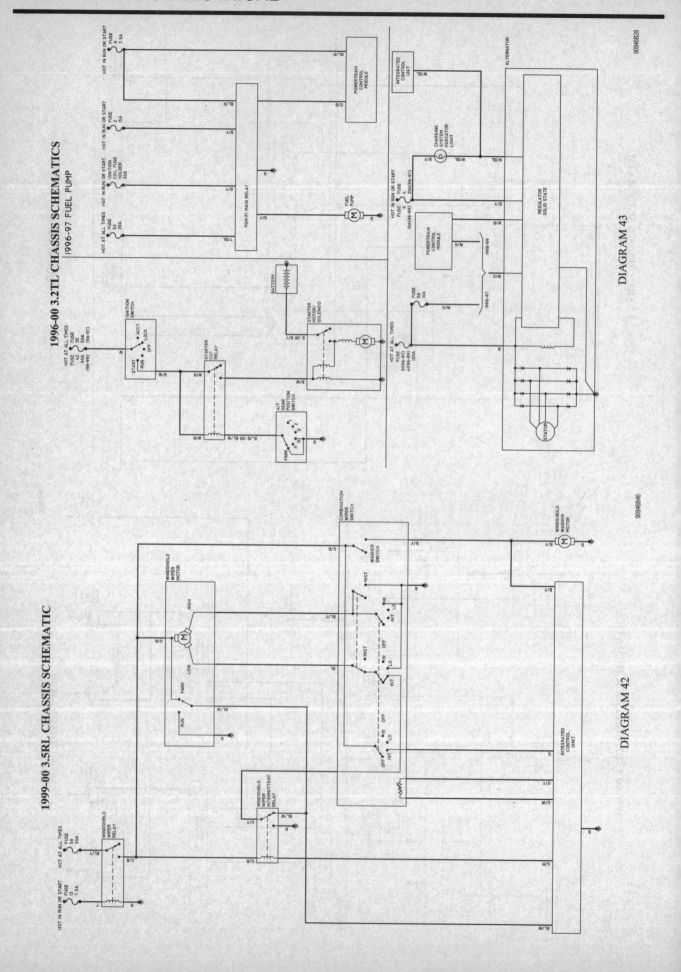

1996-00 3.2TL CHASSIS SCHEMATICS
|1996-97 FUEL PUMP

DIAGRAM 43

1999-00 3.5RL CHASSIS SCHEMATIC

DIAGRAM 42

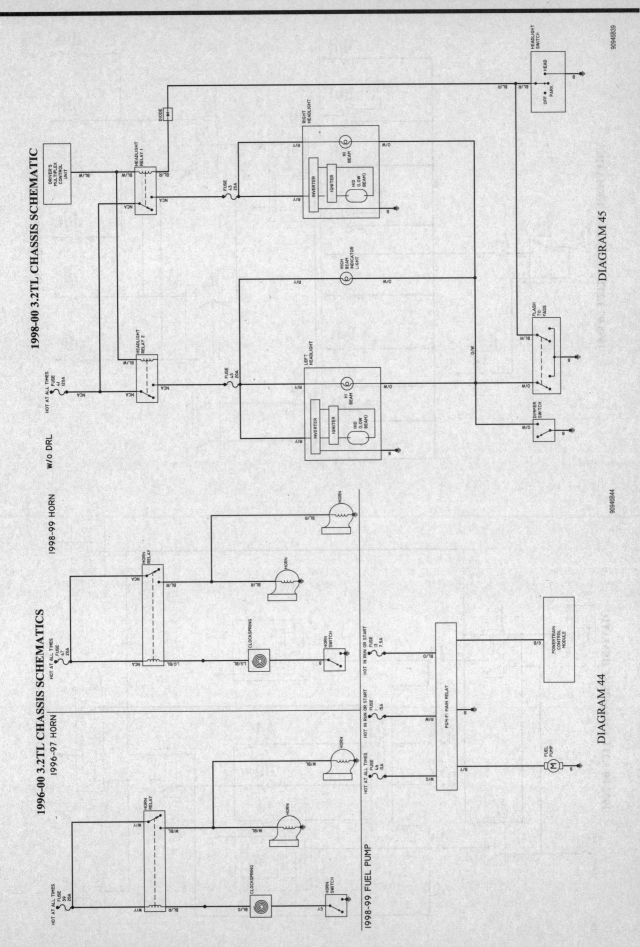

1998-00 3.2TL CHASSIS SCHEMATIC

DIAGRAM 45

1996-00 3.2TL CHASSIS SCHEMATICS

DIAGRAM 44

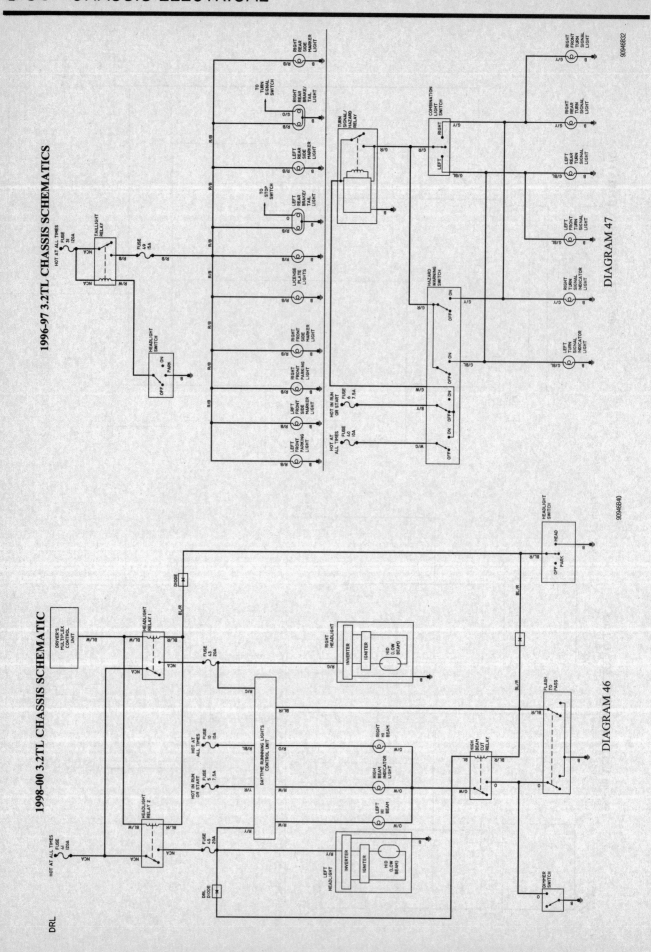

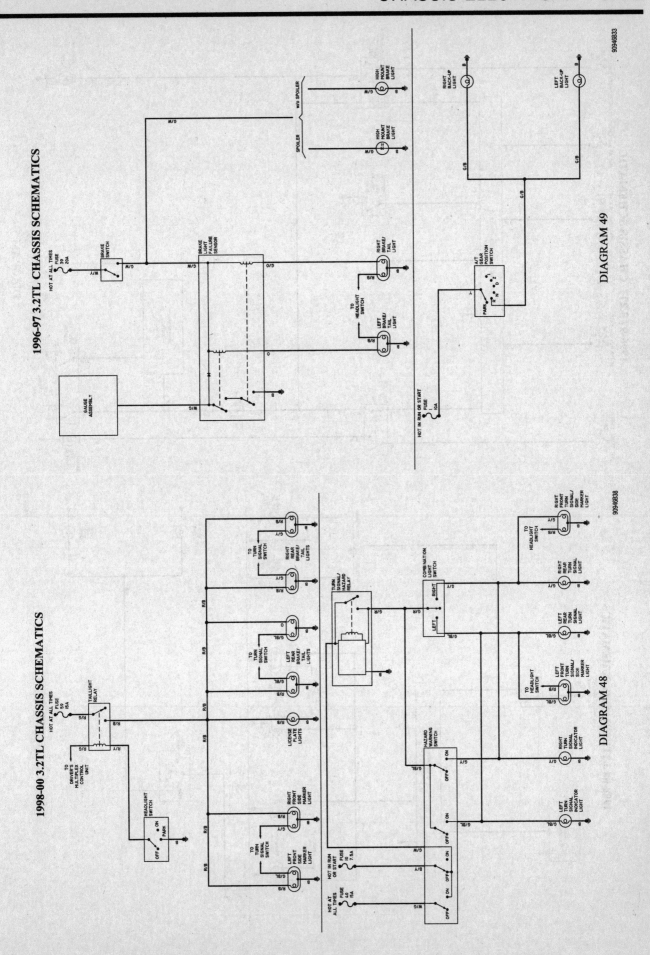

1996-97 3.2TL CHASSIS SCHEMATICS

DIAGRAM 49

1998-00 3.2TL CHASSIS SCHEMATICS

DIAGRAM 48

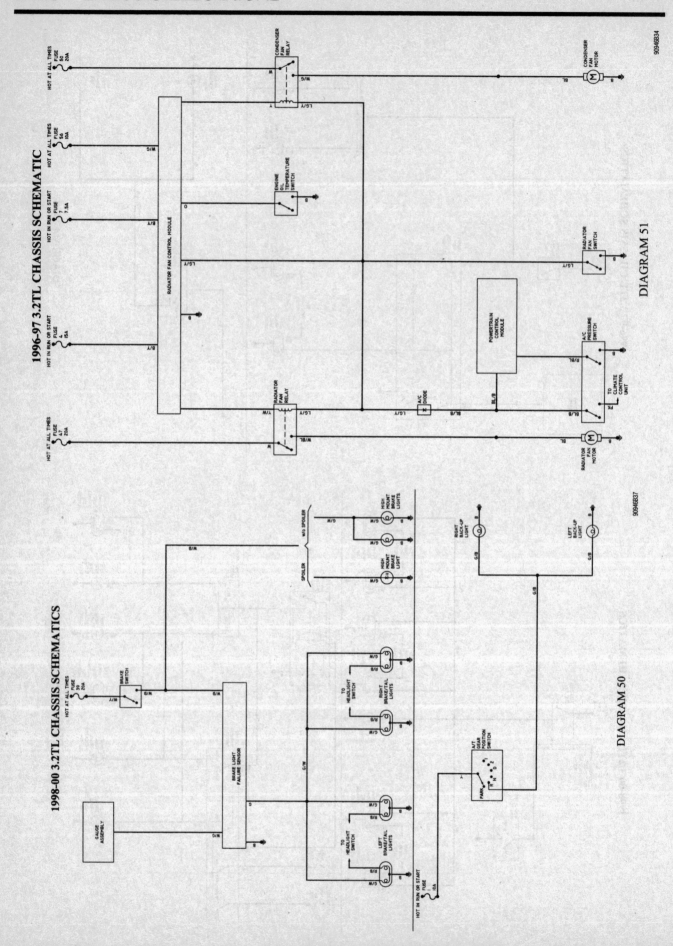

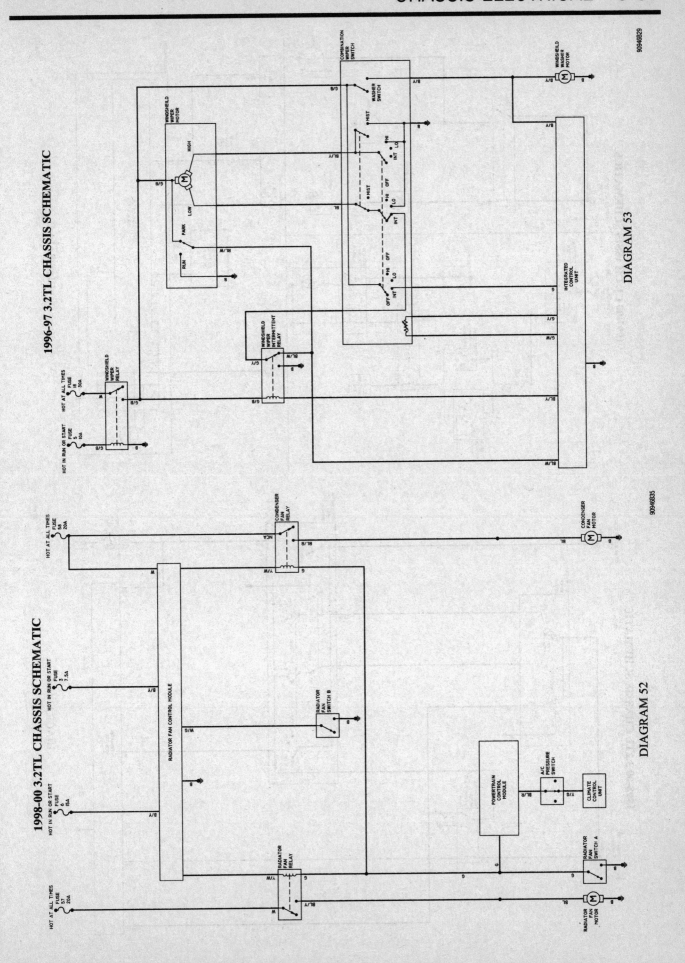

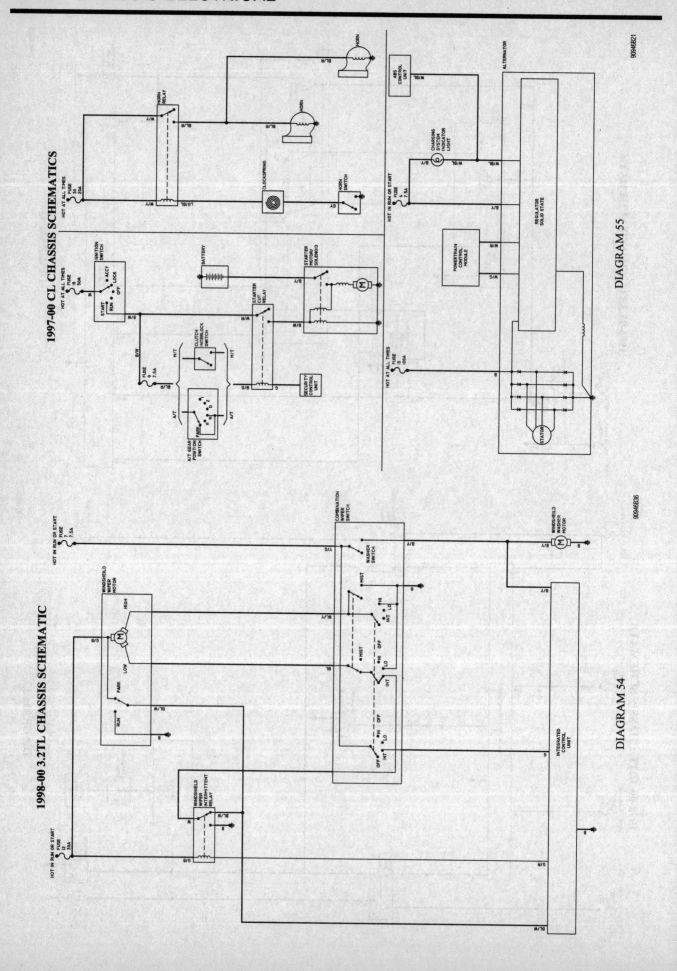

1997-00 CL CHASSIS SCHEMATICS

DIAGRAM 55

1998-00 3.2TL CHASSIS SCHEMATIC

DIAGRAM 54

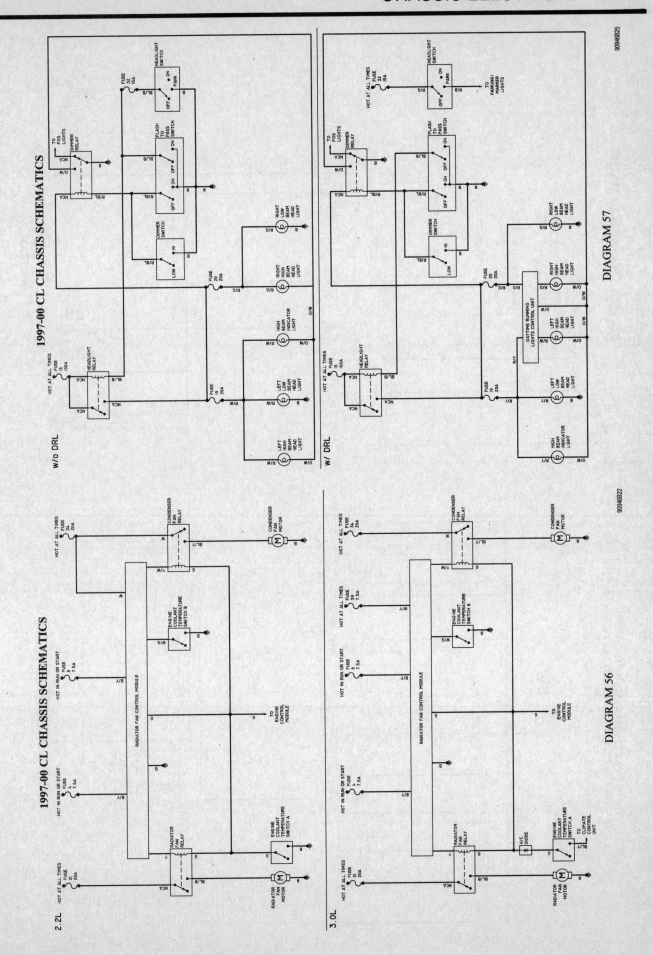

1997-00 CL CHASSIS SCHEMATICS

DIAGRAM 57

1997-00 CL CHASSIS SCHEMATICS

DIAGRAM 56

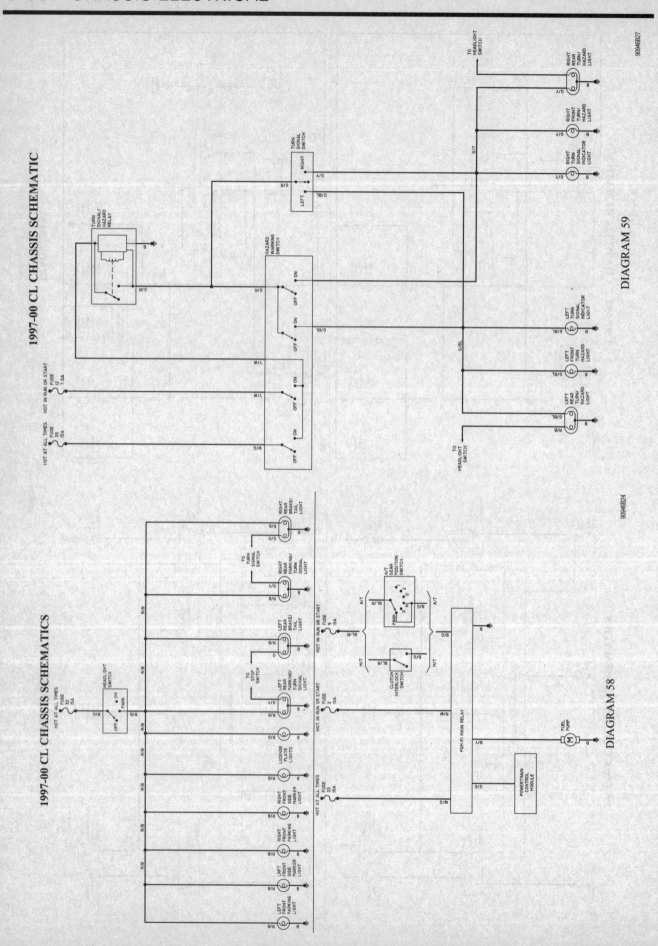

1997-00 CL CHASSIS SCHEMATIC

DIAGRAM 59

1997-00 CL CHASSIS SCHEMATICS

DIAGRAM 58

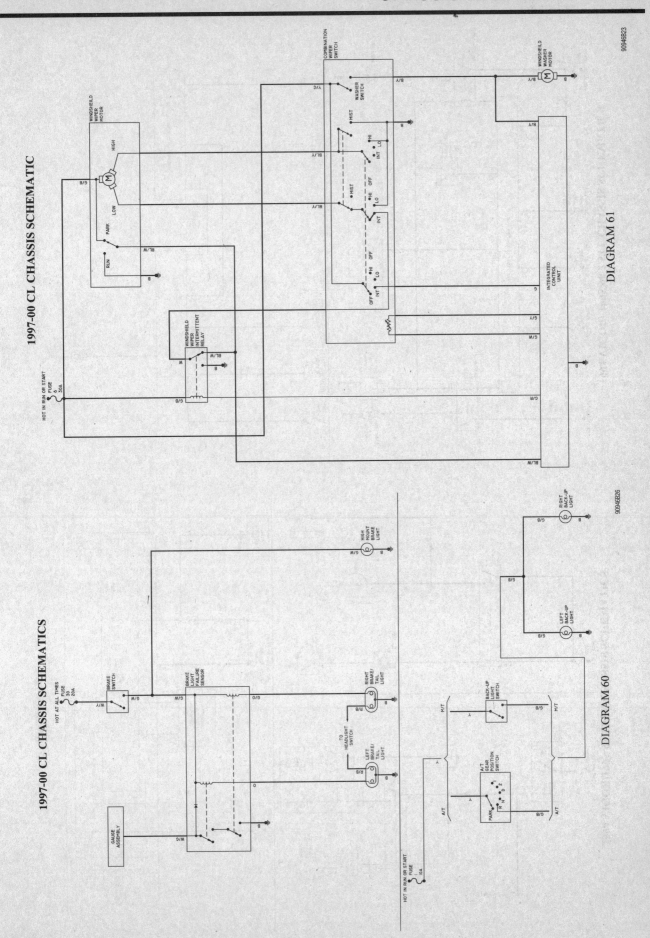

1997-00 CL CHASSIS SCHEMATIC

DIAGRAM 61

1997-00 CL CHASSIS SCHEMATICS

DIAGRAM 60

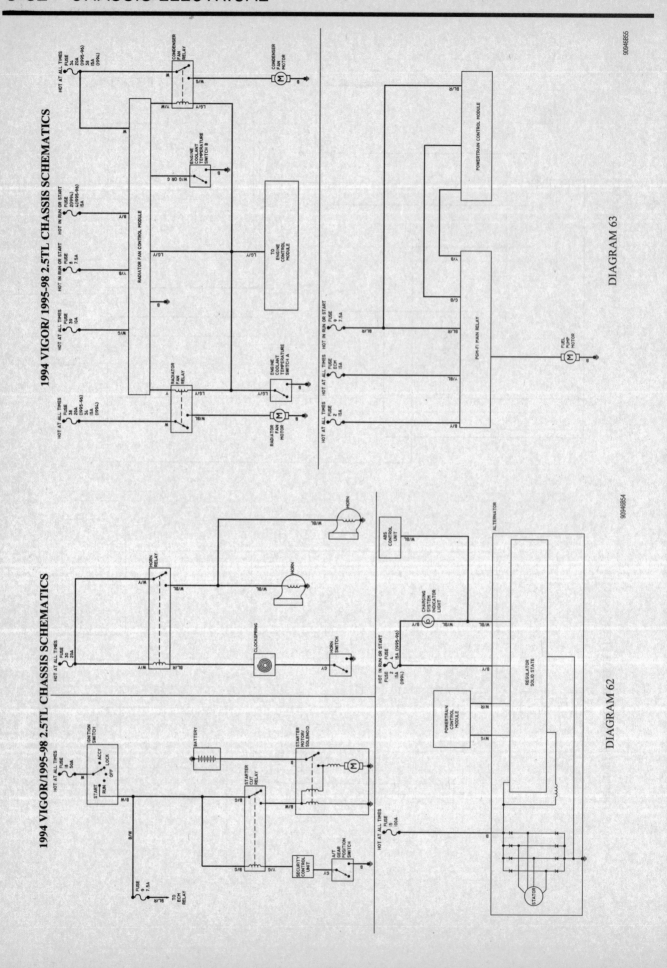

1994 VIGOR/1995-98 2.5TL CHASSIS SCHEMATICS

DIAGRAM 63

1994 VIGOR/1995-98 2.5TL CHASSIS SCHEMATICS

DIAGRAM 62

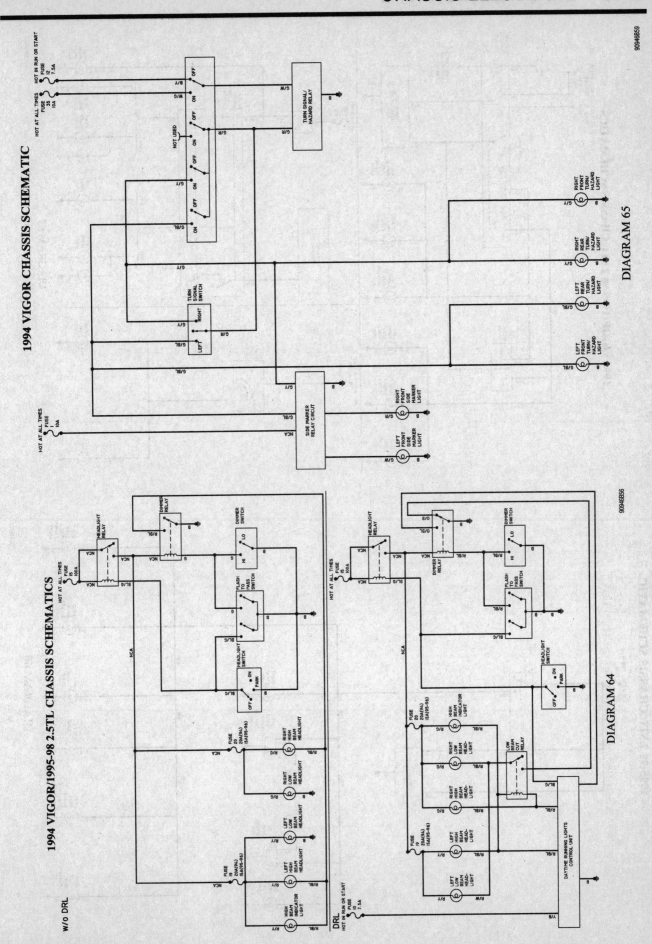

1994 VIGOR CHASSIS SCHEMATIC

DIAGRAM 65

1994 VIGOR/1995-98 2.5TL CHASSIS SCHEMATICS

DIAGRAM 64

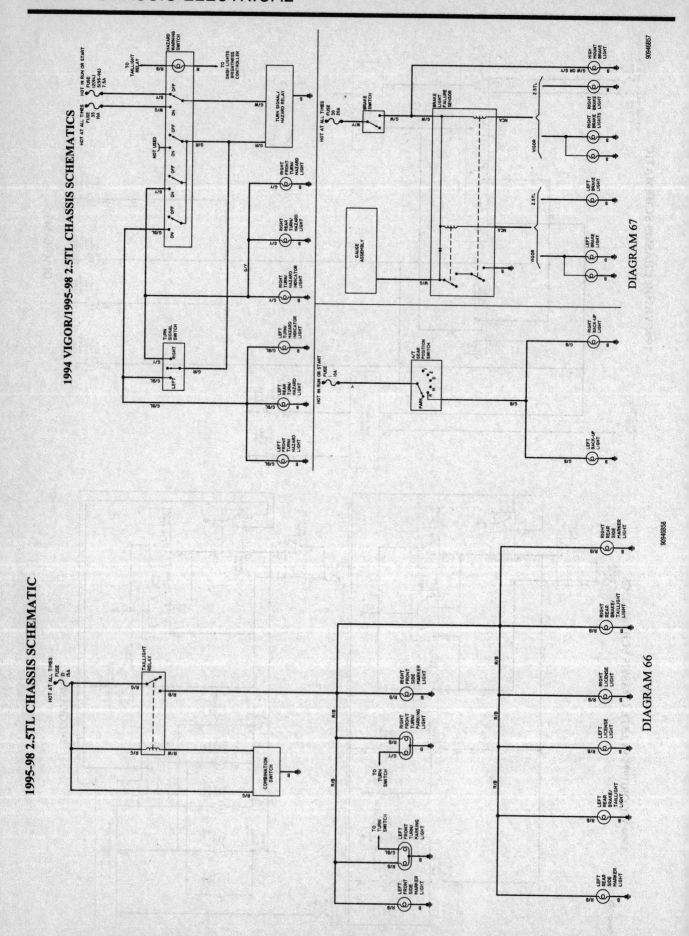

1994 VIGOR/1995-98 2.5TL CHASSIS SCHEMATICS

DIAGRAM 67

1995-98 2.5TL CHASSIS SCHEMATIC

DIAGRAM 66

7
DRIVE TRAIN

MANUAL TRANSAXLE

Understanding the Manual Transaxle

Because of the way an internal combustion engine breathes, it can produce torque, or twisting force, only within a narrow speed range. Most modern, overhead valve pushrod engines must turn at about 2500 rpm to produce their peak torque. By 4500 rpm they are producing so little torque that continued increases in engine speed produce no power increases. The torque peak on overhead camshaft engines is generally much higher, but much narrower.

The manual transaxle and clutch are employed to vary the relationship between engine speed and the speed of the wheels so that adequate engine power can be produced under all circumstances. The clutch allows engine torque to be applied to the transaxle input shaft gradually, due to mechanical slippage. Consequently, the vehicle may be started smoothly from a full stop. The transaxle changes the ratio between the rotating speeds of the engine and the wheels by the use of gears. The gear ratios allow full engine power to be applied to the wheels during acceleration at low speeds and at highway/passing speeds.

In a front wheel drive transaxle, power is usually transmitted from the input shaft to a mainshaft or output shaft located slightly beneath and to the side of the input shaft. The gears of the mainshaft mesh with gears on the input shaft, allowing power to be carried from one to the other. All forward gears are in constant mesh and are free from rotating with the shaft unless the synchronizer and clutch is engaged. Shifting from one gear to the next causes one of the gears to be freed from rotating with the shaft and locks another to it. Gears are locked and unlocked by internal dog clutches which slide between the center of the gear and the shaft. The forward gears employ synchronizers; friction members which smoothly bring gear and shaft to the same speed before the toothed dog clutches are engaged.

Back-up Light Switch

For back-up light switch replacement, please refer to the procedure located in Section 6 of this manual.

Transaxle Assembly

REMOVAL & INSTALLATION

➡The radio may have a coded theft protection circuit. Make sure you have the code before disconnecting the battery, removing the radio fuse, or removing the radio.

Integra

▶ See Figures 1 thru 12

1. Disconnect the negative battery cable, then the positive battery cable.
2. Drain the transaxle oil into a suitable container. Install the drain plug with a new washer.
3. Remove the air cleaner case and the air intake tube.
4. Detach the backup light switch connector and the transaxle ground wire.
5. Remove the lower radiator hose clamp from the transaxle hanger.
6. Remove the wiring harness clips.
7. Disconnect the starter motor cables and the Vehicle Speed Sensor (VSS) connector.
8. Remove the clutch pipe bracket and slave cylinder. Do not operate the clutch pedal once the slave cylinder has been removed.
9. Remove the three upper transaxle mounting bolts and the lower starter mounting bolt.

Fig. 1 Remove the air cleaner case assembly

Fig. 2 Remove of the transaxle hanger bolt(s)

Fig. 3 Unfasten the retaining bolts, then remove the slave cylinder

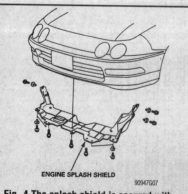

Fig. 4 The splash shield is secured with quite a few retainers

Fig. 5 View of the front suspension components

Fig. 6 Unfasten the mounting bolts, then remove the intermediate shaft

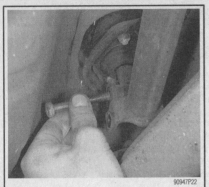

Fig. 7 Once the retainers are removed, you can remove the extension rod

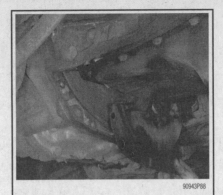

Fig. 8 Removing the clutch cover

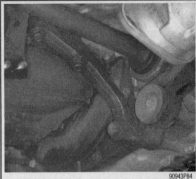

Fig. 9 Engine stiffener location and mounting

Fig. 10 The transaxle mount is secured with a large bolt

Fig. 11 Transaxle mounting bolt locations

Fig. 12 Carefully pull the transaxle away from the engine assembly

10. Safely raise and support the vehicle.

11. Unfasten the retainers, then remove the engine splash shield.

12. Disconnect the heated Oxygen (O_2S) sensor connector.

13. Remove and discard the two nuts attaching exhaust pipe "A" to the hanger bracket.

14. Remove and discard the nuts attaching exhaust pipe "A" to the exhaust manifold, then discard the exhaust gaskets.

15. Remove and discard the three nuts attaching the exhaust system to the catalytic converter, then discard the exhaust gasket. Remove exhaust pipe "A" from the vehicle.

16. Remove the cotter pins and castle nuts from the front lower ball joints. Separate the ball joints from the lower control arms. Discard the cotter pins.

17. Remove the right strut fork pinch bolt and lower nut and bolt, then remove the strut fork from the vehicle.

18. Pry the right halfshaft out of the differential, then discard the set ring on the inner joint.

19. Pry the left halfshaft out of the intermediate shaft, discard the set ring on the inner joint.

20. Tie plastic bags over the halfshaft joints to keep the splines of the joints clean.

21. Remove the intermediate shaft mounting bolts, and remove the intermediate shaft.

22. Remove the set ring from the intermediate shaft and install a new set ring.

23. Disconnect the extension rod and the shift rod:

24. If equipped with a Variable Valve Timing and Electronic Lift Control (VTEC) engine, perform the following:

    a. Remove the heat shield.

    b. Disconnect the shift extension rod from the transaxle case.

    c. Slide the boot on the shift rod back to expose the clip and spring pin. Remove the clip from the shift rod.

    d. Drive out the spring pin with a punch and disconnect the shift control rod. Note that on reassembly, install the clip back into place after driving the spring pin in.

25. Remove the rear engine stiffener, and, if equipped with a VTEC engine, remove the front engine stiffener.

26. Remove the clutch cover.

27. Remove the engine stiffener.

28. Remove the right front mount/bracket. Discard the long self–locking bolt.

29. Place a transaxle jack under the transaxle and a jackstand under the engine.

30. Remove the transaxle mount.

31. Remove the transaxle mounting bolts and the bolts from the rear mounting bracket. Discard the self–locking bolts from the rear mounting bracket.

32. Pull the transaxle assembly away from the engine until it clears the main shaft, then lower it on the transaxle jack.

To install:

33. Install the dowel pins to the clutch housing.

34. Apply a suitable super high temperature grease to the following components:

    a. The release fork bolt.

    b. The spline of the transaxle input shaft.

    c. The inside of the release bearing and the sleeve on the transaxle input shaft where the release bearing rides.

    d. The tips of the release fork and where the slave cylinder pin rides on the release fork.

35. Install the release fork boot.

36. Place the transaxle assembly on the transaxle jack and raise it to engine level.

37. Install the transaxle mounting bolts and new rear mount bracket bolts. Tighten the transaxle mounting bolts to 47 ft. lbs. (64 Nm) and the rear mount bolts to 87 ft. lbs. (118 Nm).

38. Raise the transaxle and install the transaxle mount. First tighten the mounting nuts and bolt to the transaxle to 47 ft. lbs. (64 Nm), then tighten the mounting bolt to 54 ft. lbs. (74 Nm).

39. Install the three upper transaxle mounting bolts and the lower starter

bolt. Tighten the upper transaxle mounting bolts to 47 ft. lbs. (54 Nm), then tighten the lower starter bolt to 33 ft. lbs. (44 Nm).

40. Install the right front mount/bracket. Tighten the new self locking bolt to 61 ft. lbs. (83 Nm), and tighten the other mounting bolts to 33 ft. lbs. (44 Nm).

41. Install the clutch cover. Tighten the 6x1mm bolts to 9 ft. lbs. (12 Nm), tighten the 8x1.25mm bolts to 17 ft. lbs. (24 Nm). If equipped with a B18B1 engine, tighten the 12x1.25mm bolt to 42 ft. lbs. (57 Nm).

42. Install the rear engine stiffener and the front engine stiffener, if equipped. Tighten the bolts attaching the stiffener(s) to the transaxle to 42 ft. lbs. (57 Nm). Tighten the bolts attaching the stiffener(s) to the engine to 17 ft. lbs. (24 Nm).

43. Remove the transaxle jack and the jackstand from the engine.

44. Install the shift rod to the transaxle, then install the spring pin and clip. Install the shift rod boot to the shift rod, making sure the drain hole is facing down.

45. Install the extension rod and tighten the attaching bolt to 16 ft. lbs. (22 Nm).

46. If removed, install the heat shield. Tighten the mounting bolts to 56 inch lbs. (9.8 Nm).

47. Install new set ring to the intermediate shaft and the halfshafts.

48. Install the intermediate shaft and tighten the mounting bolts to 29 ft. lbs. (39 Nm).

49. Turn the right steering knuckle fully outward and slide the halfshaft into the differential unit until you feel the spring clip engage. Turn the left steering knuckle fully outward and slide the halfshaft onto the intermediate shaft until you feel the spring clip engage.

50. Install the right strut fork. Tighten the pinch bolt to 32 ft. lbs. (43 Nm) and tighten the fork lower nut and bolt to 47 ft. lbs. (64 Nm).

51. Connect the lower ball joints to the lower control arms, tighten the castle nuts to 36–43 ft. lbs. (49–59 Nm). Install new cotter pins.

52. Install exhaust pipe "A" using new gaskets and locknuts. Tighten the nuts attaching the exhaust pipe to the exhaust manifold to 40 ft. lbs. (54 Nm). Tighten the nuts attaching the exhaust system to the catalytic converter to 25 ft. lbs. (33 Nm). Tighten the exhaust pipe hanger nuts to 12 ft. lbs. (16 Nm).

53. Install the engine splash shield.

54. Apply a suitable super high temperature grease to the tip of the slave cylinder and install the slave cylinder to the transaxle. Tighten the mounting bolts to 16 ft. lbs. (22 Nm). Install the clutch bracket pipe and tighten the mounting bolts to 56 inch lbs. (9.8 Nm).

55. Install the front wheels and lower the vehicle.

56. Attach the VSS sensor and the starter motor connectors.

57. Connect the lower radiator hose clamp to the transaxle hanger.

58. Connect the transaxle ground cable and the backup light switch connector.

59. Install the air cleaner housing assembly with the air intake tube.

60. Refill the transaxle with the proper type and amount of lubricant.

61. Connect the positive, then the negative battery cables.

62. Check the operation of the clutch and smooth operation of the shifter.

63. Check the front wheel alignment and road test the vehicle.

64. Enter the radio security code.

2.2CL and 2.3CL

▶ **See Figures 13 thru 28**

1. Disconnect the negative battery cable, then the positive cable. Remove the battery.

2. Drain the transaxle fluid into a suitable container.

3. Remove the air cleaner, air duct and resonator assembly.

4. Remove the starter. For more information, please refer to Section 2 of this manual.

5. Tag and remove all wiring from the transaxle.

6. Shift the transaxle into reverse.

7. Remove the cable bracket and the cables from the transaxle.

8. Unfasten the bolts and remove the clutch damper bracket.

9. Unfasten the retaining bolts, disconnect and plug the fluid line, then remove the slave cylinder.

10. Remove the two upper transaxle mounting bolts.

11. Remove the engine splash shield.

12. Disconnect the shock absorber from the lower arm.

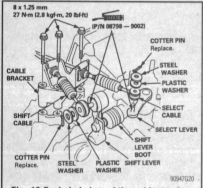

Fig. 13 Exploded view of the cables and brackets

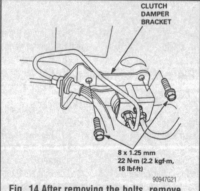

Fig. 14 After removing the bolts, remove the clutch damper bracket

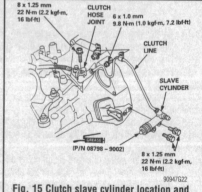

Fig. 15 Clutch slave cylinder location and mounting

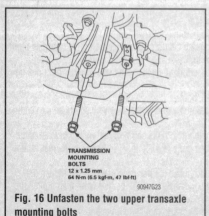

Fig. 16 Unfasten the two upper transaxle mounting bolts

Fig. 17 Unfasten the retaining bolts and clips, then remove the splash shield

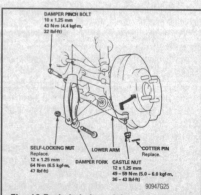

Fig. 18 Exploded view of damper fork and lower control arm

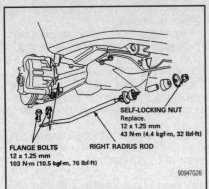

Fig. 19 Right radius rod and flange bolt location & mounting

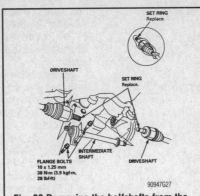

Fig. 20 Removing the halfshafts from the transaxle

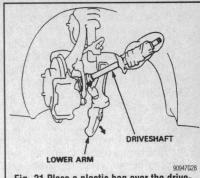

Fig. 21 Place a plastic bag over the driveshaft to keep dirt out of the joint and splines

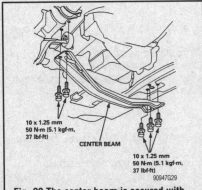

Fig. 22 The center beam is secured with five bolts

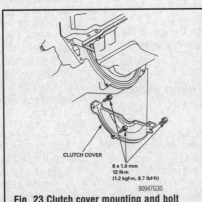

Fig. 23 Clutch cover mounting and bolt tightening specifications

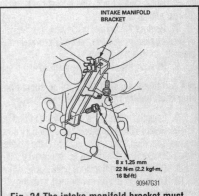

Fig. 24 The intake manifold bracket must be removed

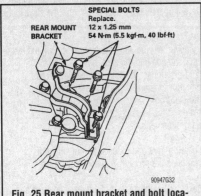

Fig. 25 Rear mount bracket and bolt location

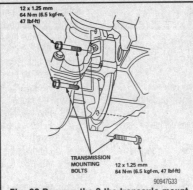

Fig. 26 Remove the 3 the transaxle mounting bolts

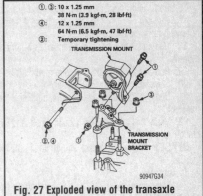

Fig. 27 Exploded view of the transaxle mount and bolt tightening specifications

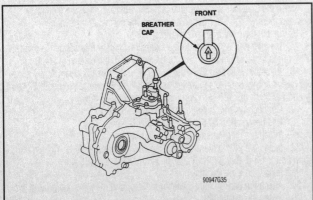

Fig. 28 Install the breather cap in the proper position as shown

13. Separate the lower ball joint from the knuckle assembly.

14. Remove the radius rod.

15. Swing the hub assemblies outward and remove the halfshafts and intermediate shaft from the transaxle..

16. Remove the center beam from the sub-frame.

17. Remove the clutch cover.

18. Remove the intake manifold bracket.

19. Remove the three bolts from the rear bracket.

20. Use a suitable jack to raise the transaxle slightly, then remove the mounting bracket.

21. Remove the three lower transaxle-to-engine mounting bolts.

22. Pull the transaxle away from the engine. Do not damage the clutch hydraulic lines.

To install:

23. Be sure the two dowels are installed in the clutch housing.

24. Grease the release fork and bearing.

25. Install the transaxle in the reverse order of the removal procedure.
26. Tighten the following components as specified:
   - Transaxle-to-engine bolts to 47 ft. lbs. (64 Nm)
   - Rear mount bracket bolts to 40 ft. lbs. (54 Nm)
   - Intake manifold bracket bolts to 16 ft. lbs. (22 Nm)
   - Center beam bolts to 37 ft. lbs. (50 Nm)
27. Refill the transaxle with the recommended amount and type of lubricant.
28. Properly position the breather cap.
29. Enter the radio security code.

Legend

1. Disconnect the positive, then the negative battery cables.
2. Unbolt the strut bar from the bulkhead and shock towers.
3. Drain the transaxle fluid and replace the plug with a new washer.
4. Remove the control box, but do not disconnect the vacuum lines.
5. Detach the wiring from the neutral switch, back-up light switch, and the reverse lockout solenoid connector.
6. Unfasten the transaxle housing bolts and the clutch hose bracket from the rear engine hanger.
7. Remove the front exhaust pipe and catalytic converter. On Legends with 6–speed transaxle, remove the twin three-way catalytic converters and their brackets.
8. Remove the converter heat shield and bracket.

➡**A suitable extension shaft puller, should be used to remove the extension shaft before removing the transaxle.**

9. Lock the transaxle by shifting it into first gear.
10. Remove the extension shaft secondary cover and the 36mm sealing bolt. Use an extension shaft puller to remove the extension shaft from the rear of the transaxle case. The differential is not removed with the transaxle.
11. Disconnect the transaxle linkage extension and the shift rod.
12. Disconnect the oil cooler lines from the oil pump pipes.
13. Remove the release fork cover and the clutch slave cylinder.
14. Support the steering rack with a suitable jack, and remove the rack cover plate. Reinstall the steering rack bolts to hold the rack in the vehicle.
15. Remove the exhaust pipe bracket.
16. Remove the transaxle rear mount and bracket assembly.
17. Pull out on the clutch fork to release it from the throw-out bearing. Don't remove it from the clutch housing.
18. Use a jack to take up the transaxle's weight. Remove the transaxle mid mounts.
19. Remove the transaxle housing mounting bolts.
20. Remove the engine stiffener and the clutch housing cover.
21. Remove the transaxle mounting bolts and the 26mm shim under the transaxle.
22. Verify that all linkages, vacuum lines, and wiring harnesses have been disconnected.
23. Slide the transaxle back and off the input shaft, and lower it from the vehicle.
To install:
24. Make sure that the transaxle mounting dowel pins are seated in the clutch housing.
25. Clean and lightly lubricate the input shaft and release fork contact points with molybdenum grease and install the fork.
26. Install the extension shaft in place. Use a new set ring on the shaft and lightly lubricate the splines with molybdenum grease. Install the sealing bolt and secondary cover.
27. Install the transaxle and start all of the bolts. Install the 26mm transaxle shim. Tighten the 12mm bolts to 55 ft. lbs. (75 Nm).
28. Install the clutch cover and engine stiffener bolts. Tighten the stiffener bolts to 16 ft. lbs. (22 Nm), and the clutch cover bolts to 9 ft. lbs. (12 Nm).
29. Install the mid mounts and the exhaust bracket. Tighten the 10mm bolts to 29 ft. lbs. (39 Nm), 10mm nuts to 36 ft. lbs. (49 Nm).
30. Install the transaxle rear mount and bracket assembly. Tighten the mount bolts to 29 ft. lbs. (39 Nm).
31. Install the shift linkage and extension rod. Make sure the hole in the shift rod boot is facing down.
32. Install the release fork and the slave cylinder.
33. Install the release fork cover and connect the oil cooler hoses.
34. With the transaxle in gear, install the extension shaft using the special tool. Coat the extension shaft with molybdenum grease and use a new set ring. Make sure the shaft snaps into place on the set ring.
35. Pack the shaft area with molybdenum grease, but keep the thread area clean. Apply liquid gasket to the sealing bolt threads and install the bolt and cover.
36. Support the steering rack with a jack and remove the bolts. Install the rack cover plate and tighten the bolts to 28 ft. lbs. (39 Nm). These bolts thread into aluminum and must have the special Dacro®coating to avoid corrosion.
37. On six-speed Legends, install the twin three-way catalytic converters and brackets.
38. Install the heat shield and the exhaust pipe and catalytic converter. Use new locking nuts and gaskets. Torque the exhaust flange nuts to 40 ft. lbs. (55 Nm) and the catalyst flange nuts to 26 ft. lbs. (34 Nm).
39. Install the clutch hose bracket.
40. Install the upper transaxle mounting bolts and torque to 55 ft. lbs. (75 Nm).
41. Reconnect the neutral position switch, backup light switch, and the reverse lockout solenoid connectors.
42. Install the control box.
43. Install the strut bar.
44. check that all linkages, vacuum lines, and wiring harnesses have been reconnected.
45. Refill the transaxle with the proper type and amount of fluid
46. Connect the positive, then the negative battery cables.
47. Check the clutch operation and adjust if necessary. Shift the transaxle through the gear range and check for smooth operation.

Vigor

1. Disconnect the positive, then the negative battery cables. Remove the battery and the battery tray.
2. Remove the ABS relay box, but do not disconnect the harness.
3. Remove the heat shield, distributor and the control box. Do not disconnect the vacuum lines from the control box.
4. Detach the transaxle ground wire and the back-up light switch connector.
5. Remove the clutch slave cylinder and the transaxle housing mounting bolts with the 26mm shim. Do not operate the clutch pedal once the slave cylinder has been removed.
6. Remove the mount beam and bracket.
7. Remove the secondary cover and the 33mm sealing bolt. Pull the extension shaft out using a puller that threads into the shaft bore.
8. Remove the exhaust and disconnect the shift and extension rods.
9. Remove the transaxle mount nuts and support the housing with a jack. Remove the mounts and the housing bolt.
10. Remove the clutch cover and the housing bolt.
11. Remove the transaxle from the vehicle.
To install:
12. Lubricate the release bearing, fork and guide with molybdenum grease and make sure the dowel pins are properly placed in the clutch housing.
13. While fitting the transaxle to the engine, turn the release lever up and make sure the fork engages the release bearing on the clutch.
14. Make sure the transaxle is properly fitted and install the lower transaxle bolts. Tighten the bolts to 47 ft. lbs. (65 Nm).
15. If the transaxle or differential is being replaced, measure the gap between them with a feeler gauge and select the correct 26mm shim.
16. Install the front transaxle mounts.
17. Install a new set ring onto the extension shaft and lubricate the shaft with a high temperature molybdenum grease. Install the extension shaft.
18. Pack the shaft area with grease but keep the threads clean. Apply a liquid gasket compound to the threads and install the 33mm sealing bolt. Tighten the bolt to 58 ft. lbs. (80 Nm) and install the secondary cover.
19. Connect the shift linkage and the extension rod.
20. Use new gaskets and install the exhaust pipe.
21. Install the rear transaxle mount and bracket.
22. Install the 26mm shim and the remaining transaxle bolts. Tighten the shim bolt to 55 ft. lbs. (75 Nm) and the rest to 47 ft. lbs. (65 Nm).
23. Install the slave cylinder.
24. Attach the backup light switch connector and the transaxle ground wire.
25. Install the distributor.

26. Install the heat shield and the ABS relay box.

27. Install the battery and connect the positive, then the negative battery cables.

28. Refill the transaxle with the proper type and amount of fluid and check the clutch operation.

29. Check the ignition timing and test drive to check the transaxle smoothness.

Halfshaft

➡The following procedures cover vehicles equipped with manual or automatic transaxles.

REMOVAL & INSTALLATION

▶ **See Figures 29, 30 and 31**

➡The outer CV-joint cannot be removed from the halfshaft. Replacement of a CV-joint boot requires removal of the halfshaft. If the outer CV-joint has failed the entire shaft must be replaced as an assembly.

1. With the vehicle on the ground, raise the locking tab on the spindle nut and loosen it with a suitable socket.

2. Disconnect the negative battery cable.

3. Raise and safely support the vehicle and remove the spindle nut and front wheels.

4. Drain the differential or transaxle lubricant.

5. Remove the strut fork nut and strut pinch bolt. Remove the strut fork.

6. Remove the lower ball joint nut, then separate the lower ball joint using a suitable ball joint removal tool.

7. Pull the knuckle outward and remove the halfshaft outboard CV-joint from the knuckle using a plastic mallet.

8. Using a small prybar with a 3.5 x 7mm tip, carefully pry out the inboard CV-joint approximately ½ in. (13mm) in order to force the spring clip out of the groove in the differential side gears.

✳✳ WARNING

Be careful not to damage the oil seal. Do not pull on the inboard CV-joint, it may come apart.

9. Pull the halfshaft out of the differential or the intermediate shaft. Replace the spring clip on the end of the inboard joint.

10. Be sure to mark the roller grooves during disassembly to ensure proper positioning during reassembly.

11. Remove the front and rear boot retaining bands, then separate the inboard joint from the halfshaft assembly.

12. Mark the spider gear and the driveshaft so they can be installed in their original positions.

13. Remove snapring, spider gear, then remove the stopper ring.

14. Be sure to mark the position on the shaft where the dynamic strut goes, to ensure it will be reinstalled in its original position. Remove the inboard CV-joint boot, dynamic strut, then the outboard CV-joint boot.

To install:

15. Wrap the spline with vinyl tape to prevent damage to the boots. Install the outboard boot, dynamic strut, and inboard boot, then remove the vinyl tape.

16. Install the stopper ring onto the halfshaft groove, then install the spider gear in its original position by aligning the marks.

17. Fit the snapring into the halfshaft groove.

18. Pack the outboard joint boot with CV-joint grease only. Do not use a substitute, or mix types of grease.

19. Fit the rollers to the spider gear with their high shoulders facing outward. Reinstall the rollers in their original positions on the spider gear.

20. Pack the inboard joint boot with a suitable CV-joint grease.

21. Fit the inboard joint onto the halfshaft. Hold the halfshaft assembly so the inboard joint points up to prevent it from falling off.

22. With the boots installed, adjust the CV-joints in or out to place the inner boot ends in the original positions.

23. Install the new boot bands on the boots and bend both sets of locking tabs. Lightly tap on the locking tabs to ensure a good fit.

24. Always use a new set ring whenever the driveshaft is being installed. Be sure the driveshaft locks in the differential side gear groove and that the CV-joint stub–axle bottoms in the differential or the intermediate shaft.

25. Tighten the ball joint nut to the proper specification for your vehicle, as follows:
   - Integra, 2.2CL, 2.3CL, 3.0CL and 2.5TL: 36–43 ft. lbs. (49–59 Nm)
   - Legend, 3.2TL and 3.5RL: 54 ft. lbs. (75 Nm)
   - Vigor: 36 ft. lbs. (50 Nm)

26. Install and tighten the lower strut nut and bolt to 47 ft. lbs. (65 Nm), for all models except the 3.2TL. For the 3.2TL, tighten the lower strut nut and bolt to 50 ft. lbs. (70 Nm).

27. Install and tighten the upper pinch bolt to 32 ft. lbs. (44 Nm) for all models except the 3.2TL. For the 3.2TL, tighten the upper pinch bolt to 36 ft. lbs. (49 Nm).

28. With the vehicle on the ground, tighten the spindle nut to the proper specification for your vehicle, as follows, then stake the nut with a new cotter pin:
   - Integra, 2.2CL, 2.3CL and 3.0CL: 134 ft. lbs. (182 Nm)
   - 2.5TL: 181 ft. lbs. (245 Nm)
   - Legend, 2.5TL, 3.2TL and 3.5RL: 242 ft. lbs. (355 Nm)
   - Vigor: 180 ft. lbs. (250 Nm)

29. Refill the transaxle or differential with the correct amount and type of fluid.

30. Reconnect the battery cable and enter the radio security code.

CV-JOINT OVERHAUL

▶ **See Figures 32 thru 45**

These vehicles use several different types of joints. Engine size, transaxle type, whether the joint is an inboard or outboard joint, even which side of the vehicle is being serviced could make a difference in joint type. Be sure to properly identify the joint before attempting joint or boot replacement. Look for identification numbers at the large end of the boots and/or on the end of the metal retainer bands.

Fig. 29 Carefully pry the inboard joint from the transaxle

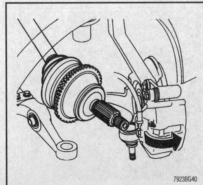
Fig. 30 Pull the hub assembly from the outboard joint

Fig. 31 Pulling the halfshaft from the vehicle

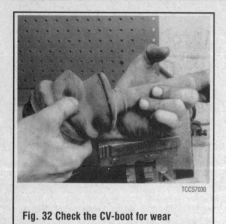

Fig. 32 Check the CV-boot for wear

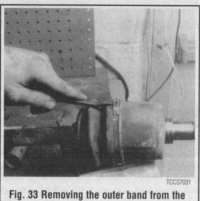

Fig. 33 Removing the outer band from the CV-boot

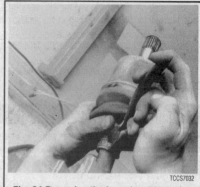

Fig. 34 Removing the inner band from the CV-boot

Fig. 35 Removing the CV-boot from the joint housing

Fig. 36 Clean the CV-joint housing prior to removing boot

Fig. 37 Removing the CV-joint housing assembly

Fig. 38 Removing the CV-joint

Fig. 39 Inspecting the CV-joint housing

Fig. 40 Removing the CV-joint outer snapring

Fig. 41 Checking the CV-joint snapring for wear

Fig. 42 CV-joint snapring (typical)

Fig. 43 Removing the CV-joint assembly

Fig. 44 Removing the CV-joint inner snapring

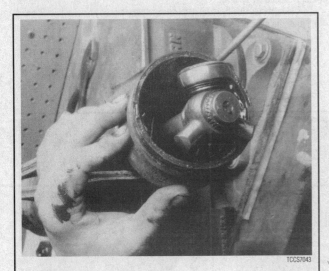

Fig. 45 Installing the CV-joint assembly (typical)

The 3 types of joints used are the Birfield Joint, (B.J.), the Tripod Joint (T.J.) and the Double Offset Joint (D.O.J.).

➡**Do not disassemble a Birfield joint. Service with a new joint or clean and repack using a new boot kit.**

The distance between the large and small boot bands is important and should be checked prior to, and after boot service. This is so the boot will not be installed either too loose or too tight, which could cause early wear and cracking, allowing the grease to get out and water and dirt in, leading to early joint failure.

➡**The driveshaft joints use special grease; do not add any grease other than that supplied with the kit.**

Double Offset Joint (D.O.J.)

The Double Offset Joint (D.O.J.) is bigger than other joints and, in these applications, is normally used as an inboard joint.

1. Remove the halfshaft from the vehicle, as outlined earlier.
2. Side cutter pliers can be used to cut the metal retaining bands. Remove the boot from the joint outer race.
3. Locate and remove the large circlip at the base of the joint. Remove the outer race (the body of the joint).
4. Remove the small snapring and take off the inner race, cage and balls as an assembly. Clean the inner race, cage and balls without disassembling.
5. If the boot is to be reused, wipe the grease from the splines and wrap the splines in vinyl tape before sliding the boot from the shaft.
6. Remove the inner (D.O.J.) boot from the shaft. If the outer (B.J.) boot is to be replaced, remove the boot retainer rings and slide the boot down and off of the shaft at this time.

To install:

7. Be sure to tape the shaft splines before installing the boots. Fill the inside of the boot with the specified grease. Often the grease supplied in the replacement parts kit is meant to be divided in half, with half being used to lubricate the joint and half being used inside the boot.
8. Install the cage onto the halfshaft so the small diameter side of the cage is installed first. With a brass drift pin, tap lightly and evenly around the inner race to install the race until it comes into contact with the rib of the shaft. Apply the specified grease to the inner race and cage and fit them together. Insert the balls into the cage.
9. Install the outer race (the body of the joint) after filling with the specified grease. The outer race should be filled with this grease.
10. Tighten the boot bands securely. Make sure the distance between the boot bands is correct.
11. Install the halfshaft to the vehicle.

Tripod Joint (T.J.)

1. Disconnect the negative battery cable. Remove the halfshaft from the vehicle.
2. Use side cutter pliers to remove the metal retaining bands from the boot(s) that will be removed. Slide the boot from the T.J. case.
3. Remove the snapring and the tripod joint spider assembly from the halfshaft. Do not disassemble the spider and use care in handling.
4. If the boot is be reused, wrap vinyl tape around the spline part of the shaft so the boot(s) will not be damaged when removed. Remove the dynamic damper, if used, and the boots from the shaft.

To install:

5. Double check that the correct replacement parts are being installed. Wrap vinyl tape around the splines to protect the boot and install the boots and damper, if used, in the correct order.
6. Install the joint spider assembly to the shaft and install the snapring.
7. Fill the inside of the boot with the specified grease. Often the grease supplied in the replacement parts kit is meant to be divided in half, with half being used to lubricate the joint and half being used inside the boot. Keep grease off the rubber part of the dynamic damper (if used).
8. Secure the boot bands with the halfshaft in a horizontal position. Make sure distance between boot bands is correct.
9. Install the halfshaft to the vehicle and reconnect the negative battery cable.

CLUTCH

Understanding the Clutch

❊❊ CAUTION

The clutch driven disc may contain asbestos, which has been determined to be a cancer causing agent. Never clean clutch surfaces with compressed air! Avoid inhaling any dust from any clutch surface! When cleaning clutch surfaces, use a commercially available brake cleaning fluid.

The purpose of the clutch is to disconnect and connect engine power at the transaxle. A vehicle at rest requires a lot of engine torque to get all that weight moving. An internal combustion engine does not develop a high starting torque (unlike steam engines) so it must be allowed to operate without any load until it builds up enough torque to move the vehicle. Torque increases with engine rpm. The clutch allows the engine to build up torque by physically disconnecting the engine from the transaxle, relieving the engine of any load or resistance.

The transfer of engine power to the transaxle (the load) must be smooth and gradual; if it weren't, drive line components would wear out or break quickly. This gradual power transfer is made possible by gradually releasing the clutch pedal. The clutch disc and pressure plate are the connecting link between the engine and transaxle. When the clutch pedal is released, the disc and plate contact each other (the clutch is engaged) physically joining the engine and transaxle. When the pedal is pushed inward, the disc and plate separate (the clutch is disengaged) disconnecting the engine from the transaxle.

Most clutches utilize a single plate, dry friction disc with a diaphragm-style spring pressure plate. The clutch disc has a splined hub which attaches the disc to the input shaft. The disc has friction material where it contacts the flywheel and pressure plate. Torsion springs on the disc help absorb engine torque pulses. The pressure plate applies pressure to the clutch disc, holding it tight against the surface of the flywheel. The clutch operating mechanism consists of a release bearing, fork and cylinder assembly.

The release fork and actuating linkage transfer pedal motion to the release bearing. In the engaged position (pedal released) the diaphragm spring holds the pressure plate against the clutch disc, so engine torque is transmitted to the input shaft. When the clutch pedal is depressed, the release bearing pushes the diaphragm spring center inward. The diaphragm spring pivots the fulcrum, relieving the load on the pressure plate. Steel spring straps riveted to the clutch cover lift the pressure plate from the clutch disc, disengaging the engine drive from the transaxle and enabling the gears to be changed.

The clutch is operating properly if:

1. It will stall the engine when released with the vehicle held stationary.
2. The shift lever can be moved freely between 1st and reverse gears when the vehicle is stationary and the clutch disengaged.

Driven Disc and Pressure Plate

REMOVAL & INSTALLATION

➡The radio may have a coded theft protection circuit. Make sure you have the code before disconnecting the battery, removing the radio fuse, or removing the radio.

Integra

▶ **See Figures 46 thru 54**

1. Before servicing the vehicle, refer to the precautions in the beginning of this section.
2. Disconnect the negative battery cable.
3. Remove the manual transaxle assembly from the vehicle.
4. Insert the a suitable clutch alignment shaft with the suitable clutch alignment disc part and handle part. Use a feeler gauge and measure the clearance between the pressure plate spring fingers and the clutch alignment disc. There should be a maximum of 0.02 in. (0.6mm) of clearance for a new pressure plate with 0.03 in. (0.8mm) limit for a used pressure plate.
5. Remove the clutch alignment disc.
6. Install a suitable flywheel holder tool to aid in the removal of the pressure plate and clutch disc.
7. Matchmark the flywheel and pressure plate for easy reassembly. Remove the pressure plate bolts in a criss-cross pattern 2 turns at a time to prevent warping the plate.
8. Remove the pressure plate, then the clutch disc with the alignment shaft

To install:

9. If the flywheel was removed, align the hole in the flywheel with the crankshaft dowel pin and install the mounting bolt finger-tight.

90947P34

Fig. 46 View of the transaxle, once it is separated from the engine

90947P41

Fig. 47 Loosen the pressure plate bolts in a criss-cross pattern. This will prevent the plate from bending during the removal procedure

90947P43

Fig. 48 Remove the pressure plate and clutch disc from the flywheel

90947P60

Fig. 49 Clutch disc and alignment tool removal

90947P59

Fig. 50 Inspect the clutch disc for signs of uneven wears

90947P49

Fig. 51 Always check the rear main seal for oil leaks that may contaminate the friction surface of the clutch disc. Replace the seal if a leak is detected

Fig. 52 Notice the surface of this flywheel. Surface irregularities such as these are caused by constant overheating of the flywheel surface. While machining the surface may be possible, it is advised that the clutch be replaced

Fig. 53 This is how the clutch alignment tool should appear after it has been inserted into the pilot bearing

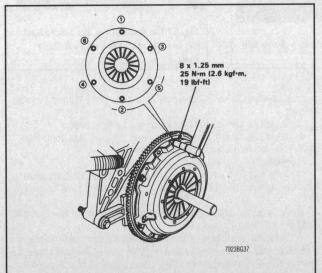

Fig. 54 Pressure plate bolt tightening sequence—Integra shown

10. Install the flywheel holder, then tighten the flywheel mounting bolts in a criss-cross pattern in several steps. The mounting bolt final torque should be 76 ft. lbs. (103 Nm).

11. Apply a suitable high temperature grease part to the splines of the clutch disc, then install the clutch disc using the clutch alignment shaft.

12. Install the pressure plate, tighten the mounting bolts to 19 ft. lbs. (25 Nm), in the proper sequence shown in the accompanying figure.

13. Remove the flywheel holding tool and the clutch alignment shaft

14. Insert the clutch alignment shaft with the clutch alignment disc and handle. Use a feeler gauge and measure the clearance between the pressure plate spring fingers and the clutch alignment disc. There should be a maximum of 0.02 in. (0.6mm) of clearance for a new pressure plate with 0.03 in. (0.8mm) limit for a used pressure plate.

15. Install the transaxle assembly.

16. Connect the negative battery cable and enter the radio security code.

2.2L, 2.3L CL

▶ See Figures 55 thru 66

1. Raise and safely support the vehicle.

2. Remove the starter motor.

3. Disconnect the hydraulic coupling for the slave cylinder at the transaxle by sliding the sleeve on the tube towards the slave cylinder and applying a slight pulling force to the tube.

4. Remove the transaxle.

5. Mark the assembled position of the clutch and pressure plate to the flywheel if it is to be reinstalled.

➡The clutch pressure plate is only held in place by the retaining bolts. No dowel pins are used, therefore the pressure plate must be supported when removing the retaining bolts.

6. Loosen the pressure plate bolts evenly until the pressure plate spring pressure is released, then finish removing the bolts while supporting the clutch and pressure plate assembly.

7. Remove the clutch and pressure plate from the vehicle.

8. Inspect the flywheel, slave cylinder and other components for wear or damage.

To install:

9. Clean the pressure plate and flywheel surfaces.

10. Install the clutch disc using an appropriate clutch aligning tool.

➡If the clutch disc and pressure plate are being reused, align the marks made during disassembly.

11. Install an appropriate flywheel holding tool to hold the flywheel.

12. Install the pressure plate and start the retaining bolts.

13. Tighten the retaining bolts evenly and in sequence to 13–18 ft. lbs. (18–26 Nm).

Fig. 55 Loosen and remove the clutch and pressure plate bolts evenly, a little at a time . . .

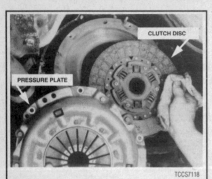

Fig. 56 . . . then carefully removing the clutch and pressure plate assembly from the flywheel

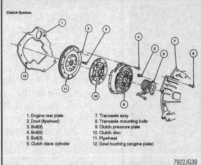

Fig. 57 Exploded view of the clutch disc, pressure plate and related component mounting

1. Engine rear plate
2. Dowl (flywheel)
3. Bolt(8)
4. Bolt(6)
5. Bolt(3)
6. Clutch slave cylinder
7. Transade assy
8. Transade mounting bolts
9. Clutch pressure plate
10. Clutch disc
11. Flywheel
12. Dowl bushing (engine plate)

Fig. 58 Check the pressure plate for excessive wear

Fig. 59 Be sure that the flywheel surface is clean, before installing the clutch

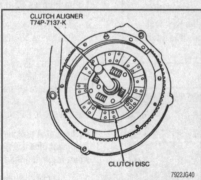

Fig. 60 Insert an alignment tool through the clutch disc to ensure that it is centered after the pressure plate is installed

Fig. 61 Typical clutch alignment tool, note how the splines match the transaxle's input shaft

Fig. 62 Use the clutch alignment tool to align the clutch disc during assembly

Fig. 63 The pressure plate-to-flywheel bolt holes should align

Fig. 64 You may want to use a threadlocking compound on the clutch assembly bolts

14. Remove the clutch aligner tool.
15. Reinstall the transaxle.
16. Reconnect the slave cylinder tube coupling by pushing the male coupling into the slave cylinder female coupling.
17. Lower the vehicle.
18. Reconnect the negative battery cable.
19. Bleed the hydraulic clutch system, if required.
20. Check the clutch system for proper operation.

Legend

1. Disconnect the negative battery cable.
2. Raise and support the vehicle.
3. Remove the transaxle from the vehicle, as outlined earlier.
4. Matchmark the flywheel and pressure plate for reassembly. Remove the pressure plate bolts in a criss-cross pattern 2 turns at a time to prevent warping the plate.
5. Inspect the pressure plate and clutch disk for signs of wear.
6. Inspect the flywheel for scoring and wear. Use a dial indicator to make sure it is flat and resurface or replace, as necessary.

To install:

7. Make sure the flywheel and the end of the crankshaft are clean before assembly. Tighten the flywheel bolts, in a criss-cross pattern, to 76 ft. lbs. (105 Nm).
8. Apply grease to the splines of the clutch disc, and install the clutch disc using a clutch alignment shaft.
9. Install the release bearing on the pressure plate, then install the pressure plate. When installing the pressure plate, align the mark on the outer edge of the flywheel with the alignment mark on the pressure plate. Failure to align these marks will result in imbalance.

Fig. 65 Be sure to use a torque wrench to tighten all bolts

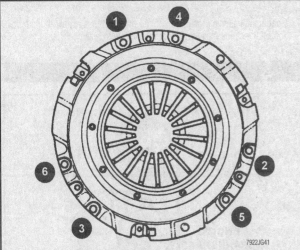

Fig. 66 Tighten the pressure plate bolts gradually and in the sequence shown to ensure correct clutch operation

10. Tighten the pressure plate bolts using an alignment shaft to center the friction disc. After centering the disc, tighten the bolts 2 turns at a time, in a criss-cross pattern to avoid warping the diaphragm springs; torque to 19 ft. lbs. (26 Nm).

11. Jack the transaxle into place and make sure the mainshaft is properly aligned with the disc spline and that the aligning pins are in place.

12. Install the transaxle and tighten the mounting bolts to 55 ft. lbs. (75 Nm).

13. Install and connect the slave cylinder and its hydraulic line. Fill the reservoir with fluid.

14. Verify that all wiring harnesses, vacuum lines, and linkages are connected properly.

15. Reconnect the negative battery cable.

16. Check the clutch adjustment and road test the vehicle.

Vigor

1. Disconnect the negative battery cable.
2. Remove the transaxle from the vehicle, as outlined earlier.
3. Remove the slave cylinder with the hydraulic hose still connected. Remove the boot from the clutch case and remove the release fork with the bearing.
4. Matchmark the flywheel and pressure plate for easy reassembly. Remove

the pressure plate bolts in a criss-cross pattern 2 turns at a time to prevent warping the plate.

5. Inspect the flywheel for scoring and wear. Use a dial indicator to make sure it is flat and reface or replace, as necessary.

To install:

6. Make sure the flywheel and the end of the crankshaft are clean before assembly. Tighten the flywheel bolts, in a criss-cross pattern, to 76 ft. lbs. (103 Nm).

7. Apply grease to the splines of the clutch disc, and install the clutch disc using a clutch alignment shaft.

8. Install the release bearing on the pressure plate, then install the pressure plate. When installing the pressure plate, align the mark on the outer edge of the flywheel with the alignment mark on the pressure plate. Failure to align these marks will result in imbalance. After installing the pressure plate, make sure the release bearing does not come off.

9. Tighten the pressure plate bolts using a pilot shaft to center the friction disc. After centering the disc, tighten the bolts 2 turns at a time, in a criss-cross pattern to avoid warping the diaphragm springs; tighten to 19 ft. lbs. (26 Nm).

10. Install the transaxle, make sure the mainshaft is properly aligned with the disc spline and the aligning pins are in place, before tightening the case bolts.

ADJUSTMENTS

Clutch Pedal Free-Play

➡ The clutch is self-adjusting to compensate for wear.

1. Loosen the locknut at the base of the clutch switch.
2. Loosen the locknut at the rear of the pedal pin.
3. Turn the pushrod in or out to obtain the specified amount of pedal play.
4. Tighten the locknut located to the rear of the pedal pin.
5. Turn the clutch switch until it contacts the pedal shaft.
6. Turn the clutch switch one turn farther.
7. Tighten the locknut on the switch.
8. Loosen the locknut on the clutch interlock switch.
9. Measure the clearance between the clutch pedal and the floor board with the clutch pedal depressed.
10. Allow the clutch pedal to rise from the floor until it is 0.59–0.79 inch. (15–20 mm) above the full bottom measurement.
11. Adjust the interlock switch so that the engine will start from this position.
12. Turn the interlock switch three quarters to one turn further.
13. Tighten the locknut to secure the position of the clutch interlock switch.

Master Cylinder

REMOVAL & INSTALLATION

✵✵ WARNING

Do not spill brake fluid on any of the vehicles painted surfaces. It will damage the paint!

1. Use a suitable siphon or a clean turkey baster to remove the brake fluid from the clutch master cylinder.
2. Disconnect the clutch pipe from the master cylinder.
3. Remove the reservoir hose from the master cylinder reservoir.
4. Pull out the cotter pin on the pedal rod.
5. Pull the pedal pin out of the yoke.
6. Unfasten the retaining nuts, then remove the clutch master cylinder.

✵✵ WARNING

Do not spill brake fluid on the clutch master cylinder damper.

7. Installation is the reverse of removal.

➡ Use only DOT 3 or 4 brake fluid to refill the clutch hydraulic system.

8. Fill and bleed the clutch system, using a suitable DOT 3 or 4 brake fluid.

Slave Cylinder

REMOVAL & INSTALLATION

▶ **See Figure 67**

1. Locate the slave cylinder.
2. Remove the flare fitting and steel line from the slave cylinder assembly.
3. Remove the slave cylinder from the clutch housing by removing the attaching bolts.
4. Installation is the reverse of the removal procedure

➡ **Use only DOT 3 or 4 brake fluid to refill the clutch hydraulic system.**

5. Fill and bleed the clutch system, using a suitable DOT 3 or 4 brake fluid..

HYDRAULIC SYSTEM BLEEDING

➡ **Use only DOT 3 or 4 brake fluid from a clean, sealed container, in the clutch master and slave cylinders. As brake fluid will damage the vehicle's paint, clean up any spills immediately.**

1. Fit a flare or box end wrench onto the slave cylinder bleeder screw.
2. Attach a rubber tube to the slave cylinder bleeder screw and suspend it into a clear drain container partially filled with brake fluid.
3. Fill the clutch master cylinder with brake fluid.
4. Open the bleeder screw and press the clutch pedal to the floor.
5. Close the bleeder screw.

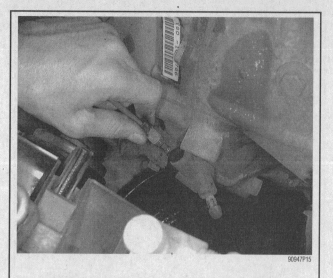

90947P15

Fig. 67 Disconnecting the hydraulic line from the slave cylinder

6. Release the clutch pedal and recheck the reservoir fluid level. Top off if necessary.
7. Continue the above procedure until no more bubbles appear in the tube.
8. Top off the clutch master cylinder reservoir with brake fluid.

AUTOMATIC TRANSAXLE

Understanding the Automatic Transaxle

The automatic transaxle allows engine torque and power to be transmitted to the front wheels within a narrow range of engine operating speeds. It will allow the engine to turn fast enough to produce plenty of power and torque at very low speeds, while keeping it at a sensible rpm at high vehicle speeds (and it does this job without driver assistance). The transaxle uses a light fluid as the medium for the transaxle of power. This fluid also works in the operation of various hydraulic control circuits and as a lubricant. Because the transaxle fluid performs all of these functions, trouble within the unit can easily travel from one part to another. For this reason, and because of the complexity and unusual operating principles of the transaxle, a very sound understanding of the basic principles of operation will simplify troubleshooting.

TORQUE CONVERTER

▶ **See Figure 68**

The torque converter replaces the conventional clutch. It has three functions:
1. It allows the engine to idle with the vehicle at a standstill, even with the transaxle in gear.
2. It allows the transaxle to shift from range-to-range smoothly, without requiring that the driver close the throttle during the shift.
3. It multiplies engine torque to an increasing extent as vehicle speed drops and throttle opening is increased. This has the effect of making the transaxle more responsive and reduces the amount of shifting required.

The torque converter is a metal case which is shaped like a sphere that has been flattened on opposite sides. It is bolted to the rear end of the engine's crankshaft. Generally, the entire metal case rotates at engine speed and serves as the engine's flywheel. The case contains three sets of blades. One set is attached directly to the case. This set forms the torus or pump. Another set is directly connected to the output shaft, and forms the turbine. The third set is mounted on a hub which, in turn, is mounted on a stationary shaft through a one-way clutch. This third set is known as the stator. A pump, which is driven by the converter hub at engine speed, keeps the torque converter full of transaxle fluid at all times. Fluid flows continuously through the unit to provide cooling. Under low speed acceleration, the torque converter functions as follows:

The torus is turning faster than the turbine. It picks up fluid at the center of the converter and, through centrifugal force, slings it outward. Since the outer edge of the converter moves faster than the portions at the center, the fluid picks up speed.

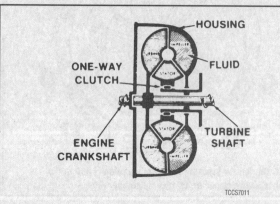

TCCS7011

Fig. 68 The torque converter housing is rotated by the engine's crankshaft, and turns the impeller—The impeller then spins the turbine, which gives motion to the turbine shaft, driving the gears

The fluid then enters the outer edge of the turbine blades. It then travels back toward the center of the converter case along the turbine blades. In impinging upon the turbine blades, the fluid loses the energy picked up in the torus.

If the fluid was now returned directly into the torus, both halves of the converter would have to turn at approximately the same speed at all times, and torque input and output would both be the same.

In flowing through the torus and turbine, the fluid picks up two types of flow, or flow in two separate directions. It flows through the turbine blades, and it spins with the engine. The stator, whose blades are stationary when the vehicle is being accelerated at low speeds, converts one type of flow into another. Instead of allowing the fluid to flow straight back into the torus, the stator's curved blades turn the fluid almost 90° toward the direction of rotation of the engine. Thus the fluid does not flow as fast toward the torus, but is already spinning when the torus picks it up. This has the effect of allowing the torus to turn much faster than the turbine. This difference in speed may be compared to the difference in speed between the smaller and larger gears in any gear train. The result is that engine power output is higher, and engine torque is multiplied.

As the speed of the turbine increases, the fluid spins faster and faster in the direction of engine rotation. As a result, the ability of the stator to redirect the

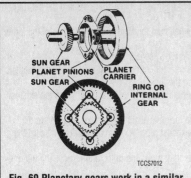

Fig. 69 Planetary gears work in a similar fashion to manual transaxle gears, but are composed of three parts

Fig. 70 Planetary gears in the maximum reduction (low) range. The ring gear is held and a lower gear ratio is obtained

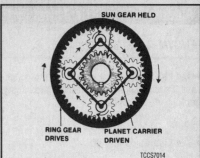

Fig. 71 Planetary gears in the minimum reduction (drive) range. The ring gear is allowed to revolve, providing a higher gear ratio

fluid flow is reduced. Under cruising conditions, the stator is eventually forced to rotate on its one-way clutch in the direction of engine rotation. Under these conditions, the torque converter begins to behave almost like a solid shaft, with the torus and turbine speeds being almost equal.

PLANETARY GEARBOX

▶ **See Figures 69, 70 and 71**

The ability of the torque converter to multiply engine torque is limited. Also, the unit tends to be more efficient when the turbine is rotating at relatively high speeds. Therefore, a planetary gearbox is used to carry the power output of the turbine to the driveshaft.

Planetary gears function very similarly to conventional transaxle gears. However, their construction is different in that three elements make up one gear system, and, in that all three elements are different from one another. The three elements are: an outer gear that is shaped like a hoop, with teeth cut into the inner surface; a sun gear, mounted on a shaft and located at the very center of the outer gear; and a set of three planet gears, held by pins in a ring-like planet carrier, meshing with both the sun gear and the outer gear. Either the outer gear or the sun gear may be held stationary, providing more than one possible torque multiplication factor for each set of gears. Also, if all three gears are forced to rotate at the same speed, the gearset forms, in effect, a solid shaft.

Most automatics use the planetary gears to provide various reductions ratios. Bands and clutches are used to hold various portions of the gearsets to the transaxle case or to the shaft on which they are mounted. Shifting is accomplished, then, by changing the portion of each planetary gearset which is held to the transaxle case or to the shaft.

SERVOS AND ACCUMULATORS

▶ **See Figure 72**

The servos are hydraulic pistons and cylinders. They resemble the hydraulic actuators used on many other machines, such as bulldozers. Hydraulic fluid enters the cylinder, under pressure, and forces the piston to move to engage the band or clutches.

The accumulators are used to cushion the engagement of the servos. The transaxle fluid must pass through the accumulator on the way to the servo. The accumulator housing contains a thin piston which is sprung away from the discharge passage of the accumulator. When fluid passes through the accumulator on the way to the servo, it must move the piston against spring pressure, and this action smooths out the action of the servo.

HYDRAULIC CONTROL SYSTEM

The hydraulic pressure used to operate the servos comes from the main transaxle oil pump. This fluid is channeled to the various servos through the shift valves. There is generally a manual shift valve which is operated by the transaxle selector lever and an automatic shift valve for each automatic upshift the transaxle provides.

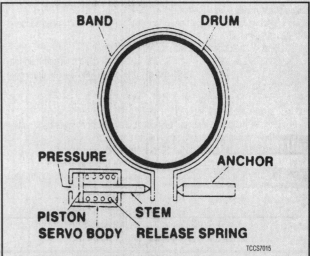

Fig. 72 Servos, operated by pressure, are used to apply or release the bands, to either hold the ring gear or allow it to rotate

➡**Many new transaxles are electronically controlled. On these models, electrical solenoids are used to better control the hydraulic fluid. Usually, the solenoids are regulated by an electronic control module.**

There are two pressures which affect the operation of these valves. One is the governor pressure which is effected by vehicle speed. The other is the modulator pressure which is effected by intake manifold vacuum or throttle position. Governor pressure rises with an increase in vehicle speed, and modulator pressure rises as the throttle is opened wider. By responding to these two pressures, the shift valves cause the upshift points to be delayed with increased throttle opening to make the best use of the engine's power output. Most transaxles also make use of an auxiliary circuit for downshifting. This circuit may be actuated by the throttle linkage the vacuum line which actuates the modulator, by a cable or by a solenoid. It applies pressure to a special downshift surface on the shift valve or valves. The transaxle modulator also governs the line pressure, used to actuate the servos. In this way, the clutches and bands will be actuated with a force matching the torque output of the engine.

Fluid Pan

For automatic transaxle fluid pan removal and installation, please refer to Section 1 of this manual.

Back-up Light Switch

For back-up light switch replacement, please refer to the procedure located in Section 6 of this manual.

Automatic Transaxle Assembly

REMOVAL & INSTALLATION

➡The radio may have a coded theft protection circuit. Make sure you have the code before disconnecting the battery, removing the radio fuse, or removing the radio.

Integra

◆ **See Figures 73 thru 86**

1. Disconnect the negative battery cable, then the positive battery cable.
2. Remove the air cleaner housing assembly with intake air tube.
3. Disconnect the starter cables and remove the cable holder from the starter.
4. Disconnect the transaxle ground cable from the transaxle hanger.
5. Disconnect the lockup control solenoid valve connector and the shift control solenoid valve connector. Remove the harness clamp on the lockup control solenoid harness from the harness stay.
6. Disconnect the Vehicle Speed Sensor (VSS), main shaft speed sensor and the counter shaft speed sensor connectors.
7. Remove the upper transaxle mounting bolts.
8. Remove the drain plug from the transaxle, then drain the used fluid into a sealable container. Properly dispose of the used fluid. Reinstall the drain plug with a new sealing washer.
9. Remove the splash shield.
10. Remove the front wheels.
11. Remove the cotter pins and castle nuts from the front lower ball joints. Separate the ball joints from the lower control arms.
12. Remove the right strut fork bolt, discard the nut.
13. Remove the right strut pinch bolt, then remove the strut fork.
14. Pry the right halfshaft out of the differential, discard the set ring on the inner joint.

15. Pry the left halfshaft out of the intermediate shaft, discard the set ring on the inner joint.
16. Tie plastic bags over the halfshaft joints to keep the splines of the joints clean.
17. Detach the heated Oxygen (O_2S) sensor connector.
18. Unfasten the nuts and bolts connecting exhaust pipe "A" to the catalytic converter. Discard the gasket and the locknuts.
19. Remove and discard the nuts attaching exhaust pipe "A" to the exhaust hanger.
20. Unfasten and discard the locknuts attaching exhaust pipe "A" to the exhaust manifold, then remove exhaust pipe "A" from the vehicle. discard the exhaust gaskets.
21. Remove the intermediate shaft mounting bolts, and remove the intermediate shaft.
22. Remove the set ring from the intermediate shaft and install a new set ring.
23. Remove the shift cable cover, then remove the shift cable by removing the control lever. Discard the lockwasher.

✳✳ WARNING

Do not bend the shift control cable when removing it.

24. Remove the right front mount/bracket and discard the two long attaching bolts.
25. Detach the end of the throttle control cable from the throttle control drum.
26. Disconnect the transaxle cooler hoses from the joint pipes. Turn the ends of the cooler hoses up to prevent fluid from flowing out, then plug the joint pipes.
27. Remove the engine stiffener and the torque converter cover.
28. Remove the eight drive plate bolts, one at a time, while rotating the crankshaft pulley.
29. Place a suitable transaxle jack under the transaxle, then raise the transaxle just enough to take the weight off of the mounts, then remove the transaxle mount.
30. Remove the transaxle mounting bolts and rear engine mounting bolts.

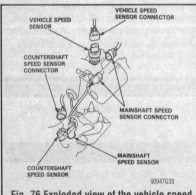

Fig. 73 Remove of the intake duct and air cleaner as an assembly

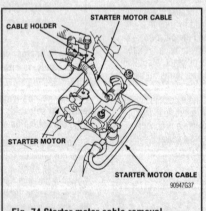

Fig. 74 Starter motor cable removal

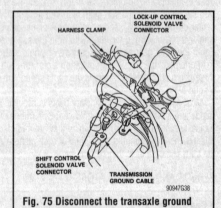

Fig. 75 Disconnect the transaxle ground cable from the hanger

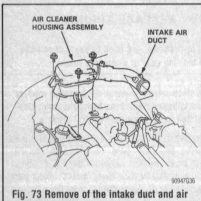

Fig. 76 Exploded view of the vehicle speed sensor

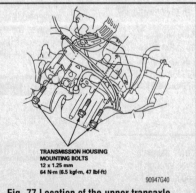

Fig. 77 Location of the upper transaxle mounting bolts

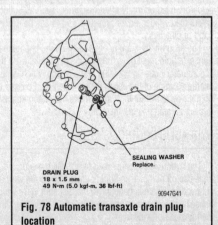

Fig. 78 Automatic transaxle drain plug location

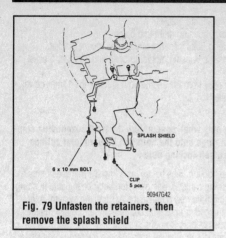

Fig. 79 Unfasten the retainers, then remove the splash shield

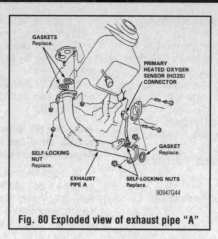

Fig. 80 Exploded view of exhaust pipe "A"

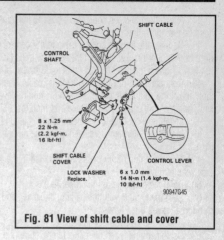

Fig. 81 View of shift cable and cover

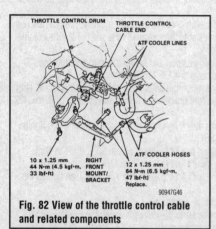

Fig. 82 View of the throttle control cable and related components

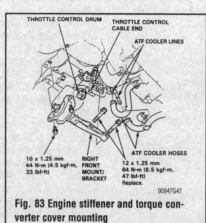

Fig. 83 Engine stiffener and torque converter cover mounting

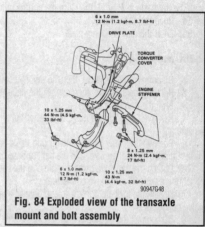

Fig. 84 Exploded view of the transaxle mount and bolt assembly

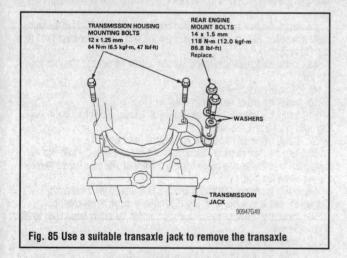

Fig. 85 Use a suitable transaxle jack to remove the transaxle

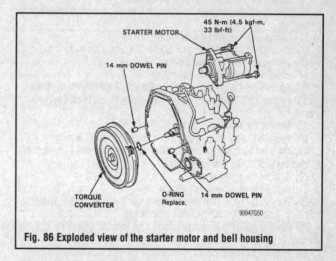

Fig. 86 Exploded view of the starter motor and bell housing

31. Pull the transaxle away from the engine until it clears the 14mm dowel pins, then lower it on the transaxle jack.

32. Remove the starter from the transaxle.

To install:

33. Flush the ATF cooler.

34. Install the starter to the transaxle, tighten the bolts to 33 ft. lbs. (45 Nm). Install the 14mm dowel pins to the torque converter housing.

35. Place the transaxle on a transaxle jack, and raise to engine level.

36. Fit the transaxle to the engine, then install the transaxle housing mounting bolts and the two rear engine mounting bolts with new washers. Tighten the transaxle housing mounting bolts to 43 ft. lbs. (59 Nm) and the rear engine mounting bolts to 86.8 ft. lbs. (118 Nm).

37. Install the transaxle mount. Tighten the bolt to 54 ft. lbs. (74 Nm) and the nuts to 47 ft. lbs. (64 Nm).

38. Install the three transaxle upper mounting bolts, tighten the bolts to 54 ft. lbs. (74 Nm).

39. Remove the transaxle jack.

40. Attach the torque converter to the drive plate with the eight retaining bolts, then tighten the bolts to 104 inch lbs. (12 Nm). Rotate the crankshaft as necessary to tighten the bolts to ½the specified torque, then the final torque, in a criss-cross pattern. After tightening the last bolts, check that the crankshaft rotates freely.

41. Install the torque converter cover, tighten the three 6x1mm bolts, to 104 inch lbs. (12 Nm) and tighten the 10x1.25 bolt to 33 ft. lbs. (44 Nm).

42. Install the engine stiffener. Tighten the bolt attaching the engine stiffener to the transaxle to 32 ft. lbs. (43 Nm). Tighten the bolts attaching the stiffener to the engine to 17 ft. lbs. (24 Nm).

43. Tighten the crankshaft pulley bolt to 130 ft. lbs. (177 Nm).

44. Attach the transaxle cooler inlet hose to the joint pipe. Leave the drain hose on the return line.

45. Connect the throttle control cable to the control drum and install the right front mount/bracket. Tighten the two new bolts (12x1.25mm) to 47 ft. lbs. (64 Nm). Tighten the two 10x1.25 bolts to 33 ft. lbs. (44 Nm).

46. Connect the control lever and shifter cable, using a new lockwasher, then install the shift cable cover. Tighten the control lever bolt to 10 ft. lbs. (14 Nm), and the shift cable cover bolts to 104 inch lbs. (12 Nm).

47. Install new set ring to the intermediate shaft and the halfshafts.

48. Install the intermediate shaft, tighten the mounting bolts to 29 ft. lbs. (39 Nm).

49. The remaining components are installed in the reverse order from which they were removed.

50. Refill the transaxle to the proper level.

51. Start the engine, with the parking brake set, and shift the transaxle through all gears three times.

52. Check and adjust the shift cable as necessary.

53. Let the engine reach operating temperature (the cooling fan comes on) with the transaxle in **P** or **N**, then turn the engine off and check the fluid level.

54. Road test the vehicle.

55. Enter the radio security code.

2.2CL and 2.3CL

1. Disconnect the negative, then the positive battery cables.

2. Remove the set plate, then remove the battery from the vehicle.

3. Shift the transaxle into **N**.

4. Remove the air intake hose, air cleaner housing, and the resonator assembly.

5. Remove the battery cable and ground cable bracket from the battery base. Remove the battery base and the battery base bracket.

6. Detach the transaxle ground cable and the speed sensor connectors. Disconnect the solenoid valve connectors.

7. Detach the lock-up control solenoid valve and shift control solenoid valve connectors.

8. Disconnect the throttle cable from the throttle control lever.

9. Detach the mainshaft speed sensor connector.

10. Disconnect the transaxle cooler hoses from the joint pipes and plug the hoses.

11. Disconnect the starter cables and remove the starter.

12. Detach the Countershaft Speed Sensor (CSS) connector.

13. Unplug the Vehicle Speed Sensor (VSS) connector.

14. Install a suitable hoist to the engine.

15. Remove the 4 upper bolts attaching the transaxle to the engine block.

16. Loosen the 3 bolts attaching the front engine mount bracket to the engine.

17. Remove the transaxle mount.

18. Raise and safely support the vehicle. Remove the front wheels.

19. Drain the transaxle fluid and reinstall the drain plug with a new washer and tighten to 36 ft. lbs. (50 Nm).

20. Remove the splash shield.

21. Remove the subframe center beam.

22. Remove the cotter pins and lower arm ball joint nuts, then separate the ball joints from the lower arms using a suitable tool. Discard the cotter pins.

23. Remove the right damper pinch bolt, then separate the damper fork and damper.

24. Remove the bolts and nut, then remove the right radius rod.

25. Using a small prytool, carefully pry the right and left halfshafts out of the differential. Remove the right and left halfshafts. Tie plastic bags over the halfshaft ends to prevent damage to the CV boots and splines.

26. Remove the bolts mounting the intermediate shaft, then remove the intermediate shaft from the differential.

27. Remove the torque converter cover and shift cable cover.

28. Remove the shift control cable by removing the lockbolt. Remove the shift cable lever from the control shaft. Don't disconnect the control lever from the shift cable. Wire the shift cable out of the work area and be careful not to kink it.

29. Remove the 8 drive plate bolts one at a time while rotating the crankshaft pulley.

30. Place a suitable jack under the transaxle and raise the jack just enough to take weight off of the mounts.

31. Remove the intake manifold bracket.

32. Remove the transaxle housing mounting bolts.

33. Remove the mounting bolts from the rear engine mount bracket.

34. Remove the 4 transaxle housing mounting bolts and 3 mount bracket nuts.

35. Pull the transaxle away from the engine until it clears the 14mm dowel pins, then lower it using the jack.

To install:

➡**Use new self-locking nuts when assembling the front suspension components. Install new set rings onto the halfshaft inboard joint splines. Replace any color-coded self-locking bolts.**

36. Flush the transaxle cooling lines before installing the transaxle using a suitable a pressurized flushing canister. Use only Honda biodegradable flushing fluid. Other types of flushing fluid may damage the A/T cooling system. After flushing is complete, dry the cooler lines with compressed air for two minutes, or until flushing agent stops draining from the system.

37. Be sure the 2, 14mm dowel pins are installed into the torque converter housing.

38. Install the torque converter onto the transaxle mainshaft with a new hub O-ring. Install the starter motor onto the transaxle case and tighten the mounting bolts to 33 ft. lbs. (44 Nm).

39. Raise the transaxle into position and install the transaxle housing mounting bolts. Tighten the bolts to 47 ft. lbs. (65 Nm).

40. Install the rear engine mounting bolts and tighten to 40 ft. lbs. (54 Nm).

41. Install the intake manifold bracket and tighten the bolts to 16 ft. lbs. (22 Nm).

42. Install the upper bolts attaching the transaxle to the engine and tighten the bolts to 47 ft. lbs. (64 Nm).

43. Tighten the front engine mount bracket bolts to 28 ft. lbs. (38 Nm).

44. Install the transaxle mount and loosely install the nuts and bolt that attach the mount. Tighten the nuts first to 28 ft. lbs. (38 Nm), then tighten the bolt to 47 ft. lbs. (64 Nm).

45. Remove the jack from the transaxle.

46. Attach the torque converter to the drive plate with the 8 bolts. Tighten the bolts in 2 steps in a crisscross pattern: first to 54 inch lbs. (6 Nm), and finally to 108 inch lbs. (12 Nm). Check for free rotation after tightening the last bolt.

47. Install the shift control cable and control cable holder. Tighten the shift cable lockbolt to 10 ft. lbs. (14 Nm). Tighten the shift cable cover bolts to 13 ft. lbs. (18 Nm).

48. Install the torque converter cover and tighten the bolts to 108 inch lbs. (12 Nm).

49. Remove the engine hoist.

50. Install the radius rod and damper fork.

51. Install the intermediate shaft into the differential and tighten the mounting bolts to 28 ft. lbs. (38 Nm).

52. Install a new set ring on the end of each halfshaft.

53. Turn the right steering knuckle fully outward and slide the axle into the differential until the set ring snaps into the differential side gear. Repeat the procedure on the left side.

54. Install the damper fork bolts and ball joint nuts to the lower arms. Tighten the ball joint nut to 40 ft. lbs. (55 Nm) and install a new cotter pin.

55. Install the subframe center beam and tighten the center beam bolts to 28 ft. lbs. (39 Nm).

56. Install the splash shield.

57. Install the front wheels and lower the vehicle.

58. Attach the speed sensor connector.

59. Support the right front knuckle with a floor jack, until the weight of the vehicle is held by the jack. Tighten the damper fork pinch bolt to 32 ft. lbs. (44 Nm). Tighten the radius rod bolts to 76 ft. lbs. (105 Nm), and the radius rod nut to 32 ft. lbs. (44 Nm). Hold the damper fork bolt with a wrench, and tighten the nut to 40 ft. lbs. (55 Nm). Remove the floor jack.

60. Connect the cables to the starter.

61. Reconnect the throttle control cable.

62. Connect the lock-up control solenoid valve and shift control solenoid valve connectors.

63. Attach the speed sensor connectors and the transaxle ground cable.

64. Connect the transaxle cooler inlet hose to the joint pipe. Attach a drain hose to the return line.

65. Install the battery base stay and the battery base.

66. Install the resonator assembly, the air cleaner assembly, and the air intake hose.

67. Install the battery and connect the positive, then the negative battery cables to the battery.

68. Refill the transaxle with the proper type and amount of automatic transaxle fluid.

    a. With the flusher drain hose attached to the cooler return line.

    b. Place the transaxle in **P**, run the engine for 30 seconds, or until approximately 1 quart of fluid is discharged. Immediately shut off the engine. This completes the cooler flushing process.

    c. Remove the drain hose and reconnect the cooler return line.

    d. Refill the transaxle to the proper level with automatic transaxle fluid.

69. Start the engine, set the parking brake, and shift the transaxle through all gears 3 times. Check for proper shift cable adjustment.

70. Let the engine reach operating temperature with the transaxle in **P** or **N**. Then, shut off the engine and check the fluid level.

71. Road test the vehicle.

72. After road testing the vehicle, loosen the front engine mount bracket bolts, then retighten them to 28 ft. lbs. (39 Nm).

73. Check and adjust the vehicle's front end alignment.

74. Enter the radio security code.

3.0CL

1. Disconnect the negative battery cable, then the positive cable.

2. Remove the battery and tray.

3. Remove the clamps securing the battery cables to the base.

4. Remove the intake air duct and the air cleaner assembly.

5. Raise the vehicle and drain the transaxle fluid. Replace the drain plug with a new washer.

6. Remove the starter wiring and harness clamps, remove the breather and radiator hoses from the retainer.

7. Detach the wiring connectors from the transaxle assembly.

8. Disconnect the cooler lines and point them up to prevent fluid drainage.

9. Remove the bolt and nut securing the rear stiffener and remove the stiffener.

10. Remove the bolts securing the transaxle to the engine.

11. Remove the front mounting bracket bolts.

12. Remove the engine under cover.

13. Disconnect the lower shock absorber mounting and the lower ball joints from the control arms.

14. Remove the bolts securing the radius rods to the lower arms.

15. Remove the halfshafts. Keep the splined ends of the shafts clean.

16. Mark the position of the sub-frame on the main-frame and remove it.

17. Remove the engine brace from the rear of the engine.

18. Remove the shift cable cover, bracket and cable.

19. Remove the 8 bolts securing the drive plate to the torque converter.

20. Attach a chain hoist to the engine and raise it slightly.

21. Place a jack under the transaxle.

22. Remove the transaxle mount bracket.

23. Remove the intake manifold support bracket.

24. Remove the rear mount bracket.

25. Pull the transaxle back slightly until it comes off the dowels and lower it from the vehicle. Do not let the torque converter fall out of the transaxle.

To install:

26. If removed, install the torque converter using a new O-ring.

27. Install the dowel pins in the torque converter housing.

28. Raise the transaxle to the engine and install the rear mount bracket. Tighten the 8mm bolt to 16 ft. lbs. (22 Nm) and the 12mm bolts to 40 ft. lbs. (54 Nm).

29. Install the transaxle-to-engine bolts. Tighten the bolts to 47 ft. lbs. (64 Nm).

30. Connect the breather tube with the dot facing up and install the transaxle mount bracket. Tighten the nuts to 28 ft. lbs. (38 Nm) and the through-bolt to 40 ft. lbs. (54 Nm).

31. Install the driveplate-to-torque converter bolts. Tighten them to 108 inch lbs. (12 Nm) in a crisscross pattern.

32. Install the shift cable, bracket and cover.

33. Install the engine brace on the rear of the engine.

34. Install the halfshafts.

35. Install the sub-frame after aligning the matchmarks. Tighten the rear bolts to 47 ft. lbs. (64 Nm) and the front bolts to 76 ft. lbs. (103 Nm).

36. Install the front mount. Tighten the bolts to 28 ft. lbs. (38 Nm).

37. Connect the shock absorbers and the radius rods to the lower control arms.

38. Install the engine under cover.

39. Attach all the wiring connectors.

40. Connect the starter wiring and install the harness clamps.

41. Install the battery.

42. Install the air cleaner assembly and intake duct.

43. Refill the transaxle with the proper amount and type of automatic transmission fluid.

Vigor and 2.5TL

▶ **See Figure 87**

1. Shift the transaxle into **P**.

2. Disconnect the negative, then the positive battery cables, then remove the battery and battery tray.

3. Without disconnecting the wires, remove the ABS relay box and set it aside.

4. Remove the heat shield and sub-ground cable.

➡ **The distributor may be removed for better access to the transaxle case bolts.**

5. Remove the emission control equipment box from the firewall without disconnecting the vacuum hoses.

6. Remove the torque converter cover and rotate the crankshaft as required to remove the eight torque converter flexplate bolts.

7. Disconnect the transaxle wiring harnesses and tag them for reassembly.

8. Remove the transaxle ground cable.

9. Remove the upper transaxle bolts and the 26mm shim.

10. Raise and support the vehicle.

11. Remove the guard plate and remove the plug to drain the transaxle fluid.

12. Remove the transaxle left side mount and bracket.

13. Disconnect the oil cooler hoses.

14. The differential stays on the vehicle. Remove the secondary cover and the 33mm sealing bolt and install an extension shaft removal tool. Disconnect the differential extension shaft from the transaxle.

➡ **Suitable extension shaft puller and installation tools are needed to disconnect the extension shaft from the differential.**

15. Remove the front exhaust pipe "A" and its mounting brackets.

16. Remove the shift cable cover and disconnect the shift cable from the control shaft. Remove the cable mounting bracket and wire the cable up and out of the way.

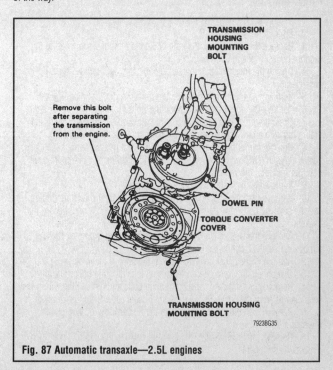

Fig. 87 Automatic transaxle—2.5L engines

7923BG35

17. Place a transaxle jack securely under the transaxle and raise it to take the weight off the mounts.

18. Use an offset wrench to remove the mid–mounts and the mid–mount spacer.

19. Remove the transaxle case bolts. Remove the torque converter cover mounting bolt located on the converter housing. Do not remove the torque converter cover.

20. Slide the transaxle back and away from the engine. Carefully lower it from the vehicle.

To install:

21. Flush the transaxle cooler lines.

22. Install the torque converter onto the mainshaft using a new O-ring. Install the mounting pins into the transaxle case.

23. Install a new set ring on the extension shaft and lightly lubricate the splines with high temperature molybdenum grease. Pack the opening in the drive pinion with high temperature molybdenum grease.

24. Install the transaxle and start all of the bolts. Don't forget the 26mm shim between the transaxle and differential. Tighten the 12mm bolts to 54 ft. lbs. (75 Nm). Tighten the torque converter cover bolt to 9 ft. lbs. (12 Nm).

25. Install the mid–mounts and brackets. Tighten the bolts to 28 ft. lbs. (39 Nm) and the nuts to 32 ft. lbs. (43–44 Nm).

26. Install a new set ring, and install the extension shaft using an extension shaft installer. Be sure the shaft snaps into place.

27. Pack the shaft area with molybdenum grease, but keep the thread area clean. Apply liquid gasket to the sealing bolt threads and tighten the bolt to 58 ft. lbs. (78–80 Nm). Install the cover.

28. Install the transaxle left side mount and bracket. Tighten the mount bolts to 47 ft. lbs. (65 Nm). Tighten the bracket bolts to 40 ft. lbs. (54 Nm).

29. Install the torque converter bolts and tighten them in 2 steps in a criss-cross pattern to 104 inch lbs. (12 Nm). Install the torque converter cover and tighten the bolts to 104 inch lbs. (12 Nm).

30. The remaining components are installed in the reverse order from which they were removed.

31. Connect all the wiring harnesses and the battery cables. Refill the transaxle with fresh fluid.

32. When all parts have been installed, start the engine and shift through all the gears 3 times to fill all the passages with fluid, then check the shift cable and adjust as needed. When the engine is fully warmed up, stop the engine and check the fluid level.

33. Enter the radio security code.

Legend, 3.2TL and 3.5RL

▶ **See Figure 88**

1. Disconnect the negative, then the positive battery cables.

2. Shift the transaxle into **P**.

3. Remove the control box from the bulkhead without disconnecting the vacuum hoses. Place the control box out of the way.

4. Detach the transaxle sub–harness connectors, and remove the sub–harness clamp.

5. Remove the three bolts securing the transaxle dipstick pipe bracket.

6. Remove the upper transaxle mounting bolts.

7. Drain the fluid from the transaxle into a sealable container. Install the drain plug with a new washer and tighten the plug to 36 ft. lbs. (49 Nm).

8. Pull the carpet back under the passenger seat to expose the secondary heated Oxygen (O2S) sensor connector. Detach the connector and push it out from the inside of the vehicle.

9. Remove the heat shields from exhaust pipe "A".

10. Remove the nuts attaching exhaust pipe "A" to the exhaust manifolds and the catalytic converter. Remove the front exhaust pipe "A" and discard the gaskets.

11. Remove the O2S sensor wiring harness cover and grommet, then remove the catalytic converter. Discard the nuts and gasket.

12. Remove the exhaust heat shield from the floor of the vehicle.

13. Disconnect the transaxle cooler hoses, then plug the hoses and pipes.

14. Remove the shift cable cover mounting bolts and remove the wiring harness clamps from the cover. Remove the shift cable cover from the transaxle.

15. Remove the shift cable holder from the holder base, do not lose the washers.

16. Remove the locknut attaching the shift cable to the control lever, then remove the shift cable.

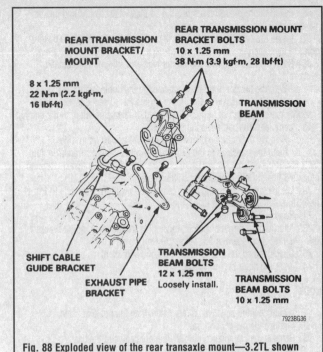

Fig. 88 Exploded view of the rear transaxle mount—3.2TL shown

17. Remove the transaxle dipstick pipe from the torque converter housing.

18. Remove the lower plate from under the rack and pinion, then install the two rack and pinion mounting bolts.

19. Remove the shift cable guide bracket from the transaxle beam.

20. Remove the transaxle beam, rear transaxle mount racket/mount and exhaust pipe hanger.

21. Be sure that the transaxle is in park, then remove the 36mm sealing bolt from the transaxle.

22. Install a suitable extension shaft puller onto the end of the extension shaft. Using the extension shaft puller, disconnect the extension shaft from the differential. Pull the extension shaft out enough to remove the set ring.

➡ **Do not try to remove the extension shaft, it cannot be removed from the transaxle this way.**

23. Place a transaxle jack under the transaxle and raise the transaxle to take the weight off of the mounts.

24. Remove the stop holder, the mid mount stops and the mid mounts.

25. Remove the engine stiffener.

26. Remove the torque converter covers.

27. Remove the six drive plate bolts one at a time while rotating the crankshaft.

➡ **If necessary, remove the spark plugs while removing the drive plate bolts.**

28. Remove the transaxle mounting bolts.

29. Pull the transaxle away from the engine until it clears the dowel pins, then lower it on the transaxle jack.

To install:

30. Flush the transaxle cooling lines before installing the transaxle using a suitable a pressurized flushing canister. Use only Honda biodegradable flushing fluid. Other types of flushing fluid may damage the A/T cooling system. After flushing is complete, dry the cooler lines with compressed air for two minutes, or until flushing agent stops draining from the system.

31. Install the torque converter to the transaxle with a new O-ring. Install the two dowel pins to the torque converter housing.

32. Clean the extension shaft opening on the differential side. Keep the extension shaft opening clean of foreign material.

33. Apply a suitable super high temperature grease to the splines on the extension shaft, then install a new set ring to the groove.

34. Raise the transaxle into position and attach the transaxle to the engine. Install the housing mounting bolt with the 26mm shim. Do not install the transaxle housing bolt on the engine stiffener side at this time.

35. Attach the torque converter to the drive plate with the six bolts. Rotate the crankshaft as necessary to tighten the bolts to 120 inch lbs. (13 Nm), then tighten the bolts in a criss-cross pattern to 20 ft. lbs. (26 Nm). After tightening the bolts check that the crankshaft rotates freely.

36. Install the torque converter covers and tighten the bolts to 104 inch lbs. (12 Nm).

37. Install the engine stiffener. Tighten the 8mm bolts loosely and tighten the transaxle housing bolt to 16 ft. lbs. (22 Nm), then tighten the rest of the bolts to 16 ft. lbs. (22 Nm).

38. Install the transaxle housing mounting bolts to the transaxle side. Tighten the bolts to 47 ft. lbs. (64 Nm).

39. Install the mid mounts, then the mid mount stops. Tighten the 8mm bolts loosely, then install the stop holder.

40. Tighten the mid mount 10mm bolts to 28 ft. lbs. (38 Nm) and tighten the 8mm bolts to 16 ft. lbs. (22 Nm). Tighten the new nuts attaching the mid mounts to 35 ft. lbs. (48 Nm) and tighten the nuts attaching the stop holder to 40 ft. lbs. (54 Nm).

41. Remove the transaxle jack from the transaxle.

42. Install the transaxle beam to the rear transaxle mount bracket/mount.

Tighten the two bolts loosely, then install them with the exhaust pipe bracket on the rear cover and body.

43. Tighten the three transaxle beam bolts to 28 ft. lbs. (38 Nm).

44. Tighten the three rear transaxle mount bracket bolts to 28 ft. lbs. (38 Nm).

45. Tighten the two bolts attaching the mount it the beam to 40 ft. lbs. (54 Nm).

46. Install the shift cable guide to the transaxle beam and tighten the bolt to 7.2 ft. lbs. (9.8 Nm).

47. Install the extension shaft using the extension shaft installation tool. Be sure that the extension shaft locks into the secondary gear and the differential.

48. Fill the secondary gear with a suitable super high temperature grease. Applying sealer to the threads of the 36mm sealing bolt, then install the bolt and tighten to 58 ft. lbs. (78 Nm).

49. Remove the two bolts from the rack and pinion necessary to install the lower plate, then install the lower plate and the attaching bolts. Tighten the lower plate attaching bolt to 28 ft. lbs. (38 Nm) and tighten the rack and pinion bolts to 43 ft. lbs. (59 Nm).

TORQUE SPECIFICATIONS

Components	Ft. Lbs.	Nm
Automatic Transaxle		
Transaxle-to-engine mounting bolts		
All models except Integra	47	64
Integra		
1994-95		
Lower Bolts	43	58
Upper Bolts	54	73
1997-00		
Lower Bolts	47	64
Upper Bolts	46	62
Rear transaxle mounting bolts	87	118
Rear transaxle mounting nuts	47	64
Engine Stiffeners		
Transaxle	47	64
Engine	17	23
Front mounting bracket		
Short	33	45
Long	47	64
Torque converter cover	108 inch lbs.	12
Drive plate-to-torque converter	108 inch lbs.	12
Manual Transaxle		
Engine-to-transaxle bolt		
Lower		
Locking bolt	87	118
Non-locking bolts	47	64
Upper		
Long starter bolt	47	64
Short bolt	33	45
Transaxle mount		
Right		
Engine bracket to mount	47	64
Mount bolts	54	73
Engine stiffener		
Short bolt	17	23
Long bolt	42	57
Clutch cover bolts		
Short bolt	144 in-lbs.	16
Left lower bolt	42	57
Right lower bolt	17	23

50. Connect the shift cable control lever to the control shaft, then install the washer and nut. Tighten the nut to 104 inch lbs. (12 Nm).

51. Install the shift cable holder to the shift cable holder base with the mounting washers. Install the attaching bolts and tighten the bolts to 104 inch lbs. (12 Nm).

52. Install the shift cable cover and tighten the mounting bolts to 104 inch lbs. (12 Nm).

53. Connect the cooler feed hose to the pipe.

54. Install the ATF dipstick pipe with a new O-ring on the torque converter housing.

55. Install the transaxle subharness clamp to the harness.

56. Install the exhaust heat shield to the floor of the vehicle and tighten the bolts to 86 inch lbs. (9.8 Nm).

57. Install the catalytic converter with a new gasket. Install the wiring harness and the grommet to the vehicle, then install the harness cover. Tighten the cover bolts to 86 inch lbs. (9.8 Nm).

58. Install exhaust pipe "A" with new gaskets and new nuts. Tighten the nuts attaching the pipe to the manifolds to 40 ft. lbs. (54 Nm) and tighten the nuts attaching the exhaust pipe to the catalytic converter to 16 ft. lbs. (22 Nm). Tighten the catalytic converter rear attaching nuts to 24 ft. lbs. (32 Nm).

59. Install the heat shields to exhaust pipe "A" and tighten the nuts to 104 inch lbs. (12 Nm).

60. Attach the secondary heated O2S sensor connector, located under the passenger front seat.

61. Install the transaxle upper mounting bolts and tighten the bolts to 47 ft. lbs. (64 Nm).

62. Install the transaxle dipstick pipe bracket bolts and tighten the bolts to 104 inch lbs. (12 Nm).

63. Connect the transaxle subharness connectors.

64. Install the control box and tighten the mounting bolts to 104 inch lbs. (12 Nm).

65. Connect the positive, then the negative battery cable.

66. Fill the transaxle with the recommended type and amount of fluid.

   a. Leave the flusher drain hose attached to the cooler return line.

   b. With the transaxle in park, run the engine for 30 seconds, or until approximately one quart of fluid is discharged. As soon as one quart of fluid drains, shut off the engine. This completes the cooler flushing process.

   c. Remove the drain hose and reconnect the cooler return line.

   d. Refill the transaxle to the proper level with the recommended type and amount of fluid.

67. Let the engine reach proper operating temperature (the radiator fan comes on) with the transaxle in **N**(neutral) or **P**(park). Turn the engine **OFF** and check the fluid level.

68. Enter the radio security code.

Halfshafts

REMOVAL & INSTALLATION

For halfshaft replacement and overhaul, please refer to the procedure located under manual transaxle, in this section

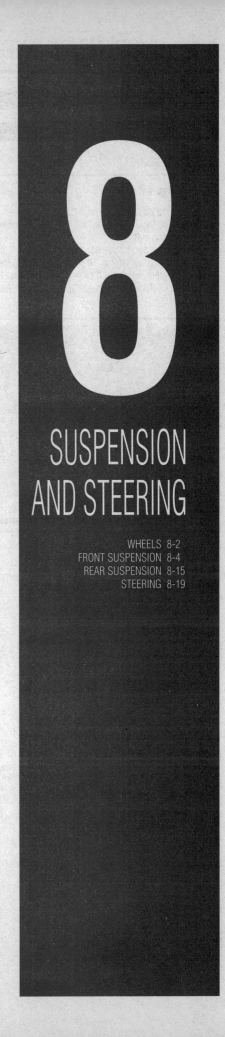

8

SUSPENSION AND STEERING

WHEELS

Wheel Assembly

REMOVAL & INSTALLATION

▶ **See Figures 1 thru 8**

1. Park the vehicle on a level surface.
2. Remove the jack, tire iron and, if necessary, the spare tire from their storage compartments.
3. Check the owner's manual or refer to Section 1 of this manual for the jacking points on your vehicle. Then, place the jack in the proper position.
4. If equipped with lug nut trim caps, remove them by either unscrewing or pulling them off the lug nuts, as appropriate. Consult the owner's manual, if necessary.

5. If equipped with a wheel cover or hub cap, insert the tapered end of the tire iron in the groove and pry off the cover.
6. Apply the parking brake and block the diagonally opposite wheel with a wheel chock or two.

➡ **Wheel chocks may be purchased at your local auto parts store, or a block of wood cut into wedges may be used. If possible, keep one or two of the chocks in your tire storage compartment, in case any of the tires has to be removed on the side of the road.**

7. If equipped with an automatic transmission/transaxle, place the selector lever in **P** or Park; with a manual transmission/transaxle, place the shifter in Reverse.
8. With the tires still on the ground, use the tire iron/wrench to break the lug nuts loose.

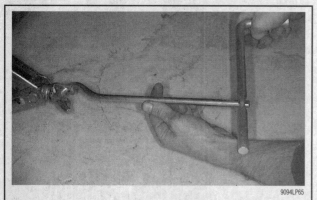

Fig. 1 Connect the spare tire jack handle as shown

9094LP65

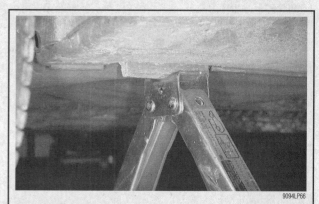

Fig. 2 Place the jack at the proper lifting point on your vehicle

9094LP66

TCCA8P01

Fig. 3 Before jacking the vehicle, block the diagonally opposite wheel with one or, preferably, two chocks

TCCA8P02

Fig. 4 With the vehicle still on the ground, break the lug nuts loose using the wrench end of the tire iron

TCCA8P03

Fig. 5 After the lug nuts have been loosened, raise the vehicle using the jack until the tire is clear of the ground

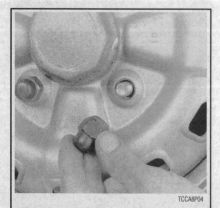

TCCA8P04

Fig. 6 Remove the lug nuts from the studs

TCCA8P05

Fig. 7 Remove the wheel and tire assembly from the vehicle

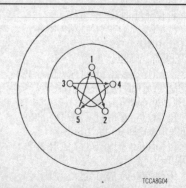

TCCA8G04

Fig. 8 Typical wheel lug tightening sequence

➡If a nut is stuck, never use heat to loosen it or damage to the wheel and bearings may occur. If the nuts are seized, one or two heavy hammer blows directly on the end of the bolt usually loosens the rust. Be careful, as continued pounding will likely damage the brake drum or rotor.

9. Using the jack, raise the vehicle until the tire is clear of the ground. Support the vehicle safely using jackstands.

10. Remove the lug nuts, then remove the tire and wheel assembly.

To install:

11. Make sure the wheel and hub mating surfaces, as well as the wheel lug studs, are clean and free of all foreign material. Always remove rust from the wheel mounting surface and the brake rotor or drum. Failure to do so may cause the lug nuts to loosen in service.

12. Install the tire and wheel assembly and hand-tighten the lug nuts.

13. Using the tire wrench, tighten all the lug nuts, in a crisscross pattern, until they are snug.

14. Raise the vehicle and withdraw the jackstand, then lower the vehicle.

15. Using a torque wrench, tighten the lug nuts in a crisscross pattern to 80 ft. lbs. (108 Nm). Check your owner's manual or refer to Section 1 of this manual for the proper tightening sequence.

✳✳ WARNING

Do not overtighten the lug nuts, as this may cause the wheel studs to stretch or the brake disc (rotor) to warp.

16. If so equipped, install the wheel cover or hub cap. Make sure the valve stem protrudes through the proper opening before tapping the wheel cover into position.

17. If equipped, install the lug nut trim caps by pushing them or screwing them on, as applicable.

18. Remove the jack from under the vehicle, and place the jack and tire iron/wrench in their storage compartments. Remove the wheel chock(s).

19. If you have removed a flat or damaged tire, place it in the storage compartment of the vehicle and take it to your local repair station to have it fixed or replaced as soon as possible.

INSPECTION

Inspect the tires for lacerations, puncture marks, nails and other sharp objects. Repair or replace as necessary. Also check the tires for treadwear and air pressure as outlined in Section 1 of this manual.

Check the wheel assemblies for dents, cracks, rust and metal fatigue. Repair or replace as necessary.

Wheel Lug Studs

REMOVAL & INSTALLATION

With Disc Brakes

▶ **See Figures 9, 10 and 11**

1. Raise and support the appropriate end of the vehicle safely using jackstands, then remove the wheel.

2. Remove the brake pads and caliper. Support the caliper aside using wire or a coat hanger. For details, please refer to Section 9 of this manual.

3. Remove the rotor. For details on wheel bearing removal, installation and adjustment, please refer to Section 1 of this manual.

4. Properly support the rotor using press bars, then drive the stud out using an arbor press.

➡If a press is not available, CAREFULLY drive the old stud out using a blunt drift. MAKE SURE the rotor is properly and evenly supported or it may be damaged.

To install:

5. Clean the stud hole with a wire brush and start the new stud with a hammer and drift pin. Do not use any lubricant or thread sealer.

6. Finish installing the stud with the press.

➡If a press is not available, start the lug stud through the bore in the hub, then position about 4 flat washers over the stud and thread the lug nut. Hold the hub/rotor while tightening the lug nut, and the stud should be drawn into position. MAKE SURE THE STUD IS FULLY SEATED, then remove the lug nut and washers.

7. Install the rotor and adjust the wheel bearings.

8. Install the brake caliper and pads.

9. Install the wheel, then remove the jackstands and carefully lower the vehicle.

10. Tighten the lug nuts to the proper torque.

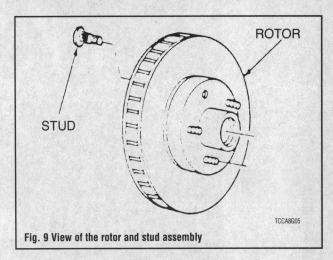

Fig. 9 View of the rotor and stud assembly

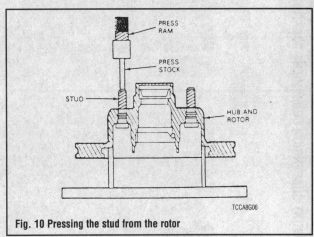

Fig. 10 Pressing the stud from the rotor

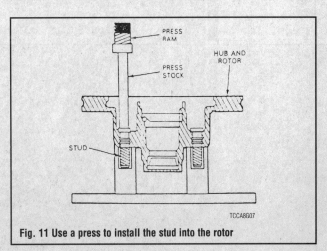

Fig. 11 Use a press to install the stud into the rotor

FRONT SUSPENSION

FRONT SUSPENSION COMPONENT LOCATIONS—INTEGRA

1. Control arm bushing
2. Sway bar bushing
3. Rack and pinion steering unit
4. Tie rod end

5. Sway bar
6. Trailing arm
7. Outer constant velocity (CV) joint
8. Ball joint

9. Control arm
10. Inner constant velocity (CV) joint
11. Intermediate shaft
12. Caliper

90948PC9

FRONT SUSPENSION COMPONENT LOCATIONS—3.2TL

1. Engine cradle mount
2. Sway bar
3. Rack and pinion steering unit
4. Tie rod ends
5. Constant velocity (CV) unit
6. Strut
7. Lower control arm
8. Lower control arm bushings
9. Trailing arm
10. Tow hook

90948PC7

Strut Assembly

REMOVAL & INSTALLATION

◆ See Figures 12, 13, 14, 15 and 16

❋❋ WARNING

The strut contains pressurized nitrogen gas. Drill a 5/64" (2.0mm) hole at the base of the strut, before disposing of it. Always wear eye protection when drilling.

1. Raise and safely support the vehicle, then remove the front wheels.
2. Support the lower suspension arm with a jack.
3. Disconnect the brake hose from the strut.

Fig. 12 Once the bottom fork bolt is removed, pull the lower control arm down to move it out of the way. This will ease strut removal

Fig. 13 Pull the strut down to remove it, once the mounting nuts have been loosened

Fig. 14 Remove the fork from the bottom of the strut by loosening the pinch bolt. Use a plastic mallet to lightly tap on the fork to remove it

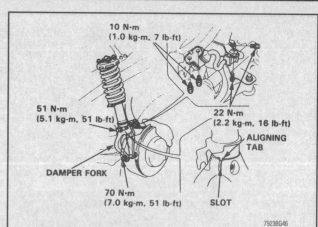

Fig. 15 Matchmark the position of the damper in the fork before removal—Legend shown

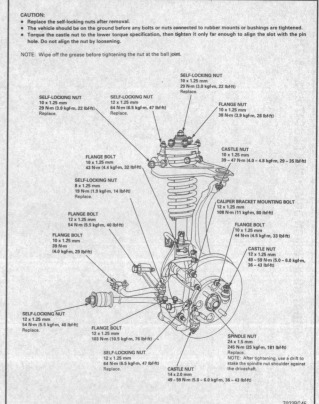

Fig. 16 Front suspension including tightening specifications—2.5TL shown, other vehicles are similar

4. Remove the lower strut mounting bolt(s). If the strut (damper) is mounted in a fork, matchmark the damper and the fork before removal.
5. Remove the upper strut assembly mounting nuts, then remove the strut assembly from the vehicle..

To install:

6. Loosely install the upper mount nuts.
7. Install the strut lower mounting bolt(s). Be sure to align the matchmark.

➥All suspension nuts and bolts should be tightened with the vehicle on the ground, or with a floor jack supporting the vehicle's weight.

8. Tighten the pinch bolt to the following specifications:
   • 2.2CL, 2.3CL, 2.5TL, 3.0CL : 47 ft. lbs. (65 Nm)
   • 3.5RL, Integra and Vigor: 32 ft. lbs. (43 Nm)
   • 3.2TL and Legend: 37 ft. lbs. (50 Nm)

9. Tighten the lower fork bolt as follows:
  • 2.2CL, 2.3CL, 2.5TL, 3.0CL, Legend and Vigor : 47 ft. lbs. (65 Nm)
  • 3.2TL, 3.5RL and Integra: 51 ft. lbs. (69 Nm)
10. Tighten the upper nuts on all models to 28 ft. lbs. (38 Nm).
11. Connect the brake hose bracket to the shock absorber.
12. Install the front wheels and lower the vehicle.
13. Check the alignment and test drive the vehicle.

OVERHAUL

▶ **See Figures 17 thru 22**

1. Raise and support the vehicle, then remove the front wheels.
2. Remove the strut (damper) from the vehicle.
3. Compress the coil spring with a suitable spring compressor.
4. Remove the locking nut from the top of the shock absorber, and remove the coil spring.

To install:

➡**Use new self-locking nuts and bolts when assembling the strut.**

5. Install the compressed coil spring on the shock absorber.
6. Assemble the upper spring seat/bearing and related components.
7. Install the mounting washer, and loosely install a new self-locking nut.
8. Hold the shock absorber piston rod with a hex wrench and tighten the self-locking nut. Tighten the self-locking nut to 22 ft. lbs. (30 Nm).

➡**All suspension nuts and bolts should be tightened with the vehicle on the ground.**

9. Install the strut in the vehicle, as outlined earlier in this section.
10. Have the front alignment checked and adjusted, if necessary.

Fig. 17 View of some of the front suspension components

Fig. 18 Remove the strut from the vehicle

Fig. 19 Compressing the coil spring with a commercially available spring compressor

Fig. 20 To remove the spring once it has been compressed, unscrew the nut at the top of the strut

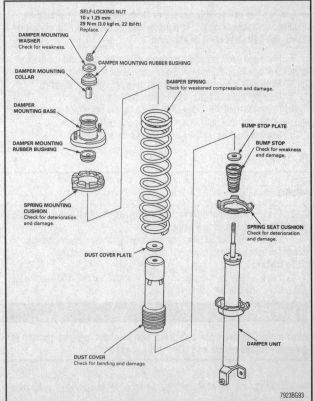
Fig. 21 Exploded view of the rear shock absorber (damper)—2.5TL shown, other vehicles are similar

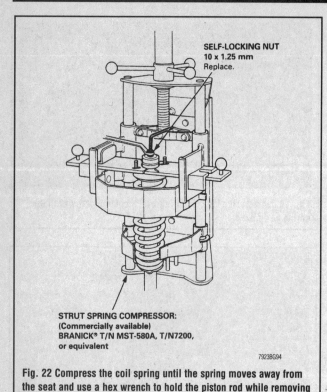

Fig. 22 Compress the coil spring until the spring moves away from the seat and use a hex wrench to hold the piston rod while removing the nut

Upper Ball Joint

INSPECTION

➡Anytime the ball joint is separated from the knuckle, it should be checked for looseness. If it is loose or can be twisted in the socket by hand, the ball joint must be replaced.

1. Raise and safely support the vehicle with jackstands under the left and right lower control arms, as far outboard and nearest to the ball joint as possible.
2. Make sure the vehicle is stable and does not rock on the stands.
3. Position a dial indicator against the wheel rim.
4. Grasp the front tire and push in on the bottom while pulling out at the top. Read the dial indicator, then reverse the push-pull procedure.
5. Replace the lower control arm if the play exceeds 0.5mm.

BOOT REPLACEMENT

Integra

1. Raise and support the vehicle safely. Remove the front wheel assemblies.
2. Remove the steering knuckle.
3. Remove the boot by prying off the snapring. Remove the 40mm clip. Check the boot for deterioration and damage, replace if necessary.
   To install:
4. Place the ball joint in position by hand. Install the ball joint into the tool and press in the new ball joint in the vise.

✳✳ WARNING

After installing the boot, check the ball joint pin tapered section for grease contamination and wipe it if necessary.

5. Install the 40mm circlip. Adjust the special tool with the adjusting bolt until the end of the tool aligns with the groove on the boot. Slide the clip over the tool and into position.
6. Install the knuckle.
7. Have the front wheel alignment checked and adjusted if necessary.

REMOVAL & INSTALLATION

▶ **See Figures 23 and 24**

➡The upper ball joint cannot be removed from the control arm. If the ball joint is damaged, the upper arm assembly must be replaced.

1. Raise and safely support the vehicle. Remove the front wheel.
2. If equipped, remove the ball joint nut cover. Remove the cotter pin and the nut connecting the upper control arm to the steering knuckle.
3. Support the lower control arm assembly with a floor jack.
4. Using a ball joint removal tool, separate the upper control arm from the steering knuckle.
5. Remove the upper control arm nuts, washers and the upper control arm from the vehicle.
   To install:
6. Replace all self-locking nuts upon installation. Clean off any dirt, oil or grease off of the threads of the fasteners. Do not tighten any nuts on any rubber mounts or bushings until the vehicle is lowered onto the ground.
7. Install the upper control arm and mounting bolts to the chassis. The upper control arms are not interchangeable.
8. Raise the steering knuckle up with a floor jack, just enough to install the upper control arm ball joint into the steering knuckle. Tighten the ball joint nut to 29–35 ft. lbs. (39–47 Nm).

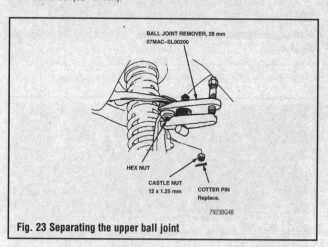

Fig. 23 Separating the upper ball joint

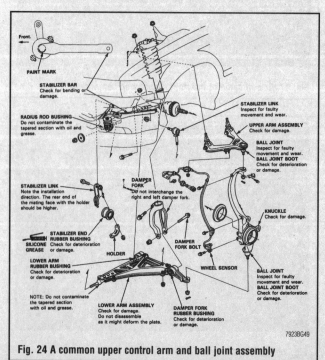

Fig. 24 A common upper control arm and ball joint assembly

9. Tighten the castle nut enough to install a new cotter pin. If removed, install the ball joint nut cover.

10. Install the front wheels, lower the vehicle, and tighten the nuts connecting the upper control arm to the chassis to 47 ft. lbs. (65 Nm).

11. Check the wheel alignment and road test the vehicle.

Lower Ball Joint

INSPECTION

Check ball joint play as follows:
1. Raise and safely support the vehicle.
2. Clamp a dial indicator onto the lower control arm and place the indicator tip on the knuckle, near the ball joint.
3. Place a prybar between the lower control arm and the knuckle.
4. Apply pressure to the bar.
5. Replace the lower control arm if the play exceeds 0.5mm.

BOOT REPLACEMENT

Integra

1. Raise and support the vehicle safely. Remove the front wheel assemblies.
2. Remove the steering knuckle.
3. Remove the boot by prying off the snapring. Remove the 40mm clip. Check the boot for deterioration and damage, replace if necessary.
To install:
4. Place the ball joint in position by hand. Install the ball joint into the tool and press in the new ball joint in the vise.
5. After installing the boot, check the ball joint pin tapered section for grease contamination and wipe it if necessary.
6. Install the 40mm circlip. Adjust the special tool with the adjusting bolt until the end of the tool aligns with the groove on the boot. Slide the clip over the tool and into position.
7. Install the knuckle.
8. Check the front wheel alignment and adjust if necessary.

REMOVAL & INSTALLATION

Integra, 2.2CL, 2.3CL, 2.5TL and 3.0CL

➡**The lower ball joint is pressed into the steering knuckle and cannot be removed.**

1. Pry up the lock tab and loosen the spindle nut. Slightly loosen the lug nuts.
2. Raise and safely support the vehicle. Remove the front wheel and spindle nut.
3. Remove the brake caliper mounting bolts and remove the caliper from the knuckle. Hang the caliper out of the way with a length of wire.
4. Remove the ABS speed sensor from the knuckle.
5. Disconnect the tie rod end from the knuckle using a ball joint remover. Be careful not to damage the joint boot.
6. Remove the cotter pin and castle nut from the lower arm ball joint. Separate the lower control arm from the knuckle.
7. Remove the cotter pin and castle nut. Separate the upper arm from the knuckle using the ball joint remover.
8. Remove the knuckle and hub by sliding the assembly off of the halfshaft. Tap the end of the halfshaft with a plastic mallet to release it from the knuckle.
9. To remove the hub and rotor assembly from the knuckle, remove the four self-locking bolts from the back of the knuckle.
10. Remove the four bolts from the hub to separate it from the brake disc.
11. The bearing can be pressed off the hub with a hydraulic press. The inner race will stay on the hub and can be removed with a bearing puller. Any time the hub and bearing are separated, the wheel bearing must be replaced with a new one.

To install:
12. Clean all the parts and examine them for wear. A worn or damaged hub will cause premature bearing failure and should be replaced.

➡**When pressing on a new bearing, be sure to press only on the inner race or the bearing will be damaged.**

13. Install the brake disc and tighten the bolts to 40 ft. lbs. (55 Nm).
14. Install the hub assembly and tighten the self-locking bolts to 33 ft. lbs. (45 Nm).

➡**Be sure that all the hub bolts are properly tightened to avoid warpage of the brake disc.**

15. Install the knuckle and hub assembly onto the halfshaft.
16. Install the knuckle on the tie rod, and the upper and lower control arms. Tighten the lower ball joint nut to 40 ft. lbs. (54 Nm), then tighten further, as required, to install a new cotter pin.
17. Tighten the upper ball joint nut to 32 ft. lbs. (44 Nm), then tighten further, as required to install a new cotter pin. Tighten the tie rod end to 36 ft. lbs. (50 Nm), then tighten further, as required to install a new cotter pin. Install the knuckle protector.
18. Install the speed sensor, sensor wire, and mounting bolts. Be careful to avoid twisting the wires.
19. Install the brake caliper, brake hoses, and mounting bolts.
20. With the wheel installed and the vehicle on the ground, tighten the spindle nut to 180 ft. lbs. (243 Nm) and stake it in place. Tighten the lug nuts to 80 ft. lbs. (108 Nm).

Legend & Vigor

1. Raise and safely support the vehicle. Remove the front wheels.
2. Remove the lower damper fork bolt.
3. Disconnect the stabilizer bar from the arm.
4. Remove the lower arm ball joint-to-steering knuckle nut.
5. Using a ball joint removal tool, separate the ball joint from the steering knuckle.
6. Disconnect the radius rod from the lower control arm and remove the arm.
To install:
7. Installation is the reverse of the removal procedure. Tighten the radius rod-to-control arm bolts to 76 ft. lbs. (105 Nm) and the chassis bolt to 39 ft. lbs. (55 Nm).
8. On Legend, tighten the ball joint nut to 54 ft. lbs. (75 Nm), then tighten further, as required to insert a new cotter pin.
9. On Vigor, tighten the lower ball joint nut to 36 ft. lbs. (50 Nm), then tighten further, as required to install a new cotter pin.

Sway Bar

REMOVAL & INSTALLATION

1. Disconnect the negative battery cable.
2. Raise and safely support the vehicle to gain access to the sway bar.
3. Unfasten the left and right sway bar link retaining nuts.
4. Remove the sway bar links from the sway bar and set aside.
5. Unfasten the sway bar insulator bracket-to-sub-frame bolts.

➡**It may be necessary to lower the sub-frame to access the sway bar**

6. Remove the sway bar from the vehicle.
To install:
7. Position the sway bar into the vehicle and secure with the mounting bracket-to-sub-frame bolts.
8. Attach the sway bar links to each side of the sway bar.
9. Reinstall the retaining nuts.
10. Carefully lower the vehicle.
11. Connect the negative battery cable.
12. Road test the vehicle and check for proper operation.

Upper Control Arm

INSPECTION

1. Raise and support the front end of the vehicle. Remove the front wheels.
2. Check for play in the upper control arm by moving the upper end of the steering knuckle.
3. If there is any play, replace the bushings in the upper control arm after removing the upper control arm.

REMOVAL & INSTALLATION

1. Raise and safely support the vehicle. Remove the front wheel.
2. Remove the cotter pin and the upper control arm-to-steering knuckle nut.
3. Using a suitable ball joint removal tool, separate the upper control arm from the steering knuckle.
4. Remove the upper control arm-to-chassis nuts, washers and the upper control arm from the vehicle.
5. To remove the bushings, remove the anchor bolts from the control arm and press the bushings out of the housing.
   To install:
6. If removed, press new bushings into the housing. Install the anchor bolts and torque the nuts to 22 ft. lbs. (30 Nm).
7. Installation is the reverse of the removal procedures. Tighten the upper control arm-to-chassis nuts to 47 ft. lbs. (65 Nm) and the upper control arm ball joint-to-steering knuckle nut to 32 ft. lbs. (42 Nm).

Lower Control Arm

REMOVAL & INSTALLATION

▶ See Figure 25

1. Raise and safely support the vehicle. Remove the front wheels.
2. Remove the lower damper fork bolt.
3. Disconnect the stabilizer bar from the arm.
4. Remove the lower arm ball joint-to-steering knuckle nut. Using a ball joint removal tool, separate the ball joint from the steering knuckle.
5. Remove the lower control arm to sub-frame mounting/pivoting bolts.
6. Disconnect the radius rod from the lower control arm and remove the arm.
   To install:
7. Installation is the reverse of the removal procedure. Tighten the radius rod-to-control arm bolts to 76 ft. lbs. (105 Nm) and the chassis bolt to 39 ft. lbs. (55 Nm).
8. On Vigor, tighten the lower ball joint nut to 36 ft. lbs. (50 Nm), then tighten further, as required, to install a new cotter pin.

Fig. 25 The lower damper fork bolt must be removed before the lower control arm can come off

CONTROL ARM BUSHING REPLACEMENT

▶ See Figures 26 and 27

➡This procedure will require the use of a press. If a press is not available, you may want to have a local shop perform this task.

1. Position the lower control arm on the press with the machined surfaces facing down.
2. Adjust the bushing driver so that it aligns itself to the inner diameter of the bushing hole, then tighten the socket bolt.
3. Position the bushing driver against the bushing.
4. Use the press as shown to remove the bushing.
   To install:
5. Align the lower control arm on the press with the machined surface facing down.
6. Align the bushing driver so that it matches the inner diameter of the bushing hole.
7. Tighten the socket bolt securely.
8. Position the bushing driver along the outer sleeve of the bushing.
9. Push the bushing into the arm using a bushing driver. Be sure the edge of the bushing reached the plate.

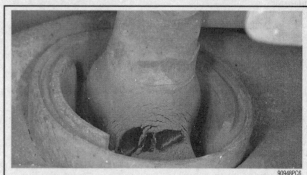

Fig. 26 This torn lower control arm bushing can cause poor handling and throw the alignment off

Fig. 27 This press is being used to push the bushing out of a lower control arm

Steering Knuckle

REMOVAL & INSTALLATION

Integra, CL, RL and TL

1. Disconnect the negative battery cable.
2. Remove the center cap or wheel cover from the rim.

3. Break loose the wheel hub retaining nut.
4. Raise and safely support the vehicle.
5. Remove the wheel and tire assembly.
6. Remove the disc brake caliper and rotor. Do not disconnect the brake line from the caliper.
7. Support the disc brake caliper with safety wire.

➡**Do not let the caliper hang by the brake hose.**

8. Remove the speed sensor from the hub assembly.
9. Remove the outer tie rod end cotter pin and remove the castellated nut. Discard the cotter pin.
10. Separate the outer tie rod end from the steering knuckle using an appropriate tie rod end remover.
11. Remove the wheel hub retaining nut.
12. Separate the halfshaft from the wheel hub.
13. Once removed, support the end of the halfshaft.
14. Remove the ball joint from the lower control arm.
15. Remove the upper ball joint from the steering knuckle.
16. Remove the steering knuckle from the vehicle.
17. Place the steering knuckle assembly onto a suitable workbench.

To install:
18. Carefully align the splines of the outer CV-joint with the splines in the hub.
19. Position the steering knuckle to the lower ball joint stud.
20. Position the steering knuckle to the lower strut tube.
21. Install a new steering knuckle to lower ball joint pinch bolt.
22. Install a new steering knuckle to strut pinch bolt.
23. Reinstall the anti-lock brake sensor and retaining bolt.
24. Reinstall the disc brake rotor and caliper assembly.
25. Reinstall a new wheel hub retaining nut.

✳✳ WARNING

Do not use an impact gun to tighten the wheel hub retaining nut or damage to the wheel bearing may result.

26. Attach the tie rod end to the steering knuckle. Install the castellated nut.
27. Install a new cotter pin.
28. Reinstall the wheel and tire assembly.
29. Connect the negative battery cable.
30. Pump the brake pedal several times to position the disc brake pads before attempting to move the vehicle.
31. Road test the vehicle and check for proper operation.

Legend

1. Pry the lock tab away from the spindle and loosen the 36mm nut. Slightly loosen the lug nuts.
2. Raise and safely support the vehicle. Remove the front wheel and spindle nut.
3. Remove the bolts retaining the brake caliper and the caliper from the knuckle. Do not allow the caliper to hang by the brake hose, support it with a length of wire.
4. Remove the disc brake rotor retaining screws if equipped. Screw both 8 x 1.25 x 12mm bolts into the disc brake removal holes and turn the bolts to press the rotor from the hub.

➡**Only turn each bolt 2 turns at a time to prevent cocking the disc excessively.**

5. Remove the tie rod from the knuckle using a tie rod end removal tool. Use care not to damage the ball joint seals.
6. Remove the cotter pin from the lower arm ball joint and the castle nut. Discard the cotter pin.
7. Remove the lower control arm from the knuckle using the ball joint removal tool.
8. Remove the cotter pin from the upper arm ball joint and the castle nut.
9. Remove the upper arm from the knuckle using the ball joint removal tool.
10. Remove the knuckle and hub by sliding the assembly off of the halfshaft.

➡**Any time the hub is removed, the wheel bearing must be replaced with a new one.**

11. On 1994 Legend, the hub can be removed with a slide hammer. Clamp the knuckle in a vise and secure the slide hammer to the wheel studs.
12. Remove the splash guard and snaprings.
13. Support the knuckle and press the bearing out towards the wheel side.
14. If the inner bearing race stayed on the hub, use a puller to remove it.

To install:
15. Clean all parts and examine for wear. A worn or damaged hub will cause premature bearing failure and should be replaced.
16. When pressing in a new bearing, install the inner snapring first and press the bearing in from the wheel side. Be sure to press only on the outer race or the bearing will be damaged.
17. Install the outer snapring and the splash guard.
18. Properly support the knuckle and press the hub into the bearing. Do not press on the wheel studs or they will press out of the hub. Be sure to support the knuckle by the inner race or the bearing will be damaged.
19. Install the knuckle in the reverse order of removal. Tighten the lower ball joint nut to 54 ft. lbs. (75 Nm) and tighten further as required to install a new cotter pin.
20. Tighten the upper ball joint nut to 32 ft. lbs. (44 Nm) and tighten further as required to install a new cotter pin. Tighten the tie rod end to 36 ft. lbs. (50 Nm) and tighten further, as required, to install a new cotter pin.
21. With the wheel installed and all 4 wheels on the ground, torque the spindle nut to 206 ft. lbs. (285 Nm) and stake it in place.

Vigor

The front wheel bearing and hub can be removed as an assembly without removing the steering knuckle.

1. Pry the lock tab away from the spindle and loosen the 36mm nut. Slightly loosen the lug nuts.
2. Raise and safely support the vehicle. Remove the front wheel and spindle nut.
3. Remove the bolts retaining the brake caliper and remove the caliper from the knuckle. Do not allow the caliper to hang by the brake hose, support it with a length of wire.
4. Remove the ABS speed sensor from the knuckle.
5. Remove the tie rod from the knuckle using a properly sized ball joint pressing tool. Use care not to damage the joint seals.
6. Remove the cotter pin from the lower arm ball joint and the castle nut. Remove the lower control arm from the knuckle using the ball joint pressing tool.
7. Remove the cotter pin from the upper arm ball joint and the castle nut. Remove the upper arm from the knuckle using the ball joint pressing tool.
8. Remove the knuckle and hub by sliding the assembly off of the halfshaft.
9. To remove the hub from the knuckle, remove the 4 self-locking bolts from the back of the knuckle. Remove the 4 bolts from the hub to remove the brake disc.

➡**Any time the hub and bearing are separated, the wheel bearing must be replaced with a new one.**

10. The bearing can be pressed off the hub with a hydraulic press. The inner race of the outer row will stay on the hub and can be removed with a bearing puller.

To install:
11. Clean all parts and examine for wear. A worn or damaged hub will cause premature bearing failure and should be replaced.
12. When pressing on a new bearing, be sure to press only on the inner race or the bearing will be damaged.
13. Install the brake disc and torque the bolts to 40 ft. lbs. (55 Nm). Do not over torque or the disc will warp.
14. Make sure the splash guard is installed on the knuckle. Install the hub assembly and torque the self-locking bolts to 33 ft. lbs. (45 Nm). Do not over torque or the hub will be distorted.
15. Install the knuckle in the reverse order of removal. Torque the lower ball joint nut to 40 ft. lbs. (54 Nm) and tighten as required to install a new cotter pin.
16. Torque the upper ball joint nut to 32 ft. lbs. (44 Nm) and tighten as required to install a new cotter pin. Torque the tie rod end to 36 ft. lbs. (50 Nm) and tighten as required to install a new cotter pin.
17. With the wheel installed and all 4 wheels on the ground, torque the spindle nut to 180 ft. lbs. (243 Nm) and stake it in place.

Front Hub and Bearings

INSPECTION

The wheel bearing end play can be checked using a dial indicator. Replace the bearings if the end play is greater than 0.002" (0.05mm).

REMOVAL & INSTALLATION

➡The following procedures for hub and wheel bearing removal and installation require the use of many special tools and a hydraulic press. Do NOT attempt this procedure without the special tools. The following tools, or their equivalents, are recommended by Acura for removing and replacing wheel bearings:

- No.07749–0010000: driver
- No.07HAD–SG00100: driver attachment
- No.07746–0010500: wheel bearing driver attachment
- No.07GAF–SD40700: hub assembly base
- No.07GAF–SE00100: hub assembly tool

Integra

▸ **See Figures 28 thru 33**

1. Raise and safely support the vehicle.
2. Remove the front wheels, then pry the lock tab away and loosen the spindle nut.
3. Remove the brake hose mounting bolts.
4. Remove the brake caliper bolts and remove the caliper from the knuckle. Do not allow the caliper to hang by the brake hose, support it with a length of wire.
5. Remove the disc brake rotor.

6. If equipped with ABS, remove the wheel sensor wire bracket, then remove the wheel sensor from the knuckle. Do not detach the wheel speed sensor connector.
7. Remove the lower ball joint.
8. Remove the upper ball joint using a suitable ball joint removal tool.
9. Pull the knuckle outward and remove the halfshaft outboard joint from the knuckle using a plastic hammer, then remove the knuckle.
10. Place the knuckle on a suitable base, take care not to distort the splash shield. Insert a disassembly tool into the hub, then using a press, remove the hub from the knuckle. Hold onto the hub to keep it from falling when pressed clear.
11. Remove the knuckle ring from the rear of the knuckle.
12. Remove the circlip from the knuckle, then remove the splash guard.
13. Place the knuckle on the disassembly base and install a driver to the bearing. Using a press, remove the bearing from the knuckle.
14. Press the wheel bearing inner race from the hub using a suitable hub disassembly tool and a bearing separator.

To install:

15. Remove the old grease from the hub and knuckle and thoroughly dry and wipe clean all components.
16. Press a new wheel bearing into the knuckle with a suitable driver attachment part, and the knuckle supported properly.
17. Install the circlip securely in the knuckle groove.
18. Install the splash guard and tighten the screws to 3.6 ft. lbs. (5 Nm).
19. Place the hub on a support, then position the knuckle on the hub. Use a suitable driver and attachment part to press the knuckle onto the hub.
20. Install the knuckle ring to the rear of the knuckle.
21. Install the knuckle/hub assembly onto the halfshaft.
22. Install the knuckle to the lower control arm and the tie rod end. Tighten the lower ball joint nut to 36–43 ft. lbs. (49–59 Nm) and tighten the tie rod end castle nut to 29–35 ft. lbs. (39–47 Nm). If necessary, further tighten the nuts to align the cotter pin holes, then install new cotter pins. Never align the cotter pin holes by loosening the nuts.

Fig. 28 Remove the dust cover from the hub

Fig. 29 Use a ratchet and socket to loosen the spindle nut

Fig. 30 Remove the nut from the spindle . . .

Fig. 31 . . . then remove the washer. Note the notch and its position in the groove on the spindle

Fig. 32 Pull the hub and bearing assembly off the spindle

Fig. 33 Pressing a sealed wheel bearing out of the hub assembly

Be careful not to damage the ball joint boots.

23. Install the knuckle to the upper control arm, then tighten the castle nut to 29–35 ft. lbs. (39–47 Nm). If necessary, further tighten the nut in order to align the cotter pin holes, then install new cotter pins. Never align the cotter pin holes by loosening the nuts.

24. Install the wheel sensor and wheel sensor wire bracket onto the knuckle (for cars with ABS only).

➡Be careful not to twist the ABS sensor wires during installation.

25. Clean the brake rotor mating surfaces, then install the disc brake rotor and its retaining screws. Tighten the screws to 7 ft. lbs. (10 Nm).

26. Install the brake caliper, caliper bracket, and mounting bolts.

27. Install the brake hose mounting bolts, tighten the mounting bolts to 7 ft. lbs. (10 Nm).

28. Install a new spindle nut and tighten the nut to 134 ft. lbs. (181 Nm). Stake the shoulder of the nut against the halfshaft.

29. Lower the vehicle and check the front wheel alignment. Road test the vehicle.

2.2CL, 2.3CL and 3.0CL

▶ See Figure 34

1. Remove the steering knuckle, as outlined earlier in this section.
2. Remove the four bolts securing the hub/rotor assembly to the knuckle.
3. Remove the brake rotor from the hub.

➡Be prepared to catch the hub/flange as it is pressed out of the bearing assembly.

4. Press the hub/flange out of the bearing assembly.
5. Press the inner race off of the hub/flange.

To install:

6. Press a new wheel bearing onto the hub/flange.
7. Install the brake rotor on the hub. Tighten the bolts to 40 ft. lbs. (54 Nm).
8. Install the hub/rotor assembly on the knuckle. Tighten the four bolts to 33 ft. lbs. (44 Nm).
9. Install the knuckle assembly.

2.5TL

1. Pry up the lock tab and loosen the spindle nut. Slightly loosen the lug nuts.

2. Raise and safely support the vehicle. Remove the front wheel and spindle nut.

3. Remove the brake caliper mounting bolts and remove the caliper from the knuckle. Hang the caliper out of the way with a length of wire.

4. Remove the ABS speed sensor from the knuckle.

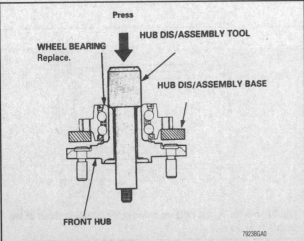

Press

HUB DIS/ASSEMBLY TOOL

WHEEL BEARING
Replace.

HUB DIS/ASSEMBLY BASE

FRONT HUB

7923BGA0

Fig. 34 Press the hub/flange out of the bearing assembly—2.2CL and 3.0CL shown

5. Disconnect the tie rod end from the knuckle using a ball joint remover. Be careful not to damage the joint boot.

6. Remove the cotter pin and castle nut from the lower arm ball joint. Separate the lower control arm from the knuckle using a ball joint remover.

7. Remove the cotter pin and castle nut. Separate the upper arm from the knuckle using the ball joint remover.

8. Remove the knuckle and hub by sliding the assembly off of the halfshaft. Tap the end of the halfshaft with a plastic mallet to release it from the knuckle.

9. To remove the hub and rotor assembly from the knuckle, remove the four self-locking bolts from the back of the knuckle. Remove the four bolts from the hub to separate it from the brake disc.

10. The bearing can be pressed off the hub with a hydraulic press. The inner race will stay on the hub and can be removed with a bearing puller. Any time the hub and bearing are separated, the wheel bearing must be replaced with a new one.

To install:

11. Clean all the parts and examine them for wear. A worn or damaged hub will cause premature bearing failure and should be replaced.

➡When pressing on a new bearing, be sure to press only on the inner race or the bearing will be damaged.

12. Install the brake disc and tighten the bolts to 40 ft. lbs. (55 Nm).

13. Install the hub assembly and tighten the self-locking bolts to 33 ft. lbs. (45 Nm).

➡Be sure that all the hub bolts are properly tightened to avoid warpage of the brake disc.

14. Install the knuckle and hub assembly onto the halfshaft.

15. Install the knuckle on the tie rod, and the upper and lower control arms. Tighten the lower ball joint nut to 40 ft. lbs. (54 Nm) and tighten as required to install a new cotter pin.

16. Tighten the upper ball joint nut to 32 ft. lbs. (44 Nm) and tighten as required to install a new cotter pin. Tighten the tie rod end to 36 ft. lbs. (50 Nm) and tighten as required to install a new cotter pin. Install the knuckle protector.

17. Install the speed sensor, sensor wire, and mounting bolts. Be careful to avoid twisting the wires.

18. Install the brake caliper, brake hoses, and mounting bolts.

19. With the wheel installed and the vehicle on the ground, tighten the spindle nut to 180 ft. lbs. (243 Nm) and stake it in place. Tighten the wheel nuts to 80 ft. lbs. (108 Nm).

3.2TL, 3.5RL, LEGEND AND VIGOR

1. Pry the lock tab away from the spindle and loosen the nut. Slightly loosen the lug nuts.

2. Raise and safely support the vehicle. Remove the front wheel and spindle nut.

3. Remove the wheel sensor from the knuckle, but do not disconnect it.

4. Remove the caliper mounting bolts. Hang the caliper out of the way with a piece of wire.

5. Remove the brake rotor retaining screws. Screw both 12mm bolts into the disc brake removal holes and turn the bolts to press the rotor from the hub. Only turn each bolt 2 turns at a time to prevent cocking the disc.

6. Remove the tie rod from the knuckle using a tie rod end removal tool. Use care not to damage the ball joint seals.

7. Remove the cotter pin from the lower arm ball joint and remove the castle nut.

➡The lower ball joints cannot be separated from the steering knuckle.

8. Remove the lower control arm from the knuckle using the ball joint removal tool.

9. Remove the cotter pin from the upper arm ball joint and remove the castle nut.

10. Remove the upper arm from the knuckle using the ball joint remover.

11. Remove the knuckle and hub by sliding the assembly off of the halfshaft. Be sure to clean any dirt or grease off of the ball joints.

12. The hub can be removed with a slide hammer. Clamp the knuckle in a vise and secure the slide hammer to the wheel studs.

13. Remove the splash guard and snaprings.

14. Support the knuckle and press the bearing out towards the wheel side.

15. If the inner bearing race stayed on the hub, use a puller to remove it.

To install:

16. Clean all parts and examine for wear and damage.

17. When pressing in a new bearing, install the inner snapring first and press the bearing in from the wheel side. Be sure to press only on the outer race or the bearing will be damaged.

18. Install the outer snapring and the splash guard.

19. Properly support the knuckle and press the hub into the bearing. Do not press on the wheel studs or they will press out of the hub. Support the knuckle by the inner race or the bearing will be damaged. Be sure to lubricate the bearings.

20. Install the knuckle/hub/bearing assembly onto the halfshaft and reassemble the knuckle to the upper and lower control arms.

21. Tighten the lower ball joint nut to 51–58 ft. lbs. (70–80 Nm) and tighten further, if necessary, to install a new cotter pin.

22. Tighten the upper ball joint nut to 29–35 ft. lbs. (40–48 Nm) and tighten further, if necessary, to install a new cotter pin. Tighten the tie rod end to 36–43 ft. lbs. (50–60 Nm) and tighten further, if necessary, to install a new cotter pin.

23. Install the disc brake rotor, caliper, mounting bolts, and brackets. Reconnect the wheel sensor bracket to the knuckle.

24. With the wheel installed and all 4 wheels on the ground. Tighten the spindle nut to specifications, then stake the nut in place.

Wheel Alignment

If the tires are worn unevenly, if the vehicle is not stable on the highway or if the handling seems poor, the wheel alignment should be checked. If an alignment problem is suspected, first check for improper tire inflation and other possible causes. These can be worn suspension or steering components, accident damage or even unmatched tires. If any worn or damaged components are found, they must be replaced before the wheels can be properly aligned. Wheel alignment requires very expensive equipment and involves minute adjustments which must be accurate; it should only be performed by a trained technician. Take your vehicle to a properly equipped shop.

Following is a description of the alignment angles which are adjustable on most vehicles and how they affect vehicle handling. Although these angles can apply to both the front and rear wheels, usually only the front suspension is adjustable.

CASTER

▶ **See Figure 35**

Looking at a vehicle from the side, caster angle describes the steering axis rather than a wheel angle. The steering knuckle is attached to the axle yoke through ball joints or king pins. The wheel pivots around the line between these points to steer the vehicle. When the upper point is tilted back, this is described as positive caster. Having a positive caster tends to make the wheels self-centering, increasing directional stability. Excessive positive caster makes the wheels hard to steer, while an uneven caster will cause a pull to one side. Overloading the vehicle or sagging rear springs will affect caster, as will raising the rear of

the vehicle. If the rear of the vehicle is lower than normal, the caster becomes more positive.

CAMBER

▶ **See Figure 36**

Looking from the front of the vehicle, camber is the inward or outward tilt of the top of wheels. When the tops of the wheels are tilted in, this is negative camber; if they are tilted out, it is positive. In a turn, a slight amount of negative camber helps maximize contact of the tire with the road. However, too much negative camber compromises straight-line stability, increases bump steer and torque steer.

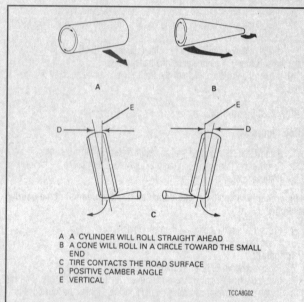

A A CYLINDER WILL ROLL STRAIGHT AHEAD
B A CONE WILL ROLL IN A CIRCLE TOWARD THE SMALL END
C TIRE CONTACTS THE ROAD SURFACE
D POSITIVE CAMBER ANGLE
E VERTICAL

TCCA8G02

Fig. 36 Camber influences tire contact with the road

TOE

▶ **See Figure 37**

Looking down at the wheels from above the vehicle, toe angle is the distance between the front of the wheels relative to the distance between the back of the wheels. If the wheels are closer at the front, they are said to be toed-in or to have negative toe. A small amount of negative toe enhances directional stability and provides a smoother ride on the highway.

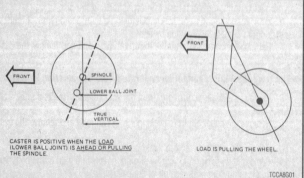

CASTER IS POSITIVE WHEN THE LOAD (LOWER BALL JOINT) IS AHEAD OR PULLING THE SPINDLE.

LOAD IS PULLING THE WHEEL.

TCCA8G01

Fig. 35 Caster affects straight-line stability. Caster wheels used on shopping carts, for example, employ positive caster

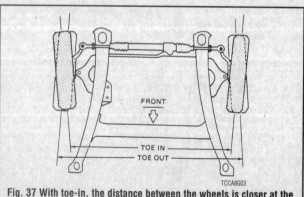

FRONT

TOE IN
TOE OUT

TCCA8G03

Fig. 37 With toe-in, the distance between the wheels is closer at the front than at the rear

REAR SUSPENSION

REAR SUSPENSION COMPONENT LOCATIONS—INTEGRA

1. Strut assembly
2. Sway bar bushing
3. Sway bar
4. Strut mount bushing
5. Crossmember
6. Lower control arm bushings
7. Lower control arm
8. Ball joint

90948P01

REAR SUSPENSION COMPONENT LOCATIONS—3.2TL

1. Rear sway bar
2. Sway bar bushing
3. Crossmember
4. Upper control arm
5. Strut assembly
6. Spindle
7. Lower control arm
8. Lower control arm bushings
9. Parking brake cable
10. Trailing arm

90948PC8

Strut Assembly

REMOVAL & INSTALLATION

Integra, 2.2CL, 2.3CL, 2.5TL, 3.0CL AND 3.2TL

▶ **See Figures 38 and 39**

✵✵ WARNING

The strut contains pressurized nitrogen gas. Drill a 5/64" (2.0mm) hole at the base of the strut, before disposing of it. Always wear eye protection when drilling.

1. Raise and safely support the vehicle and remove the rear wheels.
2. On Integra, remove the rear seat, as follows:
   a. Remove the lower cushion bolt located under the armrest.
   b. Pull the rear of the lower cushion up and lift it forward to release it from the clips.
   c. Pull down the trunk bulkhead trim and release the armrest lid clips.
   d. Remove the three bolts from the back cushion, then lift it up and forward to disengage the securing hooks.
3. On the Integra, remove the flange bolt that connects the lower arm to the trailing arm.
4. Place a floor jack under the lower arm and slightly compress the spring.
5. Remove the upper mounting nuts and the lower flange bolt.
6. Lower the jack to remove the strut. Be sure and mark the right and left struts so they can be reinstalled on the proper sides.

To install:

7. Install the struts into the vehicle. Loosely install the mounting nuts and mounting bolt, but do not tighten them until the weight of the vehicle is on the suspension.
8. Raise the rear suspension with a floor jack until the weight of the vehicle is on the strut. Tighten the upper mounting nuts to 28 ft. lbs. (39 Nm), then tighten the lower mounting bolts to 40 ft. lbs. (55 Nm). Be careful not to pinch the ABS speed sensor wire between the strut and bracket.
9. On the Integra, raise the rear suspension and install the bolt connecting the lower arm to the trailing arm.
10. Install the rear wheels and lower the vehicle.
11. Install the rear seat cushions.

3.5RL

1. Raise and safely support the vehicle and remove the rear wheels.
2. Remove the trunk side panel.
3. Remove the trim cover, then remove the upper mount nuts.
4. Remove the wheel sensor wire brackets but do not disconnect the wheel sensor connector.
5. Remove the lower shock absorber mounting bolt.
6. Lower the rear suspension and remove the shock absorber assembly from the vehicle.

To install:

7. Lower the rear suspension and position the strut assembly in the vehicle. The nut welded to the lower strut mounting should face the front of the vehicle.
8. Loosely install the upper mounting nuts.
9. Install the shock absorber lower mounting bolt.
10. Raise the vehicle until the vehicle just lifts off the safety stand and tighten the lower strut bolt and lower control arm bolt. Tighten the lower shock absorber mounting bolt to 76 ft. lbs. (103 Nm).
11. Install the wheel sensor wire bracket on cars with ABS.
12. Tighten the upper mounting nuts to 36 ft. lbs. (49 Nm).
13. Install the rear wheels, then lower the vehicle.
14. Install the trunk side panel.
15. Have the vehicle's alignment checked and adjusted, if necessary.

Vigor and Legend

1. Raise and safely support the vehicle and remove the rear wheels. 2. Remove the rear speaker and the damper assembly cap. 3. Place a floor jack under the lower arm and slightly compress the spring.
4. Remove the upper mounting nuts and the lower mounting bolt.
5. Lower the jack to remove the strut (damper) unit from the vehicle.
6. Installation is the reverse of the removal procedure. Loosely install the mounting nuts and bolt and lower the vehicle onto the wheels to torque them. Tighten the upper mounting nuts to 28 ft. lbs. (39 Nm) and the lower mounting bolt to 40 ft. lbs. (55 Nm) on Vigor, 76 ft. lbs. (105 Nm) on Legend.

OVERHAUL

1. Remove the strut (damper) unit from the vehicles. Make sure to note the spring seat and bracket positions for reassembly.
2. Install the damper into a suitable spring compressor and tighten the compressor according to manufacturer's instructions.

✵✵ CAUTION

Do not compress the spring any more than necessary.

3. Remove the locking nut from the top of the shock absorber and disassemble the damper and spring as required.

To install:

4. Reassemble the spring and strut assembly. Tighten the strut self-locking nut to 22 ft. lbs. (30 Nm).
5. Installation is the reverse of removal. Be sure to properly position the spring seat and brackets.

Control Arms

REMOVAL & INSTALLATION

▶ **See Figure 40**

➥**The control arms are not interchangeable. Note the paint markings.**

1. Remove the negative battery cable.
2. Lift and properly support the vehicle.

Fig. 38 After pulling the fork bolt out, pull the lower control arm down and out of the way

90948P91

Fig. 39 Once all bolts are removed, pull the strut from the vehicle

90948PA8

Fig. 40 Slide the upper control arm out from the fork of the spindle assembly

90948PA1

3. Remove the tire assembly.
4. Remove the Antilock Brake System (ABS) sensor wire.
5. Remove the hub assembly to lower control arm bolt.
6. On the Integra, remove the shock to lower control arm bolt.
7. Remove the lower control arm to frame bolt(s)
8. Installation is the reverse of the removal procedure.
9. Have the vehicle's alignment checked and adjusted, if necessary.

CONTROL ARM BUSHING REPLACEMENT

▶ **See Figure 27**

1. Remove the control arm from the vehicle.
2. Mark on the machined surface of the lower arm to show where the bushing is in line with the gaps on the inter ring.
3. Place the control arm on the press with the machined surface facing down.
4. Adjust the press so that the bushing driver matches the inner diameter of the bushing hole, then tighten the socket bolt securely.
5. Position the bushing driver on the bushing.
6. Apply pressure and remove the bushing.
To install:
7. Position the lower arm bushing by aligning the gap of the bushing with the mark on the control arm.
8. Install the control arm in the vehicle.

Sway Bar

REMOVAL & INSTALLATION

▶ **See Figure 41**

1. Disconnect the negative battery cable.
2. Raise and safely support the vehicle to gain access to the sway bar.
3. Unfasten the left and right sway bar link retaining nuts.
4. Remove the sway bar links from the sway bar and set aside.
5. Unfasten the sway bar insulator bracket-to-sub-frame bolts, then remove the sway bar from the vehicle.
To install:
6. Position the sway bar (stabilizer bar) into the vehicle and secure with the mounting bracket-to-sub-frame bolts.

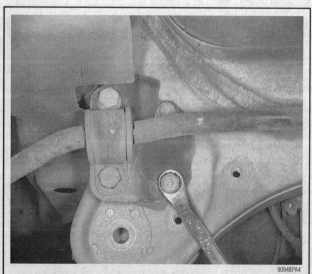

Fig. 41 Removing the sway bar-to-sub-frame bolts

90948PA4

7. Attach the sway bar links to each side of the sway bar.
8. Reinstall the retaining nuts.
9. Carefully lower the vehicle.
10. Connect the negative battery cable.
11. Road test the vehicle and check for proper operation.

Wheel Bearings

REMOVAL & INSTALLATION

Integra and Legend

1. With the vehicle on the ground, remove the hub grease cap and pry the spindle nut lock tab away from the spindle. Loosen the nut.
2. Be sure the emergency brake is disengaged.
3. Raise and safely support the vehicle and remove the rear wheels.
4. Remove the brake hose mounting bolt from the knuckle.
5. Remove the caliper with the brake hose connected, and hang it out of the way with wire.
6. Remove the caliper bracket.
7. Remove the two brake disc retaining screws, and remove the disc by pressing it off with a pair of 8mm bolts threaded into the holes between the studs. Turn each bolt 2 turns at a time.
8. Remove the spindle nut and remove the hub assembly from the knuckle. The bearing is part of the hub and the assembly is replaced as one piece.
9. Be sure to wash the bearing and spindle thoroughly in solvent before reassembly.
To install:
10. Install the hub and bearing assembly onto the spindle and install the spindle nut. Hand-tighten the spindle nut; do not final tighten it until the vehicle is on the ground.
11. Install the brake disc and tighten the disc retaining screws to 84 inch lbs. (10 Nm).
12. Install the caliper mounting bracket and tighten the bolts to 28 ft. lbs. (39 Nm).
13. Install the brake caliper and the brake hose mounting bolts. Tighten the mounting bolts to 28 ft. lbs. (38 Nm).
14. Install the brake hose mounting bolt, tighten the bolt to 16 ft. lbs. (22 Nm).
15. If applicable, install the brake caliper shield. Tighten the mounting bolts to 84 inch lbs. (10 Nm).
16. Tighten the brake disc retaining screws to 84 inch lbs. (10 Nm).
17. Install the rear wheels and lower the vehicle to the ground.
18. Install a new hub nut and tighten the nut to 134 ft. lbs. (181 Nm) for the Integra, or to 206 ft. lbs. (285 Nm) for the Legend. Stake the spindle nut, and install the grease cap.

2.2CL, 2.3CL and 3.0CL

1. Remove the rear wheel and tire assemblies.
2. Apply the parking brake.
3. Remove the grease cap the covers the spindle nut.
4. Raise the locking tab on the nut and remove it from the spindle.
5. Release the parking brake.
6. Remove the bolts securing the brake hose bracket.
7. Remove the brake caliper and hang it out of the way with wire or string.
8. Remove the brake rotor retaining screws. Install two 8 x 1.25mm bolts into the brake rotor. Tighten each screw two turns at a time to push the rotor off the hub.
9. Remove the hub/bearing unit from the spindle.
To install:
10. Install a new hub/bearing unit on the spindle.
11. Remove the two 8 x 1.25mm bolts and install the brake rotor on the hub/bearing. Tighten the two 6mm screws to 84 inch lbs. (10 Nm).

12. Install the spindle washer and a new nut on the spindle. Tighten the nut to 134 ft. lbs. (181 Nm) on the 2.2CL and 3.0CL or to 181 ft. lbs. (245 Nm) on the 2.3CL. Stake the nut to the spindle.

13. Install the brake caliper and hose bracket.

14. Install the rear wheel. Tighten the nuts to 80 ft. lbs. (108 Nm).

2.5TL, 3.2TL, 3.5RL and Vigor

1. With the vehicle on the ground, remove the hub cap and pry the spindle nut lock tab away from the spindle. Loosen the spindle nut.

2. Engage the parking brake to provide leverage to help with loosening the brake disc retaining screws.

3. Raise and safely support the vehicle and remove the rear wheels.

4. Remove the brake hose mounting bolt. Remove the caliper without disconnecting the hydraulic hose. Support the caliper with a piece of wire.

5. Remove the two disc retaining screws. Remove the disc by pressing it off with a pair of 8mm bolts threaded into the holes between the studs. Turn each bolt two turns at a time. Release the parking brake after removing the disc brake retaining screws, and before removing the brake disc.

6. Remove the spindle nut and remove the hub and bearing assembly from the knuckle. The wheel bearing is part of the hub assembly and the components are replaced as one unit.

7. Clean the bearing and spindle with solvent before reassembly. Clean the mating surfaces of the hub and brake disc.

To install:

8. Install the hub and bearing assembly onto the spindle and install a new spindle nut. Hand-tighten the spindle nut; but do not final tighten it until the vehicle is on the ground.

9. Install the brake disc and retaining screws. Install the brake caliper and the brake hose mounting bolts. Tighten the retaining screws to 84 inch lbs. (10 Nm). Tighten the caliper mounting bolts to 28 ft. lbs. (39 Nm). Tighten the hose mounting bolts to 16 ft. lbs. (22 Nm).

10. Install the rear wheels and lower the vehicle to the ground. Tighten the spindle nut, as follows:

- 2.5TL and Vigor: 181 ft. lbs. (245 Nm)
- 3.2TL: 242 ft. lbs. (355 Nm)
- 3.5RL: 180 ft. lbs. (243 Nm)

11. Stake the nut to the spindle with a punch. Install the hub cap.

STEERING

Steering Wheel

REMOVAL & INSTALLATION

▶ See Figures 42 thru 47

❋❋ CAUTION

All models covered by this manual are equipped with a Supplemental Restraint System (SRS), which uses an air bag. Whenever working near any of the SRS components, such as the impact sensors, the air bag module, steering column and instrument panel, disable the SRS, as described in Section 6.

1. Disable the SRS, as outlined in Section 6 of this manual.

2. If not already done, disconnect the negative, then the positive battery cables.

3. Remove the connector between the air bag and the cable reel.

4. Remove the bolts that hold the air bag module to the steering wheel.

5. Remove the air bag assembly, holding it away from you in case of accidental deployment.

6. Detach the connectors for the horn.

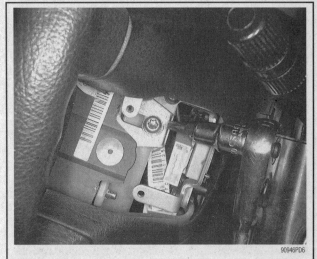

Fig. 43 A Torx® driver is required to remove these air bag mounting screws

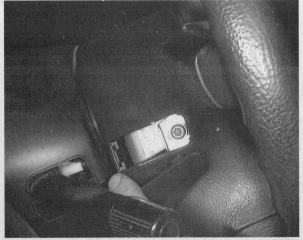

Fig. 42 Location of the 2 air bag module-to-steering wheel retainers

Fig. 44 Carefully lift the air bag module from the steering wheel

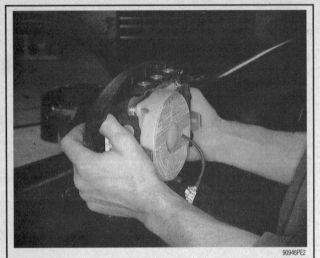

Fig. 45 Always carry a live air bag with the trim cover facing away from you

Fig. 46 Rocking the steering wheel side to side will loosen it from the shaft

7. If equipped, unplug the cruise control connector.
8. Unfasten the steering wheel nut.
9. Remove the steering wheel by rocking it slowly from side to side while pulling steadily with both hands.

To install:

10. Before installing the steering wheel, center the cable reel by pointing the arrow up. This can be done by rotating the cable reel clockwise until it stops. Then rotate the cable reel about two turns counterclockwise.
11. Install the steering wheel and make sure the wheel shaft engages the cable reel and canceling sleeve.
12. Attach all wires and harnesses.
13. Install the air bag assembly using new bolts.
14. Install all covers.
15. Connect the positive cable first and then the negative. Refer to Section 6 for more information on enabling the air bag system.
16. After installation, confirm normal system operation and that all controls are working.

Fig. 47 When installing the steering wheel on the shaft remember to line up the matchmarks you made

Combination Headlight/Turn Signal Switch

REMOVAL & INSTALLATION

▶ **See Figure 48**

1. Disable the air bag system, as outlined in Section 6.
2. Remove the lower panel of the dashboard, the knee bolster and/or the steering column covers, as necessary for your vehicle.
3. Disconnect the switch wiring harness by gently depressing the tab on the connector and pulling.
4. Remove the combination switch mounting screws, then lift our the combination switch.
5. Installation is the reverse of the removal procedure.
6. Enable the air bag system, as outlined in Section 6 of this manual.

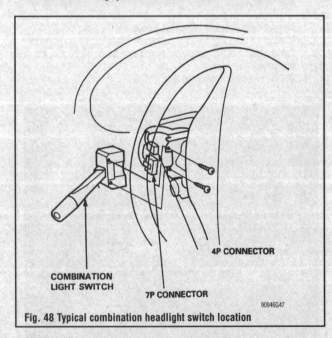

4P CONNECTOR

COMBINATION LIGHT SWITCH

7P CONNECTOR

Fig. 48 Typical combination headlight switch location

Wiper/Washer Switch

REMOVAL & INSTALLATION

▶ **See Figures 49 and 50**

1. Disable the air bag system, as outlined in Section 6 of this manual.
2. Remove the lower panel of the dashboard, the knee bolster and/or the steering column covers, as necessary for your vehicle.
3. Disconnect the harness by gently depressing the tab on the connector and pulling.

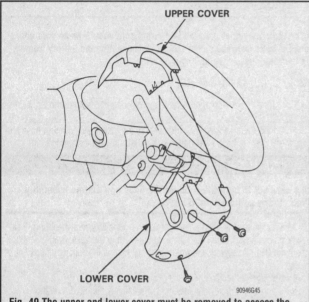

Fig. 49 The upper and lower cover must be removed to access the switch

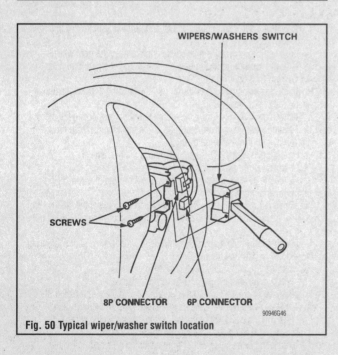

Fig. 50 Typical wiper/washer switch location

4. Unfasten the wiper switch mounting screws, then remove the switch.
5. Installation is the reverse of the removal procedure.
6. Enable the air bag system, as outlined in Section 6 of this manual.

Ignition Switch

REMOVAL & INSTALLATION

▶ **See Figures 51 and 52**

1. Disable the air bag system, as outlined in Section 6 of this manual.
2. Remove the dashboard lower cover.
3. Remove the knee bolster.
4. Unplug the connectors from the under-dash fuse block.
5. Remove the steering column upper and lower covers.

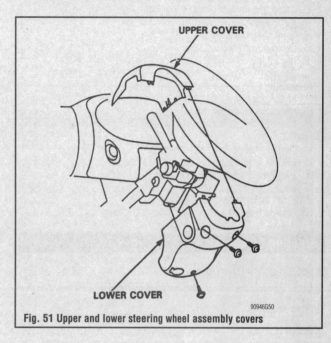

Fig. 51 Upper and lower steering wheel assembly covers

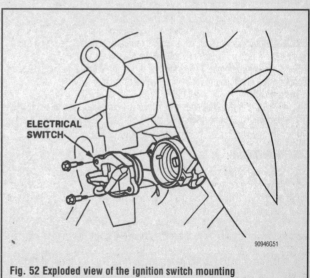

Fig. 52 Exploded view of the ignition switch mounting

6. Insert the key into the ignition, then place the ignition switch to the "O" position.

7. Remove the two screws which secure the switch to the mount.

8. Pull the ignition switch away from the mount.

9. Installation is the reverse of the removal procedure.

10. Enable the air bag system, as outlined in Section 6 of this manual.

Ignition Lock Cylinder

REMOVAL & INSTALLATION

1. Disable the air bag system, as outlined in Section 6 of this manual.
2. Remove the lower panel of the dashboard.
3. Remove the knee bolster.
4. Remove the steering column upper and lower covers.
5. Unplug the connectors from the ignition switch.
6. Remove the steering column mounting nuts.
7. Lower the steering column.
8. Center punch the shear bolts.
9. Use a 3/16" (5mm) drill bit to drill out the heads of the bolts.
10. Remove the shear bolts, then remove the lock cylinder assembly.

To install:

11. Without the key in the lock cylinder, insert it into the steering column.
12. Finger-tighten the new shear bolts.
13. Insert the key into the new lock cylinder and check for proper switch operation.
14. Tighten the shear bolts until they snap off.
15. Align the steering column and tighten the bolts.
16. Plug the harness into the ignition switch.
17. Install the steering column covers.
18. Install the dashboard panel and knee bolster.
19. Enable the air bag system, as outlined in Section 6 of this manual.

Steering Linkage

REMOVAL & INSTALLATION

Tie Rod Ends

INTEGRA

1. Raise and safely support the vehicle. Remove the front wheel.
2. Loosen the tie rod end-to-power steering gear jam nut.
3. Remove the tie rod end-to-steering knuckle cotter pin and nut.
4. Using a press type ball joint removal tool, separate the tie rod end from the steering knuckle. Take care to not damage the threads on the joint.
5. While supporting the power steering rod, remove the tie rod end, be sure to count revolutions required to remove the tie rod end.

To install:

6. Install the new tie rod end, turn it the same amount of revolutions necessary to remove it and tighten the jam nut to 42 ft. lbs. (58 Nm) and the tie rod end-to-steering knuckle nut to 29 ft. lbs. (40 Nm).

EXCEPT INTEGRA

1. Raise and safely support the vehicle. Remove the front wheels.
2. Remove the cotter pin and the nut from the tie rod end. Use a press type ball joint remover tool, separate the tie rod from the steering knuckle. Be careful to not damage the threads on the joint.
3. Disconnect the air tube at the dust seal joint. Remove the tie rod dust seal bellows clamps and move the rubber bellows back on the tie rod rack joints.
4. Straighten the tie rod lockwasher tabs at the tie rod-to-rack joint and remove the tie rod by turning it with a wrench. On some models, the lock washer is staked.

To install:

5. Reverse the removal procedure. Always use a new tie rod lockwasher and cotter pin during reassembly.

6. Torque the tie rod end-to-power steering gear to 40 ft. lbs. (55 Nm) and the tie rod end-to-steering knuckle nut to 32 ft. lbs. (44 Nm). Install a new cotter pin.

7. Fit the locating lugs into the slots on the rack and bend the outer edge of the washer over the flat part of the rod, after the tie rod nut has been properly tightened.

Power Rack and Pinion Steering Gear

REMOVAL & INSTALLATION

➡ **The radio may have a coded theft protection circuit. Make sure you have the code from the owner before disconnecting the battery, removing the radio fuse, or removing the radio.**

2.2CL, 2.3CL, 3.0CL and Integra

1. Lift the power steering reservoir and disconnect the return hose that goes to the oil cooler.
2. Connect a hose of suitable diameter to the disconnected return hose and place the end of the hose in a container to collect the power steering fluid.

✳✳ CAUTION

Take care not to spill the fluid on the body and engine assembly. Wipe off any spilled fluid at once.

3. Start the engine, let it run at idle, and turn the steering wheel from lock to lock several times. When fluid stops running out of the hose, promptly shut the engine **OFF**. Connect the return hose to the reservoir. Properly dispose of the used fluid.

4. Disconnect the negative battery cable.

5. Using cleaning solvent and a brush, wash any oil and dirt off the valve body unit and its lines, and the end of the rack.

6. Remove the steering joint cover.

7. Remove the ignition key, locking the steering wheel in the straight ahead position.

8. Remove the steering joint lower bolt and pull the joint toward the column.

9. Raise and safely support the vehicle, then remove the front wheels.

10. Remove the cotter pins and unscrew the tie rod end ball joint nuts halfway. Discard the cotter pins.

11. Break the tie rod ball joints loose from the steering knuckles, using a suitable tie rod end removal tool.

12. Remove the nuts and lift the tie rod ends out of the steering knuckles.

13. If equipped with a manual transaxle, disconnect the extension rod and the shift rod by performing the following:

   a. If equipped with a VTEC engine, remove the heat shield.

   b. Disconnect the shift extension rod from the transaxle case.

   c. Slide the boot on the shift rod back to expose the clip and spring pin. Remove the clip from the shift rod.

   d. Drive out the spring pin with a punch and disconnect the shift control rod. Note that on reassembly, install the clip back into place after driving the spring pin in.

14. If equipped with an automatic transaxle, disconnect the shift cable from the transaxle by performing the following:

   a. Remove the shift cable holder from the vehicle.

   b. Remove the shift cable cover from the transaxle.

   c. Remove the bolt attaching the control lever to the control shaft, then remove the control lever from the control shaft. Discard the lockwasher.

   d. Position the cable out of the way without bending the cable.

15. Detach the Oxygen (O_2S) sensor electrical connector.

16. Remove the catalytic converter front attaching nuts and bolts, then

remove the rear attaching nuts. Remove the catalytic converter from the vehicle. Discard the locknuts and old exhaust gaskets.

17. Remove the return clamp from the left side of the rear beam, and move the return pipe above the rack and pinion.

18. Remove the rear beam brace.

19. Remove the left tie rod end, then slide the inner tie rod all of the way to the right.

20. Disconnect the two lines from the valve body unit on the rack and pinion. Place the pipe and hose to the rear side of the rack and pinion, so they do not hinder removal of the rack and pinion.

✳✳ WARNING

After disconnecting the hose and pipe, plug or cap the hose and pipe to prevent foreign materials from entering the valve body unit.

➡**Do not loosen the cylinder pipes between the valve body unit and the cylinder.**

21. Remove the gearbox mounting bolts.

22. Pull the rack and pinion all the way down to clear the pinion shaft from the bulkhead, and remove the pinion shaft grommet.

23. Holding the rack and pinion assembly, slide the rack all of the way to the right, then place the left rack end below the rear beam.

24. Move the rack and pinion assembly to the left, and tilt the left side down to remove it from the vehicle.

To install:

25. Gently push the left inner tie rod end into the rack and pinion assembly until it reaches the end of its travel.

26. Place the right side of the rack and pinion over the rear beam and move the assembly completely to the right. Lift the left side of the rack and pinion over the rear beam.

27. Install the pinion shaft grommet, then slide the rack and pinion to the left and up into position. Be sure the pinion shaft fits the pinion shaft grommet properly by aligning the tab on the grommet with the slot in the valve body.

28. With the rack and pinion properly positioned install the mounting bolts. Tighten the left side mounting bolts to 28 ft. lbs. (38 Nm), and the right side mounting bolts to 43 ft. lbs. (58 Nm).

➡**After installing the rack and pinion, check the air hose connections for interference with adjacent parts.**

29. Center the steering rack within its stroke.

30. If applicable, be sure that the cable reel in the steering column is cantered by performing the following:

   a. Turn the steering wheel left approximately 150 degrees, to check the cable reel position with the indicator.

   b. If the cable reel is centered, the yellow gear tooth lines up with the alignment mark on the cover.

   c. Return the steering wheel right approximately 150 degrees, to position the steering wheel in the straight ahead position.

✳✳ CAUTION

Do not connect the steering joint to the pinion without the cable reel being centered. Damage to the SRS system components and personal injury may occur.

31. Slip the lower end of the steering joint onto the pinion shaft (line up the bolt hole with the groove around the shaft), and tighten the lower bolt. Tighten the bolt to 16 ft. lbs. (22 Nm).

➡**Be sure that the lower steering joint is securely in the groove in the steering pinion. If the steering wheel and rack and pinion are not centered, reposition the serration's at the lower end of the steering joint.**

32. Install the steering joint cover with the clamps and clips.

33. Connect the feed pipe to the rack and pinion valve body unit, tighten the fitting to 27 ft. lbs. Connect the return hose to the rack and pinion valve body unit and tighten the hose clamp.

34. Install the rear beam brace rod and the return pipe clamp on the rear beam. Tighten the rear beam brace rod bolts to 28 ft. lbs. (38 Nm).

35. Install the catalytic converter with new gaskets and new locknuts. Tighten the rear nuts to 25 ft. lbs. (33 Nm). Tighten the front nuts and bolts to 16 ft. lbs. (22 Nm). Connect the O2S sensor electrical connector.

36. If equipped with a manual transaxle connect the shift linkage by performing the following:

   a. Install the shifter rod and install the spring pin to attach the shifter rod to the transaxle.

   b. Install the clip over the spring pin, then cover the clip and spring pin with the boot.

   c. Install the extension rod and tighten the bolt to 16 ft. lbs. (22 Nm).

   d. Install the heat shield, if equipped and tighten the bolts to 7.2 ft. lbs. (9.8 Nm).

37. If equipped with an automatic transaxle, connect the shift cable by performing the following:

   a. Install the shift control lever to the control shaft, use a new lockwasher to secure the bolt. Tighten the bolt to 120 inch lbs. (14 Nm).

   b. Install the shift cable cover and tighten the bolts to 16 ft. lbs. (22 Nm).

   c. Attach the shift control cable holder, tighten the bolt to 104 inch lbs. (12 Nm).

38. Thread the right and left tie rod ends on to the rack and pinion an equal number of turns.

39. Connect the tie rods to the steering knuckles and install the castle nuts. Tighten the castle nuts to 29–35 ft. lbs. (39–47 Nm), tighten the nuts enough to install new cotter pins. Do not loosen the castle nuts to install the cotter pins.

40. Install the front wheels.

41. Fill the power steering reservoir with the recommended lubricant to the upper line.

42. Connect the negative battery cable and enter the radio security code.

43. Start the engine and run at a fast idle, then turn the steering lock to lock several times to bleed the air from the system.

44. Check the power steering fluid again and add, if necessary. Check the system for leaks.

45. Check and adjust the front end alignment.

2.5TL, 3.2TL, 3.5RL, Legend and Vigor

1. Disconnect the fluid return hose from the rack and put the end in a container. Start the engine and turn the steering wheel lock-to-lock several times. When fluid stops coming out, stop the engine.

2. Disconnect the negative battery cable, then disconnect the positive battery cable.

3. Raise and safely support the vehicle and remove the front wheels.

4. Remove the cotter pins and disconnect the tie rod end joints using a separator tool. Be careful to not damage the threads on the joints.

5. Loosen the steering joint bolt but do not remove it yet.

6. Remove the splash guard. The 2 long bolts also hold the rack in place, and the rack will now be partially hanging on the steering joint.

7. Carefully clean all the hydraulic fitting connections with solvent and a brush and blow them dry.

8. For 2.5TL and Vigor, disconnect the 8mm sensor line from the valve body by removing the 14mm flare nut.

9. Disconnect the hydraulic fittings and hoses.

10. Remove the hydraulic line mounting clamps from the rack.

11. Place a jack under the rack and remove the steering joint bolt. Remove the rack assembly from the vehicle.

To install:

➡**Several bolts thread into aluminum. When replacing fasteners, be sure to use bolts that have a Dacro® coating specifically designed for such applications. Using normal steel bolts could cause corrosion and loosening of the bolt.**

Use ONLY genuine Honda power steering fluid. Using any other type or brand of fluid will damage the power steering system.

12. For 2.5TL and Vigor, loosely install the right mounting bracket to hold the rack in the vehicle. The arrow stamped on the bracket should face the front of the vehicle. Install the 8mm sensor line in its clip to secure it to the rack cylinder tube.

13. For Legend and 3.2TL, fit the pinion into the steering joint and install the right side mounting rubber and bracket. Do not tighten the bolts yet.

14. Loosely connect the hydraulic lines. Install the hydraulic line cushions and clamps, then tighten the line connections.

15. Connect the four lines to the control unit. Tighten the bolts to 96 inch lbs. (11 Nm)

16. Connect the 6mm return line to 104 inch lbs. (13 Nm) and the 10mm line to 21 ft. lbs. (29 Nm)

17. Install the hoses and the hose clamps.

18. Be sure that the air bag system cable reel is centered. Turn the steering wheel left until the yellow gear tooth is visible through the lower left inspection hole. The yellow gear tooth should align with the mark on the inspection cover. Do not bolt the steering joint until the mark match.

19. Install the steering joint bolts, be sure the joint does not bind when turned, then tighten the bolts to 16 ft. lbs. (22 Nm).

20. Tighten the right side mount bolts to 28 ft. lbs. (39 Nm).

21. Install the splash guard and tighten the short bolts to 28 ft. lbs. (39 Nm). Tighten the long bolts to 43 ft. lbs. (60 Nm).

22. For 2.5TL, connect the feed line, the inlet hose, and the outlet hose to the valve body unit. Tighten the bolts to 96 inch lbs. (11 Nm). Install the 8mm sensor line to the valve body unit. Tighten the line to 18 ft. lbs. (25 Nm).

23. Connect the tie rod ends and tighten the nuts to 36–43 ft. lbs. (50–60 Nm), then tighten them enough to install a new cotter pin.

24. When installation is complete, refill the hydraulic reservoir with new steering fluid, reconnect the battery, start the engine, and turn the steering wheel lock-to-lock several times to bleed the system. Check fluid level again.

25. Check the system for leaks.

26. Check and adjust the front wheel alignment.

Power Steering Pump

REMOVAL & INSTALLATION

▶ **See Figures 53, 54, 55 and 56**

1. Place a suitable drain pan under the vehicle, then disconnect the power steering hoses from the pump to drain the fluid.

2. Remove the belt by loosening the pump adjusting bolts and mounting bolts.

3. On the 3.5RL, Legend or Vigor, remove the air cleaner cover and air intake duct.

4. Cover the alternator (Integra, 2.2CL & 2.3CL) or the crankshaft pulley (3.0CL & 3.2TL) with some rags to protect it from any spilled power steering fluid.

5. Disconnect and plug the inlet and outlet hoses from the pump.

6. Unfasten the pump mounting bolt(s), then remove the pump from the vehicle.

Do not turn the steering wheel with the pump removed.

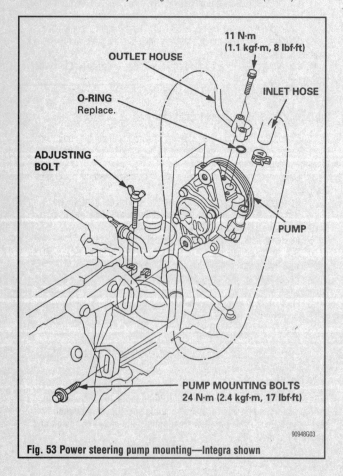

Fig. 53 Power steering pump mounting—Integra shown

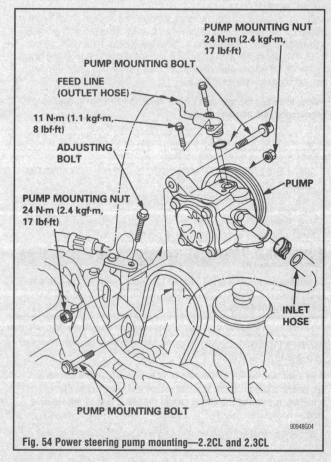

Fig. 54 Power steering pump mounting—2.2CL and 2.3CL

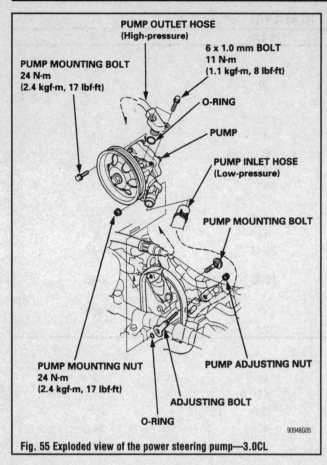

Fig. 55 Exploded view of the power steering pump—3.0CL

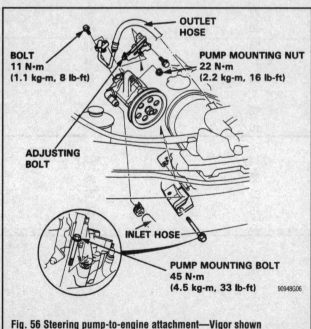

Fig. 56 Steering pump-to-engine attachment—Vigor shown

7. Cover the opening of the pump with a piece of tape to prevent any foreign material from entering the pump.

8. If you are replacing the pump and need to transfer the pulley, hold the steering pump in a suitable soft-jawed vise, hold the pulley with a suitable universal pulley holding tool, then remove the pulley nut and pulley/

9. Installation is the reverse of the removal procedure. Bleed the power steering system.

SYSTEM BLEEDING

♦ See Figure 57

✳✳ WARNING

Use only genuine Honda power steering fluid. Any other type or brand of fluid will damage the power steering pump.

1. Lift the power steering reservoir off of its mount. Disconnect the return hose from the steering rack at the reservoir. Immediately plug the reservoir inlet to prevent fluid loss and contamination. Don't disconnect the hose that connects the pump to the reservoir.

2. Insert a length of rubber tubing into the return hose and route the tubing into a drain container.

3. With the engine running at idle, turn the steering wheel lock-to-lock several times until fluid stops running out of the hose. Immediately shut the engine **OFF**.

4. After servicing, reconnect the reservoir return line. Fill the reservoir to the upper line with genuine Honda power steering fluid.

5. Run the engine at idle and turn the steering wheel lock-to-lock several times to bleed air from the system
and fill the rack valve body.

6. Recheck the fluid level and add more if necessary. Don't overfill the reservoir.

7. Check the power steering system for leaks.

8. Lower the vehicle.

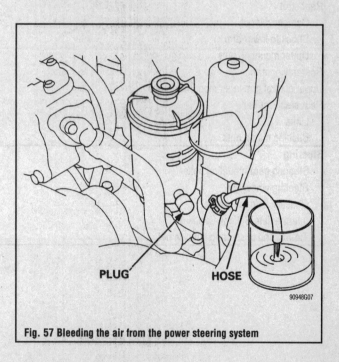

Fig. 57 Bleeding the air from the power steering system

TORQUE SPECIFICATIONS

Components	Ft. Lbs.	Nm
Front Suspension		
Strut-to-body retainers	47	64
Strut rod-to-bearing plate nut	22	30
Damper fork		
Pinch bolt	32	0
Fork-to-lower arm	47	64
Lower control arm		
Front pivot bolt	47	64
Rear pivot stud nut	61	83
Stabilizer bar		
Links	16	22
Bushing to frame nuts	16	22
Steering knuckle balljoint nut	35-44	47-60
Upper control arm		
Ball Joint nut	28-32	38-43
Integra		
Anchor bolt nut	47	64
Pivot bolt nut	22	30
Rear Suspension		
Compensator arm		
Arm to body pivot bolt	46	62
Arm to trailing arm bolt	45	61
Hub to spindle nut	134	182
Lower arm to body pivot bolt	40	54
Lower arm to trailing arm bolt	40	54
Rear strut		
Damper rod nut	22	30
Shock to lower arm	40	54
Upper mounting nuts	36	49
Rear trailing arm	47	64
Upper control arm inner moounting bolts	28	38
Rear stabilizer bar		
Links	16	22
Bushing clamp nuts	16	22
Steering		
Steering gear mounting bolts	29-32	39-43
Steering wheel nut	36	49
Chassis stiffener bracket	28	38
Intermediate Stiffener bracket	16	22
Tie-rod end to steering knuckle nut	33	45

90948C01

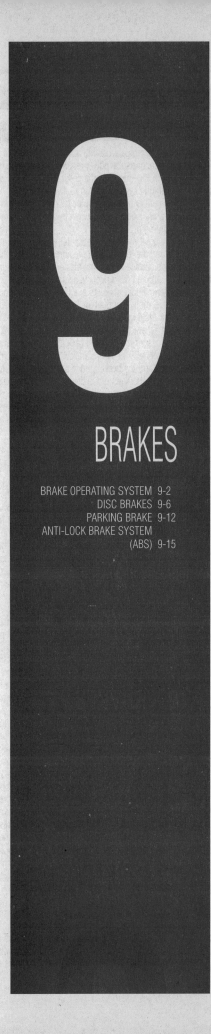

9

BRAKES

BRAKE OPERATING SYSTEM

Basic Operating Principles

Hydraulic systems are used to actuate the brakes of all modern automobiles. The system transports the power required to force the frictional surfaces of the braking system together from the pedal to the individual brake units at each wheel. A hydraulic system is used for two reasons.

First, fluid under pressure can be carried to all parts of an automobile by small pipes and flexible hoses without taking up a significant amount of room or posing routing problems.

Second, a great mechanical advantage can be given to the brake pedal end of the system, and the foot pressure required to actuate the brakes can be reduced by making the surface area of the master cylinder pistons smaller than that of any of the pistons in the wheel cylinders or calipers.

The master cylinder consists of a fluid reservoir along with a double cylinder and piston assembly. Double type master cylinders are designed to separate the front and rear braking systems hydraulically in case of a leak. The master cylinder coverts mechanical motion from the pedal into hydraulic pressure within the lines. This pressure is translated back into mechanical motion at the wheels by either the wheel cylinder (drum brakes) or the caliper (disc brakes).

Steel lines carry the brake fluid to a point on the vehicle's frame near each of the vehicle's wheels. The fluid is then carried to the calipers and wheel cylinders by flexible tubes in order to allow for suspension and steering movements.

In drum brake systems, each wheel cylinder contains two pistons, one at either end, which push outward in opposite directions and force the brake shoe into contact with the drum.

In disc brake systems, the cylinders are part of the calipers. At least one cylinder in each caliper is used to force the brake pads against the disc.

All pistons employ some type of seal, usually made of rubber, to minimize fluid leakage. A rubber dust boot seals the outer end of the cylinder against dust and dirt. The boot fits around the outer end of the piston on disc brake calipers, and around the brake actuating rod on wheel cylinders.

The hydraulic system operates as follows: When at rest, the entire system, from the piston(s) in the master cylinder to those in the wheel cylinders or calipers, is full of brake fluid. Upon application of the brake pedal, fluid trapped in front of the master cylinder piston(s) is forced through the lines to the wheel cylinders. Here, it forces the pistons outward, in the case of drum brakes, and inward toward the disc, in the case of disc brakes. The motion of the pistons is opposed by return springs mounted outside the cylinders in drum brakes, and by spring seals, in disc brakes.

Upon release of the brake pedal, a spring located inside the master cylinder immediately returns the master cylinder pistons to the normal position. The pistons contain check valves and the master cylinder has compensating ports drilled in it. These are uncovered as the pistons reach their normal position. The piston check valves allow fluid to flow toward the wheel cylinders or calipers as the pistons withdraw. Then, as the return springs force the brake pads or shoes into the released position, the excess fluid reservoir through the compensating ports. It is during the time the pedal is in the released position that any fluid that has leaked out of the system will be replaced through the compensating ports.

Dual circuit master cylinders employ two pistons, located one behind the other, in the same cylinder. The primary piston is actuated directly by mechanical linkage from the brake pedal through the power booster. The secondary piston is actuated by fluid trapped between the two pistons. If a leak develops in front of the secondary piston, it moves forward until it bottoms against the front of the master cylinder, and the fluid trapped between the pistons will operate the rear brakes. If the rear brakes develop a leak, the primary piston will move forward until direct contact with the secondary piston takes place, and it will force the secondary piston to actuate the front brakes. In either case, the brake pedal moves farther when the brakes are applied, and less braking power is available.

All dual circuit systems use a switch to warn the driver when only half of the brake system is operational. This switch is usually located in a valve body which is mounted on the firewall or the frame below the master cylinder. A hydraulic piston receives pressure from both circuits, each circuit's pressure being applied to one end of the piston. When the pressures are in balance, the piston remains stationary. When one circuit has a leak, however, the greater pressure in that circuit during application of the brakes will push the piston to one side, closing the switch and activating the brake warning light.

In disc brake systems, this valve body also contains a metering valve and, in some cases, a proportioning valve. The metering valve keeps pressure from traveling to the disc brakes on the front wheels until the brake shoes on the rear wheels have contacted the drums, ensuring that the front brakes will never be used alone. The proportioning valve controls the pressure to the rear brakes to lessen the chance of rear wheel lock-up during very hard braking.

Warning lights may be tested by depressing the brake pedal and holding it while opening one of the wheel cylinder bleeder screws. If this does not cause the light to go on, substitute a new lamp, make continuity checks, and, finally, replace the switch as necessary.

The hydraulic system may be checked for leaks by applying pressure to the pedal gradually and steadily. If the pedal sinks very slowly to the floor, the system has a leak. This is not to be confused with a springy or spongy feel due to the compression of air within the lines. If the system leaks, there will be a gradual change in the position of the pedal with a constant pressure.

Check for leaks along all lines and at wheel cylinders. If no external leaks are apparent, the problem is inside the master cylinder.

DISC BRAKES

Instead of the traditional expanding brakes that press outward against a circular drum, disc brake systems utilize a disc (rotor) with brake pads positioned on either side of it. An easily-seen analogy is the hand brake arrangement on a bicycle. The pads squeeze onto the rim of the bike wheel, slowing its motion. Automobile disc brakes use the identical principle but apply the braking effort to a separate disc instead of the wheel.

The disc (rotor) is a casting, usually equipped with cooling fins between the two braking surfaces. This enables air to circulate between the braking surfaces making them less sensitive to heat buildup and more resistant to fade. Dirt and water do not drastically affect braking action since contaminants are thrown off by the centrifugal action of the rotor or scraped off the by the pads. Also, the equal clamping action of the two brake pads tends to ensure uniform, straight line stops. Disc brakes are inherently self-adjusting. There are three general types of disc brake:

1. A fixed caliper.
2. A floating caliper.
3. A sliding caliper.

The fixed caliper design uses two pistons mounted on either side of the rotor (in each side of the caliper). The caliper is mounted rigidly and does not move.

The sliding and floating designs are quite similar. In fact, these two types are often lumped together. In both designs, the pad on the inside of the rotor is moved into contact with the rotor by hydraulic force. The caliper, which is not held in a fixed position, moves slightly, bringing the outside pad into contact with the rotor. There are various methods of attaching floating calipers. Some pivot at the bottom or top, and some slide on mounting bolts. In any event, the end result is the same.

DRUM PARKING BRAKES

Drum brakes employ two brake shoes mounted on a stationary backing plate. These shoes are positioned inside a circular drum which rotates with the wheel assembly. The shoes are held in place by springs. This allows them to slide toward the drums (when they are applied) while keeping the linings and drums in alignment. The shoes are actuated by a wheel cylinder which is mounted at the top of the backing plate. When the brakes are applied, hydraulic pressure forces the wheel cylinder's actuating links outward. Since these links bear directly against the top of the brake shoes, the tops of the shoes are then forced against the inner side of the drum. This action forces the bottoms of the two shoes to contact the brake drum by rotating the entire assembly slightly (known as servo action). When pressure within the wheel cylinder is relaxed, return springs pull the shoes back away from the drum.

Most modern drum brakes are designed to self-adjust themselves during application when the vehicle is moving in reverse. This motion causes both shoes to rotate very slightly with the drum, rocking an adjusting lever, thereby causing rotation of the adjusting screw. Some drum brake systems are designed to self-adjust during application whenever the brakes are applied. This on-board adjustment system reduces the need for maintenance adjustments and keeps both the brake function and pedal feel satisfactory.

POWER BRAKE BOOSTER

Virtually all modern vehicles use a vacuum assisted power brake system to multiply the braking force and reduce pedal effort. Since vacuum is always available when the engine is operating, the system is simple and efficient. A vacuum diaphragm is located on the front of the master cylinder and assists the driver in applying the brakes, reducing both the effort and travel he must put into moving the brake pedal.

The vacuum diaphragm housing is normally connected to the intake manifold by a vacuum hose. A check valve is placed at the point where the hose enters the diaphragm housing, so that during periods of low manifold vacuum brakes assist will not be lost.

Depressing the brake pedal closes off the vacuum source and allows atmospheric pressure to enter on one side of the diaphragm. This causes the master cylinder pistons to move and apply the brakes. When the brake pedal is released, vacuum is applied to both sides of the diaphragm and springs return the diaphragm and master cylinder pistons to the released position.

If the vacuum supply fails, the brake pedal rod will contact the end of the master cylinder actuator rod and the system will apply the brakes without any power assistance. The driver will notice that much higher pedal effort is needed to stop the car and that the pedal feels harder than usual.

Vacuum Leak Test

1. Operate the engine at idle without touching the brake pedal for at least one minute.
2. Turn off the engine and wait one minute.
3. Test for the presence of assist vacuum by depressing the brake pedal and releasing it several times. If vacuum is present in the system, light application will produce less and less pedal travel. If there is no vacuum, air is leaking into the system.

System Operation Test

1. With the engine **OFF**, pump the brake pedal until the supply vacuum is entirely gone.
2. Put light, steady pressure on the brake pedal.
3. Start the engine and let it idle. If the system is operating correctly, the brake pedal should fall toward the floor if the constant pressure is maintained.

Power brake systems may be tested for hydraulic leaks just as ordinary systems are tested.

✳✳ WARNING

Clean, high quality brake fluid is essential to the safe and proper operation of the brake system. You should always buy the highest quality brake fluid that is available. If the brake fluid becomes contaminated, drain and flush the system, then refill the master cylinder with new fluid. Never reuse any brake fluid. Any brake fluid that is removed from the system should be discarded.

Brake Light Switch

REMOVAL & INSTALLATION

▶ See Figure 1

1. Disconnect the negative battery cable.
2. Detach the brake light switch connector.
3. Loosen the holding nut.
4. Remove the brake light switch by unscrewing it in a counter-clockwise direction.

To install:

5. Screw in the brake light switch and adjust the plunger until it is fully depressed against the back of the brake pedal.
6. Back off the switch one quarter turn to allow 0.01 in (0.3mm) of clearance between the threaded and the pad.
7. Attach the brake light switch connector.
8. Connect the negative battery cable.

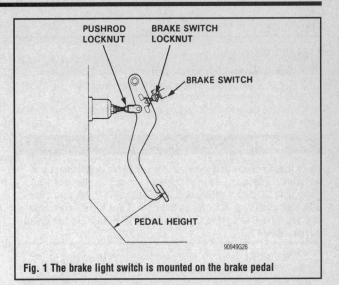

Fig. 1 The brake light switch is mounted on the brake pedal

Master Cylinder

▶ See Figure 2

✳✳ CAUTION

The Acura anti-lock brake system contains brake fluid under extremely high pressure within the pump, accumulator and modulator assembly. Do not disconnect or loosen any lines, hoses, fittings or components without properly relieving the system pressure. Use only a bleeder T-wrench 07HAA-SG00100, or equivalent, to relieve pressure. Improper procedures or failure to discharge the system pressure may result in severe personal injury and/or property damage.

Acura vehicles have a tandem master cylinder that is used to improve the safety of the vehicle. The master cylinder has one reservoir tank with two feed holes at the bottom of the tank to feed both the primary and secondary circuit.

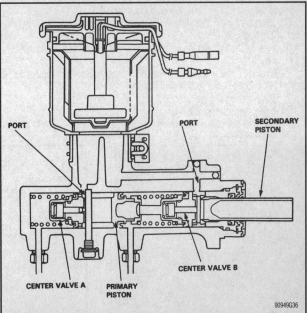

Fig. 2 Cross-sectional view of the primary and secondary circuits of a typical master cylinder

REMOVAL & INSTALLATION

▶ **See Figures 3 and 4**

1. Disconnect the negative battery cable.
2. Detach all electrical connectors from the master cylinder.
3. Remove the master cylinder reservoir cap.
4. Remove the brake fluid from the master cylinder using a siphon or clean turkey baster.

✳✳ CAUTION

Brake fluid contains polyglycol ethers and polyglycols. Avoid contact with the eyes and wash your hands thoroughly after handling brake fluid. If you do get brake fluid in your eyes, flush your eyes with clean, running water for 15 minutes. If eye irritation persists, or if you have taken brake fluid internally, IMMEDIATELY seek medical assistance.

5. On the 2.5TL, remove the check valve and the throttle cable from the four way joint bracket. Also remove the four way joint mounting bolt.
6. Use a flare nut wrench to disconnect the fluid lines from the master cylinder.

✳✳ WARNING

Be cautious not to bend the lines upon removal of the master cylinder.

7. Unfasten the mounting nuts that attach the master cylinder to the booster, then remove the master cylinder from the brake booster.
To install:
8. Install the master cylinder in the reverse order of removal.
9. Fill the master cylinder with Honda approved or equivalent DOT 3 or DOT 4 brake fluid.
10. Properly bleed the master cylinder, as outlined later in this section.

BENCH BLEEDING

If the master cylinder is off the vehicle, it can be bench bled.
1. Secure the master cylinder in a bench vise.
2. Connect 2 short pieces of brake line to the outlet fittings, bend them until the free end is below the fluid level in the master cylinder reservoirs.
3. Fill the reservoir with fresh DOT 3 or DOT 4 type brake fluid.
4. Using a wooden dowel, or equivalent, pump the piston slowly several times until no more air bubbles appear in the reservoirs.
5. Disconnect the 2 short lines, refill the master cylinder and securely install the cylinder cap.
6. If the master cylinder is on the vehicle, it can still be bled, using a flare nut wrench.
7. Open the brake lines slightly with the flare nut wrench, while pressure is applied to the brake pedal by a helper inside the vehicle.
8. Be sure to tighten the line before the brake pedal is released.
9. Repeat the process with both lines until no air bubbles come out.
10. Bleed the complete brake system, if necessary.

➡If the master cylinder has been thoroughly bled and filled to the proper level upon installation into the vehicle, it is not necessary to bleed the entire hydraulic system.

Power Brake Booster

REMOVAL & INSTALLATION

▶ **See Figure 5**

1. Disconnect the negative battery cable.
2. Detach all electrical connectors from the master cylinder.
3. Remove the brake fluid from the master cylinder, then use a flare nut wrench to disconnect.

✳✳ WARNING

Be careful not to bend the lines upon removal of the master cylinder.

4. Remove the master cylinder from the brake booster.
5. Disconnect the vacuum hoses from the brake booster.
6. On the Vigor models, remove the throttle cable clamp bolt.
7. Remove the clevis and clevis pin from the brake pedal.
8. Remove the booster mounting bolts.
9. Remove the brake booster from the engine compartment.
To install:
10. Install the power brake booster in the reverse order of removal.
11. Fill the master cylinder with Honda approved or equivalent DOT 3 or DOT 4 brake fluid.
12. Properly bleed the master cylinder.

Proportioning Valve

REMOVAL & INSTALLATION

The proportioning valve is part of the modulator control unit. Refer to that procedure, under the Anti-lock Brake System (ABS) portion of this section.

Brake Hoses and Lines

Metal lines and rubber brake hoses should be checked frequently for leaks and external damage. Metal lines are particularly prone to crushing and kinking under the vehicle. Any such deformation can restrict the proper flow of fluid and therefore impair braking at the wheels. Rubber hoses should be checked for cracking or scraping; such damage can create a weak spot in the hose and it could fail under pressure.

Any time the lines are removed or disconnected, extreme cleanliness must be observed. Clean all joints and connections before disassembly (use a stiff bristle brush and clean brake fluid); be sure to plug the lines and ports as soon as they are opened. New lines and hoses should be flushed clean with brake fluid before installation to remove any contamination.

Fig. 3 Removing the master cylinder from the brake booster

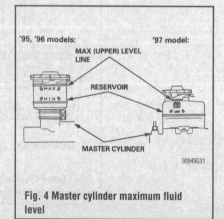

Fig. 4 Master cylinder maximum fluid level

Fig. 5 The power brake booster is the large circular canister that the master cylinder is bolted to

☀☀ CAUTION

If a brake line must be replaced, use a pre-made line or factory replacement part. Use care and a proper tubing bender when forming the new line. Use only DOT approved replacement brake hoses. If a flare must be formed, use the proper flaring tool and very carefully inspect the work. The integrity of the braking system relies on safe connections. Personal injury or death can result from a brake line failure.

REMOVAL & INSTALLATION

▶ See Figures 6, 7, 8 and 9

☀☀ CAUTION

The Acura anti-lock brake system contains brake fluid under extremely high pressure within the pump, accumulator and modulator assembly. Do not disconnect or loosen any lines, hoses, fittings or components without properly relieving the system pressure. Use only a bleeder T-wrench 07HAA-SG00100 or equivalent to relieve pressure. Improper procedures or failure to discharge the system pressure may result in severe personal injury and/or property damage.

1. Disconnect the negative battery cable.
2. Raise and safely support the vehicle on jackstands.
3. Remove any wheel and tire assemblies necessary for access to the particular line you are removing.
4. Thoroughly clean the surrounding area at the joints to be disconnected.
5. Place a suitable catch pan under the joint to be disconnected.
6. Using two wrenches (one to hold the joint and one to turn the fitting), disconnect the hose or line to be replaced.
7. Disconnect the other end of the line or hose, moving the drain pan if necessary. Always use a back-up wrench to avoid damaging the fitting.

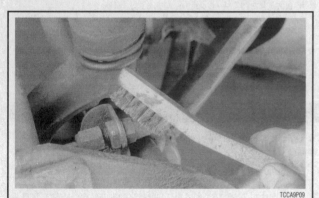

Fig. 6 Use a brush to clean the fittings of any debris

8. Disconnect any retaining clips or brackets holding the line and remove the line from the vehicle.

➡If the brake system is to remain open for more time than it takes to swap lines, tape or plug each remaining clip and port to keep contaminants out and fluid in.

To install:

9. Install the new line or hose, starting with the end farthest from the master cylinder. Connect the other end, then confirm that both fittings are correctly threaded and turn smoothly using finger pressure. Make sure the new line will not rub against any other part. Brake lines must be at least 1/2 in. (13mm) from the steering column and other moving parts. Any protective shielding or insulators must be reinstalled in the original location.

☀☀ WARNING

Make sure the hose is NOT kinked or touching any part of the frame or suspension after installation. These conditions may cause the hose to fail prematurely.

10. Using two wrenches as before, tighten each fitting.
11. Install any retaining clips or brackets on the lines.
12. If removed, install the wheel and tire assemblies, then carefully lower the vehicle to the ground.
13. Refill the brake master cylinder reservoir with clean, fresh brake fluid, meeting DOT 3 specifications. Properly bleed the brake system.
14. Connect the negative battery cable.

Bleeding the Brake System

☀☀ CAUTION

The Acura anti-lock brake system contains brake fluid under extremely high pressure within the pump, accumulator and modulator assembly. Do not disconnect or loosen any lines, hoses, fittings or components without properly relieving the system pressure, as outlined later in this section. Use only a bleeder T-wrench 07HAA-SG00100 or equivalent to relieve pressure. Improper procedures or failure to discharge the system pressure may result in severe personal injury and/or property damage.

☀☀ WARNING

Avoid spilling brake fluid on the vehicle's paint. It will damage the finish. If a spill does occur, wash it immediately with water.

The purpose of bleeding the brakes is to expel air trapped in the hydraulic system. The system must be bled whenever the pedal feels spongy, indicating that compressible air has entered the system. It must also be bled whenever the system has been opened or repaired. If you are not using a pressure bleeder, you will need a helper for this job.

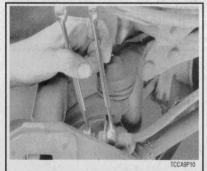

Fig. 7 Use two wrenches to loosen the fitting. If available, use flare nut type wrenches

Fig. 8 Any gaskets/crush washers should be replaced with new ones during installation

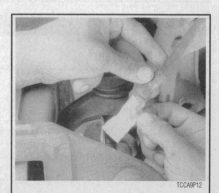

Fig. 9 Tape or plug the line to prevent contamination

✳✳ WARNING

Never reuse brake fluid which has been bled from the brake system. Brake fluid absorbs moisture which can lower its boiling point, therefore re—using old, used, or contaminated fluid can decrease the effectiveness of the braking system.

BLEEDING

▶ **See Figures 10 and 11**

➡**To bleed anti-lock brake components, please refer to the procedure located under the ABS portion of this section.**

When bleeding the brakes, air may be trapped in the brake lines or valves far upstream, as much as 10 feet from the bleeder screw. Therefore, it is very important to have a fast flow of a large volume of brake fluid when bleeding the brakes, to make sure all of the air is expelled from the system.

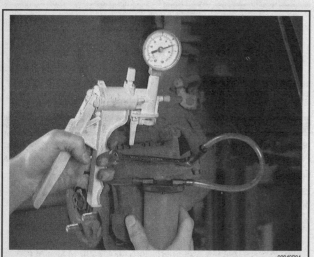

Fig. 10 A one man bleeder unit such as this one can be purchased at you local aftermarket parts supplier

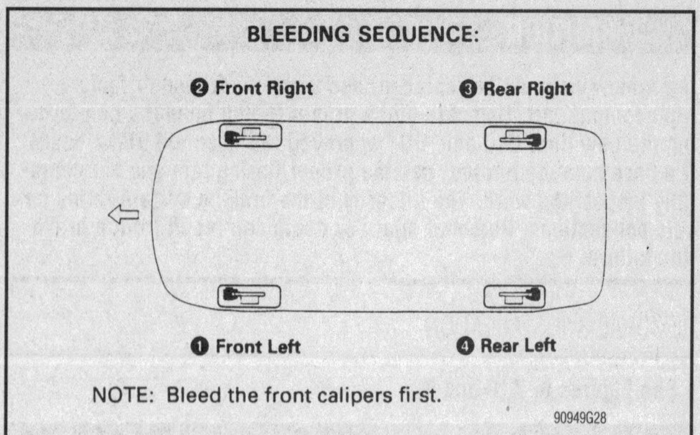

BLEEDING SEQUENCE:

❷ Front Right   ❸ Rear Right

❶ Front Left   ❹ Rear Left

NOTE: Bleed the front calipers first.

90949G28

Fig. 11 Proper brake bleeding sequence

➡**Proper manual bleeding of the hydraulic brake system will require the use of an assistant. Always follow the proper bleeding sequence listed in this section..**

1. Attach a clear plastic hose to the bleeder screw, then place the hose into a clean jar that has enough fresh brake fluid to submerge the end of the hose.
2. Have an assistant pump the brake pedal 3–4 times, and hold it down before the bleeder screw is opened.
3. Open the bleeder screw at least one full turn. When the bleeder screw opens, the brake pedal will drop.
4. Close the bleeder screw. Release the brake pedal only AFTER the bleeder screw is closed.
5. Repeat the procedure 4 or 5 times at each bleeder screw, then check the pedal for travel. If the pedal travel is not excessive, or has not been improved, enough fluid has not passed through the system to expel all of the trapped air. Make sure to watch the fluid level in the master cylinder reservoir. It must stay at the proper level so air will not re-enter the brake system.
6. Test drive the vehicle to be sure the brakes are operating correctly and that the pedal is solid.

➡**Constantly check and refill the master cylinder. Do not allow the master cylinder to run dry.**

DISC BRAKES

✳✳ CAUTION

Older brake pads or shoes may contain asbestos, which has been determined to be cancer causing agent. Never clean the brake surface with compressed air! Avoid inhaling any dust from any brake surface! When cleaning brake surfaces, use a commercially available brake cleaning fluid.

Brake Pads

REMOVAL & INSTALLATION

Front

▶ **See Figures 12 thru 19**

1. Use a siphon or clean turkey baster to remove about half of the brake fluid from the master cylinder.
2. Raise and safely support the vehicle with jackstands.
3. Remove the front wheel and tire assemblies.
4. If necessary, remove the brake hose mounting bolts from the steering knuckle.

➡**Regardless of their wear pattern, when brake pads are replaced on one side of the vehicle, they must also be replaced on the other side. It**

is advisable, however, to complete one side before beginning the other.

5. Remove the caliper bolt and pivot it up and out of the way.
6. Remove the pads and shims.
7. If the pad thickness is less than the service requirement, replace them.
8. Clean and check the brake rotor for cracks.

To install:

✳✳ WARNING

When reusing the old brake pads, be sure to install them in the same positions to prevent an increase in stopping distance.

9. Using an old pad as a cushion, push the piston into the caliper to allow enough space for the new pads. Or, you can use a large C-clamp, or other suitable tool, to completely retract the piston into the caliper.
10. Install the pad shims and the pads.
11. Apply molykote M77®or equivalent grease to both sides of the shims and the back of the pads. Do not put any on the friction material.

➡**The pad wear indicator goes on the inside.**

12. Pivot the caliper back over the pads. Be careful not to crush the boot when pivoting the down.
13. Lubricate the caliper mounting bolts.
14. Install all the mounting bolts.

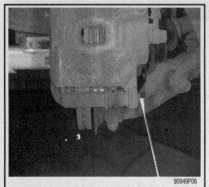

Fig. 12 Use a wrench to loosen the lower caliper mounting bolt

Fig. 13 Once the lower caliper mounting bolt has been removed . . .

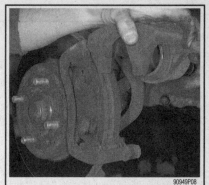

Fig. 14 . . . pivot the caliper up, out of the way for access to the pads

Fig. 15 Remove the brake pads by sliding them to the sides

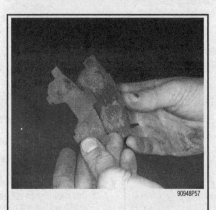

Fig. 16 Typical Acura brake pad shims

Fig. 17 Apply a suitable anti-seize lubricant to the pad mounting surface. This will enable the brake pads to slide freely throughout their service life

Fig. 18 Lubricate the caliper sliders with synthetic disc brake caliper grease

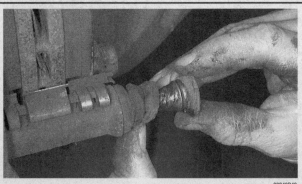

Fig. 19 Install the caliper sliders once they have been greased

15. Depress and hold the break several times to ensure they work.
16. Carefully road test the vehicle.

Rear

1. Use a siphon or clean turkey baster to remove about half of the brake fluid from the master cylinder.
2. Raise and properly support the vehicle. Remove the rear wheel and tire assemblies.
3. Remove the brake hose bracket from the rear trailing arm.
4. Remove the caliper shield.
5. Unfasten the caliper mounting bolts, then remove the caliper from the bracket.
6. Remove the pad shims.
7. Remove the brake pads. If the brake pads are worn below specifications, replace the pads.

To install:

8. Use a commercially available locknut wrench, or equivalent tool, to turn the caliper piston clockwise into position in the cylinder, then align the cutout in the piston with the tab on the inner pad by turning the piston back.
9. Clean and remove any rust from the mounting bracket and caliper assembly.
10. Clean the brake disc and check for cracks.
11. Apply Molykote M77®or equivalent grease to the back of the brake pads and shims.

➡ **Do not apply to the friction material.**

12. Install the brake pads and shims into the caliper bracket.
13. Install the brake caliper, then install and tighten the caliper mounting bolts.
14. Install the caliper shield.
15. Depress the brake pedal several times to build the pedal back up, then road test the vehicle.

INSPECTION

▶ See Figure 20

You should check the brake pads every 6,000 miles (9,600km), and any time the wheels are removed. Inspect both ends of the outer brake pad by looking in at each end of the caliper. These are the points at which the highest rate of wear normally occurs. Also, check the thickness on the inner brake pad to make sure it is not wearing prematurely. Some inboard pads have a thermal layer against the steel backing surface which is integrally molded with the pad. Do not confuse this extra layer with uneven inboard/outboard brake pad wear.

Look down through inspection hole in the top of the caliper to view the inner brake pad. Replace the pads whenever the thickness of any pad is worn within 0.030 in. (0.76mm) of the steel backing surface. For riveted brake pads, they must be replaced if the pad is worn to 0.030 (0.76mm) of any rivet head. The disc brake pads MUST be replaced in axle sets, for example, if you replace the driver's side front brake pads, you must also replace the passenger's side front brake pads. This will prevent uneven wear and other brake system problems.

1. Remove the brake pads and observe their condition.
2. Measure the thickness of the brake pad's lining material at the thinnest portion of the assembly. Do not include the pad's metal backing plate in the measurement.
3. If you can't accurately determine the condition of the brake pads by visual inspection, you must remove the caliper, then remove the brake pads.

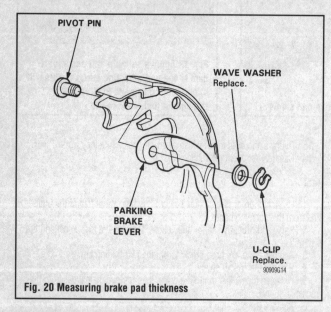

PIVOT PIN

WAVE WASHER
Replace.

PARKING
BRAKE
LEVER

U-CLIP
Replace.
90909G14

Fig. 20 Measuring brake pad thickness

Brake Caliper

REMOVAL & INSTALLATION

Front

▶ See Figures 12, 13, 14, 21, 22 and 23

➡Do not allow the master cylinder reservoir to empty. An empty reservoir will allow air to enter the brake system and complete system bleeding will be required.

1. Use a siphon or clean turkey baster to remove about half of the brake fluid from the master cylinder.
2. Raise and safely support the vehicle, then remove the tire and wheel assembly.
3. Unfasten the caliper mounting bolts, then remove the caliper.
4. Remove the brake pads and shims.
5. If the caliper is to be completely removed from the vehicle for replacement or overhaul, remove the brake hose attaching bolt, then disconnect the brake hose from the caliper and plug the hose to prevent fluid contamination or loss.
6. Remove the caliper mounting bracket bolts and lift the caliper off of the support bracket.
7. Remove the caliper and mounting bracket from the vehicle. If the caliper is only removed for access to other components or for pad replacement, support the caliper with the brake hose attached, so that there is no strain on the brake hose.

To install:

8. Completely retract the piston into the caliper using a large C-clamp or other suitable tool.
9. Clean and lubricate both steering knuckle abutments or support brackets with a coating of multi-purpose grease.
10. Position the caliper and brake pad assembly over the brake rotor. Be sure to properly install the caliper assembly into the abutments of the steering knuckle or support bracket. Be sure the caliper guide pin bolts, rubber bushings and sleeves are clear of the steering knuckle bosses.
11. Fill the master cylinder with fresh brake fluid and, if the brake hose was removed, bleed the brake system.
12. Install the wheel and tire assembly.
13. Carefully lower the vehicle, then tighten the lug nuts to the proper specifications.
14. Depress the brake pedal 3–4 times to seat the brake linings and to restore pressure in the system.

✳✳ CAUTION

Do not move the vehicle until a firm pedal is obtained.

15. Road test the vehicle and check for proper brake operation.

90949P13

Fig. 21 Never let the caliper hang by the brake hose. Always suspend if with a piece of wire so there is no tension on the hose

90949P14

Fig. 22 Use a wrench to loosen the caliper mounting bracket bolts

90949P16

Fig. 23 Once the bolts have been removed, lift the caliper mounting away from the brake rotor

Rear

▶ **See Figures 24 and 25**

> ❊❊ **CAUTION**
>
> **Never use an air hose to blow the brake dust out of a caliper. Always use an approved brake cleaning fluid.**

➡ Do not allow the master cylinder reservoir to empty. An empty reservoir will allow air to enter the brake system and complete system bleeding will be required.

1. Use a siphon or clean turkey baster to remove about half of the brake fluid from the master cylinder.
2. Raise and support the vehicle properly.

➡ If you are only lifting the rear of the vehicle, chock the front wheels.

90948P55

Fig. 24 Pull the brake caliper away from the mount

3. Remove the caliper shield mounting bolts.
4. Remove the caliper shield.
5. Unfasten the caliper mounting bolts, then remove the caliper from the bracket.
6. Remove the brake pads and shims.
7. If the caliper is to be completely removed from the vehicle for replacement or overhaul, remove the brake hose attaching bolt, then disconnect the brake hose from the caliper and plug the hose to prevent fluid contamination or loss.
8. Remove the caliper mounting bracket bolts and lift the caliper off of the support bracket.
9. Remove the caliper and mounting bracket from the vehicle. If the caliper is only removed for access to other components, support the caliper, with the brake hose attached, so that there is no strain on the brake hose.

To install:

10. Use a commercially available locknut wrench, or equivalent tool, to turn the caliper piston clockwise into position in the cylinder, then align the cutout in the piston with the tab on the inner pad by turning the piston back.
11. Position the caliper and brake pad assembly over the brake rotor. Be sure to properly install the caliper assembly into the abutments of the steering knuckle or support bracket. Be sure the caliper guide pin bolts, rubber bushings and sleeves are clear of the steering knuckle bosses.
12. Fill the master cylinder with fresh brake fluid and, if the brake hose was removed, bleed the brake system.
13. Install the wheel and tire assembly.
14. Carefully lower the vehicle. Tighten the lug nuts to the proper specifications.
15. Depress the brake pedal 3–4 times to seat the brake linings and to restore pressure in the system.

> ❊❊ **CAUTION**
>
> **Do not move the vehicle until a firm pedal is obtained.**

16. Road test the vehicle and check for proper operation.

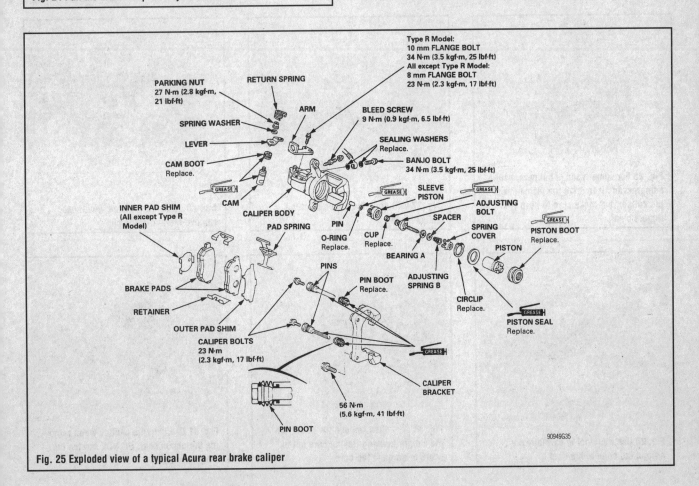

90949G35

Fig. 25 Exploded view of a typical Acura rear brake caliper

OVERHAUL

▶ **See Figures 26 thru 33**

➡Some vehicles may be equipped dual piston calipers. The procedure to overhaul the caliper is essentially the same with the exception of multiple pistons, O-rings and dust boots.

1. Remove the caliper from the vehicle and place on a clean workbench.

✳✳ CAUTION

NEVER place your fingers in front of the pistons in an attempt to catch or protect the pistons when applying compressed air. This could result in personal injury!

➡Depending upon the vehicle, there are two different ways to remove the piston from the caliper. Refer to the brake pad replacement procedure to make sure you have the correct procedure for your vehicle.

2. The first method is as follows:
   a. Stuff a shop towel or a block of wood into the caliper to catch the piston.
   b. Remove the caliper piston using compressed air applied into the caliper inlet hole. Inspect the piston for scoring, nicks, corrosion and/or worn or damaged chrome plating. The piston must be replaced if any of these conditions are found.
3. For the second method, you must rotate the piston to retract it from the caliper.
4. If equipped, remove the anti-rattle clip.
5. Use a prytool to remove the caliper boot, being careful not to scratch the housing bore.
6. Remove the piston seals from the groove in the caliper bore.
7. Carefully loosen the brake bleeder valve cap and valve from the caliper housing.

8. Inspect the caliper bores, pistons and mounting threads for scoring or excessive wear.
9. Use crocus cloth to polish out light corrosion from the piston and bore.
10. Clean all parts with denatured alcohol and dry with compressed air.
To install:
11. Lubricate and install the bleeder valve and cap.
12. Install the new seals into the caliper bore grooves, making sure they are not twisted.
13. Lubricate the piston bore.
14. Install the pistons and boots into the bores of the calipers and push to the bottom of the bores.
15. Use a suitable driving tool to seat the boots in the housing.
16. Install the caliper in the vehicle.
17. Install the wheel and tire assembly, then carefully lower the vehicle.
18. Properly bleed the brake system.

Brake Disc (Rotor)

REMOVAL & INSTALLATION

▶ **See Figures 22, 22, 34, 35, and 36**

1. Use a siphon or clean turkey baster to remove about half of the brake fluid from the master cylinder.
2. Raise and safely support the vehicle and remove the tire/wheel assembly.
3. Remove the caliper guide pin or mounting bolts.
4. Lift the caliper assembly away from the brake rotor.
5. Use a suitable piece of wire to suspend the caliper assembly from the upper control arm. This will prevent the weight of the caliper from being supported by the brake flex hose which will damage the hose.
6. If equipped, remove the rotor retaining screws.

Fig. 26 For some types of calipers, use compressed air to drive the piston out of the caliper, but make sure to keep your fingers clear

TCCA9P01

Fig. 27 Withdraw the piston from the caliper bore

TCCA9P02

Fig. 28 On some vehicles, you must remove the anti-rattle clip

TCCA9P03

Fig. 29 Use a prytool to carefully pry around the edge of the boot . . .

TCCA9P04

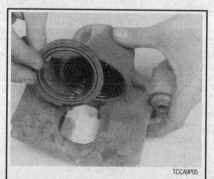
Fig. 30 . . . then remove the boot from the caliper housing, taking care not to score or damage the bore

TCCA9P05

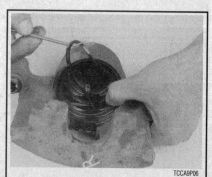
Fig. 31 Use extreme caution when removing the piston seal; DO NOT scratch the caliper bore

TCCA9P06

Fig. 32 Use the proper size driving tool and a mallet to properly seal the boots in the caliper housing

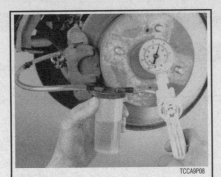

Fig. 33 There are tools, such as this Mighty-Vac, available to assist in proper brake system bleeding

Fig. 34 The use of a hand impact driver may be necessary to remove the brake rotor retaining screws

Fig. 35 Close up of the brake rotor retaining screws

Fig. 36 Remove the brake rotor by pulling it over the studs

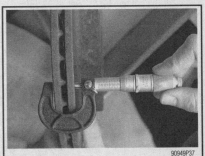

Fig. 37 Use a micrometer to measure the thickness of the brake rotor. You must discard the rotor if it is not within the manufacturer's specifications

7. Remove the brake rotor by pulling it straight off the wheel mounting studs.

To install:

8. If installing the rotor on the rear brakes, use a commercially available locknut wrench, or equivalent tool, to turn the caliper piston clockwise into position in the cylinder, then align the cutout in the piston with the tab on the inner pad by turning the piston back.

9. If installed the rotor on the front brakes, completely retract the piston into the caliper using a large C-clamp or other suitable tool.

10. Install the brake rotor onto the wheel hub.

11. Install the caliper assembly over the brake rotor and install the guide pin or mounting bolts.

12. Fill the master cylinder to the proper level with fresh brake fluid.

13. Install the tire/wheel assembly and lower the vehicle.

14. Pump the brake pedal until the brake pads are seated and a firm pedal is achieved before attempting to move the vehicle.

✳✳ CAUTION

Do not move the vehicle until a firm pedal is obtained.

15. Road test the vehicle to check for proper brake operation.

INSPECTION

▶ See Figure 37

Whenever the brake calipers or pads are removed, inspect the rotors for defects. The brake rotor is an extremely important component of the brake system. Cracks, large scratches or warpage can adversely affect the braking system, at times to the point of becoming very dangerous.

Light scoring is acceptable. Heavy scoring or warping will necessitate refinishing or replacement of the disc. The brake disc must be replaced if cracks or burned marks are evident.

If the rotor needs to be replaced with a new part, the protective coating on the braking surface of the rotor must be removed with an appropriate solvent before installing the rotor to the vehicle.

Check the run-out of the hub (disc removed). It should not be more than 0.002 inch (0.050mm). If so, the hub should be replaced.

All brake discs or rotors have markings for MINIMUM allowable thickness cast on an unmachined surface or an alternate surface. Always use this specification as the **minimum** allowable thickness or refinishing limit. Refer to a local auto parts store or machine shop, if necessary, where rotors are resurfaced.

If the rotor needs to be replaced with a new part, the protective coating on the braking surface of the rotor must be removed with an appropriate solvent before installing the rotor to the vehicle.

PARKING BRAKE

Cable

REMOVAL & INSTALLATION

Except 3.5RL

▶ See Figures 38 and 39

1. Disconnect the negative battery cable.
2. Fully release the parking brake lever.
3. Loosen the output cable adjuster nut from the parking brake cable tension equalizer. This will relieve tension from the parking brake cables allowing for easy removal.
4. On Integra models, remove the lock and clevis pin.
5. Installation is the reversal of the removal procedure.

3.5RL

▶ See Figures 40 and 41

1. Disconnect the negative battery cable.
2. Remove the parking brake switch connector.
3. With the parking brake released, disconnect the parking brake cable from the pedal.
4. Remove the parking brake pedal assembly from the vehicle by removing the mounting bolts.
5. Remove the parking brake shoes.
6. Remove the parking brake cable from the backing plate. Use a 12mm offset wrench as shown.

To install:

7. Install the parking brake cable into the backing plate.
8. Install the parking brake shoes.
9. Install the parking brake pedal assembly.

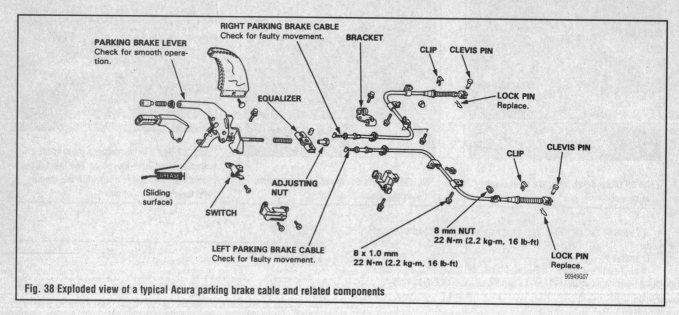

Fig. 38 Exploded view of a typical Acura parking brake cable and related components

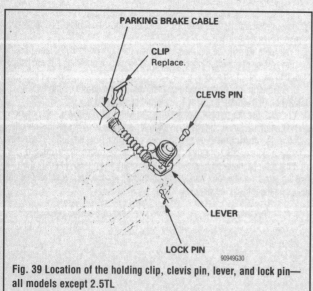

Fig. 39 Location of the holding clip, clevis pin, lever, and lock pin—all models except 2.5TL

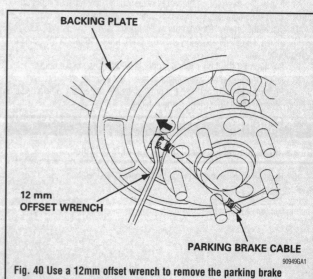

Fig. 40 Use a 12mm offset wrench to remove the parking brake cable from the backing plate

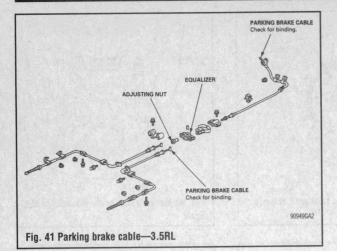

Fig. 41 Parking brake cable—3.5RL

10. Attach the parking brake cable to the pedal assembly.
11. Install the parking brake switch connector.
12. Connect the battery cable.

ADJUSTMENT

Integra, CL, and TL Models

1. Pull the parking brake with moderate force. This should position it six to ten notches up.
2. To adjust the parking brake, begin by raising the vehicle.
3. Properly support the vehicle.
4. Check that the parking brake arm on the rear brake caliper is contacting the brake caliper pin.
5. Pull the parking brake lever handle up one notch.
6. Remove the rear console.
7. Turn the adjusting nut until the wheels just begin to drag.
8. Release the parking brake lever and check that the brakes do not drag when the wheels are spun.
9. Install the rear console.

3.5RL and Vigor

1. Raise and properly support the vehicle.
2. Check to ensure that the lever of the rear brake caliper contacts the caliper pin.
3. Advance the parking brake lever or pedal one notch.
4. Lift up the console door.
5. Remove the console bottom liner.
6. Using a flexible extension and socket assembly turn the adjusting nut on the equalizer.
7. Tighten until the wheels drag slightly when turned.
8. Release the parking brake lever or pedal and check that the wheels do not drag excessively when turned.

☀ WARNING

Overtightening the parking brake may cause the brakes to drag causing excessive heat build up and brake failure.

9. If the parking brake is properly adjusted the rear brakes will be fully applied when the parking brake lever is pulled 7–11 notches for Vigor, or the pedal is depressed 6–8 clicks on the 3.5RL.
10. Lower the vehicle.

Legend

➡ **The rear brakes should be engaged when a force of 44lbs. (200Nm) is applied to the parking brake lever. It should engage the brakes between eight to twelve notches.**

1. Remove the rear cover from the console.

2. Pull the parking lever up one notch.
3. Raise and safely support the vehicle.
4. Tighten until the wheels drag slightly when turned.
5. Release the parking brake lever and check that the wheels do not drag excessively when turned.

☀ WARNING

Overtightening the parking brake may cause the brakes to drag causing excessive heat build up and brake failure.

6. If the parking brake is properly adjusted the rear brakes will be fully applied when the parking brake lever is pulled eight to twelve notches.
7. Install the rear console.
8. Install the wheels.
9. Lower the vehicle.

Parking Brake Shoes

REMOVAL & INSTALLATION

▶ **See Figures 42 thru 52**

Some models covered by this manual use a parking drum brake to hold the vehicle. These shoes are attached to a backing plate behind the rear brake rotor. To service follow the steps below.

1. Loosen the rear parking brake by lowering it to the rest position.
2. Raise the vehicle and support it with the proper jackstands.
3. Remove the rear tires.
4. Remove the two 6mm bolts.
5. Remove the rear brake disc rotor.

➡**You may need to install two 8mm bolts into the threaded holes in the rotor and tighten them. This will push the rotor from the hub and stud assembly.**

6. Inspect the brake shoe linings for contamination, cracking, glazing, or excessive wear.

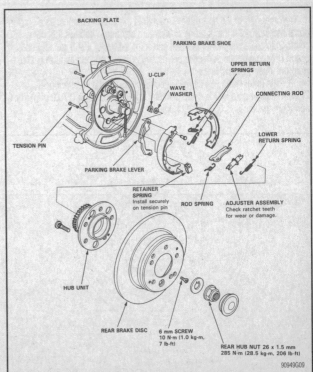

Fig. 42 Exploded view of the parking brake shoes and related components

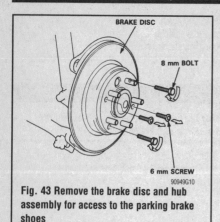

Fig. 43 Remove the brake disc and hub assembly for access to the parking brake shoes

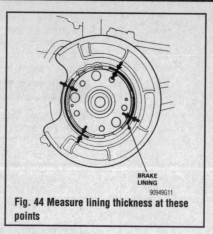

Fig. 44 Measure lining thickness at these points

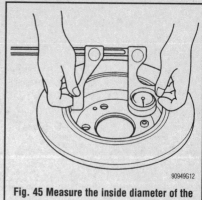

Fig. 45 Measure the inside diameter of the drum

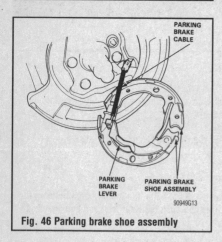

Fig. 46 Parking brake shoe assembly

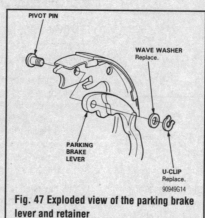

Fig. 47 Exploded view of the parking brake lever and retainer

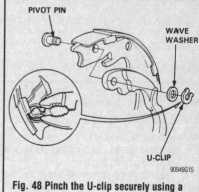

Fig. 48 Pinch the U-clip securely using a pair of pliers

7. Measure the linings of the shoes if there is any question as to the amount of life left. The lining thickness is 0.10 in (2.5mm) on a new shoe. The service limit is a minimum thickness of 0.04 in (1.0mm).

The inner part of the rear rotor is machined in the same manner as a conventional brake drum. It too is prone to wear and warping. Although it is not as common to see a warped inner drum and rotor assembly it still can and does occur. Driving with the parking brake on can quickly generate enough heat to warp the inner drum assembly.

8. The inner drum can be measured as shown in the illustration.

9. The standard inside drum diameter should be 6.69 in (170.0mm). The minimum thickness is 6.73 in (171.0mm).

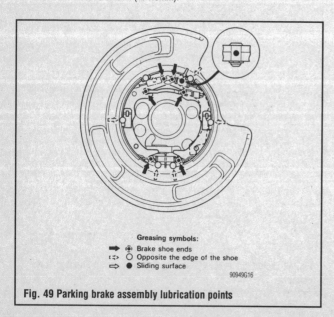

Greasing symbols:
➡ ⊙ Brake shoe ends
⇨ ○ Opposite the edge of the shoe
⇨ ● Sliding surface

Fig. 49 Parking brake assembly lubrication points

➥ **If the refinishing standard does not match the one on your drum use the maximum thickness number that is stamped on the rotor/drum as a reference. Replace the disc/drum if the specification is above the maximum specification. Also inspect the drum for sliding surface scoring, grooving or cracking.**

10. Push and turn the retainer springs to remove the tension pins.
11. Remove the return springs.
12. Remove the hub.
13. Lower the parking brake assembly from the backing plate.
14. Separate the parking brake cable and the brake lever.
15. Remove the adjuster and springs.
16. Remove the following components:
   - Wave washer.
   - Parking brake lever.
   - Pivot pin.
   - U—clip.

To install:
17. Apply a suitable brake cylinder grease to the sliding surface of the pivot pin.
18. Insert the pivot pin into the brake shoe.
19. Attach the parking brake lever and wave washer on the pivot pin.
20. Secure these components with the U-clip.

➥ **Squeeze the U-clip securely to prevent it from coming out of the brake shoe.**

21. Apply a suitable anti-seize lubricant to all of the shoe sliding surfaces on the backing plate.
22. Connect the rod spring as shown.
23. Install the brake shoe.
24. Shorten the clevises by turning the adjuster.
25. Connect the parking brake cable to the lever by sliding the cable through the eyelet.
26. The tension spring, the retainer pin and the upper return springs must be installed next.

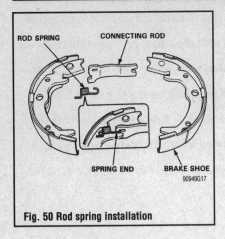

Fig. 50 Rod spring installation

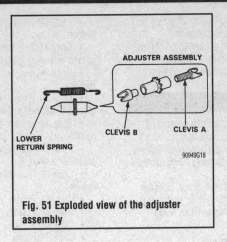

Fig. 51 Exploded view of the adjuster assembly

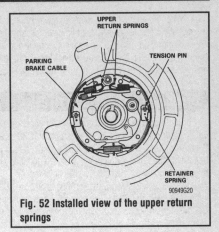

Fig. 52 Installed view of the upper return springs

27. Install the hub and torque the nut to the proper specifications.
28. Install the disc/drum assembly.
29. Install the 6mm screws.
30. Adjust the parking brake.
31. Install the rear caliper.
32. Install the wheel, then tighten the lug nuts to 80 ft. lbs. (108 Nm).

ADJUSTMENT

▶ See Figures 53 and 54

➡After the installation of new shoes it is advised that you perform a lining surface break—in and adjustment.

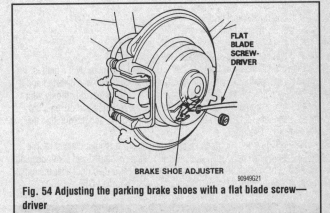

Fig. 54 Adjusting the parking brake shoes with a flat blade screw—driver

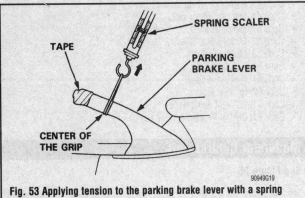

Fig. 53 Applying tension to the parking brake lever with a spring scale

1. If equipped with a console mounted parking brake lever, have an assistant pull up on the parking brake lever with a force of 18.8 lbs. (9 kg) while you drive the vehicle at a speed of 30 mph (50 km/h) for a distance of no more than ¼ (400m) miles.
2. If equipped with a parking brake pedal, while keeping the parking brake release lever pulled up, depress the parking brake pedal with a force of 66 lbs. (30 kg) while you drive the vehicle at a speed of 30 mph (50 km/h) for a distance of no more than ¼ (400m) miles.
3. After the procedure is completed, allow the brakes to cool for at least ten minutes, then perform step 1 again.
4. Allow the brakes to cool again, then check parking brake adjustment.
5. To adjust the brake shoes, turn the star wheel with a flat-bladed screwdriver.

ANTI-LOCK BRAKE SYSTEM (ABS)

General Information

When conventional brakes are applied in an emergency stop or on ice, one or more wheels may lock. This may result in loss of steering control and vehicle stability. The purpose of the Anti-lock Brake System (ABS) is to prevent lock up under heavy braking conditions. This system offers the driver increased safety and control during braking. Anti-lock braking operates only at speeds above 3 mph (5 km/h).

Under normal braking conditions, the ABS functions the same as a standard brake system with a diagonally split master cylinder and conventional vacuum assist.

If wheel locking tendency is detected during application, the system will enter anti-lock mode. During anti-lock mode, hydraulic pressure in the four wheel circuits is modulated to prevent any wheel from locking. Each wheel circuit is designed with a set of electrical valves and hydraulic line to provide modulation, although for vehicle stability, both rear wheel valves receive the same electrical signal. The system can build or reduce pressure at each wheel, depending on signals generated by the Wheel Speed Sensors (WSS) at each wheel and received at the Controller Anti-lock Brake (CAB).

Anti-lock braking systems (ABS) are available on all Acura models. When this system engages, some audible noise as well as pulses in the brake pedal may occur. Do not be alarmed; this is normal system operation.

PRECAUTIONS

Failure to observe the following precautions may result in system damage:
• Before performing electric arc welding on the vehicle, disconnect the control module and the hydraulic unit connectors.
• When performing painting work on the vehicle, do not expose the control module to temperatures in excess of 185°F (85°C) for longer than 2 hours. The system may be exposed to temperatures up to 200°F (95°C) for less than 15 minutes.
• Never disconnect or connect the control module or hydraulic modulator connectors with the ignition switch ON.
• Never disassemble any component of the Anti-Lock Brake System (ABS) which is designated unserviceable; the component must be replaced as an assembly.

- When filling the master cylinder, always use brake fluid which meets DOT-3 specifications; petroleum-based fluid will destroy the rubber parts.
- Working on ABS system requires extreme amount of mechanical ability, training and special tools. If you are not familiar have your vehicle repaired by a certified mechanic or refer to a more advanced publication on this subject.

Diagnosis and Testing

For the proper diagnostic procedure for either the entire ABS system or a single component of the system, a scan tool (DRB or equivalent) is necessary. Because of the complexity of the ABS system and the importance of correct system functioning, it is a good idea to have a qualified automotive mechanic test the system if any problems have been detected.

If the Antilock Braking System (ABS) is OK, the ABS malfunction indicator lamp (MIL) will go off after two seconds upon turning the ignition switch to the **ON** position. The ABS lamp may illuminate a second time and then go off again. This is also normal.

The ABS lamp may illuminate under the below conditions.
- When only the drive wheels spin.
- If one drive wheel is stuck.
- During vehicle spin.
- If the ABS continues to operate for a long time.
- If there is signal disturbance is detected.

The ABS lamp may or may not stay illuminated continuously if a fault is detected. It depends which Diagnostic Trouble Code (DTC) was detected and if the system corrected the problem or not. The ABS lamp may go off only after the problem is corrected and the vehicle has been restarted and driven a few miles. Remember it depends on which code was thrown and the duration that the code was detected.

This system can perform an initial diagnosis and a regular diagnosis. The initial diagnosis is performed right after the engine is started and continues until the ABS lamp goes out. The regular diagnosis is performed right after the initial diagnosis and continues until the ignition switch is turned **OFF**.

Trouble Codes

READING CODES

Reading the control module memory is one of the first steps in OBD II system diagnostics. This step should be initially performed to determine the general nature of the fault. Subsequent readings will determine if the fault has been cleared.

Reading codes can be performed using a generic scan tool, or the vehicle manufacturer's specific tester to read the control module memory.

To read the fault codes, connect the scan tool or tester according to the manufacturer's instructions. Follow the manufacturer's specified procedure for reading the codes.

CLEARING CODES

Control module reset procedures are a very important part of OBD II system diagnostics. This step should be done at the end of any fault code repair and at the end of any driveability repair.

Clearing codes can be performed by any of the methods listed below:
- Clear the control module memory with a Generic Scan Tool (GST)
- Clear the control module memory with the vehicle manufacturer's specific tester
- Turn the ignition **OFF** and disconnect the negative battery cable for at least 1 minute.

➡**Removing the negative battery cable may cause other systems in the vehicle to lose their memory. Prior to removing the cable, ensure you have the proper reset codes for radios and alarms.**

The MIL may also be de-activated for some codes if the vehicle completes 3 consecutive trips without a fault detected with vehicle conditions similar to those present during the fault.

Below are the ABS trouble codes for all 1994–00 Acura models.
- Code 11: Front right wheel sensor has an open or short to the body ground or a short to power.

- Code 12: Front left wheel sensor electrical noise or an intermittent interruption.
- Code 13: Rear right wheel sensor has an open or short to the body ground or a short to power.
- Code 14: Rear left wheel sensor electrical noise or an intermittent interruption.
- Code 15: Front right wheel sensor has an open or short to the body ground or a short to power.
- Code 16: Front left wheel sensor electrical noise or an intermittent interruption.
- Code 17: Rear right wheel sensor has an open or short to the body ground or a short to power.
- Code 18: Rear left wheel sensor electrical noise or an intermittent interruption.
- Code 21: Pulser
- Code 22: Pulser
- Code 23: Pulser
- Code 24: Pulser
- Code 31: Front right input solenoid has a short to ground or a short to wire.
- Code 32: Front right output solenoid has a short to ground or a short to wire.
- Code 33: Front left input solenoid has a short to ground or a short to wire.
- Code 34: Front left output solenoid has a short to ground or a short to wire.
- Code 35: Rear right input solenoid has a short to ground or a short to wire.
- Code 36: Rear right output solenoid has a short to ground or a short to wire.
- Code 37: Rear left input solenoid has a short to ground or a short to wire.
- Code 38: Rear left output solenoid has a short to ground or a short to wire.
- Code 41: Front right wheel lock.
- Code 42: Front left wheel lock.
- Code 43: Right rear wheel lock.
- Code 44: Left rear wheel lock.
- Code 51: Motor lock.
- Code 52: Motor stuck off.
- Code 53: Motor stuck on.
- Code 54: Fail safe relay.
- Code 61: Ignition voltage.
- Code 62: Ignition voltage.
- Code 71: Different diameter tire.
- Code 81: Central Processing Unit (CPU)

Modulator Control Unit

⬥ **See Figure 55**

The Modulator Control Unit (MCU) contains solenoid valves for each wheel. These valves are independent of each other and are positioned vertically for improved maintainability. The modulators for the rear wheels act as proportioning control valves to prevent the rear wheels from locking up in the event the anti-lock braking system is malfunctioning or not activated.

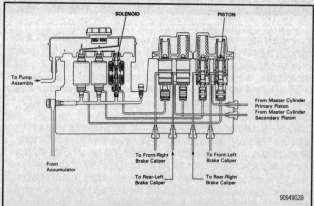

Fig. 55 Circuits of the Modular Control Unit (MCU)

REMOVAL & INSTALLATION

▶ **See Figure 56**

1. Disconnect the negative battery cable.
2. Remove the modular unit mounting bolts.
3. Detach the pump motors connectors.

✳✳ WARNING

Use a flare nut wrench on the fittings to prevent stripping of the line nuts.

4. Disconnect the brake lines.
5. Remove the modular unit from the bracket assembly.

To install:

6. Install the modular unit.
7. Connect the brake lines, using a flare nut wrench. Tighten the fittings to 11 ft. lbs. (15Nm).
8. Connect the modulator unit.
9. Attach the pump motor connectors.
10. Begin with the front wheels, start bleeding the braking system.
11. Bleed the rear wheels thoroughly after completion of the front.
12. Connect the negative battery cable.
13. After starting the engine, check to see of the ABS lamp is not on.
14. Drive the vehicle and check that the ABS light does not come on.

ABS Control Unit

The ABS control unit, or ECU, manages the entire system via inputs from various sensors and programmed decisions which are stored within the unit.

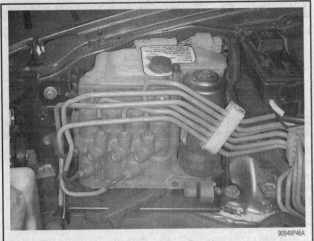

Fig. 56 View of the modulator control unit and mounting bracket

This management system includes the pump motor, various electronic solenoids, wheel sensors and an internal self-diagnostic mode. The main function of the ABS control unit is to perform calculations on the signals received from each one of the sensors at the wheels. This will enable it to control the system by actuating solenoid valves that regulate the flow and pressure of the brake fluid to each wheel. The system was designed with a sub function that gives driving signals to the pump motor as well as signals the self diagnostic mode which is a necessity for backing up the antilock braking system.

REMOVAL & INSTALLATION

Except 1997 TL Models

▶ **See Figure 57**

1. Disconnect the negative battery cable.
2. Remove the right quarter trim panel.
3. Detach the ABS control unit electrical connectors.
4. Remove the ABS control unit by removing the mounting fasteners.

To install:

5. Install the unit in the reverse order of removal.
6. Check that the ABS light comes on and then goes off once the engine has been started.
7. Drive the vehicle to ensure that the ABS light does not come on.

1997 TL Models

▶ **See Figures 58 and 59**

1. Disconnect the negative battery cable.
2. Remove the glove box.
3. Remove the mounting bolts that secure the ABS control unit mounting bracket to the firewall.
4. Shift the bracket forward to gain access to the control units connectors.
5. Detach the control unit connectors.
6. Remove the radiator fan controller module connector.
7. Unplug the connectors from the ABS control unit.
8. Remove the bracket from the car.
9. Remove the radiator fan controller and the ABS control unit mounting bolts.
10. Remove the bracket from the ABS control unit.
11. Installation of the ABS control unit is the reverse of the removal procedure.

Accumulator

REMOVAL & INSTALLATION

▶ **See Figures 60, 61 and 62**

The ABS accumulator is a pneumatic type which stores high pressure brake fluid which is fed from the pump assembly. As the ABS operates, the accumulator works in conjunction with the pump to supply extremely high pressure fluid to the modulator valve.

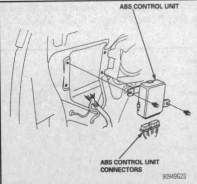

Fig. 57 Location of the typical ABS control unit—except 1997 TL models

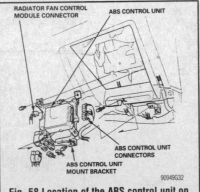

Fig. 58 Location of the ABS control unit on a 1997 TL model

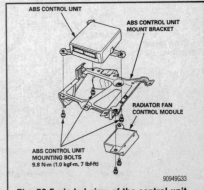

Fig. 59 Exploded view of the control unit mounting

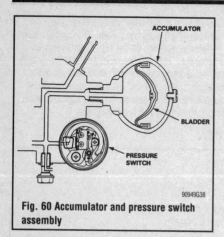

Fig. 60 Accumulator and pressure switch assembly

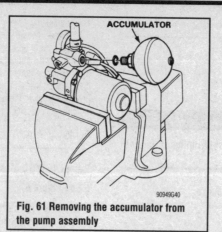

Fig. 61 Removing the accumulator from the pump assembly

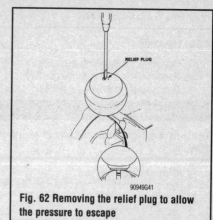

Fig. 62 Removing the relief plug to allow the pressure to escape

1. Disconnect the negative battery cable.
2. To remove the accumulator you must first remove the pump assembly, as outlined later in this section.
3. Place the pump assembly in a vise and loosen the accumulator by turning it counter clockwise with an open-end wrench.
4. The pressure in the accumulator must be released before disposing of it in the trash.
5. To relieve the accumulator pressure, perform the following:
   a. Secure the accumulator in a vise.
   b. Slowly turn the plug three to four turns.
   c. Allow five minutes for the pressure to escape.
   d. Completely remove the relief plug from the accumulator.
6. Discard the accumulator.
7. Install the accumulator assembly in the reverse order of the removal procedure.

Pump Assembly

REMOVAL & INSTALLATION

♦ See Figure 63

➡ The Antilock Brake Systems (ABS) pump assembly consists of a piston rod and cylinder body, guide, filter, and a motor. Brake fluid is pressurized and fed to a relief valve, the accumulator and modulator unit. The system pump will run until the pressure in the accumulator has reached 3,271 psi (23,000 kPa). If the pump runs continuously and the pressure

still has not reached the predescribed value, the ABS controller will stop the pump motor and trigger the ABS lamp on the dash to indicate a problem. There will also be a code stored in the controllers memory.

1. Disconnect the negative battery cable.
2. Relieve the ABS system pressure, as outlined in this section.
3. On the 3.5RL, remove the modulator unit.
4. Remove the pump motor.
5. Replace the pump motor with a new one. Do not install a used part.
To install:
6. Install the new pump into the modulator unit.
7. If removed, install the modulator unit.
8. Connect the negative battery cable.

Wheel Speed Sensor

♦ See Figure 64

Each wheel has its own wheel speed sensor which sends a small AC signal to the control module. Correct ABS operation depends on accurate wheel speed signals. The vehicle's wheels and tires must all be the same size and type in order to generate accurate signals. If there is a variation between wheel and tire sizes, inaccurate wheel speed signals will be produced.

❊❊ WARNING

It is very critical that the wheel speed sensor(s) be installed correctly to ensure continued system operation. The sensor cables must be installed, routed and clipped properly. Failure to install the sensor(s) properly could result in contact with moving parts or over extension of sensor cables. This will cause ABS component failure and an open circuit.

Acura uses a contactless type of sensor that detects the rotating speed of the wheel. It is constructed of a permanent magnet and a coil. Attached to the rotating parts are gear pulsers (aka. Tone Rings). When these pulsers turn, the magnetic flux around the coil in the wheel sensor alternates its current. This generates voltages in a frequency or wave pattern. These wave pulses are sent to the ABS control unit which identifies the speed of each of the four wheels.

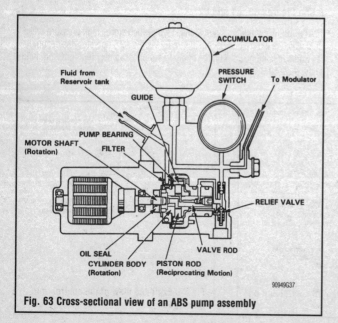

Fig. 63 Cross-sectional view of an ABS pump assembly

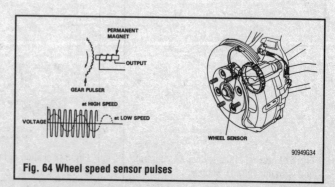

Fig. 64 Wheel speed sensor pulses

REMOVAL & INSTALLATION

▶ See Figure 65

☀☀ CAUTION

Vehicles equipped with air bag systems (SRS) have components and wiring in the same area as the front speed sensor wiring harnesses. The air bag system connectors are yellow. Do not use electrical test equipment on these circuits. Do not damage the SRS wiring while working on other wiring or components. Failure to observe correct procedures may cause the air bag system to inflate unexpectedly or render the system totally inoperative.

1. Raise and safely support the vehicle as necessary for access.
2. Make certain the ignition switch is **OFF**.
3. Detach the sensor harness connector.
4. Beginning at the connector end, remove grommets, clips or retainers as necessary to free the harness. Take careful note of the placement and routing of the harness; it must be reinstalled in the exact original position.
5. Remove the bolt holding the speed sensor to its mounting; remove the sensor. If it is stuck in place, gently tap on the side of the mounting flange with a hammer and small punch; do not tap on the sensor.
   To install:
6. Place the sensor in position; install the retaining bolts loosely. Route the harness correctly. Avoid twisting or crimping the harness; use the white line on the wires as a guide.
7. Once the harness and sensor are correctly but loosely placed, tighten the sensor mounting bolts. Tighten bolts to 16 ft. lbs. (22 Nm).
8. Working from the sensor end to the connector, install each clip, retainer, bracket or grommet holding the sensor harness. The harness must not be twisted. Tighten any bolt holding brackets to 7 ft. lbs. (10 Nm).
9. Attach the wiring connector.
10. Use the ABS checker to check for proper signal from the wheel speed sensor.
11. Carefully lower the vehicle to the ground.

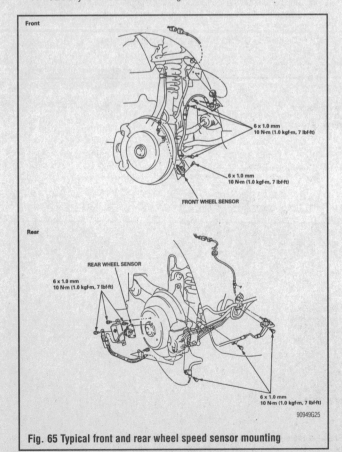

Fig. 65 Typical front and rear wheel speed sensor mounting

INSPECTION

▶ See Figure 66

1. Use a non-metallic feeler gauge to measure the gap between the sensor and the pulser.
2. Rotate the hub or axle slowly by hand, taking measurements at several locations.
3. Specifications are as follows:
   - Integra front and rear—0.016–0.039 inches (0.4–1.0mm)
   - Legend front—0.024–0.047 in. (0.6–1.2mm)
   - Legend rear—0.012–0.051 in. (0.3–1.3mm)
   - Vigor front—0.024–0.035 in. (0.6–0.9mm)
   - Vigor rear—0.020–0.035 in. (0.5–0.9mm)

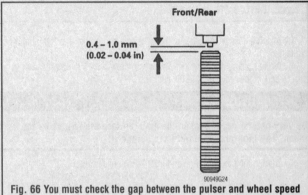

Fig. 66 You must check the gap between the pulser and wheel speed sensor

Tone Ring (Pulser)

The front ABS tone ring is an integral component of the halfshaft assemblies and therefore, cannot be serviced separately. If the front tone ring requires service, the halfshaft assembly must be replaced.

Bleeding the ABS System

The Acura anti-lock brake system contains brake fluid under extremely high pressure within the pump, accumulator and modulator assembly. Do not disconnect or loosen any lines, hoses, fittings or components without properly relieving the system pressure. Use only tool 07HAA-SG00100 or equivalent to relieve pressure.

☀☀ WARNING

Avoid spilling brake fluid on the vehicle's paint. It will damage the finish. If a spill does occur, wash it immediately with water.

☀☀ WARNING

Never reuse brake fluid which has been bled from the brake system. Brake fluid absorbs moisture which can lower its boiling point, therefore re—using old, used, or contaminated fluid can decrease the effectiveness of the braking system.

RELIEVING ABS SYSTEM PRESSURE

Integra, 2.2CL, 2.5TL, 3.2TL and 3.5RL

▶ See Figure 67

➡**This procedure covers 1994–97 vehicles. Starting in 1998, there is no provision for relieving the ABS pressure.**

1. Disconnect the negative battery cable.
2. Remove the cap from the maintenance bleeder on the modulator unit.

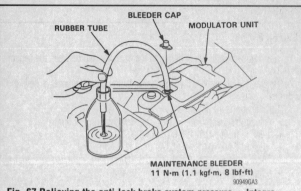

Fig. 67 Relieving the anti-lock brake system pressure— Integra, 2.2CL, 2.5TL, 3.2TL and 3.5RL

3. Attach a hose to the bleeder. Place the free end of the hose in a suitable container.

4. While holding the hose with your hand, slowly open the bleeder ⅛–¼ turn to collect the brake fluid in the container.

✳✳ CAUTION

Be very careful not to loosen the maintenance bleeder valve too much. The high-pressure fluid can burst out!

5. Tighten the bleeder fitting and install the service cap.
6. After repairs are complete, connect the negative battery cable.

Vigor and Legend

▶ **See Figure 68**

1. Disconnect the negative battery cable.
2. Remove the red service cap from the bleeder fitting on the modulator body.
3. Using Bleeder T-wrench (Special Tool No. 07HAA-SG00101), or equivalent, slowly open the bleeder screw ¼ turn to collect high-pressure fluid into the reservoir.
4. After the system pressure drops, open the bleeder 1 full turn, to completely drain the accumulator.

5. Tighten the bleeder fitting and install the red service cap.
6. After repairs are complete, connect the negative battery cable.

BRAKE LINES AND CALIPERS

The brake lines and calipers are bled in the usual fashion with no special procedures required. Refer to the bleeding procedure located earlier in this section. Make certain the master cylinder reservoir is filled before the bleeding is begun and check the level frequently.

BLEEDING HIGH PRESSURE COMPONENTS

The modulator, accumulator and power unit must be bled if any of the lines are removed or loosened during repairs or if any component is replaced. Bleeding can only be accomplished with the ABS checker (07HAJ-SG00100) and the special bleeder T-wrench (07HAA-SG00100) or their equivalents. Do not attempt to use any other procedures or tools to bleed the high pressure components.

1. Park the vehicle on level ground. Block the wheels. Place the shift selector in **P** (automatic transaxle) or **N** (manual transaxle) Make certain the ignition is in the **OFF** position.
2. Detach the 6-pin inspection connector and connect to the checker. The pink connector is usually located under the driver's or passenger seat. Connect the ABS checker.
3. Make certain the brake fluid reservoir on the modulator is filled to the upper mark. Do not reuse any fluid previously bled from the system.
4. Using the bleeder tool, bleed high pressure fluid from the port on the power unit. Close the bleeder port.
5. Start the engine and release the parking brake.
6. Select Modes 2, 3, 4 and 5 on the ABS checker, depress and hold the brake pedal firmly and press the START TEST button on the checker. There should be at least two strong kickbacks through the brake pedal.
7. If there is poor or no kickback in the pedal, turn the ignition switch **OFF**. Repeat the bleeding at the power unit and repeat the mode tests. (Steps 5 and 6, above)
8. Once proper strong pedal kickback is achieved, turn the ignition **OFF**. Check and adjust the fluid level in the modulator reservoir as necessary. Secure the cap on the reservoir.
9. Use the ABS checker to test the system in all modes.

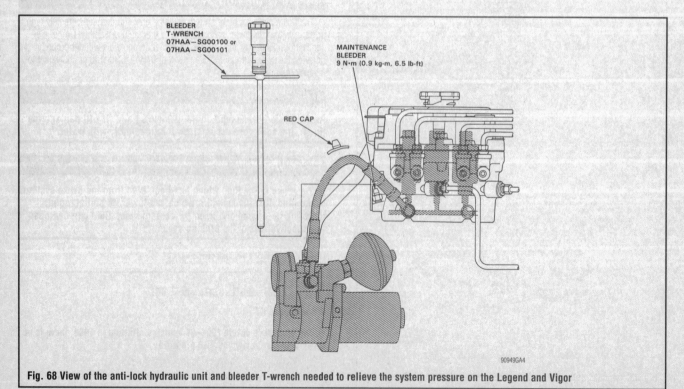

Fig. 68 View of the anti-lock hydraulic unit and bleeder T-wrench needed to relieve the system pressure on the Legend and Vigor

BRAKE SPECIFICATIONS
ACURA 2.2CL, 2.3CL, 2.5TL, 3.0CL, 3.2TL, 3.5RL, INTEGRA, LEGEND, VIGOR
All measurements in inches unless noted

Year	Model		Master Cylinder Bore	Brake Disc Original Thickness	Brake Disc Minimum Thickness	Brake Disc Maximum Runout	Brake Drum Diameter Original Inside Diameter	Brake Drum Diameter Max. Wear Limit	Brake Drum Diameter Maximum Machine Diameter	Minimum Lining Thickness Front	Minimum Lining Thickness Rear	Brake Caliper Bracket Bolts (ft. lbs.)	Brake Caliper Mounting Bolts (ft. lbs.)
1994	Integra	F	NA	0.830	0.750	0.004	—	—	—	0.06	—	—	24
		R	NA	0.350	0.310	0.006	—	—	—	—	0.06	—	24
	Legend	F	NA	1.100	1.020	0.004	—	—	—	0.06	—	—	36
		R	NA	0.350	0.300	0.006	—	—	—	—	0.06	—	17
	Vigor	F	NA	0.910	0.830	0.004	—	—	—	0.06	—	—	36
		R	NA	0.390	0.310	0.004	—	—	—	—	0.06	—	17
1995	Integra	F	NA	0.830	0.750	0.004	—	—	—	0.06	—	—	24
		R	NA	0.350	0.310	0.006	—	—	—	—	0.06	—	24
	Legend	F	NA	1.100	1.020	0.004	—	—	—	0.06	—	—	36
		R	NA	0.350	0.300	0.006	—	—	—	—	0.06	—	17
	Vigor	F	NA	0.910	0.830	0.004	—	—	—	0.06	—	—	36
		R	NA	0.390	0.310	0.004	—	—	—	—	0.06	—	17
1996	2.5TL	F	NA	0.910	0.830	0.004	—	—	—	0.06	—	80	36
		R	NA	0.350	0.300	0.004	—	—	—	—	0.06	28	17
	3.2TL	F	NA	0.910	0.830	0.004	—	—	—	0.06	—	80	36
		R	NA	0.350	0.300	0.004	—	—	—	—	0.06	28	17
	3.5RL	F	NA	0.910	0.830	0.004	—	—	—	0.06	—	80	36
		R	NA	0.350	0.300	0.004	—	—	—	—	0.06	28	17
	Integra	F	NA	0.830	0.750	0.004	—	—	—	0.06	—	80	23
		R	NA	0.350	0.310	0.004	—	—	—	—	0.06	28	17
1997	2.2CL	F	NA	0.910	0.830	0.004	—	—	—	0.06	—	80	54
		R	NA	0.390	0.310	0.004	—	—	—	—	0.06	28	18
	3.0CL	F	NA	0.980	0.910	0.004	—	—	—	0.08	—	80	54
		R	NA	0.390	0.310	0.004	—	—	—	—	0.08	28	18
	3.5RL	F	NA	0.910	0.830	0.004	—	—	—	0.06	—	80	36
		R	NA	0.350	0.300	0.004	—	—	—	—	0.06	28	17
	2.5TL	F	NA	0.910	0.830	0.004	—	—	—	0.06	—	—	36
		R	NA	0.350	0.300	0.004	—	—	—	—	0.06	28	17
	3.2TL	F	NA	0.910	0.830	0.004	—	—	—	0.06	—	80	36
		R	NA	0.350	0.300	0.004	—	—	—	—	0.06	28	17
	Integra	F	NA	0.830	0.750	0.004	—	—	—	0.06	—	80	24
		R	NA	0.350	0.310	0.004	—	—	—	—	0.06	28	17
	Integra R	F	NA	0.900	0.830	0.004	—	—	—	0.06	—	80	36
		R	NA	0.350	0.310	0.004	—	—	—	—	0.06	28	17
1998	2.3CL	F	NA	0.910	0.830	0.004	—	—	—	0.06	—	80	54
		R	NA	0.390	0.310	0.004	—	—	—	—	0.06	28	18
	3.0CL	F	NA	0.980	0.910	0.004	—	—	—	0.08	—	80	54
		R	NA	0.390	0.310	0.004	—	—	—	—	0.08	28	18

90949C01

BRAKE SPECIFICATIONS
ACURA 2.2CL, 2.3CL, 2.5TL, 3.0CL, 3.2TL, 3.5RL, INTEGRA, LEGEND, VIGOR
All measurements in inches unless noted

Year	Model		Master Cylinder Bore	Brake Disc Original Thickness	Brake Disc Minimum Thickness	Brake Disc Maximum Runout	Brake Drum Diameter Original Inside Diameter	Brake Drum Diameter Max. Wear Limit	Brake Drum Diameter Maximum Machine Diameter	Minimum Lining Thickness Front	Minimum Lining Thickness Rear	Brake Caliper Bracket Bolts (ft. lbs.)	Brake Caliper Mounting Bolts (ft. lbs.)
1998 cont.	3.5RL	F	NA	0.910	0.830	0.004	—	—	—	0.06	—	80	36
		R	NA	0.350	0.300	0.004	—	—	—	—	0.06	28	17
	2.5TL	F	NA	0.910	0.830	0.004	—	—	—	0.06	—	—	36
		R	NA	0.350	0.300	0.004	—	—	—	—	0.06	28	17
	3.2TL	F	NA	0.910	0.830	0.004	—	—	—	0.06	—	—	36
		R	NA	0.350	0.300	0.004	—	—	—	—	0.06	28	17
	Integra	F	NA	0.830	0.750	0.004	—	—	—	0.06	—	80	23
		R	NA	0.350	0.310	0.004	—	—	—	—	0.06	28	17
	Integra R	F	NA	0.900	0.830	0.004	—	—	—	0.06	—	80	36
		R	NA	0.350	0.310	0.004	—	—	—	—	0.06	28	17
1999	2.3CL	F	NA	0.910	0.830	0.004	—	—	—	0.06	—	80	54
		R	NA	0.390	0.310	0.004	—	—	—	—	0.06	28	18
	3.0CL	F	NA	0.980	0.910	0.004	—	—	—	0.08	—	80	54
		R	NA	0.390	0.310	0.004	—	—	—	—	0.08	28	18
	3.5RL	F	NA	0.910	0.830	0.004	—	—	—	0.06	—	80	36
		R	NA	0.350	0.300	0.004	—	—	—	—	0.06	28	17
	2.5TL	F	NA	0.910	0.830	0.004	—	—	—	0.06	—	—	36
		R	NA	0.350	0.300	0.004	—	—	—	—	0.06	28	17
	3.2TL	F	NA	1.100	1.020	0.004	—	—	—	0.06	—	80	36
		R	NA	0.350	0.310	0.004	①	②	②	—	③	41	17
	Integra	F	NA	0.830	0.750	0.004	—	—	—	0.06	—	—	24
		R	NA	0.350	0.310	0.004	—	—	—	—	0.06	—	24
2000	2.3CL	F	NA	0.910	0.830	0.004	—	—	—	0.06	—	80	54
		R	NA	0.390	0.310	0.004	—	—	—	—	0.06	28	18
	3.0CL	F	NA	0.980	0.910	0.004	—	—	—	0.08	—	80	54
		R	NA	0.390	0.310	0.004	—	—	—	—	0.08	28	18
	3.5RL	F	NA	0.910	0.830	0.004	—	—	—	0.06	—	80	36
		R	NA	0.350	0.300	0.004	—	—	—	—	0.06	28	17
	2.5TL	F	NA	0.910	0.830	0.004	—	—	—	0.06	—	—	36
		R	NA	0.350	0.300	0.004	—	—	—	—	0.06	28	17
	3.2TL	F	NA	1.100	1.020	0.004	—	—	—	0.06	—	80	36
		R	NA	0.350	0.310	0.004	①	②	②	—	③	41	17
	Integra	F	NA	0.830	0.750	0.004	—	—	—	0.06	—	—	24
		R	NA	0.350	0.310	0.004	—	—	—	—	0.06	—	24

NA - Not Available
F - Front
R - Rear

① Rear parking brake drum: 6.693 inches
② Rear parking brake drum maximum diameter: 6.732 inches
③ Rear pad: 0.06 inches
   Rear parking brake shoes: 0.04 inches

90949C02

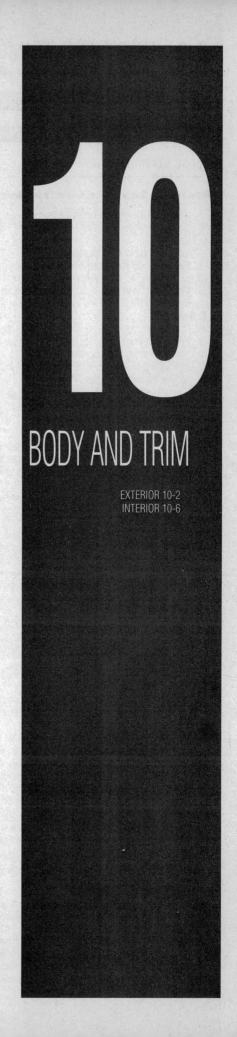

10

BODY AND TRIM

EXTERIOR

Doors

REMOVAL & INSTALLATION

➡**Front and rear doors may be removed using the same procedure.**

1. Disconnect the negative battery cable.
2. Support the door, by placing a floor jack and a piece of wood underneath the door.
3. Remove the bolts from the door stop arm.
4. Remove the connector on the main wiring harness.
5. Unplug any other applicable wiring connectors.
6. Matchmark the location of the hinges on the door.
7. Remove the hinge bolts and remove the door assembly.

To install:

8. Position the door into place and finger tighten the hinge bolts.
9. Align the door with the hinge marks made earlier and tighten the bolts.
10. Attach the wiring connectors.
11. Attach the door stop arm and tighten the bolts to 89 inch lbs. (10 Nm).
12. Remove the supporting jack.
13. Connect the negative battery cable.

ADJUSTMENT

When checking door alignment, look carefully at each seam between the door and body. The gap should be constant and even all the way around the door. Pay particular attention to the door seams at the corners farthest from the hinges; this is the area where errors will be most evident. Additionally, the door should pull in against the weatherstrip when latched to seal out wind and water. The contact should be even all the way around and the stripping should be about half compressed.

The position of the door can be adjusted in three dimensions: fore and aft, up and down, in and out. The primary adjusting points are the hinge-to-body bolts. Apply tape to the fender and door edges to protect the paint. Two layers of common masking tape works well. Loosen the bolts just enough to allow the hinge to move in place. With the help of an assistant, position the door and retighten the bolts. Inspect the door seams carefully and repeat the adjustment until correctly aligned.

The in-out adjustment (how far the door "sticks out" from the body) is adjusted by loosening the hinge-to-door bolts. Again, move the door into place, then retighten the bolts. This dimension affects both the amount of crush on the weatherstrips and the amount of "bite" on the striker.

Further adjustment for closed position and smoothness of latching is made at the latch plate or striker. This piece is located at the rear edge of the door and is attached to the bodywork; it is the piece the latch engages when the door is closed. Although the striker size and style may vary between models or from front to rear, the method of adjusting it is the same:

1. Loosen the large cross-point screw(s) holding the striker. Know in advance that these bolts will be very tight; an impact screwdriver is a handy tool to have for this job. Make sure you are using the proper size bit.
2. With the bolts just loose enough to allow the striker to move if necessary, hold the outer door handle in the released position and close the door. The striker will move into the correct location to match the door latch. Open the door and tighten the mounting bolts. The striker may be adjusted towards or away from the center of the car, thereby tightening or loosening the door fit.
3. The striker can be moved up and down to compensate for door position, but if the door is correctly mounted at the hinges this should not be necessary.

➡**Do not attempt to correct height variations (sag) by adjusting the striker.**

Additionally, some models may use one or more spacers or shims behind the striker or at the hinges. These shims may be removed or added in combination to adjust the reach of the striker or hinge.

4. After the striker bolts have been tightened, open and close the door several times. Observe the motion of the door as it engages the striker; it should continue its straight-in motion and not deflect up or down as it hits the striker.
5. Check the feel of the latch during opening and closing. It must be smooth and linear, without any trace of grinding or binding during engagement and release.

It may be necessary to repeat the striker adjustment several times (and possibly re-adjust the hinges) before the correct door to body match is produced. This can be a maddening process of loosen—tighten, check and readjust; have patience.

Hood

REMOVAL & INSTALLATION

▶ **See Figure 1**

➡**The help of an assistant is recommended when removing or installing the hood.**

1. Disconnect the negative battery cable.
2. Open and support the hood.
3. Protect the body with covers to prevent damage to the paint.
4. Use a suitable marker, or scribe marks around the hinge locations for reference during installation.
5. Unplug any electrical connections and windshield washer hoses that would interfere with hood removal.
6. While an assistant helps secure the hood, unfasten the attaching bolts, then remove the hood from the vehicle.

To install:

7. Place the hood into position. Install and partially tighten attaching bolts.
8. Adjust the hood with the reference marks and tighten the attaching bolts.
9. Check the hood for an even fit between the fenders and for flush fit with the front of the fenders. Also, check for a flush fit with the top of the cowl and fenders. If necessary, adjust the hood latch.
10. Attach any electrical connections or windshield washer hoses removed to facilitate hood removal.

9094LP02

Fig. 1 Use a suitable paint marker to matchmark the installed position of the hood brackets

ALIGNMENT

Once the hood is installed, tighten the hood-to-hinge bolts just snug. Close the hood and check for perfect seam alignment. The hood seams are one of the most visible on the car; the slightest error will be plainly obvious to an observer.

Loosen the bolts and position the hood as necessary, then snug the nuts and recheck. Continue the process until the hood latches smoothly and aligns evenly at all the seams.

➡**Do not adjust hood position by moving the latch.**

The hood bolts and the hinge mount bolts may be loosened to adjust their positions. Shims may be used behind the hinge mounts if necessary. When everything aligns correctly, tighten the bolts securely.

The elevation of the hood at the latch end may be adjusted by turning the rubber stops or cushions. These bumpers have threaded bottoms and move up or down when turned. An annoying hood rattle on bumps may be caused by these cushions being missing or out of adjustment.

Hatch

REMOVAL & INSTALLATION

➡**The help of an assistant is recommended when removing or installing the hatch.**

1. Disconnect the negative battery cable.
2. Open and support the hatch.
3. Remove the trim from the hatch.
4. Detach the hatch trim panel by pulling the trim panel forward.
5. Remove the hatch spoiler if equipped.
6. Detach the connectors and remove the wiring harness.

➡**Before removing the wiring harness, attach a string to the end of it. This will enable you to pull the harness back through upon installation.**

7. Remove the rear wiper motor.
8. Remove the upper anchor bolts from the rear seats.
9. Remove the upper quarter pillar trim panel.
10. Remove the roof trim.
11. Pull down the rear headliner.

➡**Do not use excessive force when pulling down on the rear headliner, it is fragile and will break easily.**

12. Support the hatch, and remove the support struts.

❉❉ WARNING

Do not raise the hatch too far. The edges of the glass may come in contact with the roof line.

13. Remove the mounting bolts and carefully pull the hatch from the hinges.
14. Installation is the reverse of the removal procedure.

Trunk Lid

REMOVAL & INSTALLATION

➡**The help of an assistant is recommended when removing or installing the trunk lid.**

1. Disconnect the negative battery cable.
2. Open and support the trunk lid.
3. Remove the inner trim from the trunk lid.

4. Detach the connectors and remove the wiring harness.
5. Remove the trunk lid mounting bolts and then the lid.
6. Installation is the reverse of the removal procedure.

Bumpers

REMOVAL & INSTALLATION

Integra, CL, TL, RL

FRONT

▶ **See Figures 2, 3, 4, 5 and 6**

1. On Integra, remove the turn signals. Remove the mounting screws at the sides and top of the bumpers.

Fig. 2 Bumper removal requires a Phillips head screwdriver on Integra models

Fig. 3 As always, note the size and location of each screw as you remove them

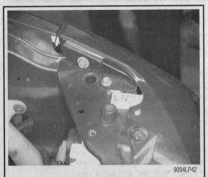

Fig. 4 The left and right side fender support brackets must also be removed

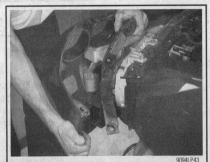

Fig. 5 As you peel the bumper away from the front of the vehicle, note the position of the attaching bracket

Fig. 6 View of the front bumper partially removed from the vehicle

2. Remove the lower clips and the bumper mounting bolts.
3. Slide the bumper off the brackets.
4. Remove the bumper brackets. Remove the corner slide and the corner slide clip screws.
To install:
5. Install the corner slide screws and the slide. Install the bumper brackets.
6. Install the bumper and check that the bumper beam hooks are set in the holes.
7. Install the bumper bolts and clips.
8. If removed, install the turn signals.

REAR

1. Open the trunk lid. Remove the mounting screws at the sides of the bumpers.
2. Remove the access panel in the trunk and disconnect the wire for the license plate light.
3. From the inside of the trunk, remove the 2 upper bumper mounting nuts.
4. From under the trunk floor, remove the clips and the under protector.
5. Remove the lower mounting nuts from beneath the trunk floor.
6. Pull the bumper off while feeding out the wiring harness.
To install:
7. Install the harness and the bumper. Install the mounting nuts and the under protector.
8. Connect the license plate light wire and replace the access cover.
9. Install the mounting screws at the sides of the bumper.

Legend

FRONT

1. Remove the covers and the turn signals. Remove the mounting bolts on the sides.
2. Remove the 4 lower skirt mounting bolts and remove the bumper by pulling up and forward.
To install:
3. Install the bumper and the bolts.
4. Install the turn signals and the covers.

REAR

1. Pull the trunk trim forward to access the 2 upper mounting nuts.
2. Remove the inner fender mounting screws and move the inner fenders away from the bumper.
3. Remove the lower mounting nuts. Remove the upper trim from the bumper and remove the 3 mounting clips.
4. Pull back the sides of the bumper and remove from the vehicle.
To install:
5. Install the bumper and the mounting clips.
6. Replace the trim.
7. Install the mounting nuts and the inner fender mounting screws.

Vigor

FRONT

1. Remove the turn signals and disconnect the harness.
2. Remove the mounting screws at the sides of the bumper. Remove the 2 lower skirt bolts and the 4 lower skirt screws.
3. Remove the 2 mounting nuts from the engine compartment. Remove the caps and the mounting bolts.
4. Slide the bumper off.
To install:
5. Install the bumper and secure in place using the mounting bolts. Install the caps.
6. Install the nuts inside the engine compartment.
7. Install the skirt bolts and screws.
8. Install the side screws and the turn signals. Connect the harness connector.

REAR

1. Pry out the caps and remove the upper mounting nuts. Remove the screws at the sides of the bumper.
2. Remove the upper trim from the bumper and remove the 3 mounting clips.
3. Remove the 2 lower mounting nuts and clip under the trunk floor. Pull back the sides of the bumper and remove by pulling forward.

To install:
4. Install the bumper, clip and mounting nuts.
5. Install the clips and trim. Install the screws and the mounting nuts. Install the caps.

Grille

REMOVAL & INSTALLATION

▶ **See Figure 7**

1. Disconnect the negative battery cable.
2. Open and support the hood.
3. Remove the grille retaining nuts/screws and any retaining clips, then remove the grille.
To install:
4. Position the grille, making sure the retaining clips are secured, then tighten the retaining screws.
5. Lower the hood.
6. Connect the negative battery cable.

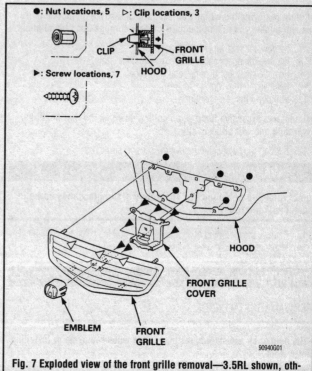

Fig. 7 Exploded view of the front grille removal—3.5RL shown, others similar

Outside Mirrors

REMOVAL & INSTALLATION

▶ **See Figures 8 and 9**

1. Disconnect the negative battery cable.
2. Remove the door panel, as outlined later in this section.
3. Remove the screw cover and the retaining screw for the mirror cover.
4. Unplug the connector for the power mirror.
5. Unfasten the three mirror retaining screws, then remove the mirror.
To install:
6. Place the mirror into position and install the retaining screws.
7. Attach the connector for the power mirror.
8. Install the mirror cover, retaining screw, and screw cover.
9. Install the door panel, as outlined later in this section.
10. Connect the negative battery cable.

Fig. 8 Remove the interior mirror trim

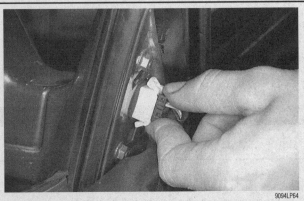
Fig. 9 Squeeze the connector harness to release the wiring from the mirror assembly

Antenna

REPLACEMENT

→ Before beginning this procedure, check with your local parts supplier as to the availability of the antenna. This part may only be sold at your local Honda/Acura dealer.

1. Remove the negative battery cable.
2. Gain access to the antenna motor.
3. Remove the trim panel.
4. Detach the connector from the motor.
5. Disconnect the antenna lead.
6. Remove the antenna nut from the top of the fender.
7. Remove the motor bracket nut.
8. Remove the motor and antenna as an assembly.
9. Remove the antenna nut spacer.
10. Connect the wiring harness to the antenna assembly.
11. Carefully pull out the antenna while an assistant turns on the radio.

To install:

12. Carefully steer the teeth of the new antenna mast cable into the antenna housing.
13. Check the engagement by gently moving the cable up and down a few times.
14. Clean and lubricate the antenna mast housing threads with a light penetrating oil.
15. Turn the radio switch off and let the power antenna's motor pull the cable down into the housing.
16. Install the bushing, spacer, and the nut.
17. The remaining steps are the reverse of the removal procedure.

Fenders

REMOVAL & INSTALLATION

▶ **See Figures 10 and 11**

1. Disconnect the negative battery cable.
2. Open the hood and support the hood with the prop rod.
3. Remove the cowl vent panels.
4. Remove the front fender splash shield(s).
5. Remove the parking lamp(s).
6. Unfasten the two front fender-to-front sidemember retaining screws
7. Remove the screw at the base of the front fender body behind the wheel opening.
8. Unfasten the screw from the rear of the front fender at the A-pillar.
9. Remove the screws from the top of the fender along the top of the apron and front sidemember.
10. Remove any shims as necessary.
11. Remove the fender from the vehicle.

To install:

12. Position the fender into place and finger tighten the screws (and shims if removed) on the top of the fender.
13. Install the remaining screws (and shims if removed) finger tight.
14. Align the fender and install shims if necessary to properly align the fender.
15. Tighten all the fender retaining screws.
16. Install the parking lamps.
17. Install the front fender splash shields.
18. Install the cowl vent panels.
19. Lower the hood.
20. Connect the negative battery cable.

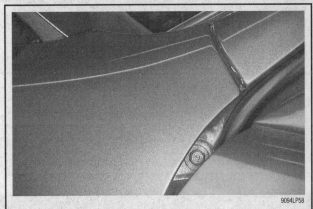
Fig. 10 Open the door to gain access to one of the fender bolts

Fig. 11 Lift the fender off of the vehicle once all fasteners are removed

Side Sill Panel

REMOVAL & INSTALLATION

▶ See Figures 12, 13 and 14

1. Remove the side sill panel by removing the necessary screws from the front and rear wheel wells.
2. Slide the panel forward and remove.
3. To remove the side sill panel clips, turn them 45°.

Fig. 12 Remove the screws from the under side of the side sill panel

Fig. 13 Pulling the side sill panel away from the rear wheel well

Fig. 14 View of side sill panel and retaining clips

To install:
4. Slide the clips onto the side sill panel.
5. Install the panel on the car by aligning the clips with the holes in the cars body.
6. Press lightly to ensure the clips have fully seated in the body.
7. Install the screws that were removed from the wheel well.

Power Sunroof

REMOVAL & INSTALLATION

1. Open the sun shade.
2. Tilt up the glass.
3. Remove the bolts and then the glass from the assembly.
4. Remove the necessary hardware to gain access to the sunshade.
5. Remove the sunshade.
6. Disconnect the negative battery cable.
7. Detach the motor wiring harness connector.
8. Remove the motor mounting bolts and then the motor.
9. Detach the drain tubes.
10. Unfasten the mounting nuts, then remove the sunroof frame from the car.
11. Installation is the reverse of the removal procedure.

INTERIOR

Instrument Cluster

REMOVAL & INSTALLATION

▶ See Figures 15, 16, 17, 18 and 19

1. Disconnect the negative battery cable.
2. Lower the steering column and remove the screws that secure the instrument cluster trim to the dash board.
3. Remove the screws that secure the instrument cluster to the dash assembly.
4. Pull the instrument cluster out of the dash.
5. Remove the wiring harnesses and speedometer cable (if applicable) from the back of the cluster.
6. Remove the instrument cluster from the dash.
To install:
7. Installation is the reverse of the removal procedure.

Fig. 15 A Phillips screwdriver is needed to remove the trim panel fasteners

Fig. 16 Remove the trim panel that surrounds the instrument cluster

Fig. 17 The clear shield can be removed by squeezing the clips along the edges

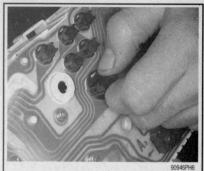

Fig. 18 To remove the instrument cluster bulbs turn the holders in the counterclockwise direction . . .

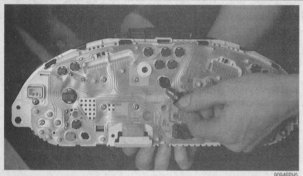

Fig. 19 . . . then pull the bulb and bulb holder from the back of the instrument cluster

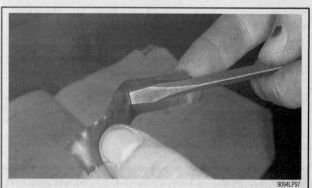

Fig. 20 Cover a small prytool with a piece of electrical tape to prevent damage to any trim pieces that may scratch easily

Dashboard

REMOVAL & INSTALLATION

▶ **See Figures 20 thru 25**

It is important to take the time to read all of the steps before beginning this procedure. There are many variations in dashboard design due to trim packages and the placement of airbags therefore this procedure was written as a guide. Do not pull or use excessive force when removing the dashboard. It is fragile and will crack easily. A good rule of thumb is if the dashboard is difficult to pull out, you most likely missed a bolt(s).

✳✳ CAUTION

Before beginning this procedure, please refer to Section 6 for proper air bag removal procedures.

1. Disconnect the negative battery cable.
2. If the vehicle is equipped with an Supplemental Restraint System (SRS), wait three (3) minutes after the battery cable has been disconnected before working on the vehicle.
3. To remove the dashboard, the following components must be removed:
   - Front seats.
   - Front and rear consoles.
   - Dashboard covers.
   - Radio
   - Sunroof switch.
   - Clock.
   - Glove Box.
   - Knee bolster.
4. Lower the steering column.
5. Remove the passenger side air bag module.
6. Detach the air temperature control cable connectors.
7. Unplug the antenna lead.

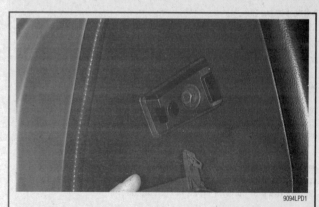

Fig. 21 Remove the side access panels, then unfasten the bolt

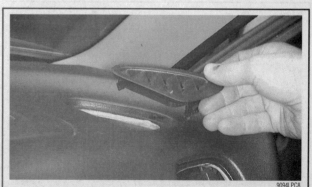

Fig. 22 Pry up on the plastic trim to remove the side window defroster vent

Fig. 23 Removal of the forward facing vents is necessary to gain access to some of the mounting bolts

Fig. 24 Free all necessary wiring from under the dash

Fig. 25 Pry the edge of the cruise control switch out, then remove the switch by hand

➡To prevent damage to the dashboard when prying, wrap your prytool with tape to pad it.

8. Detach the connectors from the fuse panel.
9. Remove the access panels located on each side of the dashboard by the door jam.
10. Remove all dashboard mounting bolts.
11. Lift and remove the dashboard from the vehicle.
12. Carefully unwind any wiring that is tangled up in the dash.
13. Installation is the reverse of the removal procedure. Make sure to fasten all retainers securely, and attach all connectors to the proper components they were removed from.

Console

REMOVAL & INSTALLATION

▶ See Figure 26

1. Disconnect the negative battery cable.
2. Detach any wiring harnesses that are tied to or integrated with in the console.
3. Remove the console mounting screws. You may need to look in the console storage bin, in the ashtray, or under trim panels to locate hidden retainers.
4. Wrap a shop cloth around the gear selector knob to prevent it from being scratched.
5. On Integra models, turn the console approximately 45°to obtain the necessary clearance for removal of the unit.
6. Remove the console.

➡This procedure can be used to remove both the front and rear consoles. It may be necessary to lift up on the parking brake lever to remove the rear console on all Integra models.

7. Installation is the reverse of the removal procedure.

Door Panels

REMOVAL & INSTALLATION

▶ See Figures 27 and 28

➡This is a general procedure. Depending on vehicle and model, the order of steps may need to be changed slightly.

1. Remove the inner mirror control knob (if manual remote) and remove the inner delta cover from the mirror mount.
2. Remove the screws holding the armrest and remove the armrest. The armrest screws may be concealed behind plastic caps which must be popped out with a non-marring tool.
3. Remove the surround or cover for the inside door handle. Again, find the hidden screw; remove it and slide the cover off over the handle.
4. If not equipped with electric windows, remove the window crank handle. This can be tricky, but not difficult. Install a piece of tape on the door pad to show the position of the handle before removal. The handle is held onto the crank axle with a spring clip shaped like the Greek letter Omega. The clip is located between the back of the crank handle and the door pad. It is correctly installed with the legs pointing away from the length of the crank handle. There are three common ways of removing the clip:
5. Use a door handle removal tool. This inexpensive slotted and toothed tool can be fitted between the crank handle and the door panel, and is used to push the spring clip free.
6. Use a rag or piece of cloth and work it back and forth between the crank

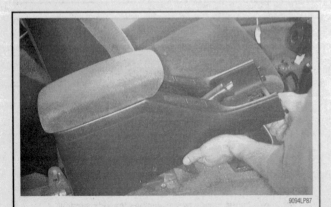

Fig. 26 Lift the console over the parking brake lever assembly

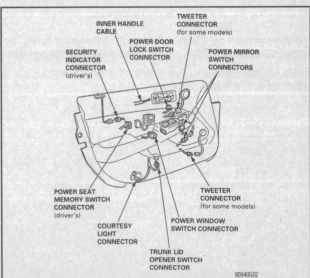

Fig. 27 View of some of the electrical connectors which may have to be detached for panel removal—3.5RL shown

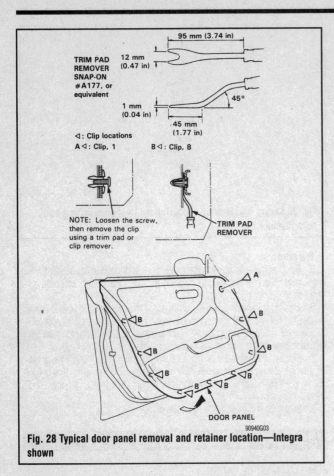

TRIM PAD
REMOVER
SNAP-ON
#A177, or
equivalent

95 mm (3.74 in)

12 mm
(0.47 in)

1 mm
(0.04 in)

45 mm
(1.77 in)

45°

◁ : Clip locations
A ◁ : Clip, 1   B ◁ : Clip, 8

NOTE: Loosen the screw,
then remove the clip
using a trim pad or
clip remover.

TRIM PAD
REMOVER

A
C
C
B
C
B
C
B
C
B
C
B
B

DOOR PANEL

90940G03

**Fig. 28 Typical door panel removal and retainer location—Integra
shown**

handle and door panel. If constant upward tension is kept, the clip will be forced
free. Keep watch on the clip as it pops out; it may get lost.

7. Straighten a common paper clip and bend a very small J-hook at the
end of it. Work the hook down from the top of the crank and engage the loop of
the spring clip. As you pull the clip free, keep your other hand over the area. If
this is not done, the clip will vanish to an undisclosed location, never to be
seen again.

8. In general, power door lock and window switches mounted on the door
pad (not the armrest) may remain in place until the pad is removed. Some cannot be removed until the door panel is off the door.

9. If the car has manual vertical door locks, remove the lock knob by
unscrewing it. If this is impossible (because they're in square housings) wait
until the panel is lifted free.

10. Using a broad, flat-bladed tool (not a screwdriver) begin gently prying
the door pad away from the door. You are releasing plastic inserts from plastic
seats. There will be 6 to 12 of them around the door. With care, the plastic
inserts can be reused several times.

11. When all the clips are loose, lift up on the panel to release the lip at the
top of the door. This may require a bit of jiggling to loosen the panel; do so
gently and don't damage the panel. The upper edge (at the window sill) is
attached by a series of retaining clips.

12. Once the panel is free, keep it close to the door and check behind it.
Disconnect any wiring for switches, lights or speakers which may be attached.

➡**Behind the panel is a plastic sheet, taped or glued to the door. This is
a water shield and must be intact to prevent water entry into the car. It
must be securely attached at its edges and not be ripped or damaged.
Small holes or tears can be patched with waterproof tape applied to
both sides of the liner.**

To install:

13. When reinstalling, connect any wiring harnesses and align the upper
edge of the panel along the top of the door first. Make sure the left-right alignment is correct; tap the top of the panel into place with the heel of your hand.

14. Make sure the plastic clips align with their holes; pop each retainer into
place with gentle pressure.

15. Install the armrest and door handle bezel, remembering to install any
caps or covers over the screws.

16. Install the window crank handle on vehicles with manual windows. Place
the spring clip into the slot on the handle, remembering that the legs should
point away from the long dimension of the handle. Align the handle with the
tape mark made earlier and put the crank over the end of the axle. Use the heel
of your hand to give the center of the crank a short, sharp blow. This will cause
the crank to move inward and the spring will engage its locking groove. The
secret to this trick is to push the crank straight on; if it's crooked, it won't
engage and you may end up looking for the spring clip.

17. Install any remaining parts or trim pieces which may have been removed
earlier. (Map pockets, speaker grilles, etc.)

18. Install the delta cover and the remote mirror handle if they were
removed.

Door Locks

REMOVAL & INSTALLATION

Power

1. Disconnect the negative battery cable.
2. Remove the door panel by removing the appropriate fasteners and wiring
harnesses.
3. Detach the wiring harness from the door lock actuator.
4. Remove the fasteners and then remove the door lock actuator.
5. Installation is the reverse of the removal procedure.

Trunk/Hatch Lock

REMOVAL & INSTALLATION

1. Disconnect the trunk lid/hatch opener cable connector.

➡**Take caution not to bend the cylinder rod and cylinder rod opener
cable.**

2. Remove the cylinder rod.
3. Remove the bolts, then remove the trunk lid/hatch latch.
4. Unfasten the lock cylinder bolts, then remove the lock cylinder.
5. Remove the lock cylinder from the cylinder rod and then take them out.
6. Installation is the reverse of the removal procedure.

Door Glass and Regulator

REMOVAL & INSTALLATION

1. Remove the door panel.
2. Remove the plastic cover from the door frame.
3. Remove the power window switch from the door panel.
4. Connect the power window switch to the door harness.
5. Fully lower the glass.
6. Pull the channel guide cover off.
7. Remove the screws from the channel guide.
8. Remove the center channel guide (if equipped).
9. Carefully remove the glass until you can see the bolts and then carefully
loosen all of them.
10. Slide the window track guide to the rear.

➡**Before removing the guide pin, scribe a line around it. This will
enable you to install it in the exact position it was removed in.**

11. Remove the glass by gently lifting it from the guide.
12. The glass can now be removed by pulling it through the window slot.

✳ CAUTION

Use extreme caution when handling window glass.

➡Check the guide pin for wear. Replace as necessary.

13. Detach the connector and remove the regulator through the hole in the door.

➡Scribe a line around the rear roller guide bolt. This mark will show where the original adjustment was at before you removed the component.

14. Remove the power window motor from the window regulator assembly.
15. Remove any clips and pull the glass run channel out.

➡It may be necessary to remove the glass stopper.

✳✳ WARNING

Grease all of the sliding surfaces of the regulator or component failure may occur.

To install:
16. Install the window motor on the regulator assembly.

➡As a check, you can connect a known good 12 volt power source to the window motor to check the operation of the entire assembly. The regulator should operate with a steady, consistent motion in either direction.

17. Install the glass run channel into the door as shown.
18. Install the regulator.
19. Install the glass.
20. Install the center channel guide.
21. Move the glass up and down to ensure free movement.
22. Attach the door wiring harness to the door.
23. Disconnect the window switch (on power controlled models) and install it into the door panel.
24. The remainder of the installation process is the reverse of removal.

Electric Window Motor

REMOVAL & INSTALLATION

▶ **See Figures 29 and 30**

1. Remove the regulator from the door assembly. Refer to the procedure in this section.
2. Except for the rear doors, drill a hole through the regulator sector gear and backplate. Install the bolt and nut to lock the sector gear in position. Be careful not to drill a hole closer than 7/16 in. (11mm) from the edge of the sector. Also, do not drill through the lift arm attaching portion of the sector gear, or the joint integrity will be jeopardized.
3. Drill out the ends of the motor attaching rivets using a 1/4 in. (6mm) bit.
4. Remove the motor and the remaining portions of the rivets from the regulator. Except for the rear doors, one rivet will not be accessible until assembly.

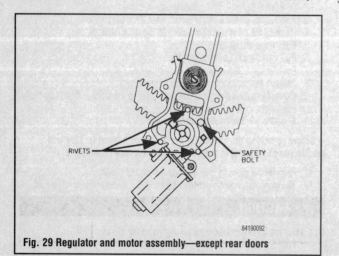

RIVETS   SAFETY BOLT

84190092

Fig. 29 Regulator and motor assembly—except rear doors

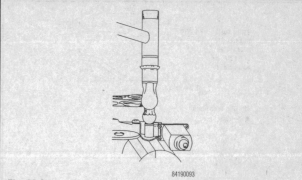

84190093

Fig. 30 Secure the rivets by collapsing the rivet ends using a ball peen hammer

To install:
5. Position the new motor to the regulator. With the aid of an assistant, install new rivets by collapsing or crushing the rivet ends using a ball peen hammer.
6. Except for the rear doors, once two of the three rivets have been installed, remove the bolt securing the sector gear to the backplate, then use an appropriate electrical source (such as the vehicle's window motor harness) to rotate the regulator, providing access to the remaining rivet.
7. Except for the rear doors, use a flat nosed rotary file to grind off one sector gear tooth from the side which does not contact the driven gear. This is necessary to reach the remaining rivet. Remove the old rivet, then install the remaining new rivet.
8. Install the regulator to the door assembly.

Windshield and Fixed Glass

REMOVAL & INSTALLATION

If your windshield, or other fixed window, is cracked or chipped, you may decide to replace it with a new one yourself. However, there are two main reasons why replacement windshields and other window glass should be installed only by a professional automotive glass technician: safety and cost.

The most important reason a professional should install automotive glass is for safety. The glass in the vehicle, especially the windshield, is designed with safety in mind in case of a collision. The windshield is specially manufactured from two panes of specially-tempered glass with a thin layer of transparent plastic between them. This construction allows the glass to "give" in the event that a part of your body hits the windshield during the collision, and prevents the glass from shattering, which could cause lacerations, blinding and other harm to passengers of the vehicle. The other fixed windows are designed to be tempered so that if they break during a collision, they shatter in such a way that there are no large pointed glass pieces. The professional automotive glass technician knows how to install the glass in a vehicle so that it will function optimally during a collision. Without the proper experience, knowledge and tools, installing a piece of automotive glass yourself could lead to additional harm if an accident should ever occur.

Cost is also a factor when deciding to install automotive glass yourself. Performing this could cost you much more than a professional may charge for the same job. Since the windshield is designed to break under stress, an often life saving characteristic, windshields tend to break VERY easily when an inexperienced person attempts to install one. Do-it-yourselfers buying two, three or even four windshields from a salvage yard because they have broken them during installation are common stories. Also, since the automotive glass is designed to prevent the outside elements from entering your vehicle, improper installation can lead to water and air leaks. Annoying whining noises at highway speeds from air leaks or inside body panel rusting from water leaks can add to your stress level and subtract from your wallet. After buying two or three windshields, installing them and ending up with a leak that produces a noise while driving and water damage during rainstorms, the cost of having a professional do it correctly the first time may be much more alluring. We here at Chilton, therefore, advise that you have a professional automotive glass technician service any broken glass on your vehicle.

WINDSHIELD CHIP REPAIR

▶ **See Figures 31 thru 45**

➡ **Check with your state and local authorities on the laws for state safety inspection. Some states or municipalities may not allow chip repair as a viable option for correcting stone damage to your windshield.**

Although severely cracked or damaged windshields must be replaced, there is something that you can do to prolong or even prevent the need for replacement of a chipped windshield. There are many companies which offer windshield chip repair products, such as Loctite's® Bullseye windshield repair kit. These kits usually consist of a syringe, pedestal and a sealing adhesive. The syringe is mounted on the pedestal and is used to create a vacuum which pulls the plastic layer against the glass. This helps make the chip transparent. The adhesive is then injected which seals the chip and helps to prevent further stress cracks from developing. Refer to the sequence of photos to get a general idea of what windshield chip repair involves.

➡ **Always follow the specific manufacturer's instructions.**

Inside Rear View Mirror

REPLACEMENT

▶ **See Figure 46**

The rear view mirror is attached to a support which is bonded to the windshield glass. If the support becomes unattached, it must be aligned and rebonded before the mirror can be mounted.

1. Mark the outside of the windshield glass using a wax pencil or crayon, then make a large diameter circle around the support location mark.

2. Clean the inside glass surface within the large marked circle using a glass cleaning solution or polishing compound. Rub the area until it is completely clean and dry.

TCCA0P00
Fig. 31 Small chips on your windshield can be fixed with an aftermarket repair kit, such as the one from Loctite

TCCA0P01
Fig. 32 To repair a chip, clean the windshield with glass cleaner and dry it completely

TCCA0P02
Fig. 33 Remove the center from the adhesive disc and peel off the backing from one side of the disc . . .

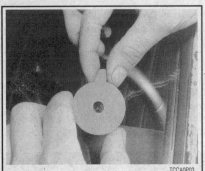

TCCA0P03
Fig. 34 . . . then press it on the windshield so that the chip is centered in the hole

TCCA0P04
Fig. 35 Be sure that the tab points upward on the windshield

TCCA0P05
Fig. 36 Peel the backing off the exposed side of the adhesive disc . . .

TCCA0P06
Fig. 37 . . . then position the plastic pedestal on the adhesive disc, ensuring that the tabs are aligned

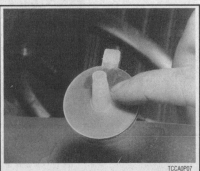

TCCA0P07
Fig. 38 Press the pedestal firmly on the adhesive disc to create an adequate seal . . .

TCCA0P08
Fig. 39 . . . then install the applicator syringe nipple in the pedestal's hole

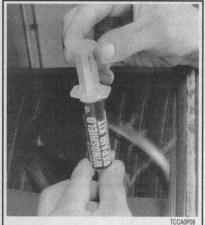

Fig. 40 Hold the syringe with one hand while pulling the plunger back with the other hand

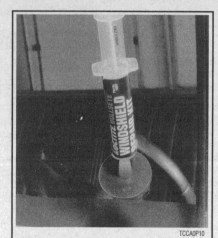

Fig. 41 After applying the solution, allow the entire assembly to sit until it has set completely

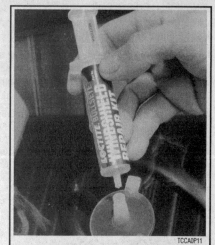

Fig. 42 After the solution has set, remove the syringe from the pedestal . . .

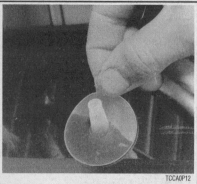

Fig. 43 . . . then peel the pedestal off of the adhesive disc . . .

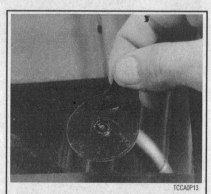

Fig. 44 . . . and peel the adhesive disc off of the windshield

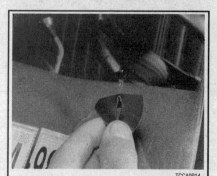

Fig. 45 The chip will still be slightly visible, but it should be filled with the hardened solution

3. Once dry, clean the area using an alcohol saturated paper towel to remove any traces of scouring powder or cleaning solution.

4. If still attached, use a Torx® bit to separate the mirror from the support, then use a piece of fine grit sandpaper to rough the bonding surface of the mirror support. If the original support is being used, all traces of adhesive must be removed prior to installation.

5. Wipe the sanded mirror support with a clean alcohol saturated paper towel, then allow to dry.

6. Follow the directions on a manufacturer's kit (Loctite® Rearview Mirror adhesive or equivalent) and prepare the support for installation.

7. When ready, position the support to the marked location, making sure the rounded end is pointed upward. Press the support to the glass for 30–60 seconds using steady pressure. After about 5 minutes, any excess adhesive may be removed with an alcohol moistened paper towel or glass cleaning solution.

8. Allow additional time to cure, if necessary, per the adhesive manufacturer's instructions, then install the rear view mirror to the support.

Seats

REMOVAL & INSTALLATION

✳✳ WARNING

When removing the seats, be careful not the damage the covers or tear the seams.

Front

1. Slide the seat forward. If necessary, remove the seat track end/bolt covers.
2. Remove the attaching bolts.
3. Slide the seat rearward.
4. Remove the seat track end covers.
5. Remove the attaching bolts.
6. Lift the seat and then detach the seat belt switch wiring harness.
7. Remove any other wiring harnesses such as the one for the seat heaters if equipped.
8. Carefully remove the seat through the front door.
9. Installation is the reverse of the removal procedure.

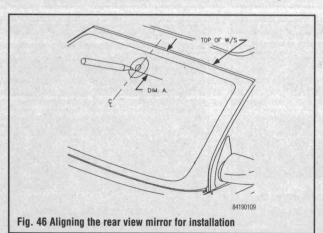

Fig. 46 Aligning the rear view mirror for installation

Rear

INTEGRA

1. Fold the seat backward using caution not to harm the seat cover.
2. Remove and fold up the trunk mat.
3. Remove the clip from the seat back hinge.
4. Push the seat backwards to disengage it from the hinge.
5. Remove the one (1) bolt that secures the seat bottom and remove it.

➡**It may be necessary to remove the seat latch from the seat back. The striker can also be removed at this time.**

✴ WARNING

Wear gloves to remove the seat latch and striker. This will prevent your hands from getting dirty and minimize the risk of damage to the upholstery.

EXCEPT INTEGRA

▶ **See Figures 47, 48 and 49**

For rear seat removal and installation, please refer to the accompanying figures.

Power Seat Motor

REMOVAL & INSTALLATION

1. Remove the negative battery cable.
2. Remove the seat.
3. Remove the connector from the power seat motor.
4. Remove the bolts that secure the power seat motor to the seat frame.
5. Remove the seat motor.
6. Installation is the reverse of the removal procedure.

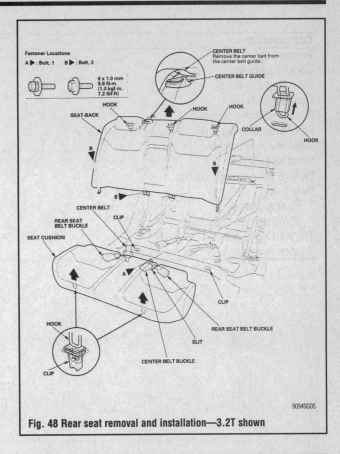

Fig. 48 Rear seat removal and installation—3.2T shown

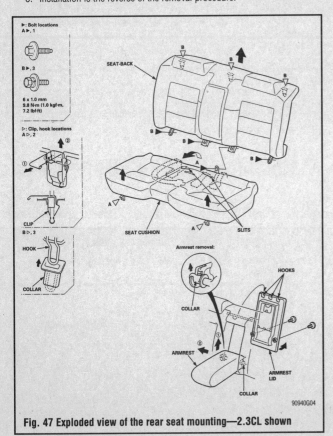

Fig. 47 Exploded view of the rear seat mounting—2.3CL shown

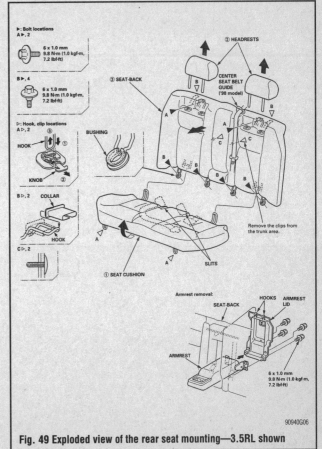

Fig. 49 Exploded view of the rear seat mounting—3.5RL shown

TORQUE SPECIFICATIONS

Components	Ft. Lbs.	Nm
Antenna nut	31-44 inch lbs.	4-5 Nm
Door hinge bolts	19-25 ft. lbs.	25-35 Nm
Door stop arm bolts	89 inch lbs.	10 Nm
Door striker bolts	4 ft. lbs.	6 Nm
Fender retaining screws	89-124 inch lbs.	10-14 Nm
Front seat retaining bolts	15-19 ft. lbs.	20-26 Nm
Grille retaining screws	11-16 inch lbs.	1.2-1.8 Nm
Hood hinge bolts	7.2 ft. lbs.	9.8 Nm
Outside mirror retaining bolts	53-71 inch lbs.	6-8 Nm
Rear seat		
Rear seat back	23-35 ft. lbs.	31-48 Nm
60/40 split rear seat back	15-19 ft. lbs.	20-26 Nm
Trunk lid hinge bolts	7.2 ft. lbs.	9.8 Nm
Window regulator-to-door glass retaining bolts	71 inch lbs.	8 Nm

90940C01

11 TROUBLE-SHOOTING

Condition   **Section/Item Number**

The following troubleshooting charts are divided into 7 sections covering engine, drive train, brakes, wheels/tires/steering/suspension, electrical accessories, instruments and gauges, and climate control. The first portion (or index) consists of a list of symptoms, along with section and item numbers. After selecting the appropriate condition, refer to the corresponding diagnostic procedure in the second portion's specified location.

INDEX

SECTION 1. ENGINE

A. Engine Starting Problems

Gasoline Engines

Engine turns over, but will not start	1-A, 1
Engine does not turn over when attempting to start	1-A, 2
Engine stalls immediately when started	1-A, 3
Starter motor spins, but does not engage	1-A, 4
Engine is difficult to start when cold	1-A, 5
Engine is difficult to start when hot	1-A, 6

Diesel Engines

Engine turns over but won't start	1-A, 1
Engine does not turn over when attempting to start	1-A, 2
Engine stalls after starting	1-A, 3
Starter motor spins, but does not engage	1-A, 4
Engine is difficult to start	1-A, 5

B. Engine Running Conditions

Gasoline Engines

Engine runs poorly, hesitates	1-B, 1
Engine lacks power	1-B, 2
Engine has poor fuel economy	1-B, 3
Engine runs on (diesels) when turned off	1-B, 4
Engine knocks and pings during heavy acceleration, and on steep hills	1-B, 5
Engine accelerates but vehicle does not gain speed	1-B, 6

Diesel Engines

Engine runs poorly	1-B, 1
Engine lacks power	1-B, 2

C. Engine Noises, Odors and Vibrations

Engine makes a knocking or pinging noise when accelerating	1-C, 1
Starter motor grinds when used	1-C, 2
Engine makes a screeching noise	1-C, 3
Engine makes a growling noise	1-C, 4
Engine makes a ticking or tapping noise	1-C, 5
Engine makes a heavy knocking noise	1-C, 6
Vehicle has a fuel odor when driven	1-C, 7
Vehicle has a rotten egg odor when driven	1-C, 8
Vehicle has a sweet odor when driven	1-C, 9
Engine vibrates when idling	1-C, 10
Engine vibrates during acceleration	1-C, 11

D. Engine Electrical System

Battery goes dead while driving	1-D, 1
Battery goes dead overnight	1-D, 2

E. Engine Cooling System

Engine overheats	1-E, 1
Engine loses coolant	1-E, 2
Engine temperature remains cold when driving	1-E, 3
Engine runs hot	1-E, 4

F. Engine Exhaust System

Exhaust rattles at idle speed	1-F, 1
Exhaust system vibrates when driving	1-F, 2
Exhaust system seems too low	1-F, 3
Exhaust seems loud	1-F, 4

Condition	Section/Item Number

SECTION 2. DRIVE TRAIN

A. Automatic Transmission

Transmission shifts erratically	2-A, 1
Transmission will not engage	2-A, 2
Transmission will not downshift during heavy acceleration	2-A, 3

B. Manual Transmission

Transmission grinds going into forward gears while driving	2-B, 1; 2-C, 2
Transmission jumps out of gear	2-B, 2
Transmission difficult to shift	2-B, 3; 2-C, 2
Transmission leaks fluid	2-B, 4

C. Clutch

Clutch slips on hills or during sudden acceleration	2-C, 1
Clutch will not disengage, difficult to shift	2-C, 2
Clutch is noisy when the clutch pedal is pressed	2-C, 3
Clutch pedal extremely difficult to press	2-C, 4
Clutch pedal remains down when pressed	2-C, 5
Clutch chatters when engaging	2-C, 6

D. Differential and Final Drive

Differential makes a low pitched rumbling noise	2-D, 1
Differential makes a howling noise	2-D, 2

E. Transfer Assembly

All Wheel and Four Wheel Drive Vehicles

Leaks fluid from seals or vent after being driven	2-E, 1
Makes excessive noise while driving	2-E, 2
Jumps out of gear	2-E, 3

F. Driveshaft

Rear Wheel, All Wheel and Four Wheel Drive Vehicles

Clunking noise from center of vehicle shifting from forward to reverse	2-F, 1
Excessive vibration from center of vehicle when accelerating	2-F, 2

G. Axles

All Wheel and Four Wheel Drive Vehicles

Front or rear wheel makes a clicking noise	2-G, 1
Front or Rear wheel vibrates with increased speed	2-G, 2

Front Wheel Drive Vehicles

Front wheel makes a clicking noise	2-G, 3
Rear wheel makes a clicking noise	2-G, 4

Rear Wheel Drive Vehicles

Front or rear wheel makes a clicking noise	2-G, 5
Rear wheel shudders or vibrates	2-G, 6

H. Other Drive Train Conditions

Burning odor from center of vehicle when accelerating	2-H, 1; 2-C, 1; 3-A, 9
Engine accelerates, but vehicle does not gain speed	2-H, 2; 2-C, 1; 3-A, 9

SECTION 3. BRAKE SYSTEM

Brakes pedal pulsates or shimmies when pressed	3-A, 1
Brakes make a squealing noise	3-A, 2
Brakes make a grinding noise	3-A, 3
Vehicle pulls to one side during braking	3-A, 4
Brake pedal feels spongy or has excessive brake pedal travel	3-A, 5
Brake pedal feel is firm, but brakes lack sufficient stopping power or fade	3-A, 6

Condition	Section/Item Number
Vehicle has excessive front end dive or locks rear brakes too easily	3-A, 7
Brake pedal goes to floor when pressed and will not pump up	3-A, 8
Brakes make a burning odor	3-A, 9

SECTION 4. WHEELS, TIRES, STEERING AND SUSPENSION

A. Wheels and Wheel Bearings

All Wheel and Four Wheel Drive Vehicles

Front wheel or wheel bearing loose	4-A, 1
Rear wheel or wheel bearing loose	4-A, 2

Front Wheel Drive Vehicles

Front wheel or wheel bearing loose	4-A, 1
Rear wheel or wheel bearing loose	4-A, 2

Rear Wheel Drive Vehicles

Front wheel or wheel bearing loose	4-A, 1
Rear wheel or wheel bearing loose	4-A, 2

B. Tires

Tires worn on inside tread	4-B, 1
Tires worn on outside tread	4-B, 2
Tires worn unevenly	4-B, 3

C. Steering

Excessive play in steering wheel	4-C, 1
Steering wheel shakes at cruising speeds	4-C, 2
Steering wheel shakes when braking	3-A, 1
Steering wheel becomes stiff when turned	4-C, 4

D. Suspension

Vehicle pulls to one side	4-D, 1
Vehicle is very bouncy over bumps	4-D, 2
Vehicle seems to lean excessively in turns	4-D, 3
Vehicle ride quality seems excessively harsh	4-D, 4
Vehicle seems low or leans to one side	4-D, 5

E. Driving Noises and Vibrations

Noises

Vehicle makes a clicking noise when driven	4-E, 1
Vehicle makes a clunking or knocking noise over bumps	4-E, 2
Vehicle makes a low pitched rumbling noise when driven	4-E, 3
Vehicle makes a squeaking noise over bumps	4-E, 4

Vibrations

Vehicle vibrates when driven	4-E, 5

SECTION 5. ELECTRICAL ACCESSORIES

A. Headlights

One headlight only works on high or low beam	5-A, 1
Headlight does not work on high or low beam	5-A, 2
Headlight(s) very dim	5-A, 3

B. Tail, Running and Side Marker Lights

Tail light, running light or side marker light inoperative	5-B, 1
Tail light, running light or side marker light works intermittently	5-B, 2
Tail light, running light or side marker light very dim	5-B, 3

C. Interior Lights

Interior light inoperative	5-C, 1
Interior light works intermittently	5-C, 2
Interior light very dim	5-C, 3

Condition	Section/Item Number

D. Brake Lights

One brake light inoperative	5-D, 1
Both brake lights inoperative	5-D, 2
One or both brake lights very dim	5-D, 3

E. Warning Lights

**Ignition, Battery and Alternator Warning Lights, Check Engine Light,
Anti-Lock Braking System (ABS) Light, Brake Warning Light,
Oil Pressure Warning Light, and Parking Brake Warning Light**

Warning light(s) remains on after the engine is started	5-E, 1
Warning light(s) flickers on and off when driving	5-E, 2
Warning light(s) inoperative with ignition on, and engine not started	5-E, 3

F. Turn Signal and 4-Way Hazard Lights

Turn signals or hazard lights come on, but do not flash	5-F, 1
Turn signals or hazard lights do not function on either side	5-F, 2
Turn signals or hazard lights only work on one side	5-F, 3
One signal light does not work	5-F, 4
Turn signals flash too slowly	5-F, 5
Turn signals flash too fast	5-F, 6
Four-way hazard flasher indicator light inoperative	5-F, 7
Turn signal indicator light(s) do not work in either direction	5-F, 8
One turn signal indicator light does not work	5-F, 9

G. Horn

Horn does not operate	5-G, 1
Horn has an unusual tone	5-G, 2

H. Windshield Wipers

Windshield wipers do not operate	5-H, 1
Windshield wiper motor makes a humming noise, gets hot or blows fuses	5-H, 2
Windshield wiper motor operates but one or both wipers fail to move	5-H, 3
Windshield wipers will not park	5-H, 4

SECTION 6. INSTRUMENTS AND GAUGES

A. Speedometer (Cable Operated)

Speedometer does not work	6-A, 1
Speedometer needle fluctuates when driving at steady speeds	6-A, 2
Speedometer works intermittently	6-A, 3

B. Speedometer (Electronically Operated)

Speedometer does not work	6-B, 1
Speedometer works intermittently	6-B, 2

C. Fuel, Temperature and Oil Pressure Gauges

Gauge does not register	6-C, 1
Gauge operates erratically	6-C, 2
Gauge operates fully pegged	6-C, 3

SECTION 7. CLIMATE CONTROL

A. Air Conditioner

No air coming from air conditioner vents	7-A, 1
Air conditioner blows warm air	7-A, 2
Water collects on the interior floor when the air conditioner is used	7-A, 3
Air conditioner has a moldy odor when used	7-A, 4

B. Heater

Blower motor does not operate	7-B, 1
Heater blows cool air	7-B, 2
Heater steams the windshield when used	7-B, 3

DIAGNOSTIC PROCEDURES

1. ENGINE

1-A. Engine Starting Problems

Gasoline Engines

1. Engine turns over, but will not start

a. Check fuel level in fuel tank, add fuel if empty.

b. Check battery condition and state of charge. If voltage and load test below specification, charge or replace battery.

c. Check battery terminal and cable condition and tightness. Clean terminals and replace damaged, worn or corroded cables.

d. Check fuel delivery system. If fuel is not reaching the fuel injectors, check for a loose electrical connector or defective fuse, relay or fuel pump and replace as necessary.

e. Engine may have excessive wear or mechanical damage such as low cylinder cranking pressure, a broken camshaft drive system, insufficient valve clearance or bent valves.

f. Check for fuel contamination such as water in the fuel. During winter months, the water may freeze and cause a fuel restriction. Adding a fuel additive may help, however the fuel system may require draining and purging with fresh fuel.

g. Check for ignition system failure. Check for loose or shorted wires or damaged ignition system components. Check the spark plugs for excessive wear or incorrect electrode gap. If the problem is worse in wet weather, check for shorts between the spark plugs and the ignition coils.

h. Check the engine management system for a failed sensor or control module.

2. Engine does not turn over when attempting to start

a. Check the battery state of charge and condition. If the dash lights are not visible or very dim when turning the ignition key on, the battery has either failed internally or discharged, the battery cables are loose, excessively corroded or damaged, or the alternator has failed or internally shorted, discharging the battery. Charge or replace the battery, clean or replace the battery cables, and check the alternator output.

b. Check the operation of the neutral safety switch. On automatic transmission vehicles, try starting the vehicle in both Park and Neutral. On manual transmission vehicles, depress the clutch pedal and attempt to start. On some vehicles, these switches can be adjusted. Make sure the switches or wire connectors are not loose or damaged. Replace or adjust the switches as necessary.

c. Check the starter motor, starter solenoid or relay, and starter motor cables and wires. Check the ground from the engine to the chassis. Make sure the wires are not loose, damaged, or corroded. If battery voltage is present at the starter relay, try using a remote starter to start the vehicle for test purposes only. Replace any damaged or corroded cables, in addition to replacing any failed components.

d. Check the engine for seizure. If the engine has not been started for a long period of time, internal parts such as the rings may have rusted to the cylinder walls. The engine may have suffered internal damage, or could be hydro-locked from ingesting water. Remove the spark plugs and carefully attempt to rotate the engine using a suitable breaker bar and socket on the crankshaft pulley. If the engine is resistant to moving, or moves slightly and then binds, do not force the engine any further before determining the problem.

3. Engine stalls immediately when started

a. Check the ignition switch condition and operation. The electrical contacts in the run position may be worn or damaged. Try restarting the engine with all electrical accessories in the off position. Sometimes turning the key on an off will help in emergency situations, however once the switch has shown signs of failure, it should be replaced as soon as possible.

b. Check for loose, corroded, damaged or shorted wires for the ignition system and repair or replace.

c. Check for manifold vacuum leaks or vacuum hose leakage and repair or replace parts as necessary.

d. Measure the fuel pump delivery volume and pressure. Low fuel pump pressure can also be noticed as a lack of power when accelerating. Make sure the fuel pump lines are not restricted. The fuel pump output is not adjustable and requires fuel pump replacement to repair.

e. Check the engine fuel and ignition management system. Inspect the sensor wiring and electrical connectors. A dirty, loose or damaged sensor or control module wire can simulate a failed component.

f. Check the exhaust system for internal restrictions.

4. Starter motor spins, but does not engage

a. Check the starter motor for a seized or binding pinion gear.

b. Remove the flywheel inspection plate and check for a damaged ring gear.

5. Engine is difficult to start when cold

a. Check the battery condition, battery state of charge and starter motor current draw.

Replace the battery if marginal and the starter motor if the current draw is beyond specification.

b. Check the battery cable condition. Clean the battery terminals and replace corroded or damaged cables.

c. Check the fuel system for proper operation. A fuel pump with insufficient fuel pressure or clogged injectors should be replaced.

d. Check the engine's tune-up status. Note the tune-up specifications and check for items such as severely worn spark plugs; adjust or replace as needed. On vehicles with manually adjusted valve clearances, check for tight valves and adjust to specification.

e. Check for a failed coolant temperature sensor, and replace if out of specification.

f. Check the operation of the engine management systems for fuel and ignition; repair or replace failed components as necessary.

6. Engine is difficult to start when hot

a. Check the air filter and air intake system. Replace the air filter if it is dirty or contaminated. Check the fresh air intake system for restrictions or blockage.

b. Check for loose or deteriorated engine grounds and clean, tighten or replace as needed.

c. Check for needed maintenance. Inspect tune-up and service related items such as spark plugs and engine oil condition, and check the operation of the engine fuel and ignition management system.

Diesel Engines

1. Engine turns over but won't start

a. Check engine starting procedure and restart engine.

b. Check the glow plug operation and repair or replace as necessary.

c. Check for air in the fuel system or fuel filter and bleed the air as necessary.

d. Check the fuel delivery system and repair or replace as necessary.

e. Check fuel level and add fuel as needed.

f. Check fuel quality. If the fuel is contaminated, drain and flush the fuel tank.

g. Check engine compression. If compression is below specification, the engine may need to be renewed or replaced.

h. Check the injection pump timing and set to specification.

i. Check the injection pump condition and replace as necessary.

j. Check the fuel nozzle operation and condition or replace as necessary.

2. Engine does not turn over when attempting to start

a. Check the battery state of charge and condition. If the dash lights are not visible or very dim when turning the ignition key on, the battery has either failed internally or discharged, the battery cables are loose, excessively corroded or damaged, or the alternator has failed or internally shorted, discharging the battery. Charge or replace the battery, clean or replace the battery cables, and check the alternator output.

b. Check the operation of the neutral safety switch. On automatic transmission vehicles, try starting the vehicle in both Park and Neutral. On manual transmission vehicles, depress the clutch pedal and attempt to start. On some vehicles, these switches can be adjusted. Make sure the switches or wire connectors are not loose or damaged. Replace or adjust the switches as necessary.

c. Check the starter motor, starter solenoid or relay, and starter motor cables and wires. Check the ground from the engine to the chassis. Make sure the wires are not loose, damaged, or corroded. If battery voltage is present at the starter relay, try using a remote starter to start the vehicle for test purposes only. Replace any damaged or corroded cables, in addition to replacing any failed components.

d. Check the engine for seizure. If the engine has not been started for a long period of time, internal parts such as the rings may have rusted to the cylinder walls. The engine may have suffered internal damage, or could be hydro-locked from ingesting water. Remove the injectors and carefully attempt to rotate the engine using a suitable breaker bar and socket on the crankshaft pulley. If the engine is resistant to moving, or moves slightly and then binds, do not force the engine any further before determining the cause of the problem.

3. Engine stalls after starting

a. Check for a restriction in the fuel return line or the return line check valve and repair as necessary.

b. Check the glow plug operation for turning the glow plugs off too soon and repair as necessary.

c. Check for incorrect injection pump timing and reset to specification.

d. Test the engine fuel pump and replace if the output is below specification.

e. Check for contaminated or incorrect fuel. Completely flush the fuel system and replace with fresh fuel.

f. Test the engine's compression for low compression. If below specification, mechanical repairs are necessary to repair.

g. Check for air in the fuel. Check fuel tank fuel and fill as needed.

h. Check for a failed injection pump. Replace the pump, making sure to properly set the pump timing.

4. Starter motor spins, but does not engage

a. Check the starter motor for a seized or binding pinion gear.

b. Remove the flywheel inspection plate and check for a damaged ring gear.

1-B. Engine Running Conditions

Gasoline Engines

1. Engine runs poorly, hesitates

a. Check the engine ignition system operation and adjust if possible, or replace defective parts.

b. Check for restricted fuel injectors and replace as necessary.

c. Check the fuel pump output and delivery. Inspect fuel lines for restrictions. If the fuel pump pressure is below specification, replace the fuel pump.

d. Check the operation of the engine management system and repair as necessary.

2. Engine lacks power

a. Check the engine's tune-up status. Note the tune-up specifications and check for items such as severely worn spark plugs; adjust or replace as needed. On vehicles with manually adjusted valve clearances, check for tight valves and adjust to specification.

b. Check the air filter and air intake system. Replace the air filter if it is dirty or contaminated. Check the fresh air intake system for restrictions or blockage.

c. Check the operation of the engine fuel and ignition management systems. Check the sensor operation and wiring. Check for low fuel pump pressure and repair or replace components as necessary.

d. Check the throttle linkage adjustments. Check to make sure the linkage is fully opening the throttle. Replace any worn or defective bushings or linkages.

e. Check for a restricted exhaust system. Check for bent or crimped exhaust pipes, or internally restricted mufflers or catalytic converters. Compare inlet and outlet temperatures for the converter or muffler. If the inlet is hot, but outlet cold, the component is restricted.

f. Check for a loose or defective knock sensor. A loose, improperly torqued or defective knock sensor will decrease spark advance and reduce power. Replace defective knock sensors and install using the recommended torque specification.

g. Check for engine mechanical conditions such as low compression, worn piston rings, worn valves, worn camshafts and related parts. An engine which has severe mechanical wear, or has suffered internal mechanical damage must be rebuilt or replaced to restore lost power.

h. Check the engine oil level for being overfilled. Adjust the engine's oil level, or change the engine oil and filter, and top off to the correct level.

i. Check for an intake manifold or vacuum hose leak. Replace leaking gaskets or worn vacuum hoses.

j. Check for dragging brakes and replace or repair as necessary.

k. Check tire air pressure and tire wear. Adjust the pressure to the recommended settings. Check the tire wear for possible alignment problems causing increased rolling resistance, decreased acceleration and increased fuel usage.

l. Check the octane rating of the fuel used during refilling, and use a higher octane rated fuel.

3. Poor fuel economy

a. Inspect the air filter and check for any air restrictions going into the air filter housing. Replace the air filter if it is dirty or contaminated.

b. Check the engine for tune-up and related adjustments. Replace worn ignition parts, check the engine ignition timing and fuel mixture, and set to specifications if possible.

c. Check the tire size, tire wear, alignment and tire pressure. Large tires create more rolling resistance, smaller tires require more engine speed to maintain a vehicle's road speed. Excessive tire wear can be caused by incorrect tire pressure, incorrect wheel alignment or a suspension problem. All of these conditions create increased rolling resistance, causing the engine to work harder to accelerate and maintain a vehicle's speed.

d. Inspect the brakes for binding or excessive drag. A sticking brake caliper, overly adjusted brake shoe, broken brake shoe return spring, or binding parking brake cable or linkage can create a significant drag, brake wear and loss of fuel economy. Check the brake system operation and repair as necessary.

4. Engine runs on (diesels) when turned off

a. Check for idle speed set too high and readjust to specification.

b. Check the operation of the idle control valve, and replace if defective.

c. Check the ignition timing and adjust to recommended settings. Check for defective sensors or related components and replace if defective.

d. Check for a vacuum leak at the intake manifold or vacuum hose and replace defective gaskets or hoses.

e. Check the engine for excessive carbon build-up in the combustion chamber. Use a recommended decarbonizing fuel additive or disassemble the cylinder head to remove the carbon.

f. Check the operation of the engine fuel management system and replace defective sensors or control units.

g. Check the engine operating temperature for overheating and repair as necessary.

5. Engine knocks and pings during heavy acceleration, and on steep hills

a. Check the octane rating of the fuel used during refilling, and use a higher octane rated fuel.

b. Check the ignition timing and adjust to recommended settings. Check for defective sensors or related components and replace if defective.

c. Check the engine for excessive carbon build-up in the combustion chamber. Use a recommended decarbonizing fuel additive or disassemble the cylinder head to remove the carbon.

d. Check the spark plugs for the correct type, electrode gap and heat range. Replace worn or damaged spark plugs. For severe or continuous high speed use, install a spark plug that is one heat range colder.

e. Check the operation of the engine fuel management system and replace defective sensors or control units.

f. Check for a restricted exhaust system. Check for bent or crimped exhaust pipes, or internally restricted mufflers or catalytic converters. Compare inlet and outlet temperatures for the converter or muffler. If the inlet is hot, but outlet cold, the component is restricted.

6. Engine accelerates, but vehicle does not gain speed

a. On manual transmission vehicles, check for causes of a slipping clutch. Refer to the clutch troubleshooting section for additional information.

b. On automatic transmission vehicles, check for a slipping transmission. Check the transmission fluid level and condition. If the fluid level is too high, adjust to the correct level. If the fluid level is low, top off using the recommended fluid type. If the fluid exhibits a burning odor, the transmission has been slipping internally. Changing the fluid and filter may help temporarily, however in this situation a transmission may require overhauling to ensure long-term reliability.

Diesel Engines

1. Engine runs poorly

a. Check the injection pump timing and adjust to specification.

b. Check for air in the fuel lines or leaks, and bleed the air from the fuel system.

c. Check the fuel filter, fuel feed and return lines for a restriction and repair as necessary.

d. Check the fuel for contamination, drain and flush the fuel tank and replenish with fresh fuel.

2. Engine lacks power

a. Inspect the air intake system and air filter for restrictions and, if necessary, replace the air filter.

b. Verify the injection pump timing and reset if out of specification.

c. Check the exhaust for an internal restriction and replace failed parts.

d. Check for a restricted fuel filter and, if restricted, replace the filter.

e. Inspect the fuel filler cap vent . When removing the filler cap, listen for excessive hissing noises indicating a blockage in the fuel filler cap vents. If the filler cap vents are blocked, replace the cap.

f. Check the fuel system for restrictions and repair as necessary.

g. Check for low engine compression and inspect for external leakage at the glow plugs or nozzles. If no external leakage is noted, repair or replace the engine.

ENGINE PERFORMANCE TROUBLESHOOTING HINTS

When troubleshooting an engine running or performance condition, the mechanical condition of the engine should be determined *before* lengthy troubleshooting procedures are performed.

The engine fuel management systems in fuel injected vehicles rely on electronic sensors to provide information to the engine control unit for precise fuel metering. Unlike carburetors, which use the incoming air speed to draw fuel through the fuel metering jets in order to provide a proper fuel-to-air ratio, a fuel injection system provides a specific amount of fuel which is introduced by the fuel injectors into the intake manifold or intake port, based on the information provided by electronic sensors.

The sensors monitor the engine's operating temperature, ambient temperature and the amount of air entering the engine, engine speed and throttle position to provide information to the engine control unit, which, in turn, operates the fuel injectors by electrical pulses. The sensors provide information to the engine control unit using low voltage electrical signals. As a result, an unplugged sensor or a poor electrical contact could cause a poor running condition similar to a failed sensor.

When troubleshooting a fuel related engine condition on fuel injected vehicles, carefully inspect the wiring and electrical connectors to the related components. Make sure the electrical connectors are fully connected, clean and not physically damaged. If necessary, clean the electrical contacts using electrical contact cleaner. The use of cleaning agents not specifically designed for electrical contacts should not be used, as they could leave a surface film or damage the insulation of the wiring.

The engine electrical system provides the necessary electrical power to operate the vehicle's electrical accessories, electronic control units and sensors. Because engine management systems are sensitive to voltage changes, an alternator which over or undercharges could cause engine running problems or component failure. Most alternators utilize internal voltage regulators which cannot be adjusted and must be replaced individually or as a unit with the alternator.

Ignition systems may be controlled by, or linked to, the engine fuel management system. Similar to the fuel injection system, these ignition systems rely on electronic sensors for information to determine the optimum ignition timing for a given engine speed and load. Some ignition systems no longer allow the ignition timing to be adjusted. Feedback from low voltage electrical sensors provide information to the control unit to determine the amount of ignition advance. On these systems, if a failure occurs the failed component must be replaced. Before replacing suspected failed electrical components, carefully inspect the wiring and electrical connectors to the related components. Make sure the electrical connectors are fully connected, clean and not physically damaged. If necessary, clean the electrical contacts using electrical contact cleaner. The use of cleaning agents not specifically designed for electrical contacts should be avoided, as they could leave a surface film or damage the insulation of the wiring.

1-C. Engine Noises, Odors and Vibrations

1. Engine makes a knocking or pinging noise when accelerating

a. Check the octane rating of the fuel being used. Depending on the type of driving or driving conditions, it may be necessary to use a higher octane fuel.

b. Verify the ignition system settings and operation. Improperly adjusted ignition timing or a failed component, such as a knock sensor, may cause the ignition timing to advance excessively or prematurely. Check the ignition system operation and adjust, or replace components as needed.

c. Check the spark plug gap, heat range and condition. If the vehicle is operated in severe operating conditions or at continuous high speeds, use a colder heat range spark plug. Adjust the spark plug gap to the manufacturer's recommended specification and replace worn or damaged spark plugs.

2. Starter motor grinds when used

a. Examine the starter pinion gear and the engine ring gear for damage, and replace damaged parts.

b. Check the starter mounting bolts and housing. If the housing is cracked or damaged replace the starter motor and check the mounting bolts for tightness.

3. Engine makes a screeching noise

a. Check the accessory drive belts for looseness and adjust as necessary.

b. Check the accessory drive belt tensioners for seizing or excessive bearing noises and replace if loose, binding, or excessively noisy.

c. Check for a seizing water pump. The pump may not be leaking; however, the bearing may be faulty or the impeller loose and jammed. Replace the water pump.

4. Engine makes a growling noise

a. Check for a loose or failing water pump. Replace the pump and engine coolant.

b. Check the accessory drive belt tensioners for excessive bearing noises and replace if loose or excessively noisy.

5. Engine makes a ticking or tapping noise

a. On vehicles with hydraulic lash adjusters, check for low or dirty engine oil and top off or replace the engine oil and filter.

b. On vehicles with hydraulic lash adjusters, check for collapsed lifters and replace failed components.

c. On vehicles with hydraulic lash adjusters, check for low oil pressure caused by a restricted oil filter, worn engine oil pump, or oil pressure relief valve.

d. On vehicles with manually adjusted valves, check for excessive valve clearance or worn valve train parts. Adjust the valves to specification or replace worn and defective parts.

e. Check for a loose or improperly tensioned timing belt or timing chain and adjust or replace parts as necessary.

f. Check for a bent or sticking exhaust or intake valve. Remove the engine cylinder head to access and replace.

6. Engine makes a heavy knocking noise

a. Check for a loose crankshaft pulley or flywheel; replace and torque the mounting bolt(s) to specification.

b. Check for a bent connecting rod caused by a hydro-lock condition. Engine disassembly is necessary to inspect for damaged and needed replacement parts.

c. Check for excessive engine rod bearing wear or damage. This condition is also associated with low engine oil pressure and will require engine disassembly to inspect for damaged and needed replacement parts.

7. Vehicle has a fuel odor when driven

a. Check the fuel gauge level. If the fuel gauge registers full, it is possible that the odor is caused by being filled beyond capacity, or some spillage occurred during refueling. The odor should clear after driving an hour, or twenty miles, allowing the vapor canister to purge.

b. Check the fuel filler cap for looseness or seepage. Check the cap tightness and, if loose, properly secure. If seepage is noted, replace the filler cap.

c. Check for loose hose clamps, cracked or damaged fuel delivery and return lines, or leaking components or seals, and replace or repair as necessary.

d. Check the vehicle's fuel economy. If fuel consumption has increased due to a failed component, or if the fuel is not properly ignited due to an ignition related failure, the catalytic converter may become contaminated. This condition may also trigger the check engine warning light. Check the spark plugs for a dark, rich condition or verify the condition by testing the vehicle's emissions. Replace fuel fouled spark plugs, and test and replace failed components as necessary.

8. Vehicle has a rotten egg odor when driven

a. Check for a leaking intake gasket or vacuum leak causing a lean running condition. A lean mixture may result in increased exhaust temperatures, causing the catalytic converter to run hotter than normal. This condition may also trigger the check engine warning light. Check and repair the vacuum leaks as necessary.

b. Check the vehicle's alternator and battery condition. If the alternator is overcharging, the battery electrolyte can be boiled from the battery, and the battery casing may begin to crack, swell or bulge, damaging or shorting the battery internally. If this has occurred, neutralize the battery mounting area with a suitable baking soda and water mixture or equivalent, and replace the alternator or voltage regulator. Inspect, service, and load test the battery, and replace if necessary.

9. Vehicle has a sweet odor when driven

a. Check for an engine coolant leak caused by a seeping radiator cap, loose hose clamp, weeping cooling system seal, gasket or cooling system hose and replace or repair as needed.

b. Check for a coolant leak from the radiator, coolant reservoir, heater control valve or under the dashboard from the heater core, and replace the failed part as necessary.

c. Check the engine's exhaust for white smoke in addition to a sweet odor. The presence of white, steamy smoke with a sweet odor indicates coolant leaking into the combustion chamber. Possible causes include a failed head gasket, cracked engine block or cylinder head. Other symptoms of this condition include a white paste build-up on the inside of the oil filler cap, and softened, deformed or bulging radiator hoses.

10. Engine vibrates when idling

a. Check for loose, collapsed, or damaged engine or transmission mounts and repair or replace as necessary.

b. Check for loose or damaged engine covers or shields and secure or replace as necessary.

11. Engine vibrates during acceleration

a. Check for missing, loose or damaged exhaust system hangers and mounts; replace or repair as necessary.

b. Check the exhaust system routing and fit for adequate clearance or potential rubbing; repair or adjust as necessary.

1-D. Engine Electrical System

1. Battery goes dead while driving

a. Check the battery condition. Replace the battery if the battery will not hold a charge or fails a battery load test. If the battery loses fluid while driving, check for an overcharging condition. If the alternator is overcharging, replace the alternator or voltage regulator. (A voltage regulator is typically built into the alternator, necessitating alternator replacement or overhaul.)

b. Check the battery cable condition. Clean or replace corroded cables and clean the battery terminals.

c. Check the alternator and voltage regulator operation. If the charging system is over or undercharging, replace the alternator or voltage regulator, or both.

d. Inspect the wiring and wire connectors at the alternator for looseness, a missing ground or defective terminal, and repair as necessary.

e. Inspect the alternator drive belt tension, tensioners and condition. Properly tension the drive belt, replace weak or broken tensioners, and replace the drive belt if worn or cracked.

2. Battery goes dead overnight

a. Check the battery condition. Replace the battery if the battery will not hold a charge or fails a battery load test.

b. Check for a voltage draw, such as a trunk light, interior light or glove box light staying on. Check light switch position and operation, and replace if defective.

c. Check the alternator for an internally failed diode, and replace the alternator if defective.

1-E. Engine Cooling System

1. Engine overheats
a. Check the coolant level. Set the heater temperature to full hot and check for internal air pockets, bleed the cooling system and inspect for leakage. Top off the cooling system with the correct coolant mixture.
b. Pressure test the cooling system and radiator cap for leaks. Check for seepage caused by loose hose clamps, failed coolant hoses, and cooling system components such as the heater control valve, heater core, radiator, radiator cap, and water pump. Replace defective parts and fill the cooling system with the recommended coolant mixture.
c. On vehicles with electrically controlled cooling fans, check the cooling fan operation. Check for blown fuses or defective fan motors, temperature sensors and relays, and replace failed components.
d. Check for a coolant leak caused by a failed head gasket, or a porous water jacket casting in the cylinder head or engine block. Replace defective parts as necessary.
e. Check for an internally restricted radiator. Flush the radiator or replace if the blockage is too severe for flushing.
f. Check for a damaged water pump. If coolant circulation is poor, check for a loose water pump impeller. If the impeller is loose, replace the water pump.

2. Engine loses coolant
a. Pressure test the cooling system and radiator cap for leaks. Check for seepage caused by loose hose clamps, failed coolant hoses, and cooling system components such as the heater control valve, heater core, radiator, radiator cap, and water pump. Replace defective parts and fill the cooling system with the recommended coolant mixture.
b. Check for a coolant leak caused by a failed head gasket, or a porous water jacket casting in the cylinder head or engine block. Replace defective parts as necessary.

3. Engine temperature remains cold when driving
a. Check the thermostat operation. Replace the thermostat if it sticks in the open position.
b. On vehicles with electrically controlled cooling fans, check the cooling fan operation. Check for defective temperature sensors and stuck relays, and replace failed components.
c. Check temperature gauge operation if equipped to verify proper operation of the gauge. Check the sensors and wiring for defects, and repair or replace defective components.

4. Engine runs hot
a. Check for an internally restricted radiator. Flush the radiator or replace if the blockage is too severe for flushing.
b. Check for a loose or slipping water pump drive belt. Inspect the drive belt condition. Replace the belt if brittle, cracked or damaged. Check the pulley condition and properly tension the belt.
c. Check the cooling fan operation. Replace defective fan motors, sensors or relays as necessary.
d. Check temperature gauge operation if equipped to verify proper operation of the gauge. Check the sensors and wiring for defects, and repair or replace defective components.
e. Check the coolant level. Set the heater temperature to full hot, check for internal air pockets, bleed the cooling system and inspect for leakage. Top off the cooling system with the correct coolant mixture. Once the engine is cool, recheck the fluid level and top off as needed.

NOTE: The engine cooling system can also be affected by an engine's mechanical condition. A failed head gasket or a porous casting in the engine block or cylinder head could cause a loss of coolant and result in engine overheating.

Some cooling systems rely on electrically driven cooling fans to cool the radiator and use electrical temperature sensors and relays to operate the cooling fan. When diagnosing these systems, check for blown fuses, damaged wires and verify that the electrical connections are fully connected, clean and not physically damaged. If necessary, clean the electrical contacts using electrical contact cleaner. The use of cleaning agents not specifically designed for electrical contacts could leave a film or damage the insulation of the wiring.

1-F. Engine Exhaust System

1. Exhaust rattles at idle speed
a. Check the engine and transmission mounts and replace mounts showing signs of damage or wear.
b. Check the exhaust hangers, brackets and mounts. Replace broken, missing or damaged mounts.
c. Check for internal damage to mufflers and catalytic converters. The broken pieces from the defective component may travel in the direction of the exhaust flow and collect and/or create a blockage in a component other than the one which failed, causing engine running and stalling problems. Another symptom of a restricted exhaust is low engine manifold vacuum. Remove the exhaust system and carefully remove any loose or broken pieces, then replace any failed or damaged parts as necessary.
d. Check the exhaust system clearance, routing and alignment. If the exhaust is making contact with the vehicle in any manner, loosen and reposition the exhaust system.

2. Exhaust system vibrates when driving
a. Check the exhaust hangers, brackets and mounts. Replace broken, missing or damaged mounts.
b. Check the exhaust system clearance, routing and alignment. If the exhaust is making contact with the vehicle in any manner, check for bent or damaged components and replace, then loosen and reposition the exhaust system.
c. Check for internal damage to mufflers and catalytic converters. The broken pieces from the defective component may travel in the direction of the exhaust flow and collect and/or create a blockage in a component other than the one which failed, causing engine running and stalling problems. Another symptom of a restricted exhaust is low engine manifold vacuum. Remove the exhaust system and carefully remove any loose or broken pieces, then replace any failed or damaged parts as necessary.

3. Exhaust system hangs too low
a. Check the exhaust hangers, brackets and mounts. Replace broken, missing or damaged mounts.
b. Check the exhaust routing and alignment. Check and replace bent or damaged components. If the exhaust is not routed properly, loosen and reposition the exhaust system.

4. Exhaust sounds loud
a. Check the system for looseness and leaks. Check the exhaust pipes, clamps, flange bolts and manifold fasteners for tightness. Check and replace any failed gaskets.
b. Check and replace exhaust silencers that have a loss of efficiency due to internally broken baffles or worn packing material.
c. Check for missing mufflers and silencers that have been replaced with straight pipes or with non-original equipment silencers.

NOTE: Exhaust system rattles, vibration and proper alignment should not be overlooked. Excessive vibration caused by collapsed engine mounts, damaged or missing exhaust hangers and misalignment may cause surface cracks and broken welds, creating exhaust leaks or internal damage to exhaust components such as the catalytic converter, creating a restriction to exhaust flow and loss of power.

2. DRIVE TRAIN

2-A. Automatic Transmission

1. Transmission shifts erratically
a. Check and if not within the recommended range, add or remove transmission fluid to obtain the correct fluid level. Always use the recommended fluid type when adding transmission fluid.
b. Check the fluid level condition. If the fluid has become contaminated, fatigued from excessive heat or exhibits a burning odor, change the transmission fluid and filter using the recommended type and amount of fluid. A fluid which exhibits a burning odor indicates that the transmission has been slipping internally and may require future repairs.
c. Check for an improperly installed transmission filter, or missing filter gasket, and repair as necessary.
d. Check for loose or leaking gaskets, pressure lines and fittings, and repair or replace as necessary.

e. Check for loose or disconnected shift and throttle linkages or vacuum hoses, and repair as necessary.

2. Transmission will not engage
a. Check the shift linkage for looseness, wear and proper adjustment, and repair as necessary.
b. Check for a loss of transmission fluid and top off as needed with the recommended fluid.
c. If the transmission does not engage with the shift linkage correctly installed and the proper fluid level, internal damage has likely occurred, requiring transmission removal and disassembly.

3. Transmission will not downshift during heavy acceleration
a. On computer controlled transmissions, check for failed sensors or control units and repair or replace defective components.

b. On vehicles with kickdown linkages or vacuum servos, check for proper linkage adjustment or leaking vacuum hoses or servo units.

NOTE: Many automatic transmissions use an electronic control module, electrical sensors and solenoids to control transmission shifting. When troubleshooting a vehicle with this type of system, be sure the electrical connectors are fully connected, clean and not physically damaged. If necessary, clean the electrical contacts using electrical contact cleaner. The use of cleaning agents not specifically designed for electrical contacts could leave a film or damage the insulation of the wiring.

2-B. Manual Transmission

1. Transmission grinds going into forward gears while driving

a. Check the clutch release system. On clutches with a mechanical or cable linkage, check the adjustment. Adjust the clutch pedal to have 1 inch (25mm) of free-play at the pedal.
b. If the clutch release system is hydraulically operated, check the fluid level and, if low, top off using the recommended type and amount of fluid.
c. Synchronizers worn. Remove transmission and replace synchronizers.
d. Synchronizer sliding sleeve worn. Remove transmission and replace sliding sleeve.
e. Gear engagement dogs worn or damaged. Remove transmission and replace gear.

2. Transmission jumps out of gear

a. Shift shaft detent springs worn. Replace shift detent springs.
b. Synchronizer sliding sleeve worn. Remove transmission and replace sliding sleeve.
c. Gear engagement dogs worn or damaged. Remove transmission and replace gear.
d. Crankshaft thrust bearings worn. Remove engine and crankshaft, and repair as necessary.

3. Transmission difficult to shift

a. Verify the clutch adjustment and, if not properly adjusted, adjust to specification.
b. Synchronizers worn. Remove transmission and replace synchronizers.
c. Pilot bearing seized. Remove transmission and replace pilot bearing.
d. Shift linkage or bushing seized. Disassemble the shift linkage, replace worn or damaged bushings, lubricate and reinstall.

4. Transmission leaks fluid

a. Check the fluid level for an overfilled condition. Adjust the fluid level to specification.
b. Check for a restricted transmission vent or breather tube. Clear the blockage as necessary and check the fluid level. If necessary, top off with the recommended lubricant.
c. Check for a porous casting, leaking seal or gasket. Replace defective parts and top off the fluid level with the recommended lubricant.

2-C. Clutch

1. Clutch slips on hills or during sudden acceleration

a. Check for insufficient clutch pedal free-play. Adjust clutch linkage or cable to allow about 1 inch (25mm) of pedal free-play.
b. Clutch disc worn or severely damaged. Remove engine or transmission and replace clutch disc.
c. Clutch pressure plate is weak. Remove engine or transmission and replace the clutch pressure plate and clutch disc.
d. Clutch pressure plate and/or flywheel incorrectly machined. If the clutch system has been recently replaced and rebuilt, or refurbished parts have been used, it is possible that the machined surfaces decreased the clutch clamping force. Replace defective parts with new replacement parts.

2. Clutch will not disengage, difficult to shift

a. Check the clutch release mechanism. Check for stretched cables, worn linkages or failed clutch hydraulics and replace defective parts. On hydraulically operated clutch release mechanisms, check for air in the hydraulic system and bleed as necessary.
b. Check for a broken, cracked or fatigued clutch release arm or release arm pivot. Replace defective parts and properly lubricate upon assembly.
c. Check for a damaged clutch hub damper or damper spring. The broken parts tend to become lodged between the clutch disc and the pressure plate. Disassemble clutch system and replace failed parts.
d. Check for a seized clutch pilot bearing. Disassemble the clutch assembly and replace the defective parts.
e. Check for a defective clutch disc. Check for warpage or lining thicknesses larger than original equipment.

3. Clutch is noisy when the clutch pedal is pressed

a. Check the clutch pedal stop and pedal free-play adjustment for excessive movement and adjust as necessary.
b. Check for a worn or damaged release bearing. If the noise ceases when the pedal is released, the release bearing should be replaced.

c. Check the engine crankshaft axial play. If the crankshaft thrust bearings are worn or damaged, the crankshaft will move when pressing the clutch pedal. The engine must be disassembled to replace the crankshaft thrust bearings.

4. Clutch pedal extremely difficult to press

a. Check the clutch pedal pivots and linkages for binding. Clean and lubricate linkages.
b. On cable actuated clutch systems, check the cable routing and condition. Replace kinked, frayed, damaged or corroded cables and check cable routing to avoid sharp bends. Check the engine ground strap for poor conductivity. If the ground strap is marginal, the engine could try to ground itself via the clutch cable, causing premature failure.
c. On mechanical linkage clutches, check the linkage for binding or misalignment. Lubricate pivots or linkages and repair as necessary.
d. Check the release bearing guide tube and release fork for a lack of lubrication. Install a smooth coating of high temperature grease to allow smooth movement of the release bearing over the guide tube.

5. Clutch pedal remains down when pressed

a. On mechanical linkage or cable actuated clutches, check for a loose or disconnected link.
b. On hydraulically actuated clutches, check the fluid level and check for a hydraulic leak at the clutch slave or master cylinder, or hydraulic line. Replace failed parts and bleed clutch hydraulic system. If no leakage is noted, the clutch master cylinder may have failed internally. Replace the clutch master cylinder and bleed the clutch hydraulic system.

6. Clutch chatters when engaging

a. Check the engine flywheel for warpage or surface variations and replace or repair as necessary.
b. Check for a warped clutch disc or damaged clutch damper hub. Remove the clutch disc and replace.
c. Check for a loose or damaged clutch pressure plate and replace defective components.

NOTE: The clutch is actuated either by a mechanical linkage, cable or a clutch hydraulic system. The mechanical linkage and cable systems may require the clutch pedal free-play to be adjusted as the clutch disc wears. A hydraulic clutch system automatically adjusts as the clutch wears and, with the exception of the clutch pedal height, no adjustment is possible.

2-D. Differential and Final Drive

1. Differential makes a low pitched rumbling noise

a. Check fluid level type and amount. Replace the fluid with the recommended type and amount of lubricant.
b. Check the differential bearings for wear or damage. Remove the bearings, inspect the drive and driven gears for wear or damage, and replace components as necessary.

2. Differential makes a howling noise

a. Check fluid level type and amount. Replace the fluid with the recommended type and amount of lubricant.
b. Check the differential drive and driven gears for wear or damage, and replace components as necessary.

2-E. Transfer Assembly

All Wheel and Four Wheel Drive Vehicles

1. Leaks fluid from seals or vent after being driven

a. Fluid level overfilled. Check and adjust transfer case fluid level.
b. Check for a restricted breather or breather tube, clear and check the fluid level and top off as needed.
c. Check seal condition and replace worn, damaged, or defective seals. Check the fluid level and top off as necessary.

2. Makes excessive noise while driving

a. Check the fluid for the correct type of lubricant. Drain and refill using the recommended type and amount of lubricant.
b. Check the fluid level. Top off the fluid using the recommended type and amount of lubricant.
c. If the fluid level and type of lubricant meet specifications, check for internal wear or damage. Remove assembly and disassemble to inspect for worn, damaged, or defective components.

3. Jumps out of gear

a. Stop vehicle and make sure the unit is fully engaged.
b. Check for worn, loose or an improperly adjusted linkage. Replace and/or adjust linkage as necessary.
c. Check for internal wear or damage. Remove assembly and disassemble to inspect for worn, damaged, or defective components.

2-F. Driveshaft

Rear Wheel, All Wheel and Four Wheel Drive Vehicles

1. Clunking noise from center of vehicle shifting from forward to reverse
a. Worn universal joint. Remove driveshaft and replace universal joint.

2. Excessive vibration from center of vehicle when accelerating
a. Worn universal joint. Remove driveshaft and replace universal joint.
b. Driveshaft misaligned. Check for collapsed or damaged engine and transmission mounts, and replace as necessary.
c. Driveshaft bent or out of balance. Replace damaged components and reinstall.
d. Driveshaft out of balance. Remove the driveshaft and have it balanced by a competent professional, or replace the driveshaft assembly.

NOTE: Most driveshafts are linked together by universal joints; however, some manufacturers use Constant Velocity (CV) joints or rubber flex couplers.

2-G. Axles

All Wheel and Four Wheel Drive Vehicles

1. Front or rear wheel makes a clicking noise
a. Check for debris such as a pebble, nail or glass in the tire or tire tread. Carefully remove the debris. Small rocks and pebbles rarely cause a puncture; however, a sharp object should be removed carefully at a facility capable of performing tire repairs.
b. Check for a loose, damaged or worn Constant Velocity (CV) joint and replace if defective.

2. Front or rear wheel vibrates with increased speed
a. Check for a bent rim and replace, if damaged.
b. Check the tires for balance or internal damage and replace if defective.
c. Check for a loose, worn or damaged wheel bearing and replace if defective.
d. Check for a loose, damaged or worn Constant Velocity (CV) joint and replace if defective.

Front Wheel Drive Vehicles

3. Front wheel makes a clicking noise
a. Check for debris such as a pebble, nail or glass in the tire or tire tread. Carefully remove the debris. Small rocks and pebbles rarely cause a puncture; however, a sharp object should be removed carefully at a facility capable of performing tire repairs.

b. Check for a loose, damaged or worn Constant Velocity (CV) joint and replace if defective.

4. Rear wheel makes a clicking noise
a. Check for debris such as a pebble, nail or glass in the tire or tire tread. Carefully remove the debris. Small rocks and pebbles rarely cause a puncture; however, a sharp object should be removed carefully at a facility capable of performing tire repairs.

Rear Wheel Drive Vehicles

5. Front or rear wheel makes a clicking noise
a. Check for debris such as a pebble, nail or glass in the tire or tire tread. Carefully remove the debris. Small rocks and pebbles rarely cause a puncture; however, a sharp object should be removed carefully at a facility capable of performing tire repairs.

6. Rear wheel shudders or vibrates
a. Check for a bent rear wheel or axle assembly and replace defective components.
b. Check for a loose, damaged or worn rear wheel bearing and replace as necessary.

2-H. Other Drive Train Conditions

1. Burning odor from center of vehicle when accelerating
a. Check for a seizing brake hydraulic component such as a brake caliper. Check the caliper piston for surface damage such as rust, and measure for out-of-round wear and caliper-to-piston clearance. For additional information on brake related odors, refer to section 3-A, condition number 9.
b. On vehicles with a manual transmission, check for a slipping clutch. For possible causes and additional information, refer to section 2-C, condition number 1.
c. On vehicles with an automatic transmission, check the fluid level and condition. Top off or change the fluid and filter using the recommended replacement parts, lubricant type and amount. If the odor persists, transmission removal and disassembly will be necessary.

2. Engine accelerates, but vehicle does not gain speed
a. On vehicles with a manual transmission, check for a slipping or damaged clutch. For possible causes and additional information refer to section 2-C, condition number 1.
b. On vehicles with an automatic transmission, check the fluid level and condition. Top off or change the fluid and filter using the recommended replacement parts, lubricant type and amount. If the slipping continues, transmission removal and disassembly will be necessary.

3. BRAKE SYSTEM

3-A. Brake System Troubleshooting

1. Brake pedal pulsates or shimmies when pressed
a. Check wheel lug nut torque and tighten evenly to specification.
b. Check the brake rotor for trueness and thickness variations. Replace the rotor if it is too thin, warped, or if the thickness varies beyond specification. Some rotors can be machined; consult the manufacturer's specifications and recommendations before using a machined brake rotor.
c. Check the brake caliper or caliper bracket mounting bolt torque and inspect for looseness. Torque the mounting bolts and inspect for wear or any looseness, including worn mounting brackets, bushings and sliding pins.
d. Check the wheel bearing for looseness. If the bearing is loose, adjust if possible, otherwise replace the bearing.

2. Brakes make a squealing noise
a. Check the brake rotor for the presence of a ridge on the outer edge; if present, remove the ridge or replace the brake rotor and brake pads.
b. Check for debris in the brake lining material, clean and reinstall.
c. Check the brake linings for wear and replace the brake linings if wear is approaching the lining wear limit.
d. Check the brake linings for glazing. Inspect the brake drum or rotor surface and replace, along with the brake linings, if the surface is not smooth or even.
e. Check the brake pad or shoe mounting areas for a lack of lubricant or the presence of surface rust. Clean and lubricate with a recommended high temperature brake grease.

3. Brakes make a grinding noise
a. Check the brake linings and brake surface areas for severe wear or damage. Replace worn or damaged parts.
b. Check for a seized or partially seized brake causing premature or uneven brake wear, excessive heat and brake rotor or drum damage. Replace defective parts and inspect the wheel bearing condition, which could have been damaged due to excessive heat.

4. Vehicle pulls to one side during braking
a. Check for air in the brake hydraulic system. Inspect the brake hydraulic seals, fluid lines and related components for fluid leaks. Remove the air from the brake system by bleeding the brakes. Be sure to use fresh brake fluid that meets the manufacturer's recommended standards.
b. Check for an internally restricted flexible brake hydraulic hose. Replace the hose and flush the brake system.
c. Check for a seizing brake hydraulic component such as a brake caliper. Check the caliper piston for surface damage such as rust, and measure for out-of-round wear and caliper-to-piston clearance. Overhaul or replace failed parts and flush the brake system.
d. Check the vehicle's alignment and inspect for suspension wear. Replace worn bushings, ball joints and set alignment to the manufacturer's specifications.
e. If the brake system uses drum brakes front or rear, check the brake adjustment. Inspect for seized adjusters and clean or replace, then properly adjust.

5. Brake pedal feels spongy or has excessive travel
a. Check the brake fluid level and condition. If the fluid is contaminated or has not been flushed every two years, clean the master cylinder reservoir, and bleed and flush the brakes using fresh brake fluid that meets the manufacturer's recommended standards.
b. Check for a weak or damaged flexible brake hydraulic hose. Replace the hose and flush the brake system.
c. If the brake system uses drum brakes front or rear, check the brake adjustment. Inspect for seized adjusters and clean or replace, then properly adjust.

6. Brake pedal feel is firm, but brakes lack sufficient stopping power or fade
a. Check the operation of the brake booster and brake booster check valve. Replace worn or failed parts.
b. Check brake linings and brake surface areas for glazing and replace worn or damaged parts.
c. Check for seized hydraulic parts and linkages, and clean or replace as needed.

7. Vehicle has excessive front end dive or locks rear brakes too easily

a. Check for worn, failed or seized brake proportioning valve and replace the valve.

b. Check for a seized, disconnected or missing spring or linkage for the brake proportioning valve. Replace missing parts or repair as necessary.

8. Brake pedal goes to floor when pressed and will not pump up

a. Check the brake hydraulic fluid level and inspect the fluid lines and seals for leakage. Repair or replace leaking components, then bleed and flush the brake system using fresh brake fluid that meets the manufacturer's recommended standards.

b. Check the brake fluid level. Inspect the brake fluid level and brake hydraulic seals. If the fluid level is ok, and the brake hydraulic system is free of hydraulic leaks, replace the brake master cylinder, then bleed and flush the brake system using fresh brake fluid that meets the manufacturer's recommended standards.

9. Brakes produce a burning odor

a. Check for a seizing brake hydraulic component such as a brake caliper. Check the caliper piston for surface damage such as rust, and measure for out-of-round wear and caliper-to-piston clearance. Overhaul or replace failed parts and flush the brake system.

b. Check for an internally restricted flexible brake hydraulic hose. Replace the hose and flush the brake system.

c. Check the parking brake release mechanism, seized linkage or cable, and repair as necessary.

4. WHEELS, TIRES, STEERING AND SUSPENSION

4-A. Wheels and Wheel Bearings

1. Front wheel or wheel bearing loose

All Wheel and Four Wheel Drive Vehicles
a. Torque lug nuts and axle nuts to specification and recheck for looseness.
b. Wheel bearing worn or damaged. Replace wheel bearing.

Front Wheel Drive Vehicles
a. Torque lug nuts and axle nuts to specification and recheck for looseness.
b. Wheel bearing worn or damaged. Replace wheel bearing.
c. Wheel bearing out of adjustment. Adjust wheel bearing to specification; if still loose, replace.

Rear Wheel Drive Vehicles
a. Wheel bearing out of adjustment. Adjust wheel bearing to specification; if still loose, replace.
b. Torque lug nuts to specification and recheck for looseness.
c. Wheel bearing worn or damaged. Replace wheel bearing.

2. Rear wheel or wheel bearing loose

All Wheel and Four Wheel Drive Vehicles
a. Torque lug nuts and axle nuts to specification and recheck for looseness.
b. Wheel bearing worn or damaged. Replace wheel bearing.

Front Wheel Drive Vehicles
a. Wheel bearing out of adjustment. Adjust wheel bearing to specification; if still loose, replace.
b. Torque lug nuts to specification and recheck for looseness.
c. Wheel bearing worn or damaged. Replace wheel bearing.

Rear Wheel Drive Vehicles
a. Torque lug nuts to specification and recheck for looseness.
c. Wheel bearing worn or damaged. Replace wheel bearing.

4-B. Tires

1. Tires worn on inside tread

a. Check alignment for a toed-out condition. Check and set tire pressures and properly adjust the toe.
b. Check for worn, damaged or defective suspension components. Replace defective parts and adjust the alignment.

2. Tires worn on outside tread

a. Check alignment for a toed-in condition. Check and set tire pressures and properly adjust the toe.
b. Check for worn, damaged or defective suspension components. Replace defective parts and adjust the alignment.

3. Tires worn unevenly

a. Check the tire pressure and tire balance. Replace worn or defective tires and check the alignment; adjust if necessary.

BRAKE PERFORMANCE TROUBLESHOOTING HINTS

Brake vibrations or pulsation can often be diagnosed on a safe and careful test drive. A brake vibration which is felt through the brake pedal while braking, but not felt in the steering wheel, is most likely caused by brake surface variations in the rear brakes. If both the brake pedal and steering wheel vibrate during braking, a surface variation in the front brakes, or both front and rear brakes, is very likely.

A brake pedal that pumps up with repeated use can be caused by air in the brake hydraulic system or, if the vehicle is equipped with rear drum brakes, the brake adjusters may be seized or out of adjustment. A quick test for brake adjustment on vehicles with rear drum brakes is to pump the brake pedal several times with the vehicle's engine not running and the parking brake released. Pump the brake pedal several times and continue to apply pressure to the brake pedal. With pressure being applied to the brake pedal, engage the parking brake. Release the brake pedal and quickly press the brake pedal again. If the brake pedal pumped up, the rear brakes are in need of adjustment. Do not compensate for the rear brake adjustment by adjusting the parking brake, this will cause premature brake lining wear.

To test a vacuum brake booster, pump the brake pedal several times with the vehicle's engine off. Apply pressure to the brake pedal and then start the engine. The brake pedal should move downward about one inch (25mm).

b. Check for worn shock absorbers. Replaced failed components, worn or defective tires and check the alignment; adjust if necessary.
c. Check the alignment settings. Check and set tire pressures and properly adjust the alignment to specification.
d. Check for worn, damaged or defective suspension components. Replace defective parts and adjust the alignment to specification.

4-C. Steering

1. Excessive play in steering wheel

a. Check the steering gear free-play adjustment and properly adjust to remove excessive play.
b. Check the steering linkage for worn, damaged or defective parts. Replace failed components and perform a front end alignment.
c. Check for a worn, damaged, or defective steering box, replace the steering gear and check the front end alignment.

2. Steering wheel shakes at cruising speeds

a. Check for a bent front wheel. Replace a damaged wheel and check the tire for possible internal damage.
b. Check for an unevenly worn front tire. Replace the tire, adjust tire pressure and balance.
c. Check the front tires for hidden internal damage. Tires which have encountered large pot holes or suffered other hard blows may have sustained internal damage and should be replaced immediately.
d. Check the front tires for an out-of-balance condition. Remove, spin balance and reinstall. Torque all the wheel bolts or lug nuts to the recommended specification.
e. Check for a loose wheel bearing. If possible, adjust the bearing, or replace the bearing if it is a non-adjustable bearing.

3. Steering wheel shakes when braking

a. Refer to section 3-A, condition number 1.

4. Steering wheel becomes stiff when turned

a. Check the steering wheel free-play adjustment and reset as needed.
b. Check for a damaged steering gear assembly. Replace the steering gear and perform a front end alignment.
c. Check for damaged or seized suspension components. Replace defective components and perform a front end alignment.

4-D. Suspension

1. Vehicle pulls to one side

a. Tire pressure uneven. Adjust tire pressure to recommended settings.
b. Tires worn unevenly. Replace tires and check alignment settings.
c. Alignment out of specification. Align front end and check thrust angle.
d. Check for a dragging brake and repair or replace as necessary.

2. Vehicle is very bouncy over bumps

a. Check for worn or leaking shock absorbers or strut assemblies and replace as necessary.
b. Check for seized shock absorbers or strut assemblies and replace as necessary.

NOTE: When one shock fails, it is recommended to replace front or rear units as pairs.

3. Vehicle leans excessively in turns
a. Check for worn or leaking shock absorbers or strut assemblies and replace as necessary.
b. Check for missing, damaged, or worn stabilizer links or bushings, and replace or install as necessary.

4. Vehicle ride quality seems excessively harsh
a. Check for seized shock absorbers or strut assemblies and replace as necessary.
b. Check for excessively high tire pressures and adjust pressures to vehicle recommendations.

5. Vehicle seems low or leans to one side
a. Check for a damaged, broken or weak spring. Replace defective parts and check for a needed alignment.
b. Check for seized shock absorbers or strut assemblies and replace as necessary.
c. Check for worn or leaking shock absorbers or strut assemblies and replace as necessary.

4-E. Driving Noises and Vibrations

Noises

1. Vehicle makes a clicking noises when driven
a. Check the noise to see if it varies with road speed. Verify if the noise is present when coasting or with steering or throttle input. If the clicking noise frequency changes with road speed and is not affected by steering or throttle input, check the tire treads for a stone, piece of glass, nail or another hard object imbedded into the tire or tire tread. Stones rarely cause a tire puncture and are easily removed. Other objects may create an air leak when removed. Consider having these objects removed immediately at a facility equipped to repair tire punctures.
b. If the clicking noise varies with throttle input and steering, check for a worn Constant Velocity (CV-joint) joint, universal (U- joint) or flex joint.

2. Vehicle makes a clunking or knocking noise over bumps
a. A clunking noise over bumps is most often caused by excessive movement or clearance in a suspension component. Check the suspension for soft, cracked, damaged or worn bushings. Replace the bushings and check the vehicle's alignment.
b. Check for loose suspension mounting bolts. Check the tightness on subframe bolts, pivot bolts and suspension mounting bolts, and torque to specification.
c. Check the vehicle for a loose wheel bearing. Some wheel bearings can be adjusted for looseness, while others must be replaced if loose. Adjust or replace the bearings as recommended by the manufacturer.
d. Check the door latch adjustment. If the door is slightly loose, or the latch adjustment is not centered, the door assembly may create noises over bumps and rough surfaces. Properly adjust the door latches to secure the door.

3. Vehicle makes a low pitched rumbling noise when driven
a. A low pitched rumbling noise is usually caused by a drive train related bearing and is most often associated with a wheel bearing which has been damaged or worn. The damage can be caused by excessive brake temperatures or physical contact with a pot hole or curb. Sometimes the noise will vary when turning. Left hand turns increase the load on the vehicle's right side, and right turns load the left side. A failed front wheel bearing may also cause a slight steering wheel vibration when turning. A bearing which exhibits noise must be replaced.
b. Check the tire condition and balance. An internally damaged tire may cause failure symptoms similar to failed suspension parts. For diagnostic purposes, try a known good set of tires and replace defective tires.

4. Vehicle makes a squeaking noise over bumps
a. Check the vehicle's ball joints for wear, damaged or leaking boots. Replace a ball joint if it is loose, the boot is damaged and leaking, or the ball joint is binding. When replacing suspension parts, check the vehicle for alignment.
b. Check for seized or deteriorated bushings. Replace bushings that are worn or damaged and check the vehicle for alignment.
c. Check for the presence of sway bar or stabilizer bar bushings which wrap around the bar. Inspect the condition of the bushings and replace if worn or damaged. Remove the bushing bracket and apply a thin layer of suspension grease to the area where the bushings wrap around the bar and reinstall the bushing brackets.

Vibrations

5. Vehicle vibrates when driven
a. Check the road surface. Roads which have rough or uneven surfaces may cause unusual vibrations.
b. Check the tire condition and balance. An internally damaged tire may cause failure symptoms similar to failed suspension parts. For diagnostic purposes, try a known good set of tires and replace defective tires immediately.
c. Check for a worn Constant Velocity (CV-joint) joint, universal (U- joint) or flex joint and replace if loose, damaged or binding.
d. Check for a loose, bent, or out-of-balance axle or drive shaft. Replace damaged or failed components.

NOTE: Diagnosing failures related to wheels, tires, steering and the suspension system can often times be accomplished with a careful and thorough test drive. Bearing noises are isolated by noting whether the noises or symptoms vary when turning left or right, or occur while driving a straight line. During a left hand turn, the vehicle's weight shifts to the right, placing more force on the right side bearings, such that if a right side wheel bearing is worn or damaged, the noise or vibration should increase during light-to-heavy acceleration. Conversely, on right hand turns, the vehicle tends to lean to the left, loading the left side bearings.

Knocking noises in the suspension when the vehicle is driven over rough roads, railroad tracks and speed bumps indicate worn suspension components such as bushings, ball joints or tie rod ends, or a worn steering system.

5. ELECTRICAL ACCESSORIES

5-A. Headlights

1. One headlight only works on high or low beam
a. Check for battery voltage at headlight electrical connector. If battery voltage is present, replace the headlight assembly or bulb if available separately. If battery voltage is not present, refer to the headlight wiring diagram to troubleshoot.

2. Headlight does not work on high or low beam
a. Check for battery voltage and ground at headlight electrical connector. If battery voltage is present, check the headlight connector ground terminal for a proper ground. If battery voltage and ground are present at the headlight connector, replace the headlight assembly or bulb if available separately. If battery voltage or ground is not present, refer to the headlight wiring diagram to troubleshoot.
b. Check the headlight switch operation. Replace the switch if the switch is defective or operates intermittently.

3. Headlight(s) very dim
a. Check for battery voltage and ground at headlight electrical connector. If battery voltage is present, trace the ground circuit for the headlamp electrical connector, then clean and repair as necessary. If the voltage at the headlight electrical connector is significantly less than the voltage at the battery, refer to the headlight wiring diagram to troubleshoot and locate the voltage drop.

5-B. Tail, Running and Side Marker Lights

1. Tail light, running light or side marker light inoperative
a. Check for battery voltage and ground at light's electrical connector. If battery voltage is present, check the bulb socket and electrical connector ground terminal for a proper ground. If battery voltage and ground are present at the light connector, but not in the socket, clean the socket and the ground terminal connector. If battery voltage and ground are present in the bulb socket, replace the bulb. If battery voltage or ground is not present, refer to the wiring diagram to troubleshoot for an open circuit.
b. Check the light switch operation and replace if necessary.

2. Tail light, running light or side marker light works intermittently
a. Check the bulb for a damaged filament, and replace if damaged.
b Check the bulb and bulb socket for corrosion, and clean or replace the bulb and socket.
c. Check for loose, damaged or corroded wires and electrical terminals, and repair as necessary.
d. Check the light switch operation and replace if necessary.

3. Tail light, running light or side marker light very dim
a. Check the bulb and bulb socket for corrosion and clean or replace the bulb and socket.

b. Check for low voltage at the bulb socket positive terminal or a poor ground. If voltage is low, or the ground marginal, trace the wiring to, and check for loose, damaged or corroded wires and electrical terminals; repair as necessary.

c. Check the light switch operation and replace if necessary.

5-C. Interior Lights

1. Interior light inoperative

a. Verify the interior light switch location and position(s), and set the switch in the correct position.

b. Check for battery voltage and ground at the interior light bulb socket. If battery voltage and ground are present, replace the bulb. If voltage is not present, check the interior light fuse for battery voltage. If the fuse is missing, replace the fuse. If the fuse has blown, or if battery voltage is present, refer to the wiring diagram to troubleshoot the cause for an open or shorted circuit. If ground is not present, check the door switch contacts and clean or repair as necessary.

2. Interior light works intermittently

a. Check the bulb for a damaged filament, and replace if damaged.

b. Check the bulb and bulb socket for corrosion, and clean or replace the bulb and socket.

c. Check for loose, damaged or corroded wires and electrical terminals; repair as necessary.

d. Check the door and light switch operation, and replace if necessary.

3. Interior light very dim

a. Check the bulb and bulb socket for corrosion, and clean or replace the bulb and socket.

b. Check for low voltage at the bulb socket positive terminal or a poor ground. If voltage is low, or the ground marginal, trace the wiring to, and check for loose, damaged or corroded wires and electrical terminals; repair as necessary.

c. Check the door and light switch operation, and replace if necessary.

5-D. Brake Lights

1. One brake light inoperative

a. Press the brake pedal and check for battery voltage and ground at the brake light bulb socket. If present, replace the bulb. If either battery voltage or ground is not present, refer to the wiring diagram to troubleshoot.

2. Both brake lights inoperative

a. Press the brake pedal and check for battery voltage and ground at the brake light bulb socket. If present, replace both bulbs. If battery voltage is not present, check the brake light switch adjustment and adjust as necessary. If the brake light switch is properly adjusted, and battery voltage or the ground is not present at the bulb sockets, or at the bulb electrical connector with the brake pedal pressed, refer to the wiring diagram to troubleshoot the cause of an open circuit.

3. One or both brake lights very dim

a. Press the brake pedal and measure the voltage at the brake light bulb socket. If the measured voltage is close to the battery voltage, check for a poor ground caused by a loose, damaged, or corroded wire, terminal, bulb or bulb socket. If the ground is bolted to a painted surface, it may be necessary to remove the electrical connector and clean the mounting surface, so the connector mounts on bare metal. If battery voltage is low, check for a poor connection caused by either a faulty brake light switch, a loose, damaged, or corroded wire, terminal or electrical connector. Refer to the wiring diagram to troubleshoot the cause of a voltage drop.

5-E. Warning Lights

1. Warning light(s) stay on when the engine is started

Ignition, Battery or Alternator Warning Light

a. Check the alternator output and voltage regulator operation, and replace as necessary.

b. Check the warning light wiring for a shorted wire.

Check Engine Light

a. Check the engine for routine maintenance and tune-up status. Note the engine tune-up specifications and verify the spark plug, air filter and engine oil condition; replace and/or adjust items as necessary.

b. Check the fuel tank for low fuel level, causing an intermittent lean fuel mixture. Top off fuel tank and reset check engine light.

c. Check for a failed or disconnected engine fuel or ignition component, sensor or control unit and repair or replace as necessary.

d. Check the intake manifold and vacuum hoses for air leaks and repair as necessary.

e. Check the engine's mechanical condition for excessive oil consumption.

Anti-Lock Braking System (ABS) Light

a. Check the wheel sensors and sensor rings for debris, and clean as necessary.

b. Check the brake master cylinder for fluid leakage or seal failure and replace as necessary.

c. Check the ABS control unit, pump and proportioning valves for proper operation; replace as necessary.

d. Check the sensor wiring at the wheel sensors and the ABS control unit for a loose or shorted wire, and repair as necessary.

Brake Warning Light

a. Check the brake fluid level and check for possible leakage from the hydraulic lines and seals. Top off brake fluid and repair leakage as necessary.

b. Check the brake linings for wear and replace as necessary.

c. Check for a loose or shorted brake warning light sensor or wire, and replace or repair as necessary.

Oil Pressure Warning Light

a. Stop the engine immediately. Check the engine oil level and oil filter condition, and top off or change the oil as necessary.

b. Check the oil pressure sensor wire for being shorted to ground. Disconnect the wire from the oil pressure sensor and with the ignition in the ON position, but not running, the oil pressure light should not be working. If the light works with the wire disconnected, check the sensor wire for being shorted to ground. Check the wire routing to make sure the wire is not pinched and check for insulation damage. Repair or replace the wire as necessary and recheck before starting the engine.

c. Remove the oil pan and check for a clogged oil pick-up tube screen.

d. Check the oil pressure sensor operation by substituting a known good sensor.

e. Check the oil filter for internal restrictions or leaks, and replace as necessary.

WARNING: If the engine is operated with oil pressure below the manufacturer's specification, severe (and costly) engine damage could occur. Low oil pressure can be caused by excessive internal wear or damage to the engine bearings, oil pressure relief valve, oil pump or oil pump drive mechanism.

Before starting the engine, check for possible causes of rapid oil loss, such as leaking oil lines or a loose, damaged, restricted, or leaking oil filter or oil pressure sensor. If the engine oil level and condition are acceptable, measure the engine's oil pressure using a pressure gauge, or determine the cause for the oil pressure warning light to function when the engine is running, before operating the engine for an extended period of time. Another symptom of operating an engine with low oil pressure is the presence of severe knocking and tapping noises.

Parking Brake Warning Light

a. Check the brake release mechanism and verify the parking brake has been fully released.

b. Check the parking brake light switch for looseness or misalignment.

c. Check for a damaged switch or a loose or shorted brake light switch wire, and replace or repair as necessary.

2. Warning light(s) flickers on and off when driving

Ignition, Battery or Alternator Warning Light

a. Check the alternator output and voltage regulator operation. An intermittent condition may indicate worn brushes, an internal short, or a defective voltage regulator. Replace the alternator or failed component.

b. Check the warning light wiring for a shorted, pinched or damaged wire and repair as necessary.

Check Engine Light

a. Check the engine for required maintenance and tune-up status. Verify engine tune-up specifications, as well as spark plug, air filter and engine oil condition; replace and/or adjust items as necessary.

b. Check the fuel tank for low fuel level causing an intermittent lean fuel mixture. Top off fuel tank and reset check engine light.

c. Check for an intermittent failure or partially disconnected engine fuel and ignition component, sensor or control unit; repair or replace as necessary.

d. Check the intake manifold and vacuum hoses for air leaks, and repair as necessary.

e. Check the warning light wiring for a shorted, pinched or damaged wire and repair as necessary.

Anti-Lock Braking System (ABS) Light

a. Check the wheel sensors and sensor rings for debris, and clean as necessary.

b. Check the brake master cylinder for fluid leakage or seal failure and replace as necessary.

c. Check the ABS control unit, pump and proportioning valves for proper operation, and replace as necessary.

d. Check the sensor wiring at the wheel sensors and the ABS control unit for a loose or shorted wire, and repair as necessary.

Brake Warning Light

a. Check the brake fluid level and check for possible leakage from the hydraulic lines and seals. Top off brake fluid and repair leakage as necessary.

b. Check the brake linings for wear and replace as necessary.

c. Check for a loose or shorted brake warning light sensor or wire, and replace or repair as necessary.

Oil Pressure Warning Light

a. Stop the engine immediately. Check the engine oil level and check for a sudden and rapid oil loss, such as a leaking oil line or oil pressure sensor, and repair or replace as necessary.

b. Check the oil pressure sensor operation by substituting a known good sensor.

c. Check the oil pressure sensor wire for being shorted to ground. Disconnect the wire from the oil pressure sensor and with the ignition in the ON position, but not running, the oil pressure light should not be working. If the light works with the wire disconnected, check the sensor wire for being shorted to ground. Check the wire routing to make sure the wire is not pinched and check for insulation damage. Repair or replace the wire as necessary and recheck before starting the engine.

d. Remove the oil pan and check for a clogged oil pick-up tube screen.

Parking Brake Warning Light

a. Check the brake release mechanism and verify the parking brake has been fully released.

b. Check the parking brake light switch for looseness or misalignment.

c. Check for a damaged switch or a loose or shorted brake light switch wire, and replace or repair as necessary.

3. Warning light(s) inoperative with ignition on, and engine not started

a. Check for a defective bulb by installing a known good bulb.

b. Check for a defective wire using the appropriate wiring diagram(s).

c. Check for a defective sending unit by removing and then grounding the wire at the sending unit. If the light comes on with the ignition on when grounding the wire, replace the sending unit.

5-F. Turn Signal and 4-Way Hazard Lights

1. Turn signals or hazard lights come on, but do not flash
a. Check for a defective flasher unit and replace as necessary.

2. Turn signals or hazard lights do not function on either side
a. Check the fuse and replace, if defective.

b. Check the flasher unit by substituting a known good flasher unit.

c. Check the turn signal electrical system for a defective component, open circuit, short circuit or poor ground.

3. Turn signals or hazard lights only work on one side
a. Check for failed bulbs and replace as necessary.

b. Check for poor grounds in both housings and repair as necessary.

4. One signal light does not work
a. Check for a failed bulb and replace as necessary.

b. Check for corrosion in the bulb socket, and clean and repair as necessary.

c. Check for a poor ground at the bulb socket, and clean and repair as necessary.

5. Turn signals flash too slowly
a. Check signal bulb(s) wattage and replace with lower wattage bulb(s).

6. Turn signals flash too fast
a. Check signal bulb(s) wattage and replace with higher wattage bulb(s).

b. Check for installation of the correct flasher unit and replace if incorrect.

7. Four-way hazard flasher indicator light inoperative
a. Verify that the exterior lights are functioning and, if so, replace indicator bulb.

b. Check the operation of the warning flasher switch and replace if defective.

8. Turn signal indicator light(s) do not work in either direction
a. Verify that the exterior lights are functioning and, if so, replace indicator bulb(s).

b. Check for a defective flasher unit by substituting a known good unit.

9. One turn signal indicator light does not work
a. Check for a defective bulb and replace as necessary.

b. Check for a defective flasher unit by substituting a known good unit.

5-G. Horn

1. Horn does not operate
a. Check for a defective fuse and replace as necessary.

b. Check for battery voltage and ground at horn electrical connections when pressing the horn switch. If voltage is present, replace the horn assembly. If voltage or ground is not present, refer to Chassis Electrical coverage for additional trouble-shooting techniques and circuit information.

2. Horn has an unusual tone
a. On single horn systems, replace the horn.

b. On dual horn systems, check the operation of the second horn. Dual horn systems have a high and low pitched horn. Unplug one horn at a time and recheck operation. Replace the horn which does not function.

c. Check for debris or condensation build-up in horn and verify the horn positioning. If the horn has a single opening, adjust the opening downward to allow for adequate drainage and to prevent debris build-up.

5-H. Windshield Wipers

1. Windshield wipers do not operate
a. Check fuse and replace as necessary.

b. Check switch operation and repair or replace as necessary.

c. Check for corroded, loose, disconnected or broken wires and clean or repair as necessary.

d. Check the ground circuit for the wiper switch or motor and repair as necessary.

2. Windshield wiper motor makes a humming noise, gets hot or blows fuses
a. Wiper motor damaged internally; replace the wiper motor.

b. Wiper linkage bent, damaged or seized. Repair or replace wiper linkage as necessary.

3. Windshield wiper motor operates, but one or both wipers fail to move
a. Windshield wiper motor linkage loose or disconnected. Repair or replace linkage as necessary.

b. Windshield wiper arms loose on wiper pivots. Secure wiper arm to pivot or replace both the wiper arm and pivot assembly.

4. Windshield wipers will not park
a. Check the wiper switch operation and verify that the switch properly interrupts the power supplied to the wiper motor.

b. If the wiper switch is functioning properly, the wiper motor parking circuit has failed. Replace the wiper motor assembly. Operate the wiper motor at least one time before installing the arms and blades to ensure correct positioning, then recheck using the highest wiper speed on a wet windshield to make sure the arms and blades do not contact the windshield trim.

6. INSTRUMENTS AND GAUGES

6-A. Speedometer (Cable Operated)

1. Speedometer does not work
a. Check and verify that the speedometer cable is properly seated into the speedometer assembly and the speedometer drive gear.

b. Check the speedometer cable for breakage or rounded-off cable ends where the cable seats into the speedometer drive gear and into the speedometer assembly. If damaged, broken or the cable ends are rounded off, replace the cable.

c. Check speedometer drive gear condition and replace as necessary.

d. Install a known good speedometer to test for proper operation. If the substituted speedometer functions properly, replace the speedometer assembly.

2. Speedometer needle fluctuates when driving at steady speeds.
a. Check speedometer cable routing or sheathing for sharp bends or kinks. Route cable to minimize sharp bends or kinks. If the sheathing has been damaged, replace the cable assembly.

b. Check the speedometer cable for adequate lubrication. Remove the cable, inspect for damage, clean, lubricate and reinstall. If the cable has been damaged, replace the cable.

3. Speedometer works intermittently
a. Check the cable and verify that the cable is fully installed and the fasteners are secure.

b. Check the cable ends for wear and rounding, and replace as necessary.

6-B. Speedometer (Electronically Operated)

1. Speedometer does not work
a. Check the speed sensor pickup and replace as necessary.
b. Check the wiring between the speed sensor and the speedometer for corroded terminals, loose connections or broken wires and clean or repair as necessary.
c. Install a known good speedometer to test for proper operation. If the substituted speedometer functions properly, replace the speedometer assembly.

2. Speedometer works intermittently
a. Check the wiring between the speed sensor and the speedometer for corroded terminals, loose connections or broken wires and clean or repair as necessary.
b. Check the speed sensor pickup and replace as necessary.

6-C. Fuel, Temperature and Oil Pressure Gauges

1. Gauge does not register
a. Check for a missing or blown fuse and replace as necessary.
b. Check for an open circuit in the gauge wiring. Repair wiring as necessary.

c. Gauge sending unit defective. Replace gauge sending unit.
d. Gauge or sending unit improperly installed. Verify installation and wiring, and repair as necessary.

2. Gauge operates erratically
a. Check for loose, shorted, damaged or corroded electrical connections or wiring and repair as necessary.
b. Check gauge sending units and replace as necessary.

3. Gauge operates fully pegged
a. Sending unit-to-gauge wire shorted to ground.
b. Sending unit defective; replace sending unit.
c. Gauge or sending unit not properly grounded.
d. Gauge or sending unit improperly installed. Verify installation and wiring, and repair as necessary.

7. CLIMATE CONTROL

7-A. Air Conditioner

1. No air coming from air conditioner vents
a. Check the air conditioner fuse and replace as necessary.
b. Air conditioner system discharged. Have the system evacuated, charged and leak tested by an MVAC certified technician, utilizing approved recovery/recycling equipment. Repair as necessary.
c. Air conditioner low pressure switch defective. Replace switch.
d. Air conditioner fan resistor pack defective. Replace resistor pack.
e. Loose connection, broken wiring or defective air conditioner relay in air conditioning electrical circuit. Repair wiring or replace relay as necessary.

2. Air conditioner blows warm air
a. Air conditioner system is discharged. Have the system evacuated, charged and leak tested by an MVAC certified technician, utilizing approved recovery/recycling equipment. Repair as necessary.
b. Air conditioner compressor clutch not engaging. Check compressor clutch wiring, electrical connections and compressor clutch, and repair or replace as necessary.

3. Water collects on the interior floor when the air conditioner is used
a. Air conditioner evaporator drain hose is blocked. Clear the drain hose where it exits the passenger compartment.
b. Air conditioner evaporator drain hose is disconnected. Secure the drain hose to the evaporator drainage tray under the dashboard.

4. Air conditioner has a moldy odor when used
a. The air conditioner evaporator drain hose is blocked or partially re-stricted, allowing condensation to build up around the evaporator and drainage tray. Clear the drain hose where it exits the passenger compartment.

7-B. Heater

1. Blower motor does not operate
a. Check blower motor fuse and replace as necessary.
b. Check blower motor wiring for loose, damaged or corroded contacts and repair as necessary.
c. Check blower motor switch and resistor pack for open circuits, and repair or replace as necessary.
d. Check blower motor for internal damage and repair or replace as necessary.

2. Heater blows cool air
a. Check the engine coolant level. If the coolant level is low, top off and bleed the air from the cooling system as necessary and check for coolant leaks.
b. Check engine coolant operating temperature. If coolant temperature is below specification, check for a damaged or stuck thermostat.
c. Check the heater control valve operation. Check the heater control valve cable or vacuum hose for proper installation. Move the heater temperature control from hot to cold several times and verify the operation of the heater control valve. With the engine at normal operating temperature and the heater temperature control in the full hot position, carefully feel the heater hose going into and exiting the control valve. If one heater hose is hot and the other is much cooler, replace the control valve.

3. Heater steams the windshield when used
a. Check for a loose cooling system hose clamp or leaking coolant hose near the engine firewall or under the dash area, and repair as necessary.
b. Check for the existence of a sweet odor and fluid dripping from the heater floor vents, indicating a failed or damaged heater core. Pressure test the cooling system with the heater set to the fully warm position and check for fluid leakage from the floor vents. If leakage is verified, remove and replace the heater core assembly.

NOTE: On some vehicles, the dashboard must be disassembled and removed to access the heater core.

GLOSSARY

AIR/FUEL RATIO: The ratio of air-to-gasoline by weight in the fuel mixture drawn into the engine.

AIR INJECTION: One method of reducing harmful exhaust emissions by injecting air into each of the exhaust ports of an engine. The fresh air entering the hot exhaust manifold causes any remaining fuel to be burned before it can exit the tailpipe.

ALTERNATOR: A device used for converting mechanical energy into electrical energy.

AMMETER: An instrument, calibrated in amperes, used to measure the flow of an electrical current in a circuit. Ammeters are always connected in series with the circuit being tested.

AMPERE: The rate of flow of electrical current present when one volt of electrical pressure is applied against one ohm of electrical resistance.

ANALOG COMPUTER: Any microprocessor that uses similar (analogous) electrical signals to make its calculations.

ARMATURE: A laminated, soft iron core wrapped by a wire that converts electrical energy to mechanical energy as in a motor or relay. When rotated in a magnetic field, it changes mechanical energy into electrical energy as in a generator.

ATMOSPHERIC PRESSURE: The pressure on the Earth's surface caused by the weight of the air in the atmosphere. At sea level, this pressure is 14.7 psi at 32°F (101 kPa at 0°C).

ATOMIZATION: The breaking down of a liquid into a fine mist that can be suspended in air.

AXIAL PLAY: Movement parallel to a shaft or bearing bore.

BACKFIRE: The sudden combustion of gases in the intake or exhaust system that results in a loud explosion.

BACKLASH: The clearance or play between two parts, such as meshed gears.

BACKPRESSURE: Restrictions in the exhaust system that slow the exit of exhaust gases from the combustion chamber.

BAKELITE: A heat resistant, plastic insulator material commonly used in printed circuit boards and transistorized components.

BALL BEARING: A bearing made up of hardened inner and outer races between which hardened steel balls roll.

BALLAST RESISTOR: A resistor in the primary ignition circuit that lowers voltage after the engine is started to reduce wear on ignition components.

BEARING: A friction reducing, supportive device usually located between a stationary part and a moving part.

BIMETAL TEMPERATURE SENSOR: Any sensor or switch made of two dissimilar types of metal that bend when heated or cooled due to the different expansion rates of the alloys. These types of sensors usually function as an on/off switch.

BLOWBY: Combustion gases, composed of water vapor and unburned fuel, that leak past the piston rings into the crankcase during normal engine operation. These gases are removed by the PCV system to prevent the buildup of harmful acids in the crankcase.

BRAKE PAD: A brake shoe and lining assembly used with disc brakes.

BRAKE SHOE: The backing for the brake lining. The term is, however, usually applied to the assembly of the brake backing and lining.

BUSHING: A liner, usually removable, for a bearing; an anti-friction liner used in place of a bearing.

CALIPER: A hydraulically activated device in a disc brake system, which is mounted straddling the brake rotor (disc). The caliper contains at least one piston and two brake pads. Hydraulic pressure on the piston(s) forces the pads against the rotor.

CAMSHAFT: A shaft in the engine on which are the lobes (cams) which operate the valves. The camshaft is driven by the crankshaft, via a belt, chain or gears, at one half the crankshaft speed.

CAPACITOR: A device which stores an electrical charge.

CARBON MONOXIDE (CO): A colorless, odorless gas given off as a normal byproduct of combustion. It is poisonous and extremely dangerous in confined areas, building up slowly to toxic levels without warning if adequate ventilation is not available.

CARBURETOR: A device, usually mounted on the intake manifold of an engine, which mixes the air and fuel in the proper proportion to allow even combustion.

CATALYTIC CONVERTER: A device installed in the exhaust system, like a muffler, that converts harmful byproducts of combustion into carbon dioxide and water vapor by means of a heat-producing chemical reaction.

CENTRIFUGAL ADVANCE: A mechanical method of advancing the spark timing by using flyweights in the distributor that react to centrifugal force generated by the distributor shaft rotation.

CHECK VALVE: Any one-way valve installed to permit the flow of air, fuel or vacuum in one direction only.

CHOKE: A device, usually a moveable valve, placed in the intake path of a carburetor to restrict the flow of air.

CIRCUIT: Any unbroken path through which an electrical current can flow. Also used to describe fuel flow in some instances.

CIRCUIT BREAKER: A switch which protects an electrical circuit from overload by opening the circuit when the current flow exceeds a predetermined level. Some circuit breakers must be reset manually, while most reset automatically.

COIL (IGNITION): A transformer in the ignition circuit which steps up the voltage provided to the spark plugs.

COMBINATION MANIFOLD: An assembly which includes both the intake and exhaust manifolds in one casting.

COMBINATION VALVE: A device used in some fuel systems that routes fuel vapors to a charcoal storage canister instead of venting them into the atmosphere. The valve relieves fuel tank pressure and allows fresh air into the tank as the fuel level drops to prevent a vapor lock situation.

COMPRESSION RATIO: The comparison of the total volume of the cylinder and combustion chamber with the piston at BDC and the piston at TDC.

CONDENSER: 1. An electrical device which acts to store an electrical charge, preventing voltage surges. 2. A radiator-like device in the air conditioning system in which refrigerant gas condenses into a liquid, giving off heat.

CONDUCTOR: Any material through which an electrical current can be transmitted easily.

CONTINUITY: Continuous or complete circuit. Can be checked with an ohmmeter.

COUNTERSHAFT: An intermediate shaft which is rotated by a mainshaft and transmits, in turn, that rotation to a working part.

CRANKCASE: The lower part of an engine in which the crankshaft and related parts operate.

CRANKSHAFT: The main driving shaft of an engine which receives reciprocating motion from the pistons and converts it to rotary motion.

CYLINDER: In an engine, the round hole in the engine block in which the piston(s) ride.

CYLINDER BLOCK: The main structural member of an engine in which is found the cylinders, crankshaft and other principal parts.

CYLINDER HEAD: The detachable portion of the engine, usually fastened to the top of the cylinder block and containing all or most of the combustion chambers. On overhead valve engines, it contains the valves and their operating parts. On overhead cam engines, it contains the camshaft as well.

DEAD CENTER: The extreme top or bottom of the piston stroke.

DETONATION: An unwanted explosion of the air/fuel mixture in the combustion chamber caused by excess heat and compression, advanced timing, or an overly lean mixture. Also referred to as "ping".

DIAPHRAGM: A thin, flexible wall separating two cavities, such as in a vacuum advance unit.

DIESELING: A condition in which hot spots in the combustion chamber cause the engine to run on after the key is turned off.

DIFFERENTIAL: A geared assembly which allows the transmission of motion between drive axles, giving one axle the ability to turn faster than the other.

DIODE: An electrical device that will allow current to flow in one direction only.

DISC BRAKE: A hydraulic braking assembly consisting of a brake disc, or rotor, mounted on an axle, and a caliper assembly containing, usually two brake pads which are activated by hydraulic pressure. The pads are forced against the sides of the disc, creating friction which slows the vehicle.

DISTRIBUTOR: A mechanically driven device on an engine which is responsible for electrically firing the spark plug at a predetermined point of the piston stroke.

DOWEL PIN: A pin, inserted in mating holes in two different parts allowing those parts to maintain a fixed relationship.

DRUM BRAKE: A braking system which consists of two brake shoes and one or two wheel cylinders, mounted on a fixed backing plate, and a brake drum, mounted on an axle, which revolves around the assembly.

DWELL: The rate, measured in degrees of shaft rotation, at which an electrical circuit cycles on and off.

ELECTRONIC CONTROL UNIT (ECU): Ignition module, module, amplifier or igniter. See Module for definition.

ELECTRONIC IGNITION: A system in which the timing and firing of the spark plugs is controlled by an electronic control unit, usually called a module. These systems have no points or condenser.

END-PLAY: The measured amount of axial movement in a shaft.

ENGINE: A device that converts heat into mechanical energy.

EXHAUST MANIFOLD: A set of cast passages or pipes which conduct exhaust gases from the engine.

FEELER GAUGE: A blade, usually metal, or precisely predetermined thickness, used to measure the clearance between two parts.

FIRING ORDER: The order in which combustion occurs in the cylinders of an engine. Also the order in which spark is distributed to the plugs by the distributor.

FLOODING: The presence of too much fuel in the intake manifold and combustion chamber which prevents the air/fuel mixture from firing, thereby causing a no-start situation.

FLYWHEEL: A disc shaped part bolted to the rear end of the crankshaft. Around the outer perimeter is affixed the ring gear. The starter drive engages the ring gear, turning the flywheel, which rotates the crankshaft, imparting the initial starting motion to the engine.

FOOT POUND (ft. lbs. or sometimes, ft.lb.): The amount of energy or work needed to raise an item weighing one pound, a distance of one foot.

FUSE: A protective device in a circuit which prevents circuit overload by breaking the circuit when a specific amperage is present. The device is constructed around a strip or wire of a lower amperage rating than the circuit it is designed to protect. When an amperage higher than that stamped on the fuse is present in the circuit, the strip or wire melts, opening the circuit.

GEAR RATIO: The ratio between the number of teeth on meshing gears.

GENERATOR: A device which converts mechanical energy into electrical energy.

HEAT RANGE: The measure of a spark plug's ability to dissipate heat from its firing end. The higher the heat range, the hotter the plug fires.

HUB: The center part of a wheel or gear.

HYDROCARBON (HC): Any chemical compound made up of hydrogen and carbon. A major pollutant formed by the engine as a byproduct of combustion.

HYDROMETER: An instrument used to measure the specific gravity of a solution.

INCH POUND (inch lbs.; sometimes in.lb. or in. lbs.): One twelfth of a foot pound.

INDUCTION: A means of transferring electrical energy in the form of a magnetic field. Principle used in the ignition coil to increase voltage.

INJECTOR: A device which receives metered fuel under relatively low pressure and is activated to inject the fuel into the engine under relatively high pressure at a predetermined time.

INPUT SHAFT: The shaft to which torque is applied, usually carrying the driving gear or gears.

INTAKE MANIFOLD: A casting of passages or pipes used to conduct air or a fuel/air mixture to the cylinders.

JOURNAL: The bearing surface within which a shaft operates.

KEY: A small block usually fitted in a notch between a shaft and a hub to prevent slippage of the two parts.

MANIFOLD: A casting of passages or set of pipes which connect the cylinders to an inlet or outlet source.

MANIFOLD VACUUM: Low pressure in an engine intake manifold formed just below the throttle plates. Manifold vacuum is highest at idle and drops under acceleration.

MASTER CYLINDER: The primary fluid pressurizing device in a hydraulic system. In automotive use, it is found in brake and hydraulic clutch systems and is pedal activated, either directly or, in a power brake system, through the power booster.

MODULE: Electronic control unit, amplifier or igniter of solid state or integrated design which controls the current flow in the ignition primary circuit based on input from the pick-up coil. When the module opens the primary circuit, high secondary voltage is induced in the coil.

NEEDLE BEARING: A bearing which consists of a number (usually a large number) of long, thin rollers.

OHM: (Ω) The unit used to measure the resistance of conductor-to-electrical flow. One ohm is the amount of resistance that limits current flow to one ampere in a circuit with one volt of pressure.

OHMMETER: An instrument used for measuring the resistance, in ohms, in an electrical circuit.

OUTPUT SHAFT: The shaft which transmits torque from a device, such as a transmission.

OVERDRIVE: A gear assembly which produces more shaft revolutions than that transmitted to it.

OVERHEAD CAMSHAFT (OHC): An engine configuration in which the camshaft is mounted on top of the cylinder head and operates the valve either directly or by means of rocker arms.

OVERHEAD VALVE (OHV): An engine configuration in which all of the valves are located in the cylinder head and the camshaft is located in the cylinder block. The camshaft operates the valves via lifters and pushrods.

OXIDES OF NITROGEN (NOx): Chemical compounds of nitrogen produced as a byproduct of combustion. They combine with hydrocarbons to produce smog.

OXYGEN SENSOR: Use with the feedback system to sense the presence of oxygen in the exhaust gas and signal the computer which can reference the voltage signal to an air/fuel ratio.

PINION: The smaller of two meshing gears.

PISTON RING: An open-ended ring with fits into a groove on the outer diameter of the piston. Its chief function is to form a seal between the piston and cylinder wall. Most automotive pistons have three rings: two for compression sealing; one for oil sealing.

PRELOAD: A predetermined load placed on a bearing during assembly or by adjustment.

PRIMARY CIRCUIT: the low voltage side of the ignition system which consists of the ignition switch, ballast resistor or resistance wire, bypass, coil, electronic control unit and pick-up coil as well as the connecting wires and harnesses.

PRESS FIT: The mating of two parts under pressure, due to the inner diameter of one being smaller than the outer diameter of the other, or vice versa; an interference fit.

RACE: The surface on the inner or outer ring of a bearing on which the balls, needles or rollers move.

REGULATOR: A device which maintains the amperage and/or voltage levels of a circuit at predetermined values.

RELAY: A switch which automatically opens and/or closes a circuit.

RESISTANCE: The opposition to the flow of current through a circuit or electrical device, and is measured in ohms. Resistance is equal to the voltage divided by the amperage.

RESISTOR: A device, usually made of wire, which offers a preset amount of resistance in an electrical circuit.

RING GEAR: The name given to a ring-shaped gear attached to a differential case, or affixed to a flywheel or as part of a planetary gear set.

ROLLER BEARING: A bearing made up of hardened inner and outer races between which hardened steel rollers move.

ROTOR: 1. The disc-shaped part of a disc brake assembly, upon which the brake pads bear; also called, brake disc. 2. The device mounted atop the distributor shaft, which passes current to the distributor cap tower contacts.

SECONDARY CIRCUIT: The high voltage side of the ignition system, usually above 20,000 volts. The secondary includes the ignition coil, coil wire, distributor cap and rotor, spark plug wires and spark plugs.

SENDING UNIT: A mechanical, electrical, hydraulic or electro-magnetic device which transmits information to a gauge.

SENSOR: Any device designed to measure engine operating conditions or ambient pressures and temperatures. Usually electronic in nature and designed to send a voltage signal to an on-board computer, some sensors may operate as a simple on/off switch or they may provide a variable voltage signal (like a potentiometer) as conditions or measured parameters change.

SHIM: Spacers of precise, predetermined thickness used between parts to establish a proper working relationship.

SLAVE CYLINDER: In automotive use, a device in the hydraulic clutch system which is activated by hydraulic force, disengaging the clutch.

SOLENOID: A coil used to produce a magnetic field, the effect of which is to produce work.

SPARK PLUG: A device screwed into the combustion chamber of a spark ignition engine. The basic construction is a conductive core inside of a ceramic insulator, mounted in an outer conductive base. An electrical charge from the spark plug wire travels along the conductive core and jumps a preset air gap to a grounding point or points at the end of the conductive base. The resultant spark ignites the fuel/air mixture in the combustion chamber.

SPLINES: Ridges machined or cast onto the outer diameter of a shaft or inner diameter of a bore to enable parts to mate without rotation.

TACHOMETER: A device used to measure the rotary speed of an engine, shaft, gear, etc., usually in rotations per minute.

THERMOSTAT: A valve, located in the cooling system of an engine, which is closed when cold and opens gradually in response to engine heating, controlling the temperature of the coolant and rate of coolant flow.

TOP DEAD CENTER (TDC): The point at which the piston reaches the top of its travel on the compression stroke.

TORQUE: The twisting force applied to an object.

TORQUE CONVERTER: A turbine used to transmit power from a driving member to a driven member via hydraulic action, providing changes in drive ratio and torque. In automotive use, it links the driveplate at the rear of the engine to the automatic transmission.

TRANSDUCER: A device used to change a force into an electrical signal.

TRANSISTOR: A semi-conductor component which can be actuated by a small voltage to perform an electrical switching function.

TUNE-UP: A regular maintenance function, usually associated with the replacement and adjustment of parts and components in the electrical and fuel systems of a vehicle for the purpose of attaining optimum performance.

TURBOCHARGER: An exhaust driven pump which compresses intake air and forces it into the combustion chambers at higher than atmospheric pressures. The increased air pressure allows more fuel to be burned and results in increased horsepower being produced.

VACUUM ADVANCE: A device which advances the ignition timing in response to increased engine vacuum.

VACUUM GAUGE: An instrument used to measure the presence of vacuum in a chamber.

VALVE: A device which control the pressure, direction of flow or rate of flow of a liquid or gas.

VALVE CLEARANCE: The measured gap between the end of the valve stem and the rocker arm, cam lobe or follower that activates the valve.

VISCOSITY: The rating of a liquid's internal resistance to flow.

VOLTMETER: An instrument used for measuring electrical force in units called volts. Voltmeters are always connected parallel with the circuit being tested.

WHEEL CYLINDER: Found in the automotive drum brake assembly, it is a device, actuated by hydraulic pressure, which, through internal pistons, pushes the brake shoes outward against the drums.

MASTER

INDEX